(1588)

£6·55

£250

COURVOISIER'S BOOK OF THE BEST

Edited by
LORD LICHFIELD

Written by
SUE CARPENTER

EBURY PRESS · LONDON

Published by Ebury Press
Division of The National Magazine Company Ltd
Colquhoun House
27-37 Broadwick Street
London W1V 1FR

ISBN 0 85223 684 0

Managing Editor   Sarah Bailey
Researchers   Beth Blackshaw
                       Joanna Hill

Correspondents
America (East Coast)   Ellen Peck
         (West Coast) David Harte
Australia   Charles de Lisle
                       Orna Mulcahy
                       Sheelagh Pyle
Canada   Freda Colbourne
France   Anne-Elisabeth Moutet
Italy   Paolo Rinaldi
Far East   Claudia Cragg
Singapore   Nichole Yarkoff

Editorial Direction   Yvonne McFarlane
Art Direction   Frank Phillips
Illustrations   Natacha Ledwidge
Design   Harry Green

Computerset in Great Britain by
MFK Typesetting Ltd, Hitchin, Herts
Printed and bound in Great Britain by Butler and
Tanner Ltd, Frome and London

Courvoisier's Book of the Best is a regularly
updated guide. We would welcome your views
in writing to Courvoisier's Book of the Best,
Ebury Press, 27-37 Broadwick Street, London
W1V 1FR.

The information contained in this book was
checked as rigorously as possible before going to
press. The publisher accepts no responsibility for
any changes which may have occurred since, nor
for any other variance of fact from that recorded
here in good faith.

Contents

TRAVEL
Introduced by
PETER USTINOV

♟AIRLINES . ♟CRUISES . ♟HOTELS
♟ISLANDS ... ♟RAIL ... ♟RESORTS
♟SAFARIS ... ♟TOURS AND AGENTS

SOCIAL AND NIGHT LIFE

Introduced by

VISCOUNTESS ROTHERMERE

🏃BARS ...... 🏃PARTY ORGANIZERS
🏃CASINOS ... 🏃CLUBS ... 🏃EVENTS
🏃GUESTS .. 🏃HOSTS .. 🏃CATERERS

FASHION AND SHOPPING

Introduced by

BRUCE OLDFIELD

🏃ACCESSORIES ..... 🏃JEWELLERY
🏃DESIGNERS ... 🏃HATS ... 🏃SHOPS
🏃PRESENTS .. 🏃SHOPPING STREETS

FOREWORD
by
LORD LICHFIELD

Since I have been editing *Courvoisier's Book of the Best*, my life has taken on new – and very enjoyable – meaning! Whenever I travel, I go armed with the first volume and make a point of testing places listed and trying out new ones. And, while I am not fortunate enough to have sampled every establishment, I do constantly have the opportunity to assess international standards – particularly of airlines, hotels and restaurants. I travel 250,000 miles a year, spend 150 nights in hotels, and eat out virtually every day.

Wherever I go, people are more than willing to volunteer both information and strong views on the best of their country. Recently, I was dining in a London restaurant when a piercing shriek resounded round the room. The owner of the powerful lungs bellowed: "Do you know where to get the best socks in the world?" I have to confess that superlative socks were not uppermost in my mind, but the Fashion and Shopping section was able to provide the answer.

You may wonder whether, as well as being heckled in public places, I have been subject to bribery. There was the case of the lorry-load of fudge sent by a manufacturer who was determined to persuade me that his was the best. But I stand by my original opinion: The Toffee Shop in Penrith remains No 1.

However, this is just my opinion. The most frequent reaction I get about *Courvoisier's Book of the Best* is "How can you decide what is the best?" The answer is I am not the only arbiter. What is best for me may differ from what is best for you. Best for me represents quality and uncompromising attention to detail. But, however you define it, opinions will vary as to what deserves the accolade 'the best'.

That is why we ask more than 200 style-setters and experts to give us their personal views. When people and establishments are recommended by more than one contributor, whose opinions are informed and respected, they are surely worthy of a place in this book. Our contributors' views form a unique international record of the best – where else can you find word-of-mouth recommendations in volume form? What is more they make riveting reading! Discover, for example, what Barbara Cartland, Zsa Zsa Gabor and Margaret Thatcher have in common; how the Auberon Waugh tastebuds react to crocodile, snake and kangaroo; the secrets of Joan Collins's desert island survival kit; what makes travel a joy for Peter Ustinov.

But this is a guide. Each entry has been thoroughly researched; full addresses and telephone numbers are supplied. We cover the best of Travel, Social and Night Life, Fashion and Shopping, Food and Drink, and – a brand new section – Culture.

In a book about the best things in life, I believe the Culture section is of prime importance. This must be the most eclectic yet practical guide available to the unmissable treasures of the arts world, including the best opera, theatre, ballet, art galleries, museums, stately homes, châteaux, gardens and festivals.

LORD LICHFIELD, great nephew of the Queen Mother, was educated at Harrow and spent 7 years in the Grenadier Guards. In the Sixties he became a photographer, working for *Life, Queen* and then American *Vogue* under Diana Vreeland. Advertising and editorial work now takes him all over the world. He lives in London and Shugborough, Staffordshire. His books include the autobiographical *Not the Whole Truth, Lichfield – A Royal Album*, and *Lichfield in Retrospect*.

There are other additions to the book. Fashion expands to include shopping – from the most chic present shops to the best flea markets; the best cars, gadgets, antiques, make-up . . . and the best areas of town for smart *and* streetwise shopping. In Food and Drink, contributors eulogize about their favourite markets, from Périgueux to Tokyo. Travel includes many tips such as *when* to tip, and how to combat jetlag; and in Social and Night Life, we list not just the hippest nightspots, but the best party organizers and top events in the social calendar.

All this makes *Courvoisier's Book of the Best* more accessible to more people. The best need not be élitist. Quality is paramount, and it doesn't necessarily come with a prohibitively high price tag. As well as frequent bargains, there are many things to experience that are entirely free: Opera in the Park (in London, Sydney, New York and San Francisco), great national art collections, best beaches, glorious gardens, magnificent views, even the atmosphere of colourful local markets and the dazzle of designer stores.

Long-standing 'bests' are balanced with what is trendsetting, innovative and currently fashionable. It is not enough simply to trot out the establishments that everyone knows are excellent. All the time wonderful places crop up; new young chefs, hoteliers and fashion designers emerge. Our experts have their ears to the ground. They spot the latest trends.

For this reason, you may find some surprises in our top 10 ratings. We have not shied away from ousting old chestnuts; we give relative newcomers that are exciting, exacting and excellent a chance to shine. However, changes have not been made for change's sake. As before, the ratings were reached by consensus opinion. Entries that received many recommendations have been awarded the familiar Courvoisier symbol, the silhouette of Napoleon.

As the producers of the best and most stylishly presented cognac in the world, it was only natural for Courvoisier to initiate and support this book with such enthusiasm. Connoisseurs in one area are able to appreciate fine things on a broader scale: those who savour Courvoisier's fine cognac are attuned to the best in life.

Courvoisier's Book of the Best will continue to be regularly updated. While some establishments are undoubtedly timeless, many fluctuate. We will constantly be assessing what is best, rating new entries and sifting out dead wood – and we we come your comments and recommendations, too. Meanwhile, if you haven't already dispensed with your suitcaseful of Michelins, Gault Millaus, Fodors, Good Food and Hotel Guides, do so now, for all you need is one, all-encompassing guide: *Courvoisier's Book of the Best.*

written by

SUE CARPENTER, a freelance writer and journalist, who has wined, dined, danced and stayed in some of the best restaurants, nightclubs and hotels of the world, from Tahiti to Tokyo and San Francisco to Sydney. Her travels have provided a rich source of material for both editions of _Courvoisier's Book of the Best_. Formerly with _Harpers & Queen_, she helped write the Official Sloane Ranger books, edited _St Moritz Magazine_, and is author of _The Good Wedding Guide_.

with contributions from

ROY ACKERMAN Food expert, chef and restaurateur with a finger in many pies. Author of _The Ackerman Guide_ to British restaurants and _The Chef's Apprentice_ (also a TV series which he presented).

AZZEDINE ALAÏA Paris-based Tunisian fashion designer, known for his sculpted forms in leather and synthetics.

LADY ELIZABETH ANSON Founder of Party Planners which has organized parties for most of the British royals, as well as international clients from Mick Jagger to Baron Thyssen.

JEFFREY ARCHER Former politician; bestselling author and playwright.

GIORGIO ARMANI Italy's No 1 fashion designer, a master of tailoring.

JANE ASHER Actress and author of books on entertaining and dress. Based in London, she has written children's stories, illustrated by husband Gerald Scarfe.

TONY ASPLER Canadian wine writer and consultant.

JOSEPH BERKMANN French-based British wine expert and traveller.

MARK BIRLEY Proprietor of Annabel's in London, the world's top nightclub. Part-owner of Harry's bar and Mark's Club.

PETER BLAKE British artist who came to prominence in the 1960s as one of the leading Pop Artists of his generation.

RAYMOND BLANC French chef-owner of the acclaimed Le Manoir aux Quat' Saisons in Oxfordshire.

BILL BLASS Top American fashion and furnishings designer. One of the most fashionable people to be seen with in New York.

KYM BONYTHON Australian art gallery owner in Adelaide.

FRANK BOWLING British-born Manager of the Carlyle in New York.

SARAH BRIGHTMAN Singer, dancer and actress, acclaimed for her role in _The Phantom of the Opera_. Married to Andrew Lloyd Webber.

SEYMOUR BRITCHKY American author of the annual guide _The Restaurants of New York_, and of the restaurant periodical _Seymour Britchky's Restaurant Letter_.

MICHAEL BROADBENT MW Head of Christie's Wine Department in London. An international wine auctioneer and author of the _Great Vintage Wine Book_.

JOHN BROOKE-LITTLE CVO NORROY & ULSTER KING OF ARMS British heraldry and genealogy expert and author at the College of Arms in London.

BONNIE BROOKS-YOUNG Socialite and Senior Vice President of Holt Renfrew, Canada.

TYLER BRULE Film critic for Canadian Broadcasting Company.

MARIO BUATTA Top New York-based interior designer and chairman of the Winter Antiques Show.

JAMES BURKE British broadcaster, traveller and writer.

JOAN BURSTEIN Owner and top buyer of Browns, the leading London fashion store.

ROBERT BURTON Australian fashion designer. He trained in London and New York before returning to Sydney.

SHAKIRA CAINE Guyanan beauty and wife of Michael Caine. Based in Beverly Hills and London.

EDMUND CAPON British-born director of the Art Gallery of New South Wales in Sydney.

ROBERT CARRIER American-born cookery expert. He divides his time between London, New York and Morocco – the inspiration for his latest book _Taste of Morocco_.

BARBARA CARTLAND The world's most famous romantic novelist. She has written over 450 books and sold over 450 million worldwide.

BERNARD CENDRON Managing Director of Les Must de Cartier in Tokyo, and one of Tokyo's best party hosts.

MARINA CHALIAPIN Daughter of the Russian bass singer, Fiodor Chaliapin, she is Rome editor of _Harpers & Queen_.

JEAN-PHILIPPE CHATRIER A French actor, he is also a journalist for _Elle_ in Paris.

TINA CHOW Japanese-American model and guru of fashion, married to restaurant owner Michael Chow.

GLYNN CHRISTIAN New Zealand-born food writer and TV broadcaster, now living in England. Runs The Cookery School in London.

CRAIG CLAIBORNE American food writer who studied at the Ecole Hôtelière in Switzerland. Food editor of _The New York Times_ for nearly 30 years, author of *The New York Times Cook Book*.

MICHAEL CLARK Avant-garde dancer and choreographer, one of the innovative leaders of modern dance in Britain.

JACKIE COLLINS British novelist and author of blockbuster novels including *Hollywood Husbands* and *Rock Star*. Married to Oscar Lerman, part-owner of the Tramp nightclubs in LA and London.

JOAN COLLINS British-born film and TV star. International traveller, author and socialite.

RICHARD COMPTON-MILLER British social observer, he is editor of the William Hickey column in the *Daily Express* and wrote the insiders' guide *Who's Really Who*.

JUDITH CONNOR Journalist based in Tokyo and co-author of the *Tokyo City Guide*.

JASPER CONRAN Top British fashion designer. Trained in New York, based in London, he has outlets all over the world.

JILLY COOPER Journalist and author of many books including the bestselling novels *Riders* and *Rivals*. Married to Leo Cooper.

LEO COOPER London-based publisher specializing in military books.

OLIVIER COQUELIN Paris-born hotelier and club owner. His latest venture is The Union Square Club in New York.

SHARI CREED Wife of Tom Creed, owner of Creeds department store in Canada. She is the publisher of Creeds fashion magazine.

QUENTIN CREWE British writer, restaurateur and traveller. His books include *Great Chefs of France*, *The Last Maharaja*, and *Touch the Happy Isles*.

QUENTIN CRISP British-born author of *The Naked Civil Servant*. Based in New York, the place that fulfills his only 'vocation' – people.

ALAN CROMPTON-BATT British food expert and writer, a former Egon Ronay inspector. He is now a leading food consultant.

JOYCE DAVIDSON Canadian TV personality living in New York. She hosts a daily news and current events programme, *The Joyce Davidson Show*, on CBC.

JEAN DEMACHY Director of *Elle* in Paris.

LORD DONOUGHUE British economist, historian, politician, lecturer and author.

DON DORWOOD San Francisco-based advertising executive of MoJo MDA.

ROBERT ELMS London-based style-writer. He produces a weekly column for *Girl About Town*, and contributes to the chatter on Radio 4's *Loose Ends*.

LEN EVANS British-born wine producer, writer and restaurateur based in Australia, where he co-owns Rothbury Estate winery in the Hunter Valley.

DOUGLAS FAIRBANKS JR Son of silent-film star Douglas Fairbanks, he has acted in over 75 films himself. Also a film, TV and theatre producer, writer and businessman.

LADY MARY FAIRFAX International socialite and charity fund-raiser living in Australia.

SERENA FASS British founder of Serenissima Travel. She now heads her own tour company called The Talent Garden.

CLARE FERGUSON New Zealand-born cookery writer and traveller, her books include *Creative Vegetarian Cookery*.

MARCHESA FIAMMA DI SAN GIULIANO FERRAGAMO Eldest child of the famous Italian shoe designer Salvatore Ferragamo, she now follows in her father's footsteps as Head of Shoe Production.

DUGGIE FIELDS Artist whose work has evoked controversy and cult admiration. He lives in London and is an avid nightclubber.

DIANA FISHER British-born social writer, TV and radio personality based in Sydney.

KEITH FLOYD Flamboyant food enthusiast whose BBC TV series and books include: *Floyd on Fish*, *Floyd on France* and *Floyd on Britain and Ireland*.

LILLIAN FRANK MBE Australian hairdresser and journalist born in Burma. She has a regular social column in the *Melbourne Herald*.

LYNNE FRANKS Chairman of her own highly successful PR company in London, specializing in fashion.

DIANE FREIS American fashion designer based in Hong Kong.

MARCHESA BONA FRESCOBALDI Italian aristocrat whose Tuscany estate yields some of Italy's best wines.

INÈS DE LA FRESSANGE French house model for Chanel, and *the* Coco girl.

ANIKO GAAL Fashion/PR Director for the top fashion store, Garfinckel's, in Washington.

JOHN GALLIANO Voted British Designer of the Year in 1988, he is one of Britain's most original and influential designers.

JOHN GOLD British co-founder and host of Tramp nightclub in London.

HARVEY GOLDSMITH Top pop promotor whose clients have included Bruce Springsteen, the Rolling Stones, Stevie Wonder and Madonna.

SONDRA GOTLIEB Wife of the Canadian ambassador to Washington, she writes a column for the *Washington Post*.

LORD GOWRIE Chairman of Sotheby's in London and former Minister for the Arts.

MICHAEL GRADE Former Director of Programmes at the BBC and now Chief Executive of Channel 4 TV.

GAEL GREENE Author and restaurant critic for the influential *New York Magazine*.

SOPHIE GRIGSON Cookery writer whose column appears in the *Evening Standard*, as well as major magazines. Her books include *Food For Friends*.

LOYD GROSSMAN American-born restaurant critic, design writer and TV game-show personality.

MICHEL GUÉRARD Top French chef and restaurateur. He created cuisine minceur at Les Prés et les Sources spa, Eugénie-les-Bains, home also to his world-famous restaurant.

HELEN GURLEY BROWN Editorial Director of *Cosmopolitan*, she has guided its expansion from one edition in America to 13 worldwide.

KATHARINE HAMNETT Trendsetting British fashion designer. She studied at St Martin's School of Art in London and founded her own company in 1979.

ROBIN HANBURY-TENISON Traveller and writer, a former vice-president and gold medallist of the Royal Geographic Society, and president of Survival International. His books include *A Ride Along the Great Wall*, *Worlds Apart* and *A Question of Survival*.

ANTHONY HANSON Wine expert and a director of Haynes Hanson & Clark wine merchants.

MARCELLA HAZAN Italian food expert. Based in Venice, she has a cookery school in Bologna and a home in New York. Her books include *The Classic Italian Cookbook* and *Marcella's Kitchen*.

MARIE HELVIN Top London-based model who grew up in Hawaii. She writes on fashion and beauty and co-hosted *Frocks on the Box* for ITV.

MARGAUX HEMINGWAY Actress and former model turned documentary film-maker. She is the granddaughter of the legendary Ernest.

ANOUSKA HEMPEL Born in Australia, of Russian-German descent, she owns the glamorous Blakes Hotel in London and is also a fashion and interior designer with her own showroom in Chelsea.

BILL HERSEY British socialite living in Tokyo, where he is advisor to some 30 nightclubs. He writes a social column for *The Tokyo Weekender*.

DON HEWITSON New Zealand-born wine expert and writer who owns several top London wine bars.

DAVID HICKS Top English interior designer, whose international assignments have included Gatcombe Park, the Princess Royal's house in Gloucestershire.

TERRY HOLMES Vice-president and Managing Director of Cunard Hotels, which includes his base, The Ritz in London.

KEN HOM Acclaimed American cookery expert. With bases in California and Hong Kong, he gives cookery demonstrations, and is a restaurant and food consultant. He wrote the bestselling *Ken Hom's Chinese Cookery* and *Ken Hom's East Meets West Cuisine*, and presented a cookery series on BBC TV.

SIMON HOPKINSON Head chef at Bibendum, Sir Terence Conran's restaurant in the Michelin building in London.

THOMAS HOVING Editorial Director of the American glossy magazine *Connoisseur*.

BARRY HUMPHRIES Australian comedian whose outrageous alter egos, Sir Les Patterson and Dame Edna Everage, entertain TV and theatre audiences around the world.

CAROLINE HUNT Based in Texas, she is the head of the Rosewood Corporation which runs some of the most exclusive American hotels.

MADHUR JAFFREY Actress and writer. Her latest book is *Food for Family and Friends*.

TAMA JANOWITZ New York-based author of the bestseller *Slaves of New York*.

JEAN-MICHEL JAUDEL International businessman based in Paris. He is a member of all the best clubs and has a fine contemporary art collection.

HUGH JOHNSON International wine expert and author of the definitive *Wine*, *World Atlas of Wine*, and the annual *Pocket Wine Guide*.

STEPHEN JONES British milliner of international standing. He has created collections for designers Enrico Coveri, Claude Montana and Myrène de Prémonville.

BARBARA KAFKA American food expert and author. President of her own New York-based food consultancy.

KAREN KAIN Prima Ballerina of the National Ballet Company of Canada.

JENNY KEE Australian fashion designer who specializes in colourful fabrics and knitwear.

IMRAN KHAN Record-breaking cricketer and former captain of the Pakistan team.

ANGELA KENNEDY Fashion editor for *Good Housekeeping* magazine in London.

BETTY KENWARD Social editor of *Harpers & Queen*. At 82, she still attends every social event in Jennifer's Diary, which she has written since 1945.

LARRY KING Radio and TV chat show host of *The Larry King Show* in America.

MILES KINGTON British humorist whose column appears in *The Independent*. Author of many books, including *Let's Parlez Franglais*.

NICO LADENIS Half-Greek, Tanzanian-born chef-owner of top restaurant Simply Nico in London.

MAX LAKE Australian writer, keen cook and owner of Lakes Folly winery in the Hunter Valley.

ELEANOR LAMBERT Head of her own top fashion PR company based in New York, she initiated the Best Dressed Lists.

ELISABETH LAMBERT ORTIZ London-born food writer of award-winning cookery books such as *The Book of Latin American Cooking* and *Taste of Excellence*. She contributes regularly to *Gourmet*.

KEN LANE American costume jewellery designer. He has shops throughout America, and in London and Paris.

RENÉ LECLER Belgian-born travel writer and travel consultant for *Harpers & Queen*. His books include the discerning traveller's bible *The 300 Best Hotels in The World* and *The World Shopping Guide*.

PRUE LEITH London-based food expert and author. She runs the prestigious Leith's School of Food and Wine, Leith's Restaurant and Leith's Good Food caterers. Cookery editor of *The Guardian*.

ANNE LEWIN Top Australian lingerie designer.

DAVID LITCHFIELD Writer and publisher of *The Ritz Newspaper*.

ALASTAIR LITTLE Top British chef whose namesake restaurant is among the most fashionable in London.

ANDREW LLOYD WEBBER Acclaimed composer of such box-office blockbusters as *Evita, Cats, Starlight Express* and *The Phantom of the Opera*.

JULIAN LLOYD WEBBER Accomplished cellist who has played with all the major British orchestras, as well as touring worldwide.

SAUL LOCKHART An American editor and writer who has lived in Hong Kong for 20 years. His 9 books include the *Insight Guide to Hong Kong* and *A Diver's Guide to Asian Waters*.

SIMON LOFTUS Director of top wine merchants, Adnams of Southwold, and author of their wine list.

EDWARD LUCIE-SMITH London-based art expert and critic.

JOANNA LUMLEY Actress and former model, she is currently working on an autobiography.

LORD McALPINE OF WEST GREEN Conservative party treasurer in Britain and a director of Sir Robert McAlpine construction. He owns an antiquities business in London and a wildlife park in Australia.

SEAN MACAULAY British journalist; film editor of *i*D magazine and avid club-goer.

MARK McCORMACK Chairman of International Management Group, the world's biggest sports management and sponsorship group.

LADY MACDONALD OF MACDONALD Author of many cookery and entertaining books, including *The Harrods Book of Entertaining*. She and her husband run the highly acclaimed Kinloch Lodge Hotel in Scotland.

SKYE MACLEOD National PR Manager for the top Australian department store, David Jones.

STEVEN HENRY MADOFF Executive editor of *Art News* in New York.

DEREK MALCOLM Film critic for *The Guardian* and *Cosmopolitan*.

MARIUCCIA MANDELLI Italian head of design at Krizia in Milan. A well-known social figure.

STANLEY MARCUS American chairman emeritus of top Dallas store Neiman-Marcus. He is also a lecturer and marketing consultant.

GEORGE MELLY Professional blues singer and modern art enthusiast, based in London. He presented the arts show *Gallery* on Channel 4.

CLIFF MICHELMORE Widely travelled British TV and radio broadcaster and producer.

ISSEY MIYAKE Top Japanese fashion designer known for his innovative use of synthetic fabrics.

DAVID MLINARIC British interior designer and a consultant to the National Trust.

ROBERT MONDAVI Internationally renowned California wine-maker and expert.

LORD MONTAGU OF BEAULIEU Chairman of the Historic Buildings & Monuments Commission for England. He created the National Motor Museum at Beaulieu.

DUDLEY MOORE British actor, comedian, pianist and restaurateur. Based in California, he is now making a sequel to his movie hit, *Arthur*.

HANAE MORI Japanese fashion and theatrical costume designer, with shops in Tokyo, Paris and New York.

ANTON MOSIMANN Swiss-born chef-owner of Mosimann's in London. He regularly travels the world giving lectures.

STIRLING MOSS OBE Former British motor racing champion. A car and gadget fanatic, he is motoring editor of *Harpers & Queen*.

ANNE-ELISABETH MOUTET Paris correspondent for British *Elle* and *The Sunday Telegraph*, she lives in Paris.

JEAN MUIR CBE Top British fashion designer. She started her career with Jaeger in 1956 and is now one of the leading names in fashion.

MICHAEL MUSTO Nightlife columnist for *The Village Voice* in New York.

ERIC NEWBY Formerly in the fashion business, now better-known as a travel writer. His highly acclaimed books include *A Short Walk in the Hindu Kush, Slowly Down the Ganges* and *Round Ireland In Low Gear*.

ROBERT NOAH American food writer living in Paris. He runs Paris en Cuisine, a company specializing in gastronomic tours of France.

PATRICK O'CONNOR Editor of *Opera* magazine in New York.

BRUCE OLDFIELD Top British fashion designer whose clients include the Princess of Wales, Charlotte Rampling and Joan Collins. He designed for Dior and Saint Laurent before opening his own shop in London.

BENNY ONG Chinese fashion designer brought up in Singapore. He now lives in London, running his own fashion business.

COMTESSE DE PARIS Born Princesse Isabelle d'Orléans-Bragance. She edited the book *Haut de Gamme*.

SIR PETER PARKER British businessman, best known for his 8 years as chairman of British Rail. He is now chairman of the Rockware Group.

MICHAEL PARKINSON British-born broadcaster, he presented his own BBC chat show *Parkinson* for 11 years, and has worked on radio and TV in Australia.

ELISE PASCOE Australian cookery writer and consultant. A regular TV and radio broadcaster, she also lectures and writes a weekly cookery column for *The Sydney Morning Herald*.

ANNE-MARIE PERIER Daughter of actor François Perier, she is the editor of *Elle* in Paris.

STEVE PODBORSKI A World Cup downhill ski champion. He is now a TV celebrity and spokesman for many companies in Canada.

BOB PAYTON American owner of several restaurants in London, including The Chicago Pizza Pie

Factory. He recently opened the country-house hotel Stapleford Park in Leicestershire.

WOLFGANG PUCK Innovative Californian chef-owner of Los Angeles restaurants Chinois on Main and Spago.

CHARLOTTE RAMPLING British actress and former model, she lives in Paris with her children and musician husband Jean-Michel Jarre.

ROBERT RAMSAY President of Remarkable Communications, a public relations consultancy in Canada. He is also on the board for the Festival of Festivals in Toronto.

BILL RANKEN Australian PR executive, a well-known social figure and property owner.

FREDERIC RAPHAEL British novelist and writer of screenplays, biographies and reviews. Novels include *The Glittering Prizes* and *After the War*, both adapted for TV. He lives in England and the Dordogne in France.

MICHAEL RATCLIFFE Theatre critic for *The Observer*.

JANE ROARTY Australian fashion editor based in Sydney.

GEOFFREY ROBERTS Pioneer of California wines in Britain, he runs Les Amis du Vin in London.

EGON RONAY Hungarian-born restaurant critic and founder of the Egon Ronay Hotel and Restaurant guides, since taken over by the Automobile Association.

CLAUDIA ROSSI Travel consultant specializing in tours outside Australia. She is a director of Mary Rossi Travel in Sydney.

DANNI ROSSI Daughter of Mary Rossi, she works in the family travel business in Sydney.

VISCOUNTESS ROTHERMERE Married to one of the world's wealthiest men, Lady 'Bubbles' Rothermere is considered to be one of the most dynamic hostesses and party-goers on the social scene.

STEVE RUBELL Entrepreneurial founder of such innovative New York nightclubs as Studio 54, Palladium and Billy Rose's Diamond

Horseshoe. He also runs Morgans hotel.

HILARY RUBINSTEIN Literary agent and editor of *The Good Hotel Guide*.

ROBERT SANGSTER British racehorse owner and breeder. Son of pools founder Vernon Sangster and director of the family business, he lives on the Isle of Man.

VIDAL SASSOON British-born founder of the worldwide hairdressing empire, he is now based in California.

SEBASTIAN SCOTT Presenter on Channel 4's *Network 7*, and LWT's *The Six o'Clock Show*. He is also a keen clubber.

LEO SCHOFIELD Australian PR and advertising expert, food and travel writer. He edits *The Sydney Morning Herald Good Food Guide*.

JANE SEYMOUR British actress, partly based in Los Angeles, known for her many leading roles (such as Maria Callas) in TV blockbusters.

NED SHERRIN Film, theatre and TV producer, director and writer. Currently host of BBC Radio 4's hit *Loose Ends*.

DAVID SHILLING British hat designer, whose annual creations for his mother, Gertrude, have been stunning Ascot-goers for years. He also designs clothes, fabric and china.

SIR CLIVE SINCLAIR Inventor and pioneer of the personal computer. Based in London and Cambridge.

DREW SMITH British food writer, editor of *The Good Food Guide* and co-editor of *The Good Food Directory*.

LIZ SMITH Fashion editor of *The Times* in London.

YAN-KIT SO London-based Chinese cookery expert from Hong Kong. Among her bestselling books are the award-winning *Yan-Kit's Classic Chinese Cook Book* and *Wok Cookbook*.

STEVEN SPURRIER British wine expert. Founder of L'Académie du Vin, Paris's first wine school, his books include *Wine Course* and *French Country Wines*.

SUSIE STENMARK Former top Australian model who is now a Channel 7 presenter and Bondi restaurateur.

SERENA SUTCLIFFE MW London-based wine expert and writer for *Decanter* and *Lloyd's Log*. Her books include *The Wine Drinker's Handbook*, *The Pocket Guide to the Wines of Burgundy* and *A Celebration of Champagne*.

TAKI THEODORACOPULOS Greek journalist known for his acerbic column, High Life, in *The Spectator*. Based in London he travels frequently around Europe and to New York, where he writes for *Esquire*.

DAN TOPOLSKI British journalist and former Olympic rower. Son of Polish artist Feliks Topolski, he has travelled extensively in South America and Africa and has written books on his expeditions.

JEREMIAH TOWER Top American chef, a pioneer of new Californian cuisine. Brought up in Europe, he owns the acclaimed restaurant Stars in San Francisco.

SHIZUO TSUJI Head of the prestigious cookery school Ecole Technique Hôtelière Tsuji in Osaka, Japan.

MURRAY TYRELL Australian wine expert who owns a top winery in the Hunter Valley.

PETER USTINOV Multi-talented international actor, author, traveller, director and producer, star of countless films and plays. A gifted linguist he lives in Switzerland and Paris.

GIANNI VERSACE Milan-based top Italian fashion designer renowned for developing new fabrics and for his designs in leather.

ED VICTOR American literary agent who divides his year between London and New York.

AUBERON WAUGH British author, wine expert and editor of the *Literary Review*. Son of Evelyn Waugh and former diary writer for *Private Eye*.

MARCO PIERRE WHITE Acclaimed young chef-owner of Harvey's in London.

DORIAN WILD English-born gossip columnist for the Sydney *Sun-Herald* and for the Channel 9 *Today* programme. A former political journalist in Canberra, he is well-known on the social scene.

LESLEY WILD Australian publisher of *Vogue* magazine, based in Sydney.

ANNE WILLAN British food expert, writer and President of Ecole de Cuisine La Varenne in Washington.

PAULA WOLFERT New York food trends observer and cookery writer. She contributes to the leading food magazines, including *Connoisseur* and *Food & Wine*. Books include *The Cooking of South-West France*.

CAROL WRIGHT British travel and cookery writer. She is travel editor for *House & Garden*.

LYNN WYATT Dynamic Texan socialite and patron of the arts, she is a key figure on the international social and charity circuit.

BEVERLEY ZBITNOFF Canadian socialite and fashion expert.

ACKNOWLEDGEMENTS

Lord Lichfield, Sue Carpenter and the publishers would especially like to thank the following people for their invaluable help in compiling this book:

Akani, Val Archer, Patricia Catel, Mary Clarke, Nicholas J Cochrane, Renata Discacciati, Helen Dore, Jane Fann, William Feaver, Laurence Floyd, Chris Freyvogel, Anna Gendel, Fred Gill, Kathie Gill, Richard Griffiths, Angela Kennedy, Kris Lee Oakes III, Robert Levey, Nellie Lide, Ada Lorini, Felicity Somers Eve, Peter McGarrick, Pat Mills, Rodney Milnes, Lynne Morton, Harry Nicoll, Harry O'Neill, Karen Penlington, Alistair Scott, Giles Shepard, Yvonne de Valera.

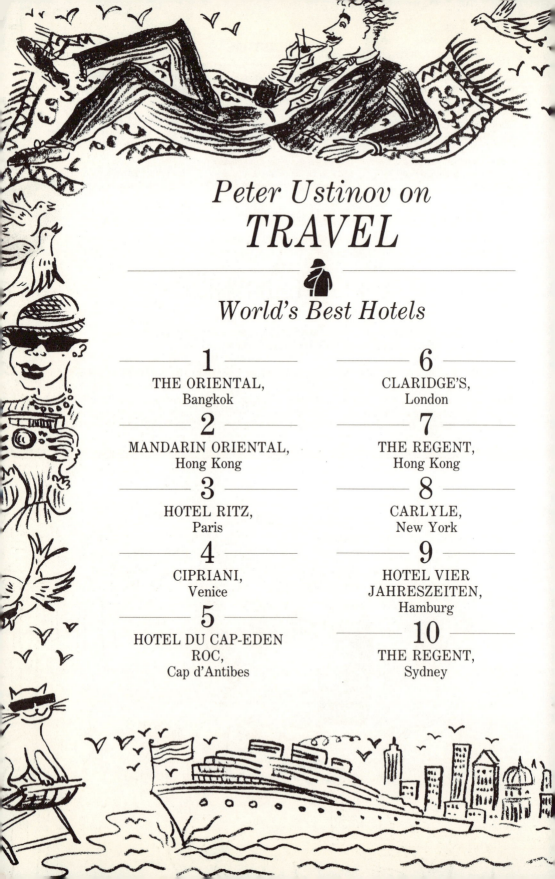

Peter Ustinov on
TRANSLATED
TRAVEL

World's Best Hotels

1
THE ORIENTAL,
Bangkok

2
MANDARIN ORIENTAL,
Hong Kong

3
HOTEL RITZ,
Paris

4
CIPRIANI,
Venice

5
HOTEL DU CAP-EDEN
ROC,
Cap d'Antibes

6
CLARIDGE'S,
London

7
THE REGENT,
Hong Kong

8
CARLYLE,
New York

9
HOTEL VIER
JAHRESZEITEN,
Hamburg

10
THE REGENT,
Sydney

E xperiencing the 'best' in travel does not simply entail staying in the best hotel. Enormous expectations often lead to disappointment, while the sudden discovery of some hidden oasis invites one to intemperate enthusiasm. In this inconsistency lies half the fascination of travel.

A comfortable flight in an Aeroflot airbus is a pleasant surprise, while Club Class in a full airliner can be a nightmare for one of even moderate corpulence whose duty-free purchases keep rolling away from his restraining foot.

The passenger in the centre seat probably has the worst time of it, since he feels impaled like a butterfly in a wall display. But the fellow near the window has to incline his head to follow the contours of the aircraft. And if the person on the aisle is anything like me, there is no room for both him and his pockets, which have to hang over the armrests. On two occasions, in lifting the pockets inboard to accommodate a passing trolley, my change has rolled over the floor, and I ended the flights in humiliation, picking up coins from under people's feet.

As airports continue to expand, there is further and further to push a trolley, with frequent changes of level, entailing the abandonment of one and the furtive search for another. In this age of high technology, with every hinge on a motor-car tested in a wind-tunnel, it is remarkable that all trolleys are whimsically different, either being impossible to steer, as at Heathrow, or else difficult to dislodge from its fellow trolleys, as in Geneva and Berlin, or else virtually non-existent, as in New York, Moscow and Munich.

However, despite such inconveniences, the joy of safe arrival remains constant, as do innumerable considerations which make travel a pleasure ... the iced tea on Thai Airways, the sheer quality of Swissair, the juice of blood oranges at Düsseldorf's Breidenbacher Hof, breakfast at Hamburg's Vier Jahreszeiten, the wonderfully thoughtful buffet in the foyer of the Four Seasons in Toronto for those leaving before crack of dawn, lunch on the roof of the Hotel Eden in Rome, and practically everything at The Oriental in Bangkok.

This chapter offers a taste of the delights experienced by other travellers. Use it as a point of departure for gathering your own collection of 'bests'.

America

♟ -America's Best- ♟

HOTELS

1 **CARLYLE,** New York
2 **THE PIERRE,** New York
3 **HOTEL BEL-AIR,** Los Angeles
4 **STANFORD COURT,** San Francisco
5 **WILLARD INTER-CONTINENTAL,** Washington, DC
6 **BEVERLY HILLS HOTEL,** Los Angeles
7 **MANSION ON TURTLE CREEK,** Dallas
8 **BEVERLY WILSHIRE,** Los Angeles
9 **THE REMINGTON,** Houston
10 **HUNTINGTON HOTEL,** San Francisco

ASPEN

One of the top ski resorts: an old mining town with an established feel, though any hint of littl' ol 19th-centuryville is countered by lines of private Learjets at the local airport. The most social resort in the USA – spot Jack Nicholson, powder skier John Denver, Don Johnson, Catherine Oxenberg, George Hamilton, Goldie Hawn, Robert Wagner, Christie Brinkley and Billy

Joel. *"Probably the most complete skiers' resort"* – **Mark McCormack.**

BOSTON

THE CHARLES HOTEL, 1 Bennett St, Cambridge, MA 02138 ☎ (617) 864 1200
A privately owned suave hotel in the trendy $90 million Charles Square development of shops and restaurants (part of the active Harvard Square with its jazz and folk clubs). Rooms are a mixture of neo-Folk Art (patchwork quilts, pine-frame four-posters) and functional. Le Pli health spa is universally held in high esteem. That, the Courtyard Café and the excellent Rarities restaurant impressed **Glynn Christian.**

♟ **RITZ-CARLTON,** 15 Arlington St, MA 02117 ☎ (617) 536 5700
Proud and dignified, the uncontested best in Boston. *"Only the Ritz-Carlton and nothing but – it's the best-run hotel in the world!"* – **Eleanor Lambert.** *"An old hotel with staff who have a sense of its tradition – and it shows"* – **Hilary Rubinstein. Bill Blass** and **Stanley Marcus** concur. Every nicety, including ice skates to guests who wish to glide across Swan Lake in the adjoining public gardens.

CHICAGO

MAYFAIR REGENT, 181 E Lake Shore Drive, IL 60611 ☎ (312) 787 8500
At the best address in town, with scintillating lake views and a penthouse restaurant for elevated locals. *"An example of*

the American hotel at its best" – **Lord Lichfield.**

RITZ-CARLTON, 160 E Pearson St at Water Tower Place, IL 60611 ☎ (312) 266 1000
A Four Seasons hotel, occupying floors 10 to 31 of the incredible 74-storey Water Tower Place complex of shops, restaurants and cinemas. You can even take the pampered pet, who can board in suitable luxury in their kennel. Votes from **Egon Ronay** and **Mark McCormack.**

DALLAS

♟ **MANSION ON TURTLE CREEK,** 2821 Turtle Creek Blvd, TX 75219 ☎ (214) 559 2100
The blueprint of Caroline Hunt's Rosewood Hotels. A cleverly converted Twenties mansion that has an established country-house ambience, with log fires, leaded windows and fresh flowers. *"Like the Bel-Air, I love the feel, the way it's run and organized"* – **Anton Mosimann.** The superb Terrace Dining Room plays host to dozens of Dallas do's.

DENVER

BROWN PALACE HOTEL, 321 17th St, CO 80202 ☎ (303) 297 3111
A staggering Victorian building. Each room is a different size and shape. *"It looks like the Flatiron Building in New York, and has wrought-iron balconies all round the lobby. It has a genuine touch of class. The food is terrific but gargantuan.*

❝ *The north shore of Maui has the best waves in the world for real high-performance windsurfing. There are 3 beaches – Kahana, Sprecklesville and Hookipa. The first is where you learn, the second is where you practise and the third is where you die!* **❞**

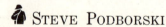 STEVE PODBORSKI

“ *The best thing that's ever happened to me is coming to America. My whole life changed, because my only pastime is people, and in America everyone talks to you everywhere you go* **”**

QUENTIN CRISP

We got there, dehydrated and exhausted, and we just said 'give us anything you recommend' and they came back with these half-cows on plates. I felt so ashamed we could only eat the corner" – **Leo Cooper.**

HAWAII

COCO PALMS RESORT HOTEL, PO Box 631, Lihue, Kauai, HI 96766
☎ (808) 822 4921
A Polynesian-style hotel where they shot the Elvis movie *Blue Hawaii*. "The most over-the-top hotel in the world! I stayed in the Top of the Palms suite, a room the size of a tennis court with Polynesian artefacts all

over it and a gold mosaic bathroom overlooking the lagoon. It was really wonderful" – **Stephen Jones.** A variety of suites and cottages, some with private garden. Seafood restaurant on the beach plus two others for Hawaiian, American and Chinese cuisine.

COLONY SURF HOTEL, 2895 Kalakaua Ave, Honolulu, HI 96815 ☎ (808) 923 5751
Small luxury hotel on the beach at the foot of Diamond Head, a dormant volcano. Their restaurant, Michel's, has been voted the most romantic in America; tuck into French/continental cuisine (with local touches) while gazing out to sea. "*Definitely one of the best hotels*" – **Lord Lichfield.**

HALEKULANI, 2199 Kalia Rd, Honolulu, HI 96815
☎ (808) 923 2311
The biggest and best hotel in Hawaii, on Waikiki Beach. Something for everyone: while shopoholics suss out the local boutiques, biz-kids can keep on plugging into the world markets (3 'phones per room). A favourite of **Viscountess Rothermere.**

HOTEL HANA-MAUI, Maui, HI 96713 ☎ (808) 248 8211
A Rosewood resort hotel with 66 bungalows sprinkled about in 4,500 acres of ranch land. Spectacular views over gardens and sea; outdoor activities and cook-outs on the beach (one of the best in the Pacific).

HOUSTON

THE REMINGTON ON POST OAK PARK, 1919 Briar Oaks Lane, TX 77027
☎ (713) 840 7600
"Fabulous – everybody flips out when they stay. Beautifully decorated, not overdone, in very good taste" – **Lynn Wyatt.** All the Rosewood thoughtful touches plus' souped-up business facilities.

LOS ANGELES

BEVERLY HILLS HOTEL, 9641 W Sunset Blvd, CA 90210
☎ (213) 276 2251
A magnificent pink stucco Spanish villa, surrounded by lawns and palm trees, dotted with cottages. The old-Hollywood hang-out, as much a landmark as the sign in the hills, where le movie monde sip cocktails from the casting couches of the Polo Lounge. *"Despite rumours of change and decline, the 'Pink Palace' is still the most amusing and typically LA hotel. Ask for*

BOUTIQUE HOTELS

America has perfected the boutique hotel, the beautiful bijou sanctum where you shall want for nothing. Properties owned by **Rosewood Hotels**, 300 Crescent Court, Suite 1000, Dallas, TX 74201 ☎ (214) 871 5400 or in the group **Small Luxury Hotels**, 339 South Robertson Blvd, Suite 103, Beverly Hills, CA 90211 ☎ (213) 659 5050 epitomize the concept. They're styled on European hotels and, of course, you'll find them elsewhere: in Sydney, the new Regent on Campbells Cove; in Japan, the Seiyo. The boutique hotel is the flip side of the soaring triple-atrium 600-room-plus anonymous international tower-block chain hotel that we all marvelled at in the 1960s and 1970s. How to recognize one? If the brochure waxes lyrical about hand-printed Fortuny fabric, baths of Roman travertine, silver by Tiffany, French-milled soaps, you're on the scent. Boutique hotels are small (200 rooms *max*, preferably under 100); often privately owned; low-rise, a building with character if not a historic conversion; fine interior design; rooms of suite proportions, each individually decorated, with private bathroom, scented goodies, etc; highly personalized service (no production-line check-in; knowing your name, likes and dislikes; own butler/valet and maid); equal attention to men and women; excellent restaurant(s), health club and communication facilities.

bungalow 11 or 12" – **Jeremiah Tower.** *"One of the greats. An institution. It's one of the treats in life to sit in the lobby and watch the world go by"* – **Michael Grade. Geoffrey Roberts, Mark McCormack** and **Viscountess Rothermere** check in for the night.

BEVERLY WILSHIRE, 9500 Wilshire Blvd, Beverly Hills, CA 90212 ☎ (213) 275 4282
Reopened earlier this year by Regent International. For **Jeremiah Tower** it's *"the one to watch with the new management"*. The old Wilshire wing has been restored to its 1930s true Hollywood elegance, while the new Beverly wing, a layer-cake of French, Mexican, Spanish and Californian floors, has had a lavish refit. The most opulent suite is the two-storey Dior, where Prince Charles has stayed. The question is who *hasn't* passed through the hotel's Louis XV gates? Here's just a few who *have*: Rudolph Nureyev, Alain Delon, Warren Beatty, the King of Tonga (who ordered McDonald's cheeseburgers), Emperor Hirohito (who ordered peeled grapes), **Lord Montagu of Beaulieu** and **Taki.**

CHATEAU MARMONT, 8221 Sunset Blvd, Hollywood, CA 90046 ☎ (213)3 656 1010
Another Hollywood landmark, a fantasy 1920s Gothic château, home from home for those in showbiz – Robert de Niro and Diane Keaton follow the train of movie stars that included

Garbo, Monroe and Valentino. 62 suites and bungalows, with kitchens and often private terraces. Good for long stays. A fine wine cellar and room-service menus, but no bar or restaurant.

L'ERMITAGE, 9291 Burton Way, Beverly Hills, CA 90210 ☎ (213) 278 3344
One of America's first boutique hotels. Suites boast blazing fires at the flick of a switch, original works of art, custom-milled soap and cologne. Roof garden with heated pool. A vote from **Eleanor Lambert.**

HOTEL BEL-AIR, 701 Stone Canyon Rd, Bel Air, CA 90077 ☎ (213) 472 1211
A heavenly pink Californian mission and private bungalows, all with terracotta tiled roofs. Gardens and courtyards full of foliage, flowers, fountains and a pond where the famous Bel-Air swans hang out. A Rosewood hotel, and a subtler sanctum than its Hills neighbours, though there's no stinting on necessities like private outdoor whirlpool baths. Piano Bar and fine Californian cuisine. Dolly Parton and Robert Wagner are frequent visitors. *"I love it for its beauty and luxury, in an idyllic and peaceful setting away from the smog"* – **Elise Pascoe.** *"It serves the most elegant breakfast"* – **Wolfgang Puck.** *"A wonderful place. I love the feel, the way it's run – it's very beautiful"* – **Anton Mosimann.** *"Spectacular setting"* – **Jeremiah Tower.** **Helen Gurley Brown, Lord**

Montagu of Beaulieu, Viscountess Rothermere and Stanley Marcus rate it most highly.

ST JAMES'S CLUB, 8358 Sunset Blvd, W Hollywood, CA 90069 ☎ (213) 650 4738
Out-boutiquing the boutiquiest of hotels, this is the latest off-shoot of the London original. Housed in the famous Art Deco Sunset Towers, with 2 fashionable restaurants (the Terrace Garden Room and the Patio) *and* heli and jet charter. Both **Jeremiah Tower** and **Jackie Collins** have been watching with interest since it's opening earlier this year.

LAS VEGAS

CAESAR'S PALACE, 3570 Las Vegas Blvd, NV 89109 ☎ (702) 734 7110
"The most fun hotel in Las Vegas – wonderfully over the top, I mean everyone dresses in Roman togas ... There are Roman statues everywhere, and the biggest pool you have ever seen. It's real Americana" – **Jackie Collins.**

NAPA VALLEY

MEADOWOOD RESORT & COUNTRY CLUB, 900 Meadowood Lane, St Helena, CA 94574 ☎ (707) 963 3646
The best country resort in the Napa. Croquet lawns, golf, tennis, a swimming pool, two restaurants – and all that luverly vino to taste. **Elise Pascoe**'s favourite *"for rest and recreation"*.

NEW ORLEANS

PONTCHARTRAIN, 2031 St Charles Ave, LA 70140 ☎ (504) 524 0581
A smallish Shangri-La for Mardi Gras. *"Old-fashioned, charming and central"* – **Lord Lichfield.**

TIPS ON TIPPING

"In Japan, the practice of tipping is extremely bad manners. In Australia, except in the big international hotels where the practice is incurable, they very courteously return your tips. You don't tip, as far as I can see, in Chinese and Russian hotels. Europe varies in its tipping practices. In India you have to have your hand constantly in your pocket. In America the nudging goes on continuously and is exceedingly tiresome. We stayed at some modest little inn and there was a bunch of flowers on the mantelpiece and a note saying 'Your cleaners Maggie and Carol thank you', with an empty envelope" – **Hilary Rubinstein.**

WINDSOR COURT HOTEL,
300 Gravier St, LA 70140
☎ **(504) 523 6000**
Owned by Anglophile Jimmy
Coleman, it's *"easily the best*
hotel in town, styled on an
English country house.
Startling art collection – a
Gainsborough, a Reynolds" –
Lord Lichfield.

NEW YORK

ALGONQUIN, 59 W 44th St,
NY 10036 ☎ **(212) 840 6800**
The old characterful hotel is
now under new ownership,
Caesar Park Hotels
International of Japan. It's had
some restoration but retains its
old-fashioned air. Hotel of the
literati, its restaurant is where
the legendary wits of the
Round Table (Dorothy Parker
et al) would sharpen their
tongues. *"I mostly stay here –*
it's very English, very old-
fashioned and very pleasant" –
Auberon Waugh. Quentin
Crewe is another fan of old.

CARLYLE, 36 E 76th St, NY
10021 ☎ **(212) 744 1600**
The best in New York, with
intelligent management
(headed by Frank Bowling,
ex-Ritz Carlton, who's *"very,*

Sharp's attention to detail,
caring year after year after
year" – **Anouska Hempel. Bill**
Blass and **Simon Hopkinson**
heartily agree.

ELYSEE, 60 E 54th St, NY
10022 ☎ **(212) 753 1066**
Small, eccentric, with named
not numbered rooms, each one
recently redecorated in a
different style. *"Very nice*
indeed. The owner is a
character and the hotel's a
character. It's where I send
personal friends who can't
afford the Carlyle; I know
they'll be looked after" – **Frank**
Bowling.

HELMSLEY PALACE, 455
Madison Ave, NY 10022
☎ **(212) 888 7000**
Owned by Leona Helmsley, a
soaring tower block of
bedrooms atop the 19th-
century Villard Mansion that
houses the lobby and dining
rooms. *"Exactly what a lot of*
people think a New York hotel
should be. It's glitzy, high-
profile and Mrs Helmsley runs
a very tight ship" – **Frank**
Bowling. *"It's like staying in a*
glorious private apartment (I
usually stay on the 48th floor),
with a fantastic view of the

and low-key, one of the top 5 in
New York" – **Frank Bowling.**

MAYFAIR REGENT, 610
Park Ave, NY 10021
☎ **(212) 288 0800**
Known to its intimates as
Dario's (Dario Mariotti is
general manager), it can't go
wrong as long as it houses
Sirio's (Le Cirque – see Food &
Drink). It's good to get
acquainted with influential
concierge Bruno Brunelli too.
Handsome and spacious, with a
rich terracotta-hued lobby, 199
rooms and almost as many
umbrellas for those who come
unprepared for showers.

MORGANS, 237 Madison Ave,
NY 10006 ☎ **(212) 686 0300**
Small, chic, clannish and club-
like, *"from a residential dump,*
Steve Rubell made it into a
very with-it hotel. As Blakes is
to London, Morgan's is to New
York" – **Frank Bowling.**
Parisian style-guru Andrée
Putman designed it in the high-
tech black-grey-white mould.
At Morgans the furniture
wears the trousers (chairs in
grey flannels, bedclothes in
Brooks Bros shirting) while
staff are decked out in Calvin
Klein and Giorgio Armani –
who stays there, incidentally,

> *66* *New York hotels? I have stayed in the lot. The food has no taste*
> *in any of them – because it is over-frozen. At one, the food was so bad*
> *we'd send out to the Italian restaurant round the corner. In a lot of*
> *American hotels they do not bother to welcome you either* *99*
>
> BARBARA CARTLAND

very good news, particularly if
you know him, he'll sort things
out for you" – **Andrew Lloyd**
Webber), loyal staff, loyal
guests. Distinguished and
classy, it's gone through a
multi-million-dollar renovation
by top designer Mark
Hampton. *"Easily the best*
hotel in New York, they haven't
lost any of their staff over the
years and they tend to know
you. The food has improved a
heck of a lot" – **ALW.** *"The*
absolute best" – **Larry King.**
"The staff are sensational, old-
fashioned, full of chat and
charm. It's the owner Peter

city. The décor is beautiful and
they don't stint on space" –
Jackie Collins.

THE LOWELL, 28 E 63rd St,
NY 10021 ☎ **(212) 838 1400**
The Art Deco landmark,
formerly a residential hotel,
has had a $25 million remodel
and is now open to all. The new
look means French and
Oriental antiques, working
fireplaces (logs $3.50 each),
Italian marble baths, kitchens
with every suite, and the
pretty Pembroke Room for
daytime nibbles. *"Very*
charming, small [60 rooms]

along with a million other
fashion-orientated people. Take
Bonnie Brooks-Young:
"Absolutely my favourite in the
world. Small, unique,
modern." **Ken Lane,** Joseph,
Azzedine Alaïa, Rod Stewart,
Brooke Shields, Bette Midler,
Mick Jagger, Cher and Farrah
Fawcett join the clan.

THE PIERRE, 5th Ave at
61st St, NY 10021
☎ **(212) 838 8000**
Peaceful and discreet, with
ultra-attentive service, it
attracts New York glamorati.

WHAT MAKES A GOOD HOTEL?

"Ambience is very important, so is food as it's certainly part of the hotel. Service – good staff – is always very important" – **Caroline Hunt.** *"Warmth, good service, and staff who stay around for a long time. The owner of the Carlyle, Peter Sharp, says it's 'Cleanliness, cleanliness and cleanliness!', but I think warmth has a great deal to do with it"* – **Frank Bowling.** *"To be great, a place needs to be terribly dependable, not wonderful one year and then sort of all right the next. It has to have that mysterious allure that creates a gathering of powerful people. Without that it will develop no myth"* – **Barbara Kafka.** *"For me it's guests who make a place – a restaurant, a hotel, a bar. You have to attract the right people because it is they who give it the atmosphere"* – **Anton Mosimann.** *"The places I like are smallish, where you sense the personal involvement of someone who cares – who has, like a monk, taken a vow, not of chastity but of hospitality. In charging VAT they are giving Value Added, not just to the bill of fare, but in a different way which makes your stay memorable"* – **Hilary Rubinstein.**

Best view over Central Park is from the elegant Presidential Suite. The Café Pierre, designed by Valerian Rybar, is a local landmark; the neo-Baroque Rotunda, with its *trompe l'oeil* sky and classical folly, is good for light lunches and tea. *"I love it and always stay here. It's still unsurpassed because the service is almost on an Eastern level"* – **Egon Ronay.** Bill Blass, **Stanley Marcus** (his best in NY), **Lord Montagu of Beaulieu, Alan**

Crompton-Batt, René Lecler, Frank Bowling and **Simon Hopkinson** are just as appreciative.

PLAZA ATHENEE, 37 E 64th St, NY 10021 ☎ (212) 734 9100 Chic little sister to the Paris PA, she's just as sophisticated, with French Regency furnishings, crystal chandeliers, marble floors and bathrooms. *"A really nice hotel. The rooms are small but really pretty, very elegant in*

🏃 **Buzzzzzzzzz** If you want to make doubly sure you're in New York when you look out of the window, go for a **view of Central Park** – from **Park Lane Hotel**, 36 Central Park South, NY 10019 ☎ (212) 371 4000 or **Hampshire House**, 150 Central Park South, NY 10019 ☎ (212) 246 7700 🏃 ..... Where do the truly private movie stars stay? At an **unnamed block** of luxury serviced apartments, at **74th and Lexington** – *that's* discreet 🏃 ..... Star stop II: many of the old greats live in hotel apartments at the **Wyndham House**, 42 W 58th St, NY 10019 ☎ (212) 753 3500. Lillian Gish, Bette Davis and Katharine Hepburn are all Wyndham girls.

★ ★ ★ ★ ★ ★ ★ ★ ★ ★ ★ ★ ★ ★ ★ ★ ★ ★ ★

soft, creamy colours – nice and sort of sexy-looking!" – **Margaux Hemingway.**

RITZ-CARLTON, 112 Central Park South, NY 10019 ☎ (212) 757 1900 Decorated by Sister Parish in the English gentlemen's club mould. Fabulous view over the Park, personal service, and it houses the mock-historic quasi-English Jockey Club dining room. To its disadvantage it has lost manager **Frank Bowling** to the Carlyle, though he still rates it in his top 5 hotels in New York (*"my old alma mater is doing well"*).

THE WESTBURY, 15 E 69th St, NY 10021 ☎ (212) 535 2000 Since its multi-million-dollar revamp, it's a New York fave. *"They always make you welcome and are happy to see you. They cosset you like a 5-year-old. They have the best concierge, Anthony Pike"* – **Inès de la Fressange.** Its clubby Polo restaurant is the place for lunch.

SAN FRANCISCO

CAMPTON PLACE, 340 Stockton St, CA 94108 ☎ (415) 781 5555 A typical boutique hotel, in an old property, impeccably decorated in rose pinks and beiges, with bleached wood, objets d'art, potted trees, fresh flowers. Popular with Britons and Australians, it's **Geoffrey Roberts**'s No 1 in San Francisco. Very fine restaurant. Mountainous breakfasts.

THE DONATELLO, Pacific Plaza Hotel, 501 Post St, CA 94102 ☎ (415) 441 7100 Another small, personal hotel. The gleaming, glossy lobby has antique furniture and contemporary art; don't overlook the mind-blowing mouth-blown Salviati glass and white marble from the very quarry where Michelangelo found his *David* (in slab form, naturally). Ristorante

TRAVEL

Donatello, with its beautiful crystal wall lamps and arched mirrors, is one of the best in town.

FOUR SEASONS CLIFT, 495 Geary St, CA 94102
☎ (415) 775 4700
Loyal following who appreciate acres of wood panelling, the Art Deco cocktail lounge, elegant French dining room, choccies and red rose on their pillow and friendly service.

🏨 **HUNTINGTON HOTEL, 1075 California St, CA 94108**
☎ (415) 474 5400
At the top of Nob Hill, with fab views and boutique hotel accoutrements (from Irish linens thru' Ming Dynasty treasures to a Rolls-Royce

Chez Jim Nassikas, hotelier extraordinary, you feel exclusive but at home. They don't forget the niceties that make your stay a pleasant one – they'll even open windows for you, something rarely done nowadays" – **Anne Willan.** *"The best in San Francisco for comfort and service"* – **Elise Pascoe. Craig Claiborne, René Lecler, Don Dorwood, Stanley Marcus** and **Egon Ronay** are of one accord. Home of the acclaimed Fournou's Ovens (see Food & Drink).

SUN VALLEY

Top ski resort in Idaho for expert skiers. Isolated, but Californians struggle to get

WASHINGTON, DC

HAY ADAMS, 1 Lafayette Sq, DC 20006 ☎ (202) 638 6600
Restored in 1985, *"an olde-worlde luxury hotel, in the top 3 because of its extraordinary service, comfort and spectacular view of the White House, overlooking Lafayette Park"* – **Aniko Gaal.** Two main restaurants – the John Hay Room (*"opulent with wood carvings and tapestries"* – **AG**) and Caspar Weinberger's lunchtime haunt, the Adams Room (*"all in luscious chintz with yellow walls and a parquet floor; it's just lovely, lovely, very fresh and spirited with elegance"* – **AG**).

> **❝** *New York is probably the most exciting fantasy place in the world, like something out of Arabian Nights when you see it from across the river, but when you get close it becomes not quite so exciting, more worrying and frightening in places – but nevertheless a fascinating and stimulating city* **❞**
>
> DOUGLAS FAIRBANKS JR

Silver Shadow courtesy car). *"The best hotel in America – the quietest, most discreet, least vulgar; they are friendly, intelligent, and it's in a lovely location"* – **David Hicks. Lord Montagu of Beaulieu** and **Don Dorwood** add their votes.

MANDARIN ORIENTAL, 222 Sansome St, CA 94104
☎ (415) 885 0999
One of the newest additions to the Mandarin Oriental fold, a 2-tower structure joined by a glass bridge. As plushy as you would expect, a strong rival to SF's top hotels. Its trump card is Silks (see Food & Drink).

🏨 **STANFORD COURT, 905 California St, CA 94108**
☎ (415) 989 3500
San F's best hotel, standing resplendent on 'Snob' Hill in Governor Leland Stanford's former family mansion, lavishly decorated with yet more of Michelangelo's marble, wood panelling, antiques, silver and chandeliers. *"The best hotel.*

here as do the bigwigs at AmEx, James D Robinson III and the Sid Basses. Favourite resort of Brooke Shields and of champion powder-hound **Margaux Hemingway,** who was brought up here. *"Jean-Claude Killy told me it has the best skiing in the US. I'll take his word for it"* – **Mark McCormack.**

VAIL

1960s resort in Colorado fashioned after an Alpine village. The accumulation of wonderful snow and trails is matched by a pile-up of names from the Social Register – ex-President Gerald Ford, Texas clans of Bass, Murchison and Wyatt, and Denver doyennes. Centralized, sleek, high up, with the fastest ski-lifts in the USA. *"A little more contrived than the other resorts. It's known as Instant Tyrol"* – **Mark McCormack.**

THE RITZ-CARLTON, 2100 Massachusetts Ave NW, DC 20008 ☎ (202) 293 2100
"A small, European-type hotel with personal attention. Its subtlety and luxury are very defined" – **Aniko Gaal.** Formerly the Fairfax Hotel, redecorated by Sister Parish, it attracts the glitterati to its oak-panelled bar and the famous Jockey Club restaurant.

🏨 **THE WILLARD INTER-CONTINENTAL, 1401 Pennsylvania Ave, DC 20004**
☎ (202) 628 9100
A golden oldie reincarnate. Built in 1816 one block down from the White House, it was one of the USA's best until it closed in 1968. Recent meticulous renovation makes it *"the most incredible hotel – I would compare it to the great ones in the world. The suites [over 60 of them] are beautifully furnished with antiques"* – **Aniko Gaal.** The Presidential Suite has black and white marble floor and

TRAVEL

columns. In the hotel's first year of rebirth it put up 11 heads of state. Home of the legendary Round Robin bar and the top-notch Willard Room (see Food & Drink).

Argentina

"It has the best beef and the most elegant women in the world. They all rush off to Paris to buy their clothes. The men don't wear top coats, they wear terribly elegant cashmere shawls. If you're lucky you'll see a llama – they're adorable-looking creatures" – **Elisabeth Lambert Ortiz.**

BUENOS AIRES

GRAN DORA, Maipu 963
☎ **(01) 312 7391**
"Very nice old-fashioned atmosphere for people up from the country. Very comfortable with good service and bang in the middle of town" – **Quentin Crewe.**

Australia

ADELAIDE

HILTON INTERNATIONAL, Victoria Sq, SA 5000
☎ **(08) 217 0711**
The best hotel in Adelaide, with pretty views over the square and beyond to the coast in one direction and the Adelaide foothills in the other. If décor is unremarkable (it has that dated modern look), the

♣ Australia's Best ♣

HOTELS

1 **THE REGENT,** Sydney
2 **THE REGENT,** Melbourne
3 **INTER-CONTINENTAL,** Sydney
4 **SEBEL TOWN HOUSE,** Sydney
5 **WINDSOR,** Melbourne
6 **SHERATON,** Brisbane

restaurant makes up for it: The Grange is one of the best in Oz. Dig into kangaroo or buffalo meat over a bottle from a cellar that boasts 400 Australian and foreign wines.

BRISBANE

♣ SHERATON BRISBANE HOTEL & TOWERS, 249 Turbot St, Qld 4000
☎ **(07) 835 3535**
One of Australia's best, superbly decorated. Glass-panelled lifts shoot up the 30-storey building as far as the rooftop restaurant. Lovely views of Brisbane River. There's also the extra-exclusive Sheraton Towers, a small hotel within the hotel, on the skyline floors (27th upwards), with its plushy Presidential Suite.

HOBART

WREST POINT CASINO, 410 Sandy Bay Rd, Tas 7000
☎ **(002) 250112**
Not super-luxe, but big rooms with 7-ft beds in a circular building. Good view of Derwent River. *"Tasmania is one of the great unexplored places, full of beautiful architecture. I always stay at the Wrest Point Casino"* – **Leo Schofield.**

MELBOURNE

HILTON INTERNATIONAL MELBOURNE ON THE PARK, 192 Wellington Parade, E Melbourne, Vic 3002 ☎ **(03) 419 3311**
Outside the city centre, overlooking Melbourne Cricket Ground and Fitzroy Gardens. *"During the cricket season all the cricket writers and players gather in the lobby in the evening. It has tremendous atmosphere – that's why it stands out for me"* – **Imran Khan.** Slick new Executive Floor. Erstwhile guests include Lady Susan Renouf, Prince Philip and Margaret Thatcher.

THE HYATT ON COLLINS, 123 Collins St, Vic 3000
☎ **(03) 657 1234**
"The swishest hotel in Australia. The bathrooms are enormous, all black marble. You want to undress immediately, get into a bathrobe, put on your shower cap, jump into the bath and use all those free oils and things. It's real luxury. You could just imagine Barbara Cartland putting on her lipstick in those bathrooms" – **Robert Burton.**

MENZIES AT RIALTO, 495 Collins St, Vic 3000
☎ **(03) 620 9111**
Curiously based in 2 Victorian buildings linked by an atrium, under the shadow of the new twin-towered Rialto, tallest building in Australia. Restored to the tune of A$40 million, it

> ❝ *I'd much rather stay in a standardized hotel than a crummy private one. I prefer the stereotyped luxury of a chain. I know people sneer at them but at least you know exactly what you're going to get. And it's so much better than going to some terrible old crumb-hole just because Oscar Wilde stayed there in 1884 ...* ❞

♣ GEORGE MELLY

> *I woke up in a hotel once, the curtains were drawn, it was black. I had no idea which country or which hotel I was in. Then I realized where I was, opened the curtains – and I was wrong!*

🕵 TERRY HOLMES

has Gothic arches and a wood-panelled ballroom.

🏨 **THE REGENT, 25 Collins St, Vic 3000 ☎ (03) 653 0000**
A 50-storey modern architectural classic, built around a sky-lit atrium. The actual hotel is based on the top 15 floors. *"It has a fantastic hollow in the middle – all black glass and little white bulbs. It's just magic!"* – **Prue Leith**. Rupert Murdoch and the Australian Open tennis stars stay. At the top are 10 suites – **Jackie Collins** stayed in the Kensington – and the best loo view in the world, with windows from floor to ceiling.

Rex Harrison, Gordon Jackson, Dave Allen, Paul Eddington. No wonder, with a VIP suite that has a sauna, Jacuzzi and a grand piano. For non-VIPs there's a communal version. Superb Ritz restaurant.

🏨 **WINDSOR, 103 Spring St, Vic 3000 ☎ (03) 653 0653**
A Victorian hotel, restored by the Oberoi International group to its original splendour. The domed Grand Dining Room boasts black marble fireplaces, glittering chandeliers and a wealth of 24-carat gold leaf. **René Lecler** and **Lillian Frank** rave about it. This is where visiting Premiers stay.

know. Adjoins the Bond Corporation building, with a view of the Governor's garden. Decorated, in true Aussie style, in the colours of the Bush. The best hotel restaurant in town is the Irwin (see Food & Drink).

MERLIN HOTEL, 99 Adelaide Terrace, WA 6000 ☎ (09) 323 0121
Sparkling 5-star hotel with a knockout lobby – pink Italian granite floor and an atrium that soars 13 storeys to a domed glass roof. Its location, 25 minutes from the business district – an age in Aussie terms – could put biz kids off, but it doesn't worry regular guest **Lord Lichfield**; he loves the restaurant Jessica's (see Food & Drink).

PARMELIA HILTON, Mill St, WA 6000 ☎ (09) 322 3622
An old favourite, for consistent service and a good position. For visiting celebs who want individual service. All the top America's Cup crews stayed.

SYDNEY

ALTONA, 56 Wunulla Rd, Point Piper, NSW 2027 ☎ (02) 327 3030
Four private serviced apartments decorated by Leslie Walford. Smart position on the waterfront with great harbour views and a swimming pool. Stars like Dame Joan Sutherland stay incognito.

THE HILTON INTERNATIONAL, 259 Pitt St, PO Box 3934, NSW 2001 ☎ (02) 266 0610
An old favourite in Sydney, recommended by **Lord Lichfield**.

🏨 **INTER-CONTINENTAL, 117 Macquarie St, NSW 2000 ☎ (02) 230 0200**
The original 3-storey Victorian

🕵 **Buzzzzzzzzz** The best getaway place is the 24-room **Cape Wilderness Lodge**, Mainland Resort, c/o Air Queensland Resorts, 62 Abbott St, St Cairns, Qld 4870 ☎ (070) 504305 on Cape York, at the very tip of northern Queensland – tropical waters, deep-sea fishing, so relaxed you might never go back to dizzy civilization again 🕵 . . . . . . Look out for the new A$80 million **Regent on Campbells Cove**, north of Sydney – a hotel biased towards the leisure rather than business market, of the new low-rise Boutique Hotel genre with 200 rooms, tiptop restaurants, its own natty shopping and eating promenade and transport into town. Due to open in spring 1989 🕵 . . . . . . **Speedy flight I** LA-Sydney United Airlines non-stop jumbo (14 hrs) which arrives at 9pm or 10pm in the evening – in time for a good kip 🕵 . . . . . . **Speedy flight II** London-Sydney British Airways one-stop at Bangkok (24 hrs 20 mins).

★ ★ ★ ★ ★ ★ ★ ★ ★ ★ ★ ★ ★ ★ ★ ★ ★ ★ ★

ROCKMAN'S REGENCY HOTEL, Corner Exhibition and Lonsdale Sts, Vic 3000 ☎ (03) 662 3900
Zazzy, smallish hotel with Sebel-like personal service that attracts celebs – Bob Hope, John McEnroe, Sean Connery,

PERTH

ANSETT INTERNATIONAL, 10 Irwin St, WA 6000 ☎ (09) 325 0481
The current best in Perth, it walks all over the others according to Aussies in the

> 66 *I love travelling the back roads of New South Wales and Western Australia or following the banks of the Darling River. One of the best things is camping at Monkeymia in WA and seeing the dolphins. My idea of heaven is driving along the long red dirt roads of WA. It's a very healing thing to do. It's my inspiration* 99
>
> JENNY KEE

building, former HQ of the NSW Government Treasury, has been preserved as part of the inner atrium, and topped with a A$150 million skyscraperful of bedrooms. Best suite is the Royal. *"The view over the harbour is absolutely terrific. The service is lovely as the Australians are such friendly people"* – **Caroline Hunt. Lord Lichfield** is also knocked out by the view: *"For me the point is you can see the Botanic Gardens."* Fine dining.

THE REGENT, 199 George St, NSW 2000 ☎ (02) 238 0000 Its brilliant position overlooking the Opera House and sparkling harbour shoots it into the top class. Suites facing the harbour have telescopes, but avoid rooms facing the motorway – drivers can see directly in. Best are the Royal Suites, on the 33rd floor. The general manager pays the greatest attention to detail and it shows: *"I love it. I consider . Ted Wright to be one of the best*

SYDNEY'S BEST BEACHES

Best voyeurs' beach: Palm Beach and **Whale Beach** – stretches of yellow sand studded with nymphets (daughters of the rich and, Southern-Hemispherically speaking, famous) and hulky surfers in zazzy board shorts ... **Best harbour beach: Balmoral ('Immoral'), Mosman** – with comforting shark netting, and teeming with trendy windsurfers ... **Best escapist beach: Stanmore Park** on the south coast ... **Best English-style beach: Manly** – *"modelled on the English seaside, it's got beach huts and fish and chip shops; terrific for kids"* – **Dorian Wild** ... Voyeur II: the **best nudist beach is Lady Jane,** *"best viewed from a boat with a pair of binoculars"* – **Dorian Wild** ... **Best gay beach: Tamarama** ('Glamarama'), a stage for macho Mr Universes (and a few topless Miss Worlds). It's the prettier, tinier neighbour of ... the well-trodden and occasionally sewage-scented **best-known beach: Bondi.** Yet, *"for all the hideousness and ugliness, it is a wonderful beach. All human life is there, that's what's so interesting"* – **Leo Schofield** ... *"When there's a moment, I dash to Bondi. I love surfing, sunbaking and playing porpoises"* – **Diana Fisher.**

hoteliers in the world" – **Lady Mary Fairfax.** *"Just terrific"* – **Prue Leith.** *"The best buffet*

breakfast in the world – they change the eggs benedict every 5 minutes; all the juices are fresh. At night it turns into the best jazz club in Sydney" – **Lord Lichfield.** *"The styling and the approach to their clients is very good"* – **Anouska Hempel.** *"The best. It's got what people want – wonderful service"* – **Leo Schofield. Jeffrey Archer** is keen, so is **Elise Pascoe:** *"Great style and service and the excellent Kables"* (see Food & Drink).

Buzzzzzzzz The Darling Harbour Development, an ambitious casino-hotel complex, is described variously as 'stunning' and 'an eyesore'. The monorail that already shoots round the development is love-hated. Worst of all, the original A$400 million budget has now near-doubled

. . . . . . Sydney's best views are from: the **gents' loo of the American Club** in Macquarie Street ... **Centrepoint Tower** – the suburbs, beaches and inlets laid out like a map ... **Sydney Opera House**, watching a cruise liner depart at night, past the green-lit big-wheel of the Harbour Bridge – just like the Art Deco posters ... the **Royal Suite of the Inter-Continental** (as the experts vouch – see above).

★ ★ ★ ★ ★ ★ ★ ★ ★ ★ ★ ★ ★ ★ ★ ★ ★ ★ ★ ★

RUSSELL HOTEL, 143a George St, NSW 2000 ☎ **(02) 241 3543** An enchanting small-shot private hotel in Sydney's olde-worlde Rocks area. It's like staying with friends in an English country home – stripped pine, Laura Ashley, and a Victorian tea room. A good hideaway for film stars.

TRAVEL

> 66 *The best way to show people Sydney is to take them out and throw them on to a boat* 99
>
> 🏃 ROBERT BURTON

🏃 **SEBEL TOWN HOUSE, 23 Elizabeth Bay Rd, Elizabeth Bay, NSW 2011**
☎ (02) 358 3244
Small, intimate hotel where visiting rock and showbiz stars are pampered. At the quiet, harbour end of razzy King's Cross it's tastefully, sombrely plushy with excellent service. Whenever a star is in town – Spandau Ballet, Dire Straits, Bob Dylan, Tina Turner, Sting, Paul Simon, Elton John, Billy Joel – fans keep vigil outside the foyer. The walls of the legendary bar are smothered with signed celeb photos.

SHERATON-WENTWORTH, 61 Phillip St, NSW 2000
☎ (02) 230 0700
Its apologetic exterior conceals a thoroughly well-run hotel with many loyal guests. Diehards swear by this one for its clubbish atmosphere and long-standing staff. Venetian concierge Tony Facciolo is one of the best-loved in the world.

REST OF AUSTRALIA

BURNHAM BEECHES COUNTRY HOUSE, Sherbrooke Rd, Sherbrooke, Vic 3789 ☎ (03) 755 1903
An Art Deco mansion built by a ship-mad family, hence the vast sun decks (terraces). The sitting room has a feel of the old *Queen Mary*, its chairs are replicas of those on the QM. Moored in a garden of English trees in the Dandenong Hills. Superb cuisine and wines.

JUPITER'S CASINO-CONRAD INTERNATIONAL, Gold Coast Highway, Broadbeach, Qld 4218
☎ (075) 921133
"The best hotel in the world. It outdoes Caesar's Palace in Las Vegas. There's nowhere else in

the whole wide world with a pool like that – tropical, with palms and fountains and two spas. There's a sort of Coliseum at the back with pillars, all in Queensland sandstone. The rooms are beautiful, the beds 9 ft wide" – **Lillian Frank.**

NOOSA HEADS, Queensland
By far the best mainland resort town – upmarket, surrounded by National Parkland, with chic shopping and eating. Visiting Europeans go during their winter, when it's too hot to hit the Barrier Reef. Lady Susan Renouf loves it. So does **Elise Pascoe**, who raves about the best hire car service, **Doug's Hire Cars**. Best hotel: **NETANYA, Hastings Street, Noosa, Qld 4567**
☎ (071) 474722.

🏃 **PEPPERS GUEST HOUSE, Ekerts Rd, Pokolbin, Hunter Valley, NSW 2321**
☎ (049) 987596
Though new and plushily fitted out, there's an established, mellow old-colonial atmosphere. Spriggy chintzy décor, swimming pool, tennis court, sauna and spa, and – naturally – a vista of vineyards. *"It's lovely, and honest – there's no cheating on the quality"* – **Elise Pascoe.**

QUEENSCLIFF HOTEL, 16 Gellibrand St, Queenscliff, Vic 3225 ☎ (052) 521066
A gracious hotel with one of Port Phillip Bay's most delightful sea views. Refined, relaxed; classic Victoriana. Run by Patricia O'Donnell, sister of Mietta of the Melbourne restaurant (see Food & Drink). Old-fashioned breakfasts go on for ever.

SHERATON AYERS ROCK, Yulara Drive, Yulara, NT 5751 ☎ (089) 562200
A wonderful sight, painted in rich Ayers Rock hues, with

COUNTRY HOTELS

If you've read 're-creates the atmosphere of an English country mansion' once, you've read it a thousand times. Country-house hotels are the absolute craze in Australia. The latest are the cliff-side **FAIRMONT RESORT**, Sublime Point Rd, Leura, Blue Mountains, NSW 2780 ☎ (047) 825222 – '. . . in the style of an English . . .' (yes, we know) plus golf, tennis, 3 lakes, pools indoor and out, health club; and **MILTON PARK**, PO Box 676, Bowral 2576 ☎ (048) 611862 – *"Lovely country-house atmosphere; we ride, play tennis, walk and just have a lovely weekend in the country"* – **Elise Pascoe.** Older favourites include **PADTHAWAY ESTATE**, Padthaway, SA 5271 ☎ (087) 655039, with lacework verandahs and its own vineyards; **ROSEVALE STATION**, south of Charleville, Qld, where you can get closer to nature, wildlife and 22,000 sheep; **PROSPECT HOUSE**, Richmond, Tasmania 7025 ☎ (002) 622207, a Georgian house with only 7 rooms and one of the best game restaurants on the island; **THE SETTLERS' COTTAGE**, 125 Avon Terrace, York, WA 6302 ☎ (096) 411096, a small, historic haven east of Perth; and **HOWQUA DALE GOURMET RETREAT**, Howqua River Rd, PO Box 114, Mansfield, Vic 3722 ☎ (057) 773503, which is just as it sounds, set in a lush valley, serving home-made dishes using local seasonal produce.

desert-toned furnishings. On a scorching site just outside the official Ayers Rock limit, it is kept cool by a series of white windsurferesque sails that form a parasol over the low-level complex. Superb pool and tennis courts and a now-flourishing garden, amid the flat flat flat of the outback.

♠ **SHERATON MIRAGE HOTEL, PO Box 172, Four Mile Beach, Port Douglas, Qld 4871 ☎ (070) 985888**
Gorgeous spanking new resort. The low-level hotel complex is surrounded by 5 acres of salt-water lagoons with walkways and islands, and can't be seen from the beach or road. There's a 200-berth marina, an 18-hole golf course, tennis courts and all ocean sports. Enormous rooms with spas; seafood restaurant. Heli or hover there from Cairns airport.

THREDBO, NSW
The best ski resort, where Aussie surfers head for winter and European pros train during their summer (June to end Sept). Best glühwein: from the Keller. Best hotel: **Thredbo Alpine** (spas, saunas, bistro, piano bar).

ISLANDS

Australia has been slow to exploit the wonders of the Great Barrier Reef, a 1,200-mile semi-submerged causeway of live coral that lies in splendour off the Queensland coast, home of 1,900 varieties of tropical fish. Until recently, most resorts remained downmarket, catering either to geriatric/18-30s package-trippers from Victoria, or to diving and snorkelling enthusiasts. (The best diving, incidentally, is off HERON ISLAND, off Gladstone.) Communications were the other major problem, now being resolved by new airstrips and swish launches. Australia's 2 major internal airlines, Ansett and Australian Airlines, and one or two entrepreneurs are still pouring millions into the development of islands to

standards that international travellers understand (eg room service, preferably 24-hour). Best time to visit is after the sea wasps (poisonous jellyfish) have gone: in the north, May to Sept; in the Whitsundays, late March to July.

BEDARRA ISLAND, c/o Australian Airlines, see Tours & Charters
Two separate resorts (Hideaway and Bedarra Bay) with 16 villas apiece. A proper Pacific island idyll, unquestionably hid away, like a private club. From the air you'd never know it existed. Units are built *around* trees so you're likely to have a palm shooting up through your bedroom. No entertainment (a mercy, since Aussie resort entertainment takes the form of toad races and bingo), just a spread of tropical goodies and a beach to yourself. Eerily quiet at night. Around A$400 a day all-in, which includes all the French champagne you can swallow – *"it's like being locked in a lolly factory"* – **Danny Rossi**. Once on the island, it's a cashless society.

HAMILTON ISLAND RESORT, PMB Post Office Hamilton Island Harbour, Qld 4803 ☎ (079) 469144
A brash, tacky but fun resort with a passenger jet-sized airstrip and a marina. Go during Race Week in April.

♠ **HAYMAN ISLAND RESORT, N Qld 4801 ☎ (079) 469100**
The best, most upmarket big-time resort, a A$120 million Ansett-owned 5-star pre-fab affair. *"You are maintained in champagne-sluiced luxury far away from the uncouth hordes of Hamilton Island"* – **Dorian Wild**. Visitors (numbers are limited) stay at the Ansett International Hotel, furnished with European antiques and Australian contemporary art, with balconied rooms overlooking the reef and a man-made lagoon the size of 5 Olympic pools. The biggest of its kind in the Southern Hemisphere (making former record-holder Hamilton's look positively pipsqueak), it holds 2 million gallons of filtered

seawater and has a freshwater pool in the centre. The first Whitsunday resort to offer 24-hour room service – the only way to ensnare rich Americans. Guests so far include Neville Wran, Bob Hawke and Sir Eric and Lady Cheadle.

♠ **LIZARD ISLAND, c/o Australian Airlines, see Tours & Charters**
The most northerly and most exclusive island in Australia, on the fringe of the Outer Reef. The main lodge faces trim lawns and a pink-white beach. *"Excellent food, small, intimate, a house-party atmosphere. No fawning attention from flunkies"* – **Claudia Rossi Hudson**. *"It's wonderful"* – **Lord Lichfield**. No playground either, just superb game fishing (hunters grapple with Black Marlin from Aug to Dec), scuba diving, snorkelling, sunbaking, and scouring the names in the visitors' book at Cook's Look: Bob Hawke, Earl Spencer (Diana's pa), Prince Charles, and Caroline Kennedy (who honeymooned here).

ORPHEUS ISLAND, Private Mail Bag, Ingham, Qld 4850 ☎ (077) 777377
Privately owned by two Italians and an Australian, it's a chic blend of Tropics and Mediterranean. No day-trippers allowed. Lots of honeymooners. Only 24 serviced units (rooms or bungalows), whitewashed, cany, airy – though the ceiling fans are hazardously low-slung. Magnificent seafood, swimming and snorkelling against a National Park backdrop. Those who have been lured into the underworld include Bob Hawke, the Duke and Duchess of Westminster and Lady Susan Renouf.

TOURS AND CHARTERS

AIR WHITSUNDAY, PO Box 166, Airlie Beach, Qld 4802 ☎ (079) 469133
For air charters, trips to the Barrier Reef and to islands.

ANSETT, 501 Swanston St, Melbourne, Vic 3000 ☎ **(03) 668 2222 (and in all Australian capital cities)** The Ansett Holiday Collection deals with the cream of dream hols – Hayman and Orpheus island, game fishing off Cairns, cruising Reef waters on the *Southern Spirit*, Australia's most luxurious yacht.

AUSTRALIAN AIRLINES, 50 Franklin St, Melbourne, Vic 3000 ☎ **(03) 665 1333 (and in all Australian capital cities)** Trips to Bedarra, Lizard, Dunk, Brampton, etc.

AUSTRALIAN AIR TOUR AND CHARTER, 1st Fl, Meriton House, 432 Chapel Rd, Bankstown, NSW 2200 ☎ **(02) 700038** Exclusive light-aircraft charter from David Le Claire. Mostly used by businessmen (first-class air fares can be halved), they've also taken passengers for a bird's-eye view of Birdsville, a look at Ayers Rock, and chasing camels over the desert. Numbers and distances no problem.

EASTERN SUBURBS SAILING CENTRE, New Beach Rd, Rushcutters Bay, NSW 2000 ☎ **(02) 328 7666** 24-ft and 36-ft yachts can be hired by the day in Sydney Harbour (until 8pm in summer to allow for twilight tipples).

HAMILTON ISLAND CHARTERS, Hamilton Island, Qld 4802 ☎ **(079) 469144** A slick fleet of cruising yachts with self-furling sails, talking depth sounders and all mod cons. Crewed motor-yachts too – Robert Holmes a' Court has hired one. The Whitsunday Passage provides perfect cruising waters.

QUICKSILVER CONNECTION, PO Box 171, Port Douglas, Qld 4871 ☎ **(070) 985373** This company provides the quickest access to the Reef. Daily cruises to the low islands and the Barrier Reef; heli trips, snorkelling and glass-bottomed boat trips.

Austria

KITZBUHEL

Medieval walled city, weekend resort for Munich café society (worth the trip for Praxmair's hot chocolate). Too low for expert skiing but good for families and **Margaux Hemingway** still likes it.

ST ANTON

Serious skiing and serious queues. Excellent tuition (over 300 hulky instructors). **Mark Birley** skis here. Best nightspot: Krazy Kanguruh.

VIENNA

IMPERIAL, Karntnerring 16, A-1015 ☎ **(01) 651765** A truly Imperial palace, built by Duke Philipp of Württemberg and opened by Emperor Franz Joseph. Bismarck, Hitler, Mussolini, Rommel and Gaddafi have stayed there; so have Wagner, Sarah Bernhardt, Placido Domingo and Luciano Pavarotti. Palatial rooms and corridors are lined with marble and adorned with chandeliers, Rococo furniture and portraits by Winterhalter. No sooner do you ring room service than a waiter waltzes in with your order and a red rose.

HOTEL SACHER, Philharmonikerstrasse 4, A-1010 ☎ **(01) 525575** *"Charming old-fashioned hotel. I had the most beautiful suite where all the furniture was white and pink – it could not have been better for me! They take a lot of trouble over you. Beautiful manners, you are welcomed in the right way and seen off in the right way – all the things that matter"* – **Barbara Cartland.** See also Food & Drink.

SCHLOSS DURNSTEIN, A-3601 Durnstein an der Donau, Wachau ☎ **(02711) 212** An old-fashioned hotel where you can indulge in figure-licking pastries while gazing from the shady terrace over the beautiful blue Danube. *"Stunning décor, great food and beautiful walks nearby"* – **Elise Pascoe.**

Brazil

"Gorgeous, glorious, wonderful Brazil. People who care about nature should go north along the Amazon. It's not comfortable, but it's the Amazon" – **Elisabeth Lambert Ortiz.** *"Marvellous for several reasons. The Baroque architecture is the best in the world, so there is something very positive and cultural to be seen. Churches have survived and whole towns, with beautiful cobbled streets, have been preserved after they were abandoned when the gold trade or economy shifted. There are superb, high-quality, cheap restaurants and hotels everywhere"* – **Robin Hanbury-Tenison.** And, of course, this is carnival country. Rio's is the most spectacular, but there are dozens more that throb throughout the land.

BAHIA

"The churches are quite spectacular; just stuffed with gold decoration" – **Quentin Crewe.** *"I don't know any churches as exciting as those in Bahia and Rio. You never saw so much gold outside of Fort Knox, and marvellous mahogany pews"* – **Elisabeth Lambert Ortiz.**

BRASILIA

"The best modern architecture in the world – amazing. The city was conceived in the 50s and built from scratch in the jungle. People were not meant to move around much so there were no traffic lights, but they had to put them in . . ." –

TRAVEL

Quentin Crewe. "*A purely artificial city, laid out in the shape of an aircraft with wings; every section is self-contained with a church and there's a garage for every flat. Any architecture buff should see it*" – **Elisabeth Lambert Ortiz**. "*Very exciting to go to – don't listen to all the stories of it being a ghost town – it's a thriving city*" – **Dan Topolski**.

MANAUS

A fascinating city 1,000 miles up the Amazon that serves as the starting point for the heart of the jungle. "*One of the most extraordinary places in the world, so strange. There was a rubber boom and everything was dragged up the river to build this city. Then the English sold the plants and the boom collapsed leaving this enormous city*" – **Quentin Crewe**.

OURO PRETO

"*The beautiful 18th-century capital of Minas Gerais state, resplendent in Baroque churches*" – **Anne Willan**. "*A lovely colonial town*" – **Dan Topolski**. "*The city was declared a national monument in 1933 and is one of the most unspoiled in the world*" – **Robin Hanbury-Tenison**. A former gold-mining centre, its name means Black Gold.

HOTEL DA ESTRADA REAL
☎ (031) 551 2122
5 miles outside the city, a modern hotel, often fully booked, that is "*very comfortable, with private wooden chalets and a swimming pool. Delightful*" – **Robin Hanbury-Tenison**.

POUSO DO CHICO REI, Rua Brig. Mosqueira 90 D
☎ (031) 551 1223
"*A perfect old colonial house so popular that it is very difficult to get in and they won't take bookings. You just have to turn up and hope*" – **Robin**

Hanbury-Tenison. Small, delightful, packed with Portuguese antiques.

PARATI

"*From Rio south to Parati the coastline is simply spectacular, like the Riviera without any houses. Parati is a very pretty, well-restored colonial town with nice people*" – **Quentin Crewe**. "*A perfect unspoilt town on the coast, the terminus of the old mule train taking gold from Ouro Preto*" – **Robin Hanbury-Tenison**.

POUSADA DO PARDIEIRO, B, Rua Comercio 74
☎ (0243) 711139
A colonial house with lovely gardens.

RIO DE JANEIRO

COPACABANA PALACE, Av Atlantica 1456
☎ (021) 542 1887
"*Obviously the best*" – **Dan Topolski**. It's certainly on the best beach, and full of beans at carnival time.

INTER-CONTINENTAL, Av Prefeito Mendes de Morais, 222 Sao Conrado, PO Box 33011☎ (021) 322 2200
A modern block on the outskirts of Rio next to Leblon and Ipanema (where The Girl came from). "*A very, very fine hotel. A choice of swimming pools*" – **Aniko Gaal**. "*The best in Rio*" – **Lord Lichfield**.

TOURS

CLASSIC TOURS, Ave NS Copacabana 1059, Office 805, Rio de Janeiro
☎ (021) 287 3390
Made-to-measure holidays within Brazil – you could embark on an expedition to Manaus, where the Amazon proper begins, a boat along the river to the island of Marajo at the delta and a stay at a lodge in the heart of the jungle.

Britain

LONDON

♣ ─Britain's Best─ ♣

	HOTELS
1	**CLARIDGE'S,** London
2	**THE CONNAUGHT,** London
3	**INVERLOCHY CASTLE,** Fort William
4	**THE BERKELEY,** London
5	**THE SAVOY,** London

🏆 **THE BERKELEY, Wilton Place, Knightsbridge, SW1**
☎ (01) 235 6000
The only one of London's best with a swimming pool (on the roof). Though the building's modern, it remains terrifically discreet, with the atmosphere of a gentleman's club and, many think, the best head porter in London. "*It remains a very good hotel, well situated and very English*" – **René Lecler**. **Douglas Fairbanks Jr** approves, as does **Lynn Wyatt**.

CAPITAL HOTEL, 22 Basil St, SW3 ☎ (01) 589 5171
"*Where I stay in London. It's very convenient – I have the penthouse apartment, which is very nice. You can't beat the food there*" – **Douglas Fairbanks Jr**. This and the 4 other apartments are decorated by Nina Campbell. Lowlier beings stay in rooms, but all savour Philip Britten's cuisine. **Ken Hom** is a particular fan.

🏆 **CLARIDGE'S, Brook St, W1**
☎ (01) 629 8860
The oldest and most dignified of the great London hotels, in operation since 1812 – though the interior is largely Art Deco, with fabulous mirrors and gleaming black and white tiled floors. Some bedrooms are perfect 1930s showpieces with enormous marble-infested

TRAVEL

> **❝** *Probably the most liveable city – it has parts of beauty and ugliness and a little of everything. It's a wonderful big city, very sophisticated and highly civilized, and also great fun. Where Venice, Rome, Hong Kong are specialized places, London is a sort of supercity, the world metropolis* **❞**

 DOUGLAS FAIRBANKS JR

bathrooms; others are more country house. *"The nearest thing to home. In the old-fashioned way, the housekeeper makes a note of whether you want three blankets, if feather pillows gave you asthma, and it's all there when you go next time. It is still run like a country house. I use it like a club and have my own table in the restaurant; the porters know my name"* – **Barbara Cartland.** *"The Rolls-Royce of London hotels . . . frightfully good service"* – **Betty Kenward** (many names from her column, *Jennifer's Diary*, lunch at the Causerie). *"Superb service and people"* – **Caroline Hunt.** A world best for **Douglas Fairbanks Jr, Frank Bowling, Jane Seymour, Lord Montagu of Beaulieu** and **Helen Gurley Brown:** *"I never stay anywhere else in London."*

 THE CONNAUGHT, Carlos Place, W1 ☎ (01) 499 7070
Distinguished, refined, small, old-fashioned and even a little dingy, it's part of the very fabric of Establishment London. For those members of its charmed circle, this is the best. **René Lecler** puts it down to *"overall quality, excellent food, politeness and very, very good management"*, while admitting it *"doesn't really want to know you if you don't belong." "I suspect it's rather like the Garrick Club,"* agrees **Frederic Raphael,** *"people are so glad to have got in, they don't actually notice if it ain't all that wonderful once they're there." "A traditional hotel which retains that tradition"* – **Hilary Rubinstein.** It slots into **Douglas Fairbanks Jr's,**

Barbara Kafka's and **Frank Bowling**'s world top ten. See also Food & Drink.

MAYFAIR HOTEL, Berkeley St, W1 ☎ (01) 629 7777
A discreet, dead-central hotel where simply *all* the big-name pop stars stay. Prince, Madonna, the Lionel Richie Band, Bruce Springsteen, Rod Stewart, Billy Joel, Elton John, Stevie Wonder, Diana Ross, Neil Diamond . . .

LE MERIDIEN, Piccadilly, W1 ☎ (01) 734 8000
Fabulously refurbished by the French group – gleaming marble lobby, glass-domed

Terrace Restaurant high above the street, and the gorgeous Edwardian oak-panelled Oak Room restaurant. *"For the grandest dining – a truly wonderful room and very good food"* – **Glynn Christian.** Guests have automatic membership of Champneys health club with its enormous faux Roman baths.

 THE RITZ, Piccadilly, W1 ☎ (01) 493 8181
Watch out for the renaissance of the Ritz under charismatic Terry Holmes. Tipped for the very top, not least because it hides the best secret garden in London. Gloriously decorated

---

WHAT ELSE MAKES A GOOD HOTEL?

"If I go to a grand hotel, I expect grand behaviour. If I am going to sleep in a back room at £2.50 a night, that is a different thing. I expect to be welcomed and seen off: if it is a good hotel, the porter should say 'Good evening, Miss Cartland' because he has been told I am arriving. They do it at the Ritz in Paris, the Oriental Bangkok and Claridge's in London. There should be quiet – hotels that are badly built are infuriating. Good service. Enough bedclothes – most hotels don't think of people who feel cold in bed and it's an awful bore if you have to keep sending for extra blankets. Flowers and fruit – I expect hotels to provide these; it is a sign of a good upper-class hotel. Hot water – you do not always get it but it is most important at £200 a night. Staff knowing you. Newspapers in the morning. All these little things count" – **Barbara Cartland.** *"Service is most important but décor comes a close second"* – **Douglas Fairbanks Jr.** *"About 65 checklist items: the first words out of the mouth of the person at the desk. Does he look you directly in the face? Do they move very fast to get you in? Is the luggage up within 10 minutes? I could go on . . ."* – **Thomas Hoving.**

> **❝** *I love London. Last time I was there it was such a novelty for me to trudge through the snowstorms. I quite liked the misery* **❞**

 ROBERT BURTON

❝ *I don't think any hotels in America could beat the best European hotels. I like all the hotels in the Savoy group – The Savoy, Claridge's, Berkeley, Connaught – they're all wonderful* **❞**

🏇 DOUGLAS FAIRBANKS JR

in fin de siècle style with pastel walls, panelling, carving and gilt. The dining room (the most beautiful in London) and wine list are exceptional though it has been debatable whether tea at the Ritz is a wonderful institution or a tourist trap. A suitably ritzy guest list includes Rex Harrison, Sophia Loren, Ginger Rogers and **Joan Collins**, who adores her suite there.

🏊 **THE SAVOY, The Strand, WC2 ☎ (01) 836 4343**
Grand old hotel overlooking Embankment Gardens and the Thames. **Frederic Raphael** and **Douglas Fairbanks Jr** support **Michael Grade**'s view: *"A river suite is undoubtedly the best in London – there's nothing to compare."* Superb Art Deco mirrors have been uncovered in the American Bar, a great post-work meeting-place. Dine in the famous yew-panelled Grill, or toy with an oyster (or his sea-mates) in the Upstairs Bar.

THE STAFFORD, St James's Place, SW1 ☎ (01) 493 0111
Father of the litter of small private hotels (see Historic Hotels box), going since 1912, and more like a club. Charming terrace bar in the cobbled mews. Head porter George has presided for over 20 years; know him and you're made.

REST OF ENGLAND

CHEWTON GLEN, New Milton, Hampshire ☎ (04252) 5341
"Enormously beautiful, a great success story, and always full" – **René Lecler**. *"A best for luxury, pampering, recreation and food"* – **Elise Pascoe**. In the New Forest, it's one of the most famous country hotels. Luxurious if unhomy, with

attentive service and exemplary cuisine that has earned toques, turrets, stars and rosettes galore.

CLIVEDEN, Taplow, Buckinghamshire ☎ (06286) 68561
While Brits turn their noses up, Japanese and Americans queue up to sample life in a real live English stately home. Former seat of the Astors, this famous Thameside house cost £3 million to turn into a hotel (sheets alone tucked in to a cool £200 a set). Liveried footmen, valets and maids carry and unpack your luggage, press your frock, and bow or curtsey, Ma'am. For décor read Splendour with a capital S.

HISTORIC HOTELS

The current outcrop of small historic hotels in London is yet another symptom of the turnaround from the big, brash, flash tower-block to the personal, tasteful home-you-wish-you-had from home. All privately owned, they pride themselves on personal service, character, a limited number of rooms – each individually and impeccably decorated down to the last tassel – and a high standard of cuisine. Top of the crop are: **THE BEAUFORT**, 33 Beaufort Gdns, SW3 ☎ (01) 584 5252 – chintz and pastel country-home appeal – nice flowers, soaps, chocs, books and a welcoming drink (no restaurant). **BLAKES**, 33 Roland Gardens, SW7 ☎ (01) 370 6701 – Anouska Hempel's swanky hotel, exotically decorated with her usual perfectionist eye for detail; a cosmopolitan oasis whose regulars include Pierre Cardin, Oscar de la Renta, Grace Jones. Ultra-stylish, expensive bar and restaurant. **DUKES HOTEL**, 35 St James's Place, SW1 ☎ (01) 491 4840 – dignified, masculine rooms downstairs, bedrooms and suites just like country drawing rooms. Good but extortionate restaurant. **HALCYON**, 81 Holland Park, W11 ☎ (01) 727 7288 – inspirational (and somewhat impractical) décor, lots of trompe l'oeil and paint effects. The Desert Room has murals and a colonial mosquito net, one suite has a parasol-filled conservatory. **Lord Lichfield** is impressed; Lauren Bacall, Bryan Ferry, Tina Turner and Richard Harris have stayed, but some suggest its non-central location may be its downfall. Fine Kingfisher restaurant. **HAZLITT'S**, 6 Frith St, W1 ☎ (01) 434 1771 – a secret corner of civilization in Soho, the cheapest at about £60 a double, no restaurant. **THE PORTOBELLO HOTEL**, 22 Stanley Gdns, W11 ☎ (01) 727 2777 – a Victorian terrace full of US and European models, and rock stars (U2, Simple Minds stayed before they hit Mayfair Hotel status; Eric Clapton still stays). Always a fight for the rooms with four-posters and for Suite 16 (round bed, Victorian bath – one of the biggest in London).

HAMBLETON HALL,
Hambleton, Oakham,
Leicestershire ☎ (0572) 56991
A Victorian hunting lodge, still
the perfect place for such
pursuits. Chef Brian Baker
continues in the tradition set by
Nick Gill, specializing in fine
fresh fish and game.

HOMEWOOD PARK, Hinton
Charterhouse, Bath, Avon
☎ (022122) 3731
If not the prettiest of houses
architecturally, the comfy
interior plus the warmth and
superb cooking from Stephen
and Penny Ross and their staff
more than make up for it.
*"Another favourite. Stephen is
a brilliant chef"* – **Roy
Ackerman.**

🕵 **HUNSTRETE HOUSE,**
Chelwood, Bristol, Avon
☎ (07618) 578
The epitome of the English
country house – Georgian,
antique-filled, with walled
garden, croquet lawn, tennis
court and heated swimming
pool. Small enough for you to
feel like a private guest. *"My
favourite. Such a relaxing
atmosphere. Thea Dupays is
fabulous the way she holds it
all together"* – **Roy Ackerman.**
René Lecler and **Jeffrey
Archer** say aye.

LE MANOIR AUX QUAT'
SAISONS, see Food & Drink

MIDDLETHORPE HALL,
Bishopthorpe, York, N
Yorkshire ☎ (0904) 641241
An elegant William and Mary
house overlooking York
racecourse. Punters put all
their money on this one.
*"Malcolm Broadbent, the
manager, runs a very good
ship. The chef is excellent.
What they've done is
tremendous – it was a total
wreck"* – **Roy Ackerman.**
*"Absolutely fabulous; great
food, people adore it"* – **Serena
Fass.**

🕵 **MILLER HOWE, Rayrigg**
Rd, Windermere, Cumbria
☎ (09662) 5236
*"Like a private country house.
Delicious food; biscuits and
Malvern water waiting for you
in your bedroom and bowls of*
*fruit in the corridor in case you
are still hungry"* – **Richard
Compton-Miller.** *"John Tovey
is a wonder. You may feel it's
over-histrionic, but it all comes
from an over-brimming
generous heart"* – **Hilary
Rubinstein.** What's more, he
can cook – *brilliantly.*

ROYAL CRESCENT
HOTEL, Royal Crescent,
Bath, Avon ☎ (0225) 319090
Superb building in the centre of
the crescent, with more rooms
in a Palladian villa round the
back. Lavish Regency suites
have four-posters, swagged
curtains and spa baths filled
from the hot springs.

SHARROW BAY, Howtown
Rd, Ullswater, Cumbria
☎ (08536) 301
The grande dame of country-
house hotels (many nippers
have modelled themselves on
her). *"They've been at it for
over 35 years and somehow
they give service out of their
hearts rather than their
pockets. There is a generosity
which extends beyond all else"*
– **Hilary Rubinstein.** *"For fun
and over-the-topness. It's like
staying with a rich auntie. Last
time we were there, some
Americans were paying with
wads of cash (they don't take
credit cards) and begging them
to find a booking for the
following year"* – **Roy
Ackerman.** King-sized feasts

with dozens of choices and
wicked puddings.

SHRUBLAND HALL
HEALTH CLINIC,
Coddenham, Suffolk
☎ (0473) 830404
The best health farm in Britain,
in a lovely country house with
gardens laid out in the style of
the Villa d'Este in Italy.
Owned by Lord and Lady de
Saumarez, it's the height of
relaxation with healthy
vegetarian food.

🕵 **STON EASTON PARK,**
Chewton Mendip, Bath, Avon
☎ (076121) 631
A grand-scale Palladian stately
(rated by **John Brooke-Little**).
Elegantly decorated and well
located for investigating the
West Country. *"Fabulously
good food; I couldn't
recommend it more highly.
Beautiful bathrooms"* – **Serena
Fass.** A favourite of **Jeffrey
Archer** and **Carol Wright:**
"Everything is perfect."

SUMMER LODGE, Evershot,
Dorset ☎ (093583) 424
*"The owners absolutely
understand what a difference it
makes to know who is turning
up, are at the door to welcome
you, make you tea and home-
made biscuits when you arrive,
perhaps clean your car . . .
their quality of hospitality goes
beyond the norm"* – **Hilary
Rubinstein.**

🕵 **Buzzzzzzzzz** Recently opened is **Stapleford
Park**, Bob Payton's Grade I listed stately with individual
designer rooms (Nina Campbell, Jane Churchill, Tiffany,
Crabtree & Evelyn, Wedgwood . . .). In huntin' country near
Melton Mowbray, Leics ☎ (057284) 522, with only 23 rooms,
croquet lawn, lake, etc, it's more like a house-party than a
hotel 🕵 . . . . . . Hurricanes hardly ever happen at Historic
House Hotels like **Hartwell House**: primed for a 1989
opening, this is the latest from Nick Cawley's 'chain'
(Bodysgallen, Middlethorpe). A Grade I 1760 building in 70
acres of Capability Brown parkland near Aylesbury, *"it will
be the best in the country"*, boasts Cawley.

★ ★

TRAVEL

THORNBURY CASTLE, Thornbury, Bristol
☎ (0454) 412647
Standards are still high since Maurice and Carol Taylor took over this Tudor castle after Kenneth Bell's retirement. "*It's a beautiful place with lovely style. Really good food – one of the best cheeseboards I've ever seen in this country, a fantastic selection including ones I'd never heard of before. All the produce is British*" – **Roy Ackerman.**

SCOTLAND

🏊 **ALTNAHARRIE INN, Ullapool, Highland**
☎ (085483) 230
A tiny inn run by Fred and Gunn Brown, where you are treated as house-guests; no choice of menu – but it's *all* dreamlike. "*Only four bedrooms and totally isolated. Gunn cooks and the food is wonderful*" – **Lady Macdonald of Macdonald.** "*You can only get to it by rowing a boat across the harbour. It's a case of bingo as to who's staying there, but the hospitality is very special*" – **Hilary Rubinstein.**

CHAMPNEYS AT STOBO CASTLE, Stobo Castle, Borders ☎ (07216) 249
A tiptop health farm retreat. "*Beautiful house and grounds in a quite spectacular valley. The most delicious food as far as calories allow*" – **Lady Macdonald of Macdonald.**

THE GLENEAGLES HOTEL, Auchterarder, Tayside ☎ (07646) 2231
Souped-up Scottish pile that will please all international golfers – a multitude of extra sporting facilities, restaurants, a hairdresser, bank, whirlpool baths, Y solarium, helipad – you name it. "*Marvellous indoor swimming pool, very good food*" – **Cliff Michelmore.** "*One of the greatest hotels in Britain. Spectacular*" – **Mark McCormack.**

GREYWALLS, Muirfield, Gullane, Lothian
☎ (0620) 842144
The best thing about this golden stone Lutyens house (a welcome incongruity in grey Scotland) is the cosy panelled library with plumped-up sofas, wall-to-wall collectors' editions of books and the proverbial roaring log fire. Golf on the famous Muirfield course and windswept walks to the sea.

🏊 **INVERLOCHY CASTLE, Fort William, Highland**
☎ (0397) 2177
Number one in Scotland, with votes from **Bob Payton** and Brooke Shields. Set in gorgeous rhododendron-filled grounds by Loch Lochy, in the shadow Ben Nevis, it's magnificent from the frescoed ceilings down to the local spring water. "*When Greta [Hobbs] is there it's great, like staying in a private castle. In the dining room, there are no staff around, but as soon as you put your fork down they appear – you feel they must be looking at you through cracks in the wall! It's just amazing ... incredibly efficient*" – **Roy Ackerman.** "*It's not only fantastic, it's probably the best in Britain*" – **Lady Macdonald of Macdonald.**

ISLE OF ERISKA HOTEL, Eriska, Strathclyde
☎ (063172) 371
Robin and Sheena Buchanan-Smith's hotel lies on a tiny but wild private island near Oban. "*Run like a country house. It's very hard to imagine that you are in a hotel after a day or so*" – **Lord Lichfield.**

KINLOCH LODGE, Sleat, Isle of Skye ☎ (04713) 214
Comfortable, homy little hotel run by Lord and **Lady Macdonald of Macdonald.** Wonderful seasonal food cooked by Lady M, who says: "*People come here for peace, quiet, walks – and drink. We have a super wine list.*"

WALES

🏊 **BODYSGALLEN HALL, Llandudno, Gwynedd**
☎ (0492) 84466
An imposing 17th-century grey stone mansion high on the hills above Conway, with 9 little self-contained cottages for shy guests. Sumptuous bedrooms, steaming scented baths and wraparound towels to sink into; scrumptious traditional food to sink your teeth into. A vote from **Roy Ackerman.**

Canada

ALTON

MILLCROFT INN, Box 89, John St, L0N 1A0
☎ (416) 791 4422
A restored mill in rural countryside just an hour from Toronto. Be sure to nab a table overlooking the waterfall.

BANFF

Top ski resort in the Canadian Rockies. Mount Norquay is famed for its steep runs, in particular the Lone Pine – one of the meanest in the world. Sunshine Village has masses of snow and you can ski across the Great Divide into BC. The nearby resort town of Lake Louise has two mountains with long runs. Best hotels, both standing like majestic castles in the middle of mountain ranges: **Banff Springs Hotel**, Banff, and **Château Lake Louise**, Lake Louise. Best dinner: the old **Post Hotel**, Lake Louise.

MONTREAL

HOTEL DE LA MONTAGNE, 1430 de la Montagne St, H3G 1Z5 ☎ (514) 288 5656
Intimate French hotel in the Arts district. Its 5-star restaurant Lutitia is a gourmet dream. "*Wonderful, old and elegant*" – **Robert Ramsay.**

RITZ-CARLTON, 1228 Sherbrooke West, H3G 1H6
☎ (514) 842 4212
Luxurious turn-of-the-century hotel near all the best boutiques, galleries and

restaurants. Its grand lobby is decorated in traditional European style.

TORONTO

FOUR SEASONS, 21 Avenue Rd, Yorkville, M5R 2G1
☎ **(416) 964 0411**
"The best hotel group. Many hotels claim they offer a high level of personal service, but the Four Seasons takes it to incredible levels so that you come to think you are the only person in the hotel. No false snobbery, they are nice to everybody" – **Robert Ramsay.** *"Always very nice"* – **Sondra Gotlieb.** Wonderful health-giving breakfasts, Truffles restaurant (see Food & Drink), and indoor and outdoor pools.

SUTTON PLACE HOTEL, 955 Bay St, M5S 2A2
☎ **(416) 924 9221**
In the heart of metro – the busy city centre – this is where Robert Redford and Kathleen Turner stay. *"One of the best hotels I've ever been in. If you're a frequent visitor you have your own bathrobe with your initials embroidered on it. It's great. I went to the hotel's English pub – it really is old, you know, with woodcuts and a big fireplace – and it was literally filled with Californian movie and TV stars – Tom Selleck, Ted Danson, Johnny Carson"* – **Joyce Davidson.**

WINDSOR ARMS HOTEL, 22 St Thomas St, M5S 2B9
☎ **(416) 979 2341**
Quiet, charming, old-fashioned and stalwart, with a loyal – though never fuddy-duddy – clientele. It boasts the finest afternoon tea in town and the Club 22 bar in the lobby which is where it's at for early-evening drinks.

VANCOUVER

PAN PACIFIC HOTEL, Suite 300, 999 Canada Place, V6C 3B5 ☎ **(604) 662 3223**
In the same 23-storey tower as the World Trade Center, it

HELI-SKIING

Instead of queuing for a lift that will eventually drop you on a piste packed with snow and punters, ski-whizzers – among them the King of Sweden, John Denver, **Margaux Hemingway** and Pierre Trudeau – prefer to pay about C$3000 a week to be chauffeur-whirled to the top of a mountainful of virgin snow and disgorged in 007 style on to its deep powder slopes. Only experienced, strong skiers can do it – terrain is totally unpredictable, and there's nothing firm to push against if you fall. The best heli-skiing is in the Bugaboos, Monashees and Cariboos in British Columbia. **CANADIAN MOUNTAIN HOLIDAYS**, PO Box 1660, Banff, Alberta T0L 0C0 ☎ (403) 762 4531 have *"the best tours available and expert guides. The heli takes you to runs like you have never seen before. It's absolutely amazing . . . breathtaking views. Skiing at its finest on top of some of the largest mountain ranges in the world. The ultimate vacation"* – **Steve Podborski.**

---

faces the spectacular Rocky Mountains and, appropriately, the Pacific Ocean. The lobby is fitted with BC bleached maple. Its restaurant, Five Sails, is justly famous.

WEDGEWOOD HOTEL, 845 Hornby St, V6Z 1V1
☎ **(604) 689 7777**
Intimate, elegant, European-style hotel with only 90 rooms. Superb service, good location in the downtown area, for those who want to remain incognito.

WHISTLER MOUNTAIN

Whistler and nearby Blackcomb Mountain offer the best skiing in Canada with the longest vertical drop in the Americas (4,278 ft). Heli-skiing and gorgeous powderbowl skiing. Trendy resort living in luxury condos, smart restaurants, ravy discos. *"Very good and very new"* – **Mark McCormack.**

TOURS

WHITEWATER ADVENTURES, 1616 Duranleau St, Vancouver V6H 3S4 ☎ **(604) 669 1110**
White-water rafting adventures of up to three days

---

down the Chilco and Nahani rivers of British Columbia. A new six-day tour down the Tatshenshini River whooshes you through glaciers, mountain streams and forests. Great for wildlife viewing.

Caribbean

ANGUILLA

A British colony, this sleepy coral island is one of the Leewards, the archipelago between Puerto Rico and Trinidad. Only 35 sq miles, it has secluded coves, sandy beaches, and turquoise seas for big game fishing.

MALLIOUHANA HOTEL, PO Box 173, Maids Bay
☎ **(809) 497 6111**
The most expensive and exclusive hotel in the Caribbean. Peace, at pushing £2,000 each a week without meals. Spectacular marble building perched on a cliff, each room with a sea view.

ANTIGUA

Largest of the Leewards, said to have a beach for every day of the year.

COPPER & LUMBER STORE, PO Box 184, St John's ☎ (809) 463 1058
A converted Napoleonic warehouse overlooking English Harbour. Bare brick walls, exposed beams, Persian rugs, Georgian antiques.

JUMBY BAY, PO Box 243, Long Island ☎ (809) 462 6000
If you want solitude or sport or fine dining or the lot, here's a 300-acre slice of paradise on a private island 2 miles north of Antigua. Ultra-comfortable villas hidden among the oleander and bougainvillaea.

MILL REEF CLUB, PO Box 133, St John's ☎ (809) 463 2081
Namesake of the racehorse *Mill Reef*, which is owned by chief club member Paul Mellon. For the in crowd, and intent on keeping it that way.

BAHAMAS

LYFORD CAY, New Providence
A private enclave for Bel Air types who are used to being locked away from the outside world – armed guards and 8-ft walls topped with military-style razor-wire keep the 'civilized' world with its pressures *out*. Some 250 pastel-coloured residences (worth $1m to $5m) house tax exiles and/or sun worshippers such as Arthur Hailey, Bernard Ashley, Sean Connery (who has 2 pads), Ringo Starr and Barbara Bach, plus Yardleys (sniff), Cadburys (munch) and Bacardis (swig).

WINDERMERE ISLAND CLUB, PO Box 25, Rock Sound, Eleuthera ☎ (809) 332 2538
The most exclusive and pretty resort, surrounded by candy-coloured beaches.

BARBADOS

Often referred to as 'Little England'. The smart part is St James Beach, on the west coast, although some smarties

are packing up to find less developed spots. The most beautiful house is **Heron Bay**, occasionally available for rent: *"There's nothing in the Caribbean of its standard. It's a great house, a sensational Palladian villa"* – **Lord Lichfield.** Those who have been Barbados-way include Paul McCartney, Mick Jagger (who rents a villa at Bathsheba on the east coast), Elton John, Princess Margaret, Omar Sharif and Bryan Ferry (who stays at the **COLONY CLUB**, St James ☎ (809) 422 2335).

CORAL REEF CLUB, St James ☎ (809) 422 2372
"One of the finest resort hotels in the Caribbean" – **René Lecler.** Cottages set in tropical gardens; endless water sports, tennis, golf, riding and polo. Formal dress is decreed on occasion.

GLITTER BAY, St James ☎ (809) 422 4111
"It's doing very well and is rather 'in' at the moment" – **Lord Lichfield.** Hot off the construction site is the grandly named Royal Pavilion, whose suites (and particularly the penthouse) are super-super-deluxe.

SANDY LANE HOTEL, St James ☎ (809) 432 1311
"One of the grander hotels on the island. The most beautiful setting and architecturally the nicest" – **Lord Lichfield.** Owned by THF, it has a private beach and golf course.

SETTLERS BEACH HOTEL, St James ☎ (809) 422 3052
Landing spot of the first settlers in Barbados. 22 self-catering villas amid coconut palms just by the beach. It's **Prue Leith**'s best on the island.

BERMUDA

Not strictly part of the Caribbean, this densely populated British outpost is way out on its own in the Atlantic, some 800 miles south-east of New York. A group of 150 coral islands.

CAMBRIDGE BEACHES, Mangrove Bay, Sandy's Parish ☎ (809) 294 0331
An original cottage colony (recently renovated) with a pink 17th-century main house, set on a peninsula with glorious ocean beaches either side. The colonial format has been much copied in the West Indies.

DOMINICA

An island with *sights*: waterfalls, sulphur springs, freshwater lakes, a gorge, botanic gardens and rain-forests. *"My favourite island in the West Indies. So beautiful and lush. It feels undiscovered, not yet destroyed by tourism.* **REIGATE HALL HOTEL** [Roseau ☎ (809) 445 4031] *is very comfortable, very good"* – **Quentin Crewe.** The secluded **PAPILLOTE WILDERNESS RETREAT** ☎ (809) 445 2287 is near the Trafalgar Triple Waterfalls and natural hot mineral baths.

DOMINICAN REPUBLIC

"The best beaches in the Caribbean – so long and completely empty. Santo Domingo has the most marvellous – and certainly the earliest – colonial architecture in all the Americas. The hotel I stayed in, **NICOLAS DE OVANDO***, Calle Las Damas 53* ☎ *687 7181, was built in 1502 for the governor. It goes up and down as a place but it's a lovely building"* – **Quentin Crewe.**

GRENADA

"One of the most up-and-coming islands. A little down at heel after the invasion, with the worst roads in the world, but there is enormous potential ... nutmeg and spices and real West Indian people. The 20th century hasn't quite got there" – **Lord Lichfield.** *"The prettiest*

capital town is St George's. A lot of it is 18th century. The trouble with most of the West Indies is the buildings get blown down in hurricanes" – **Quentin Crewe. SPICE ISLAND INN**, St George's ☎ (809) 444 4258 has luxurious suites directly on Grand Anse Beach, one of the best in the Caribbean.

GRENADINES

32 islands and cays dotted about between Grenada and St Vincent, including **Bequia, Mustique** and **Petit St Vincent**. The best winter cruising waters (under sail) in the world.

BEQUIA
6 sq miles of exclusivity, where the Queen and Bob Dylan have stayed.

MUSTIQUE
Playground of royals and super-rich, who own colonial-style houses designed by Oliver Messel. The biggest house in the Caribbean, a multi-million-dollar project, has just been built here by the American Harding Lawrence – which has shaken the old guard. The best way to stay here is to know or be related to him/Princess Margaret/Lord Glenconner/Prince Rupert Löwenstein/Lynn Wyatt/Mick Jagger/David Bowie, etc. That's what Viscount Linley, Prince Andrew, Raquel Welch and Margaux Hemingway do. Otherwise it's book way ahead for the **COTTON HOUSE** ☎ (809) 458 4621, an 18th-century former cotton storehouse made of stone and coral. *"On Mustique, public people can be private. It's relaxed, not grand, but has that fundamental Caribbean atmosphere"* – **Lord Lichfield.** The one drawback has been the poor standard of eating out. *"They have coriander, yams, aubergines, every ingredient for true Caribbean cooking, yet they import frozen steaks from Canada"* – **LL.** Plans are afoot for a new Lichfield eatery to remedy this.

PALM ISLAND
John and Mary Caldwell sailed round the world to find this little Garden of Eden and now keep a sloop for sailing parties. Local Creole cooking. **PALM ISLAND BEACH CLUB** ☎ (809) 458 4804.

PETIT ST VINCENT
Hide away here and you might never be found. Privately owned and traffic free except for Mini-mokes that scoot round the island tending to guests' every whim. As none of the 22 cottages has a 'phone, guests hoist a yellow flag to summon room service (guaranteed to vroom up within 15 minutes) or a red flag to keep the mokes at bay. **PETIT ST VINCENT RESORT** ☎ (809) 458 4801.

HAITI

LE RELAIS DE L'EMPEREUR, Petit Goave ☎ (509) 240318; **reservations** ☎ (212) 980 5140
Luxurious, private, palatial and exotic, this retreat is run by the flamboyant Olivier Coquelin. They attempt to materialize the whims of guests before they are expressed. King-size suites, private beach, olympic pool, and gardens in which Coquelin strolls with his Burmese leopard Sheba.

JAMAICA

THE HALF MOON CLUB, PO Box 80, Montego Bay ☎ (809) 953 2211
Superbly run, one of **René Lecler**'s top 3 in the Caribbean. A profusion of tropical vegetation spreading over 400 acres; a mile of private beach; an 18-hole Robert Trent Jones golf course (one of the best in the Caribbean), 13 tennis and 4 squash courts.

JAMAICA INN, Ocho Rios ☎ (809) 974 2514
A small, very elegant resort – only 45 uncluttered rooms, each with their own terrace. One of the loveliest stretches of beach, private cove, fresh-water pool.

PLANTATION INN, PO Box 2, Ocho Rios ☎ (809) 974 5601
A chi-chi resort set on twin white crescent beaches with a spectacular coral reef a short flipper away. The main inn is a perfect white colonial building with columned portico and wrought-iron balconies.

ROUND HILL, PO Box 64, Montego Bay ☎ (809) 952 5150
Elite social resort. Local-style whitewashed villas with high ceilings and verandahs, set in lush greenery. The piano in the main bar is the very same one that Noel Coward and Leonard Bernstein have played.

SANS SOUCI, PO Box 103, Ocho Rios, St Anne ☎ (09) 974 2353
Recently revamped beachside resort snuggling among the palms. Tennis club, swimming pool and a natural spring-fed mineral spa.

TRYALL GOLF & BEACH CLUB, Sandy Bay Post Office, Hanover Parish ☎ (809) 952 5110
A 2,200-acre Shangri-La centred around the 1834 Great House. The garden is dotted with villas, each with private cook, chambermaid, laundress, gardener and swimming pool. Tennis, an 18-hole golf course and water sports galore.

NEVIS

Separated from St Kitts by a 3-mile channel known as The Narrows. Sleepy, but *"very civilized"* – **Quentin Crewe.**

MONTPELIER PLANTATION INN, PO Box 474 ☎ (809) 469 5462
A super little place on the slopes of Mount Nevis. Fruit and veg are grown in the hotel grounds, bread and marmalade are home-made. *"So informal and friendly"* – **Quentin Crewe.**

ST KITTS

Forested volcanic hills slope down to exquisite sheltered

beaches, some of soft black volcanic sand.

GOLDEN LEMON, Dieppe Bay ☎ (809) 465 7260
"*Small and quite beautiful*" – **René Lecler**. An elegantly decorated haven with its own walled garden. Colonial ceiling fans, canopied beds and an open wood-floored gallery running round the 18th-century building. Where Kennedys and other faces hide away, often booking under an assumed name.

St Lucia

"*Very lush. The Pitons must be a wonder of the world – two strange volcanic mountains that shoot out of the sea, rising abruptly in a cone shape. Lord Glenconner has bought a plantation between them, which must be one of the most beautiful spots in the world*" – **Quentin Crewe**. This spot, Soufrière, is destined to become the next Mustique. However, Lord G's plans to build a private resort are far from the point of realization.

Tobago

Robinson Crusoe's island: smaller and more exclusive than its sister island, Trinidad. Miles of white sandy beaches and a tropical interior with mountains rising to 2,000 ft. **MOUNT IRVINE BAY HOTEL ☎ (809) 639 3871** has a 200-year-old converted sugar-mill restaurant. **HOTEL ROBINSON CRUSOE ☎ (809) 639 2571** is an old colonial hotel.

Virgin Islands

A cluster of 60 tiny islands east of Puerto Rico. The largest are Tortola and Virgin Gorda. Trade winds keep the climate breezy, and the waters are crystal clear.

CANEEL BAY, PO Box 120, St John, US Virgin Islands ☎ (809) 776 6111
Sister to Little Dix. The rooms and beaches are squeaky clean and spacious.

LITTLE DIX BAY, PO Box 70, Virgin Gorda, British Virgin Islands ☎ (809) 495 5555
300 acres of paradise. Stilted thatched cottages, an open-air dining room and marina.

Rentals

ALLEYNE, AGUILAR & ALTMANN, Rosebank, Derricks, St James, Barbados ☎ (809) 432 0840
Top-notch properties on Barbados for rent.

Yacht Charter

NICHOLSON'S YACHT CHARTER, English Harbour, Antigua ☎ (809) 463 1059 and CHARTER SERVICES, PO Box 9998, St Thomas, US Virgin Islands ☎ (809) 774 5300
A fine range of sailing yachts.

China

Beijing

JIANGUO, Jianguomen Wai Rd ☎ (1) 502233
Part of the Peninsula group, it's "*infinitely more convenient, far more comfortable and has far better service than the Great Wall Hotel with its huge atrium and [not entirely reliable] external lifts whizzing*

up and down. It's where everybody in the know stays, where everybody meets. A friendly, amenable hotel" – **Robin Hanbury-Tenison**.

SHANGRI-LA, 29 Zizhuyuan Rd ☎ (1) 802 1122
Hard on the heels of the Jianguo (some say it's overtaken), a 24-storey, 786-room, 40-suite, anonymously international deluxe affair. Best suite: the 4-room Royal.

Guangzhou

WHITE SWAN HOTEL, Shamian Island ☎ (20) 886968
Part of the Fok empire, this was one of the first Western-style hotels in China. By the Pearl River and the Banyan gardens, it is built around a central skylit atrium with an indoor water garden.

Xian

GOLDEN FLOWER HOTEL, 8 Chanan Xijie, Shaanxi Province ☎ 32981
By perhaps the greatest archaeological site in the world, home of the Terracotta Army – which ensures the hotel plays to full houses. "*The best hotel in all China. They have managed to create a first-class luxury hotel, which takes enormous courage and determination*" – **Robin Hanbury-Tenison**. Great restaurant (see Food & Drink) and the best breakfasts in the land – *real* bacon and eggs (local food for lunch and dinner is great, but a hearty Western breakfast is the acid test of a good hotel in China).

❝ *Shanghai is an enormous, fascinating city. It's well worth taking short train journeys on the excellent Chinese trains to places like Wuxi to look at the silk worms and to see the countryside* **❞**

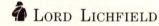 Lord Lichfield

CREWE TIPS

Quentin Crewe advises: *"Stay in a less grand hotel and order a suite for the most comfort at an inexpensive price ... The best of* **Paraguay** *is the Jesuit missions that the film [The Mission] was about. The ruins are well worth going to see ... The best travel guide, in a league of its own, is the* South American Handbook," edited by John Brooks (Travel & Trade Publications), and also voted tops by **Robin Hanbury-Tenison** and Graham Greene.

Colombia

CARTAGENA

"One of the best colonial towns in South America – it really is stunning. The fortifications are some of the best in the world" – **Quentin Crewe.** *"The best undiscovered resort on the Caribbean Sea. An intact colonial city with a good beach, modern hotels, very good food. And the city is safe to walk about in"* – **Edward Lucie-Smith.**

SAN AGUSTIN

"As good as Machu Picchu: a really exciting and beautiful place in the mountains. There are stone carvings and tombs of a pre-Inca civilization" – **Quentin Crewe.**

Ecuador

"Quito, the capital, is very high up [9,262ft] and has equal day and night because it's slap bang on the Equator. It is ringed by volcanoes, which everyone hopes are extinct. If you're romantically inclined, get up early and see them without the mist on top. Everything is so green and fertile. Not far away is the Equator. It's great romantic mad fun, especially if you have a childish streak, which I do, to put one foot on either side of the Equator and have your

picture taken" – **Elisabeth Lambert Ortiz.** *"The most peaceful little country with such an immense variety. It's possible to go from Quito to the jungle, to the top of a volcano or to the coast – all in one weekend"* – **Quentin Crewe.** *"The people are very kind. Generally a delightful place"* – **Dan Topolski.**

GALAPAGOS ISLANDS

"Go and see them before it's too late. They're threatened by pollution. Anyone who cares about nature will find them incomparable" – **Elisabeth Lambert Ortiz.** *"A must. Completely atypical tropical islands where Darwin developed his* Origin of Species. *58 islands, each containing unique flora and fauna. Huge tortoises 4 ft in diameter, iguanas, birds – blue-footed boobies, red-footed boobies, 13 different types of finch, flamingoes, albatross – a mass of things. They only let 16,000 people on the islands each year. You fly to the main island, Isla Isabela, and hire a boat. You take a guide and a cook, who dives over the side every mealtime and brings up fresh fish. You stay on the boat"* – **Dan Topolski.**

Egypt

Land of the Pharaohs, home of the Pyramids, the Sphinx, the tomb of Tutankhamun and countless other magnificent tributes to an ancient civilization, all now treated with a sad irreverence. Tourists scramble over pyramids, while guides scrape at wall paintings in tombs that have withstood their first 5,000 years but many not hold out for the next 5,000. In the Cairo Museum, the treasures of Tut's tomb are displayed offhandedly (rumour has it, in any case, that the originals were long since sold to Russia).

The Nile, an estimated 40 million years old, is Egypt's lifeblood. In this part of the Dark Continent, it rains perhaps 5 times a year. Travelling upriver from 2,320-year-old ALEXANDRIA, with its superb beaches, you reach CAIRO, a sand-tinged, crumbling, traffic-jammed bedlam, the largest city in all Africa. Sail for LUXOR, on the East Bank of the Nile, a calm winter resort with staggering temples and monuments. Just upriver at Thebes is the Valley of the Kings, where lie the tombs of Tutankhamun and Rameses VI. Past Edfu and Kom Ombo to ASWAN, salubrious and beautiful. Plant Island is its showplace for rare, exotic flora.

MENA HOUSE OBEROI, Pyramid Rd, Giza, Cairo ☎ **(02) 855444**
For claustrophobics who aren't so mad about chock-a-block Cairo. This is the old colonial weekend palace where Army and diplomatic bigwigs would meet. *"It remains one of the great success stories of hotel-keeping anywhere in the world. Fancy opening your windows in the morning and having breakfast looking at the pyramids!"* – **René Lecler.**

SALAMLEK, Kasr El-Montazah, Alexandria ☎ **(03) 860585**
A converted wing of Al-Montazah Palace, summer residence of the former Egyptian Royal family. On high ground overlooking an exquisite beach on the eastern tip of Alexandria, surrounded by colossal gardens and woods.

Nile Tours

BALES TOURS, SERENISSIMA, VOYAGES JULES VERNE, KUONI, GUERBA EXPEDITIONS and SILK CUT TRAVEL are among those who do Nile trips – see World Transport.

HELIOTOURS EGYPT, 105 Higgaz St, Heliopolis
☎ (02) 87708
Cruises arranged locally on MS *Helio*, one of the best boats on the river.

Fiji Islands

322 tropical islands, many mountainous, in the western South Pacific.

THE REGENT OF FIJI, PO Box 9081, Nadi Airport
☎ 70700
Typical tropical set-up of modern town precinct meets the jungle village: a central lofty lobby opening onto restaurants, bars and shops, set in a lush Garden of Eden dotted with simple, stylish villas. Humorous, friendly staff with bushy bushy hairdos. The barman is called Sam Meat Pie. Each day a plane glides up the beach and whisks you away to your chosen island, there to feast and imbibe champagne until nightfall.

TAVEUNI
"Beautiful, tiny, exotic, tropical island, and rather inaccessible" – **Lord Lichfield**. On the 180° longitude line, the true International Date Line (in practice, the line skirts it). The only place where you can stand with one leg in today and one in tomorrow.

TOBERUA
A 4-acre microdot, undetected by rainclouds and mosquitoes. Fresh water is brought over by barge from Fiji. Peaceful days of sunning, windsurfing, snorkelling and fishing and nights in your private thatched bure – on land or floating.

France

♟ —Europe's Best— ♟

	HOTELS
1	**HOTEL RITZ**, Paris
2	**CIPRIANI**, Venice
3	**HOTEL DU CAP-EDEN ROC**, Antibes
4	**CLARIDGE'S**, London
5	**HOTEL VIER JAHRESZEITEN**, Hamburg
6	**THE CONNAUGHT**, London
7	**HOTEL DE CRILLON**, Paris
8	**GSTAAD PALACE**, Gstaad
9	**SUVRETTA HOUSE**, St Moritz
10	**THE RITZ**, Madrid

AUCH

HOTEL DE FRANCE, place de la Libération, 32000
☎ 6205 0044
A small provincial hotel in Auch, west of Toulouse. Unprepossessing perhaps, but breakfasts from its restaurant, Daguin, entice **Jean Demachy** back: *"They wheel in a table with 5 kinds of bread, home-made croissants, 6 different jams, farm yogurt, pots and pots of freshly ground coffee, and special foie gras on toast. Sinful and marvellous."*

BIARRITZ

HOTEL DU PALAIS, 1 ave de l'Impératrice, 64200
☎ 5924 0940
So grand as to take on a surrealistic quality. Built under Napoleon III, when Empress Eugénie made Biarritz fashionable. Central, yet it stands in splendid isolation in its own; formal gardens enclosed by railings. Excellent restaurant and views over the ocean.

HOTEL MIRAMAR, ave de l'Impératrice, 64200
☎ 5924 8520
Where Princesses Stéphanie and Ira von Fürstenberg take the sea cure at the Louison Bobet thalassotherapy institute. *"The chef, André Gauzère, manages to prepare 400-calorie meals that taste like 1,500 calories!"* – **Princess Ira von Fürstenberg.**

CHAMONIX

"If you really want to ski, go to les Grands Moutets near Mont Blanc. You will get the kick of your life facing a 6,500 ft vertical drop. The famous hors-piste of Le Pas de Cheure is the corniche of ski. Les Grands Moutets are the Mecca of non-ski and snow-surf. The initiators of ski extrème and other famous ski heroes have made it their sand box" – **Olivier Coquelin.**

COURCHEVEL

Le plus chic resort for young French and British – plus **Margaux Hemingway**, Giscard d'Estaing, Roman Polanski and Roger Vadim. Private jets wing in to the Altiport. Immaculately kept runs for all levels, and the best base for off-piste skiing. Best hotel: Hôtel des Neiges. Best bar: Jack's Bar, aka La Saulire. Best clubs: La Grange; Caves de la Loze (mainly French); St Nicolas (mainly Brits).

DEAUVILLE

HOTEL ROYAL, blvd Cornuché, 14800 ☎ 3188 1641
Chic-er than its sister hotel, the Normandy, this splendid stucco palace is part of the Lucien Barrière chain which also owns the Majestic at Cannes. Stars of the American Film Festival are snapped lounging round its kidney-shaped pool. One such was Liz Taylor (who has a suite named after her). Impeccable service and a knack of always remembering your name.

EUGENIE-LES-BAINS

LES PRES ET LES SOURCES D'EUGENIE-LES-BAINS, 40320 Geaune ☎ 5851 1901
A large white country house in a tropical park, set in the famous spa in the south-west of France. For when your liver needs a holiday, or you fancy rubbing slender shoulders with the likes of Catherine Deneuve and Isabelle Adjani. *"The hotel is so elegant it feels like you're visiting friends who have excellent taste"* – **Jean Demachy.** Cuisine by Michel Guérard (see Food & Drink).

MEGEVE

Set in a wide valley, ensuring longer daylight hours than most Alpine resorts. Its where the ultra-smart natives go (it's almost exclusively French). **Inès de la Fressange** loves it. Hotter on nightlife than skiing – it's too low to be sure of snow. Best hotel: Chalet Mont d'Arbois (best food, too).

Grade. *"My favourite ski resort, perfect when you have a family. Every level of skiing and, being France, wonderful food"* – **Jane Asher.** Best lunch: buffet on the terrace of Hôtel Tarentaise in Mottaret; best dinner: Chez Kiki.

PARIS

HOTEL DE L'ABBAYE SAINT-GERMAIN, 10 rue Cassette, 75006 ☎ (1) 4544 3811
A charming little hotel only a short walk from La Coupole and Café de Flore, yet you could be in a French provincial town 50 years ago. Stay in a ground-floor bedroom, which leads into the lovely bird-filled garden.

HOTEL LE BRISTOL, 112 rue de Faubourg St Honoré, 75008 ☎ (1) 4266 9145
A glamorous hotel. Exclusive and discreet, it's where prominent Americans and diplomats stay. A favourite of former Israeli PM Menachem Begin, and of **Mark McCormack.** Terrace, gardens

"Unrivalled – one of Paris's most beautiful historic buildings, and service to match. Also one of the best places for a power breakfast" – **Jean Demachy.** *"It's got the best address and it's beautiful. I've stayed here since I used to photograph for Vogue. The nicest time to be there is during the collections. It was fascinating when La Vreeland used to hold court"* – **Lord Lichfield.** For **Alan Crompton-Batt** (who, to be fair, has links with the place), it's *"my joint best, with the Pierre in New York. I think it's a faultless hotel."* *"Excellently run, very pretty"* – **Andrew Lloyd Webber.**

L'HOTEL, 13 rue des Beaux-Arts, 75006 ☎ (1) 4325 2722
Famous as the place where Oscar Wilde died. Some rooms are a shade tasteless, a symphony in leopardskin. But it's got sex appeal; it's fun, it's different, it's Rive Gauche. A favourite of **Jane Seymour** and **Lord McAlpine:** *"The one I enjoy most – it gives one the feeling that it might have been a centre for subrosa activities."*

> ❝ *The best experience of my life was standing at the top of a glacier near Mont Blanc at about 12,000ft. There was no sound of anything whatsoever. My ears just buzzed – I'd never heard no sound before! Then I skied down – no wind, dry, clean, pure air and the view of snow-topped mountains glistening in the sun* ❞

 MICHAEL GRADE

MERIBEL-LES-ALLUES

Attractive chalet resort, excellent for families and for many smart, private British, like the Dukes of Kent and Bedford. Extensive skiing at the hub of the largest ski-lift system in Europe. *"Particularly delightful because you have access to the Trois Vallées. It's just divine, you can ski all day and never do the same run twice. The air is wonderful"* – **Michael**

and a fantasy pool like an Edwardian yacht, with polished wooden 'deck'. See also Food & Drink.

🏨 **HOTEL DE CRILLON, 10 place de la Concorde, 75008 ☎ (1) 4265 2424**
Absolutely stunning 18th-century palace, gleaming with marble, mirrors and chandeliers. Bedrooms, redecorated by Sonia Rykiel, retain their marble bathrooms that ooze super-luxe. Les Ambassadeurs (see Food & Drink) is one of the most glittering restaurants in Paris.

THE LANCASTER, 7 rue de Berri, 75008 ☎ (1) 4359 9043
A member of the Savoy group, it's discreet, personal and individual, like a private house (with beautiful leafy courtyard) where movie stars can be normal and everyone is cosseted. One contributor feels it's a shade faux, *"as if someone has actually scraped some of the pile off the carpet to make it look like an English country house"*, but most enjoy it for what it is: *"a lovely hotel, full of antiques"* – **Egon Ronay;** *"wonderful, quiet and well-organized"* – **Keith Floyd;**

"terribly cosy and has a wonderful un-hotel feeling" – **Lady Elizabeth Anson.**

HOTEL LENOX, 9 rue de l'Université, 75006
☎ **(1) 4296 1095**
A gem. Each room is decorated in country-house style with a proliferation of beams, eaves and ambience – and an extremely courteous concierge.

🏨 **HOTEL PLAZA-ATHENEE, 25 ave Montaigne, 75008**
☎ **(1) 4723 7833**
Très huitième: this could only be Paris. Lustrous silk couches, marble surfaces, a little courtyard profuse with plants. Audrey Hepburn, Herbert von Karajan, Sydney Pollack, Michael J Fox and Ben Kingsley stay; **Harvey Goldsmith, Mark McCormack, Egon Ronay** and **Lady Elizabeth Anson** admire its panache. Between 4pm and 6pm, café society meets to swap gossip in the long lobby by the courtyard.

REGENT'S GARDEN HOTEL, 6 rue Pierre Demours, 75017
☎ **(1) 4574 0730**
"One of the best-kept secrets in Paris. It's small [no more than 20 rooms], exclusive and very lovely, with a garden where you can have meals" – **Jean-Philippe Chatrier.** Norman Mailer stays here.

RESIDENCE MAXIM'S, 42 ave Gabriel, 75008
☎ **(1) 4561 9633**
The latest rabbit to spring from Pierre Cardin's hat. Vying for most luxurious hotel in Paris, the smallest room is a 500-sq ft suite, the largest a 2,500-sq ft apartment. No coffee shop here; instead a 'caviarteria' to assuage those little caviare-snack cravings, the Maximum bar, and a garden for breakfast and tea. Prices at the summit of the 'if you need to ask, this is not for you' scale.

🏨 **HOTEL RITZ, 15 place Vendôme, 75001**
☎ **(1) 4260 3830**
This is what ritziness is all about – grand glamorous décor, supremacy of setting, comfort, service and cuisine. *"The best hotel in the world. I love it because I spent my honeymoon there and my husband and I went back every year. It is the one place in the world where you can make love after luncheon, and people do not hammer on the door and ask 'are you ill?'"* – **Barbara Cartland.** *"I was very impressed when I went recently. I noticed that a lot of my old friends on the staff of the Plaza Athenée had moved there"* – **Taki.** *"It epitomizes the grand hotel – it's unashamedly luxurious and all the better for it"* – **Lord Lichfield.** *"Quite different from the Ritz in London; it's the real*

thing" – **Egon Ronay.** It's in **Frank Bowling**'s world top 10, **Barbara Kafka**'s best in Paris, and a favourite of **Joan Collins**, Barbra Streisand, **René Lecler, Lynn Wyatt** and **Lord Montagu of Beaulieu.**

HOTEL ROYAL MONCEAU, 35 ave Hoche, 75008
☎ **(1) 4561 9800**
A favourite of **Princess Ira von Fürstenberg** for its *"faultless room service, excellent Italian restaurant [Le Carpaccio] and the health spa"*. While wives are luxuriating in the spa, Les Thermes du Royal Monceau, with swimming pool, sauna, Jacuzzi, massage and La Prairie beauty institute, husbands can test the best bullshot in Paris in the bar.

Riviera

BEACH CLUB, Monte Carlo Beach Hotel, route du Bord de Mer, Roquebrune-Cap-Martin, 06190 ☎ **9378 2140**
Where Monte Coolos languish, bronzed and expensively, around the swimming pool (the beach itself is passé). Princess Stéphanie, in her Pool Position swimwear, and family hold court by their tent on the sea front, with 2 guards on standby.

LE CAP ESTEL, 06360 Eze Bord de Mer ☎ **9301 5044**
Set on a promontory with huge gardens and its own tiny beach. *"I have stayed there for 20 years. For ambience, there's no hotel in the South of France with such wonderful surroundings. A garden with pheasants, a swimming pool, and climbing geraniums. They have made little suites in the walls so when you look out you could spit in the sea if you wanted to. It is lovely"* – **Barbara Cartland. René Lecler** recommends.

CARLTON INTER-CONTINENTAL, 58 blvd de la Croisette, 06406 Cannes
☎ **9368 9168**
At Film Festival time, top producers and stars immerse themselves in the Carlton's Belle Époque luxury and hold

🕵 **Buzzzzzzzz** For nostalgia's sake, visit the old expat actors' hang-out **La Voile d'Or**, 06230 St Jean Cap Ferrat ☎ 9301 1313 (*"Some of the best food and probably one of the most incredible views in the world, but the walls are thin..."* – **Andrew Lloyd Webber**). Also **Château de la Chèvre d'Or**, rue Barri, 06360 Eze Village ☎ 9341 1212 🏨 ...... For curiosity's sake, visit **Grand Hôtel du Cap**, blvd de Général de Gaulle, 06230 St Jean Cap Ferrat ☎ 9376 0021: *"The one that everybody is intrigued about. It's been bought by a rich American for his wife, who has installed a railway down to the beach. It is quite stunning"* – **Andrew Lloyd Webber.**

★ ★

power talks over cocktails on the Terrace. Best cocktail: champagne framboise. Pandemonium reigns, with producers making deals in every nook and cranny. If you mean business, you stay here.

LE CHATEAU EZA, 06360 Eze Village, Alpes-Maritimes ☎ 9341 1224
A rustic hilltop stone château with fantastic views, run by Dominique and Danielle le Stanc. *"Absolutely idyllic hotel in one of those edge-of-the-hill villages; very beautiful"* – **Andrew Lloyd Webber.** See also Food & Drink.

🏆 **LA COLOMBE D'OR, St-Paul-de-Vence, 06570 Alpes-Maritimes ☎ 9332 8002**
An absolute delight, on the edge of a perfect medieval hill town, but impossible to penetrate unless you have *ropes* to pull. *"They're not snooty, just conscious that regular guests rebook every year and they hate to turn them down"* – **Frank Lowe.** Former guests Dufy, Matisse, Picasso, Miro, Utrillo, Braque et al would pay their bills in kind. Almost every inch of the simple whitewashed, arched and winding interior bears testimony to their work, round each corner is a new surprise – paintings, sculptures, painted glass, decorated cushions and lamp-bases. Yves Montand has made it his southern home and plays pétanque with the villagers. You can see Chagall's simple gravestone in the hilltop graveyard.

🏆 **HOTEL DU CAP-EDEN ROC, blvd Kennedy, Cap d'Antibes, 06604 Antibes ☎ 9361 3901**
Surely the most glamorous hotel imaginable – sweeping up to the grand entrance is an instant flashback to the between-wars era when Scott and Zelda Fitzgerald and Noel Coward would stay. (Now you could bump into Harrison Ford, Cher, Jacques Chirac or Madonna.) The impact of the butter-yellow château is knockout: you go up the stone stairway into an immense

---

THE RETURN OF THE LIVING MED

We asked if the Med was dead and the answer was no: concussed, perhaps, but now revived. *"The South of France is back to what it used to be; loads of English people are returning, now they can afford it. St Jean Cap Ferrat is the best place with unarguably the best situation. They haven't been allowed to develop there, so it is still a fishing village"* – **Andrew Lloyd Webber.** *"Wonderful climate, wonderful food, wonderful atmosphere"* – **Richard Compton-Miller.** People with pads there include Stavros Niarchos (and his yacht, *Atlantis II*) and Fredy Heineken (both Cap d'Antibes), Mrs David Niven, Estée Lauder and the Oscar Wyatts (all Cap Ferrat), Natasha and Joely Richardson (La Garde-Freinet), **Joan Collins** (Port Grimaud; and her boat, *Sins*), Karl Lagerfeld, **'Bubbles' Rothermere**, Michael York and Anthony Burgess (Monte Carlo), Dirk Bogarde (Grasse), Shirley Conran (Seillans), Gunther Sachs, Christina Onassis, Herbert von Karajan (and ocean racer *Helisara VI*), Mick Jagger and Elton John (St Tropez).

---

sunlit, marble-floored lobby, which opens at the far side on to beautifully tended green gardens and the sea. *"Stunning"* – **Andrew Lloyd Webber.** A world best for **Barbara Kafka, Joan Collins, Viscountess Rothermere, Mariuccia Mandelli, Marie Helvin** (*"the most romantic and glamorous hotel in the world"*), **Frank Bowling** (*"It has the most wonderful position"*) and **Joyce Davidson.**

HOTEL MAJESTIC, 14 blvd de la Croisette, 06407 Cannes ☎ 9368 9100
"The best formal resort hotel – it would need a great deal of beating" – **René Lecler.** Splendid, sparkling white, with a heated pool and palm-filled garden. Vies with the Carlton as *the* place to stay as it's so near the Palais du Festival.

🏆 **LA RESERVE DE BEAULIEU, 5 blvd General Leclerc, 06310 Beaulieu-sur-Mer ☎ 9301 0001**
Elegant apricot-tinted building decorated in light summery pastels. *"Probably the best hotel in the world"* – **Lord McAlpine.** *"A lovely hotel"* – **Andrew Lloyd Webber.**

VAL D'ISERE

Already hotting up for the 1992 Winter Olympics, this is the finest ski area in the world, according to ex-ski champ Killy, who learnt here. A largely British population hangs out at the Members' Bar of Dick's T-Bar (a nightclub that's more glam than it sounds, with outdoor lasers shining on to the mountains). Best wine bar/restaurant: Au Bout de la Rue, run by mustachioed José; tapas, and fine wines by the glass thanks to the Cruover machine.

Monaco

HERMITAGE, square Beaumarchais, 98000 Monte Carlo ☎ 9350 6731
Some think it's the best hotel in town – it has a wonderful established, old-fashioned air. **Lord Lichfield** recommends.

HOTEL DE PARIS, place du Casino, 98007 Monte Carlo ☎ 9350 8080
The landmark hotel in Monte

TRAVEL

Carlo. If its old standards of formality have slipped since the old days, and rooms are slightly dated deluxe, it still oozes gloss and glamour during the Grand Prix and Red Cross Ball week, when the jetset stay in harbourside suites, watch the motor-set and wave to the yacht-set. Fine restaurant, Louis XV (see Food & Drink).

French Polynesia

The best thing about these islands is the aerial view: the inky blue ocean, studded with green volcanic islands, each ringed with a reef that is marked by white surf. Within the reef the lagoon water is still and translucent, shaded from aquamarine to indigo. Best view from terra firma: from the top of Mount Tapioi on Raiatea. It's sadly true that the arrival town of Papeete, capital of Tahiti, is dirty and noisy. It's best to grab the first plane out to a smaller isle, or cruise around by private yacht.

BORA BORA
The only island that really caters to the rich, mainly American market, with a series of hotels and clubs set in private gardens with their own stretch of beach. Best hotel: **HOTEL BORA BORA**, BP 1015, Papeete ☎ 19689, which has also nabbed the best site on the island, on a promontory where the beach always looks magically picture-book white and palm-fringed (even though

the adjacent shoreline is shabby). Outrigger canoes, reef and motu views.

HUAHINE
The best island to cruise to – quickly, before it gets too developed. Unsophisticated, with some perfect little jewels of beaches in the south with clear-as-clear turquoise waters. Best resort: **HOTEL BALI HAI**, Huahine, c/o PO Box 26, Moorea, Tahiti ☎ (689) 561352, with its Polynesian bures set among lily ponds and bridges.

MOOREA
"One of the natural wonders of the world is the first sight of Moorea, sailing in to Cook Bay from Papeete" – **Marie Helvin**. Stay at **CLUB MED**, BP 575, Papeete, PF Tahiti, which occupies the most glorious corner of the island. Lavish feasts, their own private atoll, and all water sports on tap.

Germany

BRENNER'S PARK, An der Lichtentaler Allee,
Schillerstrasse 6, D-7570 Baden-Baden ☎ (07221) 3530 *"One of the 3 best hotels in Europe"* – **René Lecler**. A hangover from Edwardian days – people still flock to this tranquil spa to take the waters, beautify themselves at the Lancaster Beauty Farm, trot along in the coach and four, and sip tea to the strains of the string quartet. *"They have put in a marvellous swimming bath – the best in Europe"* –

Barbara Cartland. *"Superb"* – Betty Kenward.

BRISTOL HOTEL KEMPINSKI,
Kurfürstendamm 27, D-1000 Berlin 15 ☎ (030) 881091 Stay here when checking out Checkpoint Charlie.

BURGHOTEL TRENDELBURG, D-3526
Trendelburg ☎ (05675) 1021 *"Everybody's idea of what a German schloss should be. Perched high up over the Rhine, it looks a million dollars – really great!"* – **René Lecler**. Dates from the 13th century, timbered everywhere – real *Sleeping Beauty* stuff.

HOTEL VIER JAHRESZEITEN, Neuer Jungfernstieg 9-14, D-2000
Hamburg 36 ☎ (040) 34941 Among the very best in the world (as **Frank Bowling** and **Mark McCormack** will vouch) for its impeccable service, a private hotel run by Gert Prantner (unconnected with the American Four Seasons Group). Rather country house in atmosphere; lots of warm wood panelling, tapestries and elegant antique furniture.

HOTEL VIER JAHRESZEITEN KEMPINSKI,
Maximilianstrasse 17, D-8000 Munich 22 ☎ (089) 230390 A bastion of Bavarian hospitality, and the best hotel in Munich, according to **Frank Bowling**. Open since 1858, it once hosted the King of Siam, with his 1,320 pieces of luggage. Muncheners munch lunch in the top-notch Walterspiel restaurant.

❝ *The worst customs I've experienced was in Berlin when I was going to play with the Phil and they refused to believe me. We'd come in very late, everyone else had been let through and they were arguing with me. In the end I got the cello out and sat down and played. I passed the audition!* **❞**

 JULIAN LLOYD WEBBER

❝ *You get the best from Greece by having no expectations of the routine forms of excellence. You have to be a hazardist, interested in the language, because Greece is a fantasy* **❞**

🕵 FREDERIC RAPHAEL

TRAVEL

Greece

AKTI MYRINA, Myrina Beach, Myrina, Lemnos ☎ (0254) 22681
Individual stone villas clustered around a lovely beach. Relaxed, watersportif; delicious spreads laid out in the garden. *"I love it. The food is marvellous and the choice is enormous. Very informal – you dress up only if you feel like it"* – René Lecler.

ASTIR PALACE, Vouliagmeni Beach, Vouliagmeni 16671 ☎ (01) 896 0602
The only place to stay near Athens. A sophisticated, spacious resort hotel.

Hong Kong

HILTON, 2 Queen's Rd, Central ☎ 5-233111
In what must be one of the longest-surviving buildings in Hong Kong, the Hilton has a loyal following, the best health club in town, the best outdoor pool in Central, the best wine bar and an excellent restaurant. The executive floor is the place to stay.

🕵 **MANDARIN ORIENTAL, 5 Connaught Rd, Central ☎ 5-220111**
There's often only one hotel in town that feels dead right, thanks to its guests and to a confidence that comes with age and experience. In Hong Kong that place is the Mandarin. Ever-more sleekly turned out it is, for many, the best hotel in the world. However, some regulars are sad to report a difference under new management: a change of staff, more tour groups and, for one guest who was late for his confirmed reservation, they suggested a room at the Furama down the road . . . That aside, it's still No 1 meeting-place in town, at the Captain's Bar; the best whisky sours are whisked up in the Harlequin Bar at the top; accolades are showered on its (frantically expensive) restaurants – the Man Wah, the Grill and Pierrot (see Food & Drink). The multi-million-dollar revamp means the lobby is agleam with black granite and black and gold marble; rooms have Chinese furnishings and antique prints. Beds, with their soft linen sheets, must be the most comfortable in the world. *"You can't beat the kind of service in the Mandarin or Regent. They're both good because of the people – the staff and the guests. I once pushed the service bell at the Mandarin. It took 30 seconds for the boy to come and I was worried! Normally it takes 10 or 15. The best hotel in the world for me"* – **Anton Mosimann**. *"I like it for the great food in the Grill and the nearby shopping"* – **Elise Pascoe. Helen Gurley Brown, Cliff Michelmore, Jeffrey Archer, Mark Birley** and **Betty Kenward** add adulation. **Lord Lichfield**, who has tested PR departments far and wide, thinks theirs is *"second to none"*. Overall, he rates this joint No 1 with the Oriental Bangkok.

🕵 **THE PENINSULA, Salisbury Rd, Kowloon ☎ 3-666251**
Revered hotel where the original Taipans would stay, still loved by latterday CIPs (see Buzz), who enjoy gliding around in one of the Pen's 8 Rolls-Royce Silver Spirits. Most Hollywood stars have stayed at the Pen – **Douglas Fairbanks Jr**, Clark Gable, Cary Grant, Sophia Loren, Shirley MacLaine, Candice Bergen, and royals and premiers from all over the world. *"I love the Peninsula"* –

THE BATTLE FOR PERFECTION

The quest for No 1 spot is an endless one. Like the Chinese drip torture, each new hotel is drip-drip-dripping away to undermine the near-perfection previously attained by its rival(s). Where can a hotel stop and say: this is the ultimate, this is perfection? As the Regent and Shangri-La nip at the Mandarin's ankles, as it in turn hops back and forth into the top slot in alternation with its sister hotel in Bangkok, the answer must be 'never'. A hotel can *never* stop trying. Consistency is of prime importance. And that means good, caring management. All the frills are irrelevant without it. Service can't be as good without it. As **Lord Lichfield** says: *"The management really makes the difference between one good oriental hotel and another. All the top hotels have perfect oriental service. It's not unusual to find extraordinarily good waiters or houseboys because fundamentally they are trained for service. But when you get very good direction from the top, that's when you notice the difference."*

> " *I've got a passion for Hong Kong. I went last year and fell in love with it. It's the most wonderful place* "

♣ JACKIE COLLINS

TRAVEL

Madhur Jaffrey. In operation since 1928, it is now fighting back against the Regent. Its jarring '60s rooms have turned comfy chintzy country-house, it has a new business centre and the new Edwardian Grill. Expansion, adding even more facilities, will be completed in 1992. The lobby remains a favourite meeting-place and Gaddi's a prestigious restaurant (see Food & Drink).

♣ **THE REGENT, Salisbury Rd, Kowloon** ☎ 3-721 1211
Built with typical Hong Kong panache right beside what must be the most exciting harbour in the world. Where the Mandarin appeals to Brits and businessmen, the Regent is the place for Yanks and rag-

traders. Everything about it is biggest and best: the lobby has a panel of glass 146 x 60 ft, so that wherever you sit there is a stunning view. The same outlook from the restaurants serves as décor (which beats repro paintings any day). Plume and the nouvelle Cantonese restaurant Lai Ching Heen are 2 of the best in HK (see Food & Drink). The marble bathrooms are the best in HK. The octagonal pool is the biggest in HK. *"It's hyper-modern, from the façade to the rooms, and the service is so quick that your finger is barely off the phone before there's a knock at the door. The views are spectacular"* – **Thomas Hoving**. *"The best hotel I've ever stayed at . . . for location,*

comfort, amenities and service, which was just incredible for a place that size. Every time I got a cigar out there would be somebody there with a match, and as I flicked the ash, the ashtray would be whisked away" – **Michael Grade**. *"The place to stay in Hong Kong. I like it because it's right on the water; it's like sitting in front of a television screen watching every kind of boat pass by – quite incredible"* – **Jackie Collins**. In **Mariuccia Mandelli**'s top 3.

♣ **SHANGRI-LA, 64 Mody Rd, East Tsimshatsui, Kowloon** ☎ 3-721 2111
Chipping away at the foundations of the Regent and the Mandarin – converts vote it best in the city. They love the personal valet service. Confusingly, this glossy 720-room affair is part of Westin Hotels (USA) and not Shangri-La. It boasts the stupendous French restaurant Margaux (see Food & Drink).

♟ **Buzzzzzzzzz** Are you **FIT or CIP** or both? Frequent Individual Travellers and Commercially Important Persons fill the bulk of Hong Kong's 22,000-plus hotel rooms ♣ . . . . . . Vying with the Regent for the **best harbour view** is the **Hotel Victoria** – gaze from the Presidential Suite that occupies the whole of the top (40th) floor (but don't *stay* there) ♣ . . . . . . Rumour has it that the **Mandarin**, a 25-storey dwarf, is going to be **demolished** and built all over again. As skyscrapers shoot up all round it, the view is ever-more obscured (unless you prefer someone's 15th-floor office to the harbour). Watch that space ♣ . . . . . . Take a slow boat to **Macao** for the Grand Prix in Nov and stay at the **Mandarin Oriental**, Avenida da Amizade ☎ 567888 (with the best casino), the **Pousada da Sao Tiago** (pretty historical hotel converted from the Barra Fortress, with blue and white Portuguese tiles) or the **Bela Vista** (a Fawlty Towers affair loved by gweilos) ♣ . . . . . . in early 1989 the luxury **Regent of Taipei** opens in the business district ♣ . . . . . . **Caring concierges**: co-opt one of these Mr Fix-its when in Honkers – Giovanni Valenti of the Mandarin, Charlie Chang of the Excelsior or Herbert Croft at the Regent.

★ ★ ★ ★ ★ ★ ★ ★ ★ ★ ★ ★ ★ ★ ★ ★ ★ ★ ★ ★

India

AGRA

MUGHAL SHERATON, Taj Ganj, 282 001 ☎ **(0562) 64701**
Welcoming garlands of marigolds, exotic fruit and home-made biscuits in your room, charming service, an ocean of blue swimming pool – this is the way to live when taking in the Taj Mahal.

BOMBAY

THE OBEROI, Nariman Point, 400 021
☎ **(022) 202 5757**
The old Oberoi Towers is now flanked by this slick new tower-block built round a central

OBEROI MANAGEMENT SCHOOL

Even at first-class hotels in India, staff can be erratic. To ask at reception for the manager you had an appointment to meet, for example, and be told, *"Oh yes, M'dam, she will be back any day now"*, is hardly confidence-inspiring. Somehow the Oberoi International Group seem to iron out all these Eastern mysteries and provide intelligent, courteous, professional service, from the managers down to the laundry staff. It's all thanks to the Oberoi Management School in New Delhi, the only one of its kind in the subcontinent. Trainees, from the areas where there are Oberoi hotels (mainly India, plus Nepal, Egypt, etc) are hand-plucked from top universities; most have had a private education, all speak perfect English and are cultivated and self-assured. During the course they work their way through the entire hotel system from cleaning to waiting. The graduates are constantly head-hunted and match the best hoteliers in the world.

atrium, with gleaming rust-coloured polished granite floors. The marvellous penthouse Presidential Suite has pastel Shyam Ahuja dhurries and furnishings and a black granite and white marble bathroom. Efficient executive centre. The Rôtisserie is excellent and has the best wine list in India. The Bombay élite meet at the sleek Bayview Bar.

🏛 TAJ MAHAL HOTEL, Apollo Bunder, Colaba, 400 039 ☎ (022) 202 3366
The head of the Taj hotel family, presiding regally beside the Gateway of India, overlooking the glittering Arabian Sea. Stay in the refurbished old palatial part with its sweeping staircases. *"One of the best hotels I know in the world"* – **Bob Payton.** *"Very special ..."* – **Imran Khan.** *"I'd choose it because the setting is so wonderful. It's a piece of calm in the middle of that mad hubbub. I suppose it's*

an insulation – but it's a welcome one!" – **Lord Lichfield.** *"I always stay here, in the old part. It does take you away from the world a bit"* – **Madhur Jaffrey. Derek Malcolm, Charlotte Rampling** and **Quentin Crewe** are mad about it.

DELHI

HOTEL OBEROI MAIDENS, 7 Sham Nath Marg, Old Delhi 110 054 ☎ (011) 252 5464
The place to go and relax in airy, colonial splendour. Shady gardens and the best swimming towels in India – enormous black and white striped affairs.

OBEROI NEW DELHI, Dr Zakir Hussain Marg, New Delhi 110 003 ☎ (011) 699571
International travellers feel they have made a new discovery now the Oberoi's had a multi-million-dollar facelift

(old Delhi-goers always knew they liked it best). Décor is restrained, in salmon or rose pink with mahogany fittings and polished-granite floors and bathrooms. Lovely pool. *"Outstandingly the best hotel in Delhi, and the best French restaurant, La Rochelle"* – **Serena Fass.** The rooftop Taipan serves exquisite Sichuan food for a snip.

GOA

FORT AGUADA BEACH RESORT, Sinquerim, Bardez, 403 515 ☎ 4401; TAJ HOLIDAY VILLAGE ☎ 4415
An extensive resort set in fabulously lush, colourful terraced gardens overlooking a wild sweeping beach, in the laid-back Portuguese colony on the west coast of India. The main area is a hotel complex spilling over into cottages. Above it is the exclusive AGUADA HERMITAGE, built for a Commonwealth Conference (Mrs Gandhi and Margaret Thatcher were there); now smarties stay in self-contained villa luxury. Lots of Germans and antique Brits. The Taj Village has a younger clientele. A hit with **Bob Payton** and **Gianni Versace.**

JAIPUR

JAI MAHAL PALACE HOTEL, Jacob Rd, Civil Lines, 302 006 ☎ (0141) 73215
A palace only recently converted into a companion hotel to the Rambagh. Similarly beautiful.

HOTEL NARAIN NIWAS, Kanota Bagh, Narain Singh Rd, 302 004 ☎ (0141) 65448
Gorgeous decaying ochre-tinted

> 66 *India offers everything – deserts with medieval towns, tropics with waterfalls and the sea, game reserves – the choice is endless. In summer, go up to the Himalayas. Everyone should go to the highest mountains in the world – you realize what people call mountains are hillocks. It is awesome – you feel that God is up there somewhere* 99

 MADHUR JAFFREY

ERIC NEWBY'S INDIAN BUZZ ...

... The **best travel accessory** is *"a little pocket water filter which can make a cup of clean water in 15-30 seconds. It's so effective that if you pour half a pint of beer through it it comes out as water. Unfortunately it doesn't work the other way round"* ... among the **last great places unvisited** are *"certain parts of the Pamir mountains, where India, Russia, Afghanistan and China meet – but then if you get a Jules Verne brochure you'll probably find you can do it"* ... the **best clothing to wear in India** is *"a longhi if you can keep it up. When my wife and I went down the Ganges, she wore cotton trousers known as salwars and a kameez, a sort of long, loose shift."* Kit yourself out in the Indian manner at their answer to M&S, **Khadi**, Connaught Circus, New Delhi, or at one of the homespun shops found in every city.

colonial villa built in 1881. The level of luxury and service is hardly high; nor is spoken English (Q: "Where can I throw this rubbish?" A: "You want to put in freezer?" or Q: "Tea with lemon, please ..." A: "Lemon soda?"). However, you come for authentic small-scale palatial living, amid the original decorative fresco-work, four-posters, dhurries and weaponry. Breakfast on the verandah in peace, save the odd peacock screech.

RAMBAGH PALACE, Bhawani Singh Rd, 302 005 ☎ (0141) 75141
A stunning palace built in 1727 for Maharajah Sawai Jai Singh II, after whom the city is named. Lofty and cool, it is painted in creams and buttermilks, with marble floors, loggias and verandahs. Lovely gardens and an indoor pool that, in renovation, has sadly lost its mystique along with its gold mosaics. Maharajahs and visiting society drink in the colonial Polo Bar. *"Pure Rajput style – the*

ultimate in comfort and old charm" – **Olivier Coquelin**.

JODHPUR

UMAID GHAWAN PALACE, 342 006 ☎ 22316
"An unbelievable and fascinating palace, gateway of the desert. It's positively breathtaking. Once inside, don't let go of your companion – you'll never find each other again!" – **Olivier Coquelin**.

KASHMIR

KASHMIR HIMALAYAN EXPEDITIONS, Boulevard Shopping Centre, Dal Gate, Srinagar ☎ (0194) 78698
The most luxurious houseboat is *1001 Nights*, berthed on Dal Lake, with its own glorious garden. 4 bedrooms with private bath and 3 living rooms. The number of guests is matched by staff: a cook, pantry-boy, houseboy, dust-boy, log-boy, gardener and two bearers.

UDAIPUR

LAKE PALACE HOTEL, Pichola Lake ☎ 23241
Floating resplendent on a shimmering lake, this white marble palace is reminiscent of a Mississippi paddle steamer. There are little formal flower and water gardens, terraces and follies with mirrored mosaics that glint in the sun. *"The most romantic hotel in the world. There are little courtyards with orange blossom and almond trees. It is thrillingly, excitingly romantic"* – **Barbara Cartland**. *"Memorable by virtue of its position, which is magical"* – **Hilary Rubinstein**. A rapturous vote from **Olivier Coquelin**.

TOURS

COX & KINGS, 404 Deepali, 92 Nehru Place, New Delhi 110019, India ☎ (011) 641 4306
Veterans of Indian travel who once made the travel arrangements for the British Army in India. Tailor-made itineraries or set tours.

EXPLORASIA, see Transport, Tours & Agents
Brilliant treks all over India, Kashmir, Nepal, Tibet and Ladakh.

Indonesia

BALI

BALI HYATT, Sanur ☎ (0361) 8271
"The best in Bali, built in the middle of a coconut grove on a level no higher than the trees.

❝ *For me a holiday has to be in the mountains or in wilderness rather than on beaches. My ideal is the areas to the north of Pakistan that are really beautiful and untouched. The Hindu Kush, Karakoram, the Hunza Valley* ❞

 IMRAN KHAN

> **❝** *Indonesia has 30,000 islands of which only about 300 are populated. If you fly over you will see dozens and dozens of desert islands with some of the best beaches in the world* **❞**

ROBIN HANBURY-TENISON

Balinese gamelan musicians play gongs, brass kettles and metallophones – it's the most marvellous tinkling sound! The luxury of the West and the indigenous Balinese atmosphere" – **Serena Sutcliffe.** However, some travellers don't rate their bit of beach.

BALI OBEROI, Legian Beach, PO Box 351, Denpasar ☎ (0361) 51061
Beautifully laid-out complex of thatched-roof Lanai cottages and villas by a far-stretching beach, set in jungly green gardens with tropical flowers. Interesting sunken baths and little private patios. Incredible Technicolor skies and sunsets. *"One of the really wonderful hotels, away from the others. There's no roof to the bathrooms and they're surrounded by foliage"* – **Madhur Jaffrey.**

NUSA DUA BEACH HOTEL, PO Box 1028, Denpasar ☎ (0361) 71210
An impressive hotel where Ronald Reagan has stayed. Huge pool and 4 restaurants. *"It combines the best of traditional Balinese style with immaculate modern Oriental service"* – **Lord Lichfield.**

TANDJUNG SARI, PO Box 25, Denpasar ☎ (0361) 8441
A pretty little garden resort right on Sanur beach, dotted with mini thatched bamboo cottages (some privately owned), stone temples, statues of gods and goddesses, parasols and lanterns. *"A delightful hotel. Very, very beautiful on a small scale"* – **Serena Sutcliffe.**

JAKARTA

A sophisticated new **Regent** opens in 1989 on 'Embassy Row', to challenge the omnipotence of the Mandarin. Until then:

MANDARIN ORIENTAL, Jalan M H Thamrin, PO Box 3392 ☎ (021) 321307
"The only hotel you can stay in. It's much better than anywhere else in Jakarta – just the sign Mandarin makes you feel good" – **Lord Lichfield.** Barbara Cartland has stayed at this spacious oasis, too.

Ireland

ASHFORD CASTLE, Cong, Co Mayo ☎ (092) 46003
Here, big is beautiful. This vast, rambling, 13th-century castle overlooks a 68-sq mile lake, where you can fish, surrounded by 300 acres of gardens, plus a further 31,000 acres of wooded nature reserve and excellent shooting land. Ronald Reagan and other world premiers have stayed.

BALLYMALOE HOUSE, Shanagarry, Midleton, Co Cork ☎ (021) 652531
A farmhouse hotel with 400 acres of land and outbuildings, family run by Ivan and Myrtle Allen. *"My personal best. A blissful piece of paradise. It's wonderful by virtue of the involvement of the Allen family, led by the matriarch super-chef, Myrtle. Her husband, sons, daughters and grandchildren are all involved in the enterprise with an enthusiasm and a love of life that is very rare"* – **Hilary Rubinstein.** *"Smashing, friendly, a relaxed atmosphere. Myrtle is a very very good cook. It's all home cooking, with simple, lovely, well-thought-out menus. A great deal of style"* – **Roy Ackerman.**

Italy

AMALFI COAST

"Very beautiful, quite rugged. You can rest, swim, sunbathe and sightsee. You've got Amalfi, once a huge seafaring town, where the compass was invented; you're not far from Pompei, Naples, Sorrento. The bus ride along the coast is terrifying but you get used to it" – **Sophie Grigson.**

GRAND HOTEL QUISISANA, via Camerelle 2, 80073 Capri ☎ (081) 837 0788
The best hotel on the hilly isle of Capri, statuesque and historical, with antiques and individual terraces. *"Still marvellous to go to"* – **Mark Birley.**

SAN PIETRO, via Laurito 2, 84017 Positano ☎ (089) 875455
Chiselled into the cliff face, with terracotta-tiled terraces overhung by grapevines, lemon trees and bougainvillaea. Only 60 rooms, each idiosyncratically shaped according to the prevailing rock formation, spellbinding views of the coast, and an abundance of fresh seafood. A lift runs down through the cliff to a tiny private beach. *"The most exquisite suites, very discreet staff, extravagant food and magical ambience"* – **Marie Helvin.** A favourite with **Barbara Kafka** and **Marchesa Bona Frescobaldi:** *"The best place for a holiday."*

LE SIRENUSE, via C Colombo 30, 84017 Positano ☎ (089) 875066
A maze of rooms and terraces on 7 levels, with a swimming pool. *"A charming, rather old-fashioned hotel"* – **Mark Birley.**

ASOLO

**HOTEL VILLA CIPRIANI,
via Canova 298, 31011 Treviso
☎ (0423) 52166**
A 16th-century villa in the
heart of Veneto – the place to
stop off when doing Venice,
Verona and the Palladian villas.
*"Unbelievably good hotel and
restaurant in a fabulously
beautiful, unspoiled town"* –
Robin Hanbury-Tenison. *"A
hotel I particularly like"* –
**Giorgio Armani. Marchesa
Bona Frescobaldi** is another
great fan.

COMO

**VILLA D'ESTE, via Regina
40, 22010 Cernobbio, Lake
Como ☎ (031) 511471**
At the fashionable end of
Como, built in the 16th century
as a cardinal's palazzo, it's
Michael Grade's best *"for old-
world grandeur. It's right on
the lake with the most
incredible view because the
light changes, and every time
you look out the whole picture
has changed colour. The food is
out of this world and there's a
beautiful swimming pool that
juts out on to the lake. Just
divine."* Sportif too, with the
whole gamut of water sports.

CORTINA D'AMPEZZO

The St Moritz of Italy. Royals,
film stars, the Pirellis,
Buitonis, Cicognas and
Colonnas go. So does an
appreciative **Margaux
Hemingway**. Best hotels:
Miramonti Majestic; Cristallo
Palace; Hotel de la Poste.
Varied skiing with access to
more than 500 lifts in and
around the Dolomites.

FLORENCE

**HOTEL EXCELSIOR, Piazza
Ognissanti 3, 50123
☎ (055) 264201**
Old-fashioned hotel that has

hosted Sylvester Stallone and
Simon Le Bon. *"God, what a
hotel that is! It's really
wonderful! If you can get into
the top flat below the
restaurant, overlooking the
Arno, that's beautiful . . . and
prices aren't astronomical"* –
Taki.

**LOGGIATO DEI SERVITI,
Piazza SS Annuziata, 50122
☎ (055) 298280**
*"An old hotel that's been
revamped in the most exquisite
way. Very simple rooms with
high old beds and lavender-
scented sheets. Beautifully
simple bathrooms, gleamingly
clean. Marvellous cedar
ceilings; the perfume of cedar
wafts through the rooms. The
most tranquil place I've ever
been"* – **Stephen Jones.**

**PENSIONE QUISISANA E
PONTE VECCHIO,
Lungarno Archibusiere 4,
50122 ☎ (055) 216692**
The pensione made famous as
the set of *A Room with a View*
– and what a view! *"Right on
the Ponte Vecchio – it is
unbelievable. On the roof
there's a courtyard full of
plants, where they serve
breakfast there"* – **Anne Lewin.**

**VILLA SAN MICHELE, via
Doccia, 50014 Fiesole
☎ (055) 59451**
Set amid cypresses and
oleander, this former
Franciscan monastery designed
by Michelangelo has a private
frescoed chapel, cells that have
been sumptuously converted
into bedrooms and gorgeous
misty views over the red-tiled
roofs of Florence. A favourite
of **Jean Demachy** (*"the villa is
a work of art in itself"*),
Marchesa Bona Frescobaldi
(*"The best setting in the
world"*).

MILAN

**EXCELSIOR HOTEL
GALLIA, Piazza Duca
d'Aosta 9, 20124 ☎ (02) 6277**
Where the rag trade stay for
the Milan collections. *"The in
place for working fashion
people. The dining room is like

a club – all the manufacturers
buttonhole the press and buyers
and a lot of negotiating goes
on"* – **Eleanor Lambert.**

**HOTEL PRINCIPE DI
SAVOIA, Piazza della
Repubblica 17, 20124
☎ (02) 6230**
If you're in fashion and you're
not staying at the Gallia, this is
where you'll be. A larger hotel,
it's a **Harvey Goldsmith** fave.

PORTOFINO

**HOTEL SPLENDIDO, Salita
Baratta 13, 16034
☎ (0185) 69551**
Where all the Hollywood greats
used to holiday: Greta Garbo,
Humphrey Bogart, Lauren
Bacall, Elizabeth Taylor,
Richard Burton. Now part of
the James Sherwood (Orient-
Express) empire, along with
the Cipriani and the Villa San
Michele, it's attracting a big-
time international crowd again.
A typical rose-pink, green-
shuttered Riviera building with
sun-dappled terraces, set in a
glorious landscape. Traditional
herb-scented Ligurian cuisine.

ROME

**LE GRAND, via Vittorio
Emanuele Orlando 3, 00185
☎ (06) 4709**
Truly *le grand* in all its finery
of gold leaf, hand-painted
wallpaper, brocade, tapestries,
mirrors and chandeliers. Where
Douglas Fairbanks Jr and
Taki stay when in Rome.

**HOTEL DE LA VILLE, via
Sistina 69, 00187 ☎ (06) 6733**
*"The best hotel suite in Rome is
room 840. It has a terrace the
size of a football field (well,
nearly) with a panoramic view
of Rome, and a large living
room with a white grand
piano"* – **Ed Victor.**

**HOTEL HASSLER, piazza
Trinità dei Monti 6, 00187
☎ (06) 678 2651**
The best in Rome, gloriously
sited at the top of the Spanish
Steps. Though its

TRAVEL

contemporary furnishings look rather dated, it's a discreet, civilized establishment with faultless service. *"Very special – a matter not just of glamour, but a feeling that you're in the very top place"* – **René Lecler**. *"A frightfully good, old-fashioned hotel"* – **Quentin Crewe**.

LORD BYRON, via G. de Notaris 5, 00197
☎ **(06) 360 9541**
"Really excellent and small, a bit like the Carlyle or Connaught. It probably has the best hotel food in Rome apart from the Hilton" – **Andrew Lloyd Webber.**

SARDINIA

Porto Rotondo is the most exclusive resort, according to **Taki**. But **Porto Cervo** is perhaps the most ritzy, cosmopolitan resort, where God (the Aga Khan) reigns omnipotent. Here, life revolves around the water and sailing – it's one long party at Sardinia Cup time. *"Porto Cervo is still going strong"* – **Richard Compton-Miller.**

HOTEL CALA DI VOLPE, 1-07020 Porto Cervo, Costa Smeralda ☎ **(0789) 96083**
Part of the Aga Khan empire, this village-style resort is like a film set. Though modern, it blends into its rustic surroundings with chameleonic ease. *"The best by far. What is amazing is it was built less than 300 years ago. It's an architectural masterpiece. It has its own bay, a great deal of calm, and it's very well run"* – **Lord Lichfield.**

SICILY

For **Leo Schofield** it's *"my favourite place for a holiday overseas. I love it. It has a magical atmosphere and there are so many beautiful remains there – Greek, Roman and Norman – and all that Baroque architecture"*. It's wonderful to drive from Palermo to Taormina and stay at one of the best hotels in Europe, the **SAN DOMENICO PALACE**, Piazza S Domenico 5, 98039 Taormina ☎ (0942) 23701, a converted 16th-century monastery.

SIENA

A perfect medieval Tuscan city that is *"one of the most surprising places in the world. Round every corner there's something extraordinary. The square where they have the Palio is amazing, the Duomo with all that marble ... and it's on a scale I can cope with. I have trouble in Rome, and even Florence is daunting"* – **Michael Grade**. *"My absolutely favourite city. It absorbs tourists in a way other places can't. There are strict! laws about shop fronts; they're never obtrusive. One of the most beautiful main squares – it's shaped like a shell. It also has my favourite cathedral. Really delightful"* – **Sophie Grigson.**

CERTOSA DI MAGGIANO, via di Certosa 82, 53100
☎ **(0577) 288180**
A lovely tranquil hotel converted from a 13th-century monastery. The old cloisters

remain and there's a garden of olive trees. Decorated by Lorenzo Mongiardino and filled with fresh flowers, paintings and tapestries.

VENICE

"The most totally romantic magical city because it doesn't have any cars. It's unbelievably beautiful. The crowds are irrelevant, though I do actually prefer Venice in winter" – **Robin Hanbury-Tenison.**

PENSIONE ACCADEMIA, Dorsoduro 1058, 30123
☎ **(041) 521 0188**
"I love it. An intimate, small, family hotel which is a marvellous thing when it's right" – **George Melly**. *"The best place to stay if you're not doing it in grand luxe. Wonderfully old-fashioned, cultivated and central"* – **Robin Hanbury-Tenison.**

🔾 **CIPRIANI, Giudecca 10, 30100** ☎ **(041) 520 7744**
An island haven, a short glide from San Marco by private launch. *"It's where I stay a lot of the time. The only thing is that you have to keep getting in and out of a gondola and I always think I'm going to slip!"* – **Barbara Cartland**. *"I can't think of anything nicer. Superb, beautifully run, frightfully comfortable"* – **Betty Kenward**. *"The best pool in the world, an incredible exaggeration of a swimming pool. It's filled with filtered sea water so you have a little bounce for your body, but it's not so saline that it burns you. Perfectly delicious"* – **Barbara Kafka**. *"Very hard to fault, superb management"* – **Lord Lichfield**. *"An absolutely superb hotel, probably the best in the world"* – **Egon Ronay**. *"I've spent many wonderful summers here. The best place in the world for outdoor eating – gorgeous Italian melons and San Daniele ham, with a backdrop of San Giorgio island and the view across the lagoon to San Marco – I just love that place"* – **Elise Pascoe**. *"The*

> **❝** *There's no place like Tuscany. Nothing has changed in 500 years. I've just bought a farmhouse there to the south-west of Siena – the only place the English haven't overrun yet (the other side is called Chiantishire!) By far the most beautiful place in Italy* **❞**

 TAKI

one I love best in the world" – **Eleanor Lambert.** *"The apotheosis of luxury"* – **Leo Schofield.**

GRITTI PALACE, Canale Grande, 30100
☎ **(041) 522 6044**
Dripping with history, this glorious building is straight out of a Canaletto. But there are reports of less-than-charming changes to the original interior décor and disdainful service. This might have something to do with whether you speaka da lingo, for there are recommendations from **Mariuccia Mandelli** and **Barbara Kafka:** *"Only the best if you have rooms on the front,*

on the canal, then you have a wonderful view and a great big room with great style."* **Anouska Hempel** acknowledges that *"If they like you they love you, if not . . .! For me, it's Venice, it's magical, it's lovely."* **Douglas Fairbanks Jr** is another fam

Japan

KYOTO

HIRAGIYA RYOKAN, Fuyacho-Aneyakoji-agaru, Nakagyo-ku ☎ **(075) 221 1136**

A contender for best ryokan, with superb rooms overlooking traditional gardens. Past guests include Japanese novelists Yukio Mishima and Yasunari Kawabata, Angus McBean and Adrian Woodhouse.

TAWARA-YA, Nakagyo-ku, Fuyacho, Oike-Sagaru
☎ **(075) 211 5566**
A small but perfectly formed 300-year-old ryokan. About 12 bedrooms, each with their own garden. A night's stay involves the ol' tatami mat and futon routine, and not much change from 100,000 yen. *"My favourite place to stay – I love it"* – **Helen Gurley Brown.**

RYOKANS: THE ULTIMATE LUXURY

"Ryokans are the exact equivalent of Michelin 2- or 3-star hotels in France. Everything is exquisite. At the **Mukodaki,** *Higashiyama Spa, for instance, you are met by a whole row of identically dressed maids, who greet you, bowing, in unison. One maid is appointed to look after you. First you take your shoes off. You are then led to your rooms, very very simple. No bed, just a table and tatami mats, and your own garden. You are quite bossed around, made to conform exactly to Japanese ways – which is one of the things I admire. Your clothes are almost forcibly removed and you are placed in a freshly laundered kimono. A great deal of bowing and scraping goes on. You are brought tea, then marched off to the bath house. You are plonked in lots of near-boiling water where you can be massaged and scrubbed and purified. Back in your room, food is brought to you. You drink a great deal of sake and gradually pass out – which is the correct thing to do. As you fade from consciousness, the maid fusses round you a bit and you find that your futon is somehow under you and you have become prone. You wake up in the morning feeling glorious, having had none of that driving-home or going-upstairs-and-getting-undressed nonsense"* – **Robin Hanbury-Tenison.**

REST OF JAPAN

FUJIYA HOTEL, 359 Miyanoshita, Hakone
☎ **(0460) 22211**
The first Western-style hotel in Japan, its former guests include Douglas Fairbanks and Mary Pickford, Charlie Chaplin, Neil Armstrong, Prince Charles, Gandhi and Edward VIII (pre-Mrs Simpson). It's also where Emperor Hirohito learned to play golf on the Bengoku course. Lovely position near Mt Fuji.

MIYAJIMA LODGE, Miyajima ☎ **(0829) 442233**
A beautiful country inn on a little island outside Hiroshima. Prince Charles has visited and the Emperor of Japan has a house nearby. *"What a treat! An experience you never forget"* – **Anton Mosimann.**

---

66 *The great secret the Japanese have is being able to switch from the 20th century to the 16th century instantly. In the countryside, at 6pm, the whole village suddenly becomes 16th century, all in clogs and kimonos, with parasols, heading for the bath house, where they wash away the stains of civilization. Next morning they're in their pinstripe city suits, driving through the smog of central Tokyo* 99

 ROBIN HANBURY-TENISON

TRAVEL

LAND OF CONFUSION

Tokyo is the world's most confusing city for travellers – and it's no accident. The intention was that, should the alien invade, at least he wouldn't be able to find his way around. We're talking mega-CONFUSION: Tokyo (anagram of Kyoto, the old, logically laid-out capital) is a maze of incomprehensibly numbered streets; and when you *do* get a street sign, it's a maze of incomprehensible characters. So, before sallying forth, follow this anti-confusion policy:

1 Get the address and tel no (written in Japanese too)
2 Get the name of the district and, when applicable, the street (often *not* in the address – smart, eh?)
3 Find out the nearest landmark (a tall, named building is best) or street intersection
4 Know the nearest subway station/bus stop (plus, in the case of subway, the number of the nearest exit)
5 Get someone to draw you a map.

NB Don't do as one visitor did – he always carried a matchbook from his hotel as a homing device, but one taxi driver delivered him to the match factory.

IMPERIAL HOTEL, 1-1-1 Uchisaiwaicho, Chiyoda-ku ☎ (03) 504 1111
Vies with the Okura for businessmen, tends to get the younger, European set. **Anton Mosimann** recommends. Guests range from Robert Redford to Lady Mary Fairfax. Old devotees regret the loss of its original Frank Lloyd Wright façade – but at least you can see it at Meiji-mura (see Buzz).

HOTEL OKURA, 2-10-4 Toranomon, Minato-ku ☎ (03) 582 0111
A hotel of the airport-lounge era – lurid décor, piped music. However, this apparently does nothing to deter its faithful clientele, which is largely big-thinking American. **Douglas Fairbanks Jr, Joan Burstein** and **Tina Chow** rave about it; **Helen Gurley Brown** sums up: *"Wonderful sushi and tempura bars; I can stay there for*

SAPPORO
One of the best ski resorts, near Hokkaido. For hardy enthusiasts – difficult to get to, bitterly cold, but worth it to escape a billion kamikaze skiers elsewhere, and for the excellent snow. Site of the celebrated annual Snow Festival.

TOKYO

"Tokyo city's main streets have a façade, very much like Disneyland, but immediately behind, we discover – totally different – a sprawling village made up of thousands of miniature communities. This is the real dream of the city!" – **Benny Ong.**

CAPITOL TOKYU, 2-10-3 Nagata-cho, Chiyoda-ku ☎ (03) 581 4511
The favourite of Tokyoites in the know. Rudolf Nureyev, Yehudi Menuhin, Phil Collins and many other luminaries stay here when in town, while the Garden Café has become habitué Bill Hersey's adopted office. Rooms are functional, décor garish – but that's (almost) par for the course.

Buzzzzzzzzz Essential Travel Tip: get a rail card **before you leave for Japan** (not available in the country); cuts $$ off rail travel 🐾 . . . . . . ETT2: buy discount tickets from **Oshima Coin ☎** (03) 254 1111 and **Fuji Coin ☎** (03) 253 3005, both near Kanda station 🐾 . . . . . . Anti-confusion fusion: the **best meeting place** in Tokyo is in front of the **Sony Building** at the Sukiyabashi crossing in the Ginza, or in front of the **Almond Coffee Shop**, Roppongi 🐾 . . . . . . The **best old-fashioned Japanese village** is **Meiji-mura**, on a hillside near Inuyama. More than 50 buildings of the Meiji Period (1868 to 1912) plus the reconstruction of the original Frank Lloyd Wright façade of Tokyo's old Imperial Hotel 🐾 . . . . . . **Best winter spot** is **Shiga Heights** in Joshin-Etsu Kogen National Park, where you can take an open-air hot-spring bath in the company of enchanting white snow monkeys 🐾 . . . . . . **Diplomatic enclave**: the Jardine/Swire and diplomatic clan nip off at weekends to houses on the **Shimoda-Izu peninsula**. Its hot springs and beaches appeal to Ronald Reagan and Jimmy Carter too. Best ryokan is **Tatado Beach Inn ☎** (055) 82 21757 🐾 . . . . . . Keep eyes skinned for the new **Regent Park** hotel in Tokyo Bay, a synthesis of E meets W with smart health 'garden' including a fuyo-tei (hot spa).

★ ★ ★ ★ ★ ★ ★ ★ ★ ★ ★ ★ ★ ★ ★ ★ ★ ★ ★ ★

Capsules in a nutshell

If you don't mind a pimp or a drunk for a sleeping companion, slip into something a little more skimpy. Found in nightlife areas and near major commuter stations, these accommodation boxes, roughly 3ft x 6ft, are stacked on top of each other. You share with a colour TV (porn channel all inclusive), radio and alarm clock; there's air conditioning and an emergency button for the claustrophobic. The biggest capsule hotel is the 660-pigeon-hole **GREEN PLAZA**, 1-29-3 Kabukicho, Shinjuku-ku ☎ (03) 207 5411. For a minuscule 4,000-5,000 yen, it's the best bizarre stop-out you'll ever have.

several days and not go out at all." So can **David Hicks:** *"I never go out – I just stay there 3 days and then go back to the airport."*

HOTEL SEIYO, 1-11-2 Ginza, Chuo-ku ☎ (01) 535 1111 The quintessential boutique hotel, a revolution for Japan. New, small (only 80 suites and rooms), highly personalized and luxurious, it knocks spots off the others for exclusivity and 1980s-style sumptuousness. The best of East and West philosophy means: 3:1 staff:guest ratio; proper breakfasts (the chef was sent off to the USA to learn about eggs benedict and hash browns); a personal secretary

and a butler; a choice of 7 pillows; a small TV and radio in the bathrooms (which are the sleekest in Tokyo). Several top restaurants including a branch of the famous Kiccho.

Kenya

Land of safari, land of sun (8 hours a day all year round), Kenya straddles the Equator, stretching from the Indian Ocean to the shores of Lake Victoria, the largest lake in Africa. Scenery is wildly varied – hot dry bush country in the northern plains; the gaping valleys and sparkling lakes of the Great Rift Valley; the

♠ —Africa's Best— ♠

HOTELS

1 **MOUNT KENYA SAFARI CLUB**, Kenya

2 **NORFOLK HOTEL**, Kenya

3 **BIRD ISLAND LODGE**, Seychelles

4 **MOUNT NELSON HOTEL**, South Africa

5 **VICTORIA FALLS HOTEL**, Zimbabwe

gently rolling downs of the cool Central Highlands with their forests, moorlands and trout streams; rippling grass plains of the savannah; lush tropical vegetation on the coast. All that, *and* immortalized on celluloid (first *Out of Africa*, then *White Mischief*). For **Leo Cooper**, it's *"the best place in the world. I love animals and I*

was there in the Army for a long time. But it's not the best for Jilly – she's terrified of snakes and spiders."

DIANI BEACH, south of Mombasa
"The best beach in the world – the most perfect stretch of sand with palm trees and a reef. It's miraculous" – **Quentin Crewe.**

LAKE TURKANA (Lake Rudolf)
"The most beautiful lake in the world. A brilliant bluey-green jade colour, the winds blow hot and the water is icy cold and very clear" – **Quentin Crewe.** *"Remote, deserted and very beautiful"* – **Dan Topolski.** For the bluest view, fly to Eliyi Point by light aircraft, as the more adventurous young royals have done.

LAMU
A small island and former trading port with Arabia, dating back to the 10th century. *"An extraordinary, magical place, almost empty, except for the old town. There are miles of deserted beach running all round the island – it's a delight"* – **Dan Topolski.** *"My favourite place for a holiday. All the buildings are Arabic with lots of courtyards. No vehicles are allowed on the island. When you arrive by dhow at sunset, they play the Last Post and you have to stand to attention while they lower the flag"* – **Roy Ackerman.** Best hotel: **PEPONI**, Shella, PO Box 24, Lamu ☎ (0121) 3029.

MASAI MARA GAME RESERVE
One of the greatest wildlife areas in the world, where a spectacular migration of wildebeest and zebras arrives from the Serengeti,

> ❝ The idea of a package tour is anathema to both of us – we'd either commit suicide or desert. We did desert once. We took a package tour to get to Nairobi cheaply and then we defected at the airport and were never seen again ❞

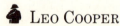 **LEO COOPER**

accompanied by numerous predators. Best hotel: **KEEKOROK LODGE**, PO Box 40075, Nairobi ☎ (02) 331635.

🏊 **MOUNT KENYA SAFARI CLUB, PO Box 35, Nanyuki** ☎ (0176) 33323
The brightest star in the vast Kenyan constellation, a cameo of old colonial days. On the slopes of Mount Kenya, it's set in 100 acres of rolling turf with ever-blooming flower-beds, ponds, a walled rose garden, vegetable and nursery gardens and a mountain stream with waterfalls. With its own airfield and satellite communications to the world, international VIPs (Bob Hope, Charlton Heston, John Travolta . . .) home in.

🏊 **NORFOLK HOTEL, PO Box 40064, Nairobi** ☎ (02) 335422
Turn-of-the-century hotel with bandas (cottages) in the gardens. The Lord Delamere Terrace is the most chic eating place in town. It even has its own private aviaries.

SAMBURU GAME RESERVE
A wild, semi-desert area bordering the Uaso Nyiro River, where zillions of animals and birds stop by for a quick one. Rare species include Grevy's zebra, oryx, reticulated giraffe, and the graceful genrenuk. Best hotel: **SAMBURU LODGE**, c/o London agents ☎ (01) 734 4246: members of the local Samburu Tribe dance daily.

TREETOPS, c/o Block Hotel Central Reservations Office, Rehema House Arcade, PO Box 47447, Nairobi ☎ (02) 335807
The famous lodge where royals and other elevated guests dine at giraffe level, above the other animals. This is an overnighter only – you transfer from your longer-stay hotel and sip cocktails at the bar, while observing a veritable menagerie swigging at the waterholes. A sheet of glass divides man and beast, for those pesky baboons have acquired more of a taste for Wallbangers than water.

SAFARIS

AIR KENYA, PO Box 30357, Nairobi ☎ (02) 501601 and **SAFARI AIR, PO Box 41951, Nairobi** ☎ (02) 501211
Flights to remote and inaccessible parts of Kenya for DIY safaris.

EAST AFRICAN WILDLIFE SAFARIS, PO Box 43747, Nairobi ☎ (02) 331228
If you want exclusive, luxury, tailor-made safaris, Jock Anderson's your man. All the best game reserves are his stamping grounds. You can fly over them on a Wing Safari and set up private camp in them, too. Jock arranged for Jackie Onassis to go private camping in the Masai Mara and ballooning over Lake Naivasha.

SILK CUT TRAVEL, Meon House, Petersfield, Hampshire ☎ (0730) 65211
16-day camel safaris with good camel:guest ratios (26:6).

TEMPO TRAVEL, 337 Bowes Rd, London N11 ☎ (01) 361 1131
Riding safaris at Sangare Ranch near Mweiga, one of the most beautiful private

properties in Kenya. Owned by Mike and Jane Prettejohn, a 6,500-acre farm with a stable of horses, mules and zebroids.

Korea

CHOSUN, 87 Sogong-dong, Chung-ku, Seoul ☎ (82) 77105
A traditional old favourite with high standards. More kudos, less flash.

HOTEL SHILLA, 2-Ga Jangchung-dong, Chung-ku, Seoul ☎ (82) 233 3131
The best in Korea, a striking modern building with top executive facilities for the ever-growing business market.

Malawi

A small tranquil country in central Africa, unspoilt, unpolluted and untamed. Its national parks and rainforests boast over 300 species of birds and over 400 types of orchid.

ROBIN HANBURY-TENISON'S TRAVEL TIPS . . .

. . . *"Tourism is taking the Western package with you,* **travel** *is experiencing the country . . .* **Research** *is essential. Read not only guide books, coffee-table books and historical books, but* **books by real travellers** *who have been there . . . Study* **maps** *– US Airforce Satellite maps are wonderful.* **Best map library:** *The Royal Geographical Society Map Room, with over 700,000 maps and 4,000 atlases.* **Best map shop:** *Edward Stanford, 12 Long Acre, London WC2* ☎ (01) 836 1321 . . . *The* **best travel accessory** *is* **a local.** *The further you get from Western civilization, the more honourable people are . . .* **Forget medicine chests** *(though John Bell & Croydon of Wigmore St's expedition cabinets are terrific fun for latent hypochondriacs); just take Lomatil for upset stomachs, aspirin and an antibiotic to zap yourself with, and make sure you have every necessary innoculation as per the latest advice . . . As for* **mosquito bites,** *a) don't scratch and b) think beautiful thoughts – it's a perfectly rational psychosomatic medicine."*

TRAVEL

CAPITAL AIR SERVICES, PO Box 14, Zomba
☎ (0265) 522679
They will fly you from Lake Malawi, with its hippos and bird island, to the Zomba Mountains and beyond.

SOCHE TOURS, PO Box 2225, Blantyre
☎ (0265) 620777
The premier grand tour operator in Malawi. Explore the Zomba Plateau in the wake of various queens and emperors, seeing forests, flowers and the Mulungosi Dam. Reel men go fly-fishing here: 3-day courses, staying at Brian and Jane Burgess's fabulous mountain home. Also mountaineering, flying and, oddly, dressage – the Burgesses keep schooled Lippizaners and run courses.

Malaysia

KUALA LUMPUR

THE REGENT, Jalan Sultan Ismail ☎ (03) 242 5588
More discreet and established than the Shangri-La. Decorated in Malaysian style with a wood-panelled lobby. A great outdoor pool and the excellent award-winning Suasa Brasserie.

SHANGRI-LA, 11 Jalan Sultan Ismail, 50250
☎ (03) 232 2388
The flashest, busiest, most spacious hotel in KL. This is where Nancy Reagan stayed with an enormous entourage. The pretty blue and rose Lafite is one of the best Western restaurants in KL; Nadaman is the best Japanese.

PENANG

EASTERN & ORIENTAL, 10 Farquhar St ☎ (04) 373804
The E&O is a classic member of the old colonial trio along with Raffles, Singapore, and the Oriental, Bangkok. Domed lobby and pretty gardens. Still loved for its place in history (it was Somerset Maugham's old hang-out) and still the place to meet for an E&O Colada or an E&O Sling. Dine in candlelit Victorian grandeur at the 1885 Grill.

MULU NATIONAL PARK
"The most beautiful place in the world. We spent 15 months there on a rainforest expedition for the Royal Geographical Society. It is just incredible, diverse, amazing. You get huge limestone cliffs, 3,000 ft high, huge caves, a vast sandstone mountain covered in tropical trees and 60 ft-high needle-sharp pinnacles of limestone. It has an immensely rich wildlife – gibbons, hornbills, amazing insects" – **Robin Hanbury-Tenison.**

TANJONG JARA BEACH HOTEL, 23009 Dungun Trengganu ☎ (09) 841801
On the unspoilt east coast stands this wooden cottage complex – with some buildings on stilts in the sea.
"Unbelievable, totally isolated, nothing but it and the jungle. The only things that live nearby are the giant turtles that go there every year to lay their eggs. You can borrow bicycles and ride off into the jungle. The Malays are among the most courteous people in the world" – **James Burke.**

Morocco

LA MAMOUNIA, Ave Bab Djedid, Marrakech
☎ (04) 48981
A Moorish extravaganza where Churchill loved to stay; now refurbished and reopened with a flourish by King Hassan II in the presence of Baroness Marie-Hélène de Rothschild, Duchesse de la Rochefoucauld, Baron de Rede and Régine (and that's just the Rs). 'Bubbles'

Rothermere loves it too. Mosaics, marble and painted cedar remain in abundance, but those who knew it in its heyday in the 1920s mourn the fact that the old magic has gone. Instead, a bombardment of colour and a flash nightclub.

EL MINZAH, 85 rue de la Liberté, Tangier ☎ (09) 35885
The best hotel in the heart of the only resort city where the Med and Atlantic meet. Here you can come to the Kasbah, set on a plateau overlooking the Straits of Gibraltar.

PALAIS JAMAI, Bab-el-Guissa, Fez ☎ (06) 34331
"The most lovely hotel with one beautiful, beautiful room – the King's Suite – which still exists just as it was. I hope nothing has changed (except the smell from the tanneries – for the better!)" – **Anouska Hempel.**
Other parts have suffered the Moroccan revamp, but the service, the food and the gardens are still sensational.

Nepal

"The best view I know in the world is at Thyangboche in the Himalayas. It's about 14,000 ft up and you look straight up the valley to Everest. There's no hotel there, just a hut and a monastery. You helicopter up from Kathmandu to Lukla [if you're privileged – the helicopter is owned by the King; otherwise it's plane or Shanks's pony], then it's a three-day walk. You go with Sherpas, who make the food and put up the tents. They scratch on your tent in the morning and a hand comes in with tea. Then there's another scratch and the hand comes in and replaces the tea with a metal bowl of warm water" – **James Burke.**

TIGER TOPS JUNGLE LODGE, Royal Chitwan National Park, Meghauli
☎ (0977) 212706
Wildlife resort in the Royal

TRAVEL

Chitwan National Park, erstwhile host to a safari-suited British royal family, and to elephant polo championships. Sleep in thatched tree-houses on stilts or in a tented camp (intrepidly deeper into the thick of things). Tiger-spotting and elephant-riding, as Prince Philip has done, on the track of rhinoceroses. Open Sept-June.

Netherlands

AMSTEL INTER-CONTINENTAL HOTEL, 1 Professor Tulpplein, 1018 GX Amsterdam ☎ (020) 226060 Super-grand hotel right on the river. The lobby has a polished marble floor and magnificent stairway leading to a balustraded balcony. Clogged with high society, who stay in suites the size of houses.

HOTEL DES INDES, Lange Voorhout 54-56, 2514 EG The Hague ☎ (070) 469553 Built in 1851 for a baron, it is loved more for its sense of the past than for zippy service. *"The one in this region I like best. A very old-fashioned grand hotel"* – **René Lecler.**

New Zealand

No Mecca for hotel-goers, gourmets or shoppers (unless it's for camping gear), but a paradise for sportif, outdoorsy types. Some of the most thrillingly beautiful scenery you'll ever see. The South Island is the most spectacular, boasting the finest walk in the world – the MILFORD TRACK (you book and pay to go on it), which winds up at MILFORD SOUND, a magnificent fjord with cruise boats that take you gasp-makingly near the sheer mountain walls and waterfalls which plummet down them. New Zealand has 70 million

sheep (and 4 million people) and on a driving holiday you'll meet most of them.

Auckland

Superb sailing around Auckland harbour. International yachties bob around the historic BAY OF ISLANDS area, catered for by ambitious new restaurants. Best hotel: the exclusive **OKIATO LODGE**, Bay of Islands, (only 4 suites, fine cuisine).

THE REGENT AUCKLAND, Albert St, Private Bag ☎ (09) 398882 The best international city hotel in the country, a new shiny high-rise, with some of the finest hotel bathrooms in the world.

Mount Cook

The highest peak (in Maori, 'Aorangi' – 'Cloud Piercer') in New Zealand with the best skiing. Uncluttered slopes. Exhilarating heli-skiing down the 8-mile Tasman Glacier. Cheap ski passes and heli-hire. Skiwis and European pros visit in July and August for training. Best (only) hotel: **THE HERMITAGE**, Private Bay, Mount Cook, South Island ☎ (05621) 809, a chalet hotel at the foot of the mountain. Here, cocktails are poured over ice from the highest, purest glaciers in the country.

Mount Ruapehu

CHATEAU TONGARIRO, Mount Ruapehu, North Island ☎ (081223) 809 The best hotel in the north, set in the mountains with marvellous views and its own ski lodge. 15 minutes from the glorious National Parkland.

Queenstown

Skiing in winter, exhilarating jet-boating on Shotover River and white-water rafting in summer. From the mountains around the lake, the Remarkables, you can shoot down metal slides into the icy water. You can also visit the Cattledrome and try your hand at milking. Best hotel: the new **QUEENSTOWN RESORT HOTEL**, Marine Parade, Queenstown Bay, Queenstown, South Island.

Taupo

HUKA LODGE, PO Box 95, Huka Falls Rd, Taupo, North Island ☎ (074) 85791 At the heart of the North Island, on the banks of the Waikato River, this latterday hunting lodge is perhaps the best hotel in New Zealand. No slacking here – you'll be fishing, deer hunting, horse-trekking, golfing, sailing, skiing, jet-boating or white-water rafting. No starving either – Huka's won a string of culinary awards (they'll even cook up what you've bagged).

Norway

"The best voyage in the world is, without doubt, the 2,500 miles on a Norwegian coastal steamer from the North Cape to Bergen, making 70 calls along the way of its 11-day journey through the Lofoten islands, in and out of the fjords. The ships act as postmen, collecting and delivering mail. You can explore lots of towns and villages, the food aboard is Norwegian and good, the accommodation first class and service super. You cross the Arctic Circle, experience the Land of the Midnight Sun and meander in and out of thousands of islands ..." – **Cliff Michelmore.**

TRAVEL

Peru

LIMA

GRAN BOLIVA HOTEL, Plaza San Martin
☎ (014) 276400
"The place to stay – it's the traditional one" – **Elisabeth Lambert Ortiz.**

MACHU PICCHU

"It's as good as it's meant to be, but not for the reasons I expected: I thought the architecture would be so pretty, but the actual setting is marvellous. You cannot believe that anyone ever thought of building there – they must have been raving. It's so high up, at 7,500 ft, with stunning views below and across to peaks. The masonry is brilliant, but I found the agriculture more fascinating. It's worth staying in the hotel up there because in the morning, before the day-trippers arrive, you have the place to yourself" – **Quentin Crewe.** *"It's an absolute must to see the ruins. They are so impressive, you feel you are in another world"* – **Elisabeth Lambert Ortiz.**

NAZCA

"There are strange lines on the desert – a monkey, a spider, a tree – drawn out on a vast scale. They are actually little trenches about 6 in deep and you have to go up in a plane to see them" – **Quentin Crewe.**

LAS DUNAS, c/o Lima offices, Las Magnolias 889, Oficina 208, San Isidro
☎ (014) 424180
A resort hotel at Ika, between Paracas and Nazca, with an English manager, a lovely pool, good restaurant and horse riding. Own airstrip for flights over the Nazca Lines.

Philippines

MANILA PENINSULA HOTEL, PO Box 307, Rizal Park, Metro Manila
☎ (02) 470011
Pure colonial grandeur, and one of very few surviving old buildings in the capital. It was used by General MacArthur as his headquarters for part of World War II. Gaze at the sunsets over Manila Bay, or dive into the swimming pool and check out the underwater music. *"A magnificent place, filled with the most marvellous antiques, carvings and paintings – it really is something!"* – **René Lecler. Auberon Waugh, Lord Lichfield** and **Mark Birley** recommend.

Portugal

AVENIDA PALACE, Rua Primeiro de Dezembro 123, Lisbon ☎ (01) 360151
"The best in Lisbon. An amazing turn-of-the-century hotel. Especially nice in winter, with an air of faded grandeur" – **Eric Newby.**

HOTEL PALACIO, Parque Estoril, Estoril
☎ (01) 268 0400
Palatial hotel near the beach with marvellous, airy, high-ceilinged halls and corridors. 18- and 9- hole golf courses. Impeccable, attentive staff. **Lord Lichfield** has stayed.

Seychelles

More than 86 islands scattered across 150,000 sq miles of the Indian Ocean make up this archipelago.

BIRD ISLAND
For bird-watchers and honeymooners – this, the most remote of the islands, is uninhabited except for millions of Sooty Terns and one hotel:

🐦 **BIRD ISLAND LODGE**, PO Box 404, Seychelles, with just 25 thatched cottages. Translucent turquoise sea, superb snorkelling.

LA DIGUE
A short boat-ride away from the second largest island, Praslin. On this one, visitors are met by ox-cart. *"The most spectacular piece of sunshine in the world. Just like a Hollywood set – there are places you think must be made of papier mâché"* – **Bob Payton.**

Singapore

🏃 **GOODWOOD PARK, 22 Scotts Rd** ☎ 737 7411
A splendid white colonial building which began life as the Teutonia Club in 1900, now modernized with perfect taste. The best suite in the East, the Brunei, is the size of a ballroom; the Sultan himself often stays. Other habitués have been the King of Malaysia, Harold MacMillan, David Frost and **Jilly Cooper.** New garden rooms open on to the 2 swimming pools. *"The best in Singapore. More personal style and service than elsewhere. A wonderful pâtisserie – you wonder how these wand-like ladies stay that way!"* – **Serena Sutcliffe.**

THE ORIENTAL, 5 Raffles Ave, Marina Sq ☎ 338 0066
This 21-storey triangular-shaped atrium affair is a fierce rival to the Shangri-La and Goodwood Park. The pool offers underwater classical music – if you can hold your breath long enough to appreciate it.

RAFFLES, 1-3 Beach Rd
☎ 337 8041
A divided field: some say it's run down, some rhapsodize that it's bliss. The only way of judging is to stay at this

legendary colonial hotel yourself. For a whiff of the past, take over the Somerset Maugham or Rudyard Kipling suite. Take a curry in the fanned coolness of the Tiffin Room and sling down a famed Singapore Sling.

SHANGRI-LA, 22 Orange Grove Rd ☎ 737 3644
A luxurious hotel with a pool, squash and tennis courts, a putting green and tropical gardens. The balconies of the Garden Wing cascade with vibrant bougainvillaea and overlook a waterfall. The new Valley Wing overflows with spacious suites.

South Africa

The best way of doing South Africa is to know people, but anyone with the loot can venture forth on gambling safaris to SUN CITY, Bophuthswana, a millionaire's playground with the largest casino south of the Equator; on gourmet safaris to JOHANNESBURG (delicious seafood from the Zoo Lake Restaurant); or on surfin' safaris to DURBAN.

The rail trail

Grab a trip on a steam locomotive before they are phased out. The best routes are the BANANA EXPRESS (Port Shepstone to Izingolweni), the APPLE EXPRESS (Port Elizabeth to Loerie), and TOOTSIE (Mossel Bay to Knysna). Best of all is the BLUE TRAIN, South Africa's answer to the Orient-Express. Streamlined and confident, it glides at a stately 40 mph from Cape Town over the Hex River Mountain Pass, across the Karoo to Johannesburg and Pretoria. Le style bleu means cuisine that is fittingly Cordon Bleu, a formidable cellar, private valets, a plushy suite, and windows tinted with pure gold to tone down the blinding glare.

CAPE OF GOOD HOPE
The most beautiful part of South Africa. On the Atlantic side of the Cape peninsula, the best beaches are CAMPS BAY, LLANDUDNO BAY and

CLIFTON BEACH – for bathing in the sun but not the sea, which is cold with dangerous undercurrents. On the Indian Ocean side, where the sea is warmer and safer, MUIZENBURG BEACH is the best.

MOUNT NELSON HOTEL, Orange St Gdns, PO Box 2608, Cape Town 8000 ☎ (021) 231000
The best hotel in town – thoughtfully run; gorgeous gardens. *"Timeless, terribly old-fashioned, very colonial – the complete antithesis to modern horrors"* – **Lord Lichfield.**

SAFARIS

SOUTH AFRICAN AIR TOURS, PO Box 8, Lanseria 1748 ☎ (011) 659 1246
Personalized South African safaris.

Spain

CARTAGENA

LA MANGA CLUB, Los Belones, Murcia ☎ (068) 569111
Swinging resort on the south-east coast of Spain, for young sportif sorts, who clock up all their bills on one card and play muchas golf and tennis.

MADRID

THE RITZ, Plaza de la Lealtad 5, 28014 Madrid ☎ (01) 521 2857
"In a lovely position looking over gardens and across to the Prado. All the rooms are very glamorous with tall ceilings. Service is excellent and outstanding; they take a lot of trouble and they give you flowers and chocolates" – **Barbara Cartland.** *"I like it because it combines extraordinary service, modern facilities and a spectacular old atmosphere. The infrastructure*

Buzzzzzzzz The **best tour operators** are – for **living it up**: Abercrombie & Kent (with an excellent 'à la carte' programme), Lindblad Travel, Voyages Jules Verne, Kuoni Travel; for **roughing it**: Encounter Overland. See World Transport ...... Hedonists go on **wine safaris** round the Stellenbosch Paarl and Franschoek Wine Estate areas of South Africa, lunching and quaffing at wonderful farms such as the former home of Cecil Rhodes and nurturing several senior hangovers a day. Tours arranged via **SARTravel**, PO Box 1111, Johannesburg 2000 ☎ (011) 774 4204 ...... There's a lot of yellow sand in Egypt; there's also the **Red Sea**. Splash in at Hurghada and sample the **best scuba diving in the world.**

★ ★

is modern but the whole spirit is of a former age. It's the only place where they have a string quartet playing Beatles songs at dinner!" – **Thomas Hoving**. A favourite of **Bruce Oldfield**. Garden terraces have flower-covered pergolas and fountains. Acres of hand-woven bespoke carpets.

MALLORCA

ANCHORAGE CLUB, The Anchorage of Bendinat, Ctra de Illetas, Calvia
☎ (071) 404151
Set in the exclusive and very beautifully designed village resort (by François Spoerry of Port Grimaud fame), a modern, clinical version of the old red-tiled, ochre-painted, green-shuttered look. The Club is owned by Prince Nawaf bin Abdul Aziz (brother of King Fahd of Saudi Arabia) and hosted by Prince Alfonso von Hohenlohe (also of the Marbella Club). The character of the village can come only from its rich itinerant population – people like King Juan Carlos, Sir Francis and Lady Dashwood and Jennifer d'Abo.

HOTEL FORMENTOR, Puerto de Pollensa, Formentor ☎ (071) 531300
Gracious, relaxed (edging towards the geriatric), set in

gorgeous hillside gardens amid acres of pines. A great sense of well-being, which the King of Spain has sampled. Paths lead down to a private beach dotted with straw umbrellas.

MARBELLA

MARBELLA CLUB HOTEL, Carretera de Cadiz
☎ (052) 771300
Hosted by Prince Alfonso von Hohenlohe, a pre-fab resort with Andalusian-style bungalows. The 3-bedroom villas have private pools. This is where the wealthy Marbella set hang out – types like Adnan Khashoggi and Baron von Thyssen (who owns a villa).

Switzerland

Swiss hotels automatically connote precision, discretion and all-round immaculateness. This is largely thanks to the legendary Ecole Hôtelière at Lausanne, which turns out the best hoteliers in the world. It is no coincidence that so many managers of the best hotels around the world have names that sound Swiss or German: they are among the far-flung alumni.

CRANS

Crans is très snob, drawing royals and aristos from Benelux, Denmark and Italy. Spectacular views over the Rhône Valley and hours more sun than most resorts. Best shopping in the Swiss Alps (rue du Golf). Best Alpine glühwein (fruity and spicy, served in silver teapot) from Des Vignettes. Best fondue and raclette from Le Cave.

GENEVA

BEAU RIVAGE, 13 quai du Mont-Blanc, CH-1201
☎ (022) 310221
Immaculate lakeside family-run hotel where the Duke of Brunswick once lived.

HOTEL DE LA PAIX, 11 quai du Mont-Blanc, CH-1201
☎ (022) 326150
5-star lakeside luxury with lovely views of Mont Blanc and distant Alpine peaks. *"A very fine hotel"* – **Frederic Raphael**.

HOTEL LE RICHEMOND, Jardin Brunswick, CH-1201 Geneva ☎ (022) 311400
Owned and run by 4 generations of Armleders, the original of whom set up the revered Ecole Hôtelière. Grand, antique-ridden hotel, refined in every respect, with eagle-eyed attention to detail.

GSTAAD

Pretty little rustic village where you're as likely to see cartloads of manure being drawn along the streets as the furred and bejewelled international jetset: Prince Rainier et famille, Audrey Hepburn, Roger Moore, Boucherons, Bulgaris and Buckleys (Pat gives the most splendid parties). *"Still for me, far, far, far above St Moritz and certainly Verbier. It keeps its own character and style"* – **Taki**. *"It's the most divine getaway holiday at the end of February"* – **Lynn Wyatt**.

THE PRIVATE JET SET

If you thought running a private yacht swallowed up a fortune, now hear this: a new Falcon 900 tri-jet (room for 12 passengers) costs US$19 million and a Gulfstream Aviation G3 (like the Aga Khan's) costs about US$5,000 an hour to operate. The super-élite who fly way above cloud nine are the Sultan of Brunei in his jumbo jet; the Saudi Arabian royals in 3 jumbos; Stavros Niarchos in his 737 (though it's on the market), Herbert von Karajan in his Falcon 10, and Christina Onassis, Georges Livanos and Gianni Agnelli all in Falcon 50s. If you fancy using a jumbo as a runaround, charter it, via Jet Aviation of Zurich or Aeroleasing of Geneva (see World Transport). It could be worth it if only for the intelligent, multi-lingual hostesses, gourmet cuisine, flowers, books and magazines that go with the package.

Civilized, sophisticated lunches take place at the Eagle Club. *"More fun and social now than St Moritz"* – **Betty Kenward.** PS The skiing's only so-so.

GSTAAD PALACE, CH-3780 Gstaad ☎ (030) 83131
A splendid affair, the hub of Alpine society in February (and February alone), when those who aren't staying at least are swaying in its Green Go disco. Excellent service. Satisfied punters include **Anton Mosimann, Taki** and **Frank Bowling.**

KLOSTERS

Small, smart, old-fashioned resort where, certainly until the recent avalanche tragedy, the Prince and Princess of Wales, the Yorks and the Gloucesters loved to ski. Best slopes at nearby Davos. Best hotels: Wynegg (excellent cuisine); Chesa Grischuna (room for only 55).

ST MORITZ

The grand Victorian resort lives on, jolted into the 1980s with a new promotional programme. Forget 'St Moritz' cigarettes – soon we'll all be wearing official resort-endorsed shades (from the Porsche sunglasses designer), carrying their luggage, drinking their (Pommery) champagne and smothering on their sunscreen. Traditionalists can relax: it still plays host to the Cresta Run (the treacherous, men-only toboggan run invented by the Brits) and to countless jetsetters (mostly with private jet in tow) – Fredy Heineken, Christina Onassis, Stavros Niarchos, the Aga Khan,

Gianni Agnelli. There's also bobsleighing, curling, heli-skiing and, on the frozen lake, racing and polo, as well as the maddest mountain sport – skikjöring, where a 'jockey' is towed, water-ski style, behind a riderless horse. Best restaurant: La Marmite (puts the haute in cuisine). Best club: Corviglia (for mountain lunches). Best nightspots: Dracula (at the Kulm) and Kings'.

BADRUTT'S PALACE, CH-7500 St Moritz ☎ (082) 21101
A winter palace with strains of baronial hunting lodge, from the wooden carved ceiling and panelling down to the antlers. The scale is monumental. *"I love it, it's filled with warmth, it looks gorgeous"* – **Anton Mosimann. Diana Fisher** is another devotee. Dancing in its famous 1970s jungle-style Kings' Club.

SUVRETTA HOUSE, CH-7500 St Moritz ☎ (082) 21121
The most discreet of the grand-scale St Moritz hotels, out of town with private ski lift, post office, etc. Where smart families have been going for generations. *"There are places in the world where everything fits. This is one. You come in and are greeted by the Müllers and you just feel at home. Very stylish, in a quiet beautiful location, and traditional, classical, creative cuisine. It's a wonderful life"* – **Anton Mosimann.**

VERBIER

Sunny, post-war trad-style chalet resort teeming with bright young Brits.

Challenging skiing – black runs and terrain for powder buffs and mogul bashers. Late-night drinks at La Luge. Best hotels: Rosalp, Rhodania (dancing in the basement Farm Club – best nightspot in the Alps), Le Mazot. **Richard Compton-Miller** approves.

ZERMATT

Romantic setting in the shadow of zer Matterhorn. Only horse-drawn sleighs and electric taxis allowed in town. Brilliant, varied skiing; some of the best heli-skiing in Europe. Best place to slope into afterwards is Elsie's Bar – Irish coffee, oysters, escargots or just drinks. Best restaurant: Le Mazot. Best discos: at Hotel Alex; Le Village and the Broken Bar at the Hotel Post. Best nightclub: Zermatt Yacht Club. Best hotels: Mont Cervin; Zermatterhof. *"I've been to Zermatt many times and it's the best"* – **Robert Sangster.**

ZURICH

BAUR AU LAC, CH-8022 Zurich ☎ (01) 221 1650
"Like the Dolder Grand, it's very up to date, but very professionally and traditionally run – the old type of hotel-keeping. Beautiful, a lovely place" – **Anton Mosimann. Mark McCormack** adds his vote.

DOLDER GRAND HOTEL, Kurhausstrasse 65, CH-8032 Zurich ☎ (01) 251 6231
Set on the mountainside just outside the city, it is *"superbly run"* – **Frank Bowling** and has *"a good atmosphere and feel"* – **Anton Mosimann.** In common

TRAVEL

66 *For me, the ideal Christmas is in St Moritz. You go out at night, you see a beautiful moon, lights … it's such a romantic atmosphere. You go to midnight mass. Snow, cold but dry, the skiing, coffee with kirsch – it's such an experience – it's the holiday season* 99

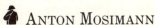 ANTON MOSIMANN

with most Swiss hotels the décor suffered a l960s/70s revamp. Sporting bankers can still chopper in, take a dip in the oscillating swimming pool, a jog in the forest, play a round of golf, a set of tennis and wind up with a triple axle on the ice before a gourmet dinner.

Tanzania

A vast country south of Kenya and equally rich in national parkland and game reserves, including the famous Serengeti National Park and the Ngorongoro Crater. *"Ngorongoro is the most awe-inspiring natural wonder. Inside are all sorts of animals – elephants, lions, rhinos, hippos, wildebeest, hyenas – just everything: it's their world and you're the alien"* – **Sir Peter Parker.**

TSAVO NATIONAL PARK
On a clear night you can observe game at illuminated watering holes and, on a clear day, you can't miss the snow-capped summit of Mount Kilimanjaro. Best hotel: **KILAGUNI LODGE**, c/o London agents ☎ (01) 541 1199.

ZANZIBAR
"Tremendous. You need to go there with a copy of White Nile, *which gives you a history of East Africa and the slave trade"* – **Dan Topolski.** On this legendary island you can visit the houses of Dr Livingstone and of the notorious slave trader Tippu Tip (not far from Topolski's hostel, incidentally). Best hotel: **BHAWANI**, PO Box 670, Zanzibar ☎ (054) 30200.

Thailand

BANGKOK

HILTON INTERNATIONAL, 2 Wireless Rd ☎ (2) 253 0123

♠ *Far East's Best* ♠

	HOTELS
1	**THE ORIENTAL,** Bangkok
2	**MANDARIN ORIENTAL,** Hong Kong
3	**THE REGENT,** Hong Kong
4	**SHANGRI-LA,** Hong Kong
5	**THE REGENT,** Bangkok
6	**THE PENINSULA,** Hong Kong
7	**TAJ MAHAL HOTEL,** Bombay
8	**HOTEL SEIYO,** Tokyo
9	**GOODWOOD PARK,** Singapore
10	**BALI OBEROI,** Bali

One of the best Hiltons in the world, a low-rise crescent-shaped building set in Nai Lert Park, over 8 prime acres of landscaped gardens by a canal. Ultra-airy and spacious to the point of appearing rather empty. The enormous Royal and Presidential suites were designed by fashion designer Valentino.

♠ **THE ORIENTAL, 48 Oriental Ave** ☎ (2) 236 0400
Current No 1 in the world, just pipping its sister in Hong Kong at the post. *"The most comfortable and one of the best hotels in the world. I stay in my pink Barbara Cartland Suite with a large number of my books in the cupboard. They have 3 suites, the Noel Coward Suite, Somerset Maugham and me – not a bad collection!"* – **Barbara Cartland.** You can't go wrong here. The Authors' Wing (1876) is full of colonial character. This is where to stay, though the modern block is supremely plush and comfortable. The Oriental Suite occupies the entire top floor, with wraparound balcony. When 'Rambo' Stallone stayed here he turned the second bedroom

into a gym. *"Bearing in mind I'm treated specially, this is the most special I've ever been treated. Breakfast arrived on a starched white cloth absolutely laden with silver, perhaps 20 types of flowers, croissants, exotic fruits, eggs, champagne, a choice of tea . . . the best breakfast I've ever had"* – **Glynn Christian.** *"Very stylish, wonderful"* – **Anton Mosimann.** More praise from **Serena Sutcliffe** – "super"; **Madhur Jaffrey** – *"I love it. A wonderful, spectacular hotel";* and **Elise Pascoe:** *"I like the nostalgic atmosphere."* See also Food & Drink.

♠ **THE REGENT, 155 Rajadamri Rd** ☎ (2) 251 6127
The old Peninsula, recently taken over by Regent, has got the Oriental worried. A fabulous property with 2 blocks built around open atria with tropical gardens, so that you can look down from open balconies at all levels. Nautical-looking doormen and bell-hops have white uniforms with brass buttons and sola topees or pill-box hats. The lobby has a ceiling of blue and gold hand-painted silk, and Thai wall decorations. Fine restaurants (see Food & Drink). *"Rather calmer than a lot of other hotels as it's not quite in the hubbub of the centre of town. It certainly is going to give the Oriental a bit of a run for it's money"* – **Lord Lichfield.** *"The best hotel service in the world"* – **Elise Pascoe.**

PHUKET

Some of the most beautiful natural beaches in the world, though the fast-growing tourist industry has already caused some areas to be spoilt – Patong Beach for example. The newest, most deluxe and expensive hotel is **AMANPURI HOTEL**, Pansea Beach ☎ (02) 250 0746, where some 20 detached pavilions house rich lotus-eaters. But the *best* resort hotels are: **PHUKET YACHT CLUB**, 23/3 Vises Rd, Nai Harn Beach ☎ (076) 214020 (with tennis court and water sports on tap); and **PANSEA HOTEL**, 118 Moo 3, Surin Beach ☎ (076) 216137, a cluster of traditional thatched cottages in a hilly coconut grove with private beach. A favourite of **Serena Sutcliffe**, who recommends their seafood buffets and Chinese food.

Turkey

Now that *Midnight Express* is of another generation, it's safe to go back to Turkey . . . and back people are *flooding*. To make things more civilized, the splendiferous **Regent of Istanbul** opens in 1989. It's housed in part of the old Moorish university; during restoration treasures kept emerging, from Moorish

mosaics to Lalique glass lampshades.

APHRODISIAS

"This ancient site is an absolute must. A wonderful site, currently being excavated. Compared with most major Greek and Italian sites it's marvellously unpoliced, so you actually have an opportunity to fantasize without being marshalled about" – **Frederic Raphael.**

PAMUKKALE

"The most extraordinary place I've ever been to – a huge hill which oozes . . . It has made enormous limestone basins full of hot spring water, which then overflow and drip and make others. An astounding sight.

You can swim in these Turkish baths. It is the most amazing natural thing I've ever seen" – **Frederic Raphael.**

Uruguay

MONTEVIDEO

HOTEL CASINO CARRASCO, Rambla Mexico ☎ (02) 501971 A city landmark. *"The best bizarre place to stay. Worth it because it's so dotty – and terribly cheap. Mad, vast pillared halls and domes and potted palms. You really feel you've stepped into the '20s. You do in Uruguay anyway because all the cars are so old – you see Model A Fords chugging by"* – **Quentin Crewe.**

PUNTA DEL ESTE

The post-Christmas (till early Feb) playground for rich Argentinians and Brazilians, and increasingly for Americans and Europeans. On one side of the peninsula is the trendy beach Brava and big waves for macho surfers; on the other side the sea is as flat as a pancake and there's miles of beach for serious sunbathing. Best hotels: **L'Auberge**, an old tower set back from the beach, serving the best waffles in town for tea; **La Posta del Cangrejo** in the trendy area of town, La Barra – bang on the beach and the hottest lunch spot. Omar Sharif has a suite here. Best café: La Fragata (still known as the Oasis) on Avenida Gorlerdo, Punta del Este's main drag. Open 24 hours a

---

AEGEAN TONIC

The Greek and Turkish islands are the holiday sailor's dream. Bodrum is the raviest port of call in Turkey. Those who rock along include Mick Jagger and Princess Margaret (both of whom stay at Ahmet Ertegun of Atlantic Records' holiday hideaway), Nureyev (who can be spied doing wheelies round town on a bicycle), Phil Collins (who can be spied doing keelies round the harbour on a chartered yacht) and David Dimbleby and Robin Day (who evidently find Turkish food preferable to that of the Beeb canteen). *"The best way to travel is to sail. Just the wind and the waves, no engine, no diesel, no noise, no telephone. The best area to sail is down the Peloponnese coast, round the Greek islands and Turkey. The joy is that you can tie up in completely unspoiled little bays; each one has a little taverna and whatever they're cooking that night is what you get. Idyllic"* – **Michael Grade.** Other old salts who love this neck of the ocean include **Douglas Fairbanks Jr** (*"Beautiful, nothing better – provided the weather is good"*), **Michael Parkinson** (*"My idea of perfect oblivion"*) and **Dan Topolski** (*"Everyone always thinks Greece is the place. But in Turkey people are nicer, there are jolly tavernas where food is better and more varied, prices are cheaper. A private or chartered yacht is the best way to travel"*).

❝ *There's nowhere 'best' to stay in Greece or Turkey, but my instinct is to stay away from the efforts they have made to please, which usually spell the end of what you enjoyed about them* ❞

 FREDERIC RAPHAEL

TRAVEL

day, it's where the young meet at the beginning of the evening for drinks and at the end for breakfast. Best casino: San Rafael.

Venezuela

HATO PINERO, Edificio General de Seguros, Piso 6, Ofic 6B, Av La Estancia, Chuao, Caracas 1060
☎ (02) 912011
A pretty ranch with *"probably the best bird-watching in the world. You can see 77 species of birds in 24 hours – and animals such as armadillos"* – **Quentin Crewe.**

Zimbabwe

BUMI HILLS SAFARI LODGE, PO Box 41, Kariba
☎ (063) 353
Fan-cooled rooms at the edge of a cliff overlooking Lake Kariba (all 5,000 sq miles of it, created by the dam built in 1961). You can go fishing, game viewing or try a Water Wilderness safari. Their boat has double beds and bathroom and is purportedly insect-proof.

VICTORIA FALLS
"Perfect – the best natural wonder in the world. I spent 3 days sitting and sleeping each night on a bench alongside the lip of the falls, waking up to the spray and thunder of the water. I just wanted to stick around. It's mesmerizing" – **Dan Topolski.** Livingstone stuck around too. He described 'scenes so lovely they must have been gazed upon by angels in their flight'. The Mosi oa Tunya ('smoke that thunders') is indeed best viewed from the air. You can join a latterday Flight of Angels: a fleet of tiny aircraft wing their way over the 5 waterfalls. Arranged by **UNITED AIR CHARTERS**, PO Box 2177, Harare

☎ (0) 21240, who also do air safaris over game parks in Zimbabwe.

⚓ **VICTORIA FALLS HOTEL, PO Box 10, Victoria Falls**
☎ (113) 203
Elegant and colonial, with lovely verandahs and gardens, it has nightly African dance displays, brilliantly staged in a floodlit amphitheatre. *"A great old hotel"* – **Hilary Rubinstein.**

World Transport

AIR CHARTER

AEROLEASING, PO Box 310, CH-1215 Geneva Airport, Switzerland ☎ (02) 984510
Air charters all over the world.

AUSTRALIAN AIR TOUR AND CHARTER, NSW, see Australia

JET AVIATION ZURICH AG, PO Box 1524, CH-8058 Zurich Airport, Switzerland
☎ (01) 816 4800
Other bases in Europe, the Middle East and USA. Worldwide charters.

AIRLINES

All airlines have their fans; here is a list of those that our contributors recommend. In general, Oriental airlines come out tops for pampering, pandering service, while Swiss, German and Scandinavian airlines are exceptional for their reliability, particularly when it comes to safety and precision timing. British Airways is the most talked-about airline for its staggering improvement under Lord King. It wins through for overall reliablity, good service, good food, and for its vast network of routes.

AIR FRANCE
Appeals to those who care about their stomachs. *"The best

food on club class to Paris. Fabulous snacks – salmon and caviare"* – **Glynn Christian.** *". . . in particular their service to Nice where they offer champagne without being asked"* – **Hilary Rubinstein.** *"The best flight I ever had was on the Sunrise Express, Paris-Tokyo non-stop. The food, the service, the whole thing was just amazing"* – **Ed Victor. Lord Montagu of Beaulieu, Betty Kenward** and **Barbara Cartland** add their votes.

AIR INDIA
"Fabulous Indian Muzak, very exotic décor and excellent food" – **Duggie Fields. Derek Malcolm** likes them too.

AIR NEW ZEALAND
"First class really is amazing because of the space. You lie on wonderful lambskins. The hospitality is very sophisticated but homespun. They've won various airline wine awards. Oh – and lots and lots of fresh fruit" – **Glynn Christian.** *"I like the feel of it"* – **Cliff Michelmore.**

AUSTRIAN AIRLINES
Punctual, courteous – and they serve delicious chocolates to all cabin classes.

⚓ **BRITISH AIRWAYS**
They're up at the top and they're sticking: *"It sounds terribly biased but they are the best – they stand out because of service"* – **Lord Montagu of Beaulieu.** *"I've had wonderful flights with BA – comfortable, excellent food and the service has moved on from that brittle 'I'm doing you a favour' thing they once had"* – **Glynn Christian.** *"There may be some airlines I don't know that are as good but there are certainly none any better"* – **Douglas Fairbanks Jr.** *"I fully expected BA not to be good but I was really knocked out when I came back from LA first class. Fabulous, really fabulous"* – **Stephen Jones.** *"The best has to be BA. I'm not just saying that to be patriotic – they have been so great with me, very very helpful. Quite apart from the cello [it travels on the seat next to him], I find they have

TRAVEL

❝ *I think the 'best airline' is really of no significance because when you have to go to a place, you've got to go on certain ones. You can't go Air France to Moscow! You're in this aluminium tube for not such a long period of time, so what the hell – it beats a bus! People who expect to find food and all of that in a tube going at 600 mph at 30,000 ft are crazy* **❞**

🎩 THOMAS HOVING

improved out of all recognition. They are even on time!" – **Julian Lloyd Webber.** *"I still think it's the best and getting better . . . they have continued to perform terrifically well. British Telecom, on the other hand, may be the worst run company I've ever come across. Lord King should take it over"* – **Bob Payton.** *"I swore 3 years ago that I would never travel BA, but it has changed. It's like another airline altogether"* – **Madhur Jaffrey.** *"What is extraordinary about BA is that they have halved the amount of staff and at the same time doubled the quality of the service. I think it's particularly good in economy, where people sometimes suffer"* – **Lord Lichfield.** *"In Europe it's the pits. Inter-continental it's the tops"* – **Harvey Goldsmith. Hilary Rubinstein, David Hicks, Derek Malcolm** and

Cliff Michelmore join the general chorus of approval.

🎩 **CATHAY PACIFIC**
Hong Kong's airline, part of the Swire Group and the best of the Oriental airlines. *"Streets ahead of any other. It's privately owned with a much freer approach, easy-going and helpful, less bureaucratic hassle"* – **Robin Hanbury-Tenison.** *"I don't think even BA can hope to match airlines like Cathay – it has Oriental service, which is second to none, and it has a higher crew:passenger ratio"* – **Lord Lichfield. Betty Kenward, Marie Helvin, Barbara Cartland** and **Derek Malcolm** are members of the appreciation society.

🎩 **CONCORDE**
"Concorde is the only decent aeroplane for me. I like planes

to be safe and fast" – **Jeffrey Archer.** *"The pilots have a fantastic sense of humour – they apologize for being 3 seconds late"* – **Terry Holmes.** *"The best for short distances, though the food is a disappointment. I take bread and champagne"* – **James Burke. Viscountess Rothermere, Margaux Hemingway, Jane Seymour** and **Joan Burstein** rave about Concorde.

JAPAN AIR LINES
"It's a tie between JAL and Air India. On JAL the food and service are excellent" – **Duggie Fields.** They're a favourite of **Margaux Hemingway** too. *"Extremely good. Extraordinary for their canapés. The level of service is fabulous"* – **Stephen Jones.**

LUFTHANSA
Teutonic precision gains them valuable points. *"Very efficient"* – **Julian Lloyd Webber.** *"Good – German punctuality comes in here"* – **Derek Malcolm.** *"Terribly efficient, terribly punctual"* – **Serena Fass.** *"I like them. The service and the food is good"* – **Madhur Jaffrey.**

MAS (MALAYSIAN AIRLINE SYSTEM)
"They struck me as totally charming. The food's nice, the stewardesses are all tiny and they take a lot of trouble. They're more inclined to put you into first class if it's not full" – **George Melly.**

🎩 **QANTAS**
In the very top league, with an impeccable safety record. *"For safety and just knowing you're going to get there, Qantas without a doubt"*

🎩 **Buzzzzzzzzz** ROYAL ATLANTIC AIR-WAYS ☎ (800) 227 1135 (USA); ☎ (01) 439 8985 (London) is the new luxury way to fly London-New York. Their 707s carry 50 instead of 180 passengers, have veritable easy chairs for seats, private compartments, a bar and a range of executive equipment including computer. Extravagant in-flight gifts, raised humidity levels to combat jetlag, 6 round trips and you get one free – all for the same price of a regular first-class trip 🎩 . . . . . . *"If you think the world can get by without you for one day, the best New York-London flight is* **BA 178**, *which leaves at 10am and arrives at 9.40pm. It always leaves on time and lands on time and there's no one in the terminal when you arrive"* – **Ed Victor** 🎩 . . . . . . *"The best seat in first class is the single seat at the front of the 747"* – **Ed Victor.**

★ ★

TRAVEL

BEST CURE FOR JETLAG

The consensus (including views from **James Burke, Madhur Jaffrey, Margaux Hemingway** and **Stanley Marcus**) advocates copious amounts of water, no alcohol, brisk exercise after the flight and locking immediately into the time zone of your destination. An all-fruit diet is another solution. Here are others' suggestions: *"Ginseng. The best is from Ortis of Belgium because they use the whole root. You can have it in liquid or capsule form – and it is the natural pure ginseng. Take two spoonfuls before you start flying and then take capsules in your bag. It is marvellous for endurance, feeling well, and it's definitely a preserver of youth"* – **Barbara Cartland** . . . *"Take another plane as soon as possible – preferably to where you came from"* – **Joan Collins** . . . *"I have a special diet I go on 4 days before departure. It works really well whichever way you're going"* – **Elise Pascoe** (send an SAE to Anti-Jet-Lag Diet, OPA, Argonne National Laboratory, 9700 S Cass Ave, Argonne, IL 60439, USA) . . . *"I walk for an hour . . . no particular place"* – **Larry King.**

– **Elise Pascoe. Robert Sangster, Diane Freis, Terry Holmes** and **Michael Parkinson** are with them all the way – as are millions of Aussies, every time they go overseas.

♣ SAS (SCANDINAVIAN AIRLINE SYSTEMS)

The airline of Denmark, Norway and Sweden. Punctual and reliable, they're the businessman's dream: no hanging around the luggage carousel – they'll send bags on to your hotel; no queues at the airport – you can check in from your hotel; limo service; business class flights at economy fares.

♣ SINGAPORE AIRLINES

A truly thoughtful airline. *"The stewardesses really are very nice to you and the food is wonderful. You can lie down upstairs and they only wake you if you want – otherwise they put a belt over you to land"* – **Prue Leith.** *"Excellent, especially for long-distance flights. They bring what you want almost before you say you want it"* – **James Burke.** *"Along with other Eastern ones, the service is so good and efficient"* – **Derek Malcolm.** *"Usually very good"* – **Diane Freis.**

♣ SWISSAIR

Very highly regarded (it's the inimitable Swiss precision, inherent also in their hoteliers and timepieces) with a comforting safety record. *"The best. Cabin service is absolutely immaculate. They are very intelligent about airline food. They understand the appetite of the airline passenger better than any other*

airline" – **Mark Birley.** *"Most attentive, excellent. The best food in the sky"* – **James Burke.** *"The best – wonderfully run. Nothing beats Swissair"* – **Lord Gowrie.** *"The other good one in Europe"* – **Lord Lichfield.** Votes too from **Lord Montagu of Beaulieu, Viscountess Rothermere** and **Serena Fass.**

THAI AIRWAYS INTERNATIONAL

"Undoubtedly the best. Much more room – you pull out the seat and can lie flat on it. The Thai girls are so sweet and the food is excellent" – **Barbara Cartland.** *"The best for luxury, service, food and in-flight perks. They do a wonderful gold spoon and fork and the best nasal spray (I get asthma). I love the Thai girls and their dress. The food is stylish and interesting"* – **Elise Pascoe.**

CRUISES

CRUISE AND CHARM, 104 rue de Faubourg St Honoré, Paris, France ☎ (1) 4266 6400 Ultra-expensive cruises aboard the good ship *Maxim's des Mer*, owned and decorated by Pierre Cardin.

BEST WAY TO TRAVEL I

"Car – with someone else driving. It's a great help not to drive. People ask how I get by. Easy – you find slaves" – **George Melly** . . . *"To fly my own Concorde"* – **Thomas Hoving** . . . *"If I had my choice and the money, I would love to go on the QE2 or, in the old days, the SS France, because you arrive totally relaxed. You don't have to go in for all this black-tie dancing stuff and you sleep like a dream"* – **Joyce Davidson** . . . *"To press a button and find I was there"* – **Jeffrey Archer** . . . *"On a horse. Riding from one place to another is outstandingly nice. If the traffic weren't so bad I would have one in London"* – **David Hicks** . . . *"Riding is the ultimate. The great thing about riding cross-country is that you travel at a pace where you can take in your surroundings and you reach places that you wouldn't otherwise dream of stopping in"* – **Robin Hanbury-Tenison** . . . *"Concorde or private jet"* – **Joan Collins** . . . *"The ideal would be a wonderful train through pretty countryside. I'd love to have a private carriage, totally comfortable and fast"* – **Imran Khan.**

BEST WAY TO TRAVEL II

"Chauffeur-driven car. I hate flying, I don't like ferries and trains are OK, but ..." – **Keith Floyd** ... *"By air – the quickest"* – **Shakira Caine** ... *"Always local transport: trucks, boats, buses. I don't like taking my own Land-Rover because it cuts me off. A motorbike might be fun because it's more transportable. I don't like to fly internally. I like to cover the land between stops"* – **Dan Topolski** ... *"Train, because I love trains. You don't go through that white-knuckle anxiety of air travel. You can look out of the window at the countryside and get a feel of the place you are in. It takes you from the heart of one city to the heart of another city"* – **Madhur Jaffrey** ... *"The only way is first class and by air"* – **Elise Pascoe** ... *"First class. Ever since I could afford it, I like first class. That's indispensable to me – wide seats, prompt service"* – **Larry King** ... *"My favourite is my own car – Alpine 310. My second is Stavros Niarchos's yacht!"* – **David Litchfield** ... *"I like travelling to the country in my own car. I think my car is the best car in the world. It's a 1962 Rolls-Royce Silver Cloud II. You're surrounded by wood and leather and you glide down the motorway"* – **Ed Victor.**

A luxurious (by Indian standards) old-fashioned train that steams round Rajasthan, packing in the sights, with overnight stops at top-class hotels. Lovely atmosphere of faded grandeur, in tiny narrow-gauge carriages that once belonged to sundry Maharajas.

Great railway journeys of the world

Top train-rides include ... The Cornish Riviera: *"The 5.40 from* **Paddington to Penzance,** *a 125, is the most beautiful train ride. I like it partly for the view and partly because Western Region really is good and they do take care of you"* – **Robin Hanbury-Tenison. Inverness to the Kyle of Lochalsh** (the ferry point for Skye), through the West Highlands – wonderful scenery, wildlife, and little station hotels. The tiny railway that runs through Indian hill plantations from **Ootacamund to Mettuppalaiyam.** The jungly north Borneo trip from **Kota Kinabalu to Tenom,** Sabah. The narrow-gauge Andean train-trek from **Cuzco to Machu Picchu,** Peru.

ROYAL VIKING LINE, 750 Battery St, San Francisco, CA 94111, USA
☎ **(415) 398 8000**
"By far the best in the world. All one class, better than first class. Any cruise is good, but the Hebridean one is very interesting" – **Lord Lichfield.** A great variety of cruise lengths (from 7 to 100 days), ports and areas – such as the Coral and Java seas, Alaska, Panama Canal-Gatun Lake and the North Cape.

SEA GODDESS CRUISES, Cunard, South Western House, Canute Rd, Southampton, England;
☎ **(0703) 634166; 30a Pall Mall, London SW1**
☎ **(01) 491 3930**
A plushy line with 2 identical small ships, more like floating clubs, carrying only 70 guests apiece. Nicely kitted out in subdued pastels, with linen and crystal. They visit the ports other ships cannot reach, such as Portofino, Puerto Banus, Patmos, Tobago Cays, Virgin Gorda and many Brazilian ports. Swimming pool, spa; occasional unscheduled stops to air the windsurfers, snorkelling equipment and speedboats (for

water-skiing) that are carried on board. Al fresco breakfasts and lunches, formal dinners and nightclub-casino.

WINDSTAR SAIL CRUISES, 7415 NW 19th St, Miami, FL 33126, USA ☎ **(305) 592 8008**
Lavish week-long cruises aboard stunning 4-masted sailing vessels – *Wind Star* in the Grenadines, *Wind Song* in French Polynesia and the new *Wind Spirit.* Norwegian officers and European hotel staff form the 84-strong crew for 150 passengers.

RAIL

BULLET TRAIN (SHINKANSEN), Japan
From Tokyo to Omiya, Morioka, Nigata and, the best route, whizzing at 130 mph through national parkland beneath Mount Fuji, through Kyoto, Nagoya, Osaka and Hiroshima to Hakata.

PALACE ON WHEELS, Central Reservation House, 36 Chandralok, Janpath, New Delhi 110001, India
☎ **(011) 322332**

TRANS-SIBERIAN EXPRESS, USSR
From Moscow, it's 8 days across the steppes of Siberia, past forests and hills thick with wild flowers, before arriving at Khabarovsk, near the Chinese border. It's a romantic notion, if rather under-patronized by the beautiful people. Book via Intourist.

TGV (Train à Grande Vitesse), France
The fastest train in the world whisks you at 168 mph from Paris to major French towns, Geneva and Lausanne. From

usual stations; must reserve a seat. *"The best train in Europe – so quick they don't need a restaurant car"* – **David Hicks**. Instead, meals are served at your seat.

VENICE SIMPLON-ORIENT-EXPRESS, Sea Containers House, 20 Upper Ground, London SE1, England ☎ (01) 928 6000
The legendary Orient-Express, sumptuously re-created in 1920s style. Dressy and elegant; gourmet cuisine and a good many cocktails murdered daily. Dig-a-dig-diggers include **Margaux Hemingway, Eric Newby, Serena Fass, Frank Bowling, Robin Hanbury-Tenison**: *"Marvellous. You have to be in the right mood, live it, throw yourself into it. It's perfectly done"* and **Lord Lichfield**: *"Wonderful. I rather wish it went on for longer. It's essential that you do stay at the Cipriani."* The 30-hour overnight trip chugs from London to Venice via the Swiss and Austrian Alps.

TOURS, VILLAS AND AGENTS

ABERCROMBIE & KENT, Sloane Square House, Holbein Place, London SW1, England ☎ (01) 730 9600; 1420 Kensington Rd, Suite 111, Oakbrook, IL 60521, USA ☎ (312) 954 2954
One of the most extensive and very best tour companies in the world. All sorts of luxury tours, staying in the best hotels. They're global, and particularly good on Africa. Marketeers for top British country-house hotels under the Pride of Britain partnership.

ALLEYNE, AGUILAR & ALTMANN, Barbados, see Caribbean

ANSETT, see Australia

ART STUDY TOURS & COUNTRY TRAVELS, c/o Serena Fass, 2 Chesil Court, Chelsea Manor St, London SW3, England ☎ (01) 352 9769
Worldwide cultural tours, organized by Serena Fass (ex-Serenissima) and accompanied by a lecturer. Egypt, Kashmir, Ladakh, Russia, etc. Also property lets in France, Portugal and Spain.

AUSTRALIAN AIRLINES, see Australia

BALES TOURS, Barrington Rd, Dorking, Surrey, England ☎ (0306) 885991
These old stalwarts do long cruises from Cairo to Aswan on their *Death on the Nile*-style steamer, *Nefertari*.

BUTTERFIELD & ROBINSON, 70 Bond St, Toronto M5B 1X3, Canada ☎ (416) 864 1354
Luxury bike tours through France and Italy: 5-star hotels, award-winning restaurants, and tours of local vineyards revive saddle-sore cyclists. Also Nile cruises, bird-watching in Ecuador and other worldwide destinations.

CARIBBEAN CONNECTION, 93 Newman St, London W1, England ☎ (01) 631 4797
Upmarket hotels and villas all over the Caribbean, especially Barbados. Yacht charter.

CLASSIC TOURS, Rio de Janeiro, see Brazil

CONTINENTAL VILLAS, 12 Grosvenor Crescent, London SW1, England ☎ (01) 245 9181
Luxury villas, mostly with pools, in the South of France, Spain, Portugal, Palm Beach and the West Indies.

COUNTRY HOMES AND CASTLES, 118 Cromwell Rd, London SW7, England ☎ (01) 370 4445
Private stays in some of the finest stately homes, castles and manors of Great Britain.

COX & KINGS, New Delhi (and worldwide), see India

CV TRAVEL, 43 Cadogan St, London SW3, England ☎ (01) 581 0851
The smartest selection of villas (and villa girls) on Corfu. The Duchess of Kent and her family have stayed in one of theirs. Also cushy villas on other Greek islands, in Turkey, the South of France, Italy, Palm Beach. Their Different World division offers exotic hotel hols mainly in Caribbean and African resorts.

EAST AFRICAN WILDLIFE SAFARIS, see Kenya

ENCOUNTER OVERLAND, 267 Old Brompton Rd, London SW5, England ☎ (01) 370 6951
For hardy types only – the best for nitty-gritty adventure expeditions in the Third World.

EXPLORASIA, 13 Chapter St, London SW1, England ☎ (01) 630 7102
Smart treks in India and Nepal. Real pioneering, well researched, involved stuff such as a rhododendron trek in Nepal, trout fishing in Kashmir. They have arranged elephant polo championships and a tailor-made trek for Prince Charles.

HELIOTOURS EGYPT, see Egypt

HEMPHILL HARRIS, 16,000 Ventura Blvd, Suite 200, Encino, CA 91436, USA ☎ (818) 906 8086
Highly exclusive tours for rich old fogeys. Guarantee the best of everything – the best rooms with the best views in the best hotels. Trips all over the world (except for their own doorstep – North America) include heli cruises, ballooning and a world tour in a private jet.

KUONI TRAVEL, Kuoni House, Dorking, Surrey, England ☎ (0306) 885044
Luxury tours around the world, including the Hemingwayesque Classic Safari in Kenya and the Concorde and Sandy Lane Spectacular (7 spectacularly expensive nights in Barbados). Also tailor-made itineraries.

LINDBLAD TRAVEL, 1 Sylvan North, PO Box 912, Westport, CT 06881, USA ☎ (203) 226 8531
Fabulously expensive trips for

the intelligent élite; conservation-loving regulars have formed an exclusive travellers' club, the Intrepids. Their Masai Mara safari has the most luxurious tented camp in Africa, staying in four-poster beds. Cruises are a speciality and among the best in the world. Over- and above-land trips too.

MARY ROSSI TRAVEL, Suite 3, 65 Berry Street, PO Box 1492, N Sydney, NSW 2060, Australia ☎ (02) 957 4511
All arrangements for upmarket globetrotters are made by Mary and 6 members of her family. Agents for Serenissima.

SERENISSIMA TRAVEL, 21 Dorset Square, London NW1, England ☎ (01) 730 9841
Incorporates Heritage tours. Chaired by John Julius Norwich, with a string of scholarly lecturers and a grand clientele. Refined cultural tours of Europe, Russia, the Middle East, South America, Africa and Asia. Not all are cocoons of luxury.

SILK CUT TRAVEL, Meon House, Petersfield, Hampshire, England ☎ (0730) 65211
Upmarket tours and cruises in South America, the Caribbean, the Far East – including a river safari in Borneo – and Africa.

SPECIALTOURS, 2 Chester Row, London SW1, England ☎ (01) 730 2297
Mainly cultural tours – Romanesque art in the Pyrenees; Moscow and Leningrad; A walk in Rajasthan, etc. Serena Fass is one of the tour leaders.

TEMPO TRAVEL, Brunswick House, 91 Brunswick Crescent, London N11, England ☎ (01) 361 1131
African safaris, trips down the Nile, to the Seychelles and Mauritius. See also Kenya.

TRAILFINDERS, 42 Earl's Court Rd, London W8, England. Europe and transatlantic ☎ (01) 937 5400; ☎ (01) 603 1515 long-haul;

☎ (01) 938 3444 first and business class
Comprehensive and knowledgeable agents on worldwide air travel. On-the-spot ticketing, insurance, immunization and medical advice, travellers' cheques and currency, maps and books.

TWICKERS WORLD, 22 Church St, Twickenham, Middlesex, England ☎ (01) 892 7606
Tours and treks to outlandish places with the accent on wildlife. Intense stuff accompanied by experts – Amazon safari, Patagonia overland, Antarctica and the Falklands, Papua New Guinea.

VACANZE IN ITALIA, Bignor, Pulborough, W Sussex, England ☎ (07987) 362
Incorporates Vacances en Campagne (☎ 366), Islands Unlimited (☎ 308) and Châteaux in France (☎ 366). Superb privately owned villas, châteaux, cottages and country houses for hire in Italy, France and England.

VOYAGES JULES VERNE, 10 Glentworth St, London NW1, England ☎ (01) 486 8751
Renowned for worming their way into hitherto uncharted (by tour companies) corners of the earth, including Albania, parts of China, Mexico and Egypt. Cultural, escorted tours.

WAYFARER HOLIDAYS, 235 Yorkland Blvd, Suite 610, Willowdale, Ontario M2J 4W9, Canada ☎ (416) 498 5566
Adventure tours around Canada and the Arctic, from whale-watching in British Columbia to the Anne of Green Gables tour around Prince Edward Island.

WORTHY INTERNATIONAL TRAVEL, 49 Graham Terrace, London SW1, England ☎ (01) 730 5501
Susie Worthy has a wealth of British aristocratic homes and country estates at her fingertips, where you can stay as a personal guest. Guided heritage tours too, and she'll

take the mystery and misery out of getting in to Ascot, Wimbledon, Henley et al.

YACHT CHARTERS

CAMPER & NICHOLSONS, BP 183, Port Pierre Canto, 06407 Cannes, France ☎ 9343 1675
Over 400 luxury crewed yachts, motor and sailing, modern and old-fashioned, steered where you will. Baron Thyssen's *Hanse* is on their books for US$84,000 a week, sleeps 12. The most expensive is *Katalina* at US$168,000 (sleeps 16); nothing much below US$5,000.

CHARTER SERVICES, US Virgin Islands, see Caribbean

HAMILTON ISLAND CHARTERS, Queensland, see Australia

NICHOLSON'S YACHT CHARTER, Antigua, see Caribbean

TOP YACHT CHARTER, Andrew Hill Lane, Hedgerley, Buckinghamshire, England ☎ (02814) 2640
Specialists in bareboat sailing around Turkey and Greece, plus some crewed boats.

WINDSOR YACHTS, c/o Navtol Agencies, 65 Broadway, 10th Fl, New York, NY 10006, USA ☎ (212) 363 7990
Brand new line to be launched early '89 by Greek-Mexican shipping magnate Ricardo Farias Nicolopulos. The Bermuda-based yachts, *Sarah* and *Diana* (with a third due in late '89), have almost 60 crew to 70 guests and can be chartered in any waters for around $2,000 a head per day.

YACHTCLUB CHARTER CO, 307 New King's Rd, London SW6, England ☎ (01) 731 0826
Smart young company operating out of Bodrum, Turkey, with a fine fleet of sailing yachts for bareboat and flotilla holidays. Also crewed old-style wooden gulets.

Viscountess Rothermere on
SOCIAL <u>AND</u> NIGHT LIFE

World's Best Nightclubs

1
ANNABEL'S,
London

2
NELL'S,
New York

3
CASTEL'S,
Paris

4
HELENA'S,
Los Angeles

5
LEXINGTON QUEEN,
Tokyo

6
NINETEEN 97,
Hong Kong

7
ROGUES,
Sydney

8
TRAMP,
London

9
LE PALACE 999,
Paris

10
THE METRO,
Melbourne

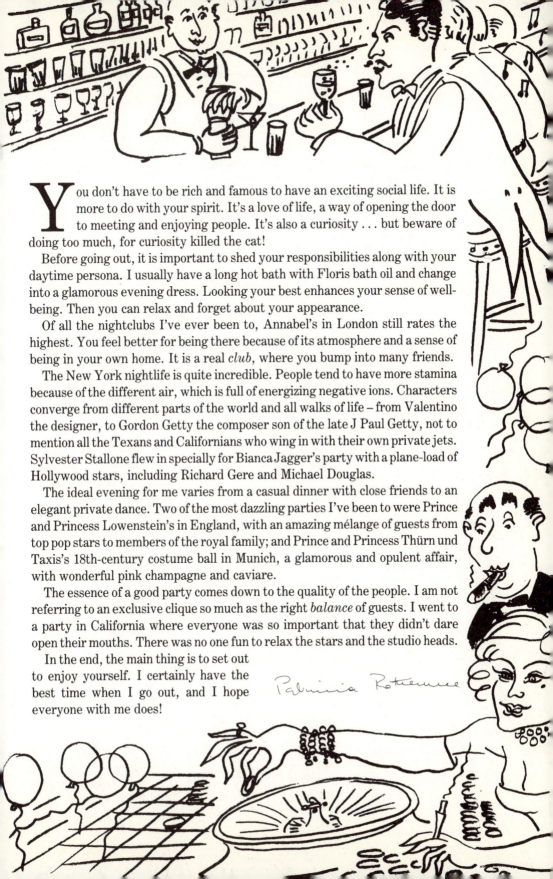

You don't have to be rich and famous to have an exciting social life. It is more to do with your spirit. It's a love of life, a way of opening the door to meeting and enjoying people. It's also a curiosity ... but beware of doing too much, for curiosity killed the cat!

Before going out, it is important to shed your responsibilities along with your daytime persona. I usually have a long hot bath with Floris bath oil and change into a glamorous evening dress. Looking your best enhances your sense of well-being. Then you can relax and forget about your appearance.

Of all the nightclubs I've ever been to, Annabel's in London still rates the highest. You feel better for being there because of its atmosphere and a sense of being in your own home. It is a real *club*, where you bump into many friends.

The New York nightlife is quite incredible. People tend to have more stamina because of the different air, which is full of energizing negative ions. Characters converge from different parts of the world and all walks of life – from Valentino the designer, to Gordon Getty the composer son of the late J Paul Getty, not to mention all the Texans and Californians who wing in with their own private jets. Sylvester Stallone flew in specially for Bianca Jagger's party with a plane-load of Hollywood stars, including Richard Gere and Michael Douglas.

The ideal evening for me varies from a casual dinner with close friends to an elegant private dance. Two of the most dazzling parties I've been to were Prince and Princess Lowenstein's in England, with an amazing mélange of guests from top pop stars to members of the royal family; and Prince and Princess Thürn und Taxis's 18th-century costume ball in Munich, a glamorous and opulent affair, with wonderful pink champagne and caviare.

The essence of a good party comes down to the quality of the people. I am not referring to an exclusive clique so much as the right *balance* of guests. I went to a party in California where everyone was so important that they didn't dare open their mouths. There was no one fun to relax the stars and the studio heads.

In the end, the main thing is to set out to enjoy yourself. I certainly have the best time when I go out, and I hope everyone with me does!

Palmina Rothermere

America

BALTIMORE

BACHELORS COTILLION,
c/o Mrs Laura Bortle, 3rd Fl,
Legal Dept, Equitable Bank
Center, 100 S Charles St, MD
21201 ☎ (301) 547 4109
The most formal and
prestigious débutante ball,
started in 1830. Held at the
Fifth Regiment Armory on the
Friday following Thanksgiving.
White-gloved paternal
gentlemen, virginal young
girls. Very *Gone With The
Wind.*

A DAY AT THE RACES

KENTUCKY DERBY, Churchill Downs, Louisville, in May
is the race everyone would like to win. Ex-Presidents,
Hollywood stars and 120,000 others trot in, then gallop off to
lunch on home-made Derby Pie, real Kentucky fried chicken
and beaten biscuits washed down by mint juleps and bourbon.
That's the first leg of the Triple Crown. The horse must go on
to win the **PREAKNESS**, Pimlico Race Course, Baltimore,
later in May and the **BELMONT STAKES**, Belmont Park,
Long Island, New York, in June. The August Meet at
SARATOGA, Saratoga Springs, is a one-month affair in up-
state New York. **BREEDERS CUP**, Los Angeles Turf Club,
Santa Anita Park, Los Angeles is a recently established race
of instant import, with the highest prize money in the world
($10 million plus).

BOSTON

Bostonians need their beauty
sleep. Virtually the only time
they emerge is for old society
balls, many of which take place
at the **Copley Plaza** in its
stunning ballroom.

CLUBS

**AXIS, 13 Lansdowne St, MA
02215** ☎ (617) 262 2437
Formerly Spit, reopened under
the same ownership as Metro.
A younger, more studenty,
arty set dive in to listen to
rock, punk, new wave and
industrial music, much of it
live. **DV8** is a smaller, livelier
club upstairs, where nightbirds
get on down to funky music.

**LINKS, 120 Boylston St, MA
02116** ☎ (617) 423 3832
Set up by DJ Michael Crane
[ex-Surf Club, NY], a dance
club modelled after a turn-
of-the-century country club,
with golf and yachting murals
and a Harvard rowing skull on
the wall.

🏊 **METRO, 15 Lansdowne St,
MA 02215** ☎ (617) 262 2424
For trainee New Yorkers. The
best boppery, it plays host to
most touring bands – Eric
Clapton, Prince, The Pogues.
The latest dance discs are spun;
laser and light shows, video
displays and robotic cameras.

EVENTS

**CONSUL'S BALL, Copley
Plaza, 138 St James Ave, MA
02216** ☎ (617) 267 5300
January. Held in honour of the
consular corps of Boston, it's
jammed with politicians and
dignitaries. By invitation only.

DEBUTANTE COTILLION,
Copley Plaza **(see above)**
June. Old-fashioned entrée into
society: white gloves,
presentations and all.

CHICAGO
CLUBS

**JAZZ SHOWCASE, 636 N
Michigan St, IL 60605**
☎ (312) 427 4300
Home of be-bop jazz, based in
the Blackstone Hotel.

**RACOON CLUB, 812 N
Franklin St, IL 60610**
☎ (312) 943 1928
The most elegant and
fashionable club in Chicago.
Real *Cotton Club* stuff with
'30s décor, small tables and
music of the era – jazz, swing –
and cabaret.

EVENTS

**DONOR'S BALL, Historical
Society, Clark St at North
Ave, IL 60614**
☎ (312) 642 4600

November. Proceeds go to the
Society's Costume Collection –
one of the best in the country –
and 450 of the most fashionable
Chicagoans pay $300 to doll
themselves up in some splendid
outfit that they may later
donate.

PASSAVANT COTILLION,
c/o Women's Board, North
Western Memorial Hospital,
250 E Superior St, IL 606ll
☎ (312) 908 3313
December. Very Social
Register. Held in the Grand
Ballroom of Chicago Hilton
Towers. Débutantes are hand
picked by committee – ex-debs
choose about 30 daughters of
other ex-debs to be presented.

HOSTS

Abra Prentice Anderson – a
Rockefeller, and benefactor of
the Prentice Women's Hospital.
Has a beautiful penthouse on
Lake Shore Drive. **Renee
Crown** – on the board of
WTTW (Chicago's public
broadcasting station), active in
the opera.

DALLAS

Society revolves around the oil
well. The caste system may be
based on business success but
the way you make the money is
paramount: it must be through
honest hard work.

CLUBS

BILLY BOB'S TEXAS, 2520 Rodeo Plaza, Fort Worth, TX 76106 ☎ (817) 429 5979
The world's largest honky-tonk club – in fact four clubs in one: rhythm 'n' blues, duelling pianos (with singalong), live concerts and local country 'n' western, played by the greats (Willie Nelson, Waylon Jennings, Merle Haggard). Real live bull-riding too.

STARCK CLUB, 703 McKinney Ave, Suite 107, TX 75202 ☎ (214) 720 0130
Designed by Philippe Starck, part-owned by Stevie Nicks of Fleetwood Mac. Unusual for Dallas, a discerning doorman picks the clientele. The black terrazzo floor is divided by a curtain 'to give a salon effect' with Italian couches one side and a 40-ft light wall at the back.

EVENTS

"It is said that 365 new restaurants and stores open in Dallas each year, and for each opening there is a social event" – **Caroline Hunt**. Winter is the hot season, when dozens of Dallas hooleys jostle for attention. After the Crystal and the Cattle Barons', the best are the Beaux Arts Ball (held by the Dallas Museum of Art), the Sweetheart Ball (run by Laura Hunt for heart research) and the Junior League Ball.

CATTLE BARONS' BALL, c/o Mrs Billy Baneaton, 6342 McCommas, TX 75214 ☎ (214) 827 5475
Held outdoors on a different ranch each June. *"For colour. People dress up in the most outlandish costumes – corny Texas gear – it's certainly theatrical"* – **Caroline Hunt**. Big money (old and new), big-name entertainment, a funfair,

and a lavish auction where people make sealed bids for each others' furs, cars and diamonds. The biggest single fund-raiser for the American Cancer Society.

CRYSTAL CHARITY BALL, 47 Highland Park Village, Suite 5, TX 75205 ☎ (214) 526 5868
"The biggest, oldest charity ball, which raises the most money. Many of the old guard, the pioneers of Dallas attend" – **Caroline Hunt**. Held each December in the outsize Anatole hotel ballroom (room for 2,300). Tickets (c. $600 a head) are sold out to the oil society virtually before they hit the printers; outsiders don't stand a chance. In aid of children's charities.

HOSTS

Caroline Hunt is the most expert hostess in Dallas, well practised from her hotel successes. **Nancy Brinker**: wife of fast-foodie polo-player Norman B., she is in the top 10 Dallas Best Dressed, and organizes a host of charity balls.

HOUSTON

The Houston season is heralded by the Museum of Fine Art's annual ball in early October. The opera opening is another major affair (see Culture).

HOST

Lynn Wyatt is the queen of Houston society. Here's her secret: *"The hostess must attend to all the details before so that when she opens the door to her first guest she feels like she's a guest too. The setting is important. Lighting creates a definite atmosphere yet most people don't give a hoot about*

it! Good food always helps. So does a theme. But in the end, it's still the people that make the party."

LOS ANGELES
BARS AND CLUBS

CLUB LINGERIE, 6507 Sunset Blvd, CA 90028 ☎ (213) 466 8557
Slick rock club with a large dance floor. Up to 4 bands a night – anything from punk rock to reggae, with a disco between sessions.

F/X, 2525 Main St, Santa Monica, CA 90405 ☎ (213) 452 4298
Restaurateur François Petit's new supper club is a Hollywood celebration, decorated with movie sets. Dennis Hopper, Lee Majors and Sean Penn join other VIPs in Le Privilege room.

 HELENA'S, 2735 W Temple St, CA 90026 ☎ (213) 384 0224
The hippest hop in LA, a membership club where the stars all go on a Friday night (and *only* on a Friday according to **Jackie Collins**): Jack Nicholson (a partner in the club), Warren Beatty, Madonna, Cher, A&M Records senior V-P Charlie Minor, Triad agent Rob Lee, etc. *"The best LA nightclub. Very small, simple décor, plain club food, typical dance music – and the best crowd in LA"* – **Steve Rubell. Wolfgang Puck** seconds that.

THE PALACE, 1735 N Vine St, Hollywood, CA 90028 ☎ (213) 462 6031
A nightclub/concert hall/restaurant based in Merv Griffin's old TV chat show set, a marvellous Art Deco landmark. 30,000 sq ft of multi-level dancing to discs and top

❝ *Good people are what make a good nightclub. Nothing else – you can have lights, sound, everything … but good people are the key* **❞**

 STEVE RUBELL

live acts such as Terence Trent D'Arby and Ry Cooder. Regular live jazz, country, punk and rock concerts, giant video screen and zany laser shows. Classy hip kids' stuff.

PIET'S PLACE, Le Mondrian Hotel, 8440 Sunset Blvd, CA 90066 ☎ (213) 474 3236
A supper club with live new-wave vaudeville and dancing. On Fridays the Kool Room is a trendy disco, Angel's Terrace an outdoor dance floor with live jazz and a fabulous view over the city; magicians perform at your table.

ROXY, 9009 Sunset Blvd, CA 90028 ☎ (213) 276 2222
The rock venue, a showcase for major touring bands, with the best lighting, sound system and stage in LA.

TRAMP, Beverly Center, 8522 Beverly Blvd, CA 90048 ☎ (213) 659 8090
Established club for the Hollywood crowd, though not as hip as Helena's. Owned by Jackie Collins's husband Oscar Lerman, much larger than London Tramp, more expensive, with cinema and private dining room. *"As inviting as its London counterpart, not least due to Jackie Collins"* – **Dudley Moore**. Other regulars include Johnny Carson, Quincy Jones, Eddie Murphy, the Pointer Sisters, Ryan O'Neal, Prince, Sylvester Stallone, Rod Stewart, Julian Lennon and the Michaels (Caine, Douglas, J. Fox).

VERTIGO, 1024 S Grand Ave, CA 90015 ☎ (213) 747 4849
Giant fashionable dance club with 4 bars, outdoor patio and late-night bistro, run by Mario Oliver (beau of Princess Stéphanie of Monaco). The doorman, whose eye was trained at Studio 54, nods the likes of Mickey Rourke and Don Johnson through the door. The best for **Wolfgang Puck**.

EVENTS

Private parties are held in restaurants like Spago, Chinois

on Main and The Bistro (see Food & Drink). The best beanos are filmbiz orientated, naturally – charity movie premières and, most crucially, **Swifty Lazar's Oscar night party:** *"Second to none. If you're not invited, leave town!"* – **Wolfgang Puck**. *"The best party of the year"* – **Jackie Collins**.

HOSTS

Wallis Annenberg, daughter of Walter, is the best. **Pamela Mason** (wife of the late James M.), **Jackie Collins, Allan Carr, Corinna** and **Freddie Fields, George Christy, Wendy** and **Leonard Goldberg** and **Marsha Weisman** are hot stuff. **Barbara** and **Marvin Davies** *"give the biggest party of the year"* – **Jackie Collins**. **Viscountess Rothermere** recommends **Wendy Stark** and **Barry Diller**.

NEW ORLEANS

The most liberal drinking laws in the States. Although clubs shut at some point in the night to clean up or reorganize, you can drink 24 hours a day. And when you leave, your drink is decanted into a 'go cup' to take away. Bourbon Street is like one big nightclub, from the seedy end (brazen brothels) to St Peter Street (live music bars).

BARS AND CLUBS

BLUE ROOM, University Place, LA 70140 ☎ (504) 529 4744
A jazzy supper club, based in the old Roosevelt Hotel. Live music.

NAPOLEON BAR, 500 Chartres St, LA 70130 ☎ (504) 524 9752
A respite from the trumpets and clarinets. Late-night drinking in the French Quarter to piped classical music.

PAT O'BRIEN'S, 718 St Peter St, LA 70116 ☎ (504) 525 4823
Civilized piano bar for jazz/pop

music with singalongs. 2 more bars – one with a juke box and one outside patio bar.

PRESERVATION HALL, 726 St Peter St, LA 70116 ☎ (504) 522 2238
Earthy home of New Orleans jazz – a small, smoky, sweaty room with sawdust on the floor, wrinkled black musicians and far too many tourists, who form endless queues to get in. Nevertheless, this is wonderful trad jazz from the heart – and so cheap at $2 for the whole evening (unless you request *When the Saints . . .* that'll cost you $5 extra). 4 bands alternate playing 7 nights a week in half-hour sets; each overheated audience tends to pile out after one set and return when they've cooled down (no re-entry charge). Bring your own food and drink.

SNUG HARBOR, 626 Frenchmen St, LA 70116 ☎ (504) 949 0696
On the edge of the French Quarter, a good place to hear local contemporary jazz. Separate restaurant.

EVENTS

MARDI GRAS
Exclusive and ultra-clandestine gentlemen's carnival organizations, known as krewes (clubs so secret that members are known only to fellow members), go through time-honoured rituals, electing kings and queens, arranging parades and masked balls. Of a week of luncheons, dinners, pageants and about 90 carnival balls, the best events are the **REX** and **COMUS** balls, both held on Mardi Gras evening itself.

NEW YORK

BARS AND CLUBS

BIG KAHUNA, 622 Broadway, NY 10012 ☎ (212) 460 9633
Has taken over from the Surf Club as the sunniest surf spot for yuppies and preppies. 1960s

♠ America's Best ♠

NIGHTSPOTS

1 **NELL'S**, New York
2 **HELENA'S**, Los Angeles
3 **PISCES**, Washington, DC
4 **LE CLUB**, New York
5 **METRO**, Boston

music, Beach Boys hits, crowded and noisy – like one big frat party.

THE BOTTOM LINE, 15 W 4th St, NY 10012
☎ (212) 228 6300
Jazz, rock 'n' pop venue, where **George Melly** and many international rock stars have played. **Harvey Goldsmith** discovered Bruce Springsteen here.

CAROLINE'S, 8th Ave and 26th St, NY 10001
☎ (212) 924 3499
The best comedy club-restaurant in the city.

Guaranteed gags from tried and tested talent – virtually all the major comedians in the USA have raised laughs here.

CBGB, 315 Bowery, NY 10002
☎ (212) 982 4052
The grandaddy of the punk scene in New York, where the likes of Blondie and Talking Heads first started turning heads. You can still catch new bands. Great sound system. Sunday afternoon concerts for under-age teenies; record shop and folk club next door.

♠ LE CLUB, 313 E 58th St, NY 10022 ☎ (212) 308 5520
Enduring, dignified private

♠ Buzzzzzzzzz The Japanese craze **karaoke** is a big noise in New York – would-be pop stars jump up on stage and sing their heart out to their fave soundtrack. Have a croon on Thursday nights at **The Lotus Blossom** ♠ . . . . . . While sophisticated New York goes trad, the kids who want frenzied excitement go to **Renegade Clubs** – thematic one-nighters like they have in London. Friday's **BLACK MARKET** (sister of BM at London's Wag Club) and Saturday's **MILKY WAY** (rap and reggae) are the best ♠ . . . . . . Revolution or evolution? The pendulum is swinging: the late-1980s version of **punk** is on its way. Shoe-shuffling jazz and comfy supper clubs don't soothe the new anti-capitalists. The complacent face of music and clubland is heading for a **shake-up.**

★ ★ ★ ★ ★ ★ ★ ★ ★ ★ ★ ★ ★ ★ ★ ★ ★ ★

ALL THAT JAZZ

The hottest jazz spots are: **MICHAEL'S PUB**, 211 E 55th St, NY 10022 ☎ (212) 758 2272 – where Woody Allen plays clarinet on Monday nights with a ragtime band, and **George Melly** has played the rest of the week ("*A nice place to play,*" he trumpets). **THE BLUE NOTE**, 131 W 3rd St, NY 10012 ☎ (212) 475 8592 – one of the oldest and best. Top names play regularly. **THE KNITTING FACTORY**, 47 E Houston St, NY 10002 ☎ (212) 219 3055 – avant-garde jazz and perform-ance art in a café setting: lovely space, innovative art. **FAT TUESDAY'S**, 190 3rd Ave, NY 10003 ☎ (212) 533 7902 – a golden oldie, good for Sunday brunch. **SWEETWATERS**, 170 Amsterdam Ave, NY 10023 ☎ (212) 873 4100 – big jazz and dance bands; restaurant too.

club, possibly even more exclusive than Doubles because it's smaller, based in a town house. Dark suits rule. Tops for **Viscountess Rothermere**.

DOUBLES, Hotel Sherry-Netherland, 783 5th Ave, NY 10022 ☎ (212) 751 9595
Exclusive private club, interior-designed (all red) by Valerian Rybar, a safe bet for older Establishment families. Very Upper East Side. Popular for private parties.

DRUMS, 333 E 60th St, NY 10022 ☎ (212) 308 2333
Groovy new live venue run by music promotor Ron Delsener, mega-rival to John Scher of

---

❝ *I don't like that New York habit of 'You're in, you're out'. I loathed that horrible Studio 54. I hated the sense that you had to be old, hideous and famous, or young and pretty to be in it. I much prefer places where they just accept you because you pay to get in* ❞

♠ GEORGE MELLY

NELL'S

♠ **NELL'S, 246 W 14th St, NY 10011 ☎ (212) 675 1567.** With its cosy gentlemen's-club-cum-country-house décor, 'Little' Nell Campbell's place is to nightlife as Ralph Lauren is to fashion and the Mansion on Turtle Creek is to hotels. Faux Establishment, anti-modernist – and a surefire success (though it peaked within its first year). The door policy's as ruthless as any (Cher and Grace Jones have been turned away); once selected, everybody *bar none* pays the $5 cover charge. You enter to the strains of live jazz, lounge on velvet sofas and chatter, or wander downstairs to dance. *"Nell makes the place work and it will continue to be a success as long as she can take the pace"* – **Duggie Fields**. *"Wonderful. It's a large peanut bar with tables and chairs and jazz. It's noisy, smoky and it's got a great atmosphere"* – **Harvey Goldsmith**. *"I love it. One of the wonderful things about Nell's is it looks as if it's been there for years. Very beautifully lit; well-designed restaurant. It's nightclub as theatre"* – **Ed Victor**. *"Very good, like a Victorian sort of living room, comfortable, old-fashioned, with lots of mirrors"* – **Michael Musto**. *"Nell's was an old electric hardware store. I used to buy screwdrivers there. Definitely the most fashionable place to go at the moment"* – **Steve Rubell. Taki, Stephen Jones, Tama Janowitz, Ken Lane, John Gold** and **Mariuccia Mandelli** add their votes, but you can't please all of the people all of the time: *"I thought it was terrible. I kept being told I was wrong. It's not what it says it is: actually it's immensely noisy, the 9-piece jazz band is mind-blowingly loud, downstairs is the hardest black funk club in New York. Victorian boudoir? It's more like a Young's pub"* – **Alan Crompton-Batt.**

Ritz. Drums form part of the décor, so dancers can beat to the rhythm of the band. Rock music Tues to Thurs, progressive jazz Fri and Sat, reggae on Sunday.

THE LONE STAR, 5th Ave at 13th St, NY 10003 ☎ (212) 242 1664
Texas comes to Manhattan. Have yourself a mighty meal and listen to the best of little ol' country rock 'n' roll. .

RITZ, 119 E 11th St, NY 10003 ☎ (212) 254 2800
The best venue for live music any night of the week. An old dance hall where touring and up-and-coming bands play rock 'n' roll, reggae, country – all sorts of music – to hip young (and grown-up) kids. Suzanne Vega was a regular; Terence Trent D'Arby has played there.

Record companies and entrepreneurs like **Harvey Goldsmith** talent-spot from upstairs tables.

SIBERIA, 804 Washington St, NY 10014 ☎ (212) 463 8521
Luxurious performance art and music venue built on many levels, with 35-ft-high ceilings. Live music from gentle jazz on a grand piano to rock bands.

S.O.B.'s, 204 Varick St, NY 10014 ☎ (212) 243 4940
Salsa or bop to Sounds Of Brazil ... the place for top international Latin-American acts. Also reggae, African, ska, etc. Carnival atmosphere, fairish food, knock-out sugar – cane alcohol and lime caipirinhas.

THE TUNNEL, 27th St and 12th Ave, NY 10001 ☎ (212) 463 8521

Already off the rails, this was one of last year's most talked-about clubs, built in an abandoned railway tunnel with the tracks still running through. Laser light shows. *"Upstairs is yuppie, straight, conservative with top 40 music; downstairs is more eclectic, creative"* – **Michael Musto.** The inner sanctum, the Rudolf Room, opens its doors only to the élite, but the Tunnel is too vast to be exclusive. **Steve Rubell** doesn't mince his words: *"Hell, I hate that place! It's like a '70s disco."* Now best when there's a private party.

THE WORLD, 254 E 2nd St, NY 10009 ☎ (212) 477 8677
Hip joint based in an old Polish wedding palace. Tacky but enormous fun, jostling with downtowners. Live blues and roots music in the Crystal Room.

ZULU LOUNGE, 1584 York Ave, NY 10028 ☎ (212) 722 0556
Set up by the owners of the Surf Club, who have dragged their tribe into the depths of Africa, midst palm trees, bamboos and Zulu masks. Small and tightly packed: 250 steamy bodies add a whiff of realism to the jungliness of it all. Recommended only for yup/prep-lovers.

EVENTS

Socialites are really *groupies*, hanging out with the Met Opera, or the Met Museum, or the Botanical Gardens, or the New York Public Library or the Morgan Library. All of these institutions embody a particular style and attract society names to match. All throw benefit dinners and auctions and balls galore. Then there are the charities: *"You can dance for a different disease every night if you want"* – **Mario Buatta**. Some of the best events are: **New York Hospital-Cornell Medical Center cabaret gala** (Sept, Waldorf Astoria, tickets from $500; stars like Debbie Reynolds and Donald O'Connor attend), the **Tiffany Ball** (aka Feathers), the **Winter Antiques Show** and the **Literary Lions dinner** (Nov, for the NY Public Library – an intellectual crowd, authors host tables). The mini-season kicks off in May, but the main bashes run from October to Christmas, chronicled in *Town & Country*.

APRIL IN PARIS BALL, American French Foundation, 250 Park Ave, Suite 624, NY 10177
☎ (212) 986 2060
October. It benefits 24 different charities. Always a theme, such as the memorable 'Circus', when Marlene Dietrich rode in on an elephant. Guests pay $400 a head but get $300 worth back in prezzies (which companies donate).

METROPOLITAN MUSEUM OF ART, Costume Institute Opening Gala (See Culture)

METROPOLITAN OPERA OPENING GALA, Lincoln Center, NY 10023
☎ (212) 870 7428
The Metropolitan Opera opens with a splash in September. The gala will set you back about $1,000 for the performance, a black-tie dinner and thrilling extras. The more private Opera Ball closes the season in May. See Culture.

GUESTS AND HOSTS

Mrs William (Pat) Buckley is the best. *"Her dinners at the Met and for Memorial Sloan-Kettering are the best – she's a great organizer"* – **Lynn Wyatt**. At the helm of all the major New York charity

---

NOT NELL'S

Nell's has launched a thousand clones. It's part of the cycle: New York re-creates what Europe already has, only it does it with more conviction, as a style statement. The rest of New York follows. Then the rest of the world follows (including Europe, re-creating New York re-creating it). Among the new relaxing, romantic, traditional, elegant, unflash supper clubs (*totally* different from Nell's they insist) are these: **MK**, 204 5th Ave, the latest from Eric [Area] Goode – an exclusive restaurant/club on several floors with library, butlers and maids. **BILLY ROSE'S DIAMOND HORSESHOE**, Century Paramount Hotel, 235 W 46th St ☎ (212) 764 5500, Steve [Palladium] Rubell's supper club. Howard Stein's **AU BAR**, 41 E 58th St ☎ (212) 308 9455, designed by naice young British girls Christina (daughter of Kokoly) Fallah, Emily Todd-Hunter and Lady Miranda Beatty. A pastiche of Bohemian Belgravia, there's a salon, a library and 'non-adolescent' music. Keep eyes peeled for Olivier Coquelin's new **UNION SQUARE CLUB**, 33 E 17th St, due Dec '88.

---

extravaganzas (and a few of her own), she is wizard at whipping up enthusiasm, a relentless doer, and mistress of the seating plan. Her right-hand women, who add gloss to any gala by their very presence, include **Mica Ertegun, Chessy Rayner, Nan Kempner, Lynn Wyatt, Paloma Picasso, Carolina Herrera** and **Susan Gutfreund** (no mean hostesses themselves). **Diana Vreeland** and **Brooke Astor** are treasured guests: *"Brooke Astor is quite rightly the crowned queen of New York"* – **Lady Fairfax.**

PARTY PEOPLE

GLORIOUS FOOD, 172 E 75th St, NY 10021
☎ (212) 628 2320
Run by Sean Driscoll, they are

the first name in catering, sweeping up all the best galas. Pat Buckley uses them a great deal, and they do the food for the grand openings at the Metropolitan Museum of Art. **Lady Elizabeth Anson** is a great admirer.

LESTER LANIN, 157 W 57th St, NY 10019 ☎ (212) 265 5208
The best oldies' dance band in the world. He was hauled across the Atlantic to play at Charles and Diana's wedding party and round the Med to serenade Vivien Duffield's guests on *Sea Goddess II.*

PEGGY MULHOLLAND, c/o 7 Dresser St, Newport, RI 02840 ☎ (212) 484 2663
Creates wildly imaginative settings and fills them with the right combination of food, music and props. She always

---

❝ *The best recipe for energy is vitamins. Ginseng is the finest energizer available. A couple of spoonfuls and one is bouncing. Also multivitamins and honey. Mrs Thatcher takes Vitamin C every day, I take 6,000 units every night and I do not have colds or flu. Zsa Zsa Gabor's secret of looking young at 68 is she gets up at 5am and swims for 2 hours, and it is go, go, go all day* **❞**

 BARBARA CARTLAND

does the Literary Lions dinner (the latest 'brought the outside inside' – birdhouses in the shape of the library, rose hedges). For the wedding of Rose Kennedy's granddaughter Victoria the theme was a Victorian Rose Garden (geddit?). Held in two tents at Southampton, Long Island – the first re-created Washington at cherry blossom time; for the second, a garden of pink roses was planted on the dance floor and there was a special gazebo with heart-shaped windows for the cake.

PETER DUCHIN, 400 Madison Ave, NY 10017 ☎ (212) 753 4393
Revered orchestra leader who plays at really big bashes.

PALM BEACH

Hardly Sin City, Palm Beach conducts its social life in a gentle, civilized manner. Few nightclubs, but in season (November to Easter) there may be as many as 100 charity receptions and balls.

EVENTS

COCONUTS, 1021 N Ocean Blvd, FL 33480 ☎ (305) 844 6659
New Year's Eve. The Coconuts is a men's club without a clubhouse. Over 50 years ago, a group of bachelors banded together to hold a New Year's Eve party to repay their social obligations. The tradition continued and a select beano is still thrown by a bunch of old coconuts, usually at the Breakers hotel. Each proposed guest has to be approved by a secret committee of Coconuts.

PRESERVATION FOUNDATION BALL, c/o Seagull Cottage, 58 Coconut Row, FL 33480 ☎ (305) 832 0731
March. Held at Mar-a-Lago, the late Marjorie Merriweather Post's madly OTT mansion, now owned by Donald and Ivana Trump. An incredible setting – 110 gilded, grotto-like

rooms of European Baroque inclination. The lovely Ivana has thrown herself winningly into the role of hostess.

HOSTS

Mary Sanford is one of the grandes dames of Palm Beach; **Sue Whitmore** and **Lewis Widener** give fab bashes.

SAN FRANCISCO

The hippest town on the West Coast. Lots of late-night activity, though drinking stops at 2am. SoMa (South of the Market) is the young, arty, clubby SoHo-cum-Rive Gauche area; NoMa is more Rive Droit.

BARS AND CLUBS

CLUB 9, 399 9th St, CA 94103 ☎ (415) 863 3290
An 'art motel' with food, dancing, a performing arts area and exhibitions, run by SoMartie Mark Rennie. Draws a select young art/museum crowd plus visiting New Yorkers.

L'ETOILE, 1075 California St, CA 94108 ☎ (415) 771 1529
An elegant bar where the wealthy go to hear Peter Mintum tinkle the ivories in vintage '40s and '50s style.

THE OASIS, 1369 Fulsom St, CA 94117 ☎ (415) 863 9178
A groovy dance club in an old motel. The swimming pool is covered over to make the dance floor. Occasional live bands.

SAN FRANCISCO MUSEUM OF MODERN ART, 401 Van Ness Ave, CA 94102 ☎ (415) 863 8800
Not a nightclub, but a meeting place for cool people on Thursday nights, when the SFMMA has open house, with late-night viewing of ever-changing exhibitions.

SESAR'S LATIN PALACE, 3140 Mission St, CA 94110 ☎ (415) 648 6611

An authentic Latin ballroom in the heart of the South American district, where all ages converge to salsa the night away.

THE STONE, 412 Broadway, CA 94113 ☎ (415) 391 8282
Though it's in NoMa, it has bags of street cred. Local hard rock and punk bands. Open till 6am (by that time it's fruit juice and a DJ).

WOLFGANG'S, 901 Columbus Ave, CA 94133 ☎ (415) 474 2995
Owned by Bill Graham, father of rock 'n' roll concerts in the US. You go for the band, not the club. Less head-banging, more cerebral goings-on take place in the basement, NOMA, where artsies gather for poetry readings, and 18-year-olds are allowed to gather for a juice until they come of age.

EVENTS

Top events are arts related – balls, dinners and fashion extravaganzas are organized by the San Francisco Symphony, Opera and the Museum of Modern Art. See also Culture.

BLACK AND WHITE BALL, c/o San Francisco Symphony Volunteer Council, Davies Symphony Hall, CA 94102 ☎ (415) 552 8000
April/May. A biennial bash in aid of the San Francisco Symphony. The originator, Anna Logan Upton, felt that as symphonies have 4 movements, so the ball should have 4 concurrent venues, and since sheet music is black and white, the theme would match. Charlotte Mailliard has taken over the running, the ball has snowballed and is now held in up to 7 venues, with continuous music in each.

HOSTS

Charlotte 'Tex' Mailliard is No 1 in both public and private entertaining. She acts as hostess for the Mayor and chairs parties for visiting dignitaries; organizes the B&W

66 *The secret of my success – if you could call it that – is other people. I've never pretended that I don't need other people. I'm like Blanche Dubois – I rely on the kindness of strangers. The best advice I've ever been given is: always think of the other person as being better than you are* 99

QUENTIN CRISP

Ball. **Ann Getty** is behind many of the major artsy charity events, to **Lady Fairfax**'s warm approval: *"I love her for her splendid use of lots of money."*

WASHINGTON, DC

The season flourishes all the time except July, Aug and Jan, when even the gossip columnists clear out. May to June and Christmas are frenetic. Washington society thrives on business meetings in the guise of formal receptions and gala dinners. With the right diplomatic contacts, you could attend 5 functions a night. The young hang out in Georgetown, or Adams Morgan, the new prettified area of restaurants and clubs.

BARS AND CLUBS

♣ THE BANK, 915 F St NW, DC 20004 ☎ (202) 393 3632
A snazzy club based in the old Equitable Bank, a 3-storey Victorian building. The ballroom has a laser show and high-energy top 40 hits, downstairs is a video gallery, up is a VIP room/champagne bar with jazz. Adorned by diplomatic brats and junior international sophisticates. Free on Wed and Thurs.

BAYOU CLUB, 31/35 K St NW, DC 20007 ☎ (202) 333 2897
Club and a concert hall mainly for established groups. Comedy acts too. Strict marine-cadet waiters (*"take your beer off the pinball machine, kid"*), dancing only when uncrowded. A university hang-out.

BLUES ALLEY, 1073 Wisconsin Ave NW, DC 20007 ☎ (202) 337 4141
Smart jazz club-cum-wine bar. Small in area, big in reputation: Sarah Vaughan, Ella Fitzgerald, Bradford and Wynton Marsalis and Dizzy Gillespie have played here.

CAFE LAUTREC, 2431 18th St NW, Adams Morgan, DC 20009 ☎ (202) 265 6436
A restaurant-jazz bar serving French cuisine; fine seafood. Outside, noses are pressed against the window to glimpse tap dancer supreme Johné Forges (from the movie *Cotton Club*) jump up on the bar and tip-tap out his routine. Live music, too.

DESIREE, 1111 29th St NW, DC 20007 ☎ (202) 342 0820
A private club in the Four Seasons Hotel, where rich diplomatic types hang out. Getting in involves being sponsored, approved, and then paying your dues – or being a hotel guest.

9.30 CLUB, 930 F St NW, DC 20004 ☎ (202) 393 0930
A London-style new-wave club where many lesser-known English bands play to a downbeat punky crowd. Lots of new acts and films.

♣ PISCES, 3040 M St NW, Georgetown, DC 20007 ☎ (202) 333 4530
The Annabel's of Washington. An elegant private dinner-dancing club decorated by Sister Parish, with grown-up clientele, music and cuisine. *"Excellent pasta; great dancing"* – **Aniko Gaal.**

RIVER CLUB, 3223 K St NW, DC 20007 ☎ (202) 333 8118
A newish dinner-dancing club

for the older smarties, wooing the Pisces set upstream.

EVENTS

Events are either wrapped up in politics or the arts (which are wrapped up in politics anyway). The **Kennedy Center Honors** (see Culture) is the do with the most cachet.

THE GRIDIRON CLUB OF WASHINGTON, c/o The Capital Hilton, 1001 16th St NW, DC 20036 ☎ (202) 783 7787
Each March the exclusive Gridiron holds an intellectual evening of satire on world politics and politicians, attended by the President, congressmen and senators (who join in the skits). *"Highly sought-after. If you get an invitation you are seen as part of the power structure"* – **Aniko Gaal.**

OPERA BALL, c/o Mrs David Humphrey, Membership Services, Washington Opera, John F Kennedy Center, DC 20566 ☎ (202) 822 4730
June. The highlight of a 3-day $1,000-plus affair for the Chairman's circle. Thursday: a congressional reception; Friday: intimate dinners at various embassies, the ball itself (at a different embassy each year); Saturday: brunch at one of the top hotels.

SYMPHONY BALL, c/o National Symphony Offices, John F Kennedy Center, DC 20566 ☎ (202) 785 8100
Held in December in aid of the Symphony and attended by any old-established 'cave-dweller' who is anyone. White tie, $350 tickets, chaired by a different embassy each year – which sets the theme for the ball.

SOCIAL AND NIGHT LIFE

A WHITE HOUSE STATE DINNER, The White House, 1600 Pennsylvania Ave, DC 20500 ☎ (202) 456 1414
An invitation to a White House dinner held in honour of a head of state (there are 1 or 2 each month) is the best you could ever muster (though whether the Reagans' successors can provide evenings of such unparalleled pzazz remains to be seen). "*A state dinner is a thrilling thing. A wonderful mixture of people – a CEO, say, a member of the government, a foreign diplomat, a scientist, a sportsman, an artist, a movie star – a full-bodied, eclectic group. The White House is beautiful, decorated with masses of flowers. After dinner, there's entertainment and everyone sits round, in a private, cosy way*" – **Lynn Wyatt.**

HOSTS

Roy Pfautch's parties see Cabinet members doing the shuffle, singing silly songs and generally letting their hair down. **Evangeline Bruce:** "*She's elegance epitomized and so are her parties*" – **Aniko Gaal. Katharine Graham**, of the *Washington Post*, is a grand party-giver: "*Her dinner parties are like old-world salons, a mix of Bohemian and intellectual. A most gracious hostess*" – **Aniko Gaal.**

Australia

ADELAIDE

ADELAIDE CASINO, North Terrace, SA 5000 ☎ (08) 212 2811
This A$160 million casino, built in a converted railway station, is a handsome cross between Monte Carlo and Las Vegas.

ADELAIDE GRAND PRIX
A sizzling event on the circuit. This one, like Monaco, is fought out on the streets, watched by

⚓ *Australia's Best* ⚓

NIGHTSPOTS

1   **ROGUES**, Sydney
2   **THE METRO,** Melbourne
3   **ROUND MIDNIGHT**, Sydney
4   **LEROX**, Adelaide
5   **MELBOURNE UNDERGROUND,** Melbourne
6   **KLUB KAKADU,** Sydney

a wild, cheering, international crowd. One of the best, despite its relative youth (b 1985), organized with professionalism and panache.

⚓ **LEROX, 9 Light Square, SA 5000 ☎ (08) 513234**
Adelaide goes avant-garde: no top 40 pop hits at this nightclub, it's all the newest, hippest, most alternative music plus regular live bands. The ceiling drips with bikes, punk dolls, wheels, loo seats, exhaust pipes . . . with splashes of paint everywhere and a parachutist crashing down. Spectacularly trendy.

BRISBANE

JUPITER'S CASINO, Gold Coast Highway, Goldbeach, Qld 4551 ☎ (075) 921133
The nearest thing to Las Vegas – only better. The A$186 million complex, open 24 hours a day, houses two gargantuan gaming rooms lined with over 100 tables and blackjack machines for which the jackpot is over A$100,000.

DARWIN

DIAMOND BEACH CASINO, PO Box 3846, NT 5794 ☎ (089) 462666
The best in Australia, taken over from John Aspinall by Peter de Savary. Caters for the very rich with high-stakes gambling for those who shun publicity.

MELBOURNE

CLUBS

THE CLUB, 132 Smith St, Collingwood, Vic 3066 ☎ (03) 417 4425
Run by ex-Skyhooks musician Bob Starkey, it's the best nightly venue for prominent local rock 'n' roll bands.

THE HIPPODROME, 14 King St, Vic 3000 ☎ (03) 614 5022
Smart club in an 18th-century building with original stained-glass windows, columns and other features. Art Deco bar. 3 floors with 3 types of music.

INDUSTRY, 453 Swanston St, Vic 3000 ☎ (03) 663 6471
Groovy underground club. Music on British independent labels is played on Fridays; some live bands.

INFLATION, 60 King St, Vic 3000 ☎ (03) 614 6122
One of the best clubs in Melbourne, like one of the (now unfashionable) New York blockbusters, built on 3 levels. Giant video screens and electronic razzmatazz attract a hip and lively crowd – on weekdays more than weekends. Upstairs is a cocktail/dance/video bar, downstairs a huge dance floor. So sophisticated.

⚓ **MELBOURNE UNDERGROUND, 22-24 King St, Vic 3000 ☎ (03) 614 7677**
The place to show visiting celebs where it's at. A comfortable club in a renovated bluestone warehouse. Masses of room, good food, and screening at the door. Very young set.

⚓ **THE METRO, 20 Bourke St, Vic 3000 ☎ (03) 663 4288**
The hottest new spot in town for young trendies. A former cinema with 5 layers to dance and drink on, the latest technology in lighting and videos. Stevie Wonder came in on the opening night. "*All the socialites, theatre people, designers and rent-a-crowd – the best of Melbourne go*" – **Lillian Frank.**

PALACE, Lower Esplanade, St Kilda, Vic 3182
☎ **(03) 534 0655**
An enormous, spacious venue in the Inflation mould. *"Still lovely, very beautiful"* – **Lillian Frank**. A fluctuating crowd goes to listen/bop to mostly live music.

EVENTS

MELBOURNE CUP, Flemingon Racecourse, Vic 3031 ☎ **(03) 376 0441**
Perhaps the greatest social occasion in Australia, the highlight of the Spring Festival, on the first Tuesday of November. The preceding week starts the major party season. *"Melbourne comes alive that week – for once. Equal best with the Epsom Derby for sheer visual appeal and because they are people's days"* – **Lady Susan Renouf**. Special luncheon for the élite and a public holiday for all.

ODYSSEY HOUSE BALL, c/o Odyssey House, 28 Bonds Rd, Lower Plenty, Vic 3093
A lavish biennial bash organized by Lillian Frank. Attended by a who's who of Melbourne. *"All the pretties and beautiful men come to my parties"* – **Lillian Frank**.

GUESTS AND HOSTS

Magnetic Melbournians include: **Sir Ian** and **Lady (Primrose) Potter** (*"she is full of the joys of life"* – **Lady Fairfax**); **Andrew Peacock** (*"Australia's most colourful politician – hugely good company, great raconteur"* – **Dorian Wild**);

Barry Humphries (*"If you have him, you're off with a bang – he won't allow people to stay stuffy for long"* – **Diana Fisher**); *Mode* columnist **Barry Everingham; Douglas** and **Margaret Carnegie** (givers and goers extraordinaire); **Hugh Morgan** (MD of Western Mining Corp); **Sir Rupert** and **Lady Clarke** (*"another favourite guest"* – **Lady Fairfax**. Top hosts too); eccentric extrovert **Captain Peter Janson**. As to hosts, *"there are 200 families in Melbourne who give good parties . . . the* **Walkers, (Lindsay) Foxes, Gandels, Wenzels, Baillieus, Lady Southey, Sarah** *and* **Baillieu Myer** *. . . Some of the 200 families are new, but it makes no difference. People accept you for what you achieve and what you can give"* – **Lillian Frank**.

PARTY PEOPLE

KEVIN O'NEILL, 123 Toorak Rd, S Yarra, Vic 3141
☎ **(03) 266 5776**
The best blossoms, possums, in the whole of Australia. 4 of their florists were flown to Perth by Alan Bond for the wedding of his daughter Susanne. Other floral credits include the Skase wedding and that of John Elliott, parties for Lady Primrose Potter and Lillian Frank. A recent rave-up was Gretel (daughter of Kerry) Packer's A$500,000 21st, for which 3 truckloads of spring blooms were sent to Sydney.

PETER ROWLAND, 3 Tivoli Rd, S Yarra, Vic 3141
☎ **(03) 240 1353**
A grand caterer and party

planner. *"His art is organizing. He is probably the best organizer in the food industry. He is clever at choosing the right team and slotting them in. In Melbourne he has a virtual monopoly. People feel if they can't say to their friends they had Peter Rowland then it wasn't quite up to standard"* – **Elise Pascoe**. He lands most of the same parties as Kevin O'Neill.

PERTH

CLUB BAYVIEW, cnr Church Lane and St Quentin Ave, Claremont, WA 6010
In a city more or less starved of nightlife, this is the best sophisticated club/disco. Haunt of Claremont and Peppermint Grove smarties. '50s décor with Venetian blinds.

PERTH CASINO & HOTEL, PO Box 500, Victoria Park, WA 6100 ☎ **(09) 362 7777**
Part of a A$270 million resort complex, the casino has been described as a cross between a squat Sydney Opera House and a supermarket. Its loss leaders, in the form of inexpensive drinks (combined with windowless rooms, dim lighting and an absence of clocks) encourage punters to play on and on and on.

SYDNEY
BARS AND CLUBS

BENNY'S BAR-RESTAURANT, 12 Challis Ave, Potts Point, NSW 2011
☎ **(02) 358 2454**
Where ragers with stamina wind up. A smoky dive that the rock industry loves.

> **❝** *My ideal night would be one spent in the company of people not entirely wrapped up in their own egos . . . Sir Clive Bossom for his enormous wit, Sir Francis Dashwood, Tim Rice, Andrew Lloyd Webber, Principessa Luciana Pignatelli for her elegance and stunning good looks, Lady Potter, Lady Rupert Clarke, the de la Rochefoucaulds and Idrina Melli* **❞**

🕵 LADY FAIRFAX

SOCIAL AND NIGHT LIFE

> **❝** *Sydney is like the London and New York of the late 1920s and early 1930s, without, of course, the delicious moneyed eccentrics of that age* **❞**

🕴 PRIMROSE DUNLOP

THE CAULDRON, 207 Darlinghurst Rd, Darlinghurst, NSW 2010 ☎ (02) 331 1523
Small, steamy pick-up joint bubbling with girls in mini skirts that rise to dizzying heights. *"A brilliant disco and one of the best meat-markets in town. As long as they like the look of you on the door, you're in"* – **Dorian Wild**.

🕴 **JAMISON STREET, (BERLIN CLUB) 11 Jamison St, NSW 2000 ☎ (02) 271937**
On Tuesdays, Jamison Street is still the best place in town to go raging (the rest of the week it's businessmen and gold chains). All the space and charm of a tram terminal – which is exactly what it was before it turned into a loud, hip dance club. Spandau Ballet and the Duran Duran boys boogied along here when in Antipodean straits, as have most touring bands. Masses of models too. Above the main dance floor is a platform for exhibitionists.

JO JO IVORY'S NEW ORLEANS RESTAURANT, 40 Macleay St, Potts Point, NSW 2011 ☎ (02) 358 1955
A late-night piano bar, with a robotic black man tinkling the ivories. *"What I'd call an adult bar. It was highly amusing the first time, but when you've heard JoJo 50,000 times, it's a bit much!"* – **Robert Burton**.

🕴 **KLUB KAKADU, 163-169 Oxford St, Darlinghurst, NSW 2010 ☎ (02) 331 4001**
One of the best of the newer-comers on the Sydney scene. Big trendy space with live music and a disco. Different theme nights attract a good-looking young bunch. **Anne Lewin** is a great fan.

🕴 **ROGUES, 165 The Laneway, Rile St, Darlinghurst, NSW 2010 ☎ (02) 336924**

The nearest Sydney gets to Annabel's, although the crowd smacks more of Stringfellow's. Fairly strict membership is enforced by man-about-town owner Peter Simpson. Dark and slick, the club has 3 bars, a high-profile dance floor, one of the best restaurants in Sydney and glamorous waitresses. *"One of the few complete clubs. Not mega-swish or mega-posh, but it's been going 10 years, not a bad innings in the mercurial Sydney nightlife scene"* – **Dorian Wild**. *"The best. I love the piano bar and I love to call in late at night for supper. They know me and spoil me"* – **Elise Pascoe**. *"People of my age like it because if you want to be noisy and jump up and down till dawn, you can; if you want to have a jolly good dinner, you can; if you want to hop into the bar and look at all the pretties flaunting themselves, you can"* – **Diana Fisher**.

🕴 **ROUND MIDNIGHT, 2 Rosslyn St, King's Cross, NSW 2011 ☎ (02) 356 4045**
The latest and coolest joint to swing into town. *"A super brasserie-style restaurant with music"* – **Diana Fisher**. The old upmarket gang from Arthur's reassemble here, alongside a flash of fashion types. When you're not right by the dance floor you could be in a gentlemen's club with all the sofas and glossy mags.

EVENTS

BLACK AND WHITE BALL, c/o Mrs Charles Parsons, 402 New South Head Rd, Double Bay, NSW 2028 ☎ (02) 327 5698
Held every October at Sydney Town Hall, for the Royal Blind Society. *"Easily the premier charity committee – it's the oldest; chairman Marno*

Parsons is a tireless worker and a very charming woman" – **Dorian Wild**. *"Stunning, dazzling, wonderful"* bubbles **Diana Fisher**.

CAUSE BALL, c/o Leo Schofield & Associates, 10th Fl, 100 William St, E Sydney, NSW 2010 ☎ (02) 357 2122
An irregular ball held by advertising agencies for a cause that fires their imagination. *"Fabulous – always a brilliant theme"* – **Diana Fisher**.

THE LEGAL FRIENDS THEMIS BALL, c/o Tania Berjbitsky, Coudert Brothers, 52 Martin Place, NSW 2000 ☎ (02) 223 1488
A recent adjunct to the Sydney social scene, started in the first inst by an ad hoc committee of law students and young lawyers. Fun young ball, top legal brass.

TAITTINGER BALL, see Black and White Ball
A newish ball from the Black and White Committee, held in October at the Great Hall of Sydney University. *"Lovely venue full of history, like going to Windsor Castle. Lovely band. Elegant, glorious flowers"* – **Diana Fisher**.

GUESTS

'My ideal dinner party' – guestwise – is a consuming preoccupation among socialites and Aussie mags and rags. Sydneysiders who sing for their supper include: **Glen-Marie Frost** – *"utterly divine to look at, a great sense of humour"* – **Dorian Wild. Harry M** and **Wendy Miller. Kerry Packer. Lady Susan Renouf** – *"for her joie de vivre"* – **Lady Fairfax. Sir James** and **Lady Rowland** (he: Governor of NSW); **Sir Roden** and **Lady Cutler** (he: former Governor of NSW) – both have quasi-royal status.

THE BEST WAY TO GET RID OF GUESTS

"Very difficult. In happier times, you simply rose and stood by the door, saying 'I shouldn't have kept you so long'. The door was opened, and they went at once" – **Quentin Crisp.** *"Be on breakfast television: 'I'm sorry, I have to get up early in the morning …'"* – **Glynn Christian.** *"Show them where the drinks are and graciously depart to bed"* – **Elise Pascoe.** *"Fall asleep on the sofa"* suggests a more kittenish **Joan Collins. Auberon Waugh** makes no compromises: *"Just make them feel unwelcome."*

Johnny Baker – every woman's favourite walker. Radio star **John Laws** – *"a charming man, accepted at the best tables in town"* – **Dorian Wild. Lord** and **Lady Portarlington.** Artist **Tim Storrier.** Theatrical producer **Wilton Morley** (son of Robert).

HOSTS

Lady Mary Fairfax, undisputed queen of private and fund-raising parties – in the role of both giver and goer (when she rolls up in her 1964 Phantom V Roller, driven by a uniformed chauffeuse). **Len Evans:** *"Fabulous, wonderful, glorious, boisterous dinner and lunch parties. In the Hunter Valley, he has the longest, most beautiful refectory table you've ever seen. He's ebullient, a great vigneron and great fun, like a mini Billy Bunter"* – **Diana Fisher. Glen-Marie** and **Robert Frost:** *"She leaves the others for dead. Very glam, warm and friendly; excellent taste. Bob has the money and Glen-Marie has the style to spend it in the right way"* –

Dorian Wild. Leo Schofield: *"Without a doubt the best dinner or luncheon host"* – **Elise Pascoe.** *"A stickler for perfection. The house is magnificent, food and wines are just marvellous"* – **Diana Fisher; Kerry** and **Ros Packer**: Daughter Gretel's 21st was a bash to remember. **Diana** and **Simon Heath:** *"A beautiful mixture of delicious people, good food, lovely French champagne, great environment and good conversation"* – **Primrose Dunlop.**

PARTY PEOPLE

ANDERS OUSBACK CATERING, 68 Victoria Rd, Drummoyne, NSW 2047 ☎ **(02) 819 6522**
Brilliant foodie hero who is concentrating his efforts increasingly into the private catering field. An ex-maître d', *"he puts together the finest ingredients in a simple but intelligent way"* – **Elise Pascoe.** *"Still the best. He did a fantastic party after the première of* Les Misérables" – **Diana Fisher.**

> **❝** *I love Sydney. It's not at all blasé. There's a terrific amount of ferment, and it lacks that sense of déjà vu you get in London. It's fresh and vigorous and full of talent. A city of the '80s* **❞**
>
>  GEORGE MELLY

TASMANIA

WREST POINT CASINO, 410 Sandy Bay Rd, Hobart, Tas 7000 ☎ **(002) 250112**
Opened in 1973, Australia's first casino is also hugely successful, with a turnover of around A$60 million. See also Travel.

♠ –Europe's Best– ♠

	NIGHTSPOTS
1	**ANNABEL'S,** London
2	**CASTEL'S,** Paris
3	**TRAMP,** London
4	**LE PALACE 999,** Paris
5	**LES BAINS,** Paris
6	**TENAX,** Florence
7	**GREEN GO,** Gstaad
8	**PLASTIC,** Milan
9	**FARM CLUB,** Verbier
10	**JIMMYZ,** Monte Carlo

Britain

LONDON

BARS AND CLUBS

♠ **ANNABEL'S, 44 Berkeley Square, W1** ☎ **(01) 629 3558**
The untoppled heroine, 25-year-old Annabel's remains, without question the world's No 1. A conventional club that is exclusive in the true sense of the word (prospective members must be proposed and seconded for the £500-a-year membership). *"It would be very hard to beat it or Mark Birley's taste – he's a perfectionist"* – **Lord Lichfield.** *"Without doubt the best in the world – my husband and I have been members since the beginning, and it's the only one of its kind. We'd almost take a trip to London just to go to Annabel's"* – **Helen Gurley Brown.** *"We*

had the party for Sarah's last night in Phantom *there. The brilliance of Annabel's is you can take a couple of young kids from the cast and some old family friends in their 70s and none of them feels uncomfortable. The Rolls-Royce of clubs; there is nowhere else in the world to touch it"* – **Andrew Lloyd Webber.** It's best for **Joan Collins**, and for **Lord Donoughue:** *"There is no other worth attending."* It's one of the best for **John Gold, Richard Compton-Miller, Shakira Caine, Taki** and **David Litchfield.** No surprises, no disappointments.

CAFE DE PARIS, 3 Coventry St, W1 ☎ (01) 437 2036
Has enjoyed a term of being the best, most coveted one-night club in town (on Weds). Red flock and gilt jaded elegance: an old restaurant in the round with a gallery for star-gazing. Laid-back jazz, blues and cha-cha entice David Bowie, Charlotte Lewis, Tina Turner, **Jasper Conran, Stephen Jones, Duggie Fields** and co. *"I still like it, though they don't let me in very often. One of the few places where everyone really will dance rather than stand around the edges drinking Japanese beer"* – **Sebastian Scott.** *"It's a social event, like going to a party. The mixture of people here is the most exciting … I'm sure it won't last"* – **David Litchfield.**

CRAZY LARRY'S, 533 King's Rd, SW10 ☎ (01) 376 5555
A smartish Sloany club with raised dance floor and candlelit tables for dinner. Robert Pereno takes over with his team of Chelsea girls on Tuesdays for Le Snog. The young, affluent bourgeoisie are still downplaying it in black polos and rolled up jeans.

FREUD'S, 198 Shaftesbury Ave, WC2 ☎ (01) 240 9933
Small subterranean minimalist bar. Sophisticated caveman décor – rough walls, green slate floor, black slate tables and changing exhibitions of modern art. Designer and fashion

---

ONE-NIGHT WONDERS

Hip kids say one-nighters are go. But what about the *argot*? So you heard of R&B, jazz, rock 'n' roll? Go back to Annabel's. Baby groovers shake a leg to go-go-grooves-salsa-soca-zouk-dirty-dance-afro-funk-psycho-rock-rare-groove-soul-hip-hop-a-go-go-funky-get-down-fusion-ska-gothic-rocksteady-glam-psychedelic-thrash-boogaloo-indie-def-jam … no kiddin'. Here's where to catch the beat:

Monday.....	**Jazz Room** at the **WAG**
Tuesday....	**Le Snog** at **Crazy Larry's**
Wednesday..	**Café de Paris**
Thursday...	**Gaz's Rockin' Blues** at **Gossip's**; **Delirium** at **Heaven**
Friday.....	**Black Market** at the **WAG**; **Mud Club**
Saturday...	house-parties; **Jongleurs**
Sunday.....	**Freud's**

NB It's an ever-changing scene, so check first in *Time Out* for what's on and what's in each week.

---

clientele, oozing stubble, leather, ripped denim and Filofaxes. *"The sort of place they throw you out of if you're wearing a city suit"* – **Sebastian Scott.** Sunday is live jazz night when a wider mix attends.

GAZ'S ROCKIN' BLUES, Gossips, 69 Dean St, W1 ☎ (01) 434 4480
The only one-night wonder (Thursdays) that's stood its ground – for 8 years. Gary (Gaz) Mayall plays ska, rhythm 'n' blues, reggae and rockabilly, and a rollicking good time is had by all. Complete mix-up of ages and styles of bopper, from quiff-heads through rastas to chic rag-traders.

HEAVEN, Under the Arches, Villiers St, Charing Cross, WC2 ☎ (01) 839 3852
The gayest nightspot in town, and the vastest gayspot in Europe. Delirium on Thursday is straights' night – stars go to hear live music plus hip-hop, rap, scratch, garage, house and deep house.

HIPPODROME, cnr Leicester Sq, WC2 ☎ (01) 437 4311
Peter Stringfellow's gaping, high-tech, high-energy club has the most impressive light show

---

in London. But massive flashy discos no longer fascinate the fashionable: tourists and passers-by are the mainstay. *"For young Madonna clones"* – **Richard Compton-Miller.** Drag shows and one-off balls.

JONGLEURS AT THE CORNET, 49-51 Lavender Gardens, SW11 ☎ (01) 877 0155
A groovy cabaret of singers, tap-dancers, jugglers and young comedians on Friday and Saturday evenings. Some of the best stand-up comics and impressionists in town – Rory Bremner, Pierre Hollins, Kit Hollerbach and co.

LIMELIGHT, 136 Shaftesbury Ave, WC2 ☎ (01) 434 1761
London's most recent big attraction with all the cool trappings (difficult doorperson, seedy VIP room, lots of one-nighters and special events). Spandau Ballet get on down. Owned by New York Limelighter Peter Gatien, it's similarly based in an old church. This one's ex-Welsh Presbyterian: 800 unorthodox, cosmopolitan citizens congregate beneath the vaulted roof to bop to LLOOOUD music. Jackson Pollock school of décor. In danger of being

boycotted – nowhere for non-members to get away from the big noise; unpredictable door policy.

MUD CLUB, Busby's, 157 Charing Cross Rd, WC2 ☎ (01) 734 6963
Fridays. Flamboyant Philip Sallon hosts this soul/go-go/hip-hop night for a clamouring crowd of trendoids and pop stars. Where many a poseur cut his teeth. Double-decker room with a balcony running round the top, big and buzzing. *"Full of Beck's and flat-tops; bluestown disco, health music – Sanatogen soul"* – **Sean Macaulay.**

151 CLUB, 151 King's Rd, U SW3 ☎ (01) 351 6826
Buzzing membership club with one small basement eatery/disco and irresistible dance music. Frequented by young City boys (still pinstriped) and their molls (going for the mean-Sloane look, Doc Martens, pouting and dishevelled).

RAFFLES, 287 King's Rd, SW3 ☎ (01) 352 0191
A pseudo-gentlemen's club in appearance – *faux* library plus disco room, where stuffed shirts must keep their jackets on to dance. Newly done-up private dining room with cornicing and mouldings. Ideal for debby parties.

RONNIE SCOTT'S, 47 Frith St, W1 ☎ (01) 439 0747
The best live jazz venue in town – archetypally dark and smoky, with tight-skirted waitresses wiggling their way round tightly packed tables. Upstairs is no longer members only. *"I've been playing there for 15 years and I love it. I love the proprietor's jokes, which haven't altered in that span. I*

like its cool detachment from its public. There's never a touch of sycophancy – in fact the contrary. Everybody is treated exactly the same. The music is the point, the food certainly isn't. I like things that last, and it's lasted for 26 years. I have very warm feelings for it, quite apart from the fact it's still *a great honour for me to appear there and to think of all the people that have walked on that stage"* – **George Melly.** *"A really good club full of real jazz fans. The best bands. Go on Tuesday or Wednesday when it's emptier"* – **Robert Elms.**

STRINGFELLOW'S, 16 Upper St Martin's Lane, WC2 ☎ (01) 240 5534
Habitués of Café de Paris/Annabel's would pour scorn on the place, but it's a perennial for flashy showbiz types. The best nightclub food, according to one chef. The best in its field, thinks **David Litchfield.**

 TRAMP, 40 Jermyn St, W1 ☎ (01) 734 0565
In the same mould as Annabel's only less refined and less expensive (£150 a year). Part-owned by Oscar Lerman, hubby of Jackie Collins, and John Gold. *"I don't go to*

TOMORROW'S CLUBLAND

While fresh-faced boppers still get a kick out of trying to get past club doormen, those who went through the Blitz Kid years – who queued up in their New Romantic ruffles to experience a new club phenomenon hosted by Steve Strange and Rusty Egan – are beginning to get that been-there-done-that feeling. They lurched round Whiskey-A-Go-Go before it became the WAG, survived the launch and sinking of the Titanic, draped themselves darkly around Batcave, went transatlantic to gawp at Area and get physical at Palladium, and raved on till Taboo burnt out. The party's over. Clubland is shifting. Enormous high-tech state-of-the-art discos: out. One-night weirdos: out. Sophisticated designer chic: *look out.* Nell in NY saw it coming. The fickle finger of fashion is pointing towards proper old-style clubs – smaller, with dining and low-key live music (jazz, salsa, piano). Clubologists mull it over: *"It's been the year of the hermit, a lot of people are sitting at home dying for a new club to happen"* – **David Shilling.** *"Nightclubs are in a slump; people got bored with clubs that jumped around. Chefs are our media stars in the way nightclub-owners were 2 years ago. Maybe a supper club will be the next big thing. The interest in food will fuse with the nightlife experience"* – **Stephen Jones.** *"I think next we might see a move back to the club with the 3-piece group, a touch of honky-tonk music"* – **John Gold.**

❝ *What makes a club good is an intangible thing. It depends upon the mixture of people – there have to be enough that know each other, that go often enough and that can relate visually. I think the amount of tourists in London discourages the club scene. After a day of wading through them, you don't want to go out with them at night* ❞

 DUGGIE FIELDS

nightclubs much but when I do I go to Tramp" – **Dudley Moore**. *"The only nightclub I've ever really liked. It has exclusivity plus seediness – a wonderful mixture. There's such a cross-section of people and the greatest charm is there's a separate dance area, so that you can talk"* – **Imran Khan**. *"For the swinging middle-aged. It is socially promiscuous in that all classes mix"* – **Richard Compton-Miller**. Mixers include Michael and **Shakira Caine**, Rod Stewart, Lady Sarah Armstrong-Jones, George Best, Pamela Stephenson, Mick Jagger, Sting, Lady Helen Windsor, **Harvey Goldsmith** and his merry bands.

WAG CLUB, 35 Wardour St, W1 ☎ (01) 437 5534
The music biz barometer, one of the coolest regular clubs in town. Black Market night on Friday is best – funky, soulful, James Brown ad nauseam, plus new, rare, re-released and bootleg music. *"Funk really hits the fan"* – **Sean Macaulay**. *"I think it's great on Monday [the Jazz Room – classic jazz and R&B with a live set each week] – the dancers in the jazz disco upstairs are unbelievable! Saturday is great too. It's just 'everybody dance' – a sweaty, hard night, like a nightclub should be"* – **Robert Elms**.

WESTWORLD
After the sad demise of La Cage (the ex-proprietor is now certified), this has taken over as the best 'club' without a home. *"It's taken the whole notion of the club a stage further – circus rides, bumper cars, films and videos – it's like a funfair. It's a huge production, the best"* – **Robert Elms**. About 6 a year, from Witchworld on Hallowe'en

night to Wetworld in a public swimming pool. See *Time Out* for where to find it.

Private Clubs

CHELSEA ARTS CLUB, 143 Old Church St, SW3 ☎ (01) 352 0973
A ramshackle country rectory and rambling garden in the heart of Chelsea – home from shabby home for struggling Bohemians. Not for *them* the Perrier luncheon. *"I like it very much because it has no pretensions to chic. I like the less glittering surface of the clubs I go to regularly"* – **George Melly**.

FRED'S, 4 Carlisle St, W1 ☎ (01) 494 3137
Baby Groucho's (no relation) meets nightclub: a compact private boîte for young media/arty types. Drink in the narrow bar, pick at tapas at the U-shaped counter, in the minuscule basement, dance to funk, soul and rap. A favourite of **Michael Clark**.

THE GROUCHO CLUB, 45 Dean St, W1 ☎ (01) 439 4685
The media drinking and dining club. Civilized and unflashily glamorous, it attracts an upbeat liter-arty set – publishers, agents, major bylines, media and music kids. *"With a group of people, this is where I'd go to eat"* – **Lord Donoughue**. *"I'm not a member but I like going to meet people there"* – **George Melly**. *"Actually, I'm not a member but I'm quite glad to know members. Huge olives – probably its greatest recommendation"* – **Sebastian Scott**. **Alastair Little** and **Stephen Jones** like it too.

MOSCOW CLUB, 62 Frith St, W1 ☎ (01) 434 1871

Groucho's racier rival has a more creative/pop video/advertising/design leaning; actors and pop stars rock up after their shows (the club's open till 1am). The narrow, black and white room feels like a train, with rows of chairs and little tables.

2 BRYDGES PLACE, WC2 ☎ (01) 836 1436
Aka Alfredo's, after the proprietor. Comfy, laid-back club in a Georgian house with a drawing room ambience, open fire, a mishmash of furniture and an even greater mishmash of members. Arty trendies like Charlotte Faber, Cosmo Fry, **Michael Clark**, Layla d'Angelo, members of the English National Opera, the odd crumbly. *"It's wonderful. Less media, more arty"* – **Robert Elms**.

CASINOS

All British casinos are private clubs.

ASPINALL'S, 20-21 Curzon St, W1 ☎ (01) 629 4400
Used to be *the* London casino when John Aspinall owned it and ran it like a gentlemen's club. Now that Peter de Savary's taken over, the old clientele are watching with interest . . .

CROCKFORD'S, 30 Curzon St, W1 ☎ (01) 493 7771
A civilized club, established 150 years ago, with none of the usual scrabble round the tables that mars flasher gaming joints. Mostly foreign clientele since it moved from St James's to Mayfair.

EVENTS

The English season kicks off with the Berkeley Dress Show

❝ *I never have to pay or wait in line. Wherever I go I just get whisked in. Half the time you don't even know where you are. You're in a car with darkened windows, next thing you're in a restaurant or a club or somebody's party* **❞**

 HARVEY GOLDSMITH

at the Savoy in April and a bevy of coming out balls in May, continues with the summer run of sporting sprees, drifts off to Scotland for August, collects its thoughts in September, then bounces back with a fresh round of charity balls in October, rising to a dizzying crescendo around Christmas.

BADMINTON HORSE TRIALS, Badminton, Avon ☎ (045421) 272
Horsies' Mecca, where Princess Anne and Captain Mark Phillips have competed. For 3 muddy days in April, spectators, clad in tree-green from head to toe, tramp round bumping into their smart

GLYNDEBOURNE, see Culture

GOODWOOD, Goodwood Racecourse, Chichester, W Sussex ☎ (0243) 774107
A delightful week of Pimm's-swilling and racing in July. Men in light suits and Panamas have a flutter; women in straw hats and frocks have more than a flutter in the strong winds that whip up over the scenic course. A favourite of **Viscountess Rothermere.**

HENLEY ROYAL REGATTA, Regatta House, Henley-on Thames, Oxfordshire ☎ (04912) 2153
The epitome of all that is English – a colourful scene of

A hardy annual held in a pink blossom-filled Grosvenor House, for Queen Alexandra Rose Day in May. Unofficially, it takes the place of the former Queen Charlotte's Ball, where débutantes were launched into society. *"The best ball of the year"* – **Betty Kenward. Viscountess Rothermere** seconds that.

ROYAL ASCOT, Ascot Racecourse, Ascot, Berkshire ☎ (0990) 22211
The crème de la crème (more like the cram de la cram) of the social racing year, held in June. The royal procession by carriage is a spectacle in itself, as are the outrageous hats, always capped by **David**

66 *There are movers and shakers and glitterati who turn up to every lighted candle. The expression 'movers and shakers' means people who literally move round the room and shake people's hands* 99

LADY ELIZABETH ANSON

county pals. You may spot the Queen having a chin-wag with the Duke of Beaufort.

COWES WEEK, Cowes Combined Clubs, 18 Bath Rd, Cowes, Isle of Wight ☎ (0983) 295744
A virtual ghost town out of season, Cowes leaps into life for the August regatta, especially when, in odd years, the prestigious Admiral's Cup series of races is held. Prince Philip and sons are there on the royal yacht *Britannia*, guarded by a Naval vessel. Streets, pubs and clubs (the Island and the Royal London are best) teem with riotous international yachties. One of the best social events, as **Viscountess Rothermere** vouches, is the **Royal Yacht Squadron Ball.**

THE DERBY, United Racecourse, Racecourse Paddock, Epsom, Surrey ☎ (03727) 26311
The most prestigious race in Britain, held in June, attended by the Queen. Tremendous sense of occasion – morning suits, black toppers, picnics, champers, mega-buck bets.

bunting, bands and blades. Stroll by the river, tuck into lavish picnics, lap up sun, champagne and Pimm's. The place to be (if not a member of Leander club) is the Stewards' Enclosure for members and guests only. Here men must wear jacket and tie; women – no trousers or skirts above the knee (nattily culotted ladies are told to leg it and for this year's fashion victims it was a *mini-disaster*).

POLO INTERNATIONAL, Guards' Club, Smiths Lawn, Windsor Great Park, Englefield Green, Egham, Surrey ☎ (0784) 34212
Royal love matches are made on the playing fields of Windsor. Here you could have followed the courtships of Charles and Diana, Andrew and Fergie (daughter of Major Ronald Ferguson, PC's polo manager). The Windsors are out in force for the international in July, the most loudly trumpeted polo event in Britain.

ROSE BALL, 1 Castelnau, Barnes, SW13 ☎ (01) 748 4824

Shilling's creation of the year for his mother Gertrude. The Royal Enclosure is *the* place to be – with your name tag, your dark morning suit (or service or national dress) and grey top hat. Women must wear a hat that covers the head. **Lady Elizabeth Anson** and **Betty Kenward** adore it.

ROYAL CALEDONIAN BALL, 94 Elms Rd, SW4 ☎ (01) 622 6074
A braw Scots affair, where reel men wear kilts, or white tie and facings, and their ladies dig out the heirloom jewels and clan sashes. Dancers descend the stairs accompanied by pipers and drums of the Scots Guards. The Duke of Atholl traditionally leads them on to the floor for the No 1 reel, often with Princess Margaret.

WIMBLEDON, All England Lawn Tennis & Croquet Club, Church Rd, Wimbledon, SW19 ☎ (01) 946 2244
The ultimate for players and spectators alike. Two weeks in June/July when it sizzles or pours, adding to the Centre Court tension. Best off-court

SOCIAL AND NIGHT LIFE

hang-out is the Members' Enclosure or IMG's hospitality tent (they manage most of the top players).

HOSTS

No 1 party-giver has to be **The Queen**, as recommended by **Viscountess Rothermere** – who also enjoys parties hosted by **Sir James Goldsmith**, **Prince** and **Princess Rupert Lowenstein**, **Mrs Andrew Sinclair** (Sonia Melchett), **Mick Jagger** and **Jerry Hall**, **Lady Rupert Neville** and **David** and **Carina Frost**. Other brilliant private party-givers include **Vivien Duffield** – *"if she gives a party you know it's going to be amazing – not just no expense spared, but no trouble spared"* – **Lord Lichfield**. Best bash was her Med cruise on *Sea Goddess II*, where the only thing the 120 celeb and aristo guests were expected to bring was an extensive wardrobe. **Lord** and **Lady Settrington** – *"Spectacular parties held in town or in Goodwood. At her last birthday party, drinks were handed out by people on stilts"* – **David Shilling** (no mean host himself with his monthly drinks parties for 100). **John Aspinall**: *"When he entertains in his own house, no one goes to more trouble or spends more money"* – **Taki**. Also tops for **Taki** are the **Marquess (Harry)** and **Marchioness (Tracey Ward) of Worcester** – *"The best young host and hostess – popular with everyone."* **Lord Glenconner**: his birthday parties on Mustique are *"quite spectacular because he has a great sense of theatre"* – **Lord Lichfield**. Charity gala-organizing supremos are **Una-Mary Parker** and **Iris Banham-Lee**. Harvey

Goldsmith masterminds the best backstage bashes.

PARTY PEOPLE

KEN TURNER, 8 Avery Row, W1 ☎ (01) 499 4952
Well known as one of the key creative forces in the world of floral decoration. Gorgeous no-holds-barred artistry. *"A wonderful, extravagant and expensive florist"* – **Lord Lichfield**.

LEITH'S GOOD FOOD, 1 Sebastian St, EC1 ☎ (01) 251 0216
It is Prue Leith's catering firm that feeds the hungry travellers on the Venice Simplon-Orient-Express. Superb personal service for weddings, banquets and cocktail parties; they can arrange the whole party package.

PARTY PLANNERS, 56 Ladbroke Grove, W11 ☎ (01) 229 9666
Lady Elizabeth Anson is the undisputed queen of party planning throughout the world. In the business for 25 years, she is involved in up to 14 parties *a day*, from a mammoth gala down to a child's birthday cake. All work is subcontracted to the best people for the job – worldwide. Everyone's vetted; even caterers have to audition. Weddings are her thing – as are post-nuptial parties, including those for the Waleses and the Yorks. **Betty Kenward** and **Diane Freis** are among Lady E's ardent fans.

SEARCY TANSLEY & CO, 124 Bolingbroke Grove, SW11 ☎ (01) 585 0505
The grandest caterers, established 150 years. They can do full party planning. Major receptions are often *chez eux*, at **30 Pavilion Road**.

Canada

MONTREAL
BARS AND CLUBS

The bars that line Crescent and Bishop Streets buzz with life. Excessive summertime strolling from one bar to the next guarantees traffic jams at 4am.

L'ESPRIT, 1234 Mountain St, H3G 1Z1 ☎ (514) 397 1711
The premier dance-club in Montreal, based in a century-old building with cathedral ceilings and multi-levels. 1,200 groovers crowd in and bop the night away to international high-energy hits.

LOLA'S PARADISE, 3604 Blvd St Laurent, H2X 2V4 ☎ (514) 282 9944
Neo-Nell's – a late-night establishment of the plush velvet boudoir variety. Restaurant-bar-café-nightclub with piano, jazz, blues and classical music. People-watching time *starts* at 3am. *"Yes it's fun! A great place to hang out"* – **Tyler Brule**.

METROPOLIS CLUB, 59 E St Catherine's St, H2X 3P5 ☎ (514) 288 5559
The largest dance club in Canada – space for 2,000 – set in an old Art Deco cinema. 6 bars, high-tech lighting, zappy dance music.

TORONTO
BARS AND CLUBS

AMSTERDAM Brasserie & Brewpub, 133 John St, M5B 2E4 ☎ (416) 595 8201
Bright, airy, stand-up bar in a

❝ *My idea of a party has always been to sit at a table with a pink light and a man saying, 'God I love you.' I've had 49 proposals. I don't like parties* **❞**

 BARBARA CARTLAND

loft-style warehouse with industrial windows, beams and skylights. Packed with young execs and *faces* (go early to avoid the queue). Home-brewed special ale and lager; great brasserie food with ever-changing menu. *"One of the hot spots. A real people-watching place to hang out"* – **Steve Podborski.**

BAMBOO, 312 Queen St W, M5V 2A2 ☎ (416) 593 5771
Wild reggae club owned by Toronto socialite Patty Habib. Outdoor deck (terrace); Thai food. *"I like it, it's kind of fun there. It has a small feel to it, and it's a little off-the-wall"* – **Steve Podborski.**

BELLAIR CAFE, 100 Cumberland St, Yorkville, M5R 1A6 ☎ (416) 964 2222
Chic restaurant-bar, haunt of the beautiful people – models and visiting pop stars inside, Ferraris and Lamborghinis double-parked outside.

LA CAGE, 2nd Fl, 279 Yonge St, M5P 1P4 ☎ (416) 364 5200
Zany cabaret/dinner club with drag shows, impersonations of some of the brassier broads of showbiz, and other tourist-aimed entertainment. *"An incredible nightclub. I was there recently and Milton Berle, Mr TV, just got up and did half an hour"* – **Joyce Davidson.**

DIAMOND CLUB, 410 Sherbourne St, M4X 1K2 ☎ (416) 927 0910
Part of the Toronto establishment. Huge dance floor with new music; androgynous coat-check/cigarette girl/guy.

EVENTS

BLACK AND WHITE POLO BALL, 4 Lansing Square, Suite 205, Willowdale, M2J 1T1 ☎ (416) 494 0600
A grand ball for 1,000 held in the first week of July in aid of the Heart and Stroke Foundation of Ontario. The weekends leading up to the ball are a wild crescendo of polo matches; the same horsy set

gallop along on the big night. *"The best event of the summer. Much more relaxed and fun than any other society ball"* – **Tyler Brule.**

VANCOUVER
BARS AND CLUBS

GRACELAND, 1250 Richards St, V6B 3G2 ☎ (604) 688 2648
The largest dance club in Vancouver, a New York-style concrete-chic affair based in a converted warehouse. The 1,600-sq ft dance floor with its 26-ft-high ceiling is jam-packed on the weekends. Music is brought in from top New York and London discos.

PELICAN BAY, 1253 Johnston St, Granville Island, V6H 3R9 ☎ (604) 683 7373
The bar in the Granville Island Hotel is a regular yuppie haunt. Wonderful views at night – one entire wall of glass looks out over the city. Also a restaurant (French/seafood) and nightclub.

RICHARDS ON RICHARDS, 1036 Richards St, V6B 3E1 ☎ (604) 687 6794
The best nightclub in the city. Always a line on Fri and Sat, when live bands play. *"An old favourite, still the in place to be"* – **Steve Podborski.**

France
PARIS
CLUBS

Clubland is not hyperactive in Paris, but the hippest kids go to one-nighters, as they do in London. The best are:

Monday	**Balajo**
Tuesday . . .	**Mix** at Le Palace 999
Wednesday..	**French Kiss** at Le Palace 999
Thursday ..	**La Fiesta** at Le Palace 999
Friday	**La Nouvelle Eve**
Saturday ..	**Régine's**

🐚 **LES BAINS, 7 rue du Bourg – l'Abbé, 75003 ☎ (1) 4887 0180**
Aka Bains-Douches. *Branché* young club, based in the old public baths, brimming with notables. **Azzedine Alaïa,** Grace Jones, Michael Douglas, Mick Jagger, Harrison Ford and Boy George go for regular dips. *"Great for the younger crowd, the real little freakies – it's news across the nation"* – **John Gold.**

BALAJO, 9 rue de Lappe, 75011 ☎ (1) 4700 0779
Fabulous Art Deco club in the Moulin Rouge tradition. The club peaked in the 1950s and is now fashionable once more, with an orchestra playing old-time dance music. It's based in the latest Bohemian *quartier* in town, le Bastille – cooler than St Germain, loftier than Les Halles. Monday nights are as streetwise as Paris gets, when retro is forgotten and modern hippery is in.

🐚 **CASTEL'S, 15 rue Princesse, 75006 ☎ (1) 4326 9022**
Paris's answer to Annabel's, albeit a poor relation. Still *the* place for glam oldies – and some youngies (from Roger Vadim to Christopher Lambert). *"It's really like home. There have been times when we've behaved like kids and ended up dead drunk on the floor at 4am and Jean Castel will bear with us"* – **Jean-Paul Belmondo.** *"It has charm; it's run more on a friends-of-Jean-Castel basis than Annabel's, where membership is rather strictly observed"* – **Mark Birley.** *"The nicest club in Paris. It's akin to Tramp, with a similar clientele and a similar ambience. Jean Castel is a charming man who knows his business well"* – **John Gold.**

NEW MORNING, 7-9 rue des Petites-Ecuries, 75010 ☎ (1) 4523 5141
A nice jazz club where bands from Europe and America play. Spacious, unsmoky, unsleazy.

LA NOUVELLE EVE, rue Fontaine, 75009 ☎ (1) 4526 7632
Friday-night club run by

Albert and Serge. 1900s vaudeville décor – OTT theatrical Rococo – sets the stage for swing, cha-cha, ramba and modern music. Appeals to the BCBG (Bon Chic Bon Genre) and US film producers.

Chattin' on the choo choo

If you're holding an extra-large party, the in place to let off steam is a railway station. The Musée d'Orsay started the craze for alternative usage of stations (though the Gare d'Orsay closed years ago). Rent a working one after the last trains leave at 12.30am – you get the platforms, the eateries *and* the trains (stationary, natch). To celebrate its 100th issue, *Actuel* magazine hired the Gare de Lyon with its fantastic fin de siècle décor and excellent brasserie Le Train Bleu, and imported an orchestra. **FRANCE R A I PUBLICITE**, 48 ave de la Grande Armée, 78017 ☎ (1) 4574 9797.

🐾 **LE PALACE 999**, 8 rue du Faubourg Montmartre, 75009 ☎ (1) 4246 1087
One of the best clubs in Paris, based in a former theatre with cupola, balconies and red neon footlights: since it's recent redecoration it's gone very Hollywood 1940s. Staff in Gaultier get-ups, Paris models, film stars and *jeunesse dorée* slink alongside the likes of **Azzedine Alaïa, Charlotte Rampling**, Terence Trent D'Arby, and Madonna. Masses of *other* attractions – magicians, jugglers, performing animals – and special nights when clubbers dress up: Mix on Tues (le look esthétique), French Kiss on Wed (fashion/music/art arrivistes) and La Fiesta (flamenco) on Thurs.

PUZZLE CASTEL, 13 rue Princesse, 75006 ☎ (1) 4634 5580 and at 6 rue Balzac, 75008 ☎ (1) 4561 9722
Offshoots of Papa Castel's designed to attract the young. Decorated by Philippe Starck and open till 5am, they act as a training ground for the grown-up version.

REGINE'S, 49 rue de Ponthieu, 75008
☎ (1) 4359 7300
Hangover jetsetty stuff, but it's enormous fun on Saturdays. Barbra Streisand, Liza Minnelli and Julio Iglesias add a touch of international stardom.

ROSEBUD, 11 bis rue Delambre, 75014
☎ (1) 4335 3854
A brilliant roomy jazz bar that stays open till all hours.

RUBY'S, 31 rue Dauphine, 75006 ☎ (1) 4633 6816
The Castel's of Paris noir, where you might meet Diana Ross, or even Mick Jagger and Jerry Hall one Ruby Tuesday. African harmonies and funk.

LE TANGO, 13 rue au Maire, 75003 ☎ (1) 4272 1778
An Afro-Latin club that's jam-packed, sweaty, abandoned – non-stop dance for dance's sake.

EVENT

PRIX DE L'ARC DE TRIOMPHE, **Hippodrome de Longchamp, Bois de Boulogne**, 75016
☎ (1) 4772 5733
October. The Arc is one of the most prestigious races in the world and the most valuable in Europe. Draws the international horsy glamorati. A whirlwind of social gatherings, the best being at the Ritz.

HOSTS

Pierre Cardin: "He gets all sorts of different people together – those who live in Paris, those passing through, opera singers, fashion and showbiz people – I love his

parties" – **Charlotte Rampling**. **Princess Caroline of Monaco**: "*A great hostess"* – **Inès de la Fressange**. The charming and witty **Nicole Wisniak**, publisher of the beautiful magazine *Egoïste* and wife of political journalist Philippe Grumbach: "*She is so good at mixing people. Her party for Helmut Newton had all sorts – Karl Lagerfeld, Françoise Sagan, Princess Caroline of Monaco, people in politics, arts...*" – **Inès de la Fressange**. **Karl Lagerfeld**, who has a spectacular 18th-century dining room and candlelit chandeliers. **Lynn Wyatt**, with her Riviera hat on, is an ambitious hostess and gives fabulous theme extravaganzas. **Eddie Barclay**, whose weddings (7 to date) are among the best parties in the South of France. **Michèle Halberstadt**, whose annual garden party for *Première* magazine (which she edits) at Cannes is a must. **Prince** and **Princess von Thurn und Taxis** (Gloria is known as TNT for her dynamite personality). With homes in New York, Paris and Munich – plus the 350-room schloss in Bavaria – they give spectacular costume and theme balls in the grand Baroque manner.

PARTY PEOPLE

The most favoured and savoured traiteurs are **DALLOYAU** (see Food & Drink) and **LENOTRE**, 44 rue d'Auteuil, 75016 ☎ (1) 4524 5252. "*Lenôtre is the most prestigious caterer – fantastic. They can serve a 2- or 3-star meal to a party of 900*" – **Steven Spurrier**. Others think Dalloyau is far superior – they cater for many 16ème deb dances (*rallyes*); what is more, their macaroons and glazed hams stuffed with pistachios have no equal.

AGNES GOLDMAN, 1 rue Meyerbeer, 75009
☎ (1) 4742 6020
Wonderful film theme parties. At her Madcap '20s bash for the Paramount Opera film theatre's 60th anniversary plus the

première of *The Untouchables*, there were acrobats, casinos (using pretend dollars), an auction and prizes such as Robert de Niro's shirt.

FRANCOISE DUMAS, 13 bis Cité de Pusy, 75017 ☎ (1) 4267 6163
"The best party organizer" – **Inès de la Fressange.** The Lady Elizabeth Anson of France, she organizes hooleys for Princess Ira von Fürstenberg and Karl Lagerfeld. Her party for *The Last Emperor* was attended by director Bernardo Bertolucci, Jacques Chirac, Lord Weidenfeld, Baroness de Rothschild, etc, and held in the ballroom of the Hôtel de Ville where Alberto Pinto had constructed a Chinese tree. Another party, for Hélène Rochas at the Musée des Arts Décoratifs, had a cruise theme; the orchestra trumpeted out the best Busby Berkeley numbers while guests arrived sporting boats, shells and even algae in their hair.

Monaco

MONTE CARLO

CASINO

MONTE CARLO CASINO, place du Casino, 98007 ☎ 9350 6931
The best – and best-loved – casino in the world. Lures the most glamorous gamblers into its beautiful Belle Epoque interior. There is an American salon for craps, blackjack and American roulette (FF10,000 to FF15,000 limit), and a European salon for French roulette and baccarat (for special clients, no limit).

CLUBS

🕴 **JIMMYZ D'HIVER (winter), place du Casino, 98007 ☎ 9350 8080; JIMMYZ D'ETE (summer), Monte Carlo Sporting Club, ave Princesse**

Grace, 98000 ☎ 9326 1414
Movable seasonal pleasure. Formerly of the Régine empire, it's still the best fun for all ages. The summer club has a motorized sliding roof that opens to reveal the sparkling night sky. **Joan Collins** has been known to pay to watch it slide back and forth all night. The Grimaldi clan attend.

LIVING ROOM, 7 ave de Spilugues, 98000 ☎ 9350 8031
A piano bar with a singer most nights and a small dance floor. Dark and noisy, a less pretentious version of Jimmyz with a grown-up clientele.

PARADISE, Monte Carlo Sporting Club, ave Princesse Grace, 98000 ☎ 9330 6161
A young Jimmyz open only in July and August.

EVENTS

BAL DE LA CROIX ROUGE, Hotel de Paris, place du Casino, 98007 ☎ 9350 8080
"The No 1 event of the season, part of the long affair of summer" – **Lynn Wyatt.** One of the glossiest, most international events in the world. Le monde jets or floats in for a week of private, commercial and charitable partying, culminating in this extravaganza. The bejewelled crowd include the Monégasque royals, Roger Moore, Audrey

Hepburn, Princess Michael of Kent, the di Portanovas (all the way from Houston). The cabaret has starred Frank Sinatra, Elton John, Liza Minnelli and Sammy Davis Jr.

LE BAL DE LA ROSE, Relations Publiques, Societé des Bains de Mer, place du Casino, 98000 ☎ 9350 8080
A chic ball in March given by Prince Rainier and Princess Caroline for the Princess Grace Foundation. Each year a rose from a different country is featured. The royals, Karl Lagerfeld, **Inès de la Fressange,** the Guccis and other fashion fiends tuck into a magnificent dinner in La Salle des Etoiles and dance amid rosy décor.

MONACO GRAND PRIX
The most social Grand Prix on the circuit, held in May. The entire town turns into the racing arena, presided over by the Grimaldis and a glittering entourage of playboys, socialites, film and pop stars. *"Monaco comes alive for those few days and you can't help being caught up in the urgency of the moment – the colour, the sound, the people, the action"* – **Stirling Moss.** Non-stop partying culminates in cocktails at the Hôtel de Paris (also a prime place to stay, in a balconied room overlooking the course (provided you don't expect a lie-in).

GOLDDIGGERS OF PUERTO BANUS

If you're going to hang loose in Puerto Banus, in Spain, mingling with the bejewelled and medallioned, you've got to be seen in the right places at the right time. The day starts at 2pm on Victor's beach (not before unless you want to admit to social failure – what a dull night *you* must have had). At sundown you disappear until 11pm (before denotes no cable TV in your timeshare apartment). First stop is Sinatra's bar, then on to OLIVIA VALERE ("The *club, the best. International, glitzy, Régine-ish, Annabel's-ish – dressed-to-kill stuff*" says **David Shilling**; or to IPANEMA ("*young and crowded, for people who are born to party*" – **DS**). PS Take **Sebastian Scott**'s advice: "*Do try and have a tan before you get there or you'll look very silly.*"

SOCIAL AND NIGHT LIFE

Hong Kong

BARS AND CLUBS

BROWNS WINE BAR, 1/F Tower Two, Exchange Square, Central ☎ 5-237003
Michael Parry's bubbly wine bar is stuffed to the gills at lunch time with Ex Sq brokers and at night with Honkers' young Turks. Regular imbibers include long-time HK roués Jeremy 'Swerve' Stewardson, John Birt, Murray Burton et al, who enjoy chatting with the jet-fresh English waitresses.

CANTON, 164 Canton Rd, Tsimshatsui ☎ 3-721 0209
Sophisticated, funky, flamboyant, this disco has super-space-age videos and lighting, and the best sound system in Hong Kong. Like all discos on the Kowloon side it's packed out with Chinese trendies with cool haircuts (10,000 have squeezed into a space for 2,000). Hong Kong-siders aren't keen on the crush (nor the price of the beer).

CAPTAIN'S BAR, Mandarin Hotel, 5 Connaught Rd, Central ☎ 5-220111
The place to begin the evening – weekdays only. Viscount Evelyn Errington, Bill Wyllie, 'Wild' Warren Kibon (dynamic Kiwi entrepreneur), Simon Swallow, Simon de Courcy-Hughes (when in town), Jenkin 'Jenks' Hyles and practically everyone who works in Central hit it between 6 and 7.30.

🐾 **DUDDELL'S, G/F, 1 Duddell St, Central ☎ 5-845 2244**
An instant hit when it opened last year thanks to a clued-up team: Ric Mayo (of Casablanca and Hollywood East fame) is manager; David S. Davies and designer Jens Munk are major shareholders. Upstairs is a brick and wood bistro-style eatery with great home cooking and a 3-piece band. A change of tempo downstairs: all-black décor, crystal chandeliers and dramatic pink flower arrangements, with Sixties and nostalgic music. Resident

magician Dr Penguin p-p-p-picks up laughs.

FACES, New World Hotel, Salisbury Rd, Kowloon ☎ 3-694111
Civilized club, where you can drink champagne in a quiet nook with a group and not be trapped in the thick of it.

HOLLYWOOD EAST, Hotel Regal Meridien, Mody Rd, Tsimshatsui ☎ 3-722 6620
Part of the Wang empire, a razzy Chinese disco with constantly changing theme décor and high-tech equipment.

HOT GOSSIP, World Finance Centre, Canton Rd, Tsimshatsui ☎ 3-721 6884
A Juliana's offshoot, competing with its TST neighbours for the highest-tech disco equipment. Videos, lasers and imported technicians.

🐾 **JOE BANANAS, 23 Luard Rd, Wanchai ☎ 5-291811**
The trendiest expats go to JB's

NED KELLY'S LAST STAND, 11a Ashley Rd, Kowloon ☎ 3-660562
"An Australian bar named after the bush ranger. It has jazz every night of the week, which the Americans would call Dixieland and the English would call traditional. It's a lot of fun" – **Saul Lockhart.**

RAFFLES, 2/F, Bank of America Tower, Harcourt Rd, Central ☎ 5-218131
Civilized British-style membership day and night club. Sitting room with buttonback armchairs, large restaurant, health club – aerobics, sauna, Jacuzzi – and a dance floor. Also a sailing yacht members can hire.

CASINOS

MACAO CASINO, Lisboa Hotel, Avenida da Amizade ☎ 77666
The best low-life casino in the Far East, with the best fung

IN THE GWEILO GROOVE

Lan Kwai Fong is the grooviest area for expat socializing, tucked away off Wellington Road, Central. **CALIFORNIA BAR AND GRILL**, 30-32 D'Aguilar St ☎ 5-211345, **CAMARGUE**, 5 Lan Kwai Fong ☎ 5-257997 and **NINETEEN 97**, 9 Lan Kwai Fong ☎ 5-260303 are the favourite hang-outs for well-heeled, cliquish young expats. The fishing fleet (single girls out to hook their man) stream in. The eatery, California, shows soundless videos and hosts ravy discos on Wed, Fri and Sat nights. Nineteen 97 is run and staffed by Europeans – the majority of the transient fleet put in here for a stint of waitressing. Excellent for cheapo champagne cocktails (10 permutations) from 5.30-7.30pm. Expensive restaurant upstairs, bistro and disco downstairs. The cosy club-restaurant Camargue, owned by Alexander Egert (who founded Nineteen 97), is the spot for old LKF hands. **DISCO DISCO** ☎ 5-248809 and **THE DATELINE**, 7 Wellington St ☎ 5-246683 are high-energy largely gay bar-discos.

---

after DPs (dinner parties) or junk trips. A buzzy pub-like place where predominantly Brits (black-tied bankers, Forces boys, fishing fleet) line up to get in. Disco music – mainly '60s and '70s – keeps the joint a-jumping 'til all hours.

shui. Money makes Macao go round and hordes of Chinese speed over from HK to keep the roulette wheel spinning (and nip off to massage parlours in between times). This is serious, not glamorous, stuff: *"It may be the best, but it's really sleazy – it's cheek-by-jowl and 10 to a table on Wednesday afternoons at 2 o'clock"* – **Saul Lockhart.**

MANDARIN ORIENTAL CASINO, Avenida da Amizade ☎ 567888
Run by casino king Stanley Ho, this is the only dressy casino in Macao. Minimum stakes are HK\$50 and HK\$100 (as opposed to the usual HK\$5 or HK\$10). *"The poshest. Beautifully laid out and a very classy hotel, so the hordes don't go"* – **Saul Lockhart.**

EVENTS

In Hong Kong, as in Tokyo, social life equals business life. There is no divide. The most socially high-profile Chinese women are also top-flight businesswomen, mothers, and dynamos for their husbands. Nevertheless, there is a season, which runs from Sept to Dec. Colonials lie low or flee after the Rugby Sevens in April, when the going gets hot and muggy, and revive in September to do the party rounds.

HONG KONG BALLET BALL, 60 Blue Pool Rd, Happy Valley ☎ 5-737398
Held at end of year at the Regent, where the creative genius of Banqueting Manager Timothy Cumming (ex-Mandarin, ex-Oriental Bangkok) makes it the most glittering and sought-after affair of the year. The Ladies' Committee of the HK Ballet organizes the event. Always a theme; last year's was A Night in Manhattan.

NEW YEAR'S EVE
Highlight of the year, when colonials wind up at Jardine's outdoor party for the Gun. Kilted gweilos reel frenetically to stave off the frost, helped by mulled wine. At midnight the cannon fires and the Chinese police break into a wailing Auld Lang Syne on their pipes. Everyone goes wild for 10 minutes and then hops thankfully on to a ferry, which transports them back to

HK: PRIVATE CLUBS

Clubs are an important and well-used part of HK social life. It's more *in* (though less exclusive) to belong to the **AMERICAN CLUB**, 47/F Exchange Square, Tower Two, Central ☎ 5-842 7400 than the Hong Kong Club, mainly because you can actually get in. Has its own country club in Tai Tam on the south side of the island (*"Very nice, especially on Sunday for champagne brunch. You can sit outside and look over the South China Sea"* – **Diane Freis**). **HONG KONG CLUB**, Jackson Rd, Central ☎ 5-258251 still has the super-cachet, though former strict rulings against Chinese and anyone under 30 have been relaxed; members can't quite get used to its new-found airport-lounge look. **FOREIGN CORRESPONDENTS' CLUB**, 2 Albert Rd, Central ☎ 5-211511 is full of character (only 2 storeys; billiards) *and* characters – 120 journalists (some of them correspondents left over from Vietnam days), plus business and legal boys. **ROYAL HONG KONG GOLF CLUB**, Fan Kan Rd, Fan Ling, New Territories ☎ 0-901211: the most expensive golf club in HK. 3 extensive courses here, plus a small 9-holer in Deepwater Bay. **SHEK O COUNTRY CLUB**, Shek O ☎ 5-94429 is a snooty, old-established club with mainly oldish gweilo members. The place for cruising-yacht owners is **ABERDEEN MARINA CLUB**, 8 Deepwater Bay Rd, Aberdeen ☎ 5-558321 – a ritzy money-minded complex with the best marina in Asia. Billiards, bridge, a marvellous mah jong room, swimming, tennis, Casablanca nightclub – the works. Room service to yachts, packed champagne lunches. **ROYAL HONG KONG JOCKEY CLUB**, Sports Rd, Happy Valley ☎ 5-837811, with its country annexe at Bees River, New Territories. They used to say that in HK hierarchy, the Jockey Club came first, Hong Kong Club second and the Government third. Things haven't changed much.

Central and the warmth of a nightclub. At 4am they repair to the Mandarin Grill for breakfast. It's hardly worth going home, since New Year's Day starts with two private binges – eggnogs at the Peninsula (10am-noon) followed by eggnogs at the Mandarin (noon-2pm). Lord Kadoorie gives his *own* ultra-prestigious party for those who have contributed to the community; he gives a speech like the Queen's, reviewing the achievements of the year.

RSPCA BALL, c/o RSPCA, Harcourt Rd, Central ☎ 5-280501
A glamorous spring event organized by the Appeals Committee under the auspices

of Christine Liao (who took over from vivacious Lady Fiona Roberts). The theme is always an animal and a colour – Pink Panther, Black and White Penguin, and in 1988 (presented by Cartier) the Golden Diamond Panther Ball.

RUGBY SEVENS
The *other* highlight, held in April, a tremendous weekend when supporters fly in from Tokyo and Singapore, consume vast quantities of alcohol along with lavish picnics and arrive late for work on Monday (sometimes by a day or two).

GUESTS

David Li: more English than the English, a great mucker of

SOCIAL AND NIGHT LIFE

Kai-Yin Lo's (they were Cambridge undergrads together). **David** and **Susanna Tang**, frightfully pukka Shanghainese. **Bill Wyllie**, Aussie business whizz kid. **Sir Denys** and **Lady Roberts** have officially left HK for Brunei, but they're still asked back for the best private parties. Rags-to-riches billionaire **Li Ka-shing. Wilfred Koo**, eligible bachelor son of Daniel K (owner of Shui Hing dept stores). **Michael Kadoorie**, Chairman of Hong Kong and Shanghai Hotels (the Peninsula Group).

HOSTS

Fashion businesswoman **Joyce Ma** and her sister **Bonnie Fung**. Kai-Yin Lo: the best dinner parties in HK, with big international names. **Lydia Dunn**, a Shanghainese who has anglicized her name. **Stanley Ho**: he gives a select banquet in Macao each year, with extraordinary delicacies such as monkeys' brains and snake soup.

Italy

FLORENCE

CLUBS

MANILA, piazza Matteucci, Campi Bisenzio, 50013
☎ (055) 894121
An avant-garde club for the hip and chic, kitted out like a garage with cars and garage lights.

🏃 **TENAX, via Pretese 47, 50126**
☎ (055) 373050
The best club in Italy. A restored warehouse – vast (8,600 sq ft), sparse, on 2 floors. The upper floor has train seating and videos. New wave music and occasional bands such as Echo & the Bunnymen. The utterly cool clientele wear Comme des Garçons and Jean-Paul Gaultier – in fact one utterly cool client *is* Jean-Paul

Gaultier. Also an admiring **Stephen Jones**. Gianni Agnelli cruises in too.

HOSTS

Gioia Marchi Falck – a Milanese living in Florence, married to Marchesa Bona Frescobaldi's brother. Her tennis tournaments in aid of cancer research are ace. And of course **Marchesa Bona Frescobaldi**, who is great friends with the British royals and has hosted Prince Charles.

MILAN

CLUBS

NEPENTHA, piazza Armando Diaz 1, 20123
☎ (02) 873652
Straight and simple, where all the smart middle-of-the-via Milanese feel safe.

🏃 **PLASTIC, viale Umbria 120, 20135** ☎ (02) 743674
The trendiest club in Milan, teeming with young fashion designers. Modern, black and slick, apart from the incongruous Venetian glass chandeliers.

HOSTS

Those who do good works (and hold smart thrashes) in the name of art include **Inge Feltrinelli** and **Donna Giulia Maria Mozzoni Crespi**, innovator and founder of FAI, the foundation for restoration of Italian places, both natural and artistic.

ROME

BARS AND CLUBS

ACROPOLIS, via Schiaparelli 29-31, 00197 ☎ (06) 870504
Large disco, revamped in Grecian style. The cool young yuppie crowd wear jeans and Timberland shoes. All the big rock and pop stars play here when in Rome.

BELLA DONNA, via Tuscolana 695, 00174
☎ (06) 766 6893
Fun disco-piano bar with cabaret, live music and 'ballo liscio' – waltzing, tango, etc.

HEMINGWAY, piazza delle Coppelle 10, 00186
☎ (06) 654 4135
Ultra-popular all-night music bar. 3 rooms – one in Victorian style with wooden detailing, one in green marble with molto mirrors and one kitted out like a Greek taverna.

NOTORIOUS, via S Nicola da Tolentino 22, 00187
☎ (06) 474 6888
One of the hippest clubs with a big celebrity following – it's always in the Roman newspapers. Restaurant, disco and cabaret.

OPEN GATE, via San Nicola da Tolentino 4, 00187
☎ (06) 475 0464
Gleaming all-white piano bar/club/disco with a red and black restaurant. Frequented by aristocratic Rome.

IL TARTARUGHINO, via della Scrofa 2, 00186
☎ (06) 678 6037
A piano bar where smart older Romans and politicians gather. In summer, it closes in Rome and follows its regulars to Sardinia.

EVENT

FOX HUNT BALL, c/o Società Romana Caccia alla Volpe, via Montoro 8, 00186
☎ (06) 656 1569
Held in a different élite venue each year – the last was at the Circolo della Caccia in the Palazzo Borghese. *Strictly* by invitation. The most exclusive ball. Immaculately turned-out revellers flock in from all over Europe.

HOSTS

Mariuccia Mandelli still places **Marta Marzotto** as *"the best hostess and the most powerful social woman in Italy"*. However, others in the know find she's faded from the scene. **Maria Pia Fanfani**, president of the Croce Rossa Italiana in Rome, gives excellent benefit balls. **Contessa Donatella Pecci-Blunt** unites politicos and pals in her lovely house.

Japan

TOKYO

BARS AND CLUBS

♠ *Far East's Best* ♠

	NIGHTSPOTS
1	**LEXINGTON QUEEN**, Tokyo
2	**NINETEEN 97**, Hong Kong
3	**JOE BANANAS**, Hong Kong
4	**BUBBLES**, Bangkok
5	**DUDDELL'S**, Hong Kong
6	**VENICE**, Tokyo
7	**RUMOURS**, Singapore
8	**EASTWEST EXPRESS**, Singapore
9	**LE CLUB**, Tokyo
10	**BROWN SUGAR**, Bangkok

Tokyo has probably more up-to-the-minute nightspots than any other city, all designed to the hilt, a rhapsody in distressed concrete. The trendy nightlife areas are ROPPONGI, AKASAKA and HARAJUKU. The brassier SHINJUKU and GINZA have a zillion nightspots. Ginza is hostess bars and restaurants, the Kabukicho area of Shinjuku is glossy/seedy gay and transvestite clubs (Japanese-style family entertainment).

BOHEMIA, T-K Bldg, B1F-B2F, 3-17-25 Nishi Azabu, Minato-ku ☎ (03) 401 8143
A Technicolor *Absolute*

Beginners-style nightclub in the basement of fashion designer Takeo Kikuchi's building which was designed by English architect Nigel Coates. On the 2nd floor is the Snooker Bar, a spoof gentlemen's club, that cued a craze for the game in Tokyo. On the ground floor is TK's boutique kitted out like a prep-school boy's bedsit.

CAFE DE ROPE, 6-1-8 Jingumae, Shibuya ☎ (03) 406 6845
The original gaijin-meets-Japan hot-spot, a see-and-be-seen café on the fashion strip Omotesando, stuffed with immensely tall, chic models from the West.

CAFFE BONGO, Parco, 15-1 Udagawa-cho, Shibuya-ku ☎ (03) 464 5111
A surreal café on the ground floor of the store Parco. A silver aeroplane wing and engine jut out above the window; inside it's a bizarre mélange of nostalgic, minimalist and classical (mosaics, Roman statues) – part Sistine Chapel, part blank brick wall. Where you start or end the evening.

CAY BAR, B1 Spiral Bldg, 5-6-23 Minami-Aoyama, Minato-ku ☎ (03) 498 5790
Thai-style restaurant in the basement of the state-of-the-art Spiral Building on Omotesando. Occasional live bands – big acts like Sade have been known to

give impromptu performances. A favourite of **Tina Chow**.

CHARLESTON, 3-8-11 Roppongi, Minato-ku ☎ (03) 402 0372
A café-bar for pre- or post-prandial drinks. Hoorayish expat hang-out with a clubby atmosphere. Japanese girls trip along in tribes, hoping to latch on to eligible gaijin.

♠ **LE CLUB, Plaza Kay B1, 5-1-1 Minami Azabu, Minato-ku ☎ (03) 444 6901**
"Super-chic interior; very fashionable with a yuppie clientele" – **Bernard Cendron**.

DEJA-VU, Tohgensha Bldg, 1F, 3-15-24 Roppongi, Minato-ku ☎ (03) 403 8777
Chic little late-late-night bar where rowdy brokers and bankers gather for post-dinner snifters and to try and get to know the young American female owner a little better.

FRANK LLOYD WRIGHT BAR, Imperial Hotel, 1-1-1 Uchisaiwai-cho, Chiyoda-ku ☎ (03) 504 1111
Like Hong Kong's Captain's Bar: foreign boys crowd in for pre-prandials. A better bet than the small ads for seeking out an elusive expat.

HENRY AFRICA, 3-15-23 Roppongi, Minato-ku ☎ (03) 403 9751
An alternative (or extra) to Charleston and Maggie's

VENICE, TOKYO

OK, so Tokyo Bay isn't quite the sparkling Aegean, and you'll have to ignore the Expressway, but the waterfront is now the hippest social hang-out in town. New zoning laws have caused a boom in harbourside cafés and restaurants, and on Mon, Wed and Fri evenings you can take an hour's cruise around the rivers and bay for a skimpy Y2,500 including drinks. Once back on terra firma, the best watering holes are **VENICE, TOKYO**, 2-2-18 Shibaura, Minato-ku ☎ (03) 452 3009 for cocktails and dancing and, next door, **TANGO** ☎ (03) 798 1311, where tables are set up outside brasserie-style for drinks and haute café-bar cuisine. This and **INK STICK SHIBAURA FACTORY**, a warehouse-based club with live music and tango (only open for scheduled events), were started by club supremo Isao Matsuyama.

Revenge – each a yen's throw from the other.

INK STICK, B1, Casa Grande Miwa Bldg, 7-5-11 Roppongi, Minato-ku ☎ (03) 401 0429
The nightclub-bar that David Bowie and cult musician Ryuichi Sakamoto hit when in town. Occasional impromptu performances by visiting rock stars. Mr Ink Stick (Isao Matsuyama) has branched out to Tokyo's waterfront (see Venice, Tokyo).

♠ LEXINGTON QUEEN, B1, 3rd Goto Bldg, 3-13-14 Roppongi, Minato-ku ☎ (03) 401 1661
The Lex is the grooviest late-night club. Proprietor Bill Hersey knows everyone and throws wonderful beanos for visiting celebs – Michael Jackson, Madonna, Bob Geldof, Eric Clapton, Whitney Houston, Tina Turner, Rod Stewart, David Bowie, the Carradine Brothers. In attendance are sleek models, groupies and paparazzi.

LIVE HOUSE LOLLIPOP, Nittaku Bldg, 3-8-15 Roppongi, Minato-ku ☎ (03) 478 0028
A fun late-night bar; excellent venue for live music. On the 1st floor is the Beatles Live House, where look- and sound-alikes strum to the Sixties beat.

MAGGIE'S REVENGE, Takano Bldg, 3-8-12 Roppongi, Minato-ku ☎ (03) 479 1096
Aussie Maggie's place is one of the liveliest bars in Roppongi with a boisterous foreign contingent.

RADIO BAR, 2-31-7 Jingumae, Shibuya-ku ☎ (03) 405 5490
A high-frequency turn-out of gaijin and trendies at this buzzing cocktail bar. It's the ultimate – there is no concoction they can't make.

SAMBA CLUB, 2F, 2-7-2 Nishi Shinjuku ☎ (03) 342 8877
For a slightly older crowd, an elegant contrast to teenybopper discos. Less noisy

---

TOKYO: PRIVATE CLUBS

FOREIGN CORRESPONDENTS' CLUB, 20F, Yurakucho Denki Bldg, 1-7-1 Yurakucho, Chiyoda-ku ☎ (03) 211 3161 – an important club for top journalists and businessmen. Great meeting place for powerful Western expats. **TOKYO AMERICAN CLUB**, 212 Azabudai ☎ (03) 583 8381 – TAC by name and verging on tack by nature, with bevies of Crimplened Americans; but it's where it all happens – the Capitol Hill of Tokyo. **TOKYO CLUB**, 3-2-6 Kasumigaseki, Chiyoda-ku ☎ (03) 580 0781 – very hard to get into, particularly for gaijin (but it has reciprocal arrangements with the Oxford & Cambridge Club in London).

---

and laser-ridden, more affluent and plush.

GUESTS

Prince Takamado, grandson of the Emperor, and his **Princess. Naohiko Umewaka**, a brilliant young No actor, and his Lebanese wife **Madeleine. Hisanaga** and **Takako Shimazu** – he of Sony, she of Seibu (and she's the youngest daughter of the Emperor). Exquisite Korean sculptress **Jae Eun Choi** and her urbane architect husband **Edward Suzuki**, the Alain Delon of Japan. Fashion designer **Junko Koshino** and husband **Hiroyuki Suzuki**. Restaurateur (of Chianti and co) **Sho Kawazoe** and wife **Kabuki Jun.**

HOSTS

Fashion designer **Hanae Mori** and her husband **Ken** host about 20 parties a year. Actor **Toshiro Mifune** is a great entertainer. Head of Cartier **Bernard** (and **Tamiko**) **Cendron** give wonderful corporate parties. Dress designer **Jun Ashida**: fabulous parties – everyone goes, including the royals. Grandes dames of society, **Fumiko Tottori**, mother of Princess Takamado; **Mrs Aso**, daughter of former PM Shigeru Yoshida, and **Chie Hachisuke**, who heads all great charity projects. **Reijiro Hattori**, of Seiko, and his son and daughter-in-law

---

Yasuo and **Kumiko. Aki** and **Yoshiko Morita** (Aki is head of Sony) entertain lavishly, as do fashion designers **Matsuda** and **Yukiko Hanai. Tetsuko Kuroyonagi** – known as 'Tamanegi Chan' (the Onion Lady) because of her hairstyle – author, TV presenter and charity money-raiser. The cosmopolitan party-giving **Yasuyuki Nambu**, twice nominated Japan's most dynamic businessman.

Singapore

CLUBS

♠ EASTWEST EXPRESS, 3rd Fl, Marina Square ☎ 339 1618
This is the latest hotspot to steam into town. Restaurant-disco with private carriages and piano-shaped bar. When the owner got married last year, he held the ceremony here; all the guests applauded after the vows.

♠ RUMOURS, 3rd Fl, Forum Galleria ☎ 732 8181
One of the most *in* discos, an enormous cool grey, high-tech space with split-level dance floor, stairs everywhere and stadium seating. Super-young kids bottleneck at the door. Best cocktail: Long Island (a killer).

TOP TEN, 400 Orchard Rd
☎ 732 3077
A converted cinema with the
Manhattan skyline scudding
across the walls. Disco and live
music, superlative lighting.

**THE WAREHOUSE, 332
Havelock Rd** ☎ 732 9922
Worth going to see the new
Video Wall. Thanks to this S$2
million piece of super-high-
technology, you can join
Michael Jackson and other nifty
star dancers on screen. Your
bopping image down on the
dance floor can be projected on
to the film so that you appear
to be a part of it.

**XANADU, Shangri-La, 22
Orange Grove Rd** ☎ 737 3644
The place for locals in the
know. Sleek, super-trendy
haunt with outsize videos,
spectacular lighting and laser
shows. Bars and seats surround
the sunken dance floor.

Private Club

**SINGAPORE ISLAND
COUNTRY CLUB, Island
Club House, 180 Island Club
Rd** ☎ 459 2222
The stupendous sum of four
18-hole courses, the result of
the combined strength of the
Royal Island and Singapore
Island clubs. The membership
fee of around S$150,000 makes
it exclusively for the rich and
powerful, though on Mondays,
caddies are allowed to play.

Switzerland

Swiss nightclubs are
horrendously expensive,
particularly at the height of the
season. On a par for glitzy
clientele (rather than décor) are
the **GREEN GO**, Palace Hotel,
Gstaad ☎ (030) 83131, the
dated **KINGS' CLUB**, Palace
Hotel, CH-7500 St Moritz
☎ (082) 21101, and Gunther
Sachs's private **DRACULA
CLUB**, Kulm Hotel, CH-7500
St Moritz ☎ (082) 21151, only
open in winter. One of the best,
most exclusive clubs in the
Alps is the **FARM CLUB**,
Hotel Rhodania, 1936 Verbier
☎ (026) 70121, lined with
English aristos at Easter.

Thailand

BANGKOK

PATPONG is the centre of all
hustling, blaring, colourful,
crazy, Oriental nightlife –
straight or kinky, from jazz
clubs, discos and bars to sex
shops and massage parlours,
with plenty of deviations in
between: all you ever dreamt of
or dreaded doing. (The going
gets even more sordid/thrilling
at the resorts of Pattaya and
Patong, Phuket, where some of
the most unattractive
Westerners imaginable bar-hop
arm-in-arm with young Thai
girls.)

BARS AND CLUBS

The latest late-night drinking
spot is **Silom Plaza**. A bevy of
café-bars such as **The Junk**
spill out on to a central outdoor
area – it feels like the Med or
the Rive Gauche. A disco called
Freakout, too. Packed with
young sophisticated Thais plus
the post-Bubbles set.

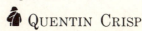 **BROWN SUGAR, 231/20
Sarasin Rd**
A bubblin' live jazz and blues
joint. A good mix of biz kids
and more arty-intellectual
types.

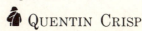 **BUBBLES, Dusit Thani,
Rama IV Rd** ☎ (2) 233 1130
A typical hotel disco, similar to
Diana's, but *always* packed
mainly because it's easier to
park. Smart but informal, chic
20s to 40s crowd.

**DIANA'S, Oriental Plaza, 48
Oriental Ave** ☎ 234 9920
An exclusive, sedate club for
those who can't stand the pace
at Brown Sugar or The Palace.
The Annabel's of Thailand, its
clientele includes the Bangkok
royals. A barrage of old school
Thais from Harrow and Eton
have accents so pukka that old
colonials imagine they *are* in
Annabel's. The only setback is
it's nigh-impossible to park.

**NASA SPACEDROME, 999
Ramkhamhang Rd**
☎ (2) 314 4024
Colossal club, consistently jam-
packed to capacity (and there's
room for 4,000 weenyboppers).
At 11pm you can have a close
encounter with a spaceship,
which glides in and hovers
above the dance floor.

**THE PALACE, Vipavadi
Rungsit Rd** ☎ (2) 253 6550
Big disco for baby Thais – a
very young, trendy and
fashion-conscious set.

**ROME CLUB
VIDEOTHEQUE, Soi
Jaruwan 90-96** ☎ (2) 233 8836
Slightly seedy, tawdry, but
very popular gay bar turned
bar for all, including celebs and
royals. At midnight, there's an
OTT transvestite show, where
the glitteringly costumed boys
mime to pop soundtracks.

> *Worrying about lack of sleep is to be avoided. People are lying
> there at 2am thinking about sleep, but they don't need to sleep so
> much. If you want to rule the world, sleep less!*
>
> QUENTIN CRISP

Bruce Oldfield on
FASHION *and* SHOPPING

World's Best Couturiers and Designers

1
YVES SAINT LAURENT,
Paris

2
GIORGIO ARMANI,
Milan

3
KARL LAGERFELD,
Paris

4
JEAN-PAUL GAULTIER,
Paris

5
REI KAWAKUBO for
COMME DES GARCONS,
Tokyo

6
CALVIN KLEIN,
New York

7
CHRISTIAN LACROIX,
Paris

8
EMANUEL UNGARO,
Paris

9
DONNA KARAN,
New York

10
ROMEO GIGLI,
Milan

Fashion means many things to many people. For me, it is not only my work, or that of other designers, but a representation of life and history seen through clothes and accessories.

Fashion is style, and different kinds of style, from the highest levels of couture chic to traditional cowboys' blue jeans, which have become the basis for a complete generation of style trends. Fashion is also an industry, and one which in many countries is not only a major contributor to trade figures, but is an ambassador of national talents and skills.

It is also the basis for huge financial empires which encompass all manner of products, from perfumes to bed-linens, carrying a designer's name and signature, and ringing up the dollars, francs and marks on cash tills around the world.

Shopping for fashion can be one of life's pleasures, and challenges, balancing one's own individual taste and desire against that of the shop owner or store buyer. A journey of discovery around the world. We can enjoy fashion in the sharp bustle of Madison Avenue or the faded elegance of Milan with its designer-owned palazzi. We can have our clothes and shoes handmade by craftsmen in London, or be among the select few who can still patronize the gilded couture salons of Paris.

I enjoy my fashion, from selecting material at the best European fabric houses to sketching the initial ideas for the collection. The first fittings, the second, even the third; one garment, the next, and the next after that – until the whole collection is ready for the catwalk, to be shown to a selection of the world's buyers and press. Finally, perhaps ten months after I looked at the first fabric swatch, I am in my own shop fitting a client, or I'm on the other side of the world doing an in-store show or talking to the television cameras.

Fashion is a continuous process, it's evolution, it's creation, and it's an intrinsic part of our lives. Enjoy buying it, and wearing it!

America

BOSTON

The best shopping areas for high fashion and hip, sporty boutiques are Newbury Street, Boylston Street in the Back Bay, ye olde Beacon Hill (cobbles and gaslights galore); and Harvard Square and Brattle Street in Cambridge.

SHOPS

CHARLES SUMNER, 16 Newbury St, MA 02116 ☎ (617) 536 6225
Bijou department store that considers itself a baby Bergdorf-Goodman. Valentino boutique, Donna Karan and a department for shoes by Rayne, Ferragamo, Jourdan and Saint Laurent.

FILENE'S, 426 Washington St, MA 02101 ☎ (617) 357 2698
"The best bargain basement in the world. Not only their own stock but also designer clothes – we're talking Christian Dior jackets, Ferragamo tasselled shoes. I can walk out with wonderful clothes at ridiculous prices" – **Glynn Christian**. If the already sensational bargains don't sell, they are slashed in price each week until they're practically given away. *"It's a nail-biting process gambling on whether the thing you want will still be there a week later"* – **GC**.

ROBERTS NEUSTADTER FURS, 69 Newbury St, MA 02116 ☎ (617) 267 2063
Furry insulation against sub-zero winters. A riot of Fendi furs for chilly nose-in-the-air but tongue-in-cheek customers.

SARA FREDERICKS, Copley Place, MA 02116 ☎ (617) 536 8766
High-class clothes for the carriage trade; good, old-fashioned service with a rather more go-ahead image of late. 8 stores, including one in Palm Beach. They stock Beene, Blass, Lagerfeld, Valentino, Ungaro and have a team of fitters and alterers.

CHICAGO

SHOPS

CITY, 213 W Institute Place, IL 60610 ☎ (312) 664 9581
The first store in the area to carry Memphis and Philippe Starck furniture. Their clothes are the wearable counterpart, mostly by Hino & Malee, a Japanese designer team based in Chicago. Also Joseph Tricot; men's clothes and Arai fabric from Japan.

MARSHALL FIELD, 111 N State St, IL 60690 ☎ (312) 781 5000
The best department store in town. All the top designers – just everything.

STANLEY KORSHAK, 940 N Michigan Ave, IL 60611 ☎ (312) 280 9520
A Chicago institution that started as a couture house 70-odd years ago and still carries the all-American stylebusters, such as Oscar de la Renta and Bill Blass. Also dressy Europeans – Krizia, Ferré, Ungaro. **Caroline Hunt** likes the branch in Dallas.

ULTIMO, 114 E Oak St, IL 60611 ☎ (312) 787 0906
The upmarket designer hunting ground for fashion-conscious men and women. A clubby kind of store with Sonia Rykiel, Lagerfeld, Armani, Muir.

DALLAS

JEWELLERY

WHITESIDE, 7805 Inwood, TX 75209 ☎ (214) 358 0089
Fine pieces and objets d'art in precious and semi-precious stones, all custom designed, many after Fabergé or in rococo high spirits.

SHOPS

In the newer cities of the USA, the mall has it all. **The Crescent** is the most stupendous and exclusive – the second largest limestone structure in the world (after the Empire State Building) with 10.5 acres of offices, hotels, shops and a gallery with changing exhibitions. **The Galleria** is the other big, fashionable mall for serious spenders, with 185 boutiques and stores, an ice rink and entertainment centre.

THE GAZEBO, 8300 Preston Rd, TX 75225 ☎ (214) 373 6661
Clothes and all the accessories that go with them. They'll call you to let you know when something you might like has come in, or bring a bag of goodies to the house for you to try. Frequent 'trunk' shows where they invite designers to show their entire collection at the store, so customers can buy direct from the designer.

LOU LATTIMORE, 4320 Lover's Lane, TX 75225 ☎ (214) 369 8585
Lovers of great clothes walk down this lane, for Chanel, YSL, Geoffrey Beene, Claude Montana, Thierry Mugler, Dolce e Gabbana, Basile and Umberto Ginochietti plus Shoe Biz, a shoe boutique with their own exclusive designs. A best for **Caroline Hunt.**

LUCY'S AT THE CRESCENT, 20200 Cedar Springs, Suite 145, TX 75201 ☎ (214) 871 8484
Mainly exclusive designer clothes imported from Britain (Lindka Cierach, Penny Green), plus their own designs. 'After-five' wear only (they start early in Dallas).

NEIMAN-MARCUS, 1618 Main St, TX 75201 ☎ (214) 741 6911
The world-famous Neiman-Marcus is one of the best and biggest-thinking stores in America. Their Christmas catalogue is chocker with indispensable priceless prezzies such as his 'n' hers diamonds ($2 million the pair), or alligator jeans at $10,000 a pair or a week's charter of the yacht *Never Say Never* (a mere $29,000). Designer collections

from Fendi and Versace to Chanel and Valentino.

SHOPPING ENGLISH COUNTRYSIDE, 2200 Cedar Springs, TX 75201
☎ (214) 871 8333
'Affordable, one-of-a-kind English antiques hand-selected by the owner (Caroline Hunt) from the manor houses and thatched cottages throughout England,' the blurb goes. Her 'philosophy of pairing the plain with the fancy' means antiques and presents are grouped in themes (for the sportsman, for the hostess) in room sets connected by a flower-filled English garden.

FREEPORT

LL BEAN, Casko St, Freeport, Maine, MI 04033
☎ (207) 865 4761; mail order 865 3111
Home of the preppy look, mainly attained by mail order. Everything you need for the great outdoors, from waders to docksiders, jumpers to chino trousers, and sporty macho accessories such as the Swiss Army Knife. *"The best single shop in the world. My favourite. I love everything they sell. It's a great antidote to most design shops where it's all black and minimalist. LL Bean sells good, old-fashioned gadgetry which I absolutely adore"* – **Loyd Grossman**.

HOUSTON

THE GALLERIA, 5075 Westheimer, TX 77056
☎ (713) 621 1907
The most exclusive shopping mall, a balconied, chandeliered extravaganza, complete with the ubiquitous ice rink and nearly 300 boutiques and stores, including Lord & Taylor, Macy's, Neiman-Marcus and Marshall Field. **Lord Lichfield** is knocked out: *"It's sensational and has a wider variety of merchandise than any mall I know."*

LOS ANGELES

DESIGNERS

BOB MACKIE, 8636 Melrose Ave, CA 90069
☎ (213) 657 7377
For spangles and sequins and showbiz pzazz, Mackie's your man. Cher dazzles in his barely there stunners. *"Incredible dresses, fantastic numbers. Very Hollywood"* – **Jackie Collins**.

🐾 **GALANOS ORIGINALS, 2254 S Sepulveda Blvd, CA 90064**
☎ (213) 272 1445
"An ivory tower designer in that he doesn't seek a lot of attention, but he delivers fabulous clothes" – **Eleanor Lambert**. Chic, beautifully handcrafted, outrageously

expensive outfits (a ready-to-wear dress could set you back $30,000). Classics in stupendous fabrics with pure silk linings – as impeccable inside as out. Beading (done by former costume beaders at MGM) is a speciality. For the thinnest of the thin – ladies like Nancy Reagan, Gloria Vanderbilt and Ann Getty.

GENE EWING/BIS, 110 E 9th St, CA 90015
☎ (213) 628 3556
Young designer whose Ewing line is smart washable silk and print numbers; Bis is all denim, fun, relaxed gear. *"One of my personal favourites, whom I believe in, but who is still not internationally known. She is a Californian designer of sports clothes with great fantasy and charm, but still very practical"* – **Eleanor Lambert**. Also at Neiman-Marcus, Bullock's and Saks.

NOLAN MILLER, 910 S Robertson Blvd, CA 90035
☎ (213) 655 7110
Exclusive designer to the Dynasty set – on and off set. He's Candy Spelling's No 1 and a hit with **Joan Collins**. Think Krystle-clear shoulder pads (no compromises here), think sex and sensation, think razzle dazzle, and you're thinking Nolan Miller.

JEWELLERY

CARITTA, 411 N Rodeo Drive, Beverly Hills, CA 90210
☎ (213) 271 7443
The glam Hollywood crowd gather here for jewels – **Jackie Collins**, Shari Belafonte-Harper et al.

FRANCES KLEIN, 310 N Rodeo Drive, Beverly Hills, CA 90210 ☎ (213) 273 0155
Prestigious, glittering jewel box of impressive antique pieces; spectacular Art Nouveau and Art Deco trinkets. *"I love it. They have a lot of estate jewellery which is reasonably priced and generally very beautifully made"* – **Dudley Moore**. Other star browsers include Sylvester Stallone and Elton John.

LA: BEST SHOPPING

Melrose is the beat of the younger, wilder, wet-behind-the-ears-but-cool crowd in LA, sons and daughters of the rich and famous. Ranges from designer boutiques like Maxfield through Retail Slut (cult vendor of punk to the US), to Olivia Newton-John's place, Koala Blue, for pastel après-workout gear . . . and yogurt. **Westwood** is the preserve of California girls and guys – UCLA student types who buy designer beach wear, surf pants and sweatshirts from Ocean Pacific. **Sherman Oaks Galleria** is the original mall that Valley Girls sprung from, but the maxi-est mall in LA is the **Beverly Center**. **Rodeo Drive**, the famous drag in Beverly Hills, is glossy, international and expensive . . . with little substance.

FRED JEWELERS, 401 N Rodeo Drive, Beverly Hills, CA 90210 ☎ (213) 278 3733
"*I like his jewellery because it's very exciting. He has wonderful designs,*" enthuses **Jackie Collins**, who wears her beloved diamond and ruby heart on a zipper.

KATHRYN POST, 1840 N Beverly Glen Blvd, CA 90077 ☎ (213) 470 7772
"*For costume jewellery. She does fake diamonds, diamonds as big as The Ritz*" – **Stephen Jones**. They're actually cubic zircons, set in sterling silver or vermeil with 18ct gold overlay. Classic Tiffany – and Harry Winston-style designs. She's done work for Bill Blass's shoes, for Cher and now the crown jewels for Eddie Murphy's movie *The Quest*.

LINGERIE

FREDERICK'S OF HOLLYWOOD, 6610 Hollywood Blvd, CA 90028 ☎ (213) 466 8506
Where you go if you *really* like it trashy. Slum it up in peek-a-boo peignoir sets, peep-hole bras, crotchless knicks and slingback mules. "*If you want to go over the top ... all the wildest things*" – **Jackie Collins.**

TRASHY LINGERIE, 402 N La Cienega Blvd, CA 90048 ☎ (213) 652 4543
8,000 ways to undress in everything from Victoriana to leather. They specialize in incredibly soft, silky leather corselets, bras and bustiers. "*Fun stuff and some very sexy stuff!*" – **Jackie Collins**. They used to get so many sightseers and tour buses stopping to ogle that you now have to be a member to get in – a matter of $2 a year. Kim Basinger peeled off their body wares in *9½ Weeks*.

SHOPS

BULLOCK'S, Beverly Center, 8500 Beverly Blvd, CA 90048 ☎ (213) 854 6655 Bullock's takes the West Coast by the

horns, its 52 branches dominating the department store scene. "*Wonderful store ... a big specialty shop like Nordstrom's*" – **Ken Lane**.

FRED HAYMAN'S GIORGIO, 273 N Rodeo Drive, Beverly Hills, CA 90210 ☎ (213) 205 2400
Still-padded shoulders pad into the famous and "*wonderful Giorgio. It's not what you think it's going to be. You expect it to be very chi-chi*" – **Jackie Collins**. Aw c'mon ... what's chi-chi about handing out free drinks and having a 'cozy fireplace' and an 'antique pool table'? Or a little yellow-and-white-striped Honda that matches the shop and runs all your deadweight goodies home? Or ferrying celebs (Barbra Streisand, Aretha Franklin, Jacqueline Bisset, OJ Simpson ...) to and from the store in a vintage '52 Roller? Or sending happy buyers a *thank-you note*? Chi-chi nothing. It's the Californian Dream.

LINA LEE, 459 N Rodeo Drive, Beverly Hills, CA 90210 ☎ (213) 556 2678
La crème de la crème of French, Italian and American designers. **Jackie Collins** and other Hollywood Wives swan in for the latest numbers.

MAXFIELD, 8825 Melrose Ave, CA 90069 ☎ (213) 274 8800
One of the coolest stockpiles of designerdom on Melrose: Yamamoto, Comme des Garçons, Alaïa, Jean-Paul Gaultier, Karl Lagerfeld, Katharine Hamnett, Joseph, Romeo Gigli, Byblos, Dolce & Gabbana and Stephen Sprouse are all here *en force*. It knocks out **Jackie Collins** and **Jeremiah Tower**: "*Most interesting and far-out clothes and objects of black and white.*"

NORDSTROM'S, 1835 Hawthorne Blvd, Redondo Beach, CA 90278 ☎ (213) 542 9440
A department store that has "*really come along in the last few years – an extraordinary collection of good stuff*" – **Ken Lane**.

NEW ORLEANS

SHOPS

The best shopping is round Canal Street and at Lakeside Mall in Metairie.

ENRICO, 201 St Charles Ave, LA 70130 ☎ (504) 582 1188
The men's equivalent of Tabbi (see below), run by Tabbi's hubbi. Clothes are specially made in Italy and a private collection is flown in from England. Also the universal Armani.

TABBI, 333 Canal Place, Suite 209, LA 70130 ☎ (504) 524 0516
The best shop for women's designer clothes, mainly Italian and a few French.

YVONNE LA FLEUR, 8131 Hampson St, LA 70118 ☎ (504) 866 9666
A whole lotta lace. Known for her custom-made hats and headpieces, especially concoctions of handmade lace. Has hatted-out movies (*Pretty Baby, Chanel Solitaire*) and the stars – Liz Taylor, Linda Gray, Nastassja Kinski, Brooke Shields. Exquisite handmade lace lingerie too.

NEW YORK

ACCESSORIES

BARRY KIESELSTEIN-CORD at Bergdorf-Goodman, see Shops
Precious jewellery and belts, displayed in a 1,000-sq ft shoplet at Bergdorf-Goodman, and at Neiman-Marcus. One of his cult items is the chunky Western unpolished gold belt buckle. Illustrious clients include the Reagans, Frank Sinatra, Jack Nicholson, Marisa Berenson, Anjelica Huston, Lionel Richie, Mick Jagger, Eddie Murphy, Diana Ross, Farrah Fawcett ...

LA CRASIA, 389 5th Ave, NY 10016 ☎ (212) 532 7414
Marvellous, wicked gloves by Sachiko, couturier for the

hands. Gold and silver gloves, frogged, fringed, fur-trimmed and encrusted ones . . .

JOHNNY FARAH, 41 Wooster St, NY 10013 ☎ **(212) 777 7711** A style leader for belts and bags. He was one of the first to use exotic skins. *"He sets trends"* – **Aniko Gaal.**

JUDITH LIEBER, 20 W 33rd St, NY 10001 ☎ **(212) 736 4244; and at Saks Fifth Avenue (see Shops)** *"Wonderful handbags, very expensive ($2,000 or $3,000). She does them in the shape of animals"* – **Helen Gurley Brown.** *"Terribly good-looking bags. Lightweight canvas with the best stripe design – her initials and a crest; fabulous little crocodile bags. Also small leather goods"* – **Eleanor Lambert.**

🐧 *America's Best* 🐧

	DESIGNERS
1	**CALVIN KLEIN**
2	**DONNA KARAN**
3	**GEOFFREY BEENE**
4	**BILL BLASS**
5	**GALANOS**
6	**OSCAR DE LA RENTA**
7	**RALPH LAUREN**
8	**MICHAEL KORS**
9	**STEPHEN SPROUSE**
10	**CARMELO POMODORO**

🐧

COUTURE

ARNOLD SCAASI COUTURE, 681 5th Ave, NY 10022 ☎ **(212) 755 5105** Although American designers are turning more towards couture, Scaasi is the only true couturier in the Paris tradition. His forté is great-occasion dressing, triumphant fantasies in taffeta and tulle. Clients are Social Register-meets-showbiz: Ivana Trump, Charlotte Ford, Mrs Adnan Khashoggi, Jackie Onassis, Barbra Streisand, Joan Rivers. Lots of débutante and wedding dresses. Also ready-to-wear at **530 7th Ave, NY 10018** ☎ **(212) 245 2683.**

DESIGNERS

ADOLFO, 36 E 57th St, NY 10022 ☎ **(212) 688 4410** Still charming the society molls and turning out natty little Coco-inspired suits. 'Darling Dolf' is Nancy Reagan's pet designer. *"What he does, he does very well. I'd go for classic knit suits"* – **Helen Gurley Brown.** At his shows, his following make a point of wearing the *same* latest suit, like a class in uniform.

🐧 **BILL BLASS, 550 7th Ave, NY 10018** ☎ **(212) 221 6660** Gorgeous evening wear designed by the man who is American's No 1 fashion accessory, draped on the arm of the best society dames. Answering the bugle call, his dresses are embroidered, embellished, beaded, sequinned and spangled to the hilt. Vest-like little sheaths with bow waists, girlish puffy minis all dripping in bugles and beads. His colour statements are just as dazzling. In the top line for **Liz Smith, Viscountess Rothermere** et al.

CAROLINA HERRERA, 19 E 57th St, NY 10022 ☎ **(212) 355 3055** Society queen turned dress designer to like-minds. Snobbish little luncheon ensembles, accomplished evening luxuries. *"Her dresses are very refined-looking, her construction excellent. Her daywear is more dressy, more city than sportswear"* – **Caroline Hunt.**

🐧 **DONNA KARAN, 550 7th Ave, 14th Fl, NY 10018** ☎ **(212) 398 1558** The Karan sarong may no longer be big news, but her pared-down style is a modern classic. Low-key neutral-toned jersey, wool and cashmere co-ordinates – a body, a skirt, pants, a shawl-collared swing jacket, et voilà. Also tights, headbands and the full clothing accessories line. *"One of the bright stars focusing on the American lifestyle – simplicity, openness, freedom of movement. Her clothes are not restricting. She has taken comfort and practicality to a stylized conclusion"* – **Aniko Gaal.** *"I love her whole capsule collection – the idea of wrap skirts, a few taut little tops, a coat . . . and her colour schemes are so beautifully muted and worked out. She has been much ripped-off"* – **Liz Smith.** *"She's*

ARE YOU WEARING KLEIN UNDERWEAR?

🐧 **CALVIN KLEIN, 205 W 39th St, NY 10018** ☎ **(212) 719 2600.** 'Nothing comes between me and my Calvins' . . . Famed for those ads for his jeans (stretched round Brooke Shields's bottom) and underwear (his is snugly the best), he's always body-conscious yet casual, and utterly American. Recently, he slipped into something a little more comfortable: lingerie-like evening wear in a feminine silk-satin-and-lace look. Autumn sees both slender pants and hip-hugging flares. Some of the best lean 'n' mean menswear. *"There can be no talk of American style without mentioning Calvin Klein. He has superb dash and panache. He has recently created a couture collection for Berdorf-Goodman – perhaps this is a turning point for American fashion"* – **Aniko Gaal.** *"My favourite designer – he's classic, sexy, sophisticated and young. I buy day and evening wear – a couple of drop-dead sexy dresses"* – **Helen Gurley Brown. Eleanor Lambert** is an admirer.

FASHION AND SHOPPING

> **66** *America has had a great effect on the way we all dress. They're adventurous, not afraid of glamour, they do good sharp clothes that have sex appeal. They may not be totally and utterly original but they have a lot of class* **99**
>
> 🦔 LIZ SMITH

very hot" – **Jackie Collins**. *"I'm a great fan and I think she's going to go far, far, far beyond even what she's doing now"* – **Eleanor Lambert.**

FLORA KUNG, 214 W 39th St, NY 10018 ☎ (212) 302 3600 A Korean designer based in the Big Apple. No design leader, but she does do *"wonderful printed silk daywear"* – **Helen Gurley Brown.**

🦔 **GEOFFREY BEENE, 550 7th Ave, NY 10018** ☎ **(212) 398 0800** A quiet noise, but an established figure, highly regarded on the fashion scene. An uncluttered look, strong on colour and fabric (some costing $300 a yard). Spare, lean, easy, 'energized' clothes in tune with that perennial US fashion basic – the working woman. *"A designer who simply doesn't care whether lots of people know about him, but he wants a few devotees to care about the perfectionism of his design"* – **Eleanor Lambert. Stanley Marcus** votes him best designer. He's one of the best in the US for **Liz Smith** and **Helen Gurley Brown.**

GLORIA SACHS, 550 7th Ave, NY 10018 ☎ (212) 921 1460 Specializes in combining fab prints (paisleys, etc) and fabrics, in contemporary sportswear. *"She has an absolutely divine sense for richness in texture and colour and pays meticulous attention to detail. She puts classic on another level"* – **Aniko Gaal.**

MARY McFADDEN, 264 W 35th St, NY 10001 ☎ **(212) 736 4078** Fortuny pleating revisited. *"One of the best because of the wonderful fabrics she uses. Her clothes are so beautiful and packable; practical and elegant"* – **Caroline Hunt.**

NORMA KAMALI, 11 W 56th St, NY 10019 ☎ (212) 957 9797 Known for her T-shirt/ sweatshirt numbers, and her high-tech rubberized black swimwear, she's more like the Europeans – now doing Forties fitted suits. Jackie Collins and Princess Stéphanie of Monaco are erstwhile admirers. *"Her clothes are rather sexy, they really cling to the body"* – **Ken Lane**. *"One of our best, most original designers. No matter what, she's a presence"* – **Eleanor Lambert.**

🦔 **OSCAR DE LA RENTA, 550 7th Ave, NY 10018** ☎ **(212) 354 6777** Darling of café society, known for his extravagant evening clothes that swank into balls and premières. Loves ornamentation, hand-beading. His top-drawer clothes-horses include Marella Agnelli, Babe Paley, Nancys Reagan and Kissinger, Lee Radziwill, Marie-Hélène de Rothschild and **Viscountess Rothermere.**

PERRY ELLIS, 575 7th Ave, NY 10018 ☎ (212) 921 8500 Continuing the Perry Ellis look, which is not unlike the Ralph Lauren look with an added dash of youth and American sexiness. Casual sportswear; large long jackets topping easy trousers and the occasional hint of plunge blouse. Natural fibres, lovely linens, neutral hues.

🦔 **RALPH LAUREN, see Shops**

ZORAN, 214 Sullivan St, NY 10012 ☎ (212) 674 6087

Zoran is understatement personified, the very zero line of underexaggeration. A cashmere slip of a skirt, a swansdown sweater. *"It's a whole dress ethic, a purist's dream, simple shapes in top-quality luxury fabrics"* – **Liz Smith**. *"Once you get the habit you can't kick it – he's an addiction"* – **Eleanor Lambert.**

Young Designers

ANGEL ESTRADA at Bergdorf-Goodman, see Shops The American answer to Galliano or Gigli. Born in Barcelona, he blends Euro and US styles. The swathes, drapes and softness are there, but clothes are briefer, sexier.

🦔 **CARMELO POMODORO, 575 7th Ave, NY 10018** ☎ **(212) 398 9116** Along with Kors, a new name in the Klein/Karan vein of svelte city dressing. Sporty, elegant, casual daywear – an integrated collection of mix 'n' match co-ordinates. His ideal is sophisticated 1950s à la Audrey Hepburn.

CAROLYNE ROEHM, 8th Fl, 550 7th Ave, NY 10018 ☎ **(212) 921 0399** Oscar de la Renta's former assistant, now wowing the best-dressed set. *"Wonderful, the new hot stuff. She's doing beautiful creations, for both day and evening, but her strength is cocktail and evening wear. Magnificent cuts, very feminine, lots of Lessage-style French beading. She designs*

> **66** *The Americans are the masters of relaxed sportswear – that is the biggest contribution of America to the fashion industry* **99**
>
> 🦔 ANIKO GAAL

for the thin, elegant, rich woman" – **Aniko Gaal.**

DAVID CAMERON, 162 W 21st St, NY 10011 ☎ (212) 807 8157
New, zany, exciting designer is one to watch. He places fun bright colours with classics – electric blue with black – and zips galore: zipped ski pants, short biker jackets with side zips, short zippy velour dresses. Snappy trouser suits too. NB Has been in and out of business . . .

ISAIA, 240 W 38th St, NY¢ 10018 ☎ (212) 302 5396
Young, sophisticated body-conscious dressing that doubles up for day or evening. *"Witty and spirited, young, contemporary. You have to have a good figure to wear the clothes, but they're fabulous"* – **Aniko Gaal.**

JOAN VASS, 117 E 29th St, 10010 ☎ (212) 213 0405
All kinds of knitwear for all the family. *"She's just coming into focus"* recommends eagle-eyed **Eleanor Lambert.**

👤 **MICHAEL KORS, 148 W 28th St, 6th Fl, NY 10001 ☎ (212) 620 4677**

Back again after a hiccup best forgotton is the man everyone is talking about, a radical shock to the New York system. Based in the SoHo warehouse that was Andy Warhol's Factory (he was a great friend and influence), Sprouse's shop is laid out thus: on the ground floor, S label jeans and minis (under $150); next, Sprouse label post-punk clothes ($150-$400); top floor, Stephen Sprouse deluxe label ($300-$3,500). *"It's great fun, all done up in silver. I love his stuff"* – **Tama Janowitz.** Arty, pop-y, punky, subversive gear – stre-e-e-etch leopard-print leggings, micro-minis, bondage jewellery. *"He's very avant-garde, more like the London school"* – **Bill Blass.**

HATS

FRANK OLIVE, 134 W 37th St, 9th Fl, NY 10018 ☎ (212) 947 6655
Ladylike, classy, elegant hats from an enduring head-master.

JAY LORD HATTERS, 30 W 39th St, NY 10018 ☎ (212) 221 8941
The only place for men to go, Stateside. Tom Wolfe, he of the

New York with immense success. Hat with style and bravado, but never outrageous. She's designed for Calvin Klein and Perry Ellis, and did Rifat Ozbek's way-out sombreros.

JEWELLERY

A LA VIELLE RUSSIE, 781 5th Ave, NY 10022 ☎ (212) 752 1727
Wartski's counterpart across the Atlantic – a fabulous cache of Russian works of art and antique jewels, particularly Fabergé fantasies.

ANGELA CUMMINGS AT BLOOMINGDALES, 1000 3rd Ave, NY 10021 ☎ (212) 355 5900
Sleek modern jewellery in mainly silver and gold. Geometric shapes with wonderful smooth semi-precious inlays.

ERIC BEAMON, 218 W 37th St, NY 10018 ☎ (212) 947 4791
Trendy jeweller of the moment. He's done bead curtain belts for Jasper Conran, designs for Calvin Klein, Oscar de la Renta and nearly all the American greats; weighed-down charm bracelets and wacky things on ropes.

> 66 *The best hat America has ever produced is the baseball cap. It's a perfect design, like a Balenciaga, or an Olivetti typewriter. It's efficient, it's flattering and it's reasonably easy to make* 99
>
> 👤 STEPHEN JONES

Young (aged 29) purveyor of the New York Look. Sassy, sexy executive elegance for the (petite) yuppie (stretching to a size 12 was a compromise). Wool, lycra and jersey daywear; tailored jumpsuits, jackets galore. He has a penchant for blacks, browns, mustard and navy – smart tones that mean business. His philosophy is similar to Jean Muir's – a minimal wardrobe of good co-ordinating pieces that can be dressed up or down.

👤 **STEPHEN SPROUSE, 99 Wooster St, NY 10012 ☎ (212) 966 2880**

flamboyant fedora, comes here, as do Richard Avedon, Joseph Papp and Miles Davis. All manner of headgear from top hats, bowlers and deerstalkers to 10-gallon cowboys and a few plucky women's hats.

MAEVE CARR, 241 W 36th St, NY 10018 ☎ (212) 714 9140
Whimsical witticisms to set on your head. She also designs in different mode for Donna Karan. At Saks, too.

PATRICIA UNDERWOOD, 265 W 40th St, NY 10018 ☎ (212) 840 6934
A British designer working in

👤 **FRED LEIGHTON, 773 Madison Ave, NY 10021 ☎ (212) 288 1872**
The best period jewellers in the world for late-19th- and 20th-century well-wrought blockbuster rocks. Lots of estate jewellery. They sold the serpent bracelet of gold, opal, enamel and diamonds that Mucha designed and Fouquet made for Sarah Bernhardt as Cleopatra – a snip at pushing a million Swiss francs. If you escape without spending over $50,000 you've done yourself proud. The best jewellers, according to **Mariuccia Mandelli.**

HARRY WINSTON, 718 5th Ave, NY 10019
☎ (212) 245 2000; at Trump Tower, see Shops
Knockout rocks. You come to the Grand Salon more for these stupendous stones and classic styles than for innovative design. The Petit Salon in Trump Tower has less grand, more practical pieces.

JAMES ROBINSON, 15 E 57th St, NY 10022
☎ (212) 752 6166
Elegant East Side jewellers, more like a miniature department store. The very best period pieces from all over the world. *"A venerable old jewellers, but upstairs in James II they have a pot pourri of less expensive things, mostly from England"* – **Bill Blass.**

JAY FEINBERG, 42 W 39th St, NY 10018 ☎ (212) 575 8474
Creative decorative pieces, some faux, some semi-precious stones, some the real McCoy. *"He's a very talented guy"* – **Aniko Gaal.** Stocked at Saks, Bergdorf-Goodman, etc.

KENNETH JAY LANE, Trump Tower, 725 5th Ave, NY 10018 ☎ (212) 868 1780; **250A Columbus Ave, NY 10023** ☎ (212) 580 5263
King of costume jewellery, and a sparkling society figure himself. *"He is a friend, and I've been a customer for 20 years. I go there for presents. Being so busy I have little time to shop, so I just buy a dozen necklaces here"* – **Helen Gurley Brown.** Some of his most famous falsies adorned the wrists, neck and earlobes of the high priestess of style, Diana Vreeland.

ROBERT LEE MORRIS GALLERY, 409 W Broadway, NY 10013 ☎ (212) 431 9405; **ARTWEAR GALLERIES, 456 W Broadway** ☎ (212) 673 2000
Sleekly understated works of art to wear pinned to your chest or around your neck, designed by RLM and other artists. *"Very good. His jewellery is very modern, rather organic"* – **Ken Lane.** *"I love his stuff down at Artwear"* – **Tama Janowitz.**

TIFFANY, 727 5th Ave, NY 10022 ☎ (212) 755 8000
A legend in its own breakfast time. Anything with the Tiffany stamp is still a status symbol. Exclusives on designers Elsa Peretti (silver abstracts) and Paloma Picasso (chunky pieces with socking jewels of mixed colours). **Jackie Collins** thinks her designs are wonderful. So does **Bob Payton**: *"Invest in Paloma Picasso today if you want to create wealth for future generations. But any silver trinket in a powder-blue box that says Tiffany is worth twice the amount."* **Barry Humphries** goes a-prezzie-buying here too. So does **Helen Gurley Brown**, *"for expensive presents – for weddings."*

VERONIQUE CARTIER at Fred Leighton, 773 Madison Ave, NY 10021
☎ (212) 288 1872
Side by side with the Victoriana and Art Deco at Fred Leighton are ravishingly bejewelled modern pieces by Veronique, granddaughter of *the* Louis Cartier. She fashions rubies, diamonds, mother-of-pearl and startling marriages of sapphire and black steel (more expensive than gold), and signs them VC for victory.

LINGERIE

See also **Calvin Klein.**

ORA FEDER, 171 Madison Ave, NY 10016
☎ (212) 532 9236
The most exclusive lingerie in the USA. Exquisite silken smoothies and peignoir sets in heavy, creamy silk. Very Jean Harlow, biased cuts and sensational fabrics.

WIFE MISTRESS, 1044 Lexington Ave, NY 10021
☎ (212) 570 9529
Lingerie as 'cruise wear' or 'lounge wear'; a demure line in cashmere and silk kaftans, chemises and swimwear – all for wife, presumably. For mistress, bustiers in silk brocade or velvet, silk tuxedo pyjamas.

SHIRTS AND TIES

A SULKA, 301 Park Ave, NY 10022 ☎ (212) 980 5226
Fabulous silk treasure house, famed for their dressing gowns, bespoke and off-the-peg shirts, ties and underwear. They supplied Robert de Niro with his silk boxers for *The Untouchables*. They do a tie in 18ct gold thread for show-offs. Blazers and menswear too.

PEC, 45 W 57th St, NY 10019 ☎ (212) 755 0758
Famed far and wide for handmade shirts of the best quality, with mother-of-pearl buttons. All the US top cats get theirs here – Tom Wolfe, Leonard Bernstein, Dan Rather, Ernest and Julio Gallo and Laurence Rockefeller.

SHOES

BASS WEEJUNS, at major stores and shoe shops
The original and only penny loafers. The New England set love them.

BELGIAN SHOES, 60 E 56th St, NY 10022 ☎ (212) 755 7372
A men's shoe shop started up by Henri Bendel's nephew. Shiny dandy dance pumps with grosgrain bows and excellent made-to-measure monogrammed slippers.

ROGER VIVIER, 965 Madison Ave, NY 10021
☎ (212) 249 4866
The world's first and only Vivier shop – up till now Vivier has come to your feet via couturiers such as Christian Dior ('twas he who did the perfect baroque beaded, sequinned and bejewelled evening slippers in cut velvets and embroidered satin for Dior in the '50s). All the shoes, bags and scarves are designed by the spry, ingenious 81-year-old Vivier. Diana Vreeland adores her Viviers and gives cast-offs to the Met.

SUSAN BENNIS WARREN EDWARDS, 440 Park Ave, NY 10022 ☎ (212) 755 4197
Swanlike evening slippers, chintzy summer mules with

FASHION AND SHOPPING

fan-pleated fronts, scalloped fantasies in crisp, light shoe leather. **Margaux Hemingway** buys here.

VITTORIO RICCI, 645 Madison Ave, NY 10022 ☎ (212) 593 5255; **404 Columbus Ave** ☎ (212) 874 2830; **1370 Ave of the Americas** ☎ (212) 247 4630 Footwork for men and women, No 1 for **Stephen Jones**. The shop has its own designers, and shoes are fashioned in Italy.

SHOPS

ABERCROMBIE & FITCH, South Street Seaport, 199 Water St, NY 10038 ☎ (212) 809 9000 The place to be kitted out for your Hemingway-esque safari. Bush jackets and other cool garb for hot climes, custom-made in their own cloth. Also sporting books, writing instruments, antique and contemporary prints and desk accessories. One of **Harvey Goldsmith**'s favourites for clothes and one of **Mariuccia Mandelli**'s for presents.

🐾 **BARNEYS, 106 7th Ave, NY 10014** ☎ (212) 929 9000 *"The best store in the world. Fabulous, beautiful, precious. It also has the best in-store restaurant with the best seafood salad – oh my God you could die for it!"* – **Stephen Jones**. Once a men's discount store, now booming chic. Upmarket, young, where all the art/design/music/film types shop. The women's store adjacent is stacked with European designer labels. *"They buy quite differently from other shops and I always prefer their taste"* – **Anouska Hempel**. *"Like Bergdorf's, another hot store"* – **Bill Blass**. And so says **Harvey Goldsmith**.

🐾 **BERGDORF-GOODMAN, 754 5th Ave, NY 10019** ☎ (212) 753 7300 A sizzling fashion-conscious store, switched on to all the latest and best designers, and *"particularly hot at the moment"* – **Bill Blass**. Brilliant eclectic buying, beautifully laid out, and *"the chic-est store for window displays"* – **Bruce Oldfield**. *"I love it – it has a tremendous assortment"* – **Diane Freis**. *"Terrific,"* adds **Helen Gurley Brown**. **Stanley Marcus**'s best store in NY.

BIJAN, 699 5th Ave, NY 10022 ☎ (212) 758 7500 The ace menswear design and marketing phenomenon. *"The most innovative, electric and, at the same time, classic designer. He combines all those elements and adds a European and Middle Eastern flavour, but he is a classicist"* – **Eleanor Lambert**. Classics include a $2,000-plus prêt-à-porter suit with free bullet-proof lining. Bijan men include King Hussein II, King Juan Carlos, Roger Moore, Julio Iglesias, Sammy Davis Jr and Jack Nicholson. You'll know if

they're wearing a Bijan shirt – the third button down is a different colour.

BLOOMINGDALE'S, 59th St and Lexington Ave, NY 10022 ☎ (212) 705 2000 This store is a New York landmark, almost a block long. *"Fascinating and very avant-garde. It is and has been the true leader in New York for a long time"* – **Ken Lane**. *"Always a great store"* – **Harvey Goldsmith**. Where **Bruce Oldfield** marches to keep his feet happy: *"It's brilliant! I've spent about $200 there on socks."*

BROOKS BROTHERS, 346 Madison Ave, NY 10017 ☎ (212) 682 8800 An institution for American men's classics, where preps grow up to be smart financial boys. The classic button-down Oxford shirt is their bestseller. The full kit – colourful cricket-style jerseys, cotton knits, off-the-peg suits and separates. *"I buy my shoes in a very complicated way: I buy them at Brooks Bros. They are all English made, but they won't*

❝ *The current trend in shopping is a big reaction against big stores. People find it confusing and uncomfortable going into them. We live in a time when we prefer the attention you get in smaller shops* ❞

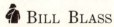 BILL BLASS

tell me by whom" – **Lord Gowrie**. The equivalent in toned-down women's wear too.

CHARIVARI, W 57th St, 10019 ☎ (212) 333 4040; branches at 2307 and 2339 Broadway, and on Columbus The ultra-modern, trendy face of fashion. An exclusive, well-edited batch of mainly European designers, men's and women's collections. Mick Jagger and Jerry Hall often drop in to the Charivari Workshop on 81st St.

– **Loyd Grossman**. Howsabout a solar-powered pith helmet (the fan on the front will keep you cool on those tiresome safaris down Madison Avenue), or an Ultimate Golf Caddy – a hovercraft for two at $7,995. **Dudley Moore** loves the branch in Beverly Hills: *"It has all the best devices that are of no use to anyone but are quite spectacularly good!"*

HENRI BENDEL, 10 W 57th St, NY 10019 ☎ (212) 247 1100 The original 'street of shops',

If you can brave the Bronx, you can cash in on superb designer clothes at half price.

LORD & TAYLOR, 424 5th Ave, NY 10018 ☎ (212) 391 3344 *"The best for typical American merchandise; good because it has so many stores across the country"* – **Bill Blass**. All the major designers, from de la Renta to Lauren. Also furniture, china, silver, etc.

MACY'S, 151 W 34th St, NY 10001 ☎ (212) 695 4400 The Western world's biggest department store, spreading over 2 million sq ft. Although it's not quite in the ranks of the prestigious Bs (Bergdorf's, Bendel's et al) it has its fair share of chi-chi browser-friendly designer boutiques and many other in-store accoutrements.

MARTHA, 475 Park Ave, NY 10022 ☎ (212) 753 1511 *"One of the best for women's wear. A specialty shop which does a fabulous business"* – **Bill Blass**. Successful, selective New York style. *The* store for anyone who is anyone. Martha collects a pantheon of top names – Bill Blass, Carolina Herrera, Valentino . . .

PAUL STUART, 350 Madison Ave, NY 10022 ☎ (212) 682 0320 Upbeat, fashion-conscious classics for men. *"Where the true New Yorker goes. His clothes are the most classic American styles. He still does the natural shoulder"* – **Bill Blass**. Also the best braces.

SAKS FIFTH AVENUE, 611 5th Ave, NY 10022 ☎ (212) 753 4000 The best-dressed bunch teeter in for the really smart clothes by famous European and American designers. *"Second to none. I like it because it's not so frenetic. I can always find someone to wait on me"* – **Helen Gurley Brown**. *"It's a big store with the view of a specialty shop"* – **Bill Blass**.

TRUMP TOWER, 725 5th Ave, NY 10022

Polo: FIRST IN THE FIELD

RALPH LAUREN/POLO, 867 Madison Ave, NY 10021 ☎ (212) 606 2100. If we're talking design/marketing phenomena, Lauren has to win the prize. Presenting the prêt-à-porter English country-house look. Home decorations and clothes for him, her and the kids mingle in this multi-million-dollar French neo-classical mansion. It's homy in the grand idiom with striking entrance, fireplace and Scarlett O'Hara staircase. *"He's amazing. He conjures up an entire way of life, that's what I love about him. Each time I go to New York I look into every corner of this amazing building, and it's always been rearranged. Everything's so pretty and inspiring and only he could have done it. He's shown us all how to appreciate real classics"* – **Liz Smith**. Paper your walls, chintz your windows, clad yourself in all-American rough 'n' tough safari savannah suits and bush shirts. Polo is his runaway-success casual menswear line. His women's wear is currently making hot fashion news. Beautiful low-key separates – narrow pants and turtle-necks topped with sheepskin waistcoats; glam evening wear – shimmering satin bustiers with flowing trousers. *"There's no questioning the success of Ralph Lauren's shop. This and Paul Stuart are the top 2 for menswear, both very American in their overall outlook"* – **Bill Blass**. *"Flourishing. I admire him."* – **Eleanor Lambert**. **Viscountess Rothermere**, Christian Lacroix and **Lord Lichfield** are Ralph-aelites.

HAMMACHER SCHLEMMER, 147 E 57th St, NY 10022 ☎ (212) 421 9000 Cult home of high-class gadgetry. *"They have the best and latest things. Sunglasses, headphones, hi-fi, percolators, solar-powered lights, croquet mallets . . . everything is tested and tested to make sure it's the best of its kind"* – **Lord Lichfield**. *"Wonderful, a sort of old-fashioned gadget pedlar"*

all cobblestones and individual boutiques, makes this more intimate and inviting than the usual stony-faced department store. It's **Lord Lichfield**'s first stop for the best pot-pourri, Agraria, and for wonderful writing paper. **Jean Muir** leaks that it has the best hose.

LOEHMANN'S, 91 W Fordham Rd, NY 10468 ☎ (212) 295 4100

☎ (212) 832 2000
Mr Trump's shrine to shopping
is 10 floors of chi-chi shops in a
knockout atrium setting with
Tarzanian waterfall that
plunges dramatically down to
oblivion beside the coffee shop.

TAILOR

**WILLIAM FIORAVANTI, 45
W 57th St, NY 10019**
☎ **(212) 355 1540**
The best tailor in America. 30
craftsmen hand-handle suits for
US captains of industry.

SAN FRANCISCO

JEWELLERY

**BARBARA WITT, 5950
Grizzly Peak Blvd, Oakland,
CA 94611** ☎ **(415) 547 3300**
Innovative designer who
interweaves carved or rough
semi-precious stones (lapis
lazuli, malachite, etc) with fine
– coloured cord macramé work.
*"Her necklaces are one of a
kind and are sought-after by
women who know they will
have great value some day.
Everything she does is on
commission. One of her fans is
Marella Agnelli [who has a
fabulous tiger's-eye necklace],
a woman of wonderful taste"* –
Eleanor Lambert.

SHOPS

**GUMPS, 250 Post St, CA
94108** ☎ **(415) 982 1616**
A smart old favourite store.
*"They carry the most beautiful
little antiques and home
furnishings, clothes and
everything. It's a true specialty
store in the olde-worlde
manner"* – **Aniko Gaal.**
Jeremiah Tower is keen too.

**I MAGNIN, 135 Stockton St,
CA 94108** ☎ **(415) 362 2100**
The first branch in the ever-
expanding group of stores. A
broad sweep of top designer
clothes and sportswear;
intuitive buying. Exclusive
Chanel in-store boutique, also
Ungaro, Valentino. A phalanx
of 'personal shoppers' will

organize your wardrobe for
you, sometimes bringing entire
collections to your house.

**MACY'S, 5th Fl, 790 Market
St, CA 94102** ☎ **(415) 397 3333**
A particularly vast branch of
Macy's known especially for the
men's department – probably
the largest in the country,
stacked on 4 floors. Wade
through Armani, Perry Ellis,
Polo, swimwear and top
designer farragoes, tuxedos
and other night-time dapperies.

**WILKES BASHFORD, 375
Sutter St, CA 94108**
☎ **(415) 986 4380**
Tops for men's garb – beautiful,
expensive suits and a funkier
department showing Gaultier,
Basile, Matsuda, Brioni and

Alexander Julian (*"my absolute
most favourite designer. He
designs the fabrics and the
clothes . . . such attention to
detail in colours and fabrics"* –
Steve Podborski). **Jeremiah
Tower** likes the store. The
women's dept is big on evening
wear. A bar on every floor.

WASHINGTON

JEWELLERY

**HELGA O, 2715 M St NW, DC
20007** ☎ **(202) 338 8739**
*"Helga Orfila's gems are
everyone's dream of faux
jewels. Exquisite selection"* –
Aniko Gaal. Also a shop at the
Willard hotel.

🕵 **Buzzzzzzzzz** The **English country look**.
Arntcha sick of it?!?! No? Right, top antique dealer **J Garvin
Mecking**'s your man. Based at 72 E 11th St, NY 10003
☎ (212) 677 4316, he *"specializes in English things, which
are still what Americans prefer. One of the best shops for
presents"* – **Bill Blass** 🕵 . . . . . . **Anglomania 2:** old
English country hand **Mario Buatta** says, *"We have had a
huge influx of young girls who have started shops that resem-
ble Colefax & Fowler . . .* **Lexington Avenue** *is filled with
them. There's* **Charlotte Moss, R. Brooke** *(after Rupert B),*
Lennox Antiques, Trevor Potts *. . . yours truly has been
doing the English country look since 1963 . . ."* 🕵 . . . . . .
Chic cheeks: **Kiehl's Pharmacy**, 109 3rd Ave, NY 10003
☎ (212) 475 3400 makes the best **bespoke make-up**. 135
years old, the shop has a swift and not-too-expensive lip (nail,
cheek, etc) service for *"excellent cosmetic products"* –
Marchesa Fiamma di San Giuliano Ferragamo 🕵 . . . . . .
For presents with a modicum of 'harmony and balance'
go-intu **Sointu**, 20 E 69th St, NY 10021 ☎ (212) 570 9449, a
showcase for contemporary and **modern classic designs**:
watches, clocks, etched crystal, porcelain, sterling silver
accessories, jewellery and table settings. *"The best gift shop"*
– **Stanley Marcus** 🕵 . . . . . . **Bookwise** contributor
Margaux Hemingway says: *"I like bookshops. The best is
Books & Co on Madison Avenue."* **Tama Janowitz** likes
Shakespeare & Co.

★ ★ ★ ★ ★ ★ ★ ★ ★ ★ ★ ★ ★ ★ ★ ★ ★ ★ ★

FASHION AND SHOPPING

SHOPS

**GARFINCKELS, 1401 F St,
DC 20004, ☎ (202) 628 7730**
The finest selection of
European and American
designers – Lacroix, Mugler,
Versace, Ferré, Lagerfeld,
Ungaro, the exclusive on
Krizia, plus Chanel and Fendi
boutiques; Carolyne Roehm, de
la Renta, Karan et al. Huge fur
salon. Old-world setting with
the best modern service. Best
men's store, too – there's
Valentino, Ungaro, Polo,
Armani and Byblos sportswear,
Charvet accessories, and Ferré
Studio. Also cosmetics, scent,
home furnishings and smart
table ware.

**RALEIGHS, 1133
Connecticut Ave NW, DC
20004 ☎ (202) 785 7000 and
branches**
The best source of menswear –
all the top international
designers. Raleighs now owns
Garfinckels. Best career
woman's selections too.

**SAKS JANDEL, 5510
Wisconsin Ave, Chevy Chase,
MD 20815 ☎ (301) 652 2250;
SAKS AT WATERGATE, 2522
Virginia Ave, DC 20037
☎ (202) 337 4200**
"Known for the finest of furs" –
Aniko Gaal. But that's not all:
there's Valentino and Saint
Laurent Rive Gauche
boutiques, a new shop, Right
Stuff, for young American
designers, plus Gucci, Chanel,
Lagerfeld and sportswear lines.
As good as the NY Saks.

Australia

MELBOURNE

DESIGNERS

**ADELE PALMER, 671
Chapel St, S Yarra, Vic 3141
☎ (03) 240 0611**
Palmer's keynote is an
insouciant style. Casual printed
cottons, sportswear and the
best jeans in Australia, Jag. All

the American film-star tough
guys 'n' gals like Redford,
Newman and Cher wear Jag.

**PRUE ACTON, Shop 10, 12
Bridge Rd, Richmond, Vic
3121 ☎ (03) 429 4122**
An original Australian
motivator in the field of
fashion, she has been awarded
an OBE. Designer basics for
day and evening: unstructured
summer suits with long gauzy
skirts; plentiful, monotone
appliqués and 'cornelli' work – a
form of buttonhole edging.

HATS

**PETER JAGO, 811 High St,
Armadale, Vic 3143
☎ (03) 509 0501**
Tailors a fine head. He does the
hats for **Robert Burton**'s
fashion shows (RB thinks he's
brilliant) and has crowned Lady
Fairfax and Judy Hirst. Jago
was commissioned to design
hats – some inspired by
Australian wild flowers – for
the Bicentennial Expo.

**WENDY MEAD HATS, Shop
11, 521 Toorak Rd, Toorak,
Vic 3142 ☎ (03) 240 9093**
Romantic, extravagant
headgear, always one step
ahead of fashion. Ready-
to-wear and custom-made one-
offs. She makes about 300 hats
for the Melbourne Cup, to
adorn heads such as the
Baillieus, Myers, Lady Stephen
and Tamie Fraser, wife of
ex-PM Malcolm. *"Even better
than before – if that's possible"*
– **Lillian Frank.**

JEWELLERY

**KOZMINSKY GALLERIES,
421 Bourke St, Vic 3000
☎ (03) 670 1277**
Fab trad source of antique
silver, crystal and estate pieces
from the last 120 years.

LINGERIE

**LA DONNA AT SHOP 3, 521
Toorak Rd, Toorak, Vic 3142
☎ (03) 241 4172**
Some of the best little silkies in
town. An exquisite treasury of

silk lingerie and resort wear by
Armonia and La Perla, plus
nightwear by both.

SHOES

**EVELYN MILES, Shop 1,
Tok-H Centre, 459 Toorak Rd,
Toorak, Vic 3142
☎ (03) 241 5844**
The best women's designer
footwear from Gianni Barbarto,
Tokio Kumagai, Robert
Clergerie, Walter Steiger,
Versace, Stephane Kélian,
Dior, Pancaldi, Charles
Jourdan, Valentino – all the
smartypants labels for real
tarting-up occasion shoes. Also
leggy accessories by Chantal
Thomass and hats by Philippe
Model.

**McCLOUD'S, 120 Queen St,
Vic 3000 ☎ (03) 673386**
Men's shoe shop that looks like
it hasn't been decorated
(unwisely) since the '30s.
However, it's a stomping
ground for English, Italian and
sturdy German shoes in kid and
hand-tooled leather for the
footwise gourmet.

SHOPS

**EMME BOUTIQUE, 507
Chapel St, S Yarra, Vic 3141
☎ (03) 241 5116**
Best imported silks, cottons
and linens from Europe and a
zany bunch of fashion lines by
Jean-Paul Gaultier, Dorothée
Bis, Piero Panchetti, Carla
Radaelli, Nigel Preston and
Charles Jourdan.

**GEORGES, 162 Collins St,
Vic 3000 ☎ (03) 630411**
This genteel establishment is
No 1 in Melbourne, now that
Figgins Diorama has closed.
Long-standing staff and equally
dyed-in-the-wool customers of
old-style elegance. The loos are
a paradisal vision with free
telephones, old sofas,
magazines, flowers, tinkling
chandeliers. Valentino, Saint
Laurent, Ungaro, Genny,
Montana, Kenzo, Rykiel,
Laurel and Liberty scarves.
Musical ensembles play on the
ground floor. A favourite store
of **Robert Burton.**

❝ Melbourne is the ultimate for fashion. The best young designers are there. The weather is more conducive to serious dressing – in Sydney it's an effort to keep cool; you take off rather than add ❞

 JANE ROARTY

HENRY BUCK'S, 320 Collins St, Vic 3000 ☎ (03) 670 9951 and branches
Men's clothes live happily in an environment of Persian carpets, polished timber and sniffy staff. A strictly classical, off-the-peg wardrobe for the conservative man. The Mecca for bow ties.

IPANEMA, 91 Bourke St, Vic 3004 ☎ (03) 654 6114
Small, stylish boutique, excellent for chic working-girl one-offs. Divine linen and cotton daywear; smart shoes and belts. One of **Robert Burton**'s favourite shops.

LE LOUVRE, 74 Collins St, Vic 3000 ☎ (03) 650 1300
Very upmarket and long-established place where formidable Melbourne matrons hoover up the best in European fashion – imports only. Glitterbug evening wear and lavish wedding gowns.

SABA, 131 Bourke St, Vic 3004 ☎ (03) 654 6176
Amid on-line visual input from fash videos of the European shows, you can sort through supercool selections from Yohji Yamamoto, Comme des Garçons, Jasper Conran and Saba himself (who produces wonderful tailored wear).

STAGGERS DIFFUSION, 37 Toorak Rd, S Yarra, Vic 3141 ☎ (03) 267 7850
Now owned by Joseph Saba (of Saba), this surreally named shop sells his own clothes and a sharp line in young international designer wear. Japanese and Italian shoes.

WAYNE WATKINS, 403 Chapel St, S Yarra, Vic 3141 ☎ (03) 241 7980
Where to get spruce, Bruce. Best in Melbourne for men's designer classics, with deeply stylish moments. Savile Row meets Milano.

PERTH
SHOES

SCARPERS, Shop 13, City Arcade, WA 6000 ☎ (09) 321 6941
The most eclectic imported feet in Perth – Robert Clergerie, Christian Dior, Rayne, Sonja Bettine, Charles Jourdan, Sergio Rossi and further Italian-crafted showy shoes.

SHOPS

COUNTRY ROAD, 162 Murray St, WA 6000 ☎ (09) 383 3893
Conservative clothes for the Aussie Sloane Ranger – dateless polished tailored gear, city separates, weekend layabout garb.

ELLE, 56 Weld St, Nedlands, WA 6009 ☎ (09) 386 6868
Takes fashion in a broad stride from classy conservatism à la YSL through to the avant-garde beatitudes of the Japs via Bruce Oldfield, Giorgio Armani and Lagerfeld. Hats, shoes, bags and costume jewellery.

R M WILLIAMS, Shop 38, Carillon Centre, Hay St Mall, WA 6000 ☎ (09) 321 7786
'The Original Bushman's Outfitters', pride of Australia, producer of some of the nation's most coveted exports. Drovers' moleskin trousers (moleys), graziers' and stockmen's shirts, kangaroo-hide plaited belts,

Akubra hats – the wide-brimmed bushie version of a trilby, and the famous Aussie oilskin Drizabone (equivalent of the Barbour). For bushboys and townies with outback swagger. About 50 stores across the continent and by mail order.

SYDNEY
DESIGNERS

CARLA ZAMPATTI, 435A Kent St, NSW 2000 ☎ (02) 264 8244
Zampatti has the Australian fashion scene wrapped up with her draped silk evening dresses and breezy day clothes. Olivia Newton-John's fave.

CHRISTOPHER ESSEX, 51 Flinders St, Darlinghurst, NSW 2010 ☎ (02) 331 3767
Razzle-dazzle come-and-get-me sequinned ballgowns. Glitterati, walk this way ... Also extravagant, feminine, frothy wedding dresses.

GEORGE GROSS, c/o Viva by George Gross and Harry Who, 19-27 Cross St Plaza, Double Bay, NSW 2028 ☎ (02) 322485
Gross likes making clothes to make women feel female – sexy and sensuous evening wear, a shade OTT. By day he is more classic and tailored, using natural fibres. The look stretches to silk jersey body suits and a lavish amount of leather and suede.

❝ I hope that the future of design in Australia is always going to be colourful, because colour represents optimism and freedom. The young designers are now just starting to stand on their own two feet and not mimic Europeans ❞

JENNY KEE

FASHION AND SHOPPING

HARRY THURSTON, Gr Fl, 91 Reservoir St, Surry Hills, NSW 2010 ☎ (02) 212 3472
One of the best menswear designers in Australia. Harry's a great character. He designs to an easy-breezy Italian tune, a sexy and bang-up-to-the-minute silhouette. Subtle and highly developed colour sense (lavenders and greys, etc). *"He goes from strength to strength"* – Skye Macleod.

HARRY WHO, c/o Viva by George Gross and Harry Who, 19-27 Cross St Plaza, Double Bay, NSW 2028 ☎ (02) 322485
Who? You may well ask if you're not from Down Under ... but Australians are just wild about Harry. A younger clientele than his partner – sculptural linens and silks for women, plus casual, stylish menswear with an easy beachboy-goes-big-city feel.

JENNY KEE, Flamingo Park, Suite 102, 2F, Strand Arcade, George St, NSW 2000 ☎ (02) 231 3027
Dynamic knitwear that has knocked the fashion world askew. An icon of originality (and much copied), her look is stupendous, bold, with rhythmic patterns in vibrant colours. Some knits are the ready-to-wear equivalent of a Ken Done painting, abounding with multicoloured squiggles of Australian images. Her fabric prints on cotton and silk have the same strength.

JILL FITZSIMON, Shop 2, Cosmopolitan Centre, Knox St, Double Bay, NSW 2028 ☎ (02) 327 7887; 591 Military Rd, Mosman, NSW 2088 ☎ (02) 960 3531
One of Sydney's top designers, she's made her name in evening wear – glorious one-of-a-kind numbers. *"Fantastic silks and appliqués. Also lovely tailored suits for the executive woman"* – Skye Macleod.

LINDA JACKSON, 52-54 Shepherd St, Chippendale, NSW 2007 ☎ (02) 699 4411
Arty-smarty bush couture using that key Aussie talent for impressionistic printing and moody painting on fabric. Best-

🌴 Australia's Best 🌴

DESIGNERS	
1	**ROBERT BURTON**
2	**GEORGE GROSS**
3	**TRENT NATHAN**
4	**JENNY KEE**
5	**WEISS**
6	**HARRY WHO**

dressed clothes-horse Alexandra Joel loves her things. See also Jewellery.

ROBERT BURTON, 104 Bathurst St, NSW 2000 ☎ (02) 267 2877
Australia's answer to couture, with all the attendant pampering service one would expect. Expensive, one-off designs for day and evening; good fabrics, impeccable cuts. A line in ready-to-wear and great accessories too. *"Classically wonderful winter range, absolutely to die for"* – Skye Macleod.

STUART MEMBERY, 188 Chalmers St, Surry Hills, NSW 2010 ☎ (02) 319 2766
High-profile trendsetter. Young, colourful, stylized clothes that play on an East meets West or some other ethnic theme. He designs the total look for women and men – sporty working gear, weekend clobber, hats, shoes, accessories.

TRENT NATHAN, 220 Henderson Rd, Alexandria, NSW 2015 ☎ (02) 550 3355
Sophisticated exec wear – great tweeds and easy-to-wear fabrics, dolled up with an Aussie sexiness. *"He has refined his image recently, become more Australian. He does wonderful houndstooth jackets"* – Skye Macleod.

WEISS, 277 Crown St, Surry Hills, NSW 2010 ☎ (02) 332 3266
Peter and Adele Weiss are international hits for their top-quality, minimal-styling knitwear (under the Pringle of Scotland label) and separates, served up in a multitude of

colours. They believe fashion should be relevant to Oz, not a rehash of styles from overseas. Shops all over Australia.

WENDY HEATHER, 312 New South Head Rd, Double Bay, NSW 2028 ☎ (02) 328 1831
Wendy is one of the painter-designers. Her original canvas was leather – the sort you wrap around your middle and call a belt. She has now branched out every which way, and designs from head to toe. *"Full of surprises. There's everything from fantastic knitwear to the perfect little black dress"* – Jane Roarty.

HATS

MORAY MILLINERY, 306 Strand Arcade, George St, NSW 2000 ☎ (02) 233 1591
The best milliner in Sydney and one of the best in Australia. Made-to-measure headgear for ladies (and gents), from neat bonnets to wild extravaganzas. *"Still the only place for hats in Sydney"* – Skye Macleod.

JEWELLERY

FINAL DETAIL, Shop 4, 2a Waters Rd, Neutral Bay, NSW 2089 ☎ (02) 902444
Stylish, mainly faux jewellery, from pearl drops to way-out sprays. Imported and Australian designs.

LINDA JACKSON, see Designers
Spellbound by opals, she calls her collection OpaLinda. Magical pieces in the mood of her fabrics. Lucent metals cut like undulating shells, set with great eyes of semi-precious stones; leaves from Australasian trees embalmed in silver or gold (sometimes with a tiny opal tucked in).

ROX GEMS AND JEWELLERY, 31 Strand Arcade, Pitt St, NSW 2000 ☎ (02) 232 7828
Spectacular costume counterfeit, Jezebel jewels and other outrageous ornament, all the way up to real gold and diamonds. Tina Turner, Boy

George, David Bowie and Olivia Newton-John have all been bejewelled at Rox. *"The best jewellery. Wonderful quality, and the most contemporary designs from New York"* – **Jane Roarty**.

LINGERIE

ANNE LEWIN at David Jones, see Shops
Australia's No 1 lingerie designer. *"Her stuff is divine – the most luxurious bits of nothing"* – **Susie Stenmark**. Also has her own shop in The Galleria, Surfers Paradise.

SHIRTS AND TAILORS

CHRIS HAND MADE SHIRTS, 4a Tank Stream Arcade, 175 Pitt St, NSW 2000
☎ **(02) 231 6094**
For just what it says. They're well known and well worth wearing. **Robert Burton** recommends.

J H CUTLER, Level 3, 33 Bligh St, NSW 2000
☎ **(02) 232 7351**
Old-fashioned English-style tailoring. John Cutler is fourth generation in the biz and doing a suit that equals Savile Row in a land bereft of men of the cloth. *"I used to get all my shirts made at Turnbull & Asser, but now J H Cutler is making shirts that are just as good"* – **Leo Schofield**.

SHOES

EDWARD MELLER, 23 Lemon Grove Shopping Centre, Chatswood, NSW 2067
☎ **(02) 419 2747; 77 Knox St, Double Bay, NSW 2028**
☎ **(02) 327 7197**
Well-made, trendy shoes that won't cost an arm and a leg. Annie Lennox trips along here.

PAPOUCCI, Shop 20, Cosmopolitan Centre, Knox St, Double Bay, NSW 2028
☎ **(02) 327 4167; 20 Bay St, Double Bay** ☎ **(02) 328 7722**
For imports (Dior, Charles Jourdan and top Italian lines)

and Australian shoes, it's the best according to **Jane Roarty**.

RAYMOND CASTLES SHOES, 21 Bay St, Double Bay, NSW 2028
☎ **(02) 327 3864**
Fab shoe store, chocker with international designer toelines. Their own range, too, which are carefree designer copies, just as nice and half the price.

SHOPS

CHRISTINE LANTAS, 43 Bay St, Double Bay, NSW 2028 ☎ **(02) 321 048**
A brilliant collection of young designers. *"The selection is huge"* – **Jane Roarty**.

DAVID JONES, Elizabeth St, NSW 2000 ☎ **(02) 266 5544 (and branches in Melbourne, Adelaide and Brisbane)**
Sydney's best and newly glossified store, the Harrods of Australia. An edited and wide-ranging collection of homegrown and foreign-label clothes – the exclusive on Chanel, Rykiel, Versace and Missoni, plus Ungaro and Valentino. Fab menswear department in the Market St branch, for the executive or the sporty or the preppy man – Louis Féraud suits, Country

Road casuals, Cuggi knitwear. The store's recent multi-million-dollar facelift was partly blown on an Italian mountain top, which had to be bought in order to obtain the desired marble (the remainder is dolling up the Adelaide branch). The Food Hall is *the* place for stocking up on goodies. And for **Anne Lewin**, *"the 7th floor is the best place to shop"*.

DORIAN SCOTT'S AUSTRALIAN FASHION DESIGNERS, 105 George St, The Rocks, NSW 2000
☎ **(02) 274090**
Dorian herself knits up fine merino classics but is even better known as the forcing-house for young Aussie talent. Her current stock of about 30 embryonics includes Susie Cooks, Amy Hamilton, Jennifer Layther, Libby Peacock and Christine Wilkie – all of whom do mostly one-offs.

FIVE WAY FUSION, 205 Glenmore Rd, Paddington, NSW 2021 ☎ **(02) 331 2828**
For a shot in the arm of European up-style dressing for men; beautiful imports from Montana, Charvet, Byblos, Armani, Cerruti, Zegna and more of the sleek crowd. *"Because I'm so big, socks and*

handkerchiefs are about the only thing I can buy off-the-peg. I get those here. They have wonderful Italian things" – **Leo Schofield.**

HAMPSHIRE & LOWNDES, 12 Cross St, Double Bay, NSW 2028 ☎ (02) 327 2834; 16 Transvaal Ave, Double Bay
The Laura Ashley of Australia. *"You can get the most wonderful things. Beautiful linen dresses and accessories, lovely linen sheets and lacy pillows"* – **Jane Roarty.**

JOHN LANE, 41 Knox St, Double Bay, NSW 2028 ☎ (02) 327 6198
Lane started at Richard Hunt and is now bringing a smart slice of Europe to Aussie men. Classics that sell to all the smarties – Michael York, Gough Whitlam, **Michael Parkinson, Robert Sangster,** Alan Bond, the Fairfaxes . . .

MARC'S, Shop T, Mid City Centre, 197 Pitt St, NSW 2000 ☎ (02) 232 2948
Top place for men's casual clothes. *"Fantastic for men – terrific American Brooks Brothers type of clothes"* – **Jane Roarty.** New branch at Oxford St, Paddington, too.

MASON'S BOUTIQUE, 45a Bay St, Double Bay, NSW 2028 ☎ (02) 329894
For the most contemporary, switched-on selection of European designers (Gigli et al). *"Very chic. The new little darlings of the fashion industry. Their clothes are very clever, new and young"* – **Anne Lewin. Jane Roarty** is also a Mason's fan.

RICHARD HUNT, 107 Pitt St, NSW 2000 ☎ (02) 232 6633
Classic menswear and beaut bow-ties. *"The best men's shop"* – **Jane Roarty.**

RHONDA PARRY, 19 Cross St, Double Bay, NSW 2028 ☎ (02) 320584
Dressing for the late-Eighties summed up in one small but big-thinking shop. The perfect minimalist formula with Issey, Yohji and the gang, plus Alaïa 5 and other Europeans – which

adds up to the most select fashion shop.

SPORTSGIRL, 13 Knox St, Double Bay, NSW 2028 ☎ (02) 327 6806 and branches
The best middle-range, fast-from-the-factory fashion gear. More-flash-than-cash own-label clobber, from Calvin Klein-style knickers through trend separates to haughty party frocks, and the whole run of accessories. Their smart range goes under the David Lawrence label.

SQUIRE SHOP, 409 New South Head Rd, Double Bay, NSW 2028 ☎ (02) 327 5726
Predominantly menswear (plus a cache of women's designer clothes at the back). Gaultier, Burani, Taverniti, Stone Island. Shirts and suits to measure.

TRELLINI MENS WEAR, 139 Elizabeth St, NSW 2000 ☎ (02) 264 6498
The manful trendspot with clients from Billy Connolly to Sting to Gough Whitlam in outrageous mood to Judy Davis in androgynous mood. Imported designer fandango – Comme des Garçons, Katharine Hamnett, Gaultier, Panchetti. Shirts are made to measure under their own label. **Robert Burton** is a fan.

WORN OUT WEST – RANCHO DE LUXE, 94A Oxford St, Paddington, NSW 2021 ☎ (02) 331 7191
Owned by stylish, suave Graham Webb, who does a unique and knockout line in '40s and '50s filmic nostalgia. He buys in second-hand period cowboy kit from the American Old West. It's Rockabilly, it's James Dean, it's Annie Get Your Gumboots. The only emporium of its kind in the continent.

SWIMWEAR

SPEEDO KNITTING MILLS, 279 Pacific Highway, Artarmon, NSW 2064 ☎ (02) 437 4011
The world's best sporting second skin, solid-gold

Olympic-medal swimwear that now has serious fashion status. Beautiful straightforward but shape-conscious maillots, two-pieces with a finger on the fashion pulse. Paula Yates and an endless list of style-steered strutters swim in a Speedo.

SURF, DIVE 'N' SKI, 466 George St, NSW 2000 ☎ (02) 267 3408
Where surfers get their beach-cred together: Billabong, Quicksilver and 100 per cent Mambo board shorts, T-shirts and Rip Curl wet suits. Other splashy brands are Hot Tuna, Lightning Bolt and Ocean & Earth.

Britain

LONDON
ACCESSORIES

CORNELIA JAMES, 55 New Bond St, W1 ☎ (01) 499 9423/629 2176
Glovemaker to the Queen. Her handsome creations come in silks, satins, leather, lace, unadorned or ornamented, to wrist or elbow, with or without fingers. Made-to-measure extravaganzas too.

J & M DAVIDSON, 4 Grosvenor St, W1 ☎ (01) 493 0068
Brill modern classic belts – in beautiful leather, crocodile, etc. All types of bags (tapestry, canvas with leather trim, trout bags) and goods.

MULBERRY CO, 11-12 Gees Court, St Christoper's Place, W1 ☎ (01) 493 2546
Great English classics – unsurpassed for the country look, solid or squidgy bags (mail bags, satchels, chic little handbags), belts and small leather goods. The total look leans towards preppy rather than Sloane. Good for presents; also a few simple clothes – knits, skirts, shirts and macs.

COUTURIERS

Couture is the big buzz word being bandied around London. Hot it may be, *haute* it isn't. Take it to mean dressy dressing, beautifully made clothes, hand embellishments, personal service. *"Couture is booming in Paris and we are never going to match that. But we have a new breed of couturier in Anouska Hempel and Victor Edelstein, who are doing some wonderful things. There's a new sense of cosmopolitan chic in British couture"* – **Liz Smith.**

♣ —Britain's Best— ♣

	COUTURIERS
1	**BRUCE OLDFIELD**
2	**VICTOR EDELSTEIN**
3	**ALISTAIR BLAIR**
4	**HARDY AMIES**
5	**CATHERINE WALKER**

♣ ALISTAIR BLAIR, at Gallery 28; Harrods, see Shops
Trained in couture Parisienne under Karl Lagerfeld, this Scot has the charmed KL touch. Impeccable collections with hat-that-matches-the-shoes-that-match-the-dress sense of detail. Likes tartan, natch, and is doing a new cashmere range for McGeorge of Scotland. The wardrobes of the Duchess of York, the Princess of Wales and Susannah Constantine boast Blair flair.

ANOUSKA HEMPEL, 2 Pond Place, SW3 ☎ (01) 589 4191
A magnificent midnight-blue showcase for this perfectionist's demi-couture collection, accessories and interior furnishings – from brocade cushions to a Biedermeier sofa. Garments for the salon or an English occasion (Ascot, a wedding, a ball), minimal shoes, maxi hats. *"Her whole shop is an experience, very original; wonderful accessories. Everything she*

touches, *from food at Blakes to fashion, is marvellous"* – **Liz Smith.**

♣ BRUCE OLDFIELD, 27 Beauchamp Place, SW3 ☎ (01) 584 1363
A designer to the Princess of Wales, favourite of everyone. His look is exhibitionist, packed with glitz, glamour and pzazz. Oldfield makes you feel like a *woman.* Short, ruched, ruffled little rustly numbers caught up shamelessly at the back; embroidery, appliqué and other couture detail. Fans **Marie Helvin, Joan Collins, Charlotte Rampling, Shakira Caine** and other international stars love to dress up here.

♣ CATHERINE WALKER, Chelsea Design Company, 65 Sydney St, SW3 ☎ (01) 352 4646
A French designer whose line of dressy day ensembles and structured ballgowns emanate good taste and an inherent sense of chic. Clothes made with care in lovely fabrics. Receiving great press – and patronage from the Princess of Wales. Darling children's clothes too at **46 Fulham Rd, SW3 ☎ (01) 581 8811.**

DAVID FIELDEN, 137 King's Rd, SW3 ☎ (01) 351 1745
"My favourite for evening wear. He hugs the body. If you're thin, he's perfect" – **Sarah Brightman.** Wedding gowns are his speciality.

EMANUEL, 26a Brook St, W1 ☎ (01) 629 5569
The careers of David and Elizabeth Emanuel took off on their big wedding number for Princess Di. Fantasy Scarlett O'Hara ballgowns and wedding dresses are still their couture forte. **Jane Seymour** is their

No 1 fan: *"Everything they do is pure fantasy."* Cocktail wear is shorter, naughtier. At **10 Beauchamp Place, SW3 ☎ (01) 584 4997** is their ready-to-wear collection.

♣ HARDY AMIES, 14 Savile Row, W1 ☎ (01) 734 2436
The Queen's couturier. The collection is now designed by Ken Fleetwood and John Wood, who still do the upper-crust English thing to a nicety, with little tweed suits, the works. Their *grande dame* clientele includes **Betty Kenward** and **Lady Elizabeth Anson**: *"I really do favour him. He gives one first-class attention."*

PATRICIA LESTER, at Harrods; Zanzis; couture ☎ (0873) 3559
Known for her gorgeous gowns of Fortuny-style pleating (only hers are finer, more fluid), plus fabulous hand-printed panné velvets. She's big news in the States – clients include Whitneys, Rockefellers and Vanderbilts, plus Baroness Marie-Hélène de Rothschild and Princess Michael of Kent. Her latest look is more structured – smoking jackets, glamour coats, ballgowns. Also at Lucienne Phillips.

♣ VICTOR EDELSTEIN, 3 Stanhope Mews W, SW7 ☎ (01) 244 7481
Tall, elegant and soigné, he is master of the society ballgown. Lavish but classy dream evening dresses in sensuous, jewel-coloured fabrics; heavenly wedding frocks. *"The best of the English evening-wear designers"* – **Stephen Jones.** Princesses Diana and Michael, Lucy Ferry, Victoria de Rothschild and Lucy Snowdon are among his coterie.

❝ *I've got so many clothes that I just keep bringing out old ones and they look like new. I am filmed the moment I step off the aeroplane, so I cannot arrive looking boggy* **❞**

 BARBARA CARTLAND

DESIGNERS

ANTONY PRICE, 34 Brook St, W1 ☎ (01) 731 0540
Still has a cult rockstar/showbiz following for glam rags. From Marie Antoinette ballgowns to daytime wide-legged trousers. He did the whole look for Bryan Ferry and co and he's one of **Marie Helvin**'s and Jerry Hall's top faves. Now does suits for biz-men.

BENNY ONG, 3 Bentinck Mews, W1 ☎ (01) 487 5954
Charming Singapore-born designer with a sensuous sense of colour. Pampering luscious evening wear and day wear with a glamorous edge. His summer collection was more sculpted than usual, in the Lacroix mould.

EDINA RONAY, 141 King's Rd, SW3 ☎ (01) 352 1085
Chic daywear from little hand-knits grow – Edina's trademark used to be ice-cream cotton knits, Fair Isles (big in TV's *Brideshead* days), bobbled, textured and patterned jerseys. Now her knits have blossomed forth with big blooms. Serious clothes line too – tailored linens, little flared skirts, wool and gabardine suits – those little ensembles that so suit the Duchess of York – expensive looks; good fabrics. *"I think she makes beautiful clothes"* – **Jane Asher.**

GEORGINA GODLEY at Whistles, see Shops
While the rest are Gigli-ing along romantically, she remains cool and intellectual. This is the lady of the Lady-gro (grown-up baby-gro) and other Godley goodies with a message. Minimal, Op Art looks, often muddy colours, fabrics from cotton towelling to silk prints. Arty, fringe clientele; Milan and New York love her.

JASPER CONRAN, 37 Beauchamp Place, SW3 ☎ (01) 589 4243
Still Britain's golden boy – everyone *loves* his polished collections, though tongues wagged over how uncannily similar his spring things were to those of his chum (and successor as Designer of the Year) John Galliano. Almost gone are the strict suits – instead softer tailoring, swirly asymmetry, half-cape jackets. Men's and women's wear for people like Lenny Henry, **Margaux Hemingway** and Paula Yates (he made her shocking red wedding dress). Nell Campbell is devoted to *"naughty little Jasper, who alters clothes to make them more outrageous for me"*. **Liz Smith** approves: *"He is using the best of our heritage with his cashmere collection, like Jean Muir did before him. I love his things."*

JEAN MUIR, 59-61 Farringdon Rd, EC1 ☎ (01) 831 0691
Queen of minimalism, her clothes have a strong identifiable look and so does she (wide eyes, dark bob). *"I think she's fabulous ... her eye for detail is marvellous, very understated, and she's very underestimated too. Her clothes are a joy to wear. You can still be your own person in them rather than have them take you over"* – **Joan Burstein.** Cuts silk jersey on the bias with a puritanical perfectionism, adds little knits and some leather. Jean Muir Studio is her cheaper line (lambswool rather than cashmere). **Liz Smith** is a fan.

SASSY SOHO

Soho's clean-up/gentrification campaign (applauded by some, bemoaned by Sohophiles **Alastair Little** and **Robert Elms** who see it going homogenized Covent Garden way) has led to the springing up of small designer shops. It's not street fashion as such, but it's individual, it's wearable, and it's a return to personal shopping. In **Lexington Street, Beau Monde**, no 43 ☎ (01) 734 6563 stocks 3 or 4 young designers at a time, Hetti Gervis hats; at **This Address**, no 51, Tina Stevens and Angie Collins do own-label designs, Willi Wear, Donna Waite, etc; on the corner, **Benedetto**, 8 Silver Place ☎ (01) 734 0089 shows Ben de Lisi's designs. **Newburgh Street** is lined with one-off shops. **Academy Soho**, no 15 ☎ (01) 439 3225, stocks men's and women's wear by Donna Twigg, Stephanie Cooper, Megan Douglas, EKO, Ozwald Boateng, etc, and shoes by Christine Ahrens; **Boyd & Storey**, no 12 ☎ (01) 494 3188 show the individual designs of Karen Boyd and Helen Storey; **F-FWD** at 14a ☎ (01) 439 0091 is designerland – watches, telephones, mugs, ashtrays, slimline Japanese gadgets. The incredible **Soho Silks**, 24 Berwick St ☎ (01) 434 3305 stocks divine French, Italian and Chinese silks, tapestry prints, embroidered tulle, wool, cashmere and 80, yes *80*, velvets. Suppliers to the RSC, BBC, ITV – you name it. For trad gents' wear gone modern, **Powell & Co**, 11 Old Compton St, W1 ☎ (01) 734 5051 is wooing young would-be-tailoreds in. Off-the-peg and made-to-measure suits, hats, braces, boxers and hair accessories (get the haircut to match in their basement salon, **Sansom & Jessett**).

♣ **JOHN GALLIANO, at Gallery 28; Harrods, see Shops**
The new darling of fashion, voted British Designer of the Year for his dream spring '88 collection. *"The big new British star, joining the ranks of excellence of the top designers"* – **Lynne Franks**. Herald of the new femininity. Fluid fabrics swinging free, hitched up or draped; masterful asymmetric cuts; shoulders bared, shawl collars, waistlines high; wide trousers of all lengths. Mouth-watering, misty colouring for spring, mud and sludge for autumn: sheer brilliance – and it costs a fortune. No matter for fans Madonna, Diana Ross, Helena Bonham-Carter, *Elle* ed Sally Brampton or Susannah Constantine. **Liz Smith** is a great admirer, too.

♣ **KATHARINE HAMNETT, 264 Brompton Rd, SW3** ☎ **(01) 584 1136; 124b King's Rd, SW3** ☎ **(01) 225 1209; 50 S Molton St, W1** ☎ **(01) 629 0827**
A favourite for street-cred separates for men and women in cotton drill, poplin, parachute silk, tailored wools and linens. Rich velvet and wool Edwardiana for autumn. **Lynne Franks** rates her in the international top 10; **John Galliano** is a fan. Her flagship branch is the Norman Foster-designed Brompton Cross shop with the empty warehouse effect, reached by a white tunnelled catwalk.

MARION FOALE, 13-14 Hinde St, W1 ☎ **(01) 935 4489**
Quality hand-knits in dreamy-hued silk, cotton and wool yarns. A touch of gentlewoman

---

THE JEAN MUIR PLAN

"The basic rule is to find your own style. It doesn't matter if it's post-punk style or a 'royal' style. It's most important to have a definite look.

I think simplicity is best, eliminating the unessential. A basic straight skirt, some lovely jumpers, a great jacket, trousers for the day and a silk pair for the evening and you're practically set for life. Have a few 'instant evening' outfits – something you can wear during the day and convert into evening wear by adding a necklace.

What you do with yourself – your face, your hair, your shoes – is as essential as what you wear. You can take the simplest short black skirt and clingy sweater, add wonderful shoes and make-up, a great necklace, a terrific thick belt and you look sensational. Yet it's just a skirt and jumper."

---

golfer, a hint of matelot. Tasteful shop in the English-country mould.

NICOLE FARHI, 25-26 St Christopher's Place, W1 ☎ **(01) 486 3416 and branches**
Known for her French Connection and Stephen Marks designs, she has now achieved own-name fame. Modern classic executive look in neutral colours – the expensive little coat-dress, the fitted suit. Exec women wanted her for weekends, too, so she designed a new casual range, Diversion.

♣ **RIFAT OZBEK, c/o 18 Haunch of Venison Yard, W1** ☎ **(01) 408 0625/491 7033**
Fashion's young Turk turns to exotic, theatrical theme dressing. He's *done* Turkey, *done* ballet, and *done* down Mehico way, and now he's doing Turkey again, tamed into a Western silhouette. Brilliant detail – frogging, braiding,

tassels, gold embellishment, embroidery, buttons, often a sense of couture militaire. Bedazzled clients include the Princess of Wales, **Marie Helvin**, Paula Yates, Charlotte Lewis, Whitney Houston, Nell Campbell and Jerry Hall. O for Ozbek is the new cheaper line – stretch lycra, cotton jersey. Stocked at Gallery 28, Browns, Harvey Nichols.

VIVIENNE WESTWOOD, Worlds End, 430 King's Rd, SW10 ☎ **(01) 352 6551**
Mother of street fashion, a true original, still going strong, still immensely influential. Punks and New Romantics started at Worlds End, so did the mini-crini and the puffball. Much of her own stuff is too way-out wacky to *wear*, but she's sobered up of late – country gear, tea-party tweeds (with caricature Victorian underpinnings). *"I think she has the most lookable-at window in London. She's the most interesting designer around today"* – **Duggie Fields**. Devotees include **Michael Clark**, Nell Campbell, Madonna, Cyndi Lauper and Donatella Getty.

WORKERS FOR FREEDOM, 4a Lower John St, W1 ☎ **(01) 734 3766**
Collectable, comfortable, peasanty gear – roomy skirts, slouchy trousers. A law unto themselves, WFF stayed

---

❝ *The dark, sombre, graphic colours so dominant in the early '80s when Japanese fashion was at its peak have given way to more colourful and structured clothes. In are bracelets, gloves and more gloves, hats, hats and hats. DMs are an apology for bad legs!* **❞**

♣ BENNY ONG

élitistly loose and large when fashion went short and sharp. Natural fabrics, neutral colours, self-coloured embroidery. *"What they have done for fashion, apart from making good street designs, is open up a quarter of London – Soho – to young designers"* – **Liz Smith**. Due to move in 1988.

HATS

Britain's hat designers now lead fashion. Top French couturiers look across the Channel for milliners to suit their heady collections. Keep on the look out for a new wave of inspired young couture milliners such as **MARINA KILLERY**, 16 Denbigh Rd, W11 ☎ (01) 727 3121 and **GILLY FORGE**, 14 Addison Ave, W11 ☎ (01) 603 3833.

DAVID SHILLING, 44 Chiltern St, W1
☎ (01) 487 3179
Born-again picture hats and flirty couture extravaganzas adorn many noble heads. Romantic ribbons-and-bows showroom.

FREDERICK FOX, 87 New Bond St, W1 ☎ (01) 629 5706
Topping couture millinery. *"He designs wonderful original models for each customer. I always wear hats on formal occasions. I think older women with greying hair blowing in the wind look absolutely idiotic"* – **Barbara Cartland**. Hats the Queen Mother and Princess Diana too.

GABRIELLA LIGENZA, 31 Luke's Mews, W11
☎ (02) 221 3403
This dynamic flame-haired Pole has been hitting the headlines with her feminine period-style hats. Great block shapes.

GRAHAM SMITH, 2 Welbeck Way, W1 ☎ (01) 486 1522
Beautiful couture hats with the Parisian touch – by appointment. Has hatted Princesses Di and Margaret, Elizabeth Taylor and Barbra Streisand. Designs a mass-market range for Kangol.

HERBERT JOHNSON, 13 New Bond St, W1
☎ (01) 408 1174
Traditional hatter to the Englishman – and woman. Jam-on trilbys and caps on the ground floor, feminine head-hugs in the basement. The rarely hatless **George Melly** knows a good hat when he sees one: *"Theirs are excellent. I love hats – gangsterish hats."* **Barry Humphries** is a fan.

JANE SMITH STRAW HATS, 131 St Philip St, SW8
☎ (01) 627 2414
Not just straw picture hats, but all manner of natty headgear, using good blocks. Jane designs for Laura Ashley. *"Lovely hats"* – **Liz Smith.**

KIRSTEN WOODWARD, Unit 26, Portobello Green Arcade, 281 Portobello Rd, W10 ☎ (01) 960 0090
Still doing Lagerfeld's witty whimsies, she goes down a wow in Paris. Inspirational pie-in-the-sky millinery to order.

The POWess's going-away hat (*old hat* – Ed) and halos for Madonna. **Liz Smith** takes her hat off to her.

LOCK & CO, 6 St James's St, SW1 ☎ (01) 930 8874
"The place for men's hats" – **Liz Smith**. Precisely that: as Lobb's is to gents' feet, so Lock's is to their heads.

STEPHEN JONES, 29-31 Heddon St, W1
☎ (01) 734 9666
Eccentric and inventive as ever, a sense of irony and wit – plus glamour – are always at play in his hats. Splashy prints (Cecil Beaton roses; suitcases for a holiday hat), asymmetrics, wriggly hats with lots of folds. Everyone loves him and his headpieces – Boy George, the Princess of Wales, Azzedine Alaïa, **Marie Helvin**, Katharine Hamnett, **Lynne Franks, Margaux Hemingway** and Liz **Smith**. He does collections for Enrico Coveri, Myrène de Prémonville, Katharine

---

HEAVENLY PRESENTS

According to **Liz Smith**, for presents, toiletries, scent, etc, the best shops are: **Penhaligon's**, 41 Wellington St, WC2 ☎ (01) 836 2150 and branches – *"She creates a wonderfully elegant shop. Everything is beautifully packaged. Her scents are straightforward smells – not too much of a cocktail"* ... **Czech & Speake**, 39c Jermyn St, SW1 ☎ (01) 439 0216, who are *"marvellous at Christmas"* ... as are **Floris**, 89 Jermyn St, SW1 ☎ (01) 930 2885. *"We are very good at that sort of thing – other countries seem to copy our style"* – **LS**. Fellow Floris fan **John Galliano** loves the Sandalwood collection. Other beautifully English prezzie treasure-stores include: **Eximious**, 10 W Halkin St, SW1 ☎ (01) 627 2888, for terrifically traditional monogrammed everything (visitors' books, hair brushes, photo albums ...) ... **Crabtree & Evelyn**, 134 King's Rd, SW3 ☎ (01) 589 6263 and branches, for scented and foodie goodies, packaged to perfection ... **General Trading Co**, 144 Sloane St, SW1 ☎ (01) 730 0411, where the Prince and Princess of Wales had no hesitation in having their wedding list – an ultra-tasteful selection of things for the home (crocks, ornaments, sofas, linen, cushions, garden furniture), plus trinkets, books, stationery ... and **The Conran Shop**, Michelin House, 81 Fulham Rd, SW3 ☎ (01) 589 7401, based in the sleekly renovated Art Deco Michelin garage, its spacious interior strategically placed with designer temptations for house and person ...

FASHION AND SHOPPING

Hamnett, Culture Shock and Claude Montana.

JEWELLERY

BUTLER & WILSON, 189 Fulham Rd, SW3 ☎ (01) 352 3045; 20 S Molton St, W1 ☎ (01) 409 2955
At the forefront of fashion-conscious costume jewellery, they help set the season's look for ears, wrists, necks and lapels. Gilt-diggers include **Shakira Caine, Stephen Jones, Dame Edna Everage, Anouska Hempel** and **Marie Helvin.**

COBRA & BELLAMY, 149 Sloane St, SW1 ☎ (01) 730 2823; at Liberty, see Shops
Tania Hunter and Veronica Manussis have a tiny trove of covetable fashion jewellery – antique and own-design. Sculpted silver pieces complement clean-cut suits. Objets d'art too.

COLLINGWOOD, 171 New Bond St, W1 ☎ (01) 499 5613
Antique and modern jewellery, specializing in Edwardian pieces. Royal warrants from the Queen, the Queen Mother and the Prince of Wales (shelling out on his wife).

DAVID MORRIS, 25 Conduit St, W1 ☎ (01) 734 5215
Some of the best modern, glossy jewels. High-fashion, high-quality, continental-style glamour.

EDITIONS GRAPHIQUES, 3 Clifford St, W1 ☎ (01) 734 3994
Tops for Art Deco and Nouveau jewels as well as objets and pictures. *"Victor Arwas is an extraordinary man. He has a great many remarkable drawings and objects and gives very honest advice. Beautifully framed work. A very good place for a slightly flash, unusual present"* – **Frederic Raphael.**

ELIZABETH GAGE, 20 Albemarle St, W1 ☎ (01) 499 2879
Young designer full of originality, highly recommended by **Eleanor Lambert** and **Liz Smith**: *"My favourite of the new jewellery shops. She uses exotic antiquities – scarabs and things that look like something out of an archaeological dig – and reworks them into elegant pieces of jewellery. She is brilliant and has had enormous success."*

GARRARD'S, 112 Regent St, W1 ☎ (01) 734 7020
Terrifically smart royal jewellers in a magnificent shop. Many a Garrard's gold cuff-link has graced a princely cuff.

JOHN JESSE & IRINA LASKI, 160 Kensington Church St, W8 ☎ (01) 229 0312
The best in Art Nouveau, Art Deco and 1940s jewellery. Jesse was one of the first devotees of Art Nouveau.

MONTY DON, 58 Beauchamp Place, SW3 ☎ (01) 584 3034
Costume jewellery designers and pioneers of the dressy multicoloured diamanté look. They now take their inspiration from the stained-glass windows of Europe's cathedrals. Tasselled Gothic-arch and trefoil earrings and brooches in brilliant hues; matt gold-plate and glass-gem medieval pieces; lustrous gold bracelets.

🐚 **S J PHILLIPS, 139 New Bond St, W1 ☎ (01) 629 6261**
Probably the best antique jewellery shop in the world, stocked with fantastically important pieces. Only the rich and brave stride through the portals. Once inside, you are privy to a powerhouse of Renaissance treasures and exquisite 18th- to 20th-century jewels. *"I can't pass his shop without gazing at the rich Renaissance heirlooms"* – **Liz Smith.**

WARTSKI, 14 Grafton St, W1 ☎ (01) 493 1141
Fabulous Fabergé. Run by A Kenneth Snowman, grandson of the original Wartski and world specialist on Fabergé, with Geoffrey Munn at his right hand to advise on the best in 19th-century jewels. *"Kenneth Snowman is a wonderful fellow, a great jeweller and a great friend"* – **Lord Gowrie.**

LINGERIE

Next (see Shops) and **Fenwick's** department stores have cottoned on to beautiful lingerie, as have **Jasper Conran** and **Juliet Dunn,** available at Harrods and Harvey Nichols. **Funn** silk stockings from Liberty are fab.

COURTENAY HOUSE, 22 Brook St, W1 ☎ (01) 629 0542
Well-bred pretties: fresh cotton, lace and silk undies, nightwear and clothes, too.

FOGAL, 36 New Bond St, W1 ☎ (01) 493 0900
For de luxe legs – great tights, stockings and socks in a zillion colours. Divine cashmere and wool leggings.

JANET REGER, 2 Beauchamp Place, SW3 ☎ (01) 584 9360
Sinful silken frillies at wicked prices. A favourite of **Jackie Collins.**

RIGBY & PELLER, 2 Hans Rd, SW3 ☎ (01) 589 9293
Serious stuff. These old stalwarts, corset-makers to the Queen, re-rose to fame during the fashion for a) the bustier and b) the exacting silhouette needed to fill an Alaïa in the right places. Made-to-measure boned satin corsets, bras in sizes you never knew existed. Princess Margaret and **Marie Helvin** are kept in their place.

THE WHITE HOUSE, 51-52 New Bond St, W1 ☎ (01) 629 3521
Lavish, ravishing and devilishly expensive, they specialize in rice-papery Irish linen – from sheets and napiery to handkerchiefs; children's whimsies and grown-ups' flimsies, hand-embroidered or plain silk in the shape of pyjamas and camisoles; silk satin negligées – mere wisps at £2,000 plus. **Betty Kenward** and **Stephen Jones** rate them uppermost for undermosts.

FASHION AND SHOPPING

STAR CARS

"*Because of my patriotism, it has to be a* **Rolls-Royce**. *Wherever you go in the world there are 3 things that are symbols of the best – Concorde, QE2 and Rolls-Royce. We are the only people who have that. We're not lucky, we're good*" – **Terry Holmes**. "*A* **Grinnall TR8 Conversion** *is a unique, hairy, wizard sports car. Bat-out-of-hell time*" – **Joanna Lumley**. (Order yours from Mark Grinnall, Westridge Farm, Heightington, Bewdley, Worcestershire ☎ (02993) 2862.) "*The most desirable car ever built must be the* **Bugatti Royale**. *There were only 6 made (in the '30s – the idea was to sell them to the crowned heads of Europe but it failed). Each one is different. One was sold last year in America for US$8 million. My personal favourites are the big Edwardian cars such as the* **1914 Alpine Rolls-Royce**. *As for modern cars, I'm pretty happy with what I've got, which is a* **Daimler**. *Also the* **Bentley Turbo R** *and a* **Mercedes**" – **Lord Montagu of Beaulieu**. "*I like travelling to the country in my own car. I think my car is the best car in the world. It's a* **Rolls-Royce Silver Cloud II – 1962**. *You're surrounded by wood and leather and you glide down the motorway*" – **Ed Victor**. "*The best car depends on what you want to use it for, its image, the whole package. The best way of getting around town is on a motorbike for speed and convenience. Otherwise, I have a* **Peugeot 205 GTI**, *which is terrific in town, a great little car. For touring I have a* **Mercedes 560 SEC** – *a Merc with a relatively short body, a 2-door coupé. It handles extremely well, is quiet, comfortable, elegant, safe*" – **Stirling Moss**.

SHIRTS AND TIES

HARVIE & HUDSON, 77 Jermyn St, SW1
☎ (01) 930 3949
Shirts that cost an arm and a leg (well over the £100 mark for silk). Minimum order, 4. Own-design striping with matching ties for City camouflage.

KATIE STEVENS, 7 Archer St, W1 ☎ (01) 437 9306
Shirtmaker to **Douglas Fairbanks Jr**: "*She's marvellous – she uses the same materials as Jermyn Street and will do copies, but she's much cheaper. I've sent lots of friends to her.*"

NEW & LINGWOOD, 53 Jermyn St, SW1 ☎ (01) 493 9621; 155 Fenchurch St, EC3 ☎ (01) 929 1582
More shirtiness, next to Turnbull & Asser in quality, with perhaps the best collars of all. Branches in Eton and Cambridge as well, to see a man through life.

T M LEWIN & SONS, 106 Jermyn St, SW1
☎ (01) 930 4291
King of tie-land. Regimental, old-school, club and association ties – 1,001 variations on a stripe. Shirts too.

THOMAS PINK, 2 Donovan Court, Drayton Gdns, SW10 ☎ (01) 373 5795; 16 Cullum St, EC3 ☎ (01) 929 1405; 35 Dover St, W1 ☎ (01) 493 6775
A relative newcomer doing the Jermyn Street thing cheaper, with a naice Chelsea/City/Mayfair clientele that pops in for a poplin shirt or pair of boxers. Mail order too.

🏆 **TURNBULL & ASSER, 71 Jermyn St, SW1**
☎ (01) 930 0502
Still voted the best bespoke shirts in London – if not the world. "*There is no greater thrill than thumbing through the shirts and ties at Turnbull . . . the rustle of all that crinkly cellophane*" – **Bob Payton**. "*They are the best, but so expensive. If you're starting afresh, and have £600 to £700 to blow, it would be good to have 10 T&A shirts, and they do last a long time*" – **Eric Newby**. "*Even if people get copies in the Far East they still go back for more from T&A. They are traditional without being stuffy – and no one makes such perfect collars*" – **Lord Lichfield**. "*I have my shirts made here, with ties to match*" – **Barry Humphries**. **John Galliano** loves 'em; he lives in his T&A cream silk scarf. **Helen Gurley Brown, Stephen Jones, Bruce Oldfield** and **Douglas Fairbanks Jr** rate them highly. **George Melly** goes for their hats.

SHOES

ALAN McAFEE, 100 New Bond St, W1 ☎ (01) 629 7975 **and branches**
New-fashioned vintage classics for men and lately for women too. Good leather brogues, Oxfords, monogrammed velvet slippers. **Barry Humphries** has shoes made here: "*They do my fitting, which is difficult.*"

HOBBS, 84 King's Rd, SW3
☎ (01) 581 2914 **and branches**
For the basic shoe wardrobe: flattie loafers, pumps and brogues, plus boots and courts.

🏆 **JOHN LOBB BOOTMAKERS, 9 St James's St, SW1** ☎ (01) 930 3664
The best traditional shoes in the world, hand-made on the premises by wrinkly craftsmen. Royal bootmakers to Princes Charles and Philip and the Queen, not to mention **Jeffrey Archer, Douglas Fairbanks Jr** ("*I have my own last, which goes back to the days of Maxwell in the '30s*") and **Leo Schofield** ("*I have my shoes made here – you wouldn't believe the expense!*"). **Lord Lichfield, Giorgio Armani** and **Liz Smith** add votes.

FASHION AND SHOPPING

🦢 MANOLO BLAHNIK, 49-51
Old Church St, SW3
☎ (01) 352 3863
The last word in shoe design,
the maestro of fancy footwork,
Manolo is No 1 in the world.
*"The modern authority in the
field of flamboyantly original
design. Others care more about
the shoe than the foot, but
Blahnik does understand
comfort"* – **Eleanor Lambert**.
Once your feet have been
cosseted by these whispers of
lusciously concocted kid, suede,
satin, brocade, velvet (sigh . . .)
it's hard to consign them to
mere shoes. Displayed in his
Roman villa-esque shop, these
oh-so-sexy shoes are the
irresistible complement to the
new couture body. *"I adore
him – such clever shoes, the
best for design"* – **Liz Smith**. *"I
love those shoes. Along with
Kurt Geiger, they're my
favourites"* – **Sarah
Brightman. Tina Chow,**
Arianna Stassinopoulos, **Marie
Helvin**, Bianca Jagger, the
Duchess of York, **Joan
Burstein, Lynne Franks,
Giorgio Armani** and
Katharine Hamnett are among
those who know the meaning of
well heeled.

MIDAS, 27a Sloane Sq, SW1
☎ (01) 730 7329; 22 Carnaby
St, W1 ☎ (01) 439 8134; Way
In at Harrods
The best source of fashion
footwear from the young
British and French designers –
Johnny Moke, Jessica Mok,
Christine Ahrens, Elizabeth
Stuart-Smith, Patrick Cox,
Robert Clergerie, Martine
Sitbon and Charles Kammer.
They carry small, special,
exclusive collections from each.
Also own-label shoes.

SHOE SHINERS

Britain's shoes are striding ahead in design terms. Free-
spirited things with their feet on the ground are creating new
looks for fashion designers as well as their own collections.
  JOHNNY MOKE, 396 King's Rd, SW10 ☎ (01) 351 2232
designs his own lasts and heel shapes and wraps toes up in
ornamented velvet, duchesse satin, reptile skins, patent and
plain leather. Moke folk include The Duchess of York, Jean-
Paul Gaultier and Romeo Gigli.
  CHRISTINE AHRENS (at Joseph, Academy Soho and
Midas) goes for buckled/strapped/laced boots and shoes, with
round or chisel toes in browns and blacks for autumn. Has
designed for Jasper Conran and David Fielden, and for films
like *Legend* and *Absolute Beginners*.
  Stomping ahead of fashion, **ELIZABETH STUART-
SMITH** (at Midas) has gone from square-toed chunky black
lace-ups (big in Japan) to thigh-high printed velvet boots.
  PATRICK COX (at Midas) put us in suede courts with
silvery steel heels this summer. Long tongues, elegant pointy
toes and heels; also round or square toes. Sombre hues for
autumn.
  Great white Hope? The designer who shuffled us through
Baroque and Rococo, **EMMA HOPE**, 33 Amwell St, EC1
☎ (01) 833 2367, gives us embroidered and encrusted courts
and slippers.
  Everything's been coming up roses for **JIMMY CHOO for
Berni Yates** (stocked at Harvey Nichols, Academy and Fenwick). Spring saw feminine suede flatties in rose-petal colours,
embossed with roses; square toes and Louis heels turn more
pointed and tall for autumn, while shades darken.

NEW & LINGWOOD, see
Shirts & Ties
Sleek expensive men's shoes in
glorious woody (beech,
chestnut) and crème caramel
tones. By far the best velvet
slippers with hand-embroidered
crests, monograms, motifs. *"A
wonderful shoe store for
brogues and classics. They also
polish shoes better than anyone
in London"* – **Ed Victor**.

Shops

THE BEAUCHAMP PLACE
SHOP, 55 Beauchamp Place,
SW3 ☎ (01) 589 4155
*"I love it. I love Beauchamp
Place, I think it says a lot for
our country. Here, Patsy Blair
edits a wardrobe for you taken
from the really good British
designers – Margaret Howell,
Edina Ronay, Jacques
Azagury – mixed with people
like Ventilo and Cerruti"* – **Liz
Smith**. The melting pot
thickens – with Betty Jackson,
Ally Capellino, Wendy
Dagworthy, Marion Foale,
Rifat Ozbek, Emmanuelle
Khanh, Richard James and
Workers for Freedom, with
accessories by J&M Davidson.
Liza Minnelli and several
Duchesses, including those of
Westminster and Kent, have
shopped here.

BROWNS, 23-27 S Molton St,
W1 ☎ (01) 491 7833
The exclusive showcase for
many leading international
designers, run by Joan
Burstein and husband. Purist
fashion sold at rocketing prices
to the cognoscenti. The large
stock of thoroughbreds includes
Azzedine Alaïa, Sonia Rykiel,
Donna Karan, Romeo Gigli,
Comme des Garçons, Byblos,
Missoni. An equally starry
clientele includes Barbra
Streisand, Liza Minnelli, **Joan
Collins, Bruce Oldfield**, Faye
Dunaway, Twiggy, **Marie
Helvin**, Lee Remick and
Jacqueline Bisset.

BURLINGTON ARCADE,
Piccadilly, W1
A beautiful bijou pink-and –
aquamarine-covered arcade
lined with deliciously British
shops (the best cashmeres,

antique jewels and objects, linen, etc). *"We are still marvellous at lovely cashmeres. I think Burlington Arcade – N Peal and S Fisher – shows the best of British"* – **Liz Smith**. *"It's the best place in the world for jerseys. I get presents for people here"* – **Helen Gurley Brown.**
   N PEAL is the undisputed best for fash cashmere in gorgeous jewel-bright or muted colours.
   LORD'S is the oldest inhabitant in the arcade (est 1774). Classic knitwear, Valerie Louthan cashmeres (snoods which double up as mini-skirts, jumpsuits) and exclusive silks, menswear, silk and leather goods. On the 1st floor at No 41 are **Georgina von Etzdorf's** bold hand-printed wispy chiffon and silk frocks, scarves, etc.
   S FISHER (also in Covent Garden) has a good British stock of bright-coloured woollens – Shetlands, cashmeres, Arans and sea island cotton polo-necks. Sound men's and women's wear for facing the elements; nice ties and socks.

FORTNUM & MASON, 181 Piccadilly, W1
☎ **(01) 734 8040**
Gourmet pilgrims (see Food & Drink) can also stock up on surprisingly tasty fashion. Ever-more designer labels – Jean Muir, Jasper Conran, Jean and Martin Pallant, Alistair Blair, MaxMara, etc. Suede gloves, jewellery (New York's hot designer Eric Beamon) and other accessories.

GALLERY 28, 28 Brook St, W1 ☎ **(01) 408 0304**
Owned by the great Dane, Peder Bertelsen (Aguecheek), who has almost sewn up the designer shop trade. An amalgam of the brash, the beautiful and the newly tailored, they stock Piero Panchetti (the pop-star look), Bertelsen-backed Blair and Galliano, Moschino (tongue-in-chic wear); Pellini jewellery; Robert Clergerie and Fausto Santini shoes.

HACKETT
So sought-after is the English Country Gentleman that he has popped his buttons and

expanded into 5 London shops plus Eton (picking 'em up early) plus Paris, Hamburg, Boston and . . . *Tokyo*. It all began in '84 with a better second-hand rail than the rest – old grandees' cast-off shooting garb, silk dressing-gowns and other young fogey fodder. *"A major major goodie – they present an image of the whole British way of life. They have warehouses full of antique luggage, they lovingly re-create old tweed jackets and tailoring . . ."* – **Liz Smith**. At 117 **Harwood Rd, SW6** ☎ **(01) 731 2790** you'll find trad formal clothes (new and 2nd-hand) – DJs, morning suits, loud accessories. At **65b New King's Rd, SW6**, daywear – cords, moleskins, shirts, tweed jackets, City boy flannels and blazers; at **65a**, off-the-peg and made-to-measure suits cut on trad lines. *"I often buy ties here. It's also good for shoes – a great place to shop"* – **Bruce Oldfield**. Mr Sportif shops at **No 1 Broxholme House, New King's Rd, SW6** – hacking jackets, jodhpurs, Barbours, riding boots, plus-fours, and Gentleman Traveller at **No 6** ☎ **(01) 371 0462** – Phileas Fogg leather suitcases, toiletries, razors, brushes.

HARRODS, Knightsbridge, SW1 ☎ **(01) 730 1234**
Where does one begin with the world's most famous store whose motto is 'Omnia, omnibus, ubique' ('Everyone, everything, everywhere')? Acres of the right stuff; since they snapped up most of the old Harvey Nicks team, fashion has taken a sharp turn for the better. Their big coup was landing the exclusive on Lacroix. Men's and children's wear, presents, accessories, furniture, fabric, books, hi-fi, scent, make-up . . . just as the motto says. The best store for **Shakira Caine, Harvey Goldsmith, Diane Freis** and **Mark McCormack**, who asks: *"How can you go wrong at Harrods?"*

HARVEY NICHOLS, 109-125 Knightsbridge, SW1
☎ **(01) 235 5000**
The store with the best window

🕵 **Buzzzzzzzzz**   The royals, James and Edward Fox, Paul Newman and Dustin Hoffman shelter under the best **handmade umbrellas**, from **Swaine Adeney Brigg & Co**, 185 Piccadilly, W1 ☎ (01) 734 4277; also riding whips, saddles, hunting horns, flask cases and car mascots such as Princess Diana's frog and Fergie's owl 🕵 . . . . . . the best (and most extortionate at £37,000 a pair) walnut **guns** are hand-built by **James Purdey & Sons**, 57 S Audley St, W1 ☎ (01) 499 5292: a sounder investment than gold but a longer waiting list to obtain. Also the best **green wellies** (Royal Hunter) 🕵 . . . . . . failing Purdey's, try **Holland & Holland**, 33 Bruton St, W1 ☎ (01) 499 4411 for top-quality made-to-measure guns with decorative engraving 🕵 . . . . . . the very best **antiques** shops line New Bond Street – **Christopher Gibbs**, 118 ☎ (01) 629 2008, a flamboyant Old Etonian dealer with unerring taste who acts for many distinguished collectors; **Partridge**, 144-146 ☎ (01) 629 0834, for important grand-scale pieces; and **Mallett & Son**, 40 ☎ (01) 499 7411, the ultimate ritzy dealer in decorative objects.

★ ★ ★ ★ ★ ★ ★ ★ ★ ★ ★ ★ ★ ★ ★ ★ ★ ★ ★ ★

LONDON: BEST SHOPPING

Smart: Establishment international designers live in and around **New Bond Street** or **Sloane Street**. Nooks of chi-chi chicery are **South Molton Street, St Christopher's Place, Covent Garden Market, King's Road, Beauchamp Place** and the newest 'in' area – **Brompton Cross**, where Fulham Road turns into Brompton Road.

Street: **Portobello Road** market (under the flyover), early on Fri and Sat, for second-hand clothes and bric-à-brac; **Brick Lane** market early on Sun for earnest scrabblers – *"Go to the Bagel Shop, which opens at 4am, and have a proper Jewish bagel with cream cheese and lox, and the strongest tea in London. Then to the market, which can be absolute junk or you can find really good furniture and clothes. Get there early because they're professionals – you need sharpened elbows and wits"* – **Robert Elms**; **Greenwich** (Sat) for junky everything and a few incredible finds; **Camden Passage**, Islington (weekends), for antiques, second-hand lace, clothes and jewellery; and trendsville **Camden Lock** market for new arty-crafty clothes and accessories (**Gianni Versace** is a fan; so is **Michael Clark** for Body Map's stall). The best source of antiques (where all the trade go) is **Bermondsey** at daybreak on Friday. **Jane Seymour** loves *any* antique markets, but particularly those in **Bath.**

displays in town, by Paul Dyson. Just about even-Stevens with Harrods these days for international designer fashion, though it's rather more palatable being smaller. Oldfield, Cerruti, Complice, Dolce & Gabbana, Conran, Muir, Byblos, Gaultier, Krizia, Montana, Maxfield Parrish, Paul Costelloe, Ozbek, Rykiel, Dior, Armani, Lauren and more, plus the trend-spot Zone. Fashion-conscious menswear from Hackett to Hilfiger. Great junk jewellery, hosiery, woolly scarves, gloves, bags, etc. Open till 8pm. *"It seems to me there is still only Harvey Nichols. It has nice things, served by people who show a reasonable interest in trying to sell them to you"* – **Lord Donoughue.**

JOSEPH BIS, 13 and 14 S Molton St, W1 ☎ (01) 493 4420; 53 King's Rd, SW3; 166 Sloane St, SW1; 130 Draycott Ave, SW3
Joseph Ettedgui is spread ever-more thickly across fashionable London. A young sporty collection of everyday wear

garnered by the city's most successful, style-stocking shopkeeper. He takes the cream of young British design and adds a dash of foreign blood like Montana. At **23 Brompton Arcade ☎ (01) 584 1857** find John Flett, John Galliano, Joe Casely-Hayford, Margaret Howell, Gabriella Ligenza hats, etc. One of the Brompton Cross batch of boutiques, **Joseph Levi's, 124 Draycott Ave**, is for black, blue or cream jeans, Chevignon jackets, J&M Davidson bags, etc. **Esprit, 6 Sloane St, SW1 ☎ (01) 245 9139** is a range of separates that reflects the easy Californian way of life.

JOSEPH POUR LA MAISON, 16 Sloane St, SW1 ☎ (01) 235 9868
Label designs for home and body. A splendid piece of furniture, a limited edition book, a vase, a coat. Azzedine Alaïa no longer reigns in solitary splendour – Martine Sitbon, Maxfield Parrish, Ozbek, Conran, Ronay et al have their place among the Filofaxes, Swatches, etc. In the

basement is L'Express, where still-stubbled chins chew on a light nouvellish snack and immaculately defined lips sip an espresso.

JOSEPH TRICOT, 18 Sloane St, SW1 ☎ (01) 235 2719 and branches
The Tricot stamp is the huge homespun knitted cover-all, with leggings, woolly skirts, fun jumpers in monochrome, zanily bright and floral ranges. Joseph cleverly spans all ages and figures – if not pockets (a little slip of a T-shirt starts around the £30s). **Marie Helvin,** Amy Irving, Koo Stark and **Joan Collins** have been Tricoted.

LIBERTY, Regent St, W1 ☎ (01) 734 1234
One of the most delectable shops in town. An immense hybrid pseudo-Tudor building with impressive interior wood panelling, it's best known for the main galleried hall full of silk scarves (over 13 miles worth sold daily at sale time) and dainty Liberty-print granny gifts (lavender bags, etc). Super-duper accessories, gorgeous leather goods, fab selection of tights and stockings. Sumptuous fabrics – tana lawn, handkerchief-fine linen, zingy oriental silks, crewelwork. Fashion is excellent in places – cashmeres, coats, menswear, etc – but a little incoherent. Own-label goods are your best buy.

LUCIENNE PHILLIPS, 89 Knightsbridge, SW1 ☎ (01) 235 2134
Frenchwoman Lucienne was one of the first to support young British designers – many of whom are now Establishment: Jean Muir, Victor Edelstein, Alistair Blair, Penny Green, Jean and Martin Pallant, Patricia Lester. Buying is slightly eccentric, but she has a loyal clientele that outshines even her designers – the Duchess of Kent, the Countess of Lichfield, Lady Attenborough, Maggie Smith, Diana Rigg, Glenda Jackson, Miriam Stoppard, Mrs Larry Hagman, Lady Teresa Manners.

FASHION AND SHOPPING

MARKS & SPENCER, Marble Arch, 458 Oxford St, W1 ☎ (01) 935 7954 and branches
Where everyone shops for *something*, though they may be reluctant to admit it. *"For all-round value and family shopping. Not very original, but I love it"* – **Jane Asher**. Great for lingerie and underwear, as **Liz Smith** notes, and for men's classics. *"You can't beat their socks and smalls, and this year I came out of their Marble Arch store with 4 perfect pairs of grey flannel trousers, each a different shade, with change from £100 in my pocket"* – **Lord Lichfield**. *"I buy my shoes here. If I find a comfortable pair, I'll buy them in every colour..."* – **Lady Elizabeth Anson**. *"This branch is dazzling"* – **Jilly Cooper**. Another fan is **Michael Clark**.

NEXT, 149 Kensington High St, W8 ☎ (01) 937 0498 and branches
Presenting switched-on fashion sense to the mass market at straightforward prices. *"One of the best stores, with an excellent affordable line of goods"* – **Lynne Franks**. Great lingerie, classic fashion, shoes, accessories, men's and children's wear. Ever expanding into the home and beyond. And now the *Directory*, the best 'mail'-order (in fact telephone) catalogue with a 48-hour delivery service.

PAUL SMITH, 41-44 Floral St, WC2 ☎ (01) 379 7133; 23 Avery Row, WC2 ☎ (01) 493 1287
One of the top names in menswear with branches worldwide (they love him in Japan). The Paul Smith look is classic updated with a shot of colour and pzazz. Zany print ties, arty boxers (he reinvented them), well-cut suits and beautifully made shirts in

LITERARY PRIZES

JOHN SANDOE, 10 Blacklands Terrace, SW3 ☎ (01) 589 9473 is the No 1 bestseller according to **Jane Asher** (*"I love it – it's a real bookshop"*), **Richard Compton-Miller** and **Frederic Raphael**: *"An almost miraculous small bookshop. He seems to have more books to the cubic inch than anyone else. Extremely resourceful in getting books, they don't take no for an answer from publishers, and they send things to you with great expedition. Really excellent."* **HATCHARD'S**, 187 Piccadilly, W1 ☎ (01) 437 3924 gains votes from **Jane Asher**, **Madhur Jaffrey** and **Margaux Hemingway**, who thinks, unreservedly: *"Book stores in London are fantastic."* **RC-M** also finds **HEYWOOD HILL**, 10 Curzon St, W1 ☎ (01) 629 0647 *"a great shop"*, as do **Lord Gowrie** and **Barry Humphries**. Votes also go to **WATERSTONE'S** everywhere, **BLACKWELL'S** in Oxford and **HEFFER'S** in Cambridge.

snappy colours that cost the shirt off your back. City boys and people like Viscount Linley love the wicked flash of individuality; ad-men, film-makers and other creative types lay it on thicker with his mix 'n' mismatch fashion wear. It's one of **Bruce Oldfield**'s favourite shops. No 41-42 is his new mini designer dept store.

REGINE, 92a Brompton Rd, SW1 ☎ (01) 589 2933; 35 Brook St, W1 ☎ (01) 409 1670; and REGINE UOMO, 80 Brompton Rd, SW3 ☎ (01) 581 5873; 37b Brook St, W1 ☎ (01) 408 0530
International designer emporia, focusing most strongly on Italy. For women – Complice, Iceberg, Chloë, Fabrice, Oscar de la Renta; for the seriously designed man, 2 floors of uninterrupted style with racks of Verri Uomo, Foncel, Missoni, Panchetti, Cerruti 1881 and Versace. The lower ground floor at No 80 is devoted entirely to **Gianfranco Ferré** ☎ (01) 581 8732, who designed his space to look like a submarine.

WHISTLES, 12 St Christopher's Place, W1 ☎ (01) 487 4484 and branches
An excellent young designer showcase with a strong identity. Lucille Lewin brings not only safe bets but also more avant-garde designs into mainstream shopping. Lolita Lempicka, Georgina Godley, Myrène de Prémonville and Junior Gaultier feature.

ZANZIS, 84 Heath St, Hampstead, NW3 ☎ (01) 431 0639
A pretty Georgian house, converted into the smartest shop in this neck of the woods, selling razzle-dazzle ballgowns and slick daywear to local Jewish American Princesses. Designers include Patricia Lester, Arabella Pollen, Monica Chong, Tomasz Starzewski.

TAILORS

ANDERSON & SHEPPARD, 30 Savile Row, W1 ☎ (01) 734 1420
"The best suits, so beautifully

> 66 *It is no good buying clothes in the medium-price range. I really believe it is Marks & Spencer or Hardy Amies – the in-between ones are always a flop* 99

 BARBARA CARTLAND

> *My clothes hero is Norman Mailer. The minute he got some money, he ordered 14 identical blue suits*

🎩 LORD GOWRIE

FASHION AND SHOPPING

cut, you can wear someone else's as I do (I never had one built for me). You can crush one in your hand like a crisp packet and it will restore itself to its original form" – **Eric Newby**. *"Along with Huntsman, probably the best traditional tailor"* – **Liz Smith**.

DOUG HAYWARD, 95 Mount St, W1 ☎ **(01) 499 5574**
"With clients like Michael Caine, Roger Moore, Jackie Stewart, Frank Muir and James Coburn, it's no wonder his shop is often described as a club. He lunches good customers at nearby Harry's Bar" – **Lord Lichfield**. Viscount Linley and **Michael Parkinson** are wised up to Doug's suits.

GIEVES & HAWKES, 1 Savile Row, W1 ☎ **(01) 434 2001**
These military tailors started with Nelson and Wellington and went on to do naval garb for the Duke of Edinburgh, mufti for Gorbachev and a morning suit for Geldof. A cavalier array of brass buttons and insignia shines out against the more sober City style. Upstairs is a baby branch of the **General Trading Co.**

HACKETT, see Shops

HENRY POOLE, 15 Savile Row, W1 ☎ **(01) 734 5985**
Oldest and biggest bespoke establishment on the Row. Livery for the Queen's footmen, suits for noblemen, the best field coats and jackets.

HUNTSMAN, 11 Savile Row, W1 ☎ **(01) 734 7441**
"Probably the best of the old-fashioned tailors" – **Liz Smith**. They still have the cutting edge over others. Costly but everlasting suits in fine cloths made for them in Scotland. Expect to cough up a good £1,500 and attend 4 fittings. **Katharine Hamnett, Bill**

Blass and **Eric Newby** recognize their worth. Also the best riding coats.

JOHN KENT, 11 Old Burlington St, W1 ☎ **(01) 734 2687**
When he left Hawes & Curtis after 17 years, he took with him the royal warrant as tailor to the Dukes of Edinburgh and York and Prince Edward.

STOVEL & MASON, 32 Old Burlington St, W1 ☎ **(01) 629 6924**
Trusted tailor to **Douglas Fairbanks Jr**: *"I do my shopping in London. As Paris is to women's fashion, so London is to men's."*

TOMMY NUTTER, 19 Savile Row, W1 ☎ **(01) 734 0831**
Dandy tailoring – classics turned up swaggeringly loud, but avoiding the Oscar Wilde bit. Fabrics like brocade make evening waistcoats into a piece of period finery. *"If I want anything really special or ornate, I go to Tommy Nutter"* – **Lord Lichfield.**

Canada

MONTREAL

DESIGNERS

JEAN CLAUDE POITRAS, 400 Maisonneuve, Suite 1150, H3A 1L4 ☎ **(514) 849 8331**
A designer of faultless taste, who calls the tune in Montreal. He dresses Mila Mulroney, the Prime Minister's wife. *"One of my favourites"* – **Bonnie Brooks-Young.**

SERGE ET REAL, 1359 Ave Greene, Westmount, H3Z 2A5 ☎ **(514) 933 3600**
Serge Senéchal and Réal Bastien do custom-made clothes for wealthy women –

Canadian couture. Réal started out as a theatrical costumier, now he brings a sense of theatre to chi-chi Montreal. A small prêt-à-porter line too.

SHOPS

LES CREATEURS, 1444 Sherbrooke St W, H3G 1K4 ☎ **(514) 284 2102**
A characterful wonderland of wit, tops for the younger Parisian lights – Jean-Paul Gaultier, Azzedine Alaïa, etc. Also, new Japan in the shape of Junko Koshino and the spaciness of Jean Charles de Castelbajac. A refreshing antidote to monotonous businesswoman chic.

GREGE, 2130 Crescent St, H3G 2B8 ☎ **(514) 843 6228**
Nicole and Patrick Loth stock the more avant-garde designers – Yamamoto, Comme des Garçons, Dolce & Gabbana, Kenzo, selling to a star-studded clientele. Tina Turner was said to have 'phoned in her Christmas shopping order from the other side of the continent. *"Really fun stuff – they have a lot of the Montreal designers"* – **Tyler Brule.**

HOLT RENFREW, 1300 Sherbrooke St, H3G 1P7 ☎ **(514) 842 5111**
The most beautiful shop in Canada. Arnold Scaasi adores it. Upmarket, classy fashion store with a very crisp, wised-up designer selection. Young French designers like Myrène de Prémonville are here alongside well-established names – Ferré, Lagerfeld, Montana, Armani, Donna Karan, plus Canadians Alfred Sung and Jean Claude Poitras. *"Absolutely gorgeous. Very Art Deco; a standard place to shop. I love it"* – **Tyler Brule.**

LILY SIMON, 1320 Beaubian St E, H2G 1K8 ☎ **(514) 273 1771**
For chic traditionalists it's the

FASHION AND SHOPPING

only place to shop – for all the die-for designers.

OGILVY'S, 1307 St Catherine St W, H3G 1P7 ☎ (514) 842 7711
Smart store, still upholding the tradition of a bagpiper wailing through its halls at noon. Catherine Hill of Chez Catherine, Toronto, has an exclusive Valentino boutique here. *"The very best. It's had a multi-million-dollar facelift. This place is unbelievable"* – **Tyler Brule.**

L'UOMO, 1452 Peel St, H3R 1S8 ☎ (514) 844 1008
Terrific men's store on trendy Peel Street. *"Wonderful – a great selection of clothes by Basile, Byblos and many others"* – **Tyler Brule.**

VERRI UOMO, 1472 Peel St, H3T 1T1 ☎ (514) 842 8400
Verri beautiful men's shop for the suavest Italian designers.

TORONTO
DESIGNERS

ALFRED SUNG, 55 Avenue Rd, M5V 2T3 ☎ (416) 968 8688
The best Canadian designer for easy, go-ahead separates in pared-away style. There's an echo of Armani ideals, with a loosened sense of cut and a good eye for colour. Beautiful cocktail numbers, too. *"He's original. You don't look like anyone else when you wear his stuff. It's sexy and elegant"* – **Joyce Davidson.**

MAGGY REEVES, 108 Cumberland St, M5R 1A6 ☎ (416) 921 9697
Romantic, swish tailoring, sophisticated evening and cocktail wear in rich European fabrics. *"One of the last great couturiers in Toronto. Her clothes are works of art"* – **Karen Kain. A Sondra Gotlieb** favourite.

ROGER EDWARDS, 339 Queen St E, M5A 1S9 ☎ (416) 368 3706
The finest leather creations in

North America. Eddie Murphy, Linda Evans and other haute celebs don his leatherwear. The Duchess of York proved a great fan at a private showing during her visit to Canada last year.

WAYNE CLARK, Suite 500A, 49 Spadina, M5V 2J1 ☎ (416) 591 6991
The best designer for magnificent high-society get-ups – serious glamour, lavishments of lace and velvet. A distinct look, feminine and alluring, and often in jet black. *"Spectacular evening wear; my absolute favourite"* – **Bonnie Brooks-Young. Karen Kain's** and **Joyce Davidson's** too.

CANADA: BEST SHOPPING

MONTREAL: In what were once the stately homes of rich colonials on **Sherbrooke Street**, high fashion now jostles with smart art galleries and fancy antique joints. TORONTO: **Yorkville**, with **Hazelton Lanes** mini-mall, **Avenue Road** and **Cumberland Street**, is the chi-chi pseudo-villagey smart area to shop, eat, drink and promenade in your furs; nearby, glossy big-time **Bloor Street** boasts the best stores. *"That whole area is so wonderful – it's all so close, you can just walk around"* – **Sondra Gotlieb**. There's also miles of underground shopping mall to lose yourself in – you never know where you might pop up. VANCOUVER: **South Granville** wins hands down – boutiques like Bacci's, Boboli, Mondo Uomo, Elegance and Numero Uno line the street. *"The fashion Mecca. The blocks from 9th to 14th Ave are best"* – **Beverley Zbitnoff**.

WINSTON KONG, 158 Cumberland St, M5R 1A8 ☎ (416) 924 8837
He's been producing haute couture for haute Canada for 20 years. Beautifully civilized clothes for special occasions. Queenly gala and wedding numbers.

Young Designers

BENT BOYS, 312 Adelaide St W, M5V 1R2 ☎ (416) 977 9868
New young avant-garde *female* design team. *"These two girls are designing a lot of new things along the lines of Ghost and Callaghan. Really fun, wild, trendy wear"* – **Bonnie Brooks-Young.**

DEAN AND DAN, c/o Ports International, 207 Queens Quay W, Suite 403, M5J 1A7 ☎ (416) 865 0102
Twins who trained at Parsons School of Design in New York. Own-label wear is crazy gear à la Gaultier; their collection for Ports International is more career-woman classics in beautiful natural fibres.

EMILY ZARB, Zarb Garb, 140 Marycroft Ave, Woodbridge, L4L 5Y4 ☎ (416) 860 1123
"An incredible new Canadian designer. She designs wonderful things for Saks right now" – **Bonnie Brooks-Young**.

Her look is a racy version of the exec woman.

SHOES

DAVIDS, 66 Bloor St W, M5S 1L9 ☎ (416) 920 1000
A step in the right direction: a large shop with the best, most elegant, shoes in Canada, for men and women. Bags and accessories, too.

SHOPS

ALAN CHERRY, 711 Yonge St, M4Y 2B4 ☎ (416) 967 1115
From designer furs to couture ensembles to designer wedding gowns, Alan stocks it all. And the most beautiful windows on the block show it all.

CHEZ CATHERINE, 55 Avenue Rd, M5R 3L2 ☎ (416) 967 5666
Owner Catherine Hill is a walking advertisement for the gorgeous day and evening gowns stocked in her boutique. Top international designer stuff (some of which is exclusive to her in Toronto) – Valentino, Basile, Ferré, Versace, Lagerfeld.

CLOTHESLINES, 50 Bloor St W, 2nd Level, M4W 1A1 ☎ (416) 920 9340
Husband-and-wife team Bernard McGee and Shirley Wickerbrod have a fresh, clever sense of what works. And what works here is their famous, classic, beautifully draped gabardine trench coat. *"I have some great classic suits and, of course, a trench coat. You really feel you're wearing quality"* – **Karen Kain.**

CLUB MONACO, 403 Queen St W, M5V 2A5 ☎ (416) 979 5633 and branches nationwide
Alfred Sung's young, cult, sportswear line – the famous khaki chinos and jodhpurs, jeans, bomber jackets, huge shirts, chamois leather separates, delicious cotton and wool jumpers and socks in masses of colourways – creamy yellows, pinks, apricots, cornflower, indigo . . . *"A wonderful line. Every teenager owns at least one item from the stores"* – **Tyler Brule.**

CREEDS, 45 Bloor St W, M4W 1A4 ☎ (416) 923 1000
A Canadian institution, family owned for 3 generations. Creeds started as a furrier and still do marvellous plushy furs that fans flock from all over North America for. Designer-wise they have slinks to go with the minks: exclusive boutiques for Ungaro, Krizia and Joan & David shoes; Montana, Chanel; and Scene International for trendy young designers such as François and Marithe Girbaud. *"The renovation looks wonderful. Scene International is a fun new boutique"* – **Tyler Brule.**

FAB, 274 Queen St W, M5V 2A1 ☎ (416) 979 7813

Trendy shop stocking Maggie Callaghan, Girbaud and other young designers. Covetable coloured cowboy boots too.

FETOUN'S, 97 Scollard St, M5R 1G4 ☎ (416) 923 3434
Owner Fetoun 'Fifi' Yousif is the glamorous socialite wife of Saudi millionaire Bahnam Yousif. This boutique is *the* place for Christian Lacroix and everyone else who is haute couture and in the news. The raspberry-coloured boutique contains an ornate bedroom for clients who are overwhelmed with the strain of buying.

HARRY ROSEN, 82 Bloor St W, M5S 1L9 ☎ (416) 972 0556
The largest store for men in the city, finished in sleek green marble with stylish glass detail. For the definitive business attire. Clothes for the female executive too.

HAZELTON LANES, 55 Avenue Rd, M5R 3L2 ☎ (416) 968 8600
In the heart of chi-chi Yorkville is this neat, chic, glassy, walk-around complex boasting the best European designer shops (from Saint Laurent to Lagerfeld), Alfred Sung, Roots, Chez Catherine, Joan & David shoes and Sharon Batten – each in their own mini hall of fame. *"Still the very best. They have everything"* – **Tyler Brule.**

HOLT RENFREW, 50 Bloor St W, M4W 1A1 ☎ (416) 922 2333
Beautiful, glossy store blazoned with glass and marble, an ultra-contemporary encore to the Art Deco palace in Montreal. The first exclusive Armani boutique in Canada, designed by him and decorated with his furnishings; also Saint Laurent and Calvin Klein boutiques. Brilliant fur salon, plus all the fashion greats bought with a discerning eye – Donna Karan, Polo, Liz Claiborne, Callaghan, Emily Zarb and Ghost. *"I love shopping here. It is beautifully laid out with exquisite boutiques and designer touches. We get the best designers. Why would I want to go anywhere else?"* – **Bonnie**

Brooks-Young. A hit with **Karen Kain,** too. The Vancouver branch has Gucci and Louis Vuitton boutiques.

IRA BERG, 1510 Yonge St, M4T 1Z6 ☎ (416) 922 9100
The place to get gowns for gala premières under designer labels like Genny and Byblos; fancy footwear too from Fratelli Rossetti. *"A real old favourite. It's been around for years. A favourite of my mother's too!"* – **Tyler Brule.**

ROOTS, 195 Avenue Rd, M5R 2J3 ☎ (416) 927 8585
Don Green and Michael Budman started a great tradition when they went back to their Roots. Earthy leather shoes, leather coats and athletic shoes and gear that every teenager owns. Now Roots have dug themselves in all over the world.

SPORTING LIFE, 2665 Yonge St, M4P 2J6 ☎ (416) 485 1611
The only sports store that has its own policeman controlling the parking lot because such crowds descend upon it. Everything from serious equipment – skis, tennis rackets – to serious sports-cred gear – designer sunglasses and sportswear by Bogner (hand-painted suits), Steinebronn, Sun Ice, Descente, Head, Rossignol, Fila, Ellesse, Obermeyer, Mondi, Fischer, Ralph Lauren . . . phew. *"I almost never go shopping, but I do love to shop at the ultimate sporting goods store. The service is wonderful as is the selection"* – **Steve Podborski.** *"The best store for sporting goods. They have everything"* – **Tyler Brule.**

VANCOUVER

BACCI, 2788 Granville St, V64 3J3 ☎ (604) 732 7317
Hip boutique with Memphis furniture and trompe-l'œil fitting rooms. Switched-on fashion by Byblos, Genny, Callaghan, Complice and Montana, swanky shoes by Fratelli Rossetti, Diego Della

Valle and Casadei. One of the best for **Beverley Zbitnoff.**

BOBOLI, 2776 Granville St, V6H 3J3 ☎ (604) 736 3458
The poshest nook in town, owned by stylemongers Catherine Guadagnuolo and Margaret Ross. *"The very best store, the jewel in the crown of civilized South Granville"* – **Beverley Zbitnoff.** The shop is super-cool with its black façade, huge windows – and the very best wrapping, in glossy black boxes with gold bows. It's about *lifestyle.* On the women's side, a polished terracotta floor and leather sofa in radical plum make one want to move in immediately; instead it's home to MaxMara and other top Italian lines. On the men's side, the herringbone-patterned steel floor sets the Euro-style tone for togs by Reporter, Barba's, Lubram and Trenchcoat.

EXQUISITE BOUTIQUE, 780 Park Royal N, V7T 1H9 ☎ (604) 922 5211
Exclusive little shop lorded over by Peggy Chroust, who never stocks more than one or two of anything. Evening glamour gowns, little suits and silk dresses, all imported from Europe – Louis Féraud, Jobis, Laborne. An old favourite.

GEORGE STRAITH'S, 900 W Georgia St, V6C 2W6 ☎ (604) 685 3301
Classy home of European classics – Liberty prints, Bally shoes, Chester Barrie, Burberry, Ballantyne, Valentino, Brioni, Hermès, plus fine French lingerie. This shop is a branch of the main store in Victoria, at 921 Government St.

LEONE'S, 757 W Hastings, V6C 1A1 ☎ (604) 683 1133
A veritable designers' den with a loyal following. Overflowing with numeros by Versace, Mondrian, Alberta Ferretti, Armani, Valentino, Debbie Schuchat and Wayne Clark.

MARK JAMES, 2941 W Broadway, V6K 2G6 ☎ (604) 734 2381
Italian style is hot in

Vancouver: after flipping through the Armanis and Versaces (who rub shoulders gracefully with Girbaud, Marcel Dachet and C-17) you can slink through to Mark James's new Italian restaurant for a nibble of minimal insalata.

PAPPAS FURS, 449 Hamilton St, V6B 2P9 ☎ (604) 681 6391
The very best furs on the West Coast, worn by the most modish women and the most macho men – including Sylvester Stallone. The Pappas family stock divinely covetable designer coats by Christian Dior, Grovesnor and Balenciaga, as well as their own sensational designs.

France

PARIS

ACCESSORIES

See also **Chanel** and **Yves Saint Laurent.**

HERMES, 24 rue du Faubourg St Honoré, 75008 ☎ (1) 4265 9648
The ultimate scarf. The ultimate handbag. Not to mention the ultimate window display – and a museum of original designs, historic carriages and curiosities such as Napoleon's overnight case. The rave revival enjoyed a couple of years ago has subsided. However, the silk square, snaffled and swagged, the calf or crocodile bag and the leather luggage will never die. The famous Kelly bag now has a rival – the Jane Birkin bag, designed for another faithful customer. **Mark Birley, Inès de la Fressange**, Catherine Oxenberg, **Tina Chow** and Diana Vreeland know quality when they see it.

LOUIS VUITTON, 78b ave Marceau, 75008 ☎ (1) 4720 4700
The familiar beige-on-brown LV canvas luggage speaks –

and holds – volumes. The Kevler sports line (made from the same stuff as aircraft nose cones) withstands earthquakes. Their latest line is quite different – no initials, no gimmicks, just beautiful leather (or *cuir épi*).

COUTURE

"Paris is definitely the centre of fashion again. It's the excitement of Lacroix, Ungaro and Saint Laurent, all of whom seem to be better this year. There's nothing that stimulates a designer like the success of another designer" – **Bill Blass.** *"The great thing about the Paris couturiers is that they are totally inspiring and are keeping all these craftsmen at work, keeping couture alive"* – **Liz Smith.**

♣ CHANEL COUTURE, 31 rue Cambon, 75001 ☎ (1) 4261 5455 and 42 ave Montaigne, 75008 ☎ (1) 4723 7412
Karl Lagerfeld wittily re-interprets the whole Chanel look. This season he went more sleek, elegant and grown-up than ever, and led the big swing back to trousers. Nevertheless, under Lagerfeld, Chanel has been growing ever-more youthful. It caused ripples of apprehension last summer – well, teenybop Gigi schoolgirl and floral gypsy are a little hard to take if you're a (chic, *bien sur*) mother of 3. But would the snuggest, shortest-ever round-necked suits have pleased Mademoiselle herself? I should

♣ —France's Best— ♣

	COUTURIERS
1	YVES SAINT LAURENT
2	KARL LAGERFELD at CHANEL
3	CHRISTIAN LACROIX
4	UNGARO
5	GIVENCHY

Coco. The *spirit* is there. The signature's there, too – the contrast braiding, the gilt chains and buttons, the camellia. Disciples include Simone Veil, Paloma Picasso, Princess Caroline, Queen Noor of Jordan, Ann Getty and Jackie Onassis. **Inès de la Fressange** tells how to wear Chanel: "*Avoid the put-together look. Mix jeans and silk, gilt chains and sneakers, a tailored jacket with a T-shirt.*" **Liz Smith** says: "*I love what Lagerfeld has done for the Chanel label – he's a genius. I like him at Chanel best of all.*" KL is undoubtedly supreme within the restraints of the old couture house. Accessories are unbeatable: "*All their accessories are tops – I use them all except shoes*" – **Lynne Franks**. Conversely, that's what **Shakira Caine** likes best; so does **Liz Smith**: "*The most comfortable shoes of all – they must have a good, generous last.*" "*I'm hooked on Chanel accessories*", says **Helen Gurley Brown**.

CHRISTIAN DIOR, 30 ave Montaigne, 75008
☎ **(1) 4723 5444**
Well-bred understated elegance – wearable suits, sleek cocktail wear – designed by Marc Bohan. He was a long-time friend of Princess Grace, and the Monaco princesses have always dressed here. Stéphanie trained at his atelier before swimming off on her own. Jerry Hall is a fan of Dior's fab mixed-pelt furs. Dynamic menswear designed by Dominique Morlotti, who dresses François Léotard and France's (nattier) answer to Wogan, Patrick Sabatier. Luscious lingerie and hosiery, too.

♣ EMANUEL UNGARO, 2 ave Montaigne, 75008
☎ **(1) 4723 6194**
An individualist who's currently in high favour. Effervescent dressy outfits in sugar-bright colours, zazzy prints, jewel-like brocades; but the effect is sleek and sophisticated, a little less heady than Lacroix. "*Elegance epitomized – in a spirited way.*

How ever unattractive a woman is, when she puts on a dress by Ungaro, she immediately feels attractive and elegant" – **Aniko Gaal**. "*I've bought one Ungaro dress and I always feel great when I put that on*" – **Jane Asher**. Also touched with the Ungaro wand are **Joan Collins**, Anouk Aimée (an ex of Emanuel lui-même), Nastassja Kinski and Princess Ira von Fürstenberg.

♣ GIVENCHY, 3 ave Georges V, 75008 ☎ **(1) 4723 8136**
Refined, restrained day and evening wear à la Audrey Hepburn (who received a Fashion Oscar for her faithfulness to this designer for 30 years) and à la Wallis Simpson (whose death sparked a revival in her elegant 1930s/1940s look). Mme Mitterrand too remains true to M Givenchy, who, suave at 61, is still plying the pencil and scissors. "*Still a great couturier*" – **Liz Smith**. Ready-to-wear at 8 ave Montaigne.

Stephen Jones says...
"*I think people read fashion magazines and then go off to M&S and buy an acrylic polo. It's a good price and it's more suitable for their lives than a Lacroix crinoline. There are 3 levels of fashion – show level, magazine level and street level. Fashion is sold because people want something new and exciting. But fashion is secondary to flattery. What's the point of wearing something fashionable that makes you look ugly? Take short skirts – if you've got appalling legs, why wear them?*"

VIVE LACROIX

♣ CHRISTIAN LACROIX, 73 rue du Faubourg St Honoré, 75008 ☎ **(1) 4265 7908.** The new national hero. Prince of the puffball, lord of the lampshade skirt, führer of the flower power revival: his wit and frivolity are infectious, his influence far-reaching. On came Lacroix and designers from Paris to New York tossed out their shoulder pads, their mean, clean, black body-hugs and went short, baby-doll, multicoloured, frou-frou. "*I'm a charter member of the Christian Lacroix fan club. I do think he's the most exciting designer to arise in the last few years – and even the last 20 years or more, because he's brought a whole new spirit that's naughty and intellectual and romantic*" – **Eleanor Lambert**. This is the man credited with giving couture its new lease of life, attracting a totally new, younger clientele – Lucy Ferry, Madonna, Bond girl Maryam D'Abo, Bette Midler, Faye Dunaway – for whom FF50,000 is a mere bagatelle. Embellishment is the key – embroidery, beading, pompoms, quilting, tassels, lace – sometimes all at once. His Luxe collection is semi-couture at half the price; the newly-launched prêt-à-porter received rave reviews. "*I think what he's done is really wonderful. Lagerfeld was always the young pretender to Saint Laurent but Lacroix has stepped in*" – **Stephen Jones**. A more dyed-in-the-wool **Liz Smith** ventures: "*Extraordinarily original, there is no question that he is enormously talented. But he hasn't taken over from Lagerfeld or even Givenchy.*"

PRIVATE COUTURE

Working apart from the great Paris designers is the serene **MADAME GRES**, place Vendôme, 1 rue de la Paix, 75002 ☎ (1) 4261 5815. At touching 90, still produces classic couture. The first to make silk jersey her medium, she perpetuates the Grecian goddess look of mathematical purity and fluid form. **Eleanor Lambert** recommends her for *"handmade fashion at its most subtle and most pure. Her show is highest level in taste and fashion."* **EL** has another secret couturier at a third of the price of YSL: English-born **HELENE HAYES**, 42 ave Montaigne, 75008 ☎ (1) 4720 4494 has kitted out Mercedes Kellogg, Mrs Oscar Hammerstein, Mrs John Heinz and Anna (Mrs Rupert) Murdoch. Dazzling evening gowns with intricate workmanship – lantern sleeves slashed to reveal bright satin, lace insertions threaded with black velvet ribbon, silk or sequin flowers.

JEAN-LOUIS SCHERRER, 51 ave Montaigne, 75008 ☎ (1) 4359 5539
Luscious cocktail and evening wear dripping with detail, embroidery, jewels. Dresses the crowned and coroneted heads of Europe, politicians' wives, names such as Mme Giscard D'Estaing and Christine Ockrent. Scherrer's daughter Laetitia models for him. Prêt-à-porter at 90 rue du Faubourg St Honoré.

VALENTINO, 19 ave Montaigne, 75008 ☎ (1) 4723 6417
Shows in Paris. See Italy.

♀ **YVES SAINT LAURENT, 5 ave Marceau, 75016** ☎ (1) 4723 7271
Though temporarily eclipsed in the frenzy over Lacroix, Saint Laurent returned the challenge with his couture tribute to Post-Impressionism, which showed just who was master. If embellishment is the buzz word, he turned it into a refined art. He remains the all-hallowed originator of modern fashion. *"Still the best. There are certain things we all have in our wardrobes that were first created by Saint Laurent. The dinner jacket for women, Le Smoking, the safari jacket, the short leather skirt with tunic (I still have mine after 4 years). He does the definitive look"* –

Liz Smith. *"Unassailable. He has reached such a position that he can't really be knocked off it"* – **Stephen Jones**. It is his sleek-lined classics, like the beautiful navy suit, that keep him at the top. *"Nobody does the cocktail hour better than YSL,"* – **Bonnie Brooks-Young.** Shakira Caine, Catherine Deneuve, Paloma Picasso, **Viscountess Rothermere, Tina Chow, Marie Helvin,** Diana Vreeland

> ## Bill Blass says . . .
>
> *"I think the influence of the fantasy of Lacroix's imaginative costumes will create another way of dressing which will be much more strict and fundamental. When you have an onslaught of one look, it prompts another look which gives the contrast."*

and the Duchess of York are YSL devotees. **Liz Smith** also thinks his ready-to-wear line Saint Laurent Rive Gauche is *"marvellous"*. **Ed Victor** swears by his menswear: *"I buy virtually all my clothes at YSL. Because he is tall, he designs for tall men."*

DESIGNERS

♟ **AZZEDINE ALAIA, 17 rue du Parc-Royal, 75003** ☎ (1) 4272 1919
Alaïa sticks to his'look and his fans stick to him. Still king of body-hugging stretch fabrics, knits and leather that sexily skim and caress the curves of the female form. Models and model-shaped stars still adore Alaïa's pared-down minimalism – Grace Jones, Beatrice (Betty Blue) Dahl, Cher, Tina Turner, Raquel Welch, Marie Helvin, Andrée Putman, Paloma Picasso. One of his earliest and unlikeliest fans is Madame Grès, who thinks he's the best cutter in Paris today. **Liz Smith** says: *"He's got his little niche carving up jersey. He really got us reshaping our bodies. He's not as buzz as he was, but every designer has to be allowed to develop his theme."*

CERRUTI 1881, 3 place de la Madeleine, 75008 ☎ (1) 4265 6872
Shows in Paris. See Italy.

♟ **CLAUDE MONTANA, 131 rue St Denis, 75002** ☎ (1) 4296 5033
The old Montana trademark of power shoulders has given way to the new flowing, sculptural silhouettes, baggy pants, plain fabrics. His colouring, tailoring and above all his handling of leather are still superb. **Stephen Jones** votes his leather goods tops. *"I love Montana most definitely for weekend wear"* – **Bonnie Brooks-Young.**

♟ **KARL LAGERFELD, 17-19 rue du Faubourg St Honoré, 75008** ☎ (1) 4266 6464
Individual, flippant and somehow detached from fashion, the great man wears tinted glasses, a little pony tail, flirts behind a snap-top fan and lives in 18th-century grandeur. *"I still think Lagerfeld is the best worldwide. He responds to a need for newness and he is the most versatile designer. He designs each for what it is. He designs Chanel in a very French manner. He has total irreverence for luxury – for*

♠ —France's Best— ♠

DESIGNERS

1. **JEAN-PAUL GAULTIER**
2. **AZZEDINE ALAIA**
3. **KARL LAGERFELD**
4. **CLAUDE MONTANA**
5. **LOLITA LEMPICKA**

Fendi he cuts up mink and sable like it was card. It takes a very special person to design all 3 labels with such style" – **Aniko Gaal**. The third label, of course, goes under his own name. **Stephen Jones** thinks *"his crown has been stolen by Lacroix"*. However, for **Lynn Wyatt**, Paloma Picasso, Princess Caroline of Monaco and **Marchesa Bona Frescobaldi** he remains king – at his best when ruling at Chanel.

KENZO, 3 place des Victoires, 75001
☎ (1) 4236 5686
Japanese by birth, Parisian in spirit. Ever true to his wearable, colourful, floral, patterned look, which darts into high fashion periodically. Smart jackets and trousers, fabulous scarves and shawls. More directional on menswear. Grace Jones, Jane Birkin and Dolph Lundgren buy here.

SONIA RYKIEL, 6 rue de Grenelle, 75006
☎ (1) 4222 4322
Sublime knitwear. There's a definite Rykiel look: understated, brilliantly co-ordinated, with a drop-waisted line, fine stripes and light texture that hark back to the 1920s, golden age of tricot. Her Graphics collection of pared-down knitwear comes in cheaper fibres. **Joan Burstein** and **Bruce Oldfield** are admirers.

THIERRY MUGLER, 130 rue du Faubourg St Honoré, 75008
☎ (1) 4256 1928
Purveyor of the high-class tart look. Expect sensational suits, structured clothes for superwomen, sophistication, satire – and zips. Think Amanda Lear, think Brigitte Nielsen, think Grace Jones – they say it all. And beware his shows, which can test the sensibilities: one featured bare-breasted black slave girls and Iman with stage-frightened tiger cub in tow.

Young Designers

ADELINE ANDRE, 28 rue Boissy d'Anglas, 75008
☎ (1) 4266 0472
A woman of resolution. She turned down a job as Marc Bohan's right hand at Dior to develop her own logic of dress. Simple, fluid designs using transparent, floaty material. Lovely evening wear.

JEAN-MARC SINAN, 45 ave Georges V, 75008
☎ (1) 4720 5144
New young designer who landed a coveted 8-page spread in *Elle* last year before anyone else had heard of him. A Turkish émigré, he is a more wearable – if less imaginative – version of Alaia. Tailored, structured, mini. Pioneer of black/brown and black/khaki colour combinations, and le Business Bag.

♣ **LOLITA LEMPICKA, 13 bis rue Pavée, 75004**
☎ (1) 4804 9696
A relative newcomer with an impressive following that includes Paloma Picasso, Kim Basinger and Annie Lennox. Curvy, feminine, tailored suits and coat-dresses (she does made-to-measure) in good strong colours. Inspired by the 1940s.

LORIS AZZARO, 65 rue du Faubourg St Honoré, 75008
☎ (1) 4266 9206
Elegant couture evening wear, originally influenced by the '30s/'40s/'50s, now rather more original. Farrah Fawcett and Princess Ira von Fürstenberg are fans. His costume jewellery is a contender for the most beautiful in Paris.

MARTINE SITBON, 161 rue St Honoré, 75001
☎ (1) 4260 9474
A Frenchified version of street cred. She's currently going through a 1960s revival flared to the hilt, and a waif-like period look. Very *in* among the young Parisian set. She is also

---

GAULT FOR IT

♣ **JEAN-PAUL GAULTIER, 70 galerie Vivienne, 75002**
☎ (1) 4296 8220. Gaultier, French Designer of the Year, is big news again. His offbeat approach to street dressing has come down to earth a shade – though he retains his Gallic humour. Inventive tailoring that is cock-eyed yet fits like a dream. A Gaultier suit is a coveted article – exquisite cut, incredible seaming. While everyone else went brief and bright, he pre-empted their next collections with flowing trousers, scarf shoulders using a muddy palette. His Junior line – less wacky, half the price – distils his style but retains his sharpness of design. Hats? Dream toppings from the same wellspring of irreverent genius. Menswear? Nutty but eminently wearable coats and suits. Aside from all that, JPG deserves the award for best show, best shop. His catwalk parades dovetail theatre and fashion into a bizarre amuseument arcade, held in a massive glass stadium. His shop is ancient Pompeii meets ancient Greece meets ship's boiler room. A cement floor is inlaid with expanses of mosaic, a crucifix of videos are set like portholes into the ground.

FASHION AND SHOPPING

ERTE'S DESIGNER COGNAC

Fashion-conscious consumers have been golloping down designer water till the springs run dry and swilling a zillion different designer beers. Now the very best drinks cabinets have a new bottle in their midst: the first ever designer cognac, **Cognac Courvoisier Collection Erté**. Famous for his Art Nouveau-style designs (including work for *Harper's Bazaar*, the Folies Bergère, Broadway and Hollywood), 96-year-old Erté has designed an ethereal teardrop-shaped label in the same golden russet tones as the cognac. It seems Courvoisier is Erté's tried-and-tested tipple. He says: *"The marvellous nose of Cognac Courvoisier wheels away in spirals just like my drawings. It has been the source of inspiration for the creation of a great number of my works."*

the new high-hoper for Chloë, designing with a more '50s eye.

MYRENE DE PREMONVILLE, 52 blvd Richard le Noir, 75011
☎ (1) 4807 2325
The English and Americans are raving about her, though some of her fickle compatriots think her passé already. Recent themes were ornamented baroque and '40s Hollywood (wide trousers, fitted silk jackets). Curvy body shapes, frivolous skirts, embroidered jackets. *"She does ladies' tailoring in a way no one else does it. She flatters the female form using very, very clever proportions"* – **Stephen Jones.**

HATS

JEAN BERTHET, 13 rue Tronchet, 75008
☎ (1) 4265 3587
A classic name for classic titfers, a-hatting since 1949. Kits out **La Comtesse de Paris.** *"Still the best. His technique is fabulous"* – **Stephen Jones.**

PHILIPPE MODEL, 33 place du Marché St Honoré, 75008
☎ (1) 4296 8902
The most inventive and polished hatter in town. Crowning glories for fantasy figures like Princess Caroline of Monaco, plenty of dressing-up-box brouhaha. *"Really very zany"* – **Liz Smith.**

JEWELLERY

BOUCHERON, 26 place Vendôme, 75001
☎ (1) 4260 3282
Quite simply, *haute joaillerie.* A glittering favourite of **Joan Collins, Margaux Hemingway** and Queen Noor of Jordan.

CHANEL, 31 rue Cambon, 75001 ☎ (1) 4261 8335
The originators of costume jewellery – chains and chains of gilt and pearls, wonderful stone-encrusted decorations. **Marie Helvin** and **Lynne Franks***: "The best jewellery – way and above even antique jewellery."*

JAR ROSENTHAL, 7 place Vendôme, 75001
☎ (1) 4296 3366
He makes everything to order, for top-drawer necks, wrists and fingers – such as Baroness Marie-Hélène de Rothschild's. *"A marvellous designer, very original. Extraordinary colours, precious stones. Very tasteful"* – **Ken Lane.**

MICHEL PERINET, 420 rue St Honoré, 75008
☎ (1) 4261 4916
One-off pieces from the period 1880-1950, mainly Art Deco and Nouveau in style.

POIRAY, 62 rue St Honoré, 75008 ☎ (1) 4265 3101; **8 rue de la Paix, 75002**
☎ (1) 4261 7058
A new jewellery business set

up by Cartier heiress Nathalie Hocq. A modern, distinctive style using cabuchon stones and semi-precious stones in gold.

VAN CLEEF & ARPELS, 24 place Vendôme, 75001
☎ (1) 4261 0236
One of the old guard along with Boucheron, greatly respected if perhaps lacking strong artistic direction.

LINGERIE

Nina Ricci, Vickie Tiel, Elisabeth Attali and Christian Dior (see Couture) do luscious lingerie.

CHANTAL THOMASS, 188 rue de Rivoli, 75001
☎ (1) 4296 3065
Fêted in Paris for her lingerie – sinuous silks and satins to cocoon the body. Also chic sheer, lacy and patterned tights and stockings. Feminine lingerie-look evening wear too.

SHIRTS

CHARVET, 28 place Vendôme, 75001
☎ (1) 4260 3070
The Turnbull & Asser of France. True specialists with the most incredible fabrics, including zillions of crisp white cotton piqués. They have the rights to make up all the Dufy prints, which they do in his innocent colours on huge silk scarves. Masters of a very particular style of collar, appreciated by **Bill Blass.** They used to sew the shirts of Charles de Gaulle and Giscard d'Estaing. *"The best nightshirts and pyjamas"* – **Tina Chow.** Accessories too.

LANVIN, 22 rue du Faubourg St Honoré, 75008
☎ (1) 4265 1440
Classic, old-fashioned shirts that last a fair chunk of a lifetime. *"They're the best, properly made shirts in very good fabrics. I've got Lanvin shirts going back more than 20 years. The buttonholes are beautifully done"* – **Mark Birley.**

FASHION AND SHOPPING

SHOES

CHARLES JOURDAN, 86 ave des Champs-Elysées, 75008 ☎ (1) 4562 2923
Recently launched an exclusive range of shoes with the couture touch by designers such as Lagerfeld, Marc Bohan for Dior, Enrico Coveri and Guy Paulin. Otherwise good for courts from flatties to stilettos, verging on the tarty. **Joan Collins** is a fan.

MAUD FRIZON, 81-83 rue des Saints Pères, 75006 ☎ (1) 4222 0693
The Manolo of Paris for butter-wouldn't-melt-like-my-leather shoes. Her suedes are divine and everything fits like a glove. She makes her own soles, which is unusual. *"Very good, but apt to care more about the shoe than the foot"* – **Eleanor Lambert**. Nevertheless, **Joan Collins, Jean Muir, David Shilling, Anouska Hempel** and **Aniko Gaal** care about Maud's shoes. Her bags are at 7 rue de Grenelle.

ROBERT CLERGERIE, 5 rue du Cherche-Midi, 75006 ☎ (1) 4544 6871
Becoming the darling of the fashionable foot brigade. Court shoes with high, sculpted heels, exquisite suede lace-ups. Modern, different, but not wacky. *"They're absolutely wonderful, fabulous shoes"* – **Anouska Hempel.**

WALTER STEIGER, 49 rue du Faubourg St Honoré, 75008 ☎ (1) 4265 1440
A classicist who knows how to take a simple pump and make it shine. Fashionable everyday shoes. **Jackie Collins** and **Liz Smith** like a Steiger – or 2.

SHOPS

AGNES B, 6 rue du Jour, 75001 ☎ (1) 4508 5656; **menswear at No 3; children's at No 2**
Fashion editor turned designer, she produces chic, easy separates. Hardy perennials like the striped T-shirt plus newer fashion lines. *"She has*

Best antiques

The chi-chi area of the Rive Gauche, around rue Bonaparte and rue Jacob, is full of delightful little antique boutiques. The top 3 are **Didier Aaron**, 118 rue du Faubourg St Honoré, 75008 ☎ (1) 4742 4734 (the premier Paris dealer in 17th- and 18th-century furniture); **Madeleine Castaing**, 21 rue Bonaparte, 75006 ☎ (1) 4354 9171 (dealer and decorator who loves the ornate Second Empire style. An extraordinary woman, who wears a wig with elastic under the chin); **Aveline & Cie**, 20 rue du Cirque, 74008 ☎ (1) 4266 6029 (grand, mainly 18th-century stock. Super-cachet).

---

the knack of middle-market items that every young woman needs: the short black skirt at a third of the price of the top designers. She has a huge following and somehow has her finger on the right look" – **Liz Smith**. Kevin Kline is a monster fan of Agnès B in

Madison Ave: *"so comfortable, so stylish yet inconspicuous that I now wear her all the time."* So do Brian and Lucy Ferry and Nastassja Kinski.

ELISABETH DE SENNEVILLE, 3 rue de Turbigo, 75001 ☎ (1) 4233 9083; **10 rue Guichard, 75016; 55 rue Bonaparte, 75006**
Young designer who has gone more diverse than ever, kitting out body and home. She does casual, elegant wear for the working woman, men's and children's wear, shoes, bags, china, glassware, even carpets. Now branching out to the States.

GALERIES LAFAYETTE, 40 blvd Haussmann, 75009 ☎ (1) 4282 3456
An Art Nouveau cavern with a stained-glass roof encompassing little designer shoplets (*all* the best concessions), *branché* own-label jerseys, scarves and accessories, and everything else you'd ever need – all with a dash more style than just any old store. **La Comtesse de Paris** recommends.

MUSEE DES ARTS DE LA MODE, 107 rue de Rivoli, 75001 ☎ (1) 4297 4728
Attached to the fabulous costume/fashion museum is a little treasure trove selling

---

PARIS: BEST SHOPPING

Smart: Around **rue du Faubourg St Honoré** and **avenue Montaigne** reside the Holy Chic – Lacroix, Lagerfeld, YSL, Chanel, Scherrer, Ungaro, Dior, Guy Laroche; **place des Victoires** and its environs house the more outlandish: Jean-Paul Gaultier, the Japs; **Le Marais** is the branché area full of hideaway one-off shops in little back streets – designers like Azzedine Alaïa and Lolita Lempicka, costume and antique jewellery. The **St Germain des Près** area buzzes with young boutiques. **Place Vendôme** is dripping in diamonds.
Street: The famous **Puce** – flea market – is at Porte de Clignancourt, for everything second-hand under the sun. Here, at Marché Biron, you can buy the best 1920s and antique couture in immaculate condition (and seriously expensive) from Madame Geneviève Autran. **Gianni Versace** is a Puce fan. Get up early for other good markets at **Porte de Vanves, Porte de Montreuil** and **Marché' d'Aligre** in the 12e.

perennial classics, repros of the first Hermès scarf and first Chanel chain, plus Schiaparelli and other blasts from the past. Also pieces by young French hot cakes like Lempicka.

PISANTI, 5 rue St Honoré, 75008 ☎ (1) 4266 2372
If you wondered how those chic soigné French women remained thus, Jacqueline Pisanti is one answer. She stocks her own collection at half the price of a Valentino, plus Byblos and other Italian designers. Her couture-trained fitters make sure you walk out properly adjusted. *"It's the look of couture at a third of the price"* – **Anne-Elisabeth Moutet.**

Hong Kong

DESIGNERS

DIANE FREIS, Shop 258 Ocean Terminal, Kowloon ☎ 3-721 4342; 271 World Commerce Bldg, Harbour City; 2B Connaught Centre; G25-26 Prince's Bldg; and branches
Ubiquitous in the South China Sea, she specializes in the one-size (that's tall, slim size) uncrushable georgette dress. A romantic jungle of patterned prints, shirred waists, frills and flounces. Soft pastel nighties and lingerie too. Jimmy Carter and his wife visit the factory, Mrs Thatcher sends for Carol's dresses; Diana Ross, Shirley MacLaine and Victoria Principal step out in a Freis.

EDDIE LAU, Shop C, GF, Mandarin Oriental Hotel, Central ☎ 5-223997
The Honkers size-10 party crowd patronize him for his 14-yard skirts on his extravagant ball dresses. Day clothes are more restrained. Sells *little* silk numbers through Chinese Arts & Crafts.

JENNY LEWIS, Shop 214 Ocean Centre, Canton Rd, Tsimshatsui ☎ 3-723 3071; Shop ME2 Peninsula Hotel;

HK: BEST SHOPPING

Hong Kong is a tax-free port for just about everything. It's a shopper's seventh heaven for jade, pearls, gold, silk, linen, embroidery, clothes, hi-fi, cameras and much more going cheap.

Smart: On HK Island, the **Mandarin**'s shops are first-class if extra-expensive; there's a bridge across to **Prince's Building** opposite; Queen's Road has **The Landmark** (a **Diane Freis** fave), with the best European designers. Kowloon has the most impressive shopping centres like **Harbour City** and **Ocean Terminal** (tops for **Diane Freis** and where you'll find perhaps the best dealers of Oriental antiques in the world, Charlotte Horstmann & Gerald Godfrey).

Street: The best Chinese goods can be found at **Chinese Arts & Crafts** or one of the many department stores (see Shops). On HK Island, **Wing On Lane** is excellent for fabric – silks, Swiss linen, shirting – do double-check that 'peeore siyook, madam' is genuine. Bargaining is de rigueur. The **Lanes** between Queen's Road Central and Des Voeux Road bristle with little stalls for all sorts of bargains and fakery. **Stanley Market** is brill – good and cheap for everything (from canteens of cutlery to Reeboks to silk by the yard at a snip), a ritual gweilo haunt on a Sunday (shop, lunch at Stanley's, shop). On Kowloon, **Nathan Road** and all roads off to the east are bursting with jewellery, embroidery and electrical goods. Go for the ones recommended in the HKTA's *Official Guide to Shopping* ... Check out too the invaluable *Complete Guide to Hong Kong Factory Bargains* by Dana Goetz.

Shop 5, GF, Swire House; and branches
English designer who beads and embroiders à la antique Chinese (she also owns a Chinese Imperial textile collection). Victoria Principal, Zsa Zsa Gabor and Stephanie Powers wear her clothes.

RAGENCE, Shop 21, GF, Swire House, Central ☎ 5-214646
Most promising young Chinese designer. Innovative, even weird (he leans towards Yohji and co), he sells internationally.

RENE OZORIO, Star House, Kowloon ☎ 3-698631
Oriental/Portuguese man of the cloth (silks and luscious brocades). Simply structured evening and cocktail wear.

FURS

About 1 in 6 women in HK own

---

a fur coat. HK offers stupendous bargains – and made-to-measure thrown in.

JINDO FURS, 308-309 World Finance Centre, Harbour City, Tsimshatsui ☎ 3-699208; Shop B101, Kowloon Hotel, 19-21 Nathan Rd
A Korean company doing extravagantly individual ready-

Shopalong hassle-free

Mary-Lou Galpin of **RIGGS SHOPPERS**, Room 702/703, Ocean Centre ☎ 3-696607 will nip down to the local shops for you and pick up a nice batch of bargains. Or she will pick you up and drive you around the best shops, haggling for the best prices along the way.

to-wear and made-to-order furs. If you want a Saga or Blackglama mink, it's here. The place is also piled with drifts of top-quality pelts; you choose your own and have them made up to your design or a photo.

SIBERIAN FUR STORE, 21 Chatham St, Kowloon ☎ 3-667039; 29 Des Voeux Rd, Central ☎ 5-221380
The very best in Honkers. This is the place to bring your *Vogue* pix of Fendi furs and have them made up to perfection.

SINGER FURS, 163B Tai Shoh Gallery, Ocean Terminal, Kowloon ☎ 3-677340
Marvelette minkies, great puffed-up jackets, and slim-priced leather coats.

JEWELLERY

You'll find freshwater pearls, pearls, coral, plus all the precious stones and gold a-plenty. For certified authentic jade, go to one of the Chinese emporia (see Shops). In general, if you want a bargain, look first in smart shops to note the quality before branching out to Kowloon; cheap prices indicate inferior goods rather than a great buy. HK is the perfect place for having stones set to your design in double-quick time. **Jackie Collins** has found *"great jewellery stores"* in HK: *"On Nathan Road, Kowloon there's* **Larry's** *and* **Henry's***. They do a mixture of traditional and modern and have extremely wonderful designs."*

K S SZE & SONS, Shop 5F, Mandarin Oriental Hotel, Central ☎ 5-242803
Mr Sze and his progeny will make anything you desire to new designs or old, or to their own. Exquisite inlaid work.

KAI-YIN LO, 2F, 6 On Lan St, Central ☎ 5-248238; Mandarin Oriental Hotel; Peninsula Hotel
Just about the only jewellery designer of international repute in the Far East. Kai-Yin (her name means 'dazzling

revelation') has sold her creations to Arianna Stassinopoulos, Natalia Makarova, Ann Getty, Imelda Marcos, Hanae Mori, various Hearsts and British royals. She works semi-precious rocks – tourmaline, agate and jade – into new designs, adding antique slivers of wrought bone or carved beads.

MIRADOR JEWELLERY, 3A, G/F, Carnarvon Rd, Kowloon ☎ 3-699730
Bring-and-buy jewellers who will make up little dazzlers from jewels in the shop, or from any you happen to have. They specialize in stringing along big ropes of beautiful pearls of the Orient.

S P H DE SILVA, Central Bldg, Pedder St, Central ☎ 5-225807
The best pearls in the Colony, by the river and rope. Ranji de Silva is one of the most trustworthy (key HK term in the jewellery trade) in terms of quality and prices for jade (can be tricky – there's little of the real McCoy around), diamonds and all kinds of glittering prizes. They make up and copy specific prize pieces such as a Tiffany dazzler.

SHIRTS·AND TAILORS

Tailors are two-a-cent in Hong Kong, and everyone has their favourite, trusted man. For **Jackie Collins**, it's Ying Ping, *"a very fast tailor at the Peninsula hotel".*

A'MAN HING CHEONG, M-4, Mandarin Oriental Hotel, Central ☎ 5-223336
One of the best tailors, who will forge a Savile Row suit or a Jermyn Street shirt remarkably well. High prices and a quick turnover. *"Wonderful. He does anything you want. He copies very good suits and makes them look even better"* – **Barry Humphries.**

DAVID'S SHIRTS, M-7 Mandarin Oriental Hotel,

Central ☎ 5-242979; 33 Kimberley Rd, G/F, Tsimshatsui ☎ 3-679556
Some of the best made-to-measure shirts in the colony. **Mark Birley** gets his here.

MANSEN GARMENT CO, Great George Bldg, 11 Great George St, Central ☎ 5-768492
Cheapo shirts (about HK$130) in good-quality Japanese cotton. You wander round choosing your cloth, followed by the shirtmaker, who cuts off snippets as you go. Only for those who're stopping off for a few days as they take their time – comparatively.

MEE YEE TAILOR, Yip On Factory Estate, Wai Yip St, Kowloon ☎ 3-756 1450
Excellent dinner shirts made to order. For those who have problems with regular shirts where the piqué finishes above the navel, he'll make one that's piqué all the way. Detachable collars, too.

SAM'S TAILOR, Burlington Arcade, 92-94 Nathan Rd, Kowloon ☎ 3-679423
A tailor of world renown. Some love him, some knock him, but there's no doubt that he's quick, cheap and has a huge variety of material and styles. Caters for everyone, from Princes Philip, Charles, and Rainier of Monaco (shirts) to Jardine Johnnies (red satin boxers).

SHOES

MAYER SHOES, M-23 Mandarin Oriental Hotel, Central ☎ 5-243317
The best (though most expensive) made-to-measure shoes in the South China Sea. If it's got a skin, they can turn it into a shoe. Or a bag. Or a camera case, as they have done for **Lord Lichfield.**

PARIS SHOES AND LEATHERWEAR, Shop D5/6, Basement, Sheraton Hotel, Kowloon ☎ 3-723 7170
The amazing 10-hour made-to-measure shoe (both), bag, briefcase – leather anythings, including clothes. For the jet-

jetsetter. But don't expect *too* much from a 10-hour shoe.

SHOPS

The best Chinese store is **Chinese Arts & Crafts** (see listing), but there are endless cheapo stores jammed with similar, utterly Chinese everyday goodies – from embroidered pillow-cases to little black red-edged notebooks to padded silk Mao jackets. **Chinese Merchandise Emporium** (Queen's Rd, Central and Argyle Centre, Kowloon), **China Products** (Yee Wo St and Hennessy Rd, Causeway Bay; Argyle St, Kowloon) and **Yue Hwa Chinese Products Emporium** (Nathan Rd, Kowloon) are among the best.

BOUTIQUE BAZAAR, Rm 110, 11/F The Landmark, Central ☎ 5-242036
This boutique is owned by the glamorous Annie Ng. Evening wear of the wham-bam-sequinned-femme kind. Farouche sparklers that are the design equivalent of a bazooka – knock 'em dead. Slightly more subdued daywear.

CHARADE BOUTIQUE, Shop 120, Edinburgh Tower, The Landmark, Central ☎ 5-258888
Korean owner Nancy Miller does her own beaded thing for the cocktail hour. Jindo Furs from Korea; Saga and other minks at competitive prices. Also antique and repro Korean chests, beds, etc, at sister store, Gallery 69 (Shop 123).

CHINESE ARTS & CRAFTS, Star House, Kowloon ☎ 3-674061; Silvercord Bldg, 30 Canton Rd; Shell House, Wyndham St, Central; and branches
The best store for mainland China's more capitalistic offerings – bales of inexpensive Chinese silk (plain colours are better than prints); jade, lapis and other precious and semi-precious jewellery; Kai-Yin Lo's beaded bags and belts; classic cashmere jerseys; porcelain tableware and ornaments; exquisite, 10-times-

cheaper-than-Irish-linen embroidered or appliquéd tablecloths and pillow-cases. Quality is strictly government controlled. Eddie Lau's slick little silk dresses are here at in-store boutiques. Also glorious, madly desirable silk undies for peanuts.

JOYCE BOUTIQUE, 214 Gloucester Tower, The Landmark, Central ☎ 5-235236
Owned by Joyce Ma, of the powerful Shanghainese shipping/ banking/department store (Wing On) family. The very best designer boutique, a small stable of top European designer togs with the likes of de la Renta thrown in for graciously modern party gowns. Lagerfeld as Lagerfeld *and* as Fendi furs, Missoni and more. Bags, belts and shoes, too. Joyce also owns the Yamamoto, Miyake and Armani boutiques in town.

LEATHER CONCEPT, 11/F 20 Hing Yip St, Kowloon ☎ 3-899338
A factory shop, which could prove difficult to find (ask your concierge to write the address down in Chinese for the taxi driver). However, it's worth trying for the best leather in the Colony. Their own designer is Hannah Pang; they also have knockout bargains like Calvin Klein leather trousers (c. HK$1,000).

Italy

FLORENCE

ACCESSORIES

BELTRAMI, via Calzaiuoli 31r, 50100 ☎ (055) 214030
Head-to-toe fetish leather, all in that ultra-well-made Italian idiom. Coats, shoes, bags, suits off-the-peg or made-to-measure. Exquisite shoes and boots are snapped up by rich transatlantics, Jenny Gucci and **Anouska Hempel.**

CELLERINI, via del Sole 37r, 50123 ☎ (055) 282533
The Florentine equivalent of Hermès for lush leather and scarves. Smart home-made bags, belts and luggage hand-stitched in their workshops. **Marchesa Bona Frescobaldi**'s favourite for handbags.

HATS

MESSERI, Por Santa Maria 4, 50123 ☎ (055) 296563
Distinguished hats for titled heads such as that of **Marchesa Bona Frescobaldi**. Garden-party and racing-day crowning glories.

JEWELLERY

FARAONE-SETTEPASSI, via Tornabuoni 25r, 50123 ☎ (055) 215506
Have decked out the Florentine nobility since 1860 in pomp and circumstance pieces. Classic gem-encrusted gold and more modern showpieces.

PICCINI, Ponte Vecchio 23, 50125 ☎ (055) 294768
The little shoplets on the Ponte Vecchio are wall-to-wall jewels. Piccini are old, established, exquisite. Rivulets of rubies, emeralds, diamonds, sapphires – the very best stones – crafted to order.

LINGERIE

GARBO, Borgo Ognissanti 2r, 50123 ☎ (055) 295338
Womanly wonders, fantasy foundations and angelic embroidery by a team of ladies on the premises who make and stitch the lot. Pristine, embroidered blouses and ornamental wedding gowns.

LORETTA CAPPONI, Borgo Ognissanti 12, 20123 ☎ (055) 213668
Seduction here with the seal of approval of **Marchesa Bona Frescobaldi** and Jenny Gucci. It's a contest with Garbo to see who's the best in town for heavenly lacy silkies.

FASHION AND SHOPPING

SHOES

**SALVATORE FERRAGAMO,
via Tornabuoni 12-16r, 50100
☎ (055) 292123**
Salvatore himself, once cobbler
to the cognoscenti, is long
gone, but his children carry on
the famous business. The
world's best narrow-fitting shoe
and **Marchesa Bona
Frescobaldi**'s favourites. Also
clothes to accessorize the
shoes.

SHOPS

**LUISA VIA ROMA, via Roma
19-21r, 50100 ☎ (055) 217826**
Stocks the raffish and refined
avant-garde: Miyake, Kenzo,
Gaultier, Comme des Garçons.
Kudos is a Luisa carrier bag.
At their branch in via del Corso
they sell their own designs in
the same free spirit.

**OSCAR PARISOTTO, via
Calimala 33-35r, 50123
☎ (055) 214598**
Oscar is the wizard of a certain
look, irrevocably Italian with
shades of London street – and
they call it Il Look Parisotto.

**PUCCI BOUTIQUE, via dei
Pucci 6, 50122 ☎ (055) 283061**
Remember Emilio? Marchese
Pucci? You will if you wore
Pucci prints in the 1950s and
'60s. The Marchese is still bold-
printing with style on draped
and flowing silks, foulards à la
Botticelli, and the '60s revival
means a re-flowering of Pucci.
Also wonderful men's tailoring,
women's clothing and
accessories. *"It's one of the
most beautiful buildings in
Florence, the Palazzo Pucci.
They do the best bow ties"* –
Stephen Jones.

**REGALI PARENTI, via dei
Tornabuoni 93r, 50125
☎ (055) 214438**
The best shop for presents,
thinks **Marchesa Bona
Frescobaldi**. Jewellery,
trinkets, silver and gold ware,
porcelain and crystal.

**VALDITEVERE, Lungarno
Soderini 1, 50124
☎ (055) 282707**
Ultra fashionable. An unfailing

line of cotton, linen and silken
chic. **Marchesa Bona
Frescobaldi** shops here with
her aristo friends.

MILAN

ACCESSORIES

**PRADA FRATELLI, Galleria
Vittorio Emanuele II 63,
20121 ☎ (02) 876979**
Contemporary city look in
natty little leather bits and

MARIO GRIGNAFFINI,
via Santi 4, 0412
Fontanellato
☎ (0521) 821354;
workshop: via Fontanino
13. An excellent,
reasonably priced tailor,
based 10 miles west of
Parma, discovered by
Eric Newby: *"He works
with his wife and, unlike a
lot of Savile Row tailors,
sews everything by hand.
He doesn't even need to
copy, just to see the sort of
thing you like. If you
want to look like an
Englishman, you have to
go on at him – though he
should know by now, and
has made some lovely
tweed suits and a fine
evening suit for me. No
English spoken but
someone will oblige on
your behalf."*

bobs, bags, luggage and shoes,
with an exotic specialization in
turtle-skin and elephant hide.
Famous for their dolly little
quilted patent leather circle
bags hung on acres of loopy
chain – so Coco!

DESIGNERS

**BYBLOS, via Senato 35,
20121 ☎ (02) 702959**
International fash fans are
raving about this label. Young
clothes with a dash of English
eccentricity provided by the
design team, London RCA
grads Alan Cleaver and Keith
Varty. Dandified hippie looks.
A great men's collection too.
Stocked also at Max Davoli, via
Marghera 45; Gio Moretti, via
della Spiga 4.

**CERRUTI 1881, at major
stores**
Classic but contemporary good
looks for men and women, the
epitome of good taste. Revered
most for superb menswear –
wonderful day and dinner suits,
impeccably tailored; beautifully
wide-cut trousers; the best
blazers in the world; casual
lounge-around togs. **Bruce
Oldfield** places them next to
Armani and they're tops for
Anouska Hempel. They put
together a mean wardrobe for
Jack Nicholson in *The Witches
of Eastwick*.

**DOLCE & GABBANA, c/o
Marisa Boutique, via Sant'
Andrea 1, 20122 ☎ (02) 795015**
Young buzz design team.
Earthy, peasant girl looks in

BEST BOOKSHOPS

In Florence, it is **BM Libreria**, Borgognissanti 4r, 50123
☎ (055) 294575: one of the widest selections of English books
in Europe, they speak 5 languages and have a shipping service. What is more, they are a positive fount of info on what's
'in' in Tuscany; they profess to know everything from the best
guide and car-hire driver to the best estate agents. In Milan,
Gianni Versace's top bookshop is **Milano Libri**, via Verdi 2,
20121 ☎ (02) 875871; for **Marchesa Fiamma di San Giuliano
Ferragamo**, it's **Idea Books**, via Vigevano 41, 20144
☎ (02) 839 0284 – who stock Italian, English, French, German, Japanese and Chinese books.

FASHION AND SHOPPING

long gauzy skirts, drapy or clinging tops. Dark colours, soft lines. Stocked at **Adriana Mode di Vascellia, via della Spiga 22, 20121 ☎ (02) 708458** (a favourite shop of **Marchesa Fiamma di San Giuliano Ferragamo**) and Italy-wide.

FENDI, via Sant' Andrea 16, 20121 ☎ (02) 791617; via della Spiga 11, 20121 ☎ (02) 799544 For leatherware and furs. See Rome.

🔱 **GIANFRANCO FERRE, via della Spiga 11-13, 20121 ☎ (02) 794864; menswear ☎ (02) 700385** An innovative designer with an architectural approach to design that usually finds expression in sharp, to-the-point city clothes for day, luxurious ease for night. Alive, fun, with a keen colour sense. Dressed-down rumpled menswear.

Who's designing who

Many top name designers are really someone else as well. Here's your undercover checklist of who's who: Gigli is the man behind Callaghan; Soprani designs Basile; Enrico Coveri also designs Touche. The French are in on the act too: Lacroix succeeds Versace as design supremo for Genny (nothing succeeds like success); flamboyant young Eric Bergère, late of Hermès, designs Erreuno now that Armani has relinquished that hold.

🔱 **GIANNI VERSACE, via della Spiga 4, 20121 ☎ (02) 705451; menswear: via Montenapoleone ang Verri 9, 20121 ☎ (02) 790281** Master of creative cutting and sewing techniques, making his mark all over again in the wake of Lacroix – what bravura! Uninhibited use of print and colour, short sculpted sticky-

🔱 —*Italy's Best*— 🔱

	DESIGNERS
1	**GIORGIO ARMANI**
2	**ROMEO GIGLI**
3	**GIANNI VERSACE**
4	**GIANFRANCO FERRE**
5	**VALENTINO**

out skirts that sway from side to side teamed with little fitted jackets. Best for impeccably cut dresses and chic suits. Exemplary menswear too, best in Europe for originally textured fabrics – crocodile-creased and oversewn suits, nobbly jackets, shirts with a sheeny stripe or mottle. "*One of the best men's designers. The only thing I wear these days. He makes you look elegant and very discreet. Everything is so well cut and flattering. For Asian men like myself who are not very tall – about the size of most Italian men – he does terrific clothes*" – **Ken Hom.**

🔱 **GIORGIO ARMANI, via Sant' Andrea 9, 20121 ☎ (02) 792757; EMPORIO ARMANI, via Durini 24, 20122 ☎ (02) 781094; MANI, via Durini 23 ☎ (02) 794248; Armani Bimbo, via Durini 27 ☎ (02) 794248** No 1 in Italy, consistently voted designer of the year by the fashion press, who *adore* him. "*Definitely my favourite Italian designer, streets ahead of the others. He takes men's tailoring and, without going all frilly or soppy about it, makes it so soft and gentle for women. His mix of colours is just wonderful – écru, mouth-watering soft pink, pearl grey ... an incrediby romantic look*" – **Liz Smith.** This autumn, he added an exotica of jewel-bright hues and embossed fabrics. De-structured jackets are his forte. Sensuous, understated and *understanding* – of women's desire to keep abreast of fashion without losing their heads to it. His more affordable, younger, sportier

range is **Emporio Armani**. Fab children's wear and, of course, menswear, where he started. "*I look at some of Armani's jackets and just die for the lapel! His clothes are so beautifully cut and executed*" – **John Galliano**. He's **Bruce Oldfield**'s favourite designer; **Wolfgang Puck**'s too.

KRIZIA, via della Spiga 23, 20121 ☎ (02) 708429 Mariuccia Mandelli is everyone's fave lady designer whose talents stretch to the new Krizia Uomo and Krizia Baby and beyond to kitchen appliances and ceramic tiles. Known for embellished knits and slightly outlandish high fashion. Short boleros, wide trousers, skimpy dresses.

LUCIANO SOPRANI, via Sant' Andrea 14, 20121 ☎ (02) 798327 More of the Italian ideal – superb tailoring with wearability and ease. Cool classics, lately softened up a shade, for men and women.

MISSONI, via Montenapoleone 1, 20121 ☎ (02) 700906 Some of the best knitwear in the world, created by true artists. Marvellous mixing of a broad palette – cornflower, mulberry, mauve, yellow thrown in together. Also Uomo and Baby lines, plus textiles by the bolt, quilts and bedspreads, etc. "*I like their sweaters – they're wonderful*" – **Harvey Goldsmith. Stephen Jones** and **Joan Burstein** are admirers.

MOSCHINO, c/o via Cappuccini 14, 20122 ☎ (02) 761 0200 The wild boy of Milan, into zips, bustiers, safety pins, corsets, crazy hats, crocheted-bedspread skirts, appliqué, horror-story colour and fabric mixes. His 'Inès de la Mélange' with its windmill buttons and Disneyland headgear poked fun at Chanel; Lagerfeld got the joke. "*Really good scarves, humorous and charming*" – **Stephen Jones.**

🔱 **ROMEO GIGLI, c/o via della Spiga 46, 20121 ☎ (02) 799978**

The most important new influence in Italian fashion. Anti-Milan in spirit, he calls his clothes elemental. He paints a moodier palette (lately warmed up with more rich, glowing hues), and cuts in nonconformist, asymmetric, romantic, drapier shapes. *"Really important, he's taken over as No 1"* – **Stephen Jones**. *"The best young designer,"* agrees **Marchesa Fiamma di San Giuliano Ferragamo**. Menswear too. Stocked at **Cose, via della Spiga 8, 20121 ☎ (02) 790703; Pupi Solari, via Mascheroni 12, 20100 ☎ (02) 463325**

UMBERTO GINOCCHIETTI, c/o via Montenapoleone 5, 20121 ☎ (02) 790856
Pretty knitwear. He clicks his needles to a young, modern rhythm, weaving wonderful patterns, using silk and linen mixes. Stocked at **Spiga 31, via della Spiga 31, 20121 ☎ (02) 793502 and Taragano, via Beccaria 4, 20121 ☎ (02) 878411.**

HATS

BORSALINO, corso Vittorio Emanuele II 5, 20121 ☎ (02) 869 0805; galleria Vittorio Emanuele II 92, 20121 ☎ (02) 874244
See Rome.

JEWELLERY

GUIDA PENNISI, via Manzoni 29, 20121 ☎ (02) 862232
Antique neck décor of the Deco kind. Fabulously worked pieces sparkling with great gawking gems to lust after. A slim file of the élite shop here. **Gianni Versace** declares them best jewellers.

SUBERT, via San Pietro all' Orto 26, 20121 ☎ (02) 793220
Eclectic baubles from the '30s and '40s, when they went in for show-stopping glamour.

LINGERIE

ARS ROSA, via Montenapoleone 8, 20121 ☎ (02) 793822
Swoonworthy satin and silk dream wear to send shivers down your spine. Deeply feminine dainties in hand-embroidered silk. Finely crafted wedding dresses and lingerie for the trousseau. Dinky babes' and children's foundations and nightwear.

DONINI BIANCHERIA, via Verri 10, 20121 ☎ (02) 702568
Embroidery extraordinaire: Italians just can't get enough of their wildly accomplished workmanship, here to be found on pure and simple silks and cottons.

STIRLING MOSS'S BEST CARS …

"There's an intangible quality in cars, it's about image. They are like women – you make up your mind what type you like to be seen with. The **ultimate car** *is the* **Ferrari***. The* **GTO***, made a couple of years ago in a limited edition of 200, sold for about £87,000; now you could make 100% profit. The GTO is a superb car – superb braking, acceleration, cornering – and an image. Ferraris have quite a noisy 12-cylinder engine, but it's a fantastic noise, a unique, superb sound – a noise you enjoy to hear. I like quiet cars, yet the noise of a Ferrari I find very exciting … Porsche is reliable, has good performance and road-holding, everything a sporty car should have, and everything a Ferrari has … but it isn't a Ferrari … The* **best family car** *is a* **Renault Espace***, which handles like a car but has the capacity of a van. Nice to drive, an enormous amount of space, very adaptable … The* **best convertible** *is a* **Peugeot 205** *or* **BMW 325i."***

LA PERLA, at Valentina, via Manzoni 44, 20121 ☎ (02) 796028
Catherine Deneuve, Princess Stéphanie, Sophia Loren, Jackie Onassis and Mme Mitterrand buy sleek undies by La Perla. Pleated, printed and plain silk camisoles, bras, basques, hosiery, swimwear – and scent as well.

PRATESI, via Montenapoleone 21, 20121 ☎ (02) 783950
Stacks of satin knickers, silky smalls and other skimpies of pure silk, cotton and lace to wear next to your designer dresses.

SHOES

ROSSETTI FRATELLI, via Montenapoleone 9, 20121 ☎ (02) 791650
The best shoes in Italy, a major step towards Latin elegance. They're working with the finest leather too. **Mariuccia Mandelli** and **Ed Victor** keep apace. *"Wonderful"* – **Liz Smith**.

SHOPS

CAFFE MODA DURINI, via Durini 14, 20122 ☎ (02) 791188
The top fashion store in the city, the latest prêt-à-porter from Ferré, Valentino, Krizia, Enrico Coveri and knitlets from Missoni. A few foreigners too.

COIN, piazza Cinque Giornate 1, 20122 ☎ (02) 782583
Run by the old Venetian family (with branches Italy-wide). Smashing little in-store designer boutiques for all your Italian and French faves. Plus, the full complement of dept store goodies.

MILA SCHON, via Montenapoleone 2, 20121 ☎ (02) 701803
Known as the Jean Muir of Italy, this Milanese designer of exotic Austro-Hungarian extraction presides at the classy end of the market. An elegant collection of wearables.

LA RINASCENTE, via Santa Radegonda 3, 20121 ☎ (02) 88521
The best store in Italy. A pricy emporium that's tops for Italian goodies for the whole bouncing family. Largely signature designer stuff, emblazoned with a *name* – Versace, Armani, Ferré et al. Great accessories – whatever's new in jewels, belts, scarves.

TAILORS

BOMBINO at Mila Schön, via Montenapoleone 2, 20121 ☎ (02) 701803
Made-to-measure suits (**Bill Blass** ranks them next to Huntsman of Savile Row) tailored with precision by Signor Bombino.

CARACENI, via Fatebenefratelli 16, 20121 ☎ (02) 655 1972
The first name in tailoring. Some of the most elegant men in the world trot along here for their made-to-measure suiting – Gianni Agnelli and the hyper-discriminating Karl Lagerfeld among them. If you lean towards the Latin (as against

---

ITALY: BEST SHOPPING

Smart: In FLORENCE, **via dei Tornabuoni** is the one, replete with Gucci, Valentino, Fendi, Armani, Versace, Ferragamo and the other classics. The more avant-garde edge live on the tiny streets that riddle the city – **via Porta Rossa, via della Vigna Nuova, via Roma, via Condotta**. In MILAN, **via della Spiga** is the ritziest street for all levels of Italian fashion. **Via Montenapoleone** is the more established street for the major international names; **via Sant' Andrea** is fash-full too. In ROME, **via Condotti, via del Corso and via Borgognona** are where shopping starts and finishes: all the best tailors, shirt-makers, fash shops, plus Bulgari, Gucci and Fendi a-plenty.

Street: in FLORENCE, **San Lorenzo** market is fab for new cut-price fashion – leather wallets, bags, shoes, lambswool jerseys and scarves, stylish bits and bobs; in MILAN, the best markets for antiques and some clothes are in **via Madonnina**, in the young trendy Brera district (third Sat of the month) and along the canals of Porta Ticinese, known as the **Naviglio** (last Sun of the month) – fave of **Gianni Versace**. For new clothes, go to **Fiera di Senegallia**, around via San Luca (every Sat) and **viale Papiniano**, where you can sometimes find knock-down designer gear. The best markets in ROME, for mainly new clothes, are at **Porta Portese** (Sat) and **Campo dei Fiori.**

Anglo-Saxon) look, they're best in the world.

ROME

ACCESSORIES

GUCCI, via Condotti 8, 00187 ☎ (06) 678 9340
One of the world's most famous shops – knockout leather feverishly branded, stamped, adorned and inbred with the notorious double G, snaffles and red-and-green-striped ribbon. Also non-emblemed shoes, bags, wallets, belts, baby-soft scarves and stoles, umbrellas, and, at **via Condotti 77 ☎ (06) 679 6147**, men's and women's clothes.

COUTURE

🐾 **VALENTINO, via Gregoriana 24, 00187 ☎ (06) 67391**
Dressing-up for the seductive screen goddess. A technical wizard in the realms of stand-up ruffles, enormous bows, etc. Jewel-bright hues.

Big fans are **Shakira Caine, Lynn Wyatt, Anouska Hempel** and **Joan Collins**, who is always spottable at his shows. **Marchesa Bona Frescobaldi** would walk miles for his shoes, designed by René Caovilla, and she'd go all the way to Bologna to **Papillon Boutique Valentino, Galleria Cavour 7a, 40124 ☎ (051) 234386**, her favourite fashion store, for the full Valentino range. "*I do like Valentino,*" says **Lord Donoughue**, "*but not for me!*"

FURS

FENDI, via Borgognona 39, 00187 ☎ (06) 679 7641
The most inspired, wittiest, most sumptuous furs in the world, designed by the irrepressible Karl Lagerfeld. **Marchesa Bona Frescobaldi** and **Aniko Gaal** wholeheartedly go along with that. Sacrilegious slicing of fabulous pelts, from mink T-shirts to lacquered golden sables, fur-cuffed evening gowns to floor-sweeping drama coats in fitch,

squirrel or fox. And now fake fur finery. Every one will knock 'em dead – and that goes for your bank manager too.

HATS

BORSALINO, via IV Novembre 157b, 00187 ☎ (06) 679 4192
Classic hats for men and women: homburgs, fedoras in the best felts, velours. Also men's clothes.

JEWELLERY

BUCCELLATI, via Condotti 31, 00187 ☎ (06) 679 0329
Perhaps the best silversmiths and goldsmiths alive today. Their jewels are a hit with **Joan Collins.**

BULGARI, via Condotti 10, 00187 ☎ (06) 679 3876
World-famous jewellery designers for important pieces with Renaissance, neo-classical and other historical influences. The best, say **Mariuccia Mandelli** and **Giorgio Armani**. Beautiful collars of crystal and gold studded with gems.

MASENZA, via del Corso 410, 00186 ☎ (06) 679 1344
Creative designers who have the edge on setting and style, though their stones are not quite up to Massoni's.

MASSONI, Largo Goldoni 48, 00187 ☎ (06) 679 0182
No glitz, glam or fuss – just straight, simple, stunning

> *❝ I like a few Italian things off the hook. You know they weren't made for you. I'm sick of clothes that look as though they fit ❞*

BARRY HUMPHRIES

silver and classic finery using serious stones.

LINGERIE

BLANCHE DE SANVOISIN, via Crispi 109, 00187 ☎ (06) 679 5365
Bijou, effete, irresistible shop, best of the best for the Italian trousseau, The most luxuriously linens and silks, hand-embroidered and made-to-measure by the modern continuation of medieval artisans.

SHIRTS

RADICONCINI, via del Corso 139, 00186 ☎ (06) 679 1807
The absolute best in shirts. These swanky tops come by the dozen, handmade to measure, with *hand-embroidered* monograms, no less.

SHOES

DAL CO, via Vittoria 65, 00187 ☎ (06) 678 6536
Best of the best in Italy, famed for their masterful handling of snakeskin. Diana Vreeland recognized the quality.

MARIO VALENTINO, via Frattina 84a, 00187 ☎ (06) 679 1246
Exquisite coquettish evening slippers.

POLLINI, via Frattina 24, 00198 ☎ (06) 678 9028
Siren shoes and gorgeous little boots in silken leather.

SHOPS

BALESTRA, via Sistina 67, 00187 ☎ (06) 679 2917
A charmingly old-fashioned shop with beautifully worked timeless designer pieces that discriminating donnas love. Elegant menswear too.

BATTISTONI, via Condotti 57, 00187 ☎ (06) 679 5527
The best of the bunch of Italian and French designer clothes and accessories. Own-label made-to-measure and ready-to-wear as well.

CAMOMILLA, piazza di Spagna 85, 00187 ☎ (06) 679 3551
Trendy storehouse for stars of stage and screen and up-to-date yups. It's the French and Jap designer clothes (Thierry Mugler, Chantal Thomass, Kenzo, Yamamoto) that gives them an upmarket edge over their blinkered all-Italian-buying rivals.

PARMA HAMS

"Parma is one of the most elegant cities. You notice a tremendous difference between the women in Parma and those in Siena, where they look as though they've been put through a washing machine. In Parma they are totally involved with clothes. At the end of the season everything – it doesn't matter if it's an Armani – is a goner. In the evening, at that lovely moment before dusk, the imbrunire, they perambulate the main streets to be seen – the passeggiata. Every country in the world where Italians have been still makes the passeggiata – even in poor old Albania they do it in their drip-dry shirts" – **Eric Newby.**

Japan

COUTURE

HANAE MORI, Omotesando, 3-6-1 Kita-Aoyama, Minato-ku ☎ (03) 400 3301
Haute couture in the European tradition by the woman known

FASHION AND SHOPPING

as The Iron Butterfly. She actually started by re-interpreting kimono silks into floating evening dresses with chiffon butterfly wings, *and* she's done costumes for *Madame Butterfly* at La Scala. Her métier is the little Ascot-style printed silk dress. Now she designs anything that moves – couture and prêt-à-porter, breakfast to ballgown, Hanae Mori tights, bed-linen, jewellery, even handkerchiefs – and it's all laid out in her own building.

DESIGNERS

"Japanese fashion is a total blank for me – I've watched it with growing horror in Paris. But it's had it's moment. What they are brilliant at is retailing" – **Liz Smith**. No one is more expert in producing a total package: the designer shop to go with the designer clothes to go with the designer accessories. Pastmasters in the art are the triumvirate of geniuses, Rei Kawakubo, Yohji Yamamoto and Issey Miyake.

COMME DES GARCONS, 5-11-5 Minami-Aoyama, Minato-ku ☎ **(03) 407 2480**
The best, most respected designer from Japan. Rei Kawakubo is the matriarch of the Jap look, creator of the holey-sweatered bag lady. While remaining purist, élitist and avant-garde, she swings gently with the tide of fashion – last spring, bias-cut asymmetric jackets with short culottes and shorts; this autumn, splashes of red. Rei's also tops for unbalanced shoes, lingerie and hats. Homme Plus is cult among men – mis-buttoned, sometimes crinkled shirts, odd little hats, clumpy sandals, brilliant suits, the lot. **John Galliano** is a keen fan:

"The clothes make me feel good." Rei designed the environment to slot her clothes into. The shop is small with a minimal stock fashionably crumpled on hangers and slung on to shelves (it took hours to arrange them thus).

ISSEY MIYAKE, Tessenkai Bldg, B1, 4-21-29 Minami-Aoyama, Minato-ku ☎ **(03) 423 1408**
Issey is the philosopher, the intellectual, the designer poet, the handsomest man in Japan. Well known for his inventive synthetics and origami cutting, you'd never guess he trained with Beene, Givenchy and Guy Laroche. Makes clothes that start as one thing and turn into something else – jackets into bags, bags back into fake fur coats. Wrong-buttoned cardigans, inside-out-seamed baggy knits, kitsch prints, unnerving colour mixes. His less expensive lines are Plantation and Issey Sports. Permanente is his collection of classics from the past 15 years. Bold outsize shirts and loose tailoring for men.

MATSUDA for MADAME NICOLE, Nicole Bldg, 3-1-25 Jingumae, Shibuya-ku ☎ **(03) 470 4821**
Known as Matsuda overseas,

he is head of the established and successful Nicole empire in Japan. Wonderful wearable suits, dresses and separates in luxury fabrics with superb detailing (insets of contrast fabric, buttons, self-coloured embroidery). A definite look, punched home by shrewd marketing and packaging. Matsuda does exquisitely detailed menswear too.

YOHJI YAMAMOTO, 3F Maison Roppongi, 6-4-9 Roppongi, Minato-ku ☎ **(03) 423 3200**
Goateed ringleader of the gang of three, champion of origami asymmetrics and ex-paramour of Rei Kawakubo, Yohji is a masterful tailor with a wry sense of whimsy. As one model has said, when you don a Yohji, you feel he made it for you alone; you put on a dress, it becomes you. Like the others, he's mellowed from merciless black to fresh colour, even pattern. His word is divine in the pop world, for Beatrice Dahl (*Betty Blue*), and for Michèle Halberstadt.

YUKIKO HANAI for MADAME HANAI, Roi Bldg, 2nd Fl, 5-5-1 Roppongi, Minato-ku ☎ **(03) 404 5791**
A designer in the Hanae Mori mould – she does the upmarket, conservative look for smart young Tokyo.

Young Designers

JUN SAITO for GRASS MEN'S at Parco Part 2, 15-1 Udagawa-cho, Shibuya-ku ☎ **(03) 463 6656**
"Sophisticated but not stuffy clothes" – **Judith Connor**. His maxim is to produce clothes that are *"decidedly masculine and yet not restricted to conservative patterns"*.

—*Japan's Best*—

DESIGNERS

1	**REI KAWAKUBO for COMME DES GARCONS**
2	**ISSEY MIYAKE**
3	**YOHJI YAMAMOTO**
4	**MATSUDA**
5	**HANAE MORI**
6	**JUNKO SHIMADA**

---

66 *When I first started designing, I had to confront the Japanese people's excessive worship of things foreign and their fixed ideas of what clothes ought to be. Today I am creating things that break national boundaries* **99**

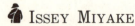 ISSEY MIYAKE

JUNKO KOSHINO, 6-5-36 Minami-Aoyama, Minato-ku ☎ (03) 498 3404
Skiwear meets Star Trek. Sculptural lean and mean looks in black leather, jersey and rubberized fabrics, to show off every contour of the body. Strong, futuristic stuff.

🐟 **JUNKO SHIMADA, Aobadai Terrace, 1-1-4 Aobadai, Meguro-ku** ☎ (03) 463 2346
Funky, fun, wearable garb which goes down a bomb with Americans.

KOSHIN SATOH for ARRSTON VOLAJU, 7-3-25 Roppongi, Minato-ku ☎ (03) 479 8151
His shows are futuristic, acrobatic theatre, with a cast of thousands. There's something for everyone in a Japanese-meets-Western hybrid style. *"I pride myself on clothes with superior construction,"* he says. *"I design for those with a free imagination."*

SHIN HOSOKAWA for PASHU, 8-11-37 Akasaka, Minato-ku ☎ (03) 479 0197
Men's and women's wear. *"Very modern, monotone fashions"* – **Judith Connor**; or as Shin himself puts it: *"Caught up in a very mechanical and unemotional world, I represent life through multiple effects achieved by colour, design and materials that are presented in a sharp, penetrating manner."*

STUDIO-V by IRIE, Hanae Mori Bldg, Omotesando, 3-6-1 Kita-Aoyama, Minato-ku ☎ (03) 406 3177
The label is something of a collective for Hanae Mori's swinging young protégés. Irie Sueo, former designer for Kenzo, was the first person working under the label.

TAKEO KIKUCHI, 6-6-22 Minami-Aoyama, Minato-ku ☎ (03) 486 6607
A hot new menswear designer, responsible for the TK Building in Nishi Azabu, where his prep-school bedsit-style shop lives alongside his nightclub Bohemia and Snooker Bar (see Social & Night Life). Witty and inventive, he aims to design

TOKYO: BEST SHOPPING

Smart: **Ginza** has the major stores – Matsuya, Mitsukoshi, Takashimaya, Isetan, Kanebo, Hankyu and Seibu (PS avoid on Sunday when the whole of Japan tries to cram into the street). **Minami-Aoyama** was the bubbling breeding ground for Yohji and the gang; designers still spring predominantly from this serious trend centre, along with **Kita-Aoyama** and **Jingumae**. Here, **Omotesando** is the sleek fashiony boulevard, with the Hanae Mori Bldg, Spiral, Vivre 21, etc; it gathers momentum in the way of chi-chi shops, crêperies, cafés and ice-cream parlours as it leads into Harajuku.
Street: No bargains *anywhere*. However, the younger, buzzier part of town is **Harajuku**, with its boutiques and stalls for shades, T-shirts, etc. Nose-to-nose weenyboppers.

clothes that are exciting to wear, for people with personality.

TOKIO KUMAGAI, 3-51-10 Sendagaya, Shibuya-ku ☎ (03) 475 5317
Darling of Paris and Tokyo alike for his nutty couture-look shoes (shops in Paris and New York), he does men's and now wonderful women's wear, too, with the same irreverent spirit that possesses the Parisians. His shoes are beautifully made and totally frivolous – inspired by Kandinsky or Pollock or mice or poetry. Kumagai says: *"My design emphasis has to be on originality."*

YUKIO KOBAYASHI for MONSIEUR NICOLE, Nicole Bldg, 1F, 3-1-25 Jingumae, Shibuya-ku ☎ (03) 478 0998
Easy menswear with great detailing. Over to Yukio himself for the design philosophy: *"Clothes are an everyday necessity which should be comfortable and practical. I prefer simple designs, so I concentrate on the intricate details, colours and subtleties that give a garment distinction."*

SHOES

See also Tokio Kumagai (Designers).

JURGEN LEHL, 1-13-18 Jingumae, Shibuya-ku ☎ (03) 405 9737

A German who has been in Japan for years – the only foreigner to make it here. Uses the ancient Japanese technique of lacquering on deerskin. Avant-garde bags for bag ladies, and clothes too.

SHOPS

BOUTIQUE YUYA, 3-10-12 Moto-Azabu, Minato-ku ☎ (03) 408 5749
The very best place to find contemporary clothes made up in traditional, out-of-this-world Japanese kimono fabrics.

LA FORET, 1-11-6 Jingumae, Shibuya-ku ☎ (03) 475 0411
Based in two buildings, an open-plan collection of young contemporary and experimental fashion boutiques, from make-up and jewellery to shoes and clothes for men and women. Jam-packed with Harajuku kids.

MATSUYA, 3-6-1 Ginza, Chuo-ku ☎ (03) 567 1211
A marvellous store displaying the whole gamut of fashion, plus, on the 7th floor, some of the world's best contemporary product design.

NUNO, Axis Bldg, B1, 5-17-1 Roppongi, Minato-ku ☎ (03) 582 7997
The best traditional fabrics. The place for beautiful hand-painted or printed silk kimono lengths.

FASHION AND SHOPPING

DESIGNER BUILDINGS

Is it a department store? Is it a shopping mall? No, it's a *building*. A building with a name (Seed, Spiral, Prime . . .) and an overall design concept. Designed to within an inch of their lives in grey, always grey, distressed concrete, marble, granite (matt rather than shiny), brushed steel, etc, these buildings deserve a position in Pseuds' Corner. It's cool to spatter English or French words around (Image, Concept, Design, Le Style, even Information – though the info's all in Japanese); floors have names and themes; each boutique, eatery, arts space and beauty salon within the building forms an integral part of the whole. These are the best: **TK BUILDING** (see Takeo Kikuchi, Designers); **SEED** (see Shops) and **WAVE**, 6-2-21 Roppongi, Minato-ku ☎ (03) 408 0111 (both part of Seibu; Wave is *the* record store with pop videos galore and compact discs you didn't know existed, plus designer goods such as the Gymnopédie collection of matt black Filos, bags, etc); **SPIRAL**, Omotesando, 5-6-23 Minami-Aoyama, Minato-ku ☎ (03) 498 1171 has a curious wide, sweeping, spiral staircase; gifty items (soaps, stationery, china) at Spiral Market, a bar (Cay), foyer café, art and exhibition spaces, video studio and beauty design centre. The slogan of **AXIS**, 5-17-1 Roppongi, Minato-ku ☎ (03) 587 2781 is 'living/design/concept'. More precinct-like; the best in modern furniture, tableware, kitchen goods, crafts, fabrics and design products – kangaroo-skin driving shoes from Le Garage (great for short hops), goose-down pillows and the most minimal-ever furniture from Cassina.

The biggest and the best store showing the latest and the cream of world fashion and design. *"Awesome. It has everything"* – **Mark McCormack**. Kudos is carried in a Seibu bag. It covers the whole fashion spectrum, from indigenous futurist stretchy black numbers to the (highly popular) English country look. Hermès, Vuitton, Rykiel, Lauren and all the foreign labels have boutiques here, as do Miyake, Comme des Garçons, Yohji and the young crew. Gaijin-size tights and great presents. And now a foreign customer helpline: ☎ (02) 286 5482.

VIVRE 21, Omotesando, 5-10-1 Jingumae, Shibuya-ku ☎ (03) 498 2221
Slick, unusually spacious hall of fashion. Shin Hosokawa, Takeo Kikuchi, Nicole and all the hip names are there. Jean-Paul Gaultier has a replica of his Paris shop (sea-green steel girders, portholes, Roman statues); next door is Koshin Satoh's sci-fi cavern with rough-hewn walls, snakeskin upholstery, serpentine lamps coiled like cobras, one wall that forms a face with green-lit eyes and snakes crawling over it.

ORIENTAL BAZAAR, Omotesando, 5-9-13 Jingumae, Shibuya-ku ☎ (03) 400 3933
For authentic, trad Japanese crafts and goods – little lacquer bowls and chopsticks, pearls, hand-blocked prints, paintings, china, furniture and ornate wedding kimonos of heavy silk brocade – to hang on the wall rather than about your person.

PARCO, 15-1 Udagawa-cho, Shibuya-ku ☎ (03) 464 5111
Stylish Japanese shopping phenomenon, a store in the Seibu group. Divided into Parts 1 (general, for good less extortionate shopping), 2 (the smallest, for one-stop Jap designer boutiques) and 3. A haven of Issier-than-thou customized shoplets where international designerdom vies for Tokyo's most taste-ridden customers. Its own exhibition space, cinema and theatre in

Part 1. To find the place sans hassle, take exit 6 from Shibuya (also for Seibu and Seed).

SEED, 21-1 Udagawa-cho, Shibuya-ku ☎ (03) 462 0111
The chic-est part of Seibu with the most original his 'n' hers lavatory signs – they're holograms. Tall, slim, grey, it's home to all the trendsetters in fashion – on 2F, 'The Express', are the young international crew – Hamnett, Betty Jackson, NO? YES!; 3F; 'The Season', 'expresses the seasonable trend dynamically' – with accessories; also a major Issey representation, cool menswear lines, the best of up-and-coming Jap fashion, fab jewellery and an English Tea House called the Café Anglais.

SEIBU, (Ginza), 2-1 Yurakucho, Chiyoda-ku ☎ (03) 286 0111 and branches

Singapore

CENTREPOINT, 176 Orchard Rd
Homesick Brits find solace at Singapore's **St Michael** (Marks & Sparks to the rest of the world). Also Charles Jourdan, Benetton and **Robinsons'** – the original 'English' department store, for exquisite presents, perfumes, tableware . . .

HILTON SHOPPING GALLERY, 581 Orchard Rd ☎ 737 2233
The best hotel shopping arcade with a handy supply of top European labels: Valentino, Ferré, Cartier, Dunhill, Gucci, Vuitton, Lanvin, Davidoff and L'Ultima shoes, plus Matsuda (for homesick Japs), antiques,

Singapore: Best Shops

In a city that is overloaded with European designer labels for the Japanese, and Japanese superstores for the locals, 2 stores excel: **C K Tang**, housing Gucci, Dunhill, YSL and other Euro labels; and **Metro** (4 branches in the Orchard area), with *branché* designer boutiques and own-label quality gear . . . much-patronized by locals. **Le Classique** is the best for local merchandise – batik shirts, carved ornaments, duty-free goods (and a policy to refund you the difference if you find the same article cheaper elsewhere). **Orchard Point**, housing over 80 shops and restaurants, is good for curios, antiques and leatherware. *The* place for jewellery and stones (prices and authenticity are regulated), is the **South Bridge Centre**. And for electronic gadgetry (plus cosmetics, furnishings and more), go to the **Funan Centre.**

paintings, jewellery, leather goods and other temptations.

SCOTTS SHOPPING CENTRE, Scotts Rd
☎ 235 5055

A S$200 million development offering some of the best shopping on the island. Etienne Aigner for clothes, handbags, shoes; a China Silk House; Diane Freis; Fellini; Ellesse sportswear. Home to the latest branch of **Tangs** department store which has taken over from the Metro Grand.

Thompson (see Silk). Lock on to **Teeraphan Wanarat** (who dresses all the society ladies in day and evening wear), **Daung Jai Bis**, **Urai Risa** and **Venick.**

JEWELLERY

The **Peninsula Plaza**, Rajadamri Rd, is home to **Bualaad Jewellery** and **Frank's Jewellery**, who bejewel high-society necks with whopping rubies and other precious stones. Also **Chailai**, a treasure trove of ethnic pieces sought out from northern Thailand by Princess

Chailai herself, and creatively restructured to her design.

LOTUS, Kannika Court, The Regent, 155-157 Rajadamri Rd
☎ (2) 250 0732

For the most exquisite Oriental trinkets and antiques, go to this beautiful boutique, managed by blue-blooded socialite Khun Ying Malinee, who knows *every*one. You must remove your shoes before stepping on the raised antique teak floor. Design – not carats – is paramount; unique antique and repro silver work, semi-precious carved stones, small presents, antique embroidery and tribal rugs.

SILK

JIM THOMPSON, 9 Surawong Rd ☎ (02) 234 4900

The best silk spot in the world for gloriously grainy and lustrous Thai silks in jewel and iridescent colours – Parma violet, purples, blues, emerald, peacock, flaming orange. New cotton furnishing fabrics too in the same vibrant palette. Enormous but elegant cushions with leopards rampant, dragons and other designs in jungular vein. Chic ready-to-wear. **Marie Helvin** thinks Jim's is world best. **Glynn Christian** finds them tops for *"Thai ties for short men."*

Thailand

BANGKOK
DESIGNERS

KAI GUERLAIN, 2-14 N Wireless Rd ☎ (02) 253 2998

Kai has run his mini-fashion dictatorship here for years, holding frequent fashion shows at the top hotels. A bit dated, but a loyal following.

Young Designers

The best of young design is to be found on the 2nd floor of the swanky new **Charn Isala Tower**, Rama V Rd – just 2 minutes' walk from Jim

Bangkok: Best Shopping

Smart: **Peninsula Plaza** is the smartest shopping centre, along with the **Regent** and **Oriental** arcades.

Street: Bangkok has taken over as the leading city for tailor-made women's clothes, completed in double-quick time – and still for a pittance. The **Siam Centre** is a maze of shoplets for cheapish young designer wear and other trend purchases. Good-quality fake designer cheap-as-cheap goods can be found around **Silom Village** in Silom Road, street 'bazaars' between **Sois 7 and 11 off Sukhumvit Road**, and the **Gaysorn** area. **Thai Home Industries**, 35 Oriental Ave, has ethnic craftware if you don't have time to hunt round the street stalls. **Chatuchak Park**, off Phalan Yothin Rd, is a weekend market for all things weird and wonderful, especially good for Thai antiques and bric-à-brac. 'Antiques' can be checked for authenticity by the Fine Arts Department ☎ (2) 233 0977 for 1,000 baht per item.

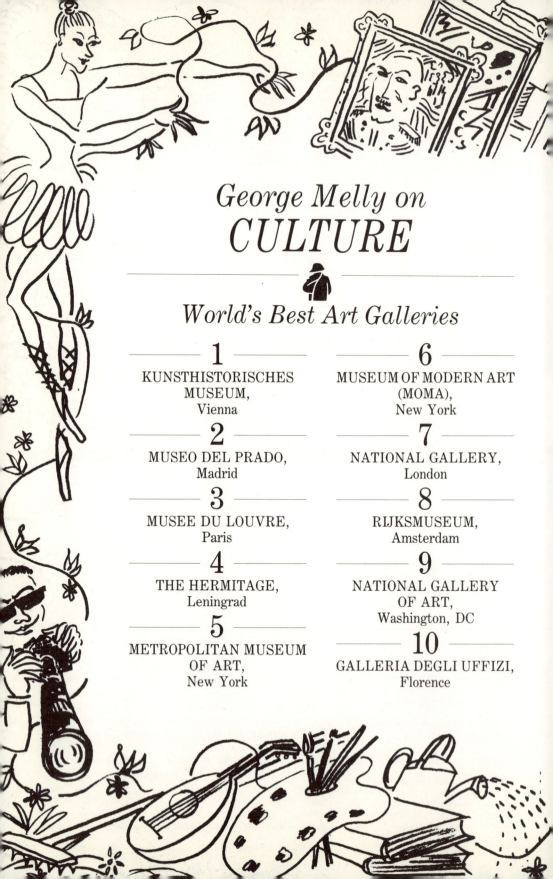

George Melly on
CULTURE

World's Best Art Galleries

1
KUNSTHISTORISCHES
MUSEUM,
Vienna

2
MUSEO DEL PRADO,
Madrid

3
MUSEE DU LOUVRE,
Paris

4
THE HERMITAGE,
Leningrad

5
METROPOLITAN MUSEUM
OF ART,
New York

6
MUSEUM OF MODERN ART
(MOMA),
New York

7
NATIONAL GALLERY,
London

8
RIJKSMUSEUM,
Amsterdam

9
NATIONAL GALLERY
OF ART,
Washington, DC

10
GALLERIA DEGLI UFFIZI,
Florence

The late and largely unlamented Field Marshal Goering once said, "When I hear the word 'culture', I reach for my revolver." The *word* may have affected him that way, but not, it would seem, the artefacts themselves. Behind the Panzer divisions, as they swept through Europe, the fatman's agents filled up many a pantechnicon of art treasures for their master's solitary delectation.

All of us, or nearly all of us, appreciate culture in one form or another. When I was in the Navy, a fellow Able Seaman, of cherubic countenance but psychopathic tendencies, used to keep the entire and intimidated mess-deck awake after he returned from a drunken and Attila-like night ashore by playing the music of Johann Sebastian Bach on his wind-up gramophone.

This section, from Hong Kong to Lugano, includes enough culture – musical, visual, theatrical, operatic, architectural, balletic, avant-garde and folkloric – to sate the most avid vulture, and turn the Field Marshal's revolver red hot.

What is so unique about this guide is that the information doesn't come from a fellow tourist, however knowledgeable, but from a citizen of the town itself – a totally different angle. Parisians or New Yorkers or Sydneysiders know more about the splendours (and miseries) of their home turf than peripatetic culture vultures.

However, there are very few people who are culturally polymathic and, just because you are away from home, there is no obligation to pay homage to culture per se. If, as a Londoner, you would never dream of visiting the National Gallery, there is not much point in trudging round the Prado. If, as a Milanese, you've never entered La Scala, why spend a fortune on a stall at the Met?

So use this section with discrimination and it will yield great treasures – and not just the obvious (the world-famous orchestra, the great national gallery), but lesser-known and equally rewarding musical or aesthetic local 'secrets'. Sometimes on a visit to, say, Rome or Copenhagen, good luck has put me in contact with an individual who could point me in a certain direction to my great advantage. This book rules out the necessity for cultural serendipity. It is an essential guide for those in search of the very best in every artistic sphere.

George Melly

America

BOSTON

ART AND MUSEUMS

BOSTON INSTITUTE OF CONTEMPORARY ART, 955 Boylston St, MA 02115
☎ (617) 266 5152
A space for displaying new painting, sculpture, video, music, dance, photography, film and performance art.

ISABELLA STEWART GARDNER MUSEUM, 280 The Fenway, MA 02115
☎ (617) 566 1401
Italian Renaissance and Dutch Baroque paintings, tapestries and sculptures, set in a replica of a Venetian palazzo with a flower-filled courtyard. *"Wonderful Old Masters in a very beautiful house"* – **Loyd Grossman**. *"An eccentric museum which I like ..."* – **Lord Gowrie**.

♣ **MUSEUM OF FINE ARTS**, 465 Huntington Ave, MA 02115 ☎ (617) 267 9300
The best art gallery in Boston: French Impressionists, the largest collection of Asiatic works under one roof, classical and decorative arts. Contemporary art in the new West Wing.

BALLET

BOSTON BALLET, Wang Center, 553 Tremont St, MA 02116 ☎ (617) 542 1323
Under the positive new artistic director Bruce Marks the Ballet is moving forward by leaps and bounds.

MUSIC

BOSTON SYMPHONY ORCHESTRA, Symphony Hall, 301 Massachusetts Ave, MA 02115 ☎ (617) 266 2378
The 108-year-old Boston Symphony is a revered institution. Under music director Seiji Ozawa, they perform over 250 concerts a year. Frequent guest conductors and soloists.

HANDEL & HAYDN SOCIETY, 295 Huntington Ave, MA 02115
☎ (617) 266 3605
Toffy music society, and the oldest continuously active performing music society in the country. Orchestral and choral pieces by various composers (not just Messrs H & H).

♣ **TANGLEWOOD FESTIVAL OF CONTEMPORARY MUSIC, Tanglewood, Lenox**, MA 01240 ☎ (413) 637 1940
The Boston Pops – the Boston Symphony move out of town for July-Aug to play mainly modern classical music here. A host of concerts and choral works by composers such as Pierre Boulez and Stravinsky.

THEATRE

AMERICAN REPERTORY THEATRE, Loeb Drama Center, 64 Brattle St, Cambridge, MA 02138
☎ (617) 547 8300
A lively company that performs classic (lots of Shakespeare and co) and contemporary drama; they have premièred several Broadway hits.

CHICAGO

ART

♣ **THE ART INSTITUTE OF CHICAGO, Michigan Ave at Adams St**, IL 60603
☎ (312) 443 3600
One of the major national art museums. A collection of almost 200,000 works, covering European painting from the Middle Ages to 1900 (a fine set of French Impressionist works), 20th-century painting and sculpture, American arts, Oriental and classical art, photographs, architectural drawings and textiles. The redesigning of 42 galleries has elevated the Art Institute's standing by several notches. Important travelling exhibitions pass this way.

MUSIC

CHICAGO OPERA THEATER, 20 E Jackson, IL 60604 ☎ (312) 663 0048
Founded in 1972, this company is highly regarded for mainly contemporary opera, sung in English. The theatre, a renovated mansion with 925 seats, is based in the grounds of a church.

CHICAGO SYMPHONY ORCHESTRA, Orchestral Hall, 220 S Michigan Ave, IL 60604 ☎ (312) 435 8122
"The best orchestra in the USA" – **Stanley Marcus**. With Sir Georg Solti directing (as he has for over 20 years), it is not surprising. Tuning up for its centenary in 1990.

FORT WORTH

♣ **KIMBELL ART MUSEUM**, 3333 Camp Bowie, TX 76107
☎ (817) 332 8451
Though not up to the Getty's budget, its modest $8 million or so a year makes it the second richest museum in the land. Mainly European art spanning the centuries of the great masters; some Oriental art.

HOUSTON

ART AND MUSEUMS

THE MENIL COLLECTION, 1511 Barnard, TX 77006
☎ (713) 525 9400
A new museum housing Dominique de Menil's private art collection of about 10,000 pieces – antiquities, Byzantine and Mediterranean art, tribal art and modern art, including Picasso, Ernst, Warhol and an impressive number of Magrittes. *"Her collection is special because of the way it's presented and mounted, and the variety"* – **Lynn Wyatt**.

MUSIC

WORTHAM THEATER CENTER, 510 Preston Ave,

TX 77002 ☎ (713) 237 1439
The new centre is home to the highly regarded Houston Grand Opera and Houston Ballet Foundation. 2 theatres – the Brown and the Cullen. Also symphony and pop music concerts. *"The theatre is structured from the inside out – they spent more money inside because of the sound system, etc. It's supposed to be comparable to La Scala"* – **Lynn Wyatt.**

THEATRE

ALLEY THEATER, 615 Texas Ave, TX 77002
☎ (713) 228 9341
Classic, modern classic and some new plays. The theatre has its own international award, given to a person outstanding in theatre or the arts, which is causing interest in dramatic circles. Arthur Miller, Jessica Tandy and Hume Cronyn are recent recipients. *"The Alley Award is becoming more and more prestigious"* – **Lynn Wyatt.**

KEY WEST

ERNEST HEMINGWAY'S HOME AND MUSEUM, 907 Whitehead St, FL 33040
☎ (305) 294 1575
A Spanish colonial house built in 1851 from coral rock. *"A house I've always craved. Photographs don't do it justice – it's a lovely house, with an exterior first-floor balcony. Rooms with shutters opening on to the gallery give endless opportunities for accidental voyeurism!"* – **Frederic Raphael.**

DESERT ISLAND SURVIVAL KIT:

JOAN COLLINS

"My books would be Everything You Ever Wanted to Know About Being Stranded on a Desert Island, *and* Savages *by Shirley Conran. My film,* Robinson Crusoe.*"*

LOS ANGELES

ART AND MUSEUMS

J PAUL GETTY MUSEUM, 17985 Pacific Coast Highway, Malibu, CA 90265
☎ (213) 459 7611
Known worldwide more for its name and incomparable wealth than its collection (Greek and Roman antiquities including the famous Getty bronze; French decorative works; master drawings, sculptures and paintings). Its present home is a peaceful classical Italianate villa, based on the Villa dei Papiri (1st century AD).

Presumably thanks to its problem of how to dispose of its money (c. $90 million must be spent a year), a new showcase designed by Richard Meier is planned for the 1990s on a 162-acre site in the hills above LA. Visitors with cars must book, via: **J Paul Getty Center, 401 Wilshire Blvd, Santa Monica, CA 90406** ☎ (213) 458 2003.

LOS ANGELES COUNTY MUSEUM OF ART, 5905 Wilshire Blvd, CA 90036
☎ (213) 857 6211
Improving and expanding into the 1990s, the County has encapsulated its 1960s buildings in shiny new structures. It is justly proud of its new Robert

---

SCREEN STARS

What would LA be without its cinemas? The best for sheer technical wizardry is **AMC Century 14 Theaters**, Santa Monica Blvd, closely followed by **UNIVERSAL CITY 18 CINEMAS**, Universal City Plaza, the largest movie-theatre complex in the US, lavishly decorated in Art Deco style. All over the city **CINEPLEX ODEONS** are to be focused on – there are 8 in LA, expensively kitted out with 10 to 18 screens, plus bars, restaurants and other luxuries. But for a whiff of old Hollywood, go to the **CHINESE THEATER**, Hollywood Blvd – the one where many a celebrity foot has left its imprint on the sidewalk. *"Any première here is always a festive occasion"* – **Wolfgang Puck.**

❝ *At their best, I prefer silent movies, because they are a distinct medium. Sound movies have to avoid being a photographed stage play. Cinema is telling a story pictorially. The appeal to the eye is more immediate and profound than the appeal to the ear, which is intellectual but not as emotional* **❞**

 DOUGLAS FAIRBANKS JR

O Anderson building, devoted to 20th-century art. Excellent collections of Indian, 18th- and 19th-century American works, plus earlier European art. *"This museum and MOCA are among the most respected museums in the world"* – **Wolfgang Puck.**

🔱 **MUSEUM OF CONTEMPORARY ART,** 250 S Grand Ave, CA 90012 ☎ (213) 621 2766
New and dynamic, MOCA is based in a rose sandstone building designed by Japanese architect Arata Isozaki. *"Probably the best new museum building anywhere. The only criticism is that it's already small for its purpose and not easily enlarged"* – **Edward Lucie-Smith.** It's certainly acquiring like crazy. A lack of greenbacks is the only drawback.

NORTON SIMON MUSEUM, 411 W Colorado Blvd, **Pasadena, CA 91105** ☎ (818) 449 6840
Based in a structure that Thomas Hoving has described as 'like a ribbon cartridge for some enormous electric typewriter'. *"The best collection of Old Masters. Better than the Getty, the LA County or anything in San Francisco"* – **Edward Lucie-Smith.** Unhappily, most of the paintings are behind 'denglas' (to protect them from UV rays).

MUSIC AND THEATRE

LA COUNTY MUSIC CENTER, 135 N Grand Ave, CA 90012 ☎ (213) 972 7200
Three buildings connected by a plaza with a fountain. The Dorothy Chandler Pavilion is the most elaborate hall (huge chandeliers, lots of mirrors), where the LA Philharmonic plays and where the Academy Awards Ceremony always used to be. (This year it was held at the even-larger Shrine Auditorium; next year who knows?) The Mark Taper Forum is an experimental

theatre in the round: new plays, new directors. The Ahmanson Theater is the baby: musicals and small plays.

NEW ORLEANS

NEW ORLEANS JAZZ AND HERITAGE FESTIVAL, PO Box 2530, LA 70176 ☎ (504) 568 0251
Over 4,000 musicians and cooks descend on the city at the end of April to give 300,000 hungry listeners an earful and a gutful of whatever suits their palate: Louisiana dishes such as file gumbo, alligator, jambalaya or turtle stew piquante, washed down by jazz, rhythm 'n' blues, Gospel, Afro-Caribbean, Cajun, blues, folk, Latin and ragtime.

PRESERVATION HALL, see Social & Night Life

NEW YORK

ART AND MUSEUMS

FRICK COLLECTION, 1 E 70th St, NY 10021 ☎ (212) 288 0700
A Louis XV/XVI-style mansion (built 1913-14), former residence of industrialist Henry Clay Frick, and home to his superb collection of European

Old Masters. *"Marvellous because it is in a house rather than a purpose-built museum. The pictures look right because they are hung on proper walls"* – **Lord Lichfield.** *"I like it because it's not that big. I get very intimidated by large galleries and museums because there's too much to take in"* – **Michael Grade. Jeffrey Archer** also gets a kick out of the Frick.

🔱 **METROPOLITAN MUSEUM OF ART,** 5th Ave/82nd St, NY 10028 ☎ (212) 879 5500
Like the Louvre, this is one to take in small doses. A tour of the majestic building with its lofty multi-domed Great Hall takes you through Egypt, including the Temple of Dendur (reassembled as it appeared on the banks of the Nile); onwards through ancient Greece and Rome; the art of Islam, Africa, Oceania and the Americas; endless European masterpieces; reconstructed rooms from Europe; and the celebrated 20th-century art wing run by William Lieberman. There's always a dazzling exhibition at the Costume Institute, and changing shows. *"Very good"* – **Lord Montagu of Beaulieu.** *"I go there all the time – I love it"* – **Margaux Hemingway.** *"A treasure"* – **Helen Gurley Brown.** A hit with **Jeffrey Archer** too. *"Too big..."* – **Auberon Waugh.** *"A wonderful collecton, you can't*

🕵 **Buzzzzzzzzz** After the best awards ceremony in the world, the Academy Awards (**Oscars** to you), it's on to **Swifty's at Spago's**: the most fashionable party to be seen at, held by *the* agent, Irving (Swifty) Lazar. *"The most important party. It's the people that make it. Everybody from Michael Jackson to George Burns"* – **Jackie Collins.** *"The best showbiz event. I go every year. It's very hard to get in – everyone wants to be invited"* – **Ken Lane** 🕵 . . . . . . Some of the **best drama** is in **Equity Waiver** theatre, which, by playing to an audience of 99 or less, are exempt from union rules. Anything goes. Experimental stuff in back rooms, *"marvellous tiny workshop productions"* – **Michael Grade.**

★ ★

FRANK RICH ON MONEY AND THE ARTS

"There's a great deal of frenzy in the New York art scene. Some of it is about creativity, some of it is about money and sometimes it's hard to tell where one begins and the other ends. The preoccupation of New York City as a whole, in the mid- to late-Eighties has been real estate.... You see the ramifications in almost everything: major museums are contemplating or have accomplished huge property additions – the Guggenheim, the Whitney, the Metropolitan Museum of Art. The entrepreneur who has big money to finance huge projects on the arts often calls the shots. I find it tragic that museums are increasingly so taken over by heavily promoted heavily commercialized blockbuster shows that the days of the museum as a place for contemplation of art on your own individual terms seems to be dying...."

London Weekend TV's *The South Bank Show*

CULTURE

beat it anywhere. The building itself I don't like" – **Duggie Fields. Bill Blass** acknowledges *"the museum is so chock-a-block you can hardly get in."* Good gift shop. **The Cloisters** at 4 Tryon Parks houses the Met's medieval collection.

♟ **MUSEUM OF MODERN ART, 11 W 53rd St, NY 10019**
☎ **(212) 708 9750**
"The Uffizi of Modernism" – **Edward Lucie-Smith.** MOMA boasts an unparalleled collection of over 100,000 works of 20th-century painting, sculpture, drawing, prints, photography, plus film, architecture, industrial and graphic design. A large number of Picassos, Matisses, Mirós and Mondrians; major works by Hopper, Wyeth, O'Keeffe, Pollock, Rothko, Rauschenberg, Johns et al.

♟ **SOLOMON R GUGGENHEIM MUSEUM, 1071 5th Ave, NY 10218**
☎ **(212) 360 3555**
A controversial Frank Lloyd Wright structure (1957-59) commissioned by Solomon Guggenheim (great-uncle of Peggy). There is a nausea-inducing spiral descent into the museum. Impressionists and modern art, strong on

Kandinsky, plus Mondrian, Braque, Klee, Chagall et al. Best for its shows. *"The most beautiful museum in the world. It displays its exhibitions in a fabulous way: it would ennoble a paper bag"* – **Stephen Jones.** *"I love going to it"* – **Margaux Hemingway.** *"I was pretty impressed. I won't forget that – it was lovely"* – **Jane Asher.**

ART FOR PARTY'S SAKE

To some people the Met is held dear for reasons other than strict art. The grand opening of the new 9-month show at Diana Vreeland's Costume Institute in early Dec marks the beginning of the NY season. An invitation (with a bill for $750 and rising) to the cocktails-dinner-ball is the deepest compliment Manhattan can bestow upon a person. *"The best, most-supported charity event. Fairly selective. A lot of international and bicoastal people go"* – **Ken Lane.** Ann Getty, the Kissingers, Estée Lauder, Brooke Astor, Bill Blass – le tout Noo York – clink glasses with global luminaries of the fashion/entertainment biz, from Diana Ross to Valentino. *"Definitely the best social event. The Kennedy Center is wonderful, but it tends to be American; the Met is international. Some people plan their lives to be in New York then"* – **Steve Rubell.** *"The best gala"* – **Bill Blass.** *"The opening is a must. Very social and exciting. There's something beautiful about having a dinner-dance where one walks through a gallery, dances in the Temple of Dendur, and dines in another part of the museum ..."* – **Lynn Wyatt.**

"It's great" – **Michael Grade**. *"Wonderful film and photographic archives"* – **Eleanor Lambert**.

WHITNEY MUSEUM OF AMERICAN ART, 945 Madison Ave, NY 10021 ☎ (212) 570 3633 Over 8,500 works of American art of the 20th century, with bold, progressive exhibitions of up-to-the-minute art. A favourite of **Eleanor Lambert**.

ordered, they're not over-priced, and they do interesting shows" – **Ken Lane**.

BALLET

Apart from the 2 main New York companies, there is the bicoastal **Joffrey Ballet**. Reconstructions of the Ballet Russe are their forte. Catch them in autumn at the City Center Theater, New York, in

associate director, and a pool of excellent athletic dancers from the School of American Ballet to draw on. Good at discovering new talent.

 NEW YORK CITY BALLET, New York State Theater, Lincoln Center, NY 10023 ☎ (212) 496 0600 The most important company in the States, set up by the legendary George Balanchine, who brought ballet to America.

> 66 *Uptown on Madison Avenue is the old-guard stomping ground for realist, landscape and genre painting. It's the kind of art that's hung over people's couches. 57th Street has its great galleries – Pace, BlumHelman, Robert Miller, David McKee – and they have very prominent artists. But generally the energy is downtown* 99
>
> STEVEN HENRY MADOFF

Commercial Galleries

PAULA COOPER, 155 Wooster St ☎ (212) 674 0766. *"has the sharpest sense of where it's at, with an intelligent and sustained commitment to her artists"* – **Edward Lucie-Smith**. **LEO CASTELLI GALLERY**, 420 W Broadway ☎ (212) 431 5160 is the best dealer of contemporary American art – Jasper Johns, Warhol, Lichtenstein, etc. *"Wonderful"* – **Lynn Wyatt**. **MICHAEL KNOEDLER & CO**, 19 E 70th St ☎ (212) 794 0550, a respected gallery for mainly contemporary art plus the odd Old Master, recommended by **Mario Buatta**. **MARLBOROUGH GALLERY**, 40 W 57th St ☎ (212) 541 4900 – the largest art gallery on 57th. European and American works by Henry Moore, Botero, Lipchitz, etc, and photographers Brandt, Brassai and Penn. **SHEPHERD GALLERY**, 21 E 84th St ☎ (212) 861 4050 is *"the best for 19th-century drawings and paintings"* – **Edward Lucie-Smith**. *"It is the best because they have a very good eye, they're very*

spring at the Los Angeles County Music Center, and the rest of the year on tour.

 AMERICAN BALLET THEATER, 890 Broadway, NY 10003 ☎ (212) 477 3030 ABT is an eclectic company, producing everything from classics to the works of new young choreographers. Dynamic and progressive, with Mikhail Baryshnikov as director, Kenneth MacMillan

His style, along with that of Jerome Robbins (of *West Side Story* fame) lives on under artistic director Peter Martins. It's perhaps true that nothing new of great note has been produced in recent years, but they boast fine dancers, mainly creamed from the School of American Ballet. *"The opening of the ballet, with dinner afterwards is a great social event. More fashionable than a charity ball"* – **Ken Lane**.

LINCOLN: LINKIN' THE ARTS

LINCOLN CENTER, Broadway between 63rd and 65th St, NY 10023 ☎ (212) 877 1800. A spectacular centre for the performing arts. On a site of 14 cultivated acres that can seat 13,666 avid artsies, it's the largest complex of its kind in the world. It encompasses: the Metropolitan Opera; the New York Philharmonic (housed at the Avery Fisher Hall); the New York City Ballet and the New York City Opera – both housed in the New York State Theater; the Lincoln Center Theater Co; the Film Society; the Chamber Music Society (housed in the Alice Tully Hall: *"Very good – it holds about 1,000 people but feels quite intimate"* – **Julian Lloyd Webber**); the School of American Ballet and the Juilliard School (of music, drama and dance, with its own theatre). Phew. Oh, and a car park for 700. **Mario Buatta** agrees with **Bill Blass, who says:** *"Between the opera, concerts and ballet it's the best."*

MUSIC

**CARNEGIE HALL, 154 W
57th St, NY 10019
☎ (212) 247 7800**
Recently restored, regilded, repainted . . . in cream, gold and red. Built in 1891 by Andrew Carnegie. The most dramatic change was the restoration of the stage dome, which had a hole cut out of it in the 1940s to allow more light for the film *Carnegie Hall*. Now *that's* Hollywood. "*A fine old opera house*" – **Helen Gurley Brown.** Its past history is one of rock and pop from Judy Garland and Frank Sinatra to the Beatles, but it now concentrates on classical.

opera devotees are not so impressed. One says, "*They seem more concerned about big-name singers than the production.*" However, 800,000 attend each season. And no one can deny the splendour of the opening gala (see Social & Night Life), nor the magic of the free operas and concerts in Central Park that set the pattern for 'Opera in the Park' worldwide.

**NEW YORK CITY OPERA, New York State Theater, Lincoln Center, NY 10023
☎ (212) 870 5570**
A dynamic young company representing the best contemporary artists – music

THEATRE

"*England has done something unthinkable by Broadway standards – it has produced hit musicals. In my view it doesn't mean a lot because almost all the shows are written by one person, Andrew Lloyd Webber. If you take away Andrew Lloyd Webber, where is the English musical? . . . When we find our Lloyd Webber, we'll see the ascendancy of the American musical again*" – **Frank Rich** – LWT's *The South Bank Show*.

BROADWAY
Broadway is not a happy beast. Productions cost so much to stage these days that Broadway only dares to put on musicals and conventional theatre that has been tried and tested and stamped and sealed with a sold-out sticker. Not only are most of the shows imported from Britain but they often get premièred elsewhere in the States to ensure their American appeal. New York audiences are tough and opinionated, the critics are avidly read; shows can close in a matter of days. You can't knock Broadway's cachet, though, and most of the shows that make it that far play to packed houses. However, with tickets so expensive (from \$40), many punters prefer to dish out their greenbacks Off-Broadway – or Off Off-Broadway. (NB Some of Broadway's major theatres are not actually *on* Broadway.)

OFF-BROADWAY
Off-Broadway refers to theatres with under 400 seats. Based in SoHo, the Village and other locations off Broadway, these theatres stage tomorrow's hits – serious dramas, comedies, new and avant-garde plays,

---

DESERT ISLAND SURVIVAL KIT:

MICHAEL GRADE

"*I would have the film* Pat and Mike, *a George Cukor comedy with Spencer Tracy and Katharine Hepburn. I must have seen it 15 or 20 times and because of the chemistry between them you can always find something new in every scene. Pure diversion! My record would have to be a Mozart opera –* Don Giovanni *– just exquisite. The book would have to be either inpenetrable or one that would cheer me up. Either James Joyce's* Ulysses *or the collected short stories of the American humorist S J Perelman.*"

**METROPOLITAN OPERA, Metropolitan Opera House, Lincoln Center, NY 10023
☎ (212) 362 6000**
A company of world renown, over 100 years old, with an 800-strong company. A tradition of producing no-holds-barred extravaganzas with the very best, crowd-pulling performers. "*You get bigger, better operas in New York at the Metropolitan*" – **Auberon Waugh**; "*tremendously popular big blockbuster shows*" confirms **Bill Blass**, but true

by Sondheim, design by Hockney, libretto by Maurice Sendak . . . Also new productions of classics like *The Magic Flute*, with English surtitles above the stage. "*Very fine. Much more adventurous than the Met*" – **Andrew Lloyd Webber**. "*A recently revitalized company doing musicals and light opera such as Brigadoon and South Pacific – they're doing very well*" – **Helen Gurley Brown.**

CULTURE

> **❝** *The main opera companies vie for the international pool of artists, so 'best' is a matter of 'Has Domingo sung better at the Met than he has at Covent Garden?' It's these international stars that keep top opera houses firmly on the map* **❞**

ANDREW LLOYD WEBBER

> 66 *I have very catholic tastes. I love all theatre, good and bad. My wife always waits to see the notices, but I just love it all* 99

    DOUGLAS FAIRBANKS JR

unconventional productions of classics. This is the cutting edge of American theatre – and cheaper than Broadway.

OFF OFF-BROADWAY
A more extreme, more experimental version of Off-Broadway.

> 66 *Where America scores is Off Off-Broadway. There's lots of experimentation throughout the States. Nearly all major cities have fringe and alternative theatre* 99

    MICHAEL GRADE

NEW YORK SHAKESPEARE FESTIVAL, 425 Lafayette St, NY 10003 ☎ (212) 598 7100
A series of excellent free Shakespeare plays (mostly directed by founder and president Joseph Papp), at the Delacorte Theater in Central Park in late-June to mid-Sept. Top actors have starred – William Hurt, Kevin Kline, Martin Sheen, Meryl Streep, Christopher Walken. First-come, first-served seating unless you're a sponsor.

PALM BEACH

ART AND MUSEUMS

HENRY MORRISON FLAGLER MUSEUM (WHITEHALL), Cocoanut Row, PO Box 969, FL 33480 ☎ (305) 655 2833
Whitehall is a stunning hybrid mansion built in 1901. It has a white pillared colonial façade, marble hall with double staircase and frescoed ceiling, gilt-edged Louis XIV music room, rich red damask and walnut Italian Renaissance library, Louis XV ballroom and an Elizabethan breakfast room – all of which must have led to an identity crisis.

NORTON GALLERY & SCHOOL OF ART, 1451 S Olive Ave, W Palm Beach, FL 33401 ☎ (305) 832 5194
Mainly modern European and American works of art. Also Chinese jades; ceramics, bronzes and sculpture. Concerts, films and lectures, plus the annual Bal des Arts, one of the highlights of the Palm Beach season.

PHILADELPHIA

ART

  PHILADELPHIA MUSEUM OF ART, 26th St and Benjamin Franklin Parkway,

PO Box 7646, PA 19101 ☎ (215) 763 8100
The neo-classical building is one of the greatest art institutions in the world, housing over 500,000 works from classical to modern times. Chinese antiquities, reconstructed period rooms, European masters, antique furniture, American painting and decorative arts, and international modern art. Their **Rodin Museum**, 22nd St and Benjamin Franklin Pky ☎ (215) 787 5431, has casts of most of his great sculptures.

SAN FRANCISCO

FILM

SAN FRANCISCO INTERNATIONAL FILM FESTIVAL, 1560 Fillmore, CA 94115 ☎ (415) 567 4641
Held in March. Movies from America, Asia, Africa, Europe and Australia, animations, documentaries, etc. Special awards and tributes bestowed on deservers in the film biz.

MUSIC

OPERA IN THE PARK, Music Concourse, Golden Gate Park
A free concert featuring the San Francisco Opera Orchestra and stars from the opening night production, held on the Sunday after the opening of the fall season.

SAN FRANCISCO OPERA, War Memorial Opera House, 301 Van Ness Ave, CA 94102 ☎ (415) 565 6431
Very highly regarded company,

> 66 *Theatre is exciting because of the immediate contact. Practically anything else – movies, television, radio – can be canned, but you can't can a live theatre performance. The knowledge that something could go wrong adds a little frisson to it all* 99

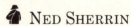

    NED SHERRIN

CULTURE

Desert Island Survival Kit:

IMRAN KHAN

"Whichever book you took you'd finish ... I'm stumped!"

where many of the world's great artists have made their début – Francis Ford Coppola, Sir Geraint Evans, Elisabeth Schwarzkopf, Sir Georg Solti. Operas are sung in their original language with English surtitles. Also recitals, concerts and visiting ballet. The opera is at the apex of high society in San Francisco, strongly supported by Ann and Gordon Getty. The Sept opening of the 3-month fall season is the West Coast event of the year – a grand dinner, gala performance and a ball.

THE SAN FRANCISCO SYMPHONY, Davies Symphony Hall, CA 94102 ☎ (415) 552 8011 One of the best orchestras in the States, under the baton of Herbert Blomstedt. A forward-thinking company, they play many new works as well as classics, and have championed young up-and-coming artists. Also hot on gala benefits, they hold a biennial Black and White Ball (see Social & Night Life) and one-off extravaganzas.

Washington, DC

Art and Museums

HIRSHHORN MUSEUM & SCULPTURE GARDEN, 7th St and Independence Ave SW, 20560 ☎ (202) 357 1300 An extensive collection of modern and contemporary art; best known for sculpture – a gardenful of Rodin, Henry Moore and co. Matisse, Degas and Daumier are there, plus Cubists, Nihilists, the New York school (from World War II onwards), etc. Works are shown in rotation every 3 months, so that you can keep going back and see a different collection each time. **Aniko Gaal** and **Lord Montagu of Beaulieu** feast their eyes.

🍴 **NATIONAL GALLERY OF ART**, 4th St and Constitution Ave NW, DC 20565 ☎ (202) 737 4215 The sleek modern East Building, designed by I M Pei (of controversial Louvre fame) houses the permanent collection of 20th-century art from Europe and America, and holds special exhibitions. A bunch of Old Masters live in the 1940s West Building. *"I love I M Pei's building. It's so dramatic, such a work of art"* – **Margaux Hemingway**. *"One of the cultural entities for the country. Under the direction of J Carter Brown it has had some of the best international exhibitions in Washington – Tutankhamen, the Treasure Houses of Britain ... An exhilarating feast for the eyes and soul"* – **Aniko Gaal**. *"Absolutely stunning, partly because they have such a good shop. Plenty of choice, beautifully displayed"* – **Serena Fass**.

PHILLIPS COLLECTION, 1600 21st St NW, DC 20009 ☎ (202) 387 2151 American and European paintings from the Impressionists to the present day: Bonnard, Braque, Cézanne, Daumier and Renoir's celebrated *Luncheon of the Boating Party*; Avery, Dove, Gatch, Marin, O'Keeffe, Prendergast. Excellent concerts and lectures that put paintings in context.

Music

THE JOHN F KENNEDY CENTER, DC 20566 ☎ (202) 872 0466 Waving the banner for the arts,

Best Fests

🍴 **SANTA FE FESTIVAL OF THE ARTS**, 628 **Paseo de Peralta, Santa Fe, NM 87501** ☎ (505) 988 3924 is the top US fest, of high international regard, held in Oct. *"Fun if you want to look at a great open-air opera house. You'd have to go far to find something as visually stunning as that. I'd love to see La Fanciulla del West by Puccini there – it could be fantastic. It's great fun to be somewhere so remote"* – **Andrew Lloyd Webber**. *"The best opera festival"* – **Wolfgang Puck.**
🍴 **SPOLETO FESTIVAL USA**, PO Box 157, Charleston, SC 29402 ☎ (803) 722 2764 is an offshoot of the original (see Italy), under the same direction of Gian Carlo Menotti. 17 warm southern days in May-June are packed with 107 performances of opera, concerts, theatre and dance. Many new or rarely performed works. The whole town gives itself to the festival. Black-tie dinners, dances, champagne bashes, a floating fiesta and fireworks on the harbour.
NEWPORT JAZZ FESTIVAL, PO Box 605, Newport, RI 02840 ☎ (401) 847 3710, Aug. *"All the international jazz greats go. It's on day and night. It's the best – I'd recommend it to anybody. It's the kind of music I love – jazz and salsa"* – **Margaux Hemingway.**

CULTURE

A MATTER OF HONORS

Artsies, the society segment, corporates, politicos and bicoastals coast in for the event of the year: the Kennedy Center Honors, a gala in December to honour a handful of greats in the performing arts world. Last year's hit list included Perry Como, Bette Davis and Sammy Davis Jr. After a reception at the White House for patrons, there's the Honors – gold medals bestowed – attended by the President and the First Lady, and a dinner-dance to which the Kennedy family turn out en force. A balcony seat for the ceremony might knock you back $4,000 – if you can get it. *"This is the most prestigious event in the Washington calendar. It is so highly sought-after that invitations, although sent, are redundant. It's a beautiful evening, a most glamorous affair"* – **Aniko Gaal**. *"The Honors are something special. A good show"* – **Lynn Wyatt**.

feeding a city of hungry culture vultures, this centre is second only to the Lincoln in New York. *"4 theatres, the opera house and the concert hall all under one roof. It's the testing ground for Broadway"* – **Aniko Gaal**. The wood-panelled Eisenhower stages major shows, the Terrace stages music, the American Film Institute Theater new films and retros; the small Theater Lab shows cabaret, comedy etc; the Opera House is base to the Washington Opera, and the Concert Hall is proud home of the National Symphony Orchestra. International companies visit, from La Scala to the Bolshoi. John Gielgud, Katharine Hepburn, Ella Fitzgerald, Liza Minnelli and Frank Sinatra have taken the stage. Even audiences make the pilgrimage from all over the States.

THEATRE

ARENA STAGE, 6th St and Maine Ave SW, DC 20024 ☎ (202) 554 9066
A complex of 3 theatres that puts on mainly new plays by American writers. Some modern classics too. The resident Arena Company does occasional tours.

NATIONAL THEATER, 1321 Pennsylvania Ave NW, DC

20004 ☎ (202) 628 6161
DC's other top theatre, for musicals, comedy and drama.

Australia

ADELAIDE

⚓ **ADELAIDE FESTIVAL, GPO Box 1269, SA 5001 ☎ (08) 216 8600**
A major international festival, *"well worth going to"* – **Andrew Lloyd Webber**. Held biennially, the next festival will be in Feb-March 1990. A blend of cultures, of classical and of contemporary works – theatre, dance, art exhibitions and classical music – with eminent conductors such as Sir Georg Solti, Michael Tilson Thomas and Pierre Boulez wielding the baton. A massive outdoor stage allows 50,000 to drink in the opening-night music spectacular. Writers' Week is one of Adelaide's special features – a gathering of over 60 international writers, who read, debate and perform. State-of-the-art cuisine at Lyrics restaurant: special festival menus are created by visiting chefs (recently, Gay Bilson from Berowra Waters, Cheong Liew, and Mark Armstrong from Pegrum's and the Macleay Street Bistro.

ADELAIDE FESTIVAL CENTRE, King William St, SA 5000 ☎ (08) 213 4788
Superb performing arts complex with regular concerts and performances. *"In terms of a modern building for music theatre it is probably the finest in the world – wonderful acoustics, wonderful sight lines, wonderfully organized"* – **Andrew Lloyd Webber**. *"Very good to play in"* – **Julian Lloyd Webber**. *"The best ballet venue"* – **Lesley Wild**.

BRISBANE

MUSEUM OF CONTEMPORARY ART, 164 Melbourne St, Qld 4101 ☎ (07) 846 2255
"MOCA is the best cultural venue, a beautiful 1930s building" – **Anne Lewin**. Opened to the public only last year, the gallery houses a large private collection of modern works; visiting exhibitions.

CANBERRA

AUSTRALIAN NATIONAL GALLERY, Parkes Place, ACT 2600 ☎ (062) 712501
The leading art gallery in the country, showing the best works by Australian artists and Aboriginal tribes. Also international works (over 70,000 pieces in total). Eerily silent lakeside terrace with striking modern sculpture.

MELBOURNE

BALLET

⚓ **AUSTRALIAN BALLET, 11 Mount Alexander Rd, Flemington, Vic 3031 ☎ (03) 376 1400**
Under the artistic directorship of Sir John Gielgud's niece, Maina Gielgud, this company performs mainly full-length classical ballets at home and abroad. On a par with the National Ballet of Canada.

FESTIVAL

SPOLETO FESTIVAL, 6th Level, 1 City Rd, S Melbourne, Vic 3205 ☎ (03) 614 4484
Latest outpost of Menotti's festival (see Italy), held in 2 weeks of Sept. Expect contemporary and classical dance, drama and musicals as well as classical music. A truly international event. Last year, singers and dancers descended from Taiwan, Japan, China, Canada, Europe and the USA.

175 miles away), this is nevertheless a highlight of the WA cultural calendar, when over 6,000 people flock to these al fresco classical concerts in Feb/Mar. Held on multi-millionaire businessman Denis Horgan's magnificent estate, where guests picnic in casual or evening wear à la Glyndebourne. The Berlin State Orchestra, Royal Danish Orchestra and Western Australian Symphony Orchestra have performed in the past. Unusual but magical

SYDNEY

ART AND MUSEUMS

AUSTRALIAN MUSEUM, 6 College St, NSW 2000 ☎ (02) 339 8111
Perhaps the best representation in the country of Australian natural history and Aboriginal artefacts.

ROBIN GIBSON GALLERIES, 278 Liverpool St, Darlinghurst, NSW 2010 ☎ (02) 331 6692
The best of contemporary Australian art – Brett Whiteley, Tim Storrier and co.

TUSCULUM, 3 Manning St, Potts Point, NSW 2011 ☎ (02) 356 2955
The new focus of architecture and design in Australia. This is the first architectural gallery in the country. Its main base is the two-storey, double-verandah villa, Tusculum, designed in 1832 by John Verge, who also designed Elizabeth Bay House.

VICTORIAN ARTS CENTRE

This spired city landmark is perhaps the largest visual and performing arts centre in the world. Based at **100 St Kilda Rd, Vic 3004 ☎ (03) 617 8211**, it houses: the National Gallery of Victoria, the Museum of Victoria, a 2,600-seat Concert Hall, 3 theatres, a Performing Arts Museum, a Children's Museum and a vast outdoor entertainment area. The complex is innovative in the fields of architecture and acoustics; it extends as far as 6 floors underground, into the old bed of the Yarra River. *"The Playhouse is the best theatre venue, the State Theatre the best opera venue – for the actual performance"* – **Lesley Wild**. The gallery contains Australian, Aboriginal and international art; its lofty Great Hall has a dramatic stained-glass ceiling.

Held mainly at the Victorian Arts Centre, plus churches and other venues.

GARDENS

Melbourne, capital of the Garden State, Victoria, has dozens of lush gardens and parks. The **ROYAL BOTANIC GARDENS, Domain Rd, S Yarra, Vic 3141 ☎ (03) 639424** are among tree – and plant-loving **Lord Lichfield**'s favourites.

evenings, where music is accompanied by the impromptu cackling of kookaburras.

PERTH ENTERTAINMENT CENTRE, Wellington St, WA 6000 ☎ (09) 322 4766
The main auditorium is the largest in Australia, and the best pop concert venue says **Lesley Wild**. Also the smaller, more intimate Concert Hall, *"a great hall"* according to **Julian Lloyd Webber.**

GARDENS

ROYAL BOTANIC GARDENS, Macquarie St, NSW 2000 ☎ (02) 231 8119
57 acres of undulating lawns, flower beds, exotic and Australian trees and a hothouse of ferns and orchids, right on the harbourside. *"It's like a park, the place to take people who think botanical gardens are all science, just to see how wonderfully well they can be landscaped. It has the perfect*

PERTH

MUSIC

LEEUWIN CONCERTS, Leeuwin Estate, Gnarawary Rd, Margaret River. Tickets: Barrack House, 262 St George's Terrace, Perth, WA 6000 ☎ (09) 322 2288
Not strictly in Perth (in fact it's

DESERT ISLAND SURVIVAL KIT:

AUBERON WAUGH

"My book is the Oxford Dictionary of Quotations. *My luxury, a vine so that I could grow grapes and make wine. The person I'd like to be stranded with? My wife is excluded, like* The Bible *and* Shakespeare. *It would have to be a female, attractive, slightly unusual and slightly mad. Also she would have to be helpful with cooking."*

CULTURE

setting right next door to the Opera House" – **Lord Lichfield**. See the view from Mrs Macquarie's Chair.

MUSIC

OPERA IN THE PARK, c/o Festival of Sydney, 175 Castlereagh St, NSW 2000 ☎ (02) 267 2311
Using the New York Central Park blueprint, this series of free opera and classical music concerts is held in the Domain, accompanied by the chomping of picnics. Some years the *1812* forms the stunning grand finale, with fireworks, cannons, and the ringing of real cathedral bells from nearby St Mary's.

SYDNEY OPERA HOUSE, Bennelong Point, Circular Quay, NSW 2001 ☎ (02) 250 7111
We all know the building, a spectacular spinnakered construction that is one of the most famous landmarks in the world. True, it's best seen from a distance – all those off-white tiles are more like a public toilet if you get too close – but from the sea or the air, its sails dazzle and gleam, mimicking the yachts on the harbour. The reverse view is equally captivating – from the Northern Foyers over the harbour. **Lesley Wild** thinks it's *"the best opera venue – for the lobby"*. **Robert Burton** is more magnanimous: *"The best theatre? I would have to say the Opera House. That's where it all happens."* Opera *and* ballet are what happens. It is home to the Australian Opera, who do English-language productions with occasional visiting stars – Dame Joan 'Wonderlungs' Sutherland often returns to her

motherland. OK, so the pit is too small for the orchestra and they can't do Wagner, but all of Sydney society turns out for the opening of the season.

Austria

ART

🎭 **KUNSTHISTORISCHES MUSEUM, Burgring 5, A-1010 Vienna ☎ (01) 934 5410**
The state collection of art, spanning classical antiquities and the great masters – no end of Bruegels and Titians, but for starters, see Benvenuto Cellini's gold salt cellar, Velázquez's *Infanta Margarita*, Hals's *Portrait of a Young Man* and Raphael's *Madonna in the Meadows*. *"The greatest place on earth for Western pictures. It is special because the Hapsburgs collected madly, sensuously, and the paintings represent all the great artists of the Western world. The collection is not overloaded by religious subject matter . . . the Hapsburgs liked the flesh. The paintings are superb, large, diverse, in excellent condition"* – **Thomas Hoving**. *"Must take an awful lot of beating – it's outstanding"* – **Lord Montagu of Beaulieu**.

MUSIC

BREGENZER FESTSPIELE, Festspiel-und-Kongresshaus, Platz der Wiener Symphoniker, A-6900 Bregenz ☎ (05574) 22811
This medieval town hosts a spirited festival (July-Aug) on Lake Constance. Performances take place on an elaborate

🎭 —Europe's Best— 🎭

ART GALLERIES

1. **KUNSTHISTORISCHES MUSEUM**, Vienna
2. **MUSEO DEL PRADO**, Madrid
3. **MUSEE DU LOUVRE**, Paris
4. **THE HERMITAGE**, Leningrad
5. **NATIONAL GALLERY**, London
6. **RIJKSMUSEUM**, Amsterdam
7. **GALLERIA DEGLI UFFIZI**, Florence
8. **STEDELIJK MUSEUM**, Amsterdam
9. **STAATSGALERIE**, Stuttgart
10. **MUSEI VATICANI**, Rome

floating stage against dramatic evening skies and firework finales. Also an indoor theatre. Opera and symphony concerts.

BRUCKNERFEST, Brucknerhaus, Postfach 57, Untere Donaulande 7, A-4010 Linz ☎ (0732) 275225
A week of predominantly Anton Bruckner recitals and concerts. Special open-air 'Cloud of Sound' performances, which envelop the audience from all sides.

🎭 **SCHUBERTIADE HOHENEMS, Postfach 100, Schweizer Strasse 1, A-6845 Hohenems ☎ (05576) 2091**
A June festival devoted to the works of Schubert. Performances are held in the

> ❝ *What makes a festival – or an opera company – is the musical director. With von Karajan at Salzburg it is he that people associate the event with, he is the dominant musical force. It's the drive and taste of such personalities; they choose the music – or they choose the people who know how to choose* ❞

🎭 PATRICK O'CONNOR

courtyard or inside the Palasthof, a Renaissance castle only open for the festival.

VIENNA

MUSIC

"Vienna is the best place for classical music" – **Stanley Marcus**. Catch the **Vienna Philharmonic**, which, along with the Berlin Phil, is the best for **Lord Donoughue**.

VIENNA FESTIVAL, Wiener Festwochen, Rathausstrasse 9, A-1010 Vienna ☎ (01) 42804 A major festival of old and modern classical music, promenade concerts, jazz, theatre, ballet, puppet shows and exhibitions, mid-May to end-June. The whole city enters into festive mood.

🏛 **VIENNA STATE OPERA, Opernring 2, A-1010 Vienna ☎ (01) 514440**

A tremendous tradition of opera in a lavish setting. This hitherto turbulent opera house is now under the directorship of the great Claudio Abbado. The central pit offers the best standing room in the world. Your chance to dance-along-a-Vienna-State-Opera comes on New Year's Eve at the **Vienna Imperial Ball**, a splendid traditional affair held in the state rooms of the Hofburg Palace. Grand dinner, much clinking of crystal at midnight, followed by formal dancing in the grand ballroom.

THEATRE

THEATER AN DER WIEN, Linke Wienzeile 6, A-1060 Vienna ☎ (01) 58830 *"Probably the most beautiful opera house in the world. Absolutely wonderful"* – **Andrew Lloyd Webber**. Sadly you can no longer hear Mozart there; instead it houses modern

---

SALZBURG FESTIVAL

🏛 **SALZBURGER FESTSPIELE, Postfach 140, Hofstallgasse 1, A-5010 Salzburg ☎ (06222) 42541** Perhaps the most famous festival in the world (end-July to end-Aug): a gathering of the musical clans, the most revered performers and conductors, both on and off stage. Home of Mozart and von Karajan, Salzburg attracts sophisticated and dressy audiences by night, all haute couture and sparkling jewels. By day it's a different scene: a scrum to buy sausages and sauerkraut from the market, a madhouse battling through droves of twee lederhosen – and dirndl-clad locals in national costume. Mozart heads the musical menu; there's an orgy of opera, orchestral concerts, recitals, theatre, open-air candlelit concerts, and puppet opera in the magical Marionette Theatre – described by *The New York Times* as 'the damndest thing'. *"Marvellous for its concerts and the quality of some of the opera"* – **Andrew Lloyd Webber**. Frank Bowling sings its praises, while for **Marchesa Bona Frescobaldi, Giorgio Armani, Lynn Wyatt** and **Mariuccia Mandelli** it's the best music festival. Tickets: first stab must be made by January; try again for left-overs in March/April. If you fail, sniff out a (villainously expensive) black-market ticket from a hotel door-man. Stay at **Hotel Osterreichischer Hof**, Schwarzstrasse 5 ☎ (0662) 72541; or out of town where **Michael Grade** stays, at the **Schloss Fuschl**, 5322 Hof-bei-Salzburg ☎ (0662) 6229 (*"An old hunting lodge on a lake. Haute cuisine making the best of what is available locally. Exquisite"* – **MG**).

---

musicals, recently those from the Lloyd Webber fount – *Cats* and *The Phantom of the Opera*.

Britain

LONDON

ART AND MUSEUMS

Some of the most spectacular shows are staged at the **ROYAL ACADEMY OF ARTS**, Burlington House, Piccadilly, W1 ☎ (01) 439 7438. Their annual Summer Exhibition (mid-May to early-Aug) of about 1,000 contemporary works is a much-loved institution and often controversial (usually for not being controversial enough). Major contemporary shows and modern retrospectives are staged by the **HAYWARD GALLERY**, South Bank Centre, Belvedere Rd, SE1 ☎ (01) 928 3144.

BRITISH MUSEUM, Great Russell St, WC1 ☎ (01) 636 1555 Renowned for its impressive collection of antiquities. It was to the BM that the Greeks lost their marbles . . . the Elgin Marbles, that is. Roll along if only to see these – and the awesome Egyptian mummies. Also prehistoric, medieval and Renaissance works, engravings and English watercolours. A new Japanese gallery is due for 1990. *"Everything is displayed marvellously"* – **Duggie Fields**. *"I love it, but you get exhausted after two rooms"* – **Serena Fass. Lord Montagu of Beaulieu** recommends.

COURTAULD INSTITUTE GALLERIES, Woburn Square, WC1 ☎ (01) 580 1015 One of the finest collections of Impressionist and Post-Impressionist paintings in existence – Renoir's *La Loge*, Van Gogh's *Man with Bandaged Ear*, and famous works by Manet, Gauguin, Seurat, Degas, Pissarro and

CULTURE

CULTURE

> **"** *The London collections in aggregate contain the greatest works of art in the world. The Courtauld, Somerset House, the Tate, the National Gallery, the Wallace Collection, the Queen's Gallery at Buckingham Palace ... you don't need hiking boots to see an extraordinary range* **"**
>
> LORD GOWRIE

Cézanne. Also Flemish, Dutch and Italian Old Masters. In summer 1989 the Institute moves to Somerset House in the Strand.

IMPERIAL WAR MUSEUM, Lambeth Rd, SE1
☎ (01) 735 8922
"One of the best museums I know of in England. The great thing is the theme – what war did to people, and what politicians did to people; it's not a sabre-rattling organization at all. It's there to remind you not to do it again" – **Keith Floyd**. War memorabilia, plus photographs and paintings of the war years. *"My favourite museum. It shows what Britain used to be all about ..."* – **Keith Floyd**.

NATIONAL GALLERY, Trafalgar Square, WC2
☎ (01) 839 3321
No 1 on the tourist circuit, a supremely fine, extensive and balanced collection of masterpieces from the Italian, Dutch and other European schools up to 1900. Their 'Quick Visit' takes in 16 golden greats including Van Eyck's *Arnolfini and his Wife*, Constable's *Hay Wain* and Turner's *Fighting Temeraire*. **Peter Blake** likes the restored Barry rooms. The new extension opens in 1991.

NATIONAL PORTRAIT GALLERY, Trafalgar Square, WC2 ☎ (01) 930 1552
Portraits that record famous sitters (from the Queen to Churchill to the Brontë sisters) rather than painters – though Rubens, Reynolds, Gainsborough and other greats are represented. The NPG constantly commissions new works of current notabilities. *"I'm very fond of it. I like the subject material"* – **Leo Cooper**. *"One of my favourites"*

– **Lord Montagu of Beaulieu**. One of **Peter Blake**'s too.

SIR JOHN SOANE'S MUSEUM, 13 Lincoln's Inn Fields, WC2 ☎ (01) 405 2107
A through-the-keyhole look at the 1813 house designed and lived in by Sir John Soane. Keyhole king **Loyd Grossman** is *"very fond of it"*; so are **Anouska Hempel** and **Sophie Grigson**. A perfect period piece with thousands of noteworthy antiques and paintings (Turner, Lawrence, Canaletto, and the famous Hogarth series, *The Rake's Progress* and *The Election*).

TATE GALLERY, Millbank, SW1 ☎ (01) 821 1313
The national collection of British and modern European art. A treasure trove of Turners, now housed under one roof (in accordance with the painter's will) in the new Clore Gallery. *"It's the most agreeable building, very relaxing, very pleasing"* – **Michael Grade**. A superb store of Stubbs, Blake, Gainsborough, Hogarth, Constable, Pre-Raphaelites; and key moderns. *"I am a great fan"* – **Jane Asher**; so is **Peter Blake**, but **Auberon Waugh** says, *"I don't much care for it,*

Buzzzzzzzzz If chill and candlelight thrill and delight you, make an appointment to visit **18 Folgate St**, Spitalfields ☎ (01) 247 4013, a Georgian house restored to the point of utter (and eerie) authenticity by its American owner, Dennis Severs ...... on Fridays after 5pm it's open house at **Feliks Topolski's studio**, Arch 158, Concert Hall Approach, SE1 ☎ (01) 928 3405. *"It's fun, like a salon, but much more relaxed"* – **Dan Topolski** ...... Kid's stuff: the **Science Museum**, Exhibition Rd, SW7 ☎ (01) 589 3456 and the next-door **Natural History Museum**, Cromwell Rd, SW7 ☎ (01) 938 9388 will keep 'em quiet ...... Que pasa **post-Boilerhouse**? Conran's new riverside **Design Museum**, due to open in spring '89 at Butler's Wharf, 45 Curlew St, SE1 ☎ (01) 403 6933, with Stephen Bayley at the helm. ...... Secret stash: **Dulwich Picture Gallery**, College Rd, SE21 is a gem say **Loyd Grossman** (*"Frightfully nice Dutch paintings"*) and **Lord Gowrie** (*"Marvellous collection of Old Masters"*) ...... Click into the **National Museum of Photography, Film and Television**, Princes View, Bradford, W Yorkshire: *"The best in the world – there's nothing to touch it"* – **Lord Lichfield**.

★ ★ ★ ★ ★ ★ ★ ★ ★ ★ ★ ★ ★ ★ ★ ★ ★ ★ ★

although they have some lovely pictures". He may prefer the Tate restaurant, renowned for its wine list. PS The Tate opens in Liverpool this year, exhibiting modern art borrowed from the London collection.

VICTORIA AND ALBERT MUSEUM, South Kensington, SW7 ☎ (01) 589 6371
Victoriana in proliferation, from paintings and drawings to costume to the original William Morris Room. Also a 20th-century gallery for design-orientated exhibitions. Views are ambivalent: *"Fabulous content, but they don't know how to display it. It's dark, gloomy and the layout makes no sense"* – **Duggie Fields.** *"I'm rather a devotee, but it doesn't have any great picture collection"* – **John Brooke-Little.** *"I love it, but it's in a bit of a muddle at the minute"* – **Serena Fass.** London waits with baited breath to see what changes the new director, Elizabeth Esteve-Coll, makes.

WALLACE COLLECTION, Hertford House, Manchester Square, W1 ☎ (01) 935 0687
A Georgian house, celebrated for its superb collection of French furniture and 18th-century French paintings – Fragonard, Watteau, Boucher. Also Dutch, Flemish, Italian, Spanish 17th-century and English 18th-century works. *"Great works of art yet no one ever goes there"* – **Lord Gowrie.** *"People don't go enough and they should"* – **John Brooke-Little.** *"My favourite gallery in London. I'm very fond of it"* – **Auberon Waugh. Lord Lichfield** is another fan.

Commercial Galleries

COLNAGHI & CO, 14 Old Bond St, W1 ☎ (01) 491 7408 for serious Old Masters – Botticelli, Rubens, Rembrandt and co. **THOS AGNEW & SON,** 43 Old Bond St, W1 ☎ (01) 629 6176 for fine Old Masters – Reynolds, Gainsborough, Turner – plus

contemporaries.
MARLBOROUGH FINE ART, 6 Albemarle St, W1 ☎ (01) 629 5161, for modern art – Henry Moore, Barbara Hepworth, John Piper; **WADDINGTON GALLERIES,** 11 Cork St, W1 ☎ (01) 437 8611 – 4 galleries of the best modern and contemporary art and sculpture from Picasso, Miró and Matisse to Elisabeth Frink and Allen Jones. **ALBEMARLE GALLERY,** 18 Albemarle St, W1 ☎ (01) 493 7968: *"My gallery, but that's not the only reason why I like it. It's a nice space, run by two men with a passion for their work rather than commodity brokers"* – **Duggie Fields. LISSON GALLERY,** 67 Lisson St, NW1 ☎ (01) 724 2739 (mainly sculpture), **NIGEL GREENWOOD,** 4 New Burlington St, W1 ☎ (01) 434 3795 and **ANTHONY REYNOLDS,** 37 Cowper St,

EC2 ☎ (01) 608 1516 are *"the best for avant-garde art"* according to **Edward Lucie-Smith,** who votes **KATE GANZ,** 49 Maddox St, W1 ☎ (01) 409 2442 *"the best dealer in Old Master drawings",* **HARARI & JOHNS,** 12 Duke St, SW1 ☎ (01) 839 7671 *"the best dealers in Old Masters"* and **ESKENAZI,** Foxglove House, 166 Piccadilly, W1 ☎ (01) 493 5464 *"the best for Chinese art".*

Ballet

🏃 **ROYAL BALLET COMPANY, Royal Opera House, Covent Garden, WC2 ☎ (01) 240 1066**

The leading company in the world, and certainly the one that has the most influence on international ballet, founded by the pioneering Dame Ninette de Valois. The brilliant founder choreographer Frederick Ashton established the lyrical English style – more dramatic, less athletic. Sensational productions of Ashton's work, that of principal choreographer Kenneth MacMillan and, of course, the classics, under the directorship of Anthony Dowell. Dancers are drawn almost exclusively from their ballet school. The active Sadler's Wells Royal Ballet comes under the same Opera House umbrella.

Film

LONDON FILM FESTIVAL, National Film Theatre, South Bank, SE1 ☎ (01) 928 3232
More of an arts event for the movie-goer in the street than

DESERT ISLAND SURVIVAL KIT:

JEFFREY ARCHER

"My film would be Brief Encounter. *It is wonderful, truly remarkable, one of the great films of all time, very old-fashioned and very moving. Celia Johnson was the most brilliant actress this century in Britain. Were she still alive, that's who I'd like to be stranded on a desert island with."*

---

the cattle (sorry, *culture*) markets of Cannes and co. 120 films – British and foreign premières, the best of the new international films, multi-million-dollar movies, low-budget Third World films, archive flicks.

Gardens

CHELSEA PHYSIC GARDEN, Royal Hospital Rd, SW3 ☎ (01) 352 5646
An idyllic walled garden founded in 1673 by the Society of Apothecaries. Blissfully solitary, since it's open only to Friends (from £16 a year) except on Wed and Sun afternoons, mid-Apr to Oct.

PARLIAMENT HILL,
Hampstead Heath, NW3
"Absolutely the outstanding best. You walk over the hill and see right across London, with all the kites flying and the trees. It's not a park, you see, it's a bit of lovely old countryside, left as it was" – **Lord Donoughue.**

RICHMOND PARK,
Richmond, Surrey
"I'm very fond of it. To have deer in London is very special" – **Jane Asher**. *"The Isabella Plantation is a breathtaking place and no one seems to know it's there. Go between the second week in May and the second week in June when the rhododendrons are in bloom"* – **Duggie Fields.**

ROYAL BOTANIC
GARDENS, Kew, Surrey
☎ (01) 940 1171
These lovely gardens will never be quite the same after last year's hurricane-force winds razed many of the oldest, rarest trees, leaving the land looking like a battle site. Of 11,000 trees, 500 were lost. However, the replanting programme has been speeded up, and the gardens remain dear: *"I love Kew. There are two huge new tropical glasshouses, very well worth seeing"* – **Duggie Fields.** For **Lord Lichfield**, *"the best time is mid-winter, when few other people go. Some of the dormant trees and winter-flowering shrubs are stunning."*

MUSIC

ENGLISH NATIONAL
OPERA, London Coliseum,
St Martin's Lane, WC2
☎ (01) 836 3161
Adventurous, stimulating,

♟ —World's Best— ♟

OPERA COMPANIES

1 **ROYAL OPERA HOUSE,** Covent Garden, London
2 **L'OPERA,** Paris
3 **LA SCALA,** Milan
4 **METROPOLITAN OPERA,** New York
5 **ENGLISH NATIONAL OPERA (ENO),** London
6 **VERONA ARENA,** Verona
7 **BAVARIAN STATE OPERA,** Munich
8 **NEW YORK CITY OPERA,** New York
9 **GERMAN OPERA,** Berlin
10 **VIENNA STATE OPERA,** Vienna

---

polished – the one opera buffs puff. The only full-time repertory company in Britain – with bags of team spirit. More casual than Covent Garden – and more penetrable. *"It would be hard to think of any opera company in the world that keeps up the standard of the ENO, doing opera in English very, very well and sometimes controversially. A fabulous operation"* – **Andrew Lloyd Webber**. *"Mostly I go to the ENO because I do love being able to understand what they're saying"* – **Jane Asher**. *"I often go to the ENO after work and get a seat in the gods"* – **Leo Cooper**. *"Although it's heresy to say it, I'm starting to prefer the ENO to Covent Garden because of their stagecraft"* – **Ed Victor**. *"Visually superior to Covent Garden"* – **Duggie Fields.**

HENRY WOOD
PROMENADE CONCERTS,
Royal Albert Hall,
Kensington Gore, SW7
☎ (01) 589 8212
The Proms are a season (July-Sept) of superb classical concerts with cheap standing room. *"They make serious music accessible to everyone. The overt enjoyment of the promenaders and the way they express it – people with their heads buried in the score conducting, others in a trance, others bobbing about – becomes part of the event"* – **Michael Grade**. The Last Night, a beloved British tradition, sees a mass of bodies swaying, singing, waving and cheering in a patriotic frenzy to *Rule Britannia* and *Land of Hope and Glory*.

ROYAL FESTIVAL HALL,
South Bank Centre, SE1
☎ (01) 928 3002
The best concert hall in Britain, where all the top dogs play. *"A lovely atmosphere and superb acoustics"* – **Sir Clive Sinclair**. Together with the smaller Queen Elizabeth Hall and Purcell Room, it presents more live music than anywhere else in the world.

ROYAL OPERA HOUSE,
Covent Garden, WC2
☎ (01) 240 1066
The grandest opera house in the country, with more cachet than cash. Dire financial straits have led to flagging esprit de corps in the past, but there are high hopes for the new regime under Jeremy Isaacs, John Sainsbury and Bernard Haitink. It's still a thrill to attend: *"I would go all the time if I could afford it. When I do go, it's Covent Garden every time"* – **Serena Fass**. *"I love its looks – it has a wonderful early-Victorian interior"* – **Lord Gowrie**. *"The place to go*

> **❝** *I feel strongly that opera should be like my area of musical theatre – the formality attached to the event can be rather boring. If you want to see a great performance of music theatre, you don't necessarily want to have to dress up* **❞**

 ANDREW LLOYD WEBBER

TICKET TRAUMAS

If you're not part of a company that block-books tickets and you don't have strings to pull, you must be *organized*. Pay a small sub to be on the opera's mailing list, fill in the forms pronto, and hey presto! Only a few lucky ones get into Glyndebourne this way, however. 95 per cent of tickets are snapped up by members of the Festival Society, for which there's a 7,000-plus waiting list. It's like trying to get into Eton; members are putting their *children* down. For Covent Garden and ENO try taking **Duggie Fields**'s advice: *"On first nights there are empty seats – people don't want to pay until the critics have passed judgement. After a favourable review comes out, tickets are impossible to get. So go on a first night."*

for the music" – **Duggie Fields**. A favourite of **Sir Clive Sinclair, Jane Asher, Leo** and **Jilly Cooper**. Three resident companies, the Royal Opera, the Royal Ballet and Sadler's Wells Royal Ballet, plus international visiting companies.

THEATRE

BARBICAN, Barbican Centre, EC2 ☎ (01) 628 8795
This modern arts complex is perplexingly complex to negotiate, but worthy of bestdom for being London home of the Royal Shakespeare Company. The largest and *"the best theatre company in the world"* declare **Stanley Marcus** and **Douglas Fairbanks Jr** (who is on the board of governors). *"I would go anywhere to see the RSC, but I don't like all those automatic doors. I'm always afraid I'll get lost like in Disneyland"* – **Michael Grade.**

CRITERION, Piccadilly Circus, W1 ☎ (01) 930 3216
One of Britain's rare underground theatres, a bijou Victorian affair, still with the original stylized wall tiles and the pink and gilt auditorium. *"A lovely, intimate theatre"* – **Michael Ratcliffe.**

DRURY LANE THEATRE ROYAL, Catherine St, WC2 ☎ (01) 836 8108
Perhaps the oldest theatre site in London – 4 theatres have

existed there since Restoration times. Now one of the best venues for musical extravaganzas – and for ghosts (look out for the man in grey...).

HAYMARKET THEATRE ROYAL, Haymarket, SW1 ☎ (01) 930 9832
A gracious Regency building, it's one of the oldest, most prestigious and beautiful theatres in London. Superior plays (Shaw, Wilde, the best

contemporaries) and actors (Derek Jacobi, Rex Harrison, Alan Bates, Maggie Smith).

HER MAJESTY'S THEATRE, Haymarket, SW1 ☎ (01) 839 2244
Now playing the almost unstoppable *The Phantom of the Opera*, this is *"another very prestigious theatre, opposite the Haymarket – the two theatres complement one another. A lot of wonderful things have played there* – West Side Story, Fiddler on the Roof ..." – **Michael Ratcliffe.**

NATIONAL THEATRE, South Bank, SE1 ☎ (01) 928 2252
Considered, in tandem with the RSC, the best large-scale theatre company in the world. A key part of the South Bank Centre, the complex has 3 theatres: Olivier, Lyttelton and the baby Cottesloe – *"I think it's the nicest modern theatre in London. You have very close contact with the performance"* – **Michael Ratcliffe**. Richard Eyre succeeds Sir Peter Hall as director this year. *"You feel the buzz when you walk in. It is an*

CULTURE

WHO HAS THE BEST THEATRE?

"London, unquestionably" came the response from **Douglas Fairbanks Jr**, backed by **Stanley Marcus**. *"Britain by 100,000 miles!"* expostulated **Jeffrey Archer**: *"How can a bunch of colonials who can't even pronounce the language hope to challenge the greatest country on earth?! We have brilliant actresses – Maggie Smith, Judi Dench, Diana Rigg – we have so many of them it's frightening. America has just one – Meryl Streep."* **Ned Sherrin** is less partisan: *"British theatre is the best at the moment because of the long tradition and the writers, directors and actors – the standard is tremendously high. Right now, the only musicals are coming out of England, though America does have the best writer of musicals in Sondheim. Apart from that, it's the economic climate: people can still afford to put on musicals here – just – which they can hardly do in America."* The only dissenters are **Auberon Waugh**: *"There are more theatres in Britain than anywhere else, but even so, there's an awful lot of rubbish..."* and **Bob Payton**: *"People who say the best theatre is in Britain are the foreigners, who want to see Alec Guinness or Diana Rigg, or Robert Morley because they saw him in a British Airways commercial."*

❝ *I like the atmosphere of English theatres. There's nothing to compare with Drury Lane or the Haymarket, Wyndham's, the Criterion or the Ambassadors. They're wonderful jewel boxes. Theatres have more the aspect of a barn in America* **❞**

🏃 NED SHERRIN

exciting centre of excellence. I love to go there despite all the grey and mauve and chrome because it's alive – the people make it" – **Michael Grade**. **Douglas Fairbanks Jr** thinks it's among the best theatres in the world.

OPEN-AIR THEATRE, Regent's Park, NW1
☎ **(01) 486 2431 (end-May to mid-Sept); ☎ (01) 935 5884 (all year)**
Pretty (and often pretty chilly) theatre that seems to grow from the grassy garden, an evocative setting for plays such as *A Midsummer Night's Dream*. The New Shakespeare Company perform 2 Shakespeares each summer season plus a trad and a children's play. Bring cushions and blankets; buy mulled wine and hot food there.

PALACE THEATRE, Shaftesbury Ave, W1
☎ **(01) 437 6834**
"*A beautiful theatre, built as an opera house by Richard D'Oyly Carte. Wonderful rich late-Victorian decoration. It's one of those large theatres that has a great feeling of intimacy*" – **Michael Ratcliffe**. Owned and newly spruced up by Andrew Lloyd Webber's Really Useful Group, whose chairman, **Lord Gowrie**, says: "*My favourite theatre, an amazing building . . .*"

THE ROYAL COURT, Sloane Square, SW1 ☎ **(01) 730 1745**
Off the main drag is this fine, often controversial, theatre which specializes in new writing. Many leading dramatists cut their teeth at this nucleus of creativity. The old rehearsal rooms have become the **Theatre Upstairs** (☎ (01) 730 2554) for more new works.

WYNDHAM'S, Charing Cross Rd, WC2 ☎ **(01) 836 3028**
Sir Charles Wyndham's theatre, with its gorgeous gilt swagged ceiling and mouldings, is still run by the same family. "*You know that if you go to Wyndham's or the Albery [which has the same family ties], it will be a play of some quality. It's a matter of tradition and history. They're like a reliable store, like Liberty's*" – **Michael Ratcliffe**.

REST OF BRITAIN

ART AND MUSEUMS

The provinces are rich in art galleries and museums. Here is a run-down of what's best in 3 of Britain's top towns for culture-vulturing of the visual kind.

BATH
Littered with museums that reflect life in Roman and Regency Britain. Wallow in the **Roman Baths** and **Roman Museum**, housing the gilded bronze head of *Minerva*, found on the site. See life as it was when Beau Nash was dandying around town at the **Pump Room**, social centre of the spa; at the authentically furnished Georgian house at **No 1 Royal Crescent**; the **Carriage Museum** (the finest in the country) and the **Holburne Museum**, Great Pulteney St ☎ (0225) 66669, a beautifully proportioned Regency building containing the Holburne family's collection of decorative and fine art, plus an excellent art library and works by contemporary craftsmen. "*It's in a whole house, typical of*

18th-century Bath, which is lovely. A nice comprehensive collection of paintings, furniture, silver, china, porcelain, carpets, all English things" – **Serena Fass**. Dedicated followers of fashion can pursue their love from the 17th century to the present day at the **Museum of Costume** in the Assembly Rooms. Don't miss the charming **American Museum** at Claverton Manor, with its collection of folk art, furniture and handmade patchwork quilts.

CAMBRIDGE
This small historic city is home to the famous university, rival to Oxford. Only some 40 years its junior (dating back to 1209), among its notable colleges are **Peterhouse** (the oldest), **St John's** (spectacular Tudor gateway and its own Bridge of Sighs), **Corpus Christi** (whose Old Court is in fact the oldest in town), **Trinity** (the largest court) and **King's**, whose awesome Gothic chapel houses Rubens's *Adoration of the Magi*. The **Fitzwilliam Museum** contains medieval illuminated manuscripts, antiquities, arms and armour, pottery, porcelain and paintings by Rembrandt, Titian, Constable and Turner. See prints of colleges and town at the **Bene't Gallery**. PS One of the loveliest walks in Britain is along the Backs, where college lawns meet the River Cam. The jewel of Cambridge's gardens is the stone-walled Fellow's Garden of Clare College.

OXFORD
A city of superlatives, Oxford is not only synonymous with the oldest and most famous university in Britain (founded c. 1167), but home to the **Museum of the History of**

Science (the finest collection of early astrological, mathematical and optical instruments in the world) and the **Ashmolean Museum** (superb collection of prints and drawings – some by Michelangelo and Raphael – Old Master paintings, Chinese art and decorative pieces). **Christ Church Picture Gallery** contains more Old Master drawings, and portraits of eminent former members of college. The little-visited **Exeter** chapel has a lovely Burne-Jones tapestry. Of the glorious golden-stone colleges, see **Merton** (whose Mob Quad and library are the oldest in Oxford), the majestic **Christ Church** (Wren's Tom Tower), **New College** (enchanting cloisters; Sir Joshua Reynolds's stained-glass windows in the ante-chapel) and **Magdalen** (cloisters, deer park and the landmark bell tower). Don't miss the 15th-century **Divinity School** in Broad Street, the oldest lecture room in the city: *"People pass by places like this, which in James I's time was the most absolute building in Christendom. It's really unusual"* – **John Brooke-Little.**

FESTIVALS

"A festival should very much feature the locality and involve the local people. The place should come alive" – **Julian Lloyd Webber**. The best fests are: **Chichester** (July), which *"revolves around the cathedral. Very good, with many local events as well as big concerts"* – **JLW. Three Choirs Festival** (Aug), the oldest music festival in Britain, alternating between the cathedrals of Worcester, Gloucester and Hereford. *"A fantastic atmosphere. It means a lot to me"* – **JLW**. The highly respected feast of music at **Aldeburgh**, Suffolk (June), founded by Benjamin Britten. **Bath** (May-June) for music, arts, fringe. **Lichfield**, Staffordshire (July): *"Apart from extravagant and elegant choral and orchestral offerings, there is a very good fringe.*

Recently, George Melly sang and Alan Bates read. Spectacular fireworks at the close" – **Lord Lichfield. Cambridge** (July-Aug), making use of its most beautiful buildings. **Cheltenham** (July) for largely contemporary music; and **Brighton** (May), the largest in England. **Henley's** 4-day festival after the rowing regatta (July) is a rather different affair: it's Royal Regatta-meets-May Ball-meets-Last Night of the Proms. Punters wear evening dress; there's dinner in tented versions of London restaurants, cabaret, dancing, and concerts on a floating stage. Culminates in a rousing *Pomp and Circumstance* and *1812* by a military band with fireworks over the river. Tickets: 27 Hart St, Henley ☎ (0491) 575751.

GLYNDEBOURNE GLORY

♣ **GLYNDEBOURNE FESTIVAL OPERA**, Lewes, E Sussex ☎ (0273) 812321. Heads the social-cultural calendar in Britain. What could be more divine? It's grand (Elizabethan country estate setting), trad Brit (evening dress, stiff upper lips ploughing through picnics even when perishing cold) *and* it has a very high standard of opera (Sir Peter Hall is Artistic Director, the London Philharmonic is the resident orchestra, top artists are creamed from all over the world). What is more, it's exclusive: the only way to guarantee tickets is to be or know a member of the Festival Society. 5 or 6 operas are presented from the end of May to mid-August. *"There is no place in the world like Glyndebourne, it's a jewel. An exquisite experience because it's small and perfect. For me its scale makes it best in the world"* – **James Burke**. *"For a total experience, it would take a lot of beating. You will certainly see something original and stimulating, the best possible directors, exciting young singers – you could be seeing the début of a really phenomenal artist"* – **Andrew Lloyd Webber**. *"The best festival in the world. It's just so wonderful"* – **Frank Bowling**. Some find the event has become unappetizingly corporate but *"you have to do it once . . . more often, given the opportunity. A Glyndebourne picnic on a summer's day is a delight"* – **Roy Ackerman**. *"A treat – the social side is fabulous. Tourists must go to see the English in their own environment"* – **Duggie Fields**. *"It's rather silly – you have to dress up in dinner jackets and it's 50 miles out of London, so it couldn't be more inconvenient. But it is extremely good, brilliant"* – **Auberon Waugh**. *"There is nothing more sublime than an evening at Glyndebourne and a picnic – it's a great ritual, wonderfully decadent and extravagant: caviare, fresh lobster, raspberry and meringue shortcake with cream and really cold Chassagne-Montrachet – marvellous"* – **Michael Grade**. Old hands arrive well before the 5pm-ish start and bag a hot spot in the garden for their interval picnic (rugs are de rigueur, tables are out). If you don't fancy sittin' in the rain, dine à la carte at the Middle and Over Wallop Restaurant, or settle for the set-price carvery/cold buffet in the Nether Wallop Restaurant. Book dinner along with the tickets (£40-£50, by post from the end of March). Only 830 seats, so get in there *faust*.

CULTURE

MUSIC

Opera North in Leeds is an independent, international opera company of high repute, ranking alongside Scottish Opera and a close second to the Royal Opera and ENO.

PAVILION OPERA, Thorpe Tilney Hall, Nr Lincoln, Lincolnshire ☎ (05267) 231
The creation of Freddie Stockdale, whose troupe tours the drawing rooms of English country houses, performing 18th- and 19th-century operas in the round. The room itself is the scenery; you are a fly on the wall watching a real-life drama. *"Tiny company of young wonderful singers accompanied by piano (which is so good that after a while you think it's an orchestra). You really focus on the opera, its action and singing. Charming and wonderful"* – **Ed Victor**. Much admired by **Lord Lichfield** and **Lord Gowrie**: *"It has reminded people that opera is an intimate art and not a great 19th-century circus."*

STATELY HOMES AND GARDENS

Most country houses are open to the public from around Easter to the end of October. The **National Trust**, 36 Queen Anne's Gate, London SW1 ☎ (01) 222 9251, owns over 200 properties and 100 gardens of historical interest or natural beauty – join the NT and get their handbook.

BLENHEIM PALACE, Woodstock, Oxfordshire ☎ (0993) 811325
Magnificent 18th-century home of the 11th Duke of Marlborough, birthplace of Sir Winston Churchill. *"The grandest from the outside"* – **Lord Montagu of Beaulieu.**

BOTANIC GARDENS, High St, Oxford ☎ (0865) 276920
Thought to be the oldest botanic gardens in Britain. *"A lovely garden by the river with hot houses. It's a rather romantic place, nobody ever goes there. You can go in summer and find only a dozen other people wandering around. It is a garden for the study of botany, so you do get every plant under the sun. It's well cared for, very casual, and it's free"* – **John Brooke-Little**. *"Small, intimate with some splendid specimens"* – **Lord Lichfield.**

BURGHLEY HOUSE, Stamford, Lincolnshire ☎ (0780) 52451
The largest Elizabethan house in existence in the UK, built by William Cecil, set in Capability Brown deer parks. *"A great discovery. It has the most wonderful silver wine coolers. The really big houses are almost too much to comprehend. Burghley is on a more manageable scale. I like houses I can relate to in today's terms. People had such a vision of life back in those days. I see myself as a Victorian [sic] anyhow. I've just been reincarnated, I think"* – **Bob Payton.**

CASTLE HOWARD, York, N Yorkshire ☎ (065384) 333
Architect Sir John Vanbrugh's dramatic neo-classical building must be the most-seen stately in Britain, since it starred as Brideshead in the TV series of Waugh's novel. Still owned by the Howard family, whose ancestral portraits – by Gainsborough, Romney and Reynolds – cover the walls. Fine sculpture collection, tapestries and furniture.

CHATSWORTH, Baslow, Derbyshire ☎ (024688) 2204
The Duke and Duchess of Devonshire's 17th-century seat, renowned for the fine Old Master drawings and paintings – though the Duke has been selling off some important drawings and prints. *"Enormously grand, beautifully proportioned classic building; magnificent Capability Brown grounds; built in the grand manner – a touch of Versailles"* – **John Brooke-Little**. *"I think the drawing room is the most beautiful room in terms of paintings and atmosphere"* –

Lord Gowrie. *"Probably the best for content – the pictures and furnishings are difficult to compare"* – **Lord Montagu of Beaulieu.**

HAREWOOD HOUSE, Harewood, Leeds, W Yorkshire ☎ (0532) 886225
Standing in one of Capability's largest and most beautiful parks is this marvellous 18th-century house. State rooms are filled with furniture by Chippendale and Robert Adam, Sèvres and Chinese porcelain, Italian and English Old Masters. Also a bird garden, with a tropical house containing some rare species.

LEEDS CASTLE, Maidstone, Kent ☎ (0622) 65400
"A really picturesque castle, surrounded by a moat with its own wonderful little 'Bridge of Sighs'" – **Auberon Waugh**. Built in 1119, it's one of the most ancient – and well-preserved – castles in the land. Used for conferences, etc.

LONGLEAT HOUSE, Warminster, Wiltshire ☎ (09853) 551
Longleat, seat of the Marquis of Bath, is probably best known for its lions – for part of the 11,000-acre grounds forms a spectacular safari park (☎ 328) with around 50 lions and tigers and other wild animals. Capability Brown's landscaping includes a chain of lakes. The house, built in 1580, is one of the earliest to show the influence of the Italian Renaissance.

OSBORNE HOUSE, York Ave, E Cowes, Isle of Wight ☎ (0983) 200022
One of Queen Victoria's residences, built in 1845 and designed by Prince Albert. *"One of the most interesting houses to visit. It's as it was when Queen Victoria died"* – **Lord Montagu of Beaulieu.**

PENSHURST PLACE, Penshurst, Tonbridge, Kent ☎ (0892) 870307
Viscount de L'Isle's country house has, apart from one of the finest medieval halls in the country (the house dates back

to 1340), a magnificent 10-acre Tudor walled garden, subdivided by yew hedges. *"The best, well-kept, formal garden" – John Brooke-Little.*

SISSINGHURST CASTLE GARDENS, Cranbrook, Kent ☎ (0580) 712850
A great – and ultra-popular – English garden, created by Vita Sackville-West in the 1930s, designed and planted with inspiration. Her famous White Garden has white pansies, white peonies, white irises, white lilies ... The house is open, too.

STOURHEAD, Stourton, Warminster, Wiltshire ☎ (0747) 840348
A country house with wildly lyrical and romantic classical grounds: rolling parkland landscaped by Henry Hoare, flowering shrubs, Palladian follies, grottoes, temples and a lake. *"Absolutely marvellous in the spring with all the azaleas. It's very pretty in autumn, too" – Serena Fass.*

THEATRE

A quick trip round the provincials reveals the best to be: **Stratford-upon-Avon** (absolute tops, HQ of the RSC and the best place to take in the Bard. *"Lovely" – Michael Grade*). The **Bristol Theatre Royal**, and the **Theatre Royal, Bath** (*"I'm very fond of them – both are very attractive" – Jane Asher*): Bristol has 2 resident companies – the Old Vic (for quality theatre, old and modern) and New Vic (studio theatre in the round for more modern and avant-garde productions; visiting guest actors). Bath shows touring productions only. The **Alhambra Theatre, Bradford** (*"recently restored at immense expense – very beautiful" – Michael Ratcliffe*). The **Citizens Theatre, Glasgow** (lots of bold, European theatre). **Crucible Theatre, Sheffield** (adventurous open-stage theatre, great musicals). **Chichester Festival Theatre, Chichester** (established works, respected rep company). The

Leicester Haymarket (highly reputed for classical works and musicals). The **Royal Exchange Theatre, Manchester** (*"the most exciting modern theatre in the country. Special in every way, unique. It's inside the enormous old cotton exchange, which was one of the biggest buildings in the world at the time [1874]. It looks like a space capsule that's landed inside a great building. It's extraordinary" – MR*).

SCOTLAND

ART AND MUSEUMS

BURRELL COLLECTION, 2060 Pollokshaws Rd, Pollok Country Park, Glasgow ☎ (041) 649 7151
Ship-owner William Burrell amassed over 800 items, from antiquities and Oriental art to

his famous decorative arts collection – tapestries, silver, ceramics ... and stained glass, which appeals to **John Brooke-Little**. Rich in Dutch and French masterpieces, particularly Degas. *"All terribly good things, beautifully displayed, very well written up – you don't get indigestion. If you want a comprehensive look at a lovely collection, it is a dream to walk around – 2 hours there and you can learn about anything" – Serena Fass.*

NATIONAL GALLERIES OF SCOTLAND, The Mound, Edinburgh ☎ (031) 556 8921
3 galleries – the **National** (fine paintings by the great masters – Raphael, Rembrandt, Van Dyck, Constable, et al, and works by Scottish artists); **Gallery of Modern Art**, Belford Rd (most major European and American 20th-century artists – Matisse to Moore, Picasso to Paolozzi),

CULTURE

FRINGE BENEFITS

🎭 **EDINBURGH INTERNATIONAL FESTIVAL, 21 Market St, Edinburgh** ☎ (031) 225 5756) is *the* all-encompassing arts festival, held in August. Opera from Finland, theatre from China, dance from Russia, music from Japan... Running concurrently are the famous **Fringe, 170 High St** ☎ (031) 226 5257 (low-budge shows of a serious/loony/musical nature by some 500 companies from all over the world), the Assembly Rooms (sharp shows that bridge Fringe and Fest), the distinguished Film Festival, TV Festival, Jazz Festival and – to remind you where you are – the Military Tattoo. Your feet won't touch the ground. *"It has to be the best. Unique because it has film and theatre and music and ballet. It transforms the town" – Dan Topolski. "It would take a very great deal to beat it. There's such a wide mix of events, and it's an incredibly beautiful city. One tends to forget how very fine it is" – Andrew Lloyd Webber. "I love the Fringe. You can end up in somebody's living room watching a Jacobean comedy – bizarre. The joy is the carnival atmosphere, non-threatening, relaxed, with vistors from all over the world just enjoying it. An amazing atmosphere" – Michael Grade.* However, lack of funds has caused the quality end of the programme to suffer; music, in particular, has slipped into a minor key. For **Julian Lloyd Webber**, it's too international: *"It's the same as London or New York. I don't get any local feel there at all – what they do are token gestures."*

CULTURE

❝ *Glasgow is one of the liveliest cities for contemporary arts, and for dance in particular* ❞

♟ MICHAEL CLARK

and the **Portrait Gallery**, Queen St (great Scots on canvas). Do see Raeburn's *Rev Robert Walker skating on Duddingston Loch* and Sargent's *Lady Agnew of Lochnaw*. A pleasing and balanced collection, enjoyed by Sassenach **Jeffrey Archer**. PS You can enjoy a pleasing, balanced lunch in the very good basement restaurant.

MUSIC

After a period of ups and downs, **Scottish Opera** is one to be reckoned with under new Musical Director John Mauceri, hot from the New York Met.

USHER HALL, Lothian Rd, ˙Edinburgh ☎ (031) 228 1155 *"My favourite hall in Britain. So nice to play there – it's one of the few halls where you feel it influences your performance"* – **Julian Lloyd Webber.**

WALES
MUSIC

BRECON JAZZ FESTIVAL, Watton Mount, Brecon ☎ (0874) 2631 Held in August, this gets *"a warm recommendation. It's beautiful countryside and a small town which really fizzes"* – **George Melly.**

♟ **WELSH NATIONAL OPERA, John St, Cardiff** ☎ (0222) 464666 Mooted by those in the know to be the best in Britain. Heartfelt, exciting, sometimes shoestring productions. Tremendous team spirit and, naturally, a great chorus. Tours take them Oxford, Birmingham and Bristol-wards.

Canada
MONTREAL

MONTREAL WORLD FILM FESTIVAL, 1455 blvd de Maisonneuve Est, H3G 1M8 ☎ (514) 879 4057 An *"up-and-coming festival"* – **Derek Malcolm**, where over 200 movies are screened.

TORONTO
BALLET

♟ **NATIONAL BALLET OF CANADA, 157 King St E, M5C 1G9** ☎ (416) 362 1041 A fine company that travels the world with their productions. The toast of New York and London with their performances of *Alice*. Prima ballerinas **Karen Kain** and Veronica Tennant match the best in the world. *"A wonderful ballet company"* – **Sondra Gotlieb**. At Christmas it's a great Toronto tradition to turn out for *The Nutcracker*.

FILM

Toronto is where both IMAX (incredible 360° screen) and CINEPLEX (the main complex is a 24-screen whopper) originated.

TORONTO FESTIVAL OF FESTIVALS, Suite 205, 69 Yorkville Ave, M4Y 2TI ☎ (416) 364 5924 One for the directors, producers and brightest stars: 10 days in Sept animated with documentaries, silent movies, international films. Julie Christie, Peter Ustinov, Paul Newman, Joanne Woodward, Jane Fonda, Sophia Loren,

Norman Mailer and Warren Beatty flock over for gala première performances (premières to N America if not the world). *"I love it when I see people running from one screening to the next. Some people take holidays during the festival just to watch all the movies"* – **Robert Ramsay**. *"It is world renowned. I go every year. It is one of the best in the world"* – **Bonnie Brooks-Young.**

VANCOUVER

DU MAURIER INTERNATIONAL JAZZ FESTIVAL, c/o Coastal Jazz & Blues Society, 203/1206 Hamilton St, V6B 259 ☎ (604) 682 0706 June-July. A broad spectrum of the world's finest jazz and blues artists (Wynton Marsalis, Miles Davis, Tito Puerte) play everything from trad to contemporary and ethnic sounds. *"An event not to be missed. A host of hot jazz acts from around the world. At every club and bandstage, known and unknown talent plays day and night to jazz-loving audiences"* – **Beverley Zbitnoff.**

Denmark

♟ **ROYAL DANISH BALLET, Royal Theatre, Kongens Nytorv, Copenhagen** ☎ (01) 141765 Under new director Frank Andersen, the Danish Ballet is regaining its stature and now ranks alongside the greats in Paris, Russia, New York and London. The RDB continues to perform the dances of the great Danish choreographer August Bournonville. The ballet school has turned out such luminaries as Peter Schaufuss, artistic director of the London Festival Ballet, Peter Martins, director of the New York City Ballet, and Erik Bruhn, director of the National Ballet of Canada. The Danish Ballet Festival was revived last year.

France

PARIS

ART AND MUSEUMS

The best international touring exhibitions are staged at the **Grand Palais**, ave du Général Eisenhower ☎ (1) 4289 5410; the **Petit Palais**, opposite, at ave Winston Churchill ☎ (1) 4265 1273, holds 2 major exhibitions each year, on top of its permanent collection of antiquities through to 19th-century art.

CENTRE GEORGES POMPIDOU, place Beaubourg, 75004 ☎ (1) 4277 1233

A young, living, cultural centre, a modern landmark in Paris famed for its Meccano-meets-ship's boiler room structure. It houses the newly extended Musée National d'Art Moderne – the national collection of art from Matisse and the Post-Impressionists up to *c.* 1945. Frequent visiting exhibitions of contemporary art and photography. *"Everybody knows it now, but it's an interesting place, both architecturally and for the taste of its exhibitions"* – **Jean-Michel Jaudel**. Excellent library. What goes on outside – buskers, mime, street theatre, student café society – is fun for young tourists, but otherwise, in the words of one Parisian, *"noisy, dirty and a pain in the neck"*.

MUSEE CARNAVALET, 23 rue de Sévigné, 75003 ☎ (1) 4272 2113

A charming 16th-century mansion in which the story of the city of Paris unravels through historical paintings, mementos of the Revolution, period furniture and objects. *"A very beautiful structure with 4 magnificent courtyards"* – **Jean-Michel Jaudel**.

♣ MUSEE D'ORSAY, 62 rue de Lille, 75007 ☎ (1) 4549 4814

A FINE LOUVRE AFFAIR

♣ MUSEE DU LOUVRE, 34 quai du Louvre, 75001 ☎ (1) 4260 3926. The enormous former palace has been incensing rather than delighting tourists over the past 2 years: disruptive restoration and construction work has offered little of aesthetic value. I M Pei's vast new glass pyramid structure, unveiled this year, sits incongruously in the main courtyard. It will act as skylight to an underground plaza with arteries to all the 200-plus galleries. Don't hold your breath: completion is due in the year 2000.

If you can get at it, there's an awesome collection of art covering Egyptian, Greek, Roman and Oriental antiquities, objets and furniture, and paintings of the European schools – including, of course, the *Mona Lisa*, behind grubby bullet-proof glass after the uncharitable attempts to wipe that smile off her face. To avoid utter exhaustion, join the ranks of Yanks in spongy running shoes – better still, take it a leetle at a time.

Beloved of **Lord Montagu of Beaulieu, Jean-Michel Jaudel, Margaux Hemingway** and **Joyce Davidson**, who marvels at its *"millions – well, hundreds – of galleries"*. What she's particularly fallen for is the **MUSEE DES ARTS DE LA MODE**, in the Louvre's **Pavillon de Marsan**, 111 rue de Rivoli, 75001 ☎ (1) 4260 3214. *"Fascinating and so beautifully done."* The first national costume museum in France, it includes couture garb donated by some of the world's great clothes-horses, and stages exhibitions of the fashion greats – Yves Saint Laurent, Christian Dior et al.

The new museum that's dazzling visitors and Parisians alike. The old fin de siècle Gare d'Orsay, a steel and glass pavilion, has been redesigned by Gae Aulenti as an immense, rich museum of 19th-century paintings and objets d'art. All highly impressive – not least for the Impressionist collection, absorbed from the Jeu de Paume. Renoir's *Moulin de la Galette* and Manet's *Déjeuner sur l'Herbe* are among the household-name paintings. Monet, Degas, Cézanne, Gauguin et al are here. *"I love it. It's very controversial: a marvellous space which people love to hate, but I love to like. It's a railway station turned cultural cathedral. As well as the Impressionists, you have the 19th-century French Victorian-style paintings"* – **Jean-Michel Jaudel.**

MUSEE GUSTAVE MOREAU, 14 rue de la Rochefoucauld, 75009

☎ (1) 4874 3850
"There are lots of little museums like this in Paris that are unheard of. This is a marvellous place, Moreau's former studio. A lot of fun" – **Jean-Michel Jaudel**. The early work of the Symbolists can be seen in this mammoth collection of 11,000 paintings and drawings.

MUSEE PICASSO, Hôtel de Salé, 5 rue de Thorigny, 75003 ☎ (1) 4271 2521

Based in a renovated 17th-century *hôtel particulier*, this is *"a marvellous place, very interesting architecturally, with lighting by Diego Giacometti, brother of the sculptor. It's beautiful. If you're a Picasso fan, it's a must"* – **Jean-Michel Jaudel**. *"Definitely my favourite museum. I like the fact that it presents one artist's work in depth. You can see fantastic paintings, statues, ceramics, book illustrations,*

CULTURE

manuscripts, all in a very beautiful cream-coloured private house. Even little owls by Picasso peek at you over doorways" – **Robert Carrier**.

MUSEE RODIN, Hôtel Biron, 77 rue de Varenne, **75007 Paris** ☎ (1) 4705 0134 *The Kiss, The Thinker*, they're all here, in the calm of Rodin's pretty 18th-century house and garden, set among flowers and fountains as the sculptor intended. Also working drawings and sketches.

Commercial Galleries

The best area for contemporary and antique art is the rue de Seine and its arteries, on the Rive Gauche. **GALERIE DU LETHE-LETAILLEUR ALAIN**, 50 rue de Seine, 75006; 1 rue Jacob, 75006 ☎ (1) 4633 2517 – best for Post-Impressionists. **GALERIE CLAUDE BERNARD**, 7 rue des Beaux-Arts, 75006 ☎ (1) 4326 9707 – *"One of the best galleries in Paris, showing the most famous, confirmed artists, ranging from Picasso and Giacometti to some*

younger artists" – **Jean-Michel Jaudel. GALERIE ALBERT LOEB**, rue des Beaux-Arts, 75006 ☎ (1) 4633 0687 – *"interesting, contemporary art at more reasonable prices"* – J-MJ; the same goes for **GALERIE JEAN BRIANCE**, rue Guenegaud. **BRAME & LA RENCEAU**, 68 blvd Malesherbes, 75008 ☎ (1) 4522 1689 is the best dealer of Impressionists.

BALLET

♟ **L'OPERA BALLET**, Palais Garnier, 8 rue Scribe, 75009 ☎ (1) 4266 5022
Under the direction of mega-étoile personality Rudolf Nureyev this ballet company is making a huge mark in the dance world. He has brought in international contemporary choreographers and dancers, plus there is an ever-brimming fount of new dancers from their excellent ballet school. Sylvie Guillem and Elisabeth Platel are the current wows of the troupe. 10-12 productions are performed each year including 3 or 4 new ones, such as the recent *Nutcracker*. Based in palatial splendour under the same roof as L'Opéra.

♟ —*World's Best*— ♟

BALLET COMPANIES

1   **L'OPERA BALLET**, Paris
2   **ROYAL BALLET**, London
3   **KIROV BALLET**, Leningrad
4   **NEW YORK CITY BALLET**, New York
5   **BOLSHOI BALLET**, Moscow
6   **AMERICAN BALLET THEATER**, New York
7   **ROYAL DANISH BALLET**, Copenhagen
8   **NATIONAL BALLET OF CANADA**, Toronto
9   **AUSTRALIAN BALLET**, Melbourne
10 **JOFFREY BALLET**, New York

MUSIC

FEP FESTIVAL ESTIVAL DE PARIS, 20 rue Geoffroy-l'Asnier, 75004 Paris ☎ (1) 4804 9801
A season (mid-July to mid-Sept) of classical music held at different churches and auditoria.

♟ **L'OPERA**, Palais Garnier, 8 rue Scribe, 75009 Paris ☎ (1) 4266 5022
The grandiose Second Empire opera house, with its magnificent staircase and clashingly striking 1960s ceiling by Chagall, is the largest in the world with room for 450 players on stage. Home to the Paris Opéra and the Opéra Ballet. Their second theatre, the Opéra Comique at **Salle Favart**, 5 rue Favart, 75009, stages smaller productions. Between the 2 theatres, they show 4-5 productions a year of both resident and visiting ballet and opera (always imported *étoiles*).

♟ **Buzzzzzzzzz** It's been a rocky road for **L'OPERA DE LA BASTILLE**, place de la Bastille: the brand-new opera house, brainchild of Jack Lang, was shelved by Chirac but finally given the green light by Mitterrand. The avant-garde building was designed by Carlos Ott. Daniel Barenboim, conductor-director of the Orchestre de Paris, will take the helm. Due to open on 14 July, 1989, for the bicentenary of Le Storming. Info: Ministère de la Culture, 3 rue de Valois, 75001 ☎ (1) 4296 1040 ♟ . . . . . . The theatre at the centre of the latest controversy (Paris *loves* a good controversy) is the **THEATRE NATIONAL DE LA COLLINE**, 15 rue Malte Brun, 75980 Paris ☎ (1) 4366 4360, an ultra-modern building, for mainly modern theatre, which opened earlier this year ♟ . . . . . . the new **CENTRE DE MUSIQUE BAROQUE**, Versailles ☎ (1) 4396 4848 stages concerts, opera and ballet in the château, the park and in town.

★ ★ ★ ★ ★ ★ ★ ★ ★ ★ ★ ★ ★ ★ ★ ★ ★ ★ ★ ★

CULTURE

THEATRE DES CHAMPS-ELYSEES, 15 ave Montaigne, 75008 ☎ (1) 4720 3637
This newly opened centre for the performing arts sees the re-blossoming of the fabulous 1913 building, with its lofty marble lobby and double staircase sweeping up to a frescoed gallery. The chic venue for opera, ballet, music and mime.

THEATRE MUSICAL DE PARIS, 2 place de Chatelet, 75001 Paris ☎ (1) 4261 1983
A trad hall for recitals, concerts, musicals and opera, drawing international artists like Jessye Norman.

VERSAILLES FESTIVAL OPERA, c/o Syndicat d'Initiative, 7 rue des Réservoirs, Versailles 78000 ☎ (1) 3950 3622
A programme of opera and concerts held for one week in May/June. The highlight is a beautiful Baroque opera staged at the Château de Versailles in the original setting and costumes. Its tiny jewel of an opera house was built by Gabriel, architect of the Place de la Concorde, for the future Louis XVI's marriage to Marie-Antoinette.

REST OF FRANCE

ART AND MUSEUMS

FONDATION MAEGHT, 06570 St-Paul-de-Vence ☎ 9332 8163
Just outside the hill village of St Paul, this pair of modern rose and white buildings houses a gallery of modern paintings and sculpture. Stained-glass windows by Ubac and Braque, a Braque mosaic, sculpture by Giacometti and works by Provence-phones Chagall, Miró, Matisse et al.

MUSEE BALZAC, Château de Saché, 37190 Azay-le-Rideau ☎ (47) 268650
"Where Balzac used to write.

Buzzzzzzzzz Azur brain seized up with all that lounging on the Côte d'Azur? Adjust the shades and mosey off to: the **Musée Matisse et d'Archéologie**, 164 ave des Arenes, Nice, for canvases, bronzes, sketches and memorabilia ...... more Henri: **Matisse's Chapel** at Vence was, the artist felt, his masterpiece – simple, whitewashed throughout, with tiny stained-glass windows and black line murals ...... the vividly mosaic'd **Musée National Fernand Léger** at Biot contains everything from ceramics to carpets (all by Léger). A treasure for **Duggie Fields**: *"The perfect place and setting"* ...... Renoir spent the last 12 years of his life at Cagnes-sur-Mer. His house and studio at Les Collettes have been perfectly preserved as the **Renoir Museum**. Stalk through the olive, orange and lemon trees to glimpse his bronze of Venus ...... **Cézanne** was considered so important in Aix that he had a street named after him; see his studio at 9 Ave Paul Cézanne, Aix-en-Provence ...... for a brush with **Courbet, visit the Musée Fabre**, 13 rue Montpelieret, Montpelier ...... Sated with Post-Impressionism? Stroll along to the gorgeous 19th-century **Villa Ethrussi de Rothschild**, blvd Denis Semeria, St Jean Cap Ferrat. The gardens, overlooking the Med, are memorable enough to have inspired Proust; the art collection includes Renaissance works, Meissen pottery, paintings by Boucher, Sisley, Monet and Renoir.

★ ★ ★ ★ ★ ★ ★ ★ ★ ★ ★ ★ ★ ★ ★ ★ ★ ★ ★ ★

It's not a rush-there-because-it's-so-amazing type of place, but it is evocative of the curious mixture of splendours and miseries of a writer's life. You see downstairs, where all his admirers gathered in his drawing room, but in order to do things they all admired, he had to retire to his little room upstairs. You realize all you need is an alcove and a drawing board and a great deal of coffee and imagination to write about courtesans until you drop" – **Frederic Raphael.**

MUSEE DES BEAUX ARTS, rue Mathieu Lalanne, 64000 Pau ☎ 5927 3302
"I love this museum because it's full of absolute junk, but it has one incredible masterpiece, the Degas painting of the

Cotton Exchange in New Orleans. If I was American I would swap pretty well anything for that painting" – **Lord Gowrie.**

MUSEE PICASSO, Château Grimaldi, place du Château, 06600 Antibes ☎ 9334 9191
Picasso turned out an astonishing number of works when he was living in Antibes in the latter half of 1946. Here they are – large-scale paintings, ceramics, lithographs and drawings inspired by Riviera life.

CHATEAUX

All the following grand Loire châteaux have superb son et lumière performances.

CULTURE

**CHATEAU D'AZAY-
LE-RIDEAU, 37190 Azay-
le-Rideau, Loir-et-Cher
☎ 4745 4204**
An elegant Renaissance
château set in beautiful
grounds by the Indre river, a
tributary of the Loire. Built in
1517 for François I. Very fine
tapestries.

**CHATEAU DE BLOIS, 41000
Blois, Loir-et-Cher
☎ 5478 0662**
A rich and varied architectural
treat, with elements from many
periods, dating back to the 13th
century with additions up until
the 17th. François I made his
mark with a magnificent
Italian-decorative-style
staircase that rises spirally in
an octagonal well.

**CHATEAU DE CHAMBORD,
41250 Bracieux, Loir-et-Cher
☎ 5420 3132**
This grand château was built in

DESERT ISLAND SURVIVAL KIT:

QUENTIN CRISP

*"The best person to be stranded with is your agent. My book
would be Proust's* A la Recherche du Temps Perdu *because it
is keyhole literature. My film? People are always asking me,
'What is the best movie you've ever seen?' and how do you
answer? Is* Cover Girl *a better movie than* Citizen Kane?
*American movies are the best because they were so dark and
dreamy and inevitable. The women were like the sphinx, so
inscrutable."*

1519 for François I (who
wanted the Loire diverted to
pass by his front gate but had
to settle for the smaller river
Cosson). It's the largest
château in the region, with 440
rooms and a 13,600-acre estate.
Don't miss the famous double
spiral staircase. Rooms may be
hired for balls.

**CHATEAU DE
CHENONCEAU, 37150 Bléré,
Loir-et-Cher ☎ 5478 0662**
Perhaps the most picturesque
of the grand Loire châteaux,
built in the centre of the Cher
river (you can take boat trips in
summer). A multi-arched
bridge and gallery stretches
across the water, and the
original keep is surrounded by
moats. Splendid formal
gardens, planted for Diane de
Poitiers, mistress of Henri II,
and Catherine de Medici.

DOING THE CANNES-CAN

**CANNES INTERNATIONAL FILM FESTIVAL, 71 rue du
Faubourg St Honoré, 75008 Paris ☎ (1) 4266 9220.** Where
do the global glitterati defect to in May? They're all doing the
Cannes-can, cruising along La Croisette, hobnobbing in lob-
bies (the Majestic's best – here a £2 million contract was
written out on a napkin between Menahem Golan and Jean-
Luc Godard for *Lear*), tattling on terraces (the Carlton's tops),
basking blondly, bronzedly and *barely* on the beach. *"The sort
of festival one terminally wants to avoid is Cannes. That kind
of event can leave one very cold"* – **Andrew Lloyd Webber**.
But 40,000 traders and punters can't be wrong; *they* know it's
red hot: *"Enormous fun even if you're not involved in the film
biz. There are lots of parties and receptions, I always seem to
wangle my way into the films. On the beach it's funny to follow
the hordes of photographers chasing one poor bare-breasted
girl . . ."* – **Dan Topolski**. There are theme parties (for *Biggles,
Hooray for Rock 'n' Roll*), yacht parties, and – the best –
parties at Maurice Tinchant's villa in the hills, graced even by
Depardieu. **Madhur Jaffrey** thinks it's all great; **David
Litchfield** gets his cultures crossed: *"The best jazz venue I've
ever been to was Cannes Film Festival, having lunch on the
beach"*; **Derek Malcolm** casts his critic's eye: *"It's a mixture
of the sacred and the profane. You may get a bum merchant
along with the greatest directors in the world."* Oh yes, *that's*
what we're here for: the *films*. The world's No 1 film festival
and market place shows 800 films round the clock, many of
them premières. The ultimate prize for best film is the coveted
Palme d'Or.

FILM

**AVORIAZ INTERNATIONAL
FANTASY FILM FESTIVAL,
c/o Promo 2000, 33 ave
MacMahon, 75017 Paris
☎ (1) 4267 7140**
Held in Jan-Feb, it's the forum
for sci-fi and horror movies,
where Spielberg first reared his
head, earning first prize in 1975
for *Duel*. You don't have to get
totally square-eyed – there's
skiing too. Princess Stéphanie
is a regular.

**DEAUVILLE FESTIVAL DU
CINEMA AMERICAIN, c/o
Promo 2000, 33 ave
MacMahon, 75017 Paris
☎ (1) 4267 7140; or Office de
Tourisme, Deauville
☎ (31) 882143**
An altogether smaller affair
than Cannes, but mega-celebs
turn out to see American (plus
James Bond) films – Liz Taylor,
Robert De Niro, Shirley
MacLaine, Timothy Dalton,
Douglas Fairbanks Jr.

MUSIC

**CHOREGIES, BP 180, 84105
Orange ☎ 9034 2424**
A 3-week season in July of
magnificent one-off opera
productions in the Théâtre
Antique, a Roman
amphitheatre. Recitals and
concerts too. Big international
names, chic dressing.

**FESTIVAL
INTERNATIONAL D'ART
LYRIQUE, Palais de l'Ancien
Archevêché, 13100 Aix-
en-Provence ☎ 4223 3482**
The best festival in France, one
of great tradition and charm,
held in July. 5 operas are
staged in the al fresco Théâtre
de l'Archevêché in the
Archbishop's Palace. Concerts
resound from churches and
courtyards in the twisty
medieval streets. France's
favourite divas Jessye Norman
and Barbara Hendricks
perform regularly. *"Very good"*
– **Andrew Lloyd Webber.**

**FESTIVAL MONDIAL DE
JAZZ D'ANTIBES, Maison du
Tourisme d'Antibes, Place
Charles-de-Gaulle, 06600
Antibes ☎ 9333 9564**
Antibes and Juan les Pins
swing even more than usual
with 2 weeks in July of big-
band jazz, top singers and
players such as Sarah
Vaughan, Ray Charles and
Fats Domino.

THEATRE

**FESTIVAL D'AVIGNON,
Bureau de Festival, BP 92,
84006 Avignon ☎ 9082 6511**
A festival (July-Aug) of drama
– experimental, comic, all-
night, ethnic, sketches – the

lot. Peter Brook's
Mahabharata was premièred
here. Also dance, lectures and
exhibitions. *"Best theatre
festival"* – **Marchesa Bona
Frescobaldi.**

Germany

ART

The **Wallraf-Richartz
Museum/Ludwig** in Cologne is
the largest art gallery in the
Rheinland, housing fine works
from the Impressionists to
contemporary art.

**ALTE PINAKOTHEK, Barer
Strasse 27, D-8000 Munich 2
☎ (089) 2380 5215**
Among the best collections of
Old Masters in the world – 65
Rubens, a number of priceless
Italians, all the German
masters. The museum opened
in 1836 in a building
commissioned by Ludwig I.

**NEUE PINAKOTHEK, Barer
Strasse 29, D-8000 Munich 40
☎ (089) 2380 5195**
A sensational new building
opposite the Alte Pinakothek,
opened in 1981 to house 18th-
and 19th-century European art.
Fine works follow the German
Romantics through to Realism.

**STAATSGALERIE, Konrad-
Adenauer-Strasse 32, D-7000
Stuttgart ☎ (0711) 212 5108**
The most impressive collection
of 19th- and 20th-century art in
Germany, from Impressionism
to the present day. Strong on
Expressionism and other 20th-
century Germans. Manet,
Renoir, Cézanne, Gauguin,
Picasso, Dali, Ernst, Beckmann
and Klee are there en force.

**STAATSGALERIE
MODERNER KUNST,
Prinzregentenstrasse 1 (Haus
der Kunst), D-8000 Munich 22
☎ (089) 292710**
A leading museum of 20th-
century art with 400 paintings
and sculptures. All major
schools are covered – Cubism,
Fauvism, Surrealism,
American Abstract
Expressionism, Pop Art,
Minimal Art, and a dozen other
isms. Good on Picasso, all the
important German moderns –
Paul Klee, Franz Marc, Max
Beckmann – and Italians –
Boccioni, de Chirico, Marini,
Burri.

> **❝** *Film should be regarded as one of the arts.
> Directors such as Buñuel and Bergman
> have made a contribution to culture and are
> as important as writers such as Kafka* **❞**

 DEREK MALCOLM

FILM

**BERLIN INTERNATIONAL
FILM FESTIVAL,
Budapester Strasse 50, D-1000
Berlin 30 ☎ (030) 25489**
The No 2 festival in Europe
(after Cannes), held in Feb.
The Golden Bear goes to the
best film. Emphasis on
retrospective and children's
films, and new German cinema.
Blockbuster receptions are held
on the first and final nights at
the Hotels Schweizerhof and
Intercontinental.

**MUNICH INTERNATIONAL
FILM FESTIVAL,
Türkenstrasse 93, D-8000
Munich 40 ☎ (089) 393011**
A rapidly expanding festival
held in June. Around 120 films

DESERT ISLAND SURVIVAL KIT:

DOUGLAS FAIRBANKS JR

"My film would be The Thief of Baghdad. *Aside from the fact
that it's my father's film, I think it shows the best use of the film
medium. As a motion picture, as a work of art, I think it is one
of the best and most beautiful films ever made. If it had sound,
I think it would be ruined. It's more like a pictorial ballet."*

CULTURE

are shown, including premières from 30 countries and highlights from Cannes. Expect new German films, unknown Russian films, documentaries, independents, galas, concerts and film buffs in their thousands.

Music

As in Italy, opera is a major enthusiasm for all. Practically every town has its opera company. Top of the ops is the BAVARIAN STATE OPERA at MUNICH, followed closely by BERLIN, then COLOGNE and FRANKFURT (which is having to perform in a theatre with less-than-perfect acoustics, after the opera house burnt down last year).

♣ **B**RAVING BAYREUTH

"There's only one festival, but you have to like Wagner. It's impossible, it's uncomfortable – the seats are such that you might as well bring along your neurosurgeon. You can't get in – I think you need a mafia hit-man to pave the way. Tickets are handed down by families to their children but if you work 3 years in advance and really plot it well – like a company takeover – you might get a pair. The people are stuffy and awful and coltish but at least it is for absolute music lovers of a hateful individual who did, despite all of his vitriol, compose some of the most magnificent music ever created. You can go to Salzburg and see social-climbing German industrialists, you can go to Glyndebourne and see flashy British social climbers, but for pure absolute excellence in music you have to suffer at Bayreuth!" – **Thomas Hoving**. Did you get that? Don't doubt the gravity or prestige of this event – nor the hardness of those straight-backed wooden seats. **Lord Gowrie** bears up: *"The most exciting experiences I've had in opera have been at Bayreuth in Wagner's opera house, which he designed. If you like Wagner, it's the temple."* In Bayreuth's first year (1876), Mahler, Saint-Saëns, Liszt, Tchaikovsky and Grieg were among the audience. The festival, still run by the Wagner family, is from end-July to end-Aug. Get a prog by end-Oct and apply for tickets by mid-Nov, from Kartenbüro, Bayreuther Festspiele, Postfach 100262, D-8580 Bayreuth 2 ☎ (0921) 20221.

MUNICH OPERA FESTIVAL, Festspielkasse, Bayerische Staatsoper, Maximilianstrasse 11, D-8000 Munich 22 ☎ **(089) 221316**
Top-notch opera and classical music is produced at various venues most of the year. In July the pace steps up for the festival, a wide programme of opera at the Nationaltheater and Altes Residenztheater – plenty of Wagner, plus Strauss, Mozart, Verdi et al.

PHILHARMONIE, Natthaikirch Strasse 1, D-1000 Berlin 30 ☎ **(030) 254880**
Home of the Berlin Philharmonic, which has the 'best sound' (along with the Vienna Phil) for **Lord Donoughue**. *"One of the best modern halls. It must hold about 3,000, but the way it's constructed makes it very intimate"* – **Julian Lloyd Webber**.

TICKETS PLEASE ...

"What you need is not so much the best festival as somebody who can get you tickets. Who do we know who's actually been to Bayreuth? I don't go to any of these festivals very much because I'm too mean to bribe and too weak to barge" – **Frederic Raphael**. No means to take over a company? No clout with the hotel doorman? Try a specialist travel agency such as **Heritage Travellers**, 21 Dorset Square, London NW1 ☎ (01) 730 9841; **Serenissima/Heritage**, 41 E 42nd St, Suite 2312, New York, NY 10017 ☎ (212) 953 7720.

Buzz round Berlin...

... Listening to the **Berlin Symphony Orchestra**, Dornickerstrasse 39a, D-1000 Berlin 20, is the ultimate for **Stanley Marcus** ... In Sept catch the Berlin festival of music, drama and ballet, a good forum for new work. Tickets: **Kartenbüro der Berliner Festspiele**, Budapester Strasse 50, D-1000 Berlin 30 ☎ (030) 2548 9250 ... **Jazz buzz**: the best jazz fest in the land is held in Nov in Berlin.

WURZBURG MOZARTFEST, Haus zum Falken, D-7800 Würzburg ☎ (0931) 37336
For Mozartmaniacs, a festival of opera, recitals and concerts held at the end of June in the Residenz, a gorgeous Baroque palace, and its gardens.

Greece

ATHENS FESTIVAL, 1 Voukourestiou St, Athens TT 133 ☎ (01) 322311
An international festival of classical Greek and modern drama, opera, ballet and concerts. Spectacular setting at the foot of the Acropolis in the AD 161 amphitheatre, the Theatre of Herodus Atticus, beneath a floodlit Parthenon. Hard marble seats, heavy night air. Tickets: no booking? Be brazen and *bribe*.

Hong Kong

HONG KONG ACADEMY FOR PERFORMING ARTS, 1 Gloucester Rd, Wanchai ☎ 5-282 6622
Since opening, this high-tech arts centre and training school (built thanks to a HK$300

million donation from the Jockey Club) has transformed the cultural scene, providing the slickest forum in town for international touring companies in the fields of music, theatre, opera and ballet. The Academy holds an annual ball at the Regent with little ballerinas lining the stairs and a ballet performance after dinner. Very smart – anything they do is brilliantly arranged.

HONG KONG FILM FESTIVAL, Hong Kong Coliseum, Annex Bldg, Parking Deck Fl, KCR Kowloon Station, 8 Cheong Wan Rd, Kowloon ☎ 3-642217
A festival, held in March, that is eagerly awaited by the movie-starved (It's not unusual for Hong Kong to be missed off the circuit, even for major films). Very much a film-goer's festival, showing the latest and best films from Asia as well as international works. **Derek Malcolm** recommends.

India

FATEHPUR SIKRI
The City of Victory was constructed as "*a huge 16th-century fortress, built by the most wonderful – and probably*

the richest – *Mogul emperor that we've had. The whole court was inside this fortress, with workshops for calligraphers, painters, bookbinders ... People go to the Taj and miss this! You go to see the grand architecture*" – **Madhur Jaffrey**. No sooner had Emperor Jahangir finished his hilltop fortress than it was abandoned, for the water supply ran dry. It remains perfectly preserved and peaceful, save the swooping eagles, the preying self-styled guides ("*you pay me nothing*" – but you'd better spend an hour in his shop) and the pleading children ("*one pen, one pen*").

Ireland

GUINNESS JAZZ FESTIVAL. Tickets: Cork Opera House, Emmet Place, Cork ☎ (021) 270022
"*My favourite festival. The reason I like it so much is it's a charming town, one gets a chance to meet a great many colleagues, it's small and you can get around, the weather always seems to be marvellous in October, and the Guinness is splendid, absolutely incredible! There is no comparison between Irish and English Guinness*" – **George Melly**.

WEXFORD FESTIVAL OPERA, Theatre Royal, High St, Wexford ☎ (053) 22240
The Glyndebourne of Ireland. A 12-day festival in October of 3 rare operas sung by young unkowns who often turn into (less-young) stars. Staged in a tiny theatre. Smarties descend from all corners of Ireland for the final long weekend. Formal

CULTURE

❝ *Jaipur is my favourite city. The idea of a unified city designed by one man appeals to me. The most pure beautiful things are the private houses, called havelis, in Shekhawati in Jaipur state. The houses are marvellously painted and frescoed – spectacular* ❞

QUENTIN CREWE

dress but devil-may-care atmosphere. Also recitals, fringe events, bands playing in the street – and pubs stay open till 3am.

Italy

FLORENCE

ART AND MUSEUMS

🏛 **GALLERIA DEGLI UFFIZI, Loggiato degli Uffizi 6, 50122 ☎ (055) 218341**
The most important collection in the world of Florentine and Sienese art from 13th century to the Renaissance. The palazzo, designed by Vasari, is crammed with drawings and prints, paintings and sculpture, works by the greatest Italian artists – Fra Angelico, Lippi, Bellini, da Vinci, Giotto, Mantegna – and the celebrated Botticelli Room, where Venus rises from the waves. And don't miss the famous 3rd-century BC *Medici Venus*.

GALLERIA DI PALAZZO PITTI, piazza dei Pitti, 50125 ☎ (055) 213440
The Renaissance palace of the Medici family. The Royal Apartments and Silver Museum offer a superb display of fine and decorative arts – furniture, silver, gold, ivory, glassware and Italian paintings. A fabulous collection of Titians and Raphaels in the Palatine Gallery. The Modern Art Gallery represents mainly Tuscan artists. One of **Jeffrey Archer**'s favourite art galleries.

MUSEO DI STORIA DELLA SCIENZA, piazza dei Giudici 1, 50122 ☎ (055) 293494
An outstanding collection (formed by the Medicis) of historic scientific instruments, many of which were used by Galileo. *"It is one of the most important museums of its kind in the world. When I took the Prince of Wales there, he was thrilled. It's a heavenly place,*

a beautiful palazzo, and the view is wonderful" – **Marchesa Bona Frescobaldi.**

MUSIC

MAGGIO MUSICALE FIORENTINO, Teatro Comunale, corso Italia 16, 50100 ☎ (055) 277 9236
The May/June festival of Florentine music is: *"The first of the Italian music festivals, now in its 52nd year, and still the biggest. Its orchestra is often conducted by the leading masters; the operatic performances have a great deal of prestige"* – **Marchesa Bona Frescobaldi.**

MILAN

ART AND MUSEUMS

ACCADEMIA DELLE BELLE ARTI, via Brera 28, 20121 ☎ (02) 806969
An 18th-century mansion containing works by some of the most important Florentine, Lombardan and Venetian painters – Lotto, Mantegna, della Francesca, Veronese.

CASTELLO SFORZESCO, 20121 ☎ (02) 870926
Houses the Municipal Museum of Art, containing Michelangelo's last work, the unfinished Rondanini *Pietà*. Also works by Lippi, Mantegna, Bellini, Tintoretto and Tiepolo.

MUSIC

🏛 **LA SCALA, Teatro alla Scala, via Filodrammatici 2, 20121 ☎ (02) 887 9211**
The famous La Scala. A brilliant company where all the greats sing – Pavarotti, Domingo et al. Mostly Italian opera, produced by the likes of Franco Zeffirelli. The season runs from Dec to July, opening on a spectacularly high note on 7 Dec, the feast day for Sant' Ambrogio, patron saint of Milan. The greatest social gaffe

is to invite someone out on the 7th. *"When nearly all the other state-subsidized cultural institutions (there are 11) have opened their seasons, La Scala provides, right on time, the event. The evening comprises songs, entertainment and society – an event with real international appeal"* – **Marchesa Bona Frescobaldi**. A favourite of **Mariuccia Mandelli** and **Gianni Versace**. *"The most magic opera house, mainly because of the enthusiasm of the audience"* – **David Litchfield.**

ROME

ART AND MUSEUMS

MUSEO BORGHESE, via Pinciana ☎ (06) 858577
Set in the Villa Borghese, in the biggest park in Rome. Powerful sculptures by Bernini – *David, Apollo and Daphne, The Rape of Proserpine*, etc – and superb paintings.

MUSEO CAPITOLINO, piazza dei Campidoglio, 00186 ☎ (06) 678 2862
The first-ever public collection of art in Europe, displaying Greek and Roman sculptures and ancient paintings.

LA GALLERIA DORIA PAMPHILI, piazza del Collegio Romano 1 ☎ (06) 679 4365
The Palazzo Doria is still owned by the Doria family, who have *"the loveliest private collection in Italy that is open to the public"* – **Marchesa Bona Frescobaldi**. Caravaggio, Carracci and Velázquez are there.

🏛 **MUSEI VATICANI, Città del Vaticano ☎ (06) 698 3333**
A maze of diverse museums occupying part of the palaces built by the popes in the 13th century. Most celebrated for the unmissable, neck-breaking Sistine Chapel with the recently restored frescoes by Michelangelo on walls and ceiling. The next-best walls in

Rome are those that Raphael frescoed, in the apartments of Giulio II. And, according to **Jeffrey Archer**, the superb picture gallery contains *"the world's finest picture – the only one I would consider stealing – Bellini's Pietà."*

VENICE

ART AND MUSEUMS

While in the region of Venice, visit the **Palladian villas of Veneto**, following the course of the Brenta river; the frescoes by Giotto in the **Cappella degli Scrovegni at Padua**; and the **Museo del Castelvecchio**, at corso Cavour 2, Verona, which has been beautifully restored by architect Carlo Scarpa.

CA' D'ORO, Canareggio, 30100 ☎ (041) 523 8790
"The most beautiful Gothic

building in Venice, now a very handsome gallery" – **Victor Hazan**. Restored over 10 years back to its gilded glory. The Galleria Franchetti has a permanent collection of antique art and mounts ever-changing exhibitions.

CA' REZZONICO, campo San Barnaba ☎ (041) 522 4543 Grand house containing Baroque furniture and a collection of 18th-century Venetian art including Tiepolo, Canaletto and Guardi.

COLLEZIONE D'ARTE MODERNA PEGGY GUGGENHEIM, Dorsoduro 701 ☎ (041) 5206288 A breath of fresh air after the riches of old Venice: Peggy Guggenheim's house has been turned into a museum containing her collection of modern art – Cubism (Picasso et al), Expressionism (including Ernst), abstract art and, above all, Surrealism.

GALLERIA DELL' ACCADEMIA, Dorsoduro, Campo della Carità ☎ (041) 22247 The place for a complete picture of the very best of Venetian art. The masters are here en force: Bellini, Giorgione (including his famous *Tempest*), Titian (including his last work, *Pietà*), Veronese, Tintoretto and Tiepolo.

PALAZZO DUCALE, piazza San Marco ☎ (041) 520 3414 The spectacular Doge's Palace, former residence of the governors of the Republic of Venice, was decorated by the major painters of the Venetian School and remains intact. *"It is unique to have a palazzo untouched like this"* – **Marchesa Bona Frescobaldi**. From here the Bridge of Sighs connects with the prisons from which Casanova made his escape.

PALAZZO GRASSI, Campo San Samuele, San Marco, 30124 ☎ (041) 523 1680 An impressive 18th-century house on the Grand Canal, recently bought and renovated for $15 million by one of Italy's latterday grand patrons, Gianni Agnelli, under his Fiat corporation. Director of arts is Pontus Hulten, late of the Centre Pompidou in Paris. The palace satisfies the most modern gallery demands and stages a major, often unusual, pioneering show in summer plus a smaller winter exhibition at Carnival time.

VENICE BIENNALE, Ca' Giustinian, San Marco, 30124 ☎ (041) 520 0311 A large, fashionable exhibition of international art, held at the Giardini Pavilion in even years (June-Oct). A rich but often chaotic show. *"The most exciting event"* – **David Litchfield**. Now a contemporary music section, too.

CHURCHES

BASILICA DI TORCELLO A 9th- to 11th-century basilica containing mosaics that make it

---

🕵 **Buzzzzzzzzz** At the Accademia, Via Ricasoli 60, Florence, find the original **David by Michelangelo**, rather smaller but in far better condition than the copies that stand outside 🕵 . . . . . . press your nose up to the **Florence Baptistery Doors** by Pisano and Ghiberti for the full glory of these relief masterpieces 🕵 . . . . . . a rich source of **Caravaggio** is the Pinacoteca Ambrosiana, piazza Pio XI 2, Milan 🕵 . . . . . . at the Museo dell'Accademia, Dorsoduro 1050, Venice see **Spring by Botticelli** 🕵 . . . . . . in Milan, Chiesa delle Grazie for **The Last Supper by Leonardo** and Palazzo e Pinacoteca di Brera for **Mantegna**'s famously foreshortened **Dead Christ** 🕵 . . . . . . the Museo Egiziano (**Egyptian Museum**), via Accademia delle Scienze, Turin is second only to Cairo's 🕵 . . . . . . Go to the following churches in Rome for spectacular sculptures: San Pietro in Vincoli – **Moses by Michelangelo**; Santa Maria della Vittoria – **The Ecstasy of St Teresa by Bernini**; San Pietro, Vatican – **Michelangelo's Pietà** 🕵 . . . . . . See the famous **Piero della Francesca** frescoes at the church of San Francesco, Arezzo; at nearby Monterchi is his **Madonna del Parto**.

★ ★

CULTURE

"one of the most significant monuments of Italian Byzantine art. Torcello is a heavenly, heavenly island" – **Marchesa Bona Frescobaldi.**

SAN GIORGIO MAGGIORE, Isola di San Giorgio
Majestic 16th-century church with paintings by Tintoretto. *"A small jewel"* – **Marchesa Bona Frescobaldi.** You can trek up the bell tower for a cherub's eye view of the city.

FILM

VENICE INTERNATIONAL FILM FESTIVAL, Ca' Giustinian, San Marco, 30124 ☎ (041) 520 0311
One of the most important festivals in Europe, held in late Aug-Sept at the Lido. It's had a slightly rocky reception in the film biz of late, but for **Mariuccia Mandelli** and **Marchesa Bona Frescobaldi** it's still the best film fest. **David Litchfield** qualifies that: *"the best for style."* **Gianni Versace** says: *"I have been to this and Spoleto for years, but I am quite selective about what I attend."* Many international films are premièred here and vie for the Golden Lion.

MUSIC

LA CHIESA SANTA MARIA DELLA PIETA
Vivaldi's music can be heard once more in this church near the Conservatorio, where the master used to teach and hold concerts. Regular concerts of his and other Baroque music.

GRAN TEATRO LA FENICE, Campo San Fantin, 30124 ☎ (041) 521 0161; 521 0336
One of Italy's oldest, most famous and glitteringly gilty opera houses, now under the

new artistic director Gianni Tangucci. The season of opera, concerts, ballet and theatre starts with a mighty splash in Nov/Dec. *"I've played here and I thought it was just sensational. It's absolutely beautiful, gold and plush. In the old days, people drew up in their gondolas. Now they just walk, but it's really pretty and romantic"* – **Jane Asher.**

REST OF ITALY

FESTIVALS

FESTIVAL DEI DUE MONDI, via del Duomo 7, Spoleto ☎ (0743) 28120; tickets also from via Margutta 17, 00187 Rome ☎ (06) 361 4041
Founded by composer Gian Carlo Menotti, this is the best music, drama and ballet festival in Italy (late June-July). It has spawned 2 Spoleto bambini, in South Carolina (see America) and Melbourne (see Australia). Opera, concerts, ballet (Baryshnikov has been) and other arts events. *"One of the best festivals; it has a very good*

atmosphere" – **Julian Lloyd Webber.** *"One of the most important events in the Italian social/cultural calendar"* for **Gianni Versace**; the best festival for theatre say **Mariuccia Mandelli, Marchesa Bona Frescobaldi** and **Giorgio Armani.** The Spoleto set eat variations on a truffle at Il Tartufo.

FESTIVAL PUCCINIANO, Torre del Lago Puccini, 55049 Viareggio ☎ (0584) 343322
A festival of Puccini operas, concerts and choral works, held in July-Aug in Tuscany. Prestigious and pretty, it draws Puccini lovers around the globe to the open-air theatre on Lake Massacciuccoli.

MUSICA NEL CHIOSTRO, Santa Croce, Batignano, Tuscany
Held in late July-early Aug, this enchanting festival run by Adam Pollock is, for **Joanna Lumley**, *"the best opera festival, held in a semi-ruined convent".*

ROSSINI OPERA FESTIVAL, via Rossini 37, 61100 Pesaro ☎ (0721) 30161
A brilliant little opera festival in celebration of Rossini, held

Buzzzzzzzzz When hiking up and down the country don't miss the **Palazzo Abbatellis**, Palermo, Sicily, a 15th-century palace restored by Carlo Scarpa; it houses the National Gallery of Sicily ...... the 13th-century **Basilica of St Francis**, Assisi, with the famous Giotto frescoes and those by Simone Martini, Cimabue's *Crucifixion* and beautiful cloisters ...... the **Museo di Capodimonte**, Naples, for its picture gallery, royal apartments and, of course, porcelain ...... **Pinacoteca Nazionale**, Bologna, for the Bolognese school of the 14th century, Renaissance and Baroque periods.

★ ★ ★ ★ ★ ★ ★ ★ ★ ★ ★ ★ ★ ★ ★ ★ ★ ★

> 66 *In Italy everyone is so enthusiastic about opera. It's like the Welsh and choral singing. Window cleaners think they are opera singers in Italy ...* 99

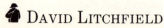

DAVID LITCHFIELD

in his birthplace. A favourite of **Giorgio Armani** and **Marchesa Bona Frescobaldi**: *"Renowned for its interpretations of the rarer works by this master of Pesaro and for the inventiveness and high calibre of its productions."* Operas by Rossini are staged during 3 weeks in Aug-Sept.

SIENESE MUSICAL WEEK, c/o Accademia Musicale Chigiana, via di Città 89, 50300 Siena ☎ (0577) 46152
A season of prestigious recitals and concerts is put on by the Accademia, *"an institution founded over half a century ago by a forward-thinking aristocrat. The Week [in Aug] is the high point of the season"* – **Marchesa Bona Frescobaldi.**

STRESA MUSICAL WEEKS, Settimane Musicale, Palazzo dei Congressi, via R Bonghi 4, 28049 Stresa ☎ (0323) 31095
Gorgeous setting in the Lakes region for this 4-week festival (Aug-Sept) of classical music by international artists and young winners of prestigious music

competitions. Some concerts take place in a beautiful Baroque palace on Isola Bella, the largest island on Lake Maggiore. Stay in company with many of the performers at **Hotel des Iles Borromées,** Lungolago Umberto I, 67 ☎ (0323) 30431.

FILM

TAORMINA ARTE, Palazzo Firenze, 98039 Taormina, Sicily ☎ (0942) 2142
A small July festival of films, music and plays in *"one of the best venues in the world. Films are screened in the open air in a huge Greek amphitheatre. It's wonderful"* – **Derek Malcolm.**

MUSIC

Opera is as much a part of Italy as spaghetti, and is devoured every bit as enthusiastically by the natives, who chatter excitedly throughout performances, telling each other the plot, and shine torches at their copy of the

score. A swarm of Italian luminaries chase the grand openings of the season up the coast . . . the spectacular Teatro di San Carlo in Naples, the Teatro Comunale of Florence . . . the crescendo culminating at La Scala, Milan. For opera and most festivals, foreigners can reserve tickets from their local Italian State Tourism office.

ARENA DI VERONA, ENTE Arena, Piazza Bra 28, 37121 Verona ☎ (045) 590109. **Tickets: Arcovolo 6 dell' Arena ☎ (045) 596517**
Romeo and Juliet's cobbledy medieval city plays host to an ultra-fashionable festival season (July-Aug) of opera and ballet in the ancient 1st-century arena with its superb acoustics. An experience: lavish productions, virtuoso performances (Placido Domingo and Maria Callas made their débuts here), passionate listeners and a glittering spectacle, lit not only by stars but by candles held by each member of the 25,000-strong audience. *"Fabulous"* – **Andrew Lloyd Webber.**

TEATRO REGIO DI PARMA, via Garibaldi, 43100 Parma ☎ (0521) 7951
A season of opera and concerts. A festival of Verdi operas is planned for July/Aug 1989 (Verdi was born in Roncole di Busseto, a village near Parma).

PALIOMANIA

The Palio must be the shortest and most dramatic horse race in the world. Lasting just over 3 minutes, it's a frenzied dash around Il Campo in which horses and riders may come crashing down. But what is less obvious to the lay spectator are the behind-scenes dramas. *"There are 17 contrade [districts] in Siena – rival mutual benevolent societies – into which the members are literally baptized. The boys grow up together. The most extreme thing they do at the time of the Palio is engage in internecine warfare with the other contrade, but not in the same way as the IRA would – they just hit one another a bit rather than blow one another to smithereens. There are two Palios a year, in July and August. 10 horses race (if you had 17, they'd all be dead) – the 7 that didn't race in the previous Palio and 3 chosen by lot. It's impossible to believe the agonies and miseries the supporters of the various contrade go through in the days preceding the event. It's as if they're in a state of religious ecstacy. When they lose, it's terrible. It is an amazing sight for tourists because it isn't put on for them. Unless you have enormous graft, it's very difficult to get a seat as a tourist. If you can't, it's standing room only, which means hours without the possibility of a pee. I had an appalling hot seat in the sun which cost L 100,000. Seats in the shade are L 150,000, and well worth the difference"* – **Eric Newby.**

Japan

KYOTO

The old capital (from 794 to 1868 – before that it was nearby Nara, well worth a day tour) is a beautiful city of temples, shrines and gardens. Historic sights not to be missed are: the IMPERIAL PALACE and the gardens of KATSURA IMPERIAL VILLA (for both you need royal permission – check with the tourist office); and the double-moated NIJO

CULTURE

CASTLE, ex-des res of the Tokugawa Shoguns. The wooden corridor is famous for its Nightingale Floor that twitters and squeaks when you tread on it (to warn of intruders). The time to hit Kyoto is for the cherry blossom, at its zenith for about 2 weeks in early-mid April, or in autumn.

TEMPLES AND GARDENS

ENRYAKU-JI TEMPLE, Mount Hiei

An ancient center of Buddhism, a haunting group of temples on this sacred mountain outside Kyoto. The eerie sound of a distant gong can be heard before you see any buildings. Here, the Inextinguishable Dharma Light has been

glowing away for the past 1,200 years. A far better place to feel spiritual than the crowded, noisy temples and shrines in the city centre. Go by local bus to Shimeidake from Kyoto station.

HEIAN SHRINE

Renowned for its gardens of cherry blossoms (confetti of the palest pink and white), irises and ponds.

KINKAKUJI TEMPLE

The Golden Pavilion is a replica of the *c.* 1400 original (in fact, nearly all Kyoto's landmark buildings are modern reconstructions as the originals were destroyed by fire). Set in lovely water gardens. The nearby Ryoanji Temple garden displays the ultimate in precision raking: the tiny pebbles are coiffed daily into perfect shape.

KIYOMIZU TEMPLE

Perhaps the most beautiful temple, in the most serene and panoramic setting in the hills overlooking Kyoto. The trees turn myriad different shades, softened by a bluey-violet haze.

TOKYO

ART AND MUSEUMS

GALLERY WHITE ART, Taihokosan Bldg 3F, 2-5-4 Ginza, Chuo-ku ☎ (03) 567 0089
One of the best contemporary Japanese art collections.

Hakone Open Air Museum

Kanagawa-ken
☎ (0460) 21161. A great collection of Japanese and Western sculpture set in gardens and galleries. On a day-trip from Tokyo you can feel both virtuous *and* indulgent: take the special open-top train, the Romance Car, from Shinjuku through spectacular scenery (fab Fuji views) to the museum, then steam all intellectual thoughts away at the nearby hot springs.

HARA MUSEUM, 4-7-25 Kitashinagawa, Shinagawa-ku ☎ (03) 445 0651
Toshio Hara is *the* authority on Japanese contemporary art. His inspiration for setting up this museum came from Europe and New York since there was no precedent in Japan. In turn, visiting experts from MOMA and the Centre Pompidou make this their first port of call.

IDEMITSU MUSEUM OF THE ARTS, International Bldg 9F, 3-1-1 Marunouchi, Chiyoda-ku ☎ (03) 213 3111
Next door to the Imperial Theatre. A great private

🕵 **Buzzzzzzzzz** The essence of Japanese culture and spirituality is embodied in the **tea ceremony** and **ikebana** (flower arranging): watch the meaningful brew-up, sippa cuppa (green) tea, and glean hints on where to place your twigs and cherry blossom at **Sakura-kai**, 3-2-25 Shimo Ochiai, Shinjuku-ku ☎ (03) 951 9043. No dainty finishing school pastime this, it is something *every* Japanese does – even the most vile and viscious Darth Vader-like riot police are obliged to do an hour of ikebana a day 🕵 . . . . . . **Sumo** dates back to the 8th century. Catch wrestlers (weighing up to 500 lbs) mid-grip at their 6.30am practices at **Takasago-beya**, 1-22-5 Yanagibashi, Taito-ku ☎ (03) 861 4600 (ask your concierge to check they'll be grappling that day) 🕵 . . . . . . The onset of the **sakura** (cherry blossom) is a time for celebration. The country comes alive with **ohana-mi** – cherry-blossom-viewing picnics – which may take place anywhere from a graveyard to a grass verge, so long as it's under a cherry tree 🕵 . . . . . . In this the **Land of the Camera**, don't miss the astonishing photography exhibitions mounted by top camera companies. The best are at **Nikon Salon, Pentax Forum** and **Zeit Photo**. PS Japanese photography mags make the cheapest **coffee-table books** in town.

★ ★ ★ ★ ★ ★ ★ ★ ★ ★ ★ ★ ★ ★ ★ ★ ★ ★ ★ ★

CULTURE

collection of traditional art, including ukiyoe, the famous Japanese prints. Industrialist Sazo Idemitsu has also amassed thousands of objects, including some of the finest Japanese and Chinese porcelain in the world.

MAGAZINE HOUSE, 3-13-10 Ginza, Chuo-ku
☎ **(03) 545 7227**
Not quite haute culture, but over 1,000 current magazines from all over the world. With all those mags *and* a coffee shop, you could be there some time.

SETAGAYA ART MUSEUM, Kinuta Koen, Setagaya-ku
A brilliant new cultural activities centre with the motto, 'Art and nature together guide man towards wholesomeness'. Architect Shozo Uchii's 3-level building is spread low across the ground to blend in with the surroundings of the Kinuta Park in Yoga. Fine contemporary exhibitions.

SUNTORY MUSEUM OF ART, Suntory Bldg 11F, 1-2-3 Moto-Akasaka, Minato-ku
☎ **(03) 470 1073**
Impressive collection of textiles, kimonos, lacquer objects, porcelain and painting. Regular changing exhibitions.

Commercial Gallery

TOLMAN COLLECTION, 2-2-18 Shiba-Daimon, Minato-ku ☎ **(03) 434 1300**
Based in a gorgeous house, this is one of the best places to buy contemporary Japanese prints. Since it's run by the American Tolman family, it means straightforward Western-style dealing. George Bush is among the many Americans who buy prints here.

Music

SUNTORY MUSIC HALL, 1-13-1 Akasaka, Minato-ku
☎ **(03) 505 1001**
More culture c/o the Japanese beerage. They have sunk a fortune into making this the

---

Fertility rites

Modesty does not prevail at Japan's top 3 fertility festivals, one held every lunar new year's day in the farming town of Yokoto in Akita prefecture, one on 15th March at the Tagata Shrine, Aichi prefecture, and one 8th April at Kawasaki's Wakamiya Hachiman Shrine. At the Tagata festival, an outsize collection of erotic talismen is carted through town, some of them straddled by kimono'd girls (a photogenic event, this). Homage is paid to the gods of the phallus in order to return a fertile harvest. It is believed that if intercourse takes place under a tree in the garden of the Tagata Shrine, the parents will have a healthy, gifted child. At Kawasaki, the Kanamara Matsuri (Festival of the Steel Phallus) is held.

---

most advanced concert hall in the world, the apotheosis of Japanese technology. Bernstein has conducted here; most leading conductors are itching to wave their batons in this hall.

Theatre

KABUKI
A theatrical art form dating back to the 17th century. Kabuki was originally developed by a woman, Okuni, but the government banned actresses from appearing publicly in 1629. The subsequent male-only tradition still holds today. The best way to find out about performances of kabuki, as well as No and bunraku, is via the weekly *Tour Companion*. The best kabuki is at **Kabuki-za Theatre**, 4-12-5 Ginza, Chuo-ku

---

☎ (03) 541 3131 (in front of Higashi Ginza station); English-language headphones and programmes.

TAKARAZUKA, Takarazuka Theatre, 1-1-3 Yuracho, Chiyoda-ku ☎ **(03) 580 1251**
A 500-strong all-girl revue, similar to the Ziegfeld Follies. Here, women play all the male roles. Outside the theatre clamour all the young 'wanabees', waiting to glimpse their heroines.

Netherlands

AMSTERDAM

The whole city of Amsterdam throbs with contemporary culture. It's part of its charm. Here, the arts are alive and kicking, accessible on all levels, never élitist. It's like one big fringe festval in summer. Street theater, experimental dance, jazz musicians and rock bands clog the streets, set up on corners, spill out of bars and give impromptu performances in the Vondelpark. Even the main concert hall, the Concertgebouw, offers regular free lunchtime concerts.

Art and Museums

REMBRANDTHUIS, Jodenbreestraat 6, 1011 NK
☎ **(020) 249486**
Former home of the man himself. Virtually all his etchings and sketches remain in tribute.

RIJKSMUSEUM VINCENT VAN GOGH, Paulus Potterstraat 7, 1071 CX
☎ **(020) 764881**
About 200 paintings and 500 drawings by Van Gogh and co (*The Sower, Vincent's Bedroom, The Potato Eaters*, a version of *Sunflowers*). Also vg VG memorabilia.

CULTURE

CULTURE

🏛 **RIJKSMUSEUM,**
Stadhouderskade 42, 1071 ZD
☎ **(020) 732121**
Not only the unsurpassed
collection of 17th-century
Dutch paintings (not to mention
16th, 18th and 19th) but also
sculpture, antique furniture,
Delft pottery, ceramics, silver,
lace, glassware, and more.
Rembrandt's *Night Watch* is
the *Mona Lisa* of the
Rijksmuseum.

🏛 **STEDELIJK MUSEUM,**
Paulus Potterstraat 13, 1071
CX ☎ **(020) 573 2911**
The national collection of
modern art from 1850,
including some fine examples of
Matisse and Picasso. Strong on
artistic developments since
1950. Changing exhibitions.

Russia

ART

🏛 **THE HERMITAGE, Palace**
Square, Leningrad
The largest art gallery in the
world, containing a rich
collection of international
artworks, jewels and objects.
The building itself is the

equally opulent Winter Palace
of the Tsars, a symphony of
gilt, marble and crystal. It has
recently set out on a £100
million programme of much-
needed expansion and
modernization. *"For me this
has the most wonderful
collection of art treasures in
the world"* – **Helen Gurley
Brown.**

Ballet and Opera

🏛 **BOLSHOI BALLET AND**
OPERA, Bolshoi Theatre, 2
Ploshchad Sverdlova, Moscow
Renowned as one of the great
classical ballet companies,
where the great Grigorovich is
artistic director. Choreography
and technique rather than
theatrical pzazz are all-
important, though their neo-
classical home is glamorous
enough with its 5-tier red and
gold auditorium (currently
being restored; performances
meanwhile at the Kremlin
Palace of Congresses).
Frequent tours beyond the
Iron Curtain. Their ballet
school provides a massive pool
of muscular dancers to draw
on. The Bolshoi has one of the
world's largest resident
orchestras and a fine opera
company.

🏛 **KIROV THEATRE OF**
OPERA AND BALLET,
Leningrad Academic Theatre,
Leningrad
Some of the most splendid
productions of classical ballet in
the world, performed under the
directionz of Vinogradov.
Choreography tends to be less
adventurous than the Bolshoi,
but the athletic dancing is
astonishing. Like the Bolshoi,
they have an important ballet
school. Baryshnikov, Nureyev
and Makarova trouped over on
the Kirov's first tours in the
1960s and never went back: 3
stars gone West. Nevertheless,
the ballet still makes frequent
tours. Opera company, too.

Spain

ART AND MUSEUMS

MUSEO DEL GRECO, El
Paseo del Transito, Toledo
☎ **(025) 224046**
*"I particularly like – in the
sense of crave – 2 houses in the
world. El Greco's and
Hemingway's (see America).
This is a town house with lots
of little interior courtyards,
and balconies on the first floor.
It has a beautiful scale and
proportions – very un-Greco-
ish, not elongated at all!"* –
Frederic Raphael.

🏛 **MUSEO DEL PRADO, Paseo**
del Prado, Madrid
☎ **(01) 468 0950**
*"Probably the greatest single
museum in the world. It has
such great works of art. I don't
think they display them
fantastically well but then I
rather like scruffy display and
the feeling of having discovered
something"* – **Lord Gowrie.**
The Prado houses the national
collection of 12th- to 19th-
century Italian art, 15th- to
18th-century Dutch, French,
English and German art, plus,
of course, the Spaniards –
Velázquez and his amigos. A
favourite of **Jeffrey Archer,
Thomas Hoving** and **Lord
Gowrie.**

HOLY WEEK IN SEVILLE
BY ERIC NEWBY

*"Holy Week, the Semana Santa, is unforgettable whatever
your religious persuasion, or lack of it. There is the constant
weird beat of the matching music-bugles, trumpets and drums
of the various cofradieras (brotherhoods] which, hooded and
accompanied by barefoot penitentes, bent double under the
weight of heavy crosses, escort the great effigies of Christ and
the Virgin through the streets. A single effigy of the Virgin
may be decked in 100,000 worth of jewels and clothing. It takes
more than 40 men to carry some of these vast floats, and the
largest procession, that of La Macarena, lasts over 12 hours.
When trhe costaleros, the men who carry these floats on their
shoulders, have finished the course, some of them have great
open wounds in their shoulders with blood pouring from
them. The whole thing is an astonishing spectacle. Watch
your belongings in Seville, a very dangerous city. Never
carry a handbag."*

Sweden

THE LITTLE ROYAL THEATRE, Drottningholm Theatre Museum, Box 27050, S-10251 Stockholm ☎ (08) 608225
"The most beautiful theatre in the world. It is a perfect 18th-century theatre with 18th-century technology. All the sets can be changed by turning cranks under the stage. It's incredibly beautiful, in Swedish taste – austere, restrained neo-classicism, which I love – rather than the very nouveau riche styles you got in England at the height of wealth and power. I would give that the prize for the place to see an opera" – **Lord Gowrie.**

Switzerland

MUSIC

FESTIVAL DE MUSIQUE MONTREUX-VEVEY, ave des Alpes 14, CH-1820 Montreux ☎ (021) 635450
A calm, glimmering lakeside setting for the classical music festival that runs from end-Aug to end-Sept, filling concert halls, châteaux and churches with its vibes.

MONTREUX JAZZ FESTIVAL, Service de Location, Case 97, CH-1820 Montreux. Tickets c/o Tourist Office ☎ (021) 631212
More famous and far more rowdy than its classical counterpart, it's a mix of jazz and rock with names like Terence Trent D'Arby and the

A FEW OF MY FAVORITA THINGS

COLLEZIONE THYSSEN, VILLA FAVORITA, 6976 Castagnola ☎ (091) 521741. Baron Heini Thyssen's art collection is the greatest private collection in the world after the Queen of England's. Here, near Lugano, you only see about a quarter of the full whack of some 550 Old Masters (Titian, Holbein, Rembrandt, Rubens, Goya, Van Eyck, Canaletto) and 800 modern works (Picasso, Gauguin, Cézanne, Renoir, Van Gogh, Degas). World powers are falling over themselves in their offers to house the full collection. The Getty wanted to build a £244 million museum; the Swiss considered building a new wing on the Villa. Then Thyssen told the Russians he'd give them his priceless collection if they knocked down the Berlin Wall. The latest is that Spain will show some 600 of his paintings (on loan for 10 years) at the Villahermosa Palace opposite the Prado, as from 1989/90. But Thyssen still hopes to find a permanent showcase in Europe. Catch the collection quick before it *evaporates*.

Beastie Boys breaking up the harmony set by Wynton Marsalis, Herbie Hancock and co. Musicians mosey in from as far as Brazil, New Orleans and Jamaica.

Thailand

BANGKOK

THE ARTIST'S GALLERY, 60 Pan Rd, Silom ☎ (2) 236 4830
In the basement below the café-restaurant Savoury is perhaps the best commercial contemporary gallery for Thai paintings and sculpture. Owner Sook Lek is an artist himself. Many of the artists exhibited are recognized internationally – Jirapat Pitpreecha, Itthi

Khongkhakul, Damrong Wong-Uparaj – yet, since few Thais are switched on to contemporary art, they sell at a snip.

GRAND PALACE
Home of the royal family. The palace and surrounding wats (temples) form a glittering, gaudy, golden and mosaic'd wonderland. The palace itself, designed by an Italian, is a perfect blend of Thai and colonial/Mediterranean styles. *"Beautiful, exquisite, very majestic. A tremendous amount of workmanship – broken teacups arranged in various floral patterns and soft pastels totally cover the building. It is gorgeous. The tile work and the Buddhas are breathtaking"* – **Diane Freis.**

JIM THOMPSON'S HOUSE, 6 Soi Kasemsan 2, Rama 1 Rd
A delightful taste of old Thailand. Silk king Jim Thompson (see Fashion) transported 6 trad Thai houses from the ancient capital, Ayutthaya, and reconstructed them to form one rambling canal-side house. The beautiful polished teak structures on stilts contain his impressive collection of fine art, porcelain and furniture.

DESERT ISLAND SURVIVAL KIT:

DUDLEY MOORE

"I would like a piano and Bach's 48 preludes and fugues – both books! That would keep me content till the end of my days."

CULTURE

Ken Hom on
FOOD AND DRINK

World's Best Restaurants

1
JAMIN (ROBUCHON),
Paris

2
GIRARDET,
Crissier, Switzerland

3
LE BERNARDIN,
New York

4
MICHEL GUERARD,
Eugénie-les-Bains, France

5
FOOK LAM MOON,
Hong Kong

6
**LE MANOIR AUX QUAT'
SAISONS,**
Great Milton, England

7
LE CIRQUE,
New York

8
LUCAS CARTON,
Paris

9
STEPHANIE'S,
Melbourne

10
KICCHO,
Osaka, Japan

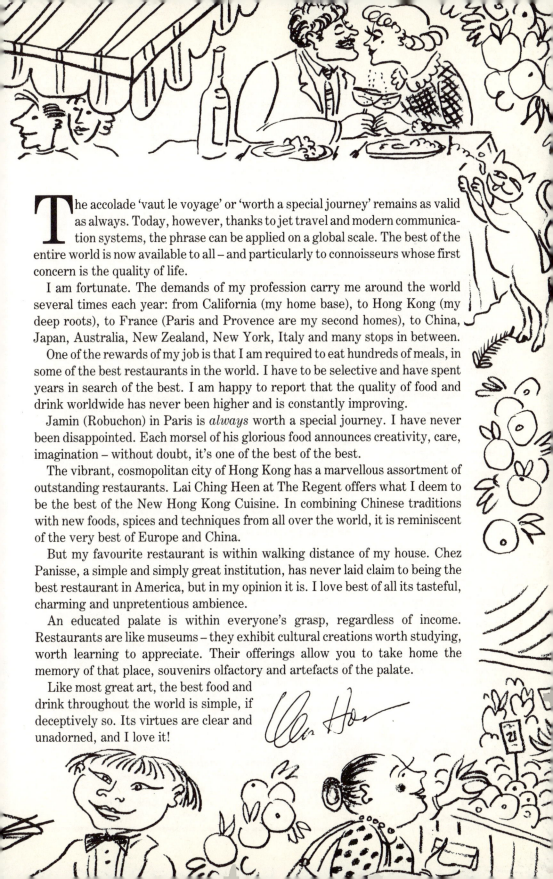

The accolade 'vaut le voyage' or 'worth a special journey' remains as valid as always. Today, however, thanks to jet travel and modern communication systems, the phrase can be applied on a global scale. The best of the entire world is now available to all – and particularly to connoisseurs whose first concern is the quality of life.

I am fortunate. The demands of my profession carry me around the world several times each year: from California (my home base), to Hong Kong (my deep roots), to France (Paris and Provence are my second homes), to China, Japan, Australia, New Zealand, New York, Italy and many stops in between.

One of the rewards of my job is that I am required to eat hundreds of meals, in some of the best restaurants in the world. I have to be selective and have spent years in search of the best. I am happy to report that the quality of food and drink worldwide has never been higher and is constantly improving.

Jamin (Robuchon) in Paris is *always* worth a special journey. I have never been disappointed. Each morsel of his glorious food announces creativity, care, imagination – without doubt, it's one of the best of the best.

The vibrant, cosmopolitan city of Hong Kong has a marvellous assortment of outstanding restaurants. Lai Ching Heen at The Regent offers what I deem to be the best of the New Hong Kong Cuisine. In combining Chinese traditions with new foods, spices and techniques from all over the world, it is reminiscent of the very best of Europe and China.

But my favourite restaurant is within walking distance of my house. Chez Panisse, a simple and simply great institution, has never laid claim to being the best restaurant in America, but in my opinion it is. I love best of all its tasteful, charming and unpretentious ambience.

An educated palate is within everyone's grasp, regardless of income. Restaurants are like museums – they exhibit cultural creations worth studying, worth learning to appreciate. Their offerings allow you to take home the memory of that place, souvenirs olfactory and artefacts of the palate.

Like most great art, the best food and drink throughout the world is simple, if deceptively so. Its virtues are clear and unadorned, and I love it!

America

BERKELEY

CHEZ PANISSE, 1517 Shattuck Ave, CA 94709 ☎ (415) 548 5525
The pioneering Alice Waters's famous Californian restaurant. Downstairs, there is a different one-off 5-course fixed-price menu *every* night. *"Truly one of the best restaurants in America. You eat whatever's on the menu of the day – it's always different, always a surprise and always extremely good"* – **Ken Hom**. *"A remarkable combination of relaxation and good food"* – **Seymour Britchky**. Upstairs is her trattoria-cum-bistro, **CAFE CHEZ PANISSE**: *"I thought it was wonderful. No bookings, excellent pasta, beautiful pizzas, wonderful Californian salads. It's not Californian cooking, it's just sensible cooking – she's a fanatic for fresh vegetables"* – **Alastair Little**. *"The best calzone [folded pizza] I have ever eaten – filled with Sonoma goat's cheese, shallots and other wondrous things – melt in the mouth!"* – **Elise Pascoe**.

BOSTON

MARKET

QUINCY MARKET, Faneuil Hall Marketplace
"Food markets don't really exist in the USA. The equivalent is the food hall or court, where there are perhaps 500 different fast food outlets peddling enchiladas and caviare and all that. The best is probably Quincy Market. You can buy half a dozen oysters or a bagel and smoked salmon or an enchilada or ice cream" – **Loyd Grossman**.

RESTAURANTS

AUJOURD'HUI, Four Seasons Hotel, 200 Boylston St, MA 02116 ☎ (617) 338 4400
Under chef Mark Baker, this deluxe dining room is wowing Bostonians. French-rooted cuisine using local produce and Oriental spices.

FANEUIL HALL MARKETPLACE
Home to all sorts of foodie delights. Not only the copper-domed Quincy Market, but some excellent restaurants such as **SEASONS**, Bostonian Hotel ☎ (617) 523 4119, an excellent American rooftop restaurant; **CRICKETS** ☎ (617) 227 3434, for fresh fish and regional foods; **SEASIDE RESTAURANT & BAR** ☎ (617) 742 8728, for surf-fresh seafood, salads etc.

LE MARQUIS DE LAFAYETTE, 1 Ave de Lafayette, MA 02150 ☎ (617) 451 2600
The elegantly chandeliered American outpost of French chef Louis Outhier, who acts as consultant. Probably the best French restaurant in Boston.

PANACHE, 798 Main St, Cambridge, MA 02139 ☎ (617) 492 9500
Zippy bistro with a creative menu. Chef-owner Bruce Frankel cooks up a mean mako shark with coriander. Fine wine list, including a round-up of the best local wines.

RARITIES, The Charles Hotel, 1 Bennett St, Cambridge, MA 02138 ☎ (617) 864 1200
First-class restaurant where many Harvard dignitaries dine. *"The most exciting food I've eaten for years. It proves you can be modern and creative, but still be generous and have fun"* – **Glynn Christian**.

RESTAURANT JASPER, 240 Commercial St, MA 02109 ☎ (617) 523 1126
"Considered the best restaurant in Boston. He has made New England food exciting, and if you think that is easy, you should have grown up there – then you would know this man is brilliant!" – **Paula Wolfert**.

RITZ-CARLTON DINING ROOM, 15 Arlington St, MA 02117 ☎ (617) 536 5700
An institution in Boston, known as the place which would not let Joseph Kennedy set foot in it. The clientele is discreet, elegant, old-style – no glitzy rock-star stuff. It's the sort of place you come to celebrate your wedding anniversary. Silver cutlery.

TURNER FISHERIES BAR & RESTAURANT, Westin Hotel, 10 Huntington Ave, MA 02116 ☎ (617) 424 7425
For fish and seafood, this is

SKINNY TIPS

"This idea that to be thin is to be beautiful is built entirely on fashion. Women get their ideas of what women should be like from glossy magazines. Fashion designers want their clothes to be shown diagrammatically – they want the seams to be straight and all the buttons to be facing you, so they put the clothes on girls of 15 and 16, and all the women think that this is the way to be. I have never heard a man praise a woman because she is skinny. Women are people and are loved by the pound!" – **Quentin Crisp**. *"Don't eat!"* – **Shakira Caine**. *"I went on a carbohydrate diet with my Dad which was absolutely marvellous. We got to eat all the pasta we wanted! The key is to exercise – really go for it. That's the key to health anyway"* – **Margaux Hemingway**. *"Eat little meals every time you feel the slightest bit hungry – that is probably every couple of hours. That way you get to the good stuff before the bad stuff can get a stranglehold"* – **Dudley Moore**. *"Do this exercise: push away your plate"* – **Joan Collins**.

"*the only place*", according to **Glynn Christian**, who finds that at other restaurants you can't book and everything is cooked in batter. They also have live jazz nightly.

CHICAGO

RESTAURANTS

AVANZARE, 161 E Huron St, IL 60611 ☎ (312) 337 8056
Eclectic, progressive Italian cooking, as its name suggests . . . raw tuna and grilled rolled aubergine, pan-fried baby artichokes with mustard sauce, baked polenta with goat's cheese. *"Great Italian food"* – **Bob Payton.**

CHARLIE TROTTER'S, 816 W Armitage St, IL 60614 ☎ (312) 248 6228
Newish restaurant in Viennese style, with a wine rack extending to the ceiling and a granite bar. Eclectic menu – American-inspired French with hints of Asia. Chic clientele.

THE EVEREST ROOM, 440 S La Salle, 40th Fl, IL 60605 ☎ (312) 663 8920
Outstanding French restaurant with great views over West Chicago. Fresh, light cuisine from the Alsace region.

LE FRANCAIS, 269 S Milwaukee Ave, Wheeling, IL 60606 ☎ (312) 541 7470
A neo-country inn where seasonal foodie masterpieces are prepared by owner-chef Jean Banchet. One of **Craig Claiborne**'s top restaurants.

MORTONS, 1050 N State St, IL 60610 ☎ (312) 266 4820
The best-quality meat in Chicago, vast red slabs of prime beef, chomped in company with the prime cut of the eating population. "The *place for really good steaks*" – **Bob Payton.**

LES NOMADES, 222 E Ontario St, IL 60611 ☎ (312) 649 9010
A private dining club, but you can get in if you know a

♣ –America's Best– ♣

RESTAURANTS

1 **LE BERNARDIN,** New York

2 **LE CIRQUE,** New York

3 **COYOTE CAFE,** Santa Fe

4 **CHANTERELLE,** New York

5 **CHINA MOON CAFE,** San Francisco

6 **JEAN-LOUIS AT WATERGATE,** Washington, DC

7 **CHEZ PANISSE,** Berkeley

8 **ARIZONA 206,** New York

9 **SPAGO,** Los Angeles

10 **STARS,** San Francisco

♣   ♣

member. All the top brass in Chicago belong. *"I consider it the best bistro in America. Wonderful, wonderful French bourgeois country food"* – **Paula Wolfert.**

RITZ-CARLTON DINING ROOM, 160 E Pearson St, IL 60611 ☎ (312) 266 1000
As sumptuous and impressive as its Boston sister. Impeccable French cuisine.

SHAW'S CRAB HOUSE, 21 E Hubbard St, IL 60611 ☎ (312) 527 2722
Fresh fish and seafood restaurant with occasional jazz trios playing.

DALLAS

RESTAURANTS

ACTUELLE, 2800 Routh St, TX 75201 ☎ (214) 855 0440
Top-quality restaurant with a glass atrium and muted colour scheme. New American cuisine with ethnic influences.

BEAU NASH, Hotel Crescent Court, 400 Crescent Ct, TX 75201 ☎ (214) 871 3240
"The American chef serves

Italian/fresh American food. It's very successful and more informal than many of the other Dallas restaurants" – **Caroline Hunt.** Expect romantic glorified pizzaland à la Wolfgang Puck (who is a consultant), but don't think 'informal', Dallas-style, precludes a dress code.

THE HARD ROCK CAFE, 2601 McKinney Ave, TX 75204 ☎ (214) 827 8282
Stood in one Hard Rock queue, stood in 'em all? No way. This is *"the greatest, the supreme court of rock 'n' roll. It's a real trip"* – **Harvey Goldsmith.**

MANSION ON TURTLE CREEK, 2821 Turtle Creek Blvd, TX 75219 ☎ (214) 559 2100
Superb food – American regional specialities – in the most elegant setting in town (see also Travel). Ritzy soap opera clientele. Owner **Caroline Hunt** says: *"The chef here, Dean Fearing, is one of the outstanding chefs in the US, a pioneer of Dallas cuisine. His speciality is tortilla soup – a meal in itself."*

♣ ROUTH STREET CAFE, 3005 Routh St, TX 75201 ☎ (214) 871 7161
Fine American southwestern food under French wraps; real foodie stuff. The prix-fixé menu changes daily. *"One of the best"* – **Caroline Hunt**. *"It continues to earn its reputation as one of the great restaurants of America. It's getting better and better"* – **Stanley Marcus**. It has given birth to the buzzy **BABY ROUTH, 2708 Routh St, TX 75201 ☎ (214) 871 2345**. *"The type of cuisine established by its parent is maintained, but it's cheaper, younger and noisier than the more luxe original"* – **SM**. Grilled prawns and apple-smoked bacon club sandwiches, pumpkin-ginger crème brûlée with snickerdoodle cookies.

SONNY BRYAN'S, 2202 Inwood Rd, TX 74235 ☎ (214) 357 7120
The best barbecue in Dallas. Also great sandwiches and take-away goodies.

FOOD AND DRINK

TRENDS IN AMERICAN CUISINE

"Whereas before most of the food influences came from Europe, lots of young Americans are now becoming chefs. This means there is now more regional food based on American influences. One of the most popular which is being eaten all over the States is southwestern cuisine. This takes the typical Mexican – or Latin-type food and updates it, using the same seasonings – lots of chilli and tortillas" – **Caroline Hunt**. *"Of all the trends in cooking, southwestern is one of my favourites. St Estèphe in Manhattan Beach has the best southwestern food in Los Angeles; each dish pleases the eye as much as the stomach"* – **Wolfgang Puck**. *"A kind of cooking based on fresh ingredients is definitely developing. North American flavours – which include Mexican and Central American influences – and European techniques"* – **Seymour Britchky**. *"There is more Caribbean influence – fruits such as gourds, root vegetables, seasonings"* – **Barbara Kafka**.

HOUSTON

CADILLAC BAR, 1802 Shepherd St, TX 77007
☎ (713) 862 2020
"The drinks – beer and neon-green margaritas – are passed from hand to hand by groups four-deep at the bar. The polyglot group is half-Mexican, half-larger-than-life cowboys. We had at our table a great basket of mesquite-barbecued quail, replenished as quickly as we could tuck them in, using our hands. Unforgettable!" – **Anne Willan.**

LOS ANGELES

CAFES AND BARS

LE DOME, 8720 Sunset Blvd, CA 90069 ☎ (213) 659 6919
Bar-bistro that pulls a razzy pop-star and latterday starlet set round its circular bar. *"It's had a fine revival. At lunchtime it's the power place for the movie crowd. Exciting"* – **Jeremiah Tower**. *"When I need to unwind from a hectic night in the restaurant, I can always find company at Le Dome, along with a glass of good wine and a satisfying late supper"* – **Wolfgang Puck**. **Jackie Collins, Robert**

Sangster and **Harvey Goldsmith** are Dome-loving types.

POLO LOUNGE, Beverly Hills Hotel, 9641 W Sunset Blvd, CA 90201
☎ (213) 276 2251
Still playing to packed houses – any international star who's passing through will check in for a pre- or post-prandial cocktail. Also the place for power breakfasts. *"Bernice is the captain in the morning. She's a formidable woman and is well plugged in to who's in and who's out, who gets the boot and who doesn't. There are A and B tables and you know you've arrived in Hollywood when Bernice recognizes you. You may have been going there for 20 years but suddenly she'll move you from a B to an A"* – **Michael Grade**. The Polo's tops with **Lord Lichfield.**

RESTAURANTS

THE BISTRO, 246 N Canon Drive, Beverly Hills, CA 90210
☎ (213) 273 5663
Golden oldies glow within the ersatz walls of the Paris bistro from *Irma la Douce*, given to the restaurant by one of its original backers, Billy Wilder. It has played host to Frank

Sinatra, Jack Lemmon, Tony Curtis, the Reagans and some marvellous Hollywood hooleys.

BISTRO GARDEN, 176 N Canon Drive, Beverly Hills, CA 90210 ☎ (213) 550 3900
A Bistro clone, with a racier image than the original. Movie greats lunch in the Riviera-style garden. A favourite of **Robert Sangster, Lord Lichfield** and **David Shilling.**

CHASEN'S, 9039 Beverly Blvd, CA 90048
☎ (213) 271 2168
Impressive, expensive '30s starlet, famous for its hobo steaks and chilli. James Stewart, David Frost, **Mark McCormack** and Richard Nixon love to plough through a hobo – a slab of sirloin, cooked to Chasen's own special 50-year-old recipe, sliced finely and served with melting butter on sourdough bread.

CHINOIS ON MAIN, 2709 Main St, Santa Monica, CA 90405 ☎ (213) 392 9025
The Franco-Oriental brainchild of that eclectic sorcerer Wolfgang Puck. *"The product of a true genius of the culinary art. I think the Mongolian lamb is my special favourite"* – **Dudley Moore**. *"Puck trying to do an East meets West is actually terrific. A wonderful place to be in – a great environment"* – **Ken Hom**. Diners are generally the same bunch that munch at Spago.

CITRUS, 6703 Melrose Ave, CA 90038 ☎ (213) 857 0034
Chef-owner Michel Richard is the man behind *"the best food in Los Angeles right now"* – **Jeremiah Tower**. It's also the coolest restaurant on the coolest street in LA, jam-packed with glossy showbizzos and yuppies. An open patio (with canvas pull-over roof) forms the dining room. Exciting French-Californian cuisine – local shrimp and crab ravioli, terrine of endive and foie gras with brioche, cassis cake. *"The best restaurant I ate in when I was in LA. It's typical LA – cool, smart, Californian cuisine, good wine list"* – **Geoffrey Roberts.**

CITY RESTAURANT, 180 S La Brea Ave, CA 90036
☎ (213) 938 2155
Modern, unusual dishes in similar surroundings. "*A place I really liked. The best décor and atmosphere for me. It's huge, with white rough walls; the roof is very high and you've got a lot of room to breathe. Beautiful crockery – square, multi-coloured plates with a different-coloured plate for each dish. Good service, and a fabulous display of American desserts which looks very impressive*" – **Alastair Little**.

THE IVY, 113 N Robertson Blvd, CA 90048
☎ (213) 274 8303
Masters of mesquite grilling – a Californian cuisine trademark – and a menu rich in fish, chicken and veal. Catherine Oxenberg loves it. **Jeremiah Tower** likes their seaside spin-off, **Ivy by the Shore**, 1541 Ocean Ave, Santa Monica: "*A wonderful setting for lunch on a Sunday afternoon. Very amusing; friendly staff.*"

LITA GRAY, 926 S La Brea Ave, CA 90036
☎ (213) 939 6813
Brand new bistro-cum-bakery-cum-espresso bar, opened this autumn by Mark Peel (ex-Spago and Ma Maison) and his pastry-chef wife Nancy Silverton. Based in a delightful 1927 house built by Lita Gray (wife of Charlie Chaplin), the 3-in-1 eatery forms 3 sides of a square around a courtyard with a fountain. The bistro serves Californian cuisine Chinese-style on a central platter. Nancy bakes 2,000 loaves of heavenly bread a day.

MICHAEL'S, 1147 3rd St, Santa Monica, CA 90403
☎ (213) 451 0843
Michael McCarty creates New Californian-cum-French cuisine using the very best ingredients.

MORTONS, 8800 Melrose Ave, CA 90069
☎ (213) 276 5205
The place to see a galaxy of stars, would-bes and has-beens. Marinated and grilled meats; scrumptious puddings such as

chocolate truffle cake. "*An industry restaurant. Great ambience and a wonderful mix of people*" – **Jackie Collins**. **Harvey Goldsmith**, Catherine Oxenberg and **Frank Bowling** join the throng. **Jeremiah Tower** is ambivalent: "*Everything you could want in LA but good food.*"

L'ORANGERIE, 903 N La Cienega Blvd, CA 90069
☎ (213) 652 9770
"*Stunning. The fish is flown in from the Mediterranean every few days – it's just exquisite. Great wine. Unpretentious and wonderful*" – **Michael Grade**. "*Very pretentious but quite beautiful décor and the food is very good. A certain mood of New-World formality*" – **Jeremiah Tower**. Confused?

THE REGENCY CLUB, 10900 Wilshire Blvd, CA 90024
☎ (213) 208 1443
This exclusive dining club and bar now boasts the legendary Joachim Splichal as its chef.

Formerly of Max au Triangle, he is now making the Regency a gourmet's paradise. It will set you back $5,000 initial membership fee plus $110 a month to get your foot in the door. Arianna Stassinopoulos is a fan. Now that Splichal's there, "*it could have spectacular food*", speculates **Jeremiah Tower**.

LA SERRE, 12969 Ventura Blvd, Studio City, CA 91604
☎ (818) 990 0500
Chic French restaurant which prompts **Vidal Sassoon** to say: "*To choose a favourite restaurant in Beverly Hills is tantamount to suicide. Just imagine what the other restaurants will do to my food! But just over Coldwater Canyon is La Serre, and there you can have a magnificent bouillabaisse. They fly the fish in from Marseilles ... need I say more?*"

🍴 **SPAGO, 1114 Horn Ave, CA 90069** ☎ (213) 652 4025
Wolfgang Puck's cult palm-

🍴 **Buzzzzzzzzz** I'd walk a million miles for one of your 🍴...... CHOCOLATE AND RASPBERRY ICE CREAMS from **Robin Rose Ice Cream**, Rodeo Collection, 429 N Rodeo Drive, Beverly Hills: "*It just knocks you for six. Fresh raspberries folded through the richest, most decadent chocolate ice cream you could imagine*" – **Elise Pascoe** 🍴...... STEAKS, from **The Palm**, 9001 Santa Monica Blvd, West Hollywood: "*When I am tired of all the crazy food people like to serve up, and feel like a really good steak, I head straight here*" – **Wolfgang Puck** 🍴...... CHOCO-LATE TURTLES: "*I'm not a big enough ... well I'm lying – I'm a big chocolate freak, but the best chocolates are Turtles made by Fanny May – caramel with nuts and chocolate*" – **Bob Payton** 🍴...... SUSHI, from **Katsu** in Los Feliz, LA: "*On a Sunday night, after a weekend of parties, food and wine, I love to go here – it's inspired and wonderfully fresh*" – **Wolfgang Puck** 🍴...... bottles of MINERAL WATER: **Calistoga**, from California (voted by **Barbara Kafka**); **Crystal Geyser**, from the West Coast; **Vintage** from the East Coast; **Poland Spring**, from Maine: "*the best still water*" – **Gael Greene**.

★ ★

FOOD AND DRINK

Petit-monde cuisine?

"As communications become more and more sophisticated, cuisine becomes more and more eclectic. Modern cuisine is moving towards international cuisine – you still have the regional element, but you can also have Californian asparagus the day after it's cut, Japanese and Indian spices and so on ... It's wonderful, like having a piano with 20 notes added. You can create a new song. It's a discovery, it's enriching our cuisine" – **Raymond Blanc.**

---

studded and tented parlour is the original nouvelle pizzeria, with wild mushroom, smoked duck sausage and other innovative toppings. *"The best pizza joint in LA. It's run brilliantly, it has great ambience and a terrific mix of people. Any night you could see Joan Rivers or Dudley Moore or Michael Caine or Billy Wilder"* – **Jackie Collins.** For **Dudley Moore**, this and Chinois on Main are: *"The best restaurants in the world. Spago has wonderful food, beautifully cooked and prepared."* Further votes from **Paula Wolfert, Mark McCormack, Shakira Caine** and **Barry Humphries**. *"Very much the scene of the older powers. There have been rumours about the quality, but Puck is still the genius of LA"* – **Jeremiah Tower.** *"When I went, the place was filled with paparazzi. All I wanted to do was watch what the chef was doing, which was mesquite-grilled fish"* – **Clare Ferguson.**

72 MARKET ST, 72 Market St, Venice, CA 90291
☎ (213) 392 8720
"I could also mention my own restaurant, where I've had some of the best dishes ever –

warm scallop salad, spinach salad, curried lentil soup with mint and yogurt, crab cakes..."* – **Dudley Moore.**

THE SUGAR SHACK, 8751 W Pico Blvd, CA 90035
☎ (213) 271 7887
Jamaican restaurant frequented by Michael J Fox, Paul-Michael Glaser (Starsky to you) and Penny Marshall. *"My favourite. It used to be a Polynesian restaurant and then they just went mad with spray cans, painted it with red and green stripes inside, and turned it into this Caribbean restaurant. It's really great fun"* – **Stephen Jones.**

TRUMPS, 8764 Melrose Ave, CA 90069 ☎ (213) 855 1480
Another hit with celebs, showing ever-changing contemporary art. *"Very Valley people,"* observes **Jeremiah Tower.** Airy, modern base for adventurous cuisine – Pacific Western salmon tartar and other creations. *"When a friend wants to have lunch at Trumps, I always make time. Their wonderful eclectic menu attracts people all day long"* – **Wolfgang Puck.** *"I had a stunning entrée here, a salad I shall never forget. It was Japanese inspired, made with fresh Californian tomatoes, avocados, enoki mushrooms and chives. I adored that"* – **Elise Pascoe.**

VALENTINO, 3115 Pico Blvd, Santa Monica, CA 90405
☎ (213) 829 4313
Piero Selvaggio's Italian restaurant has been given a beautiful new image and an accomplished young team of chefs. Exquisite southern Italian cuisine. *"There is no place outside Italy like Valentino. The ambience is warm and inviting, the food innovative and the wine cellar quite remarkable"* – **Wolfgang Puck.**

WEST BEACH CAFE, 60 N Venice Blvd, Venice, CA 90291 ☎ (213) 823 5396
Young arty types flock in from a hard day's sunning and surfing and lap up fresh California cuisine and

wonderful seafood. Exhibitions of contemporary paintings and sculpture, too. *"Innovative, unique and wonderful at lunch. Simple and avant-garde"* – **Jeremiah Tower.**

Shops

"There are two great delis in LA; **NATE 'N' ALS,** 414 N Beverly Drive ☎ (213) 274 0101 *and* **ART'S DELI,** 12224 Ventura Blvd, Studio City ☎ (818) 769 9808 *which is over the hill in the valley. I prefer Art's but the whole community is divided between the 2"* – **Michael Grade.**

IRVINE RANCH MARKET, Beverly Center, 142 S San Vicente, CA 90048
☎ (213) 657 1931
The place for *"the widest variety of meat, fish, produce and specialty items"* – **Wolfgang Puck.** The manager expounds further: *"We put Harrods to shame! We import the best from all over the world – peaches, apricots, nectarines, strawberries and seedless avocados that are an immaculate conception. It's summer all year round here!"*

Napa Valley

AUBERGE DU SOLEIL, 180 Rutherford Hill Rd, Rutherford CA 94573
☎ (707) 963 1211
Sophisticated Californian-French cuisine. *"They use local ingredients and concentrate on that ... fresh garden vegetables and fresh fish"* – **Robert Mondavi.** *"Spectacular setting for California, and very comfortable for a retreat. Top marks!"* – **Jeremiah Tower.** *"If you want to be grand..."* – **Geoffrey Roberts.**

DOMAINE CHANDON, PO Box 2470, Yountville, CA 94599 ☎ (707) 944 8844
"Stunning. The most beautiful grounds, with lakes, swans, ducks and all manner of birdlife, beautiful lawns, winding paths and overhanging trees with lovely Japanese

lanterns hanging in them, all lit up like fairyland. An excellent menu and the best of the world's wines" – **Elise Pascoe.**

MIRAMONTE, 1327 Railroad Ave, St Helena, CA 94574 ☎ (707) 936 3970
"Very good – typically Californian-French cuisine. The wines are very very good" – **Robert Mondavi.**

MUSTARD'S GRILL, 7399 St Helena Highway, CA 94558 ☎ (707) 944 2424
Probably the best restaurant in the Napa Valley. *"Very much the local scene. Everyone, however grand, ends up there sooner or later. The place to see the wine-makers"* – **Jeremiah Tower.** More fine Californian cooking; especially good seafood. A favourite of **Geoffrey Roberts, Robert Mondavi** and **Don Hewitson.** *"Young and fresh, with a woman chef"* – **Barbara Kafka.**

TRA VIGNE, 1050 Charter Oak, CA 94574 ☎ (707) 963 4444
Another Puck clone. *"The latest hot restaurant in Napa Valley. What I call nouvelle Italian, very good pizzas, pasta, etc"* – **Geoffrey Roberts.**

NEW ORLEANS

BISTRO AT MAISON DE VILLE, 733 Rue Toulouse, LA 70130 ☎ (504) 561 5858
A little bistro that's full of Noo Orluns character – part of the Hotel Maison de Ville, which has been restored to its original *Angel Heart*-et-al state. Susan Spicer updates creole and Cajun with an international eclectic touch. Soft-shell crab and creole mustard salad, grilled shrimp with coriander, cod cakes with tomato coulis.

BRENNANS, 417 Royal St, LA 70130 ☎ (504) 525 9713
Even 12 dining rooms can't contain the tourist throng in comfort, but you have to go, *"for the most comprehensive breakfast in the world –*

absinthe frappé, eggs benedict, grits . . ." – **Lord Lichfield.**

COMMANDER'S PALACE, 1403 Washington Ave, LA 70130 ☎ (504) 899 8221
"Old-guard, consistently good. They have wonderful brunches. It's one of the great New Orleans experiences – that and K'Paul's" – **Paula Wolfert.** *"I discovered a wonderful dessert there, the creole bread pudding. It's a soufflé, nice and light, with a whisky sauce"* – **Elise Pascoe.**

🍤 **K'PAUL'S LOUISIANA KITCHEN, 416 Chartres St, LA 70130 ☎ (504) 942 7500**
Cult centre of Cajun cuisine, cooked up by its godfather, Paul Prudhomme. Cajun encompasses the spices of the bayou kitchen, the fish and stews of creole, the best and freshest local ingredients and the eclectic polish of New American cuisine. K'Paul's is informal and downbeat, but the food inspired enough to lure the most exalted of eaters. **Lord Lichfield** loves their blackened red fish. *"One of the best 3 restaurants in America"* – **Craig Claiborne.** *"A meal of a lifetime; it's just wonderful"* –

Bob Payton. A vote from **Egon Ronay** too. In the summer of odd-numbered years, K'Paul's moves to another town, where the queues mark its arrival. Look out for them in London in 1989. 1991 just might be Paris.

NEW YORK
CAFES AND BARS

See also **Elaine's** and **Odeon** (Restaurants). The **Oak Room** at **The Algonquin** (see Travel) is an old-fashioned drinking institution with consistently good cabaret and dinner too. **Café Carlyle** at **The Carlyle** (see Travel) is a similar set-up with Cole Porteresque entertainment.

WESTIN PLAZA HOTEL, 768 5th Ave, NY 10019 ☎ (212) 759 3000
The Plaza has 2 noteworthy bars. Oak Bar: *"A very old bar with great murals of old New York on the walls and a tall mahogany ceiling. It has a very friendly atmosphere"* – **Craig Claiborne.** Trader Vic's: for the best scorpions.

THE BEST SEAFOOD FOR MILES

GINO'S, 3019 Grand Caillou Rd, Houma, LA 70360 ☎ (504) 876 4896 *"might well be the best shellfish restaurant in the world,"* sighs **Miles Kington.** *"Nobody has heard of Gino's. Well, nobody has heard of Houma either. I went there on Annie Miller's boat trip on the swamps (the best swamp boat trip in the world). Gino's is a square, flat, one-storey structure, its ceiling festooned with caps belonging to oil companies in the Gulf. Gino's speciality is shrimp and crab pizza. It is the best pizza I have ever eaten – or perhaps the best shrimp and crab, soft and tasty, crusty and chewy. Gino's speciality is also soft-shelled crab. It was beautiful. His speciality is also broiled alligator, which I had never eaten before – in fact, it wasn't eaten much in Louisiana right then, as it had only just come off the protected list. It was wonderful. I would have eaten more of his specialities, but I didn't have room.*
'You ought to export this all over the world,' I told him.
'Japanese gentleman came in recently, and liked my pizzas so much I now send him one each week. Well, one pizza to Tokyo is a start.'"

FOOD AND DRINK

RESTAURANTS

ARCADIA, 21 E 62nd St, NY10021 ☎ (212) 223 2900
Real New American cuisine from the Anne Rosenzweig kitchen (she cooks there at least 2 days a week), using rich, strong flavours such as smoked lobster, gorgonzola, American caviare, quail and venison. Cool New Yorkers book to sit in the main dining room at the back, by the walls. *"It's American and it's wonderful. Anne Rosenzweig is terrific. A whole new way of thinking about combinations of herbs, and fresh ingredients"* – **Mario Buatta**. A hit with **Mark McCormack** too.

🍴 **ARIZONA 206, 206 E 60th St, NY 10022 ☎ (212) 838 0440**
Run by local boy Brendan Walsh, whom **Paula Wolfert** and **Jeremiah Tower** rate as one of the best young chefs in America. Southwestern cooking – like chilli-rubbed roast free-range chicken. *"He's a bit of a genius. This and the Gotham Bar & Grill are 2 of the most exciting restaurants in the city"* – **PW**.

🍴 **BELLINI, 777 7th Ave, NY 10019 ☎ (212) 265 7770**
An offshoot of Harry's Bar, run by Harry (well, Arrigo) Cipriani and his son Giuseppe. Plays to packed houses of the very chic-est kind. Smarties who enjoy conspicuous consumption sit at the front. *"I think the whole group of Cipriani restaurants are excellent"* – **Helen Gurley Brown. Bill Blass, Marchesa Fiamma di San Giuliano Ferragamo, Joan Burstein** and **Eleanor Lambert** add votes. **Mario Buatta** looks on with a decorator's eye: *"Early 20th-century chairs, very clean, modern wood tones – it's very nice."* Choose from a fixed-price menu to make the bill palatable.

🍴 **LE BERNARDIN, 155 W 51st St, NY 10111 ☎ (212) 489 1515**
The best seafood and arguably the best French restaurant in New York, awarded an almost-unheard-of 4 stars by *The New York Times. "The most exciting restaurant to open in New York in the last 10 years. Gilbert Le Coze serves dishes like fish dressed in oil. It is undercooked compared with the way fish has been served for so long. It is a big, luxurious restaurant, hung with seafaring and seafood paintings"* – **Seymour Britchky**. *"The best French restaurant I've ever been to in New York"* – **Alan Crompton-Batt**. *"The best fish restaurant in the city"* – **Olivier Coquelin**. *"I like it because they work unremittingly – bristling with anxiety to make it better each day"* – **Thomas Hoving. Mario Buatta** adds praise.

BICE, 7 E 54th St, NY 10022 ☎ (212) 688 1999
The new NY outpost of the fashionable 60-year-old Milan restaurant is overrun with glamorati. If they're not at Bellini they're here. *"It seems, once again, that America has gone crazy for Italian food"* – **Bill Blass**. *"For a change the food is good at a trendy place. It's more usual to have good people and terrible food!"* – **Steve Rubell**. *"Typically modern Italian"* – **Mario Buatta. Joan Burstein** and **Marchesa Fiamma di San Giuliano Ferragamo** join the chorus of devotees.

CAFE LUXEMBOURG, 200 W 70th St, NY 10023 ☎ (212) 873 7411
An offshoot of Odeon, offering rich French cuisine – escargots, chicken liver terrine, lemon tart. **Tama Janowitz** and **Ned Sherrin** like it.

IL CANTINORI, 32 E 10th St, NY 10003 ☎ (212) 673 6044
Expensive Italian ristorante with ye-olde-farmhouse décor. *"Most people who know Italian food in New York think this is the best restaurant"* – **Paula Wolfert**. *"That's another terrific one. It's generally quiet enough to, and I know the maître d', so it's a nice treat"* – **Tama Janowitz**.

🍴 **CHANTERELLE, 89 Grand St, NY 10013 ☎ (212) 966 6960**
Simple, old-style restaurant serving post-nouvelle cuisine that is extremely highly rated. *"Definitely one of the best restaurants in the city. You can't get in – you have to wait until 1999"* – **Paula Wolfert**. Interesting fish, a superb cheese board, home-made breads, and baby profiteroles with coffee. The Waltucks, who run it, show *"perfection and style"* – **Gael Greene**. In **Seymour Britchky**'s top 3.

CHEZ LOUIS, 1016 2nd Ave, NY 10022 ☎ (212) 752 1400
"For the best roast chicken and potatoes in New York. I call it the $50 potato – it costs $50 to eat there, and the potatoes are wonderful. They are cooked in goose fat, garlic and parsley. It's hearty bistro cooking" – **Paula Wolfert**.

🍴 **LE CIRQUE, 58 E 65th St, NY 10021 ☎ (212) 794 9292**
Sirio Maccioni is running what is still one of the buzzest restaurants in town, based in the Mayfair Regent. It may have lost its old chef to the 21 Club, but the new one, Daniel Boulud, is *sensational*. (**Jeremiah Tower** votes him one of the best rising chefs.) Eclectic French and Italian cuisine includes the famous sea scallops and truffles, carpaccio of snapper, foie gras and the best crème brûlée in town. Regulars like Lee Iacocca, Mick Jagger, Richard Nixon, **Bill Blass, Douglas Fairbanks Jr, Eleanor Lambert, Ken Lane**, Woody Allen, Jerry Zipkin and Nancy Reagan have their tables earmarked – by the door is best (but beware a door jam). *"I still feel the same about it, I hope I always will"* – **Margaux Hemingway**. *"I like it for the people, and for the pzazz and the personality of Sirio"* – **Robert Carrier**. *"Still very popular with everybody"* – **Mario Buatta**.

COACH HOUSE, 110 Waverly Place, NY 10011 ☎ (212) 777 0303
A much-loved institution, based in a historical carriage house in Greenwich Village. **Madhur Jaffrey** says go *"if you're looking for a very American,*

> *I know New York is not America, but when I went I was absolutely stunned by the quality of the ingredients and what they are doing with them*

🐜 RAYMOND BLANC

wonderful meal with European influences". Regional dishes from chef Larry Terrier include black bean soup, corn sticks and pecan pie. California wines. *"I love it"* – **Egon Ronay**.

DARBAR, 44 W 56th St, NY 10019 ☎ (212) 432 7227
An opulent, gilded and ornamented homage to India. *"The best Indian food in New York. A high-class restaurant with linen on the tables. Good service"* – **Seymour Britchky**.

DAVID K'S, 115 3rd Ave, NY 10021 ☎ (212) 371 9090
David Keh, ex-Auntie Yuan, now owns his own restaurant for nouvelle Chinoise cuisine. *"His cooking is quite pure and clean and wonderful"* – **Ken Hom**. *"It's Chinese home cooking, without MSG; healthy foods. It's been getting rave reviews"* – **Paula Wolfert**.

ELIO'S, 121 2nd Ave, NY 10028 ☎ (212) 772 2242
Café-bar with rather good fresh fish and seafood dishes. *"Like a liner of the 1930s with an Italian twist. Uncluttered. I go a lot"* – **Taki**. **Tama Janowitz** is a fan; **Ed Victor** notes the literary clientele.

FOUR SEASONS, 99 E 52nd St, NY 10022 ☎ (212) 754 9494
The lunch spot for media heads and captains of industry – and it costs nigh on a tanker of oil to eat here. *"The world's most beautiful restaurant. It's monumental with a pool in the middle. So stylish and absolutely colossal"* – **Egon Ronay**. It's most 'in' to eat not in the grander Pool Room (that's for tourists) but in the Bar Room, *"the best luncheon club in town. Certain habitués phone only when they won't be using their table that day"* – **Gael Greene**. While **Jeffrey Archer** and **Douglas Fairbanks Jr** are all for it, Seymour Britchky has knocked

it for a) coming apart and b) small portions of unappetizing food. Still, it's *"Where the upper echelon of the publishing world goes. Like a club, everybody goes there and table-hops"* – **Ed Victor**. *"They have a great new thing for light food. I like the two bosses – they're always on hand. The welcome and the service is among the best in the world"* – **Robert Carrier**. A best for **Craig Claiborne**.

GOTHAM BAR & GRILL, 12 E 12th St, NY 10003 ☎ (212) 620 4020
Glamorous and successful restaurant with incongruous *faux* Arabian décor, hung-over from a previous whim. An eclectic menu in the hands of a gifted chef, who wields the best of American ingredients around his creations (duck breast carpaccio in pesto, grilled tuna with lemon-basil pasta). *"Irresistible good taste"* – **Gael Greene**. *"One of the most exciting restaurants in the city"* – **Paula Wolfert**.

LA GRENOUILLE, 3 E 52nd St, NY 10022 ☎ (212) 752 1495
The famous restaurant has been rather fussily over-done up. The classic French haute cuisine has been at le sommet for over 20 years. However, there are warning words from **Andrew Lloyd Webber**: *"It used to be wonderful but it's so heavily old-fashioned that it's slightly going into a time warp food-wise."* **Douglas Fairbanks Jr** still rates it highly.

🐜 **LUTECE, 249 E 50th St, NY 10022 ☎ (212) 752 2225**
Still one of the very best French restaurants in town. Like all top dineries in New York, it has its cossetted regulars (**Bill Blass** is one). For everyone, *"the welcome is pleasantly unintimidating. The chef-owner, André Soltner, is a*

master of the grand tradition, with innate taste: innovative but incapable of committing nouvelle silliness"* – **Gael Greene**. *"The best French restaurant in NY. Soltner does magic things to fish and game. He does a magisterial côte de boeuf au vin rouge"* – **Robert Carrier**. *"The best restaurant in NY; it usually gets the top rating by the critics"* – **Michael Musto**.

MAURICE, Parker Meridien, 119 W 56th St, NY 10019 ☎ (212) 245 7788
Comfortable, club-like hotel dining room with seriously different modern cooking inspired by Alain Senderens. **Gael Greene** applauds *"an inventive kitchen"*.

IL MONELLO, 1460 2nd Ave, NY 10021 ☎ (212) 535 9310
"A funny little place that has some of the most extraordinary 'grandmother's' Italian food that I've ever had. One dish is so good that I can't believe it, it's so simple! They call it Papa because Papa makes it. It's seeded and peeled tomatoes, diced and stirred with breadcrumbs in olive oil and stock for an hour until it's a thick purée. It's out of this world. All their simple pastas are terribly good" – **Robert Carrier**.

MORTIMER'S, 1057 Lexington Ave, NY 10021 ☎ (212) 861 2481
"One of the most popular restaurants – a sort of club; you know most of the people there. They do rather simple 'Nanny' food" – **Ken Lane**. 'Members' of Glenn Bernbaum's exclusive 'club' include **Taki**, Pat Buckley, **Ken Lane**, Nan Kempner, Carolina Herrera, **Lynn Wyatt, Bill Blass** and **Eleanor Lambert**, but the list of celebs who have dined there is endless: **Jackie Onassis, Shirley MacLaine, Gloria**

FOOD AND DRINK

FOOD AND DRINK

Vanderbilt, Princess Margaret, King Juan Carlos, Joan Collins, George Hamilton ... The most desired table for 2 in town is 1B, by the window. *"One of my favourite places in New York, but you don't go for the food, you go to see. If you want a table and they don't know you, you need a great sense of self not to be ignored"* – **Paula Wolfert.**

ODEON, 145 W Broadway, NY 10013 ☎ (212) 233 0507
An American brasserie with tons of tubular chrome, bags of *ambience* and surprisingly fine French food. A streetwise young crowd cram into *"the best late-night spot downtown"* – **Gael Greene.** Brilliant brunches too. *"The atmosphere's wonderful"* – **Simon Hopkinson.** *"One of the most atmospheric restaurants I know"* – **Egon Ronay.** *"Good fun – a kind of Art Deco place"* – **Harvey Goldsmith. Ned Sherrin** is *"very keen"*.

🦪 **OYSTER BAR, Grand Central Terminal, Lower Level, NY 10163 ☎ (212) 490 6650**
From their bar stools beneath white-tiled vaulting, customers become rapt watching white-coated waiters whip oysters from their shells. *"Lovely. The most tremendous seafood. It's the best oyster bar in the world. The chefs are tremendously funny and lively and dance about; they're old guys who know fish like nobody else"* – **Clare Ferguson.** *"The best, and an extraordinary variety, noted for their freshness"* – **Craig Claiborne.** *"The best range of oysters, incomparable scallop stew and great California Chardonnay. My idea of bliss"* – **Michael Broadbent.** *"It's amazing. I love the clam chowder"* – **Liz Smith.** *"A wonderful list of California wines too"* – **Egon**

Ronay. *"I'm very fond of it"* – **Lord Gowrie.** *"Wonderful"* – **Paula Wolfert.**

PAMIR, 1437 2nd Ave, NY 10021 ☎ (212) 650 1095
A favourite with the Lloyd Webber clan, who rave (independently) about it: *"A great Afghan restaurant – really nice"* – **Julian LW.** *"An excellent place, they do delicious things like lamb in rosewater"* – **Andrew LW.** *"It's fabulous"* – **Sarah Brightman.**

PARIOLI ROMANISSIMO, 24 E 81st St, NY 10028 ☎ (212) 288 2391
Conscious chic, marvellous pasta. **Mario Buatta** recommends, as does **Lynn Wyatt**: *"My favourite Italian restaurant."* *"No one has rack of veal or baby birds as magnificent, and no restaurant is quite so pretentious"* – **Gael Greene.** Nor so expensive ...

PETROSSIAN, 182 W 58th St, NY 10019 ☎ (212) 245 2214
The grander restaurant counterpart to the Parisian caviare bar. An Art Deco symphony in pink, with banquettes of mink-trimmed kid. *"Here you can have a majestic best tasting of caviare, served on a pedestal"* – **Robert Carrier.** Also *"the best foie gras in New York"* – **Craig Claiborne** (and a mighty bill).

PRIMAVERA, 1578 1st Ave, NY 10028 ☎ (212) 861 8608
Popular with the Nancy Girls, it's one of the smartest, plushest Italianos in New York, with superb cucina nuova. *"Sublime porcini, intense white truffles, irresistible baby artichokes and crisp-roasted goat"* – **Gael Greene.**

🦒 **THE QUILTED GIRAFFE, AT&T Arcade, 550 Madison Ave, NY 10022 ☎ (212) 593 1221**

One of the best, most famous, but priciest restaurants in town. Newly based in the AT&T arcade, with a dining room of steel and marble, it continues to serve New American cuisine to mega-rich/expense-accounted-for jacketed-and-tied enthusiasts. *"The best food in New York"* – **Egon Ronay.** *"The food is sensational ... and the prices!"* – **Prue Leith.** *"I love it, nothing compares to it. It's so expensive it hurts"* – **Don Hewitson.** In **Craig Claiborne**'s top 3. A **Harvey Goldsmith** hang-out. Even **Andrew Lloyd Webber** sticks his neck out: *"The new ones come and they tend to go in New York – I think this is about the best. Jolly good."*

LE RELAIS, 712 Madison Ave, NY 10021 ☎ (212) 751 5108
A high-toned café that burgeons out onto the sidewalk in summer. Parisian brasserie style. *"It's cramped and frenetic. Zeffirelli might be on the next table, and all the people you saw at the party the night before – it's great"* – **Bruce Oldfield.**

ROSA MEXICANO, 1063 1st Ave, NY 10022 ☎ (212) 753 7407
Despite its location far from the border, it's one of the best Mexican restaurants in the USA. A highbrow Mex mix – from red snapper in cilantro (coriander) to freshly made tortillas and by far the best guacamole in town. **Elisabeth Lambert Ortiz** advises going down Rosa Mexicano way.

RUSSIAN TEA ROOM, 150 W 57th St, NY 10019 ☎ (212) 265 0947
Exotic, bustly café-restaurant where the café society sip Russian tea or swig vodka (one of 20 different types). *"One of my favourite places to eat."*

> ❝ *People very, very rarely have dinner in their own home because everyone works so hard. Their apartments are usually miserably small, or else they don't have any furniture* ❞

🧥 **TAMA JANOWITZ**

Wonderful blinis and caviare"
– **Helen Gurley Brown**. *"A bit
hackneyed, but I still love it"* –
Egon Ronay. *"I'm very boring
– I prefer the Russian Tea
Room to anywhere else. I like
Russian food and that mock-
Ruritanian atmosphere. If you
want to feel like the Prisoner of
Zenda it's a good place to go"* –
Loyd Grossman.

**SERYNA, 11 E 53rd St, NY
10022 ☎ (212) 980 9393**
Where smarties are stopping
off for their sushi. *"The best
Japanese restaurant in New
York and, as far as I know, in
the world, outside Japan"* –
Helen Gurley Brown. **Eleanor
Lambert** seconds that, while
Raymond Blanc is quite
overcome: *"It was brilliant. I
very rarely go silly and
emotional about food, but here
I did because everything was so
brilliantly executed. I had a
little consommé of shellfish
with Japanese seaweed, and
some raw fish – so good and
melting and clear. It was so
pure, nothing was overdone. It
was* more *than excellent"* – **RB.**

**SHUN LEE PALACE, 155 E
55th St, NY 10022
☎ (212) 371 8844**
The best Chinese, according to
Craig Claiborne; a favourite of
Ken Hom and **Harvey
Goldsmith**. Highly
orchestrated feasting on
specialities from all over China.

**SLOPPY LOUIE'S, 92 South
St, NY 10038 ☎ (212) 509 9694**
Rough 'n' ready fish restaurant
on the seaport. *"It's good
because it's fresh. You can sit
next to a truck driver or Liz
Taylor. The staff aren't really
trained, but it's a great
atmosphere and the food is very
special"* – **Terry Holmes.**

**LA TULIPE, 104 W 13th St,
NY 10011 ☎ (212) 691 8860**
Très français, très chouette.
The Parisian scene, set by a
zinc-topped bar and tables, is
completed by Sally and John
Dare's artfully arranged dishes
Herby, succulent snapper,
game with spinach and pine
kernels, typical French
gâteaux. Savoured by
Elisabeth Lambert Ortiz.

CLAIM YOUR STEAK

Nouvelle Californie may be all the rage, but a doorstep of
charred steak, oozingly red inside, is an all-American fave that
fashion can't faze. *"We have wonderful steakhouses in New
York. When French people come here, that's what they want"* –
Paula Wolfert. **PETER LUGER STEAKHOUSE**, 178
Broadway, Brooklyn, NY 10038 ☎ (718) 387 7400 is the steak
Mecca for filet mignon, porterhouses and T-bones, wolfed
down by businessmen from the finance district. *"A wonderfully atmospheric steakhouse with back-slapping waiters"* –
Egon Ronay. *"Very, very good"* – **Paula Wolfert**. **SPARKS
STEAKHOUSE**, 210 E 46th St, NY 10017 ☎ (212) 687 4855
has the best cuts of beef in Manhattan – sirloins to lay down
and die for. **Terry Holmes**'s No 1: *"Consistently good standard of food – the beef is excellent."* *"Good steaks and a
brilliant wine list. Dignified, like a gentlemen's club"* – **Don
Hewitson**. **PALM**, 837 2nd Ave, NY 10017 ☎ (212) 687 2953
has sawdust on the floor, no menus, steaks *this* thick and *that*
tender. Has the cutting edge on its sister, **PALM TOO**, 840
2nd Ave, NY 10017 ☎ (212) 697 5198.

**21 CLUB, 21 W 52nd St, NY
10019 ☎ (212) 582 7200**
Under new ownership
(acquired for a suitable $21
million), overseen by Anne
Rosenzweig (of Arcadia) and
Ken Aretsky, with Alain
Sailhac (ex-Le Cirque) running
the kitchen, this old
gentlemen's clubby chestnut is
now a force to reckon with. The
character remains the same as
do old favourites on the menu,
but a wave of wildly
imaginative dishes are hauling
in more than just the tired
expense-accounters. **Douglas
Fairbanks Jr** and **Lord
Lichfield** recommend.

Shops

**BALDUCCI'S, 424 Ave of the
Americas, NY 10011
☎ (212) 673 2600**
Brilliant family deli-grocer for
superb fresh local and exotic
produce with an Italian accent:
herbs, pastas, cheeses, candies,
fresh and smoked meats and
fish, home-made take-away
dishes and hampers. Lavish
displays, premium quality.

**BLOOMINGDALE'S,
Lexington Ave at 59th St, NY**

10022 ☎ (212) 705 2000
An amazing array of foods,
excellent bakery, and the
cream of European produce and
speciality imports. Good for
kitchen equipment, too.

**CARNEGIE DELI, 854 7th
Ave, NY 10019
☎ (212) 757 2245**
*"I wouldn't miss out on the
Jewish deli – pastrami-on-rye
sort of stuff. This is the best of
the well-known ones"* –
Madhur Jaffrey. Queues of
people can be seen on Sunday
morning and sometimes even at
midnight, waiting for their fix
of matzoh ball soup and
sandwiches. Open 6am – 4am.

**DEAN & DELUCA, 121
Prince St, NY 10012
☎ (212) 254 7774**
Chief rival to Balducci's and
Zabar's. Glamorously
presented Italian and general
deli foods, fruit and veg (many
of which are sprayed with mist
hourly) plus specialist
temptations such as edible
ferns (4 different types).

**EAT, 867 Madison Ave, NY
10021 and 1064 Madison Ave,
NY 10028 ☎ (212) 879 4017**
Owned by Eli Zabar, brother of
Saul and Stanley of Zabar's. He

makes fabulously slender baguettes, and may even whizz off to France for the day to find the right cheese.

MACY'S, 151 W 34th St, NY 10001 ☎ (212) 695 4400
One of the biggest delis in town, with all the latest foodstuffs.

WILLIAM POLL, 1051 Lexington Ave, NY 10021 ☎ (212) 288 0501
Old-established deli-caterer, the first to make fine take-away dishes. **Marcella Hazan**'s favourite chocolatier, **Barbara Kafka**'s source of smoked salmon.

ZABAR'S, 2245 Broadway, NY 10024 ☎ (212) 787 2000
"The best delicatessen, with the world's greatest variety per square inch" – **Anne Willan**. *"The best deli in the world,"* echoes **Paula Wolfert**. An institution – you can barely move for the crowds. Each week at least 30,000 customers get through 30,000 croissants, 10,000lb of coffee and 2,000lb of smoked salmon. Zabar's stock 26 kinds of salami, 30 types of honey and 42 of mustard, chicken roasted in 5 different ways and marvellous ready-cooked meals to take away. *"You must go – it's the best-known deli in the world"* – **Egon Ronay**.

PHILADELPHIA

RESTAURANTS

LE BEC-FIN, 1523 Walnut St, PA 19102 ☎ (215) 567 1000
Grandiose French restaurant run by chef-owner Georges Perrier. Gorgeous Louis XV décor (chandeliers, damask and mirrored walls), modern-classic cuisine and faultless service. A hit with **Craig Claiborne**.

RESTAURANT ODEON, 114 S 12th St, PA 19107 ☎ (215) 922 4399
New restaurant serving French country cuisine. *"Reputed to be wonderful. Everybody is talking about it"* – **Paula Wolfert**.

SAN FRANCISCO

CAFES AND BARS

🐔 **CHINA MOON CAFE, 639 Post St, CA 94109 ☎ (415) 775 4789**
"A café rather than a restaurant, run by Barbara Tropp. She's very much the current darling. Her food is wonderful. The café is full of cheery, slap-happy waitresses, very lively, for really healthy non-serious eating" – **Clare Ferguson**. *"Very, very good"* – **Paula Wolfert**.

HARRY'S BAR, 2020 Fillmore St, CA 94115 ☎ (415) 921 1000
Vibrant bar run by Harry Denton (rather than Cipriani) with live jazz and occasional rock 'n' roll bands. Kitted out in mahogany, with mirrors, and an antique bar shipped in. *"The latest yuppie and singles' bar, with great music and simple, good food"* – **Jeremiah Tower**.

SWAN OYSTER DEPOT, 1517 Polk St, CA 94109 ☎ (415) 673 1101
"Very small, but wonderful for

oysters and crab" – **Jeremiah Tower**. Shrimps, clam chowder and smoked salmon too from this seafood bar, running since 1912.

TOSCA CAFE, 242 Columbus Ave, CA 94133 ☎ (415) 986 9651
"Great after-dinner scene, involving famous film and music people. Great for everyone – old and new San Francisco" – **Jeremiah Tower**.

RESTAURANTS

BUTLER'S, 625 Redwood Highway, Mill Valley, CA 94941 ☎ (415) 383 1900
Lively new home to Square One's former chef, Heidi Insalata Krahling. Her own delectable brand of southwestern food – a mix of Californian, Italian, Mexican and Indian cuisines.

🐔 **CAMPTON PLACE, Campton Place Hotel, 340 Stockton St, CA 94108 ☎ (415) 781 5155**
Utterly tasteful hotel restaurant with first-class fresh, modern Californian cuisine. For a while it has been *"unquestionably the best*

COCKTAIL CABINET

CARIBBEAN COCKTAIL *"My favourite cocktail when in the Caribbean: cut a fresh coconut in half and remove most of the juices. Score the flesh (secret of the magic cocktail maker), add a measure of brown, powerful Barbados rum and one of the lightest most sophisticated white rum, mix in a dash of Cointreau, the juice of a lime, an orange, pineapple and grapefruit, and cane syrup to sweeten. 2 straws and a bit of sunshine – you can't beat it!"* – **Raymond Blanc**.
DRY MARTINI *"The best I ever had was at the bar at Commander's Palace, New Orleans"* – **Elise Pascoe**.
ETIENNE A good measure of Cognac Courvoisier in a long glass, topped with fresh orange juice and a dash of fresh grapefruit juice.
RAMOS GIN FIZZ *"The best come from Perry's, San Francisco. It's a very West Coast brunch-time drink, made with egg white, cream, gin, lemon and orange-flower water"* – **Bob Payton**.
MARGARITA *"The best in New York, on balance of ingredients, comes from the Gotham Bar & Grill [see New York]: really fresh lime and a great glass"* – **Gael Greene**.

restaurant in San Francisco" –
Lord Lichfield, though some
San Fran foodies are defecting
to Silks or the Portman Hotel.
Paula Wolfert and **Geoffrey
Roberts** still approve.

**ELITE CAFE, 2049 Fillmore
St, CA 94115 ☎ (415) 346 8668**
*"Delicious Cajun cuisine; their
creole gumbo is an incredible
meal in itself, and the bread
pudding with Bourbon sauce is
the best this side of Dixie.
White-coated waiters scurry
around long tables"* – **Beverley
Zbitnoff.**

**L'ETOILE, Huntington
Hotel, California St, Nob
Hill, CA 94108
☎ (415) 771 1529**
A refined pre-opera meeting-
place, and where music lovers
of a different sort go to hear
pianist Peter Mintum. *"A
restaurant with class and
charm, the best for classic
French food"* – **Jeremiah
Tower.** *"A dish I like there is
chicken forestienne – as good
as any I've had in the world"* –
Robert Mondavi.

**FLEUR DE LYS, 777 Sutter
St, CA 94109 ☎ (415) 673 7779**
One of San F's few proper,
classic French restaurants,
totally revitalized under its
new and brilliant chef, Hubert
Keller (late of Sutter 500). *"The
best French food in San
Francisco"* – **Jeremiah Tower**.
Diners bask under red silk-
screened tenting.

**FOURNOU'S OVENS,
Stanford Court Hotel, 905
California St, CA 94108
☎ (415) 989 1910**
A charming place where the
huge provençal-tiled ovens do
their magic. Recommended by
Barbara Kafka. *"A lovely
French country restaurant"* –
Anne Willan.

**THE MANDARIN,
Ghirardelli Square, 900
N Point St, CA 94109
☎ (415) 673 8812**
Sichuan and Hunan cuisine.
Owner Madame Chiang has
peppered the place with her
antiques. **Robert Mondavi**
savours specialities such as
smoked tea duck.

**PORTMAN HOTEL, 500 Post
St, CA 94108 ☎ (415) 771 8600**
*"Chef Fred Halpert, formerly
at Restaurant 101, is now
blossoming at the Portman. It
is the only hotel dining room of
the open-to-the-lobby variety
that works. Very comfortable;
often excellent food"* –
Jeremiah Tower.

🐟 **SILKS, Mandarin Oriental
Hotel, 222 Sansome St,
CA 94104 ☎ (415) 885 0999**
Superlative French restaurant
that's wowing international
foodies. Impeccable, typically
Mandarin, quality of service.
Votes from **Jeremiah Tower**
and **Lord Lichfield.**

🐟 **SQUARE ONE, 190 Pacific
St, CA 94111 ☎ (415) 788 1110**
Lofty, spacious restaurant for
eclectic/Mediterranean cuisine.
*"Real gutsy American food.
They've got the freshness of all
the Californian ingredients;
they take the best from other
parts of the world and give
them the West Coast thrill"* –
Paula Wolfert. *"Very good"* –
**Geoffrey Roberts. Serena
Sutcliffe** is impressed – not
least by the wine list.

🐟 **STARS, 150 Redwood St,
CA 94102 ☎ (415) 861 7827**
Jeremiah Tower's star success
story is one of the chief
exponents of New American
cuisine (or, as he coins it,
*"American brasserie market-
place cooking"*). He has led
sharks and lambs alike to the
mesquite grill, he's combined
oysters with spiced lamb
sausage, and fried black bean
cake with chillies and sour
cream. The bar is *the* watering-
hole in town. *"One of the most
convivial, cheerful and
comfortable restaurants I have
encountered for a long time"* –
Seymour Britchky. *"I
absolutely love it. Terrific.
Marvellous"* – **Leo Schofield**.
*"Great. I've had wonderful
nibbles there"* – **Clare
Ferguson.** *"Excellent grilled
food"* – **Marcella Hazan**. Only
one voice of dissent: *"I can't
understand all the fuss. I find
it really average. It serves
hamburgers and that's what
everyone eats there"* – **Don
Hewitson.**

**TAXI, 374 11th St, CA 94103
☎ (415) 558 8294**
Arty-trendy warehouse-
restaurant in SoMa, San F's
answer to SoHo. Fresh, grilled
Californian cooking rounded off
with sticky puds. **Jeremiah
Tower** thinks it has *"the best
champagne bar in town".*

**TRADER VIC'S, 20 Cosmo
Place, CA 94109
☎ (415) 775 6300**
The original. The most eclectic
menu in the world, with dishes
from the South Sea Islands,
Indonesia, Europe and
America, in a Polynesian
setting. *"You must be in the
Captain's Cabin. Very old-
guard crowd"* – **Jeremiah
Tower**. *"My favourite bar – I
went every day when I was
staying in SF"* – **Elise Pascoe.**
Jackie Collins is a Trader fan.

**ZUNI CAFE, 1658 Market St,
CA 94102 ☎ (415) 552 2522**
Zingy café-restaurant with
stark white décor, open kitchen
with brick oven and grill, and a
long copper bar. *"For relaxed
Italian/Californian-
southwestern dining, this is the
one. It's where the Stars staff
hang out"* – **Jeremiah Tower.**

SANTA FE

🐟 **COYOTE CAFE, 132 West
Water St, NM 87501
☎ (505) 983 1615**
Ace new place. *"Mark Miller's
long-anticipated restaurant has
thus far lived up to everyone's
expectations. It serves the most
interesting southwestern
cuisine in the country"* –
**Wolfgang Puck. Barbara
Kafka** and **Paula Wolfert** are
fans.

WASHINGTON,
DC

**FLUTES, 1025 Thomas
Jefferson St NW,
Georgetown, DC 20007
☎ (202) 333 7333**
A rather glamorous piano bar-
restaurant for champagne,
caviare and dancing in a
chandeliered room with marble

FOOD AND DRINK

columns. Also light American/ French dishes. *"It is wonderful late at night or after work"* – **Aniko Gaal.**

JEAN-LOUIS AT WATERGATE, Watergate Hotel, 2650 Virginia Ave, DC 20037 ☎ (202) 298 4488
The most elegant diner in the capital. Renowned for its wonderful, eponymous French chef, Jean-Louis Palladin, and its multi-course, prix-fixé meals (though they are fixed pretty high). *"One of the top chefs in the country. He comes from Armagnac, but he is introducing a lot of American-style nouvelle cuisine"* – **Terry Holmes. Aniko Gaal** thinks *"It's still the best in the classic French category"* and **Paula Wolfert** agrees: *"It's the best in DC; in fact he's the best chef in the country by far."*

THE JOCKEY CLUB, Ritz-Carlton Hotel, 2100 Massachusetts Ave NW, DC 20008 ☎ (202) 293 2100
More American nouvellerie. *"One of the best and most famous restaurants in the city. Tables are the perfect distance apart. You could see the Secretary of Defense or the Treasury or Nancy Reagan or Estée Lauder – it really has a spectacular clientele. Good food, too"* – **Aniko Gaal.**

OCCIDENTAL, 1475 Pennsylvania Ave NW, DC 20014 ☎ (202) 783 1475
The return of the great 19th-century restaurant where statesmen from Roosevelt to Churchill have dined, re-created with the same mahogany bar and vintage elevator car. It is once more the meeting place of literati and politicos – Nancy Reagan, Senator Baker, Ambassador Roosevelt – plus stars in town such as Baryshnikov. *"Understated elegance . . . the most wonderful grilled foie gras with wild mushrooms on a bed of warm seasonal greens with cherry vinegar sauce – it is to die for"* – **Aniko Gaal.**

PRIMI PIATTI, 2013 I St, DC 20016 ☎ (202) 223 3600
"The closest thing in

KING'S INN

THE INN AT LITTLE WASHINGTON, PO Box 300, Washington, VA 22747 ☎ (703) 675 3800
"The best restaurant I ever ate in. Probably the best fun in the US as an inn and a restaurant. It's romantic, it only has 10 rooms, and the food is incredible – people drive for 3 hours to have dinner there. It's one of the great spots in the world, at the foothills of the Blue Ridge Mountains" – **Larry King.**

Washington to a good Italian trattoria. Fun and amusing" – **Aniko Gaal.**

TWENTY-ONE FEDERAL, 1736 L St NW, DC 20036 ☎ (202) 331 9771
A new source of haute cuisine that has **Aniko Gaal** in ecstasy: *"So divine. A very clever mixture of French and American. Swordfish carpaccio with wonderful fresh fennel and herbs; appetizers prepared in exotic ways; excellent seafood. It's so special – any gourmet should go."*

WILLARD ROOM, Willard Inter-Continental, 1401 Penn Ave NW, DC 20004 ☎ (202) 628 9100
Top-class restaurant in the hotel with the mostest. Cuisine is nouvelle Americaine with regional specialities. Fine wines from 39 wine-producing states in the USA as well as France and Italy. Knock back a Bloody Mary before dinner in the Round Robin bar – a masculine room with a round bar, where all the Washington journos meet after work.

AMERICAN WINE

CALIFORNIA

Although the great winemakers such as André Tchelistcheff got there first, it was Robert Mondavi who, in building his Napa Valley winery in 1966, uncorked the torrent, and for 15 years wine splashed and foamed in every corner of

California. The wineries that are still around today are producing better wines every year, as those in the know testify: *"I like California wines. They are the best-made wines in the world, for California has the world's best winemakers. It's very unlikely you'll get a bad California wine. The climate is perfect, and their wines combine the best of European techniques, yet maintain a consistency of style that is the envy of the Europeans. And their labelling is so informative. They put a back label on; everything you need to know is there"* – **Geoffrey Roberts.**
Styles have changed. The original idea was to make the Great American Wine, the one that had the most of everything. France was going to have to learn Californian. The power game is now over though: subtlety's the new buzz. The best California wines of today have acidity, complexity and an alcohol level that means you can still remember your name after a glass or two.

Napa Valley

"Napa Valley and Bordeaux are, in my estimation, the top wine-growing areas in the world, though our climatic conditions are definitely better than they are in Bordeaux. Once you get accustomed to tasting our wine and French wine, you'll appreciate both of them. I can't say that one is better than the other . . . they have very different characteristics. They are equally pleasing. Each and

every one is different" – **Robert Mondavi.**

ROBERT MONDAVI

The perennial high-profile house of Napa. *"He fits the description of genius better than anyone I know. His aim is to top quality on an industrial scale. Inspiration and perspiration have taken him there"* – **Hugh Johnson**. *"The best red wine? California and Bob Mondavi every time!"* – **Anne Willan**. His best wines are from the grape variety the Napa Valley is chiefly famous for: Cabernet Sauvignon. His RESERVE wine is *"a gentle Titan you can drink with relish but would do well to keep for 20 years"* – **Hugh Johnson**. The coup de grace is OPUS 1, a joint venture between Mondavi and Baron Philippe de Rothschild: the best cellars simply must have it. 1979 is the best quaff now. On the white side, **Lord Gowrie** thinks Mondavi's FUME BLANC *"a great wine".*

ANDRE TCHELISTCHEFF

Dean of Napa. *"The greatest winemaker that ever turned up in the Napa Valley. He's in his eighties and looks like a schoolboy. Worshipped in the area"* – **Hugh Johnson**. The GEORGES DE LATOUR PRIVATE RESERVE CABERNETS (Beaulieu vineyard) of the '50s and '60s are thought to be his masterpieces. **Jeremiah Tower** prizes the first – 1937 – above all. **Michael Broadbent** singles out the 1946 BEAULIEU PINOT NOIR as the best Californian version of this grape he's tasted.

JOE HEITZ

Heists accolades too. He buys his grapes from friends, and the ones Martha May sells him go to make the famous MARTHA'S VINEYARD CABERNET SAUVIGNON. The 1974 was California's epic Cabernet for **Michael Broadbent** and a wine **Hugh Johnson** describes as *"dense and gutsy, with spicy, cedary and gumtree flavours, unmistakably the Mouton of the Napa Valley, even at the teeth-staining state."*

Geoffrey Roberts's best wineries

When choosing a California wine, *"look for the maker's name and not the geography: if you go to any of these makers, you'll get a good wine"*:
ROBERT MONDAVI (for Fumé Blanc)
JOSEPH PHELPS (for Cabernet Sauvignon)
TREFETHEN (for Chardonnay)
RIDGE (for Zinfandel)
HEITZ (for Martha's Vineyard)

TREFETHEN
Earns rosettes from **Hugh Johnson** among others for *"beautifully long-lived, well-balanced Chardonnay, one of the best Rieslings in the Valley, and the best winery building, in the best old barn."*

Other wineries that are rarely caught napping on them Cabernet front are **CHAPPELLET** (*"staggering, immortal Cabernet"* – **Hugh Johnson**; Bernard Portet's **CLOS DU VAL** (Bernard was brought up at Lafite, where his father was manager): **FREEMARK ABBEY** and **STAG'S LEAP** (*"certainly one of my favourites"* – **Serena Sutcliffe**).

Santa Clara

A small but important wine-producing area.

RIDGE

Comes way out on top. *"We are really trying to make the finest wine not just in California but in the world,"* Paul Draper has said, and his MONTEBELLO

California sparkle

Serena Sutcliffe bubbles: *"The most exciting movement at the moment in California is the French-American joint venture with the bubble. Domaine Chandon got there first. Then there was Piper-Sonoma, and now Mumm and Deutz. Autumn '88 sees the long-awaited Roederer new baby. French know-how and grape varieties are certainly proving themselves in California soil, and the Americans are lapping them up."*
Geoffrey Roberts, meanwhile, thinks the SCHRAMSBERG BLANC DE BLANCS is California's *"finest sparkling wine – as good as, if not better than, most champagnes."* Others prefer looking through a glass of BLANC DE NOIRS darkly.

FOOD AND DRINK

> 66 *What's new in California is they are beginning to realize they can produce truly fine wines that are drinkable when young yet will also improve with age. Outstanding, civilized wines of balance and harmony, drinkable within 5 years of production rather than the usual 7 to 10 years earliest, and 15 to 20 at best* 99

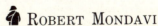 ROBERT MONDAVI

Grapie gadgetry

Elise Pascoe would be lost without her **champagne sealer**. *"I keep one in my luggage. I usually stay in the same hotels, and management get to know you, and when you're well known, the management send you champagne, and it's usually a full bottle . . ."* Both **Leo Cooper** and **Stanley Marcus** plump for a plain ol' **corkscrew** (though **SM** specifies the infallible **Screwpull**). **Stirling Moss** has just treated himself to a **Cruover machine**, like they have in wine bars, to keep an opened bottle of wine from going off.

Cabernet Sauvignon is what he is aiming to convince the world with. *"There's nothing like the Montebello"* – **Hugh Johnson**. Some have already been convinced: at a blind tasting of Latour and Montebello arranged for New York wine writers, no one spotted that the wines were from different wineries. Ridge's YORK CREEK Cabernet Sauvignon is nearly as good, and their red Zinfandels are the best in their own right (*"fine grape, marvellous wine,"* enthuses **Geoffrey Roberts**).

Sonoma Valley

SONOMA-CUTRER
The best winery, for Chardonnay only. *"It wangles unbelievable flavours from different vineyards: LES PIERRES is its Montrachet"* – **Hugh Johnson.**

CHATEAU ST JEAN
Owned by Suntory, still has a great name. White wine specialists whose Chardonnay is one of California's leaders. A fine winery to visit.

Of the rest, **JORDAN** is California's answer to Eden – *"beautiful even by Sonoma standards"* – **Hugh Johnson;** *"certainly one of the greatest Cabernet Sauvignons being made"* – **Serena Sutcliffe.** **IRON HORSE** is among the front runners in Sonoma for Cabernets, and for sparkling wine, thinks **Steven Spurrier**. **KALIN CELLARS**, in Marin County, *"produce fabulous wines, both reds and whites. They don't own vineyards; they buy grapes from Sonoma and Santa Barbara. They are particularly good at Pinot Noir, one of the most difficult wines to produce"* – **Serena Sutcliffe** (who adds: *"The other top Pinot Noir is CALERA").*

Rest of America

Wine fever is sweeping America, vines are replacing lonesome pines coast-to-coast: Texan Traminer and Michigan Merlot are realities. Vineyards and winemaking are now a mandatory part of The Great American Dream. Two areas – the Pacific North-West and New York State – have turned dream into drink on a commercial scale.

Dominus

After Opus 1 comes (from a different source) Dominus. This time, the French connection is Christian Moueix of Château Pétrus fame, in league with sisters Robin Lail and Marcia Smith of Napahook. The wine, released in 1988, prompts **Anthony Hanson** to predict: *"The most sought-after bottle of Napa Valley red wine in 1988 may well be Dominus, which is set to rival Opus I (but at a somewhat less-daunting opening price)."*

New York State

Winemaking is old-established in this area; the shock of the new here is the invasion of European grape varieties. GOLD SEAL VINEYARDS get the Lone Star award for persistent innovation: in particular, their Chardonnay and Riesling show the way.

Pacific North-West

The major forces are the states of Oregon and Washington (*"lovely whites"* – **Hugh Johnson**) and neighbouring Idaho (whose STE CHAPPELLE is *"a great Chardonnay"* – **HJ**). For **Anthony Hanson**, Oregon is of great importance as *"potentially the best source for Pinot Noir in the USA. David Lett's 1983 Pinot Noir from Eyrie Vineyards is the finest non-French Pinot I have tasted. Brian Croser of Australia and Robert Drouhin from Beaune are both reported to be investing in Oregon vineyards."*

Australia

Adelaide

Restaurants

THE BANGKOK, 217 Rundle St, SA 5000 ☎ (08) 223 5406
Foodies clamour to get a table at the hottest Thai restaurant in town. Book way in advance for a spice of the action.

THE BRIDGEWATER MILL, Mount Barker Rd, Bridgewater, SA 5155 ☎ (08) 339 4227
Owned by Brian Croser, Petaluma winemaker extraordinaire. The building, a revamped flour mill, is not as romantic as it sounds (pre-fab cement walls), but the food is exquisite and inventive. Catherine Kerry does raw tuna with tiny potato-and-chive

cakes and sour cream, mallard duck pie with Madeira glaze, kangaroo fillet with anchovy butter (kangaroo is available only in South Australia and Tasmania). And, of course, Petaluma wines.

🦘 **CHLOES, 36 College Rd, Kent Town, SA 5067**
☎ **(08) 422574**
Based in an old house, run by well-known restaurateur Nick Papazahariakis. He bones his own pheasant, quail and chicken and makes a marvellous abalone mousseline. Good crustacean creations too. Impressive, trendy, with masterly presentation.

DA LIBERO, 69 Fullerton Rd, Kent Town, SA 5067
☎ **(08) 310292**
The best Italian in Adelaide, based in a renovated cottage with courtyard for al fresco feasting. Especially good for seafood and pig-out puds.

DYNASTY, 26 Gouger St, SA 5000 ☎ **(08) 211 7036**
Luxurious, no; good food, *absolutely*. This is the best Chinese in town, with yummy yum cha (dim sum) on Sun.

🦘 **GLO-BO'S, 125 Gillies St, SA 5000** ☎ **(08) 223 6271**
The most 'in' restaurant in town. The menu hops from kangaroo to more trad meats wrapped up in inventive ways. Mainly modern Frenchified dishes. Excellent service.

JASMINE, 31 Hindmarsh Square, SA 5000
☎ **(08) 223 7837**
Some like it hot ... if you do, speed along to this brilliant Indian restaurant run by the Singhs, who grind up their own spices. Trendy, Westernized atmosphere.

MISTRESS AUGUSTINE'S, 145 O'Connell St, N Adelaide, SA 5006 ☎ **(08) 267 4479**
One of the best restaurants in Adelaide. Decorative dishes; smart, subtle surroundings.

🦘 **NEDIZ TU, 170 Hutt St, SA 5000** ☎ **(08) 223 2618**
Kate Sparrow and chef Le Tu Thai (both late of The Magic Flute) took over the old Neddy's (where Cheong Liew was chef) earlier this year. The cuisine continues in the Oriental-Occidental-antipodean vein, and you can still feast on kangaroo. Charming surroundings; lively crowd.

REST OF SA

THE BARN, Main Rd, McLarenvale, SA 5171
☎ **(08) 323 8618**
This restaurant, based in a 140-year-old former horse-changing station, is some 25 miles out of Adelaide in a premier wine-producing area. You choose your own wine (from 300 mostly, but not exclusively, local kinds). Casual dining at wooden tables; in summer you can sit in the grapevine-filled courtyard. *"The best place to eat among the vineyards. Very simple. It's a must if you want to see something of the wine-growing areas"* – **Don Hewitson.**

BRISBANE
RESTAURANTS

FOUNTAIN ROOM, Queensland Cultural Centre, South Bank, Qld 4000
☎ **(07) 840 7111**
An excellent riverside restaurant built on 3 levels within this modern cultural complex. Menus make use of the best local produce – mud crabs, fish, tropical fruits and nuts. Fine city views.

🕵️ **Buzzzzzzzzz** A brill deli/**fromagerie** is **The Village Delicatessen** in St Lucia (the university suburb of Brisbane) ☎ (07) 371 1023, run by John MacDonald, who stocks *"all the farmhouse cheeses Australia is now making and can be justifiably proud of"* – **Elise Pascoe** 🦘 . . . . . . the most delicious **tropical fruit, juice and ice cream** come from **Donna Toussaint's Fruit Factory** (shops in the marinas of Port Douglas and Surfers Paradise): *"They use wonderful old pulping machines to make ice cream from jackfruit, soursop, black persimmon, star apple, sugar cane and other exotic fruits"* – **Dorian Wild** 🦘 . . . . . . Best find in the far north of Qld is **High Falls Fruit Farm**, Mossman ☎ (070) 988148, which grows 80 different types of **tropical fruit**: *"You can see at least 11 types of banana. The restaurant is just a canopied area above a fresh-water stream, which acts as natural air-conditioning. They have some of the best grilled Barramundi, yummy papaya scones and fresh lime juice"* – **Dorian Wild** 🦘 . . . . . . Speaking of which, **limes are it**: *"any kind of lime pudding, like a lime bread and butter custard. We're into tropical fruits in a big way – fresh lychees, hairy mangostines and rambutin. And* **puddings***, as against desserts, are in, in, in"* – **Elise Pascoe** 🦘 . . . . . . on the loose in **Noosa**? For seafood, dine at **Palmer's**, 10 Hastings St ☎ (071) 473237, run by the sister of fashion designer Adele Palmer.

★ ★ ★ ★ ★ ★ ★ ★ ★ ★ ★ ★ ★ ★ ★ ★ ★ ★ ★ ★

FOOD AND DRINK

🍴 **KELVIN HOUSE, 252 Kelvin Grove Rd, Kelvin Grove, Qld 4059 ☎ (07) 356 8605**
The best restaurant in Brisbane. Tracey Christensen produces food with the distinctive flavour of Queensland – fish, seafood and tropical fruits are married in dishes like chicken breast filled with crabmeat and mango. **Elise Pascoe** dreams of the dessert, 'triple silk' – layers of dark, milk and white chocolate bavarois with a special coulis.

MICHAEL'S RESTAURANT, 164 Queen St, Qld 4000 ☎ (07) 229 4911
"A very elegant restaurant with one of the best wine lists in Australia" – **Elise Pascoe.**

RAGS, 25 Caxton St, Petrie Terrace, Qld 4000 ☎ (07) 369 6794
Charmingly set in twin terraced houses. French cuisine and a fine wine list please the **Len Evans** palate. *"Traditional Queensland interior, rather formal; very good reputation"* – **Anne Lewin.**

RUMPOLES, Cnr of North Quay and Turbot Sts, Qld 4000 ☎ (07) 229 5922
Newish restaurant with mainly starters and no full-size main courses on its adventurous, ever-changing menu (try croc-meat with wasabi cream sauce). *"Really good food and a nice atmosphere – very light breezy, décor. You eat lots of small things"* – **Anne Lewin.**

CANBERRA
RESTAURANTS

CHARLIE'S, Bunder St, ACT 2600 ☎ (062) 488338
Nouvelle-style epicure in an unusually dark setting. Interesting soups and simple dishes, all beautfully done.

FRINGE BENEFITS BRASSERIE, 54 Marcus Clarke St, ACT 2600 ☎ (062) 474042
The most fashionable hang-out in town – lots of politicians,

🍴 *Australia's Best* 🍴

RESTAURANTS

1 **STEPHANIE'S,** Melbourne

2 **BEROWRA WATERS INN,** Berowra Waters

3 **CLAUDE'S,** Sydney

4 **FANNY'S,** Melbourne

5 **KABLE'S,** Sydney

6 **PEGRUM'S,** Sydney

7 **OASIS SEROS,** Sydney

8 **LE TRIANON,** Sydney

9 **KELVIN HOUSE,** Brisbane

10 **THE LAST AUSSIE FISHCAF,** Melbourne

🍴   🍴

including the very Minister for Finance that taxed expense-account lunching. Modish food of the char-grilling, pasta and innovative salad variety.

HILL STATION RESTAURANT, Shepard St, Hume, ACT 2620 ☎ (062) 601393
Classical French cuisine cooked up by Steve Muscat for a typically political clientele. Dine in the new Garden Room.

MELBOURNE
CAFES AND BARS

SODA SISTERS, 382 Chapel St, Prahran, Vic 3181 ☎ (03) 241 4795
A '50s-style soda fountain with rollerskating waiters and waitresses, crooning Andrews Sisters and mountainous ices.

STARDUST CAFE, 97 Brighton Rd, Elwood, Vic 3184 ☎ (03) 531 2926
A '30s café with milkshakes to shake all others to their knees – chocker with cherries, chunks of chocolate and ice cream.

RESTAURANTS

The Hyatt on Collins has a trendy restaurant and glam lounge bar (see Travel).

CAFE LATIN, 55 Lonsdale St, Vic 3000 ☎ (03) 662 1985
Smart hang-out for modern Italian cuisine from Bill and Cheryl Marchetti and excellent wines.

CAFE MAXIMUS, 64 Acland St, St Kilda, Vic 3182 ☎ (03) 534 9245
Very fashionable brasserie-style Italian eatery under the same ownership as Café Latin. Trendoids of Melbourne unite.

CHAMPAGNE CHARLIE'S, 422 Toorak Rd, Toorak, Vic 3142 ☎ (03) 241 5936
Run by Francophile New Zealander Iain Hewitson, whose cuisine veers towards the Californian. *"It's like a permanent floating cocktail party with loads of reasonably priced champagnes, innovative food, an intriguing mixture of nouvelle French and tandoori. It's owned by my brother! It's still going like crazy"* – **Don Hewitson.**

CLICHY, 9 Peel St, Collingwood, Vic 3066 ☎ (03) 417 6700
Chef Hans-Verner Hartkopf offers a superb traditional French menu with a modern approach. *"A tiny little place, very good"* – **Max Lake.**

🍴 **FANNY'S, 243 Lonsdale St, Vic 3000 ☎ (03) 663 3017**
Internationally renowned, part of the Staley stable (along with Glo-Glo's and Chez Oz), and one of the best-loved restaurants in the country. *"Small and cosy, and the food is just out of this world. The best food I've ever eaten in my whole life"* – **David Hicks.** Upstairs is rather chic and smart, downstairs is a bistro with an open kitchen serving cheaper food. Lauren Bacall and Marlene Dietrich and **Len Evans** have eaten here.

FLORENTINO'S, 80 Bourke St, City, Vic 3000 ☎ (03) 662 1811

The most proper restaurant in town, with the best, old-fashioned service. Reminiscent of the dining room of a gentlemen's club – wood panelling and ramrod – stiff linen tablecloths. Excellent, traditional Italian-cum-French cuisine.

🏮 **FLOWER DRUM, 103 Little Bourke St, Vic 3000**
☎ **(03) 663 2531**
One of the best Chinese restaurants in Australia. **Barry Humphries** goes along with that: *"Awfully good. Very fresh ingredients. They do Australian fish very well."* Spacious, upmarket, expensive. **Len Evans** finds it sweet, never sour. The **New Flower Drum** in Market Lane is good, but people in the know prefer the original for atmosphere and intimacy.

GLO GLO'S, 3 Carters Ave, Toorak, Vic 3142
☎ **(03) 241 2615**
Glamorous, formal, expensive, a dressy affair (if a little passé) for very special occasions. Modern French cuisine.

HAGGER'S, 31 Russell St, Vic 3000 ☎ **(03) 639944**
Elegant and special. Habituated by rag traders, fashionable sorts and foodies, who flock to sample fine fish and seafood, and the best chocolate soufflés in town. Owner-chef Dennis Hagger and his wife Cheryl are professional but fun and zany.

KENZAN, Lower Ground Floor, Collins Place, 45 Collins St, Vic 3000
☎ **(03) 654 8933**
A Japanese restaurant beneath the Regent Hotel, with food you'd commit harakiri for.

🏮 **THE LAST AUSSIE FISHCAF, 256 Park St, S Melbourne, Vic 3205**
☎ **(03) 699 1942**
Probably the best restaurant to open last year, by a team that includes Iain Hewitson of Champagne Charlie's. According to Iain's brother, **Don Hewitson**, it's *"anything but a fish caff. It's all '50s – the menu is really good."* Milk-bar décor complete with lino floor,

chrome-edged tables, loud jukebox. Stuffed to the gills with ad and film types. Fish dishes show the influence of creole and Oriental cuisines – or simply of home. Blackened fish fillets, spicy Thai fish cakes, boudin of char-grilled seafoods, Tasmanian Pacific and Sydney Rock oysters, tempura of prawns, Tasmanian smoked salmon, caviare trio, and good ol' fish and chips. The best part of the evening is when co-owner John Flower mimes to '60s hits, leaping from bar stool to bar stool.

LYNCH'S, 133 Domain Rd, S Yarra, Vic 3141
☎ **(03) 266 5627**
Something of an institution. Owner Paul Lynch sets a distinctive style – an air of Parisian Bohemia coupled with the feeling that you are a guest as much as a customer. Original, French-based dishes. Terrace overlooking the Royal Botanic Gardens. Private dining room too.

MASK OF CHINA, 115-117 Little Bourke St, Vic 3000
☎ **(03) 662 2116**
A newcomer to Chinatown, with modern, cool grey décor and finely balanced Chiu Chow cuisine (close to Cantonese). Hot on seafood; BYO.

🏮 **MIETTA'S, 7 Alfred Place, Vic 3000** ☎ **(03) 654 2366**
One of Melbourne's best restaurants, in a grand, century-old setting with plenty of waiters hovering. Elegant seasonal epicure – warm winter salad with quail breasts, tart of King Island crab and scallops. Occasional guest chefs. Renowned for its fabulous, rare wines. The superlative cheeseboard includes Aussie cheeses. It is very much to **Len Evans's** taste, and **Robert Burton's**: *"I adore it. Everyone there is extremly well mannered, it's like a great big Victorian drawing room."* Mietta also holds a wonderful, refined New Year's Eve bash.

PICKWICK'S ON TOORAK, 176 Toorak Rd, S Yarra, Vic 3141 ☎ **(03) 240 0099**
Trendy new place to be seen,

full of Toorak cowboys (city slickers in the guise of rural grandees). Done up in chrome and black, it serves nouvellish food and great cocktails.

PIERONI'S, 172 Toorak Rd, S Yarra, Vic 3141
☎ **(03) 241 7833**
Airy, echoey place, combining Italian railway station and old palazzo – lots of shiny black marble, walls with trompe-l'oeil faded frescoes. Row upon row of tables, seating the most fashionable types in town. Light Italian nosh. A favourite of **Lillian Frank.**

ROSATI, 95 Flinders Lane, Vic 3000 ☎ **(03) 654 7005**
Designed by Piero Gesualdi, who also did Pieroni's, this is another capacious trend-spot that seats hundreds. Lively, chic, lots of clatter. **Lillian Frank** loves it here.

SHARK FIN INN, 50 Little Bourke St, Vic 3000
☎ **(03) 662 2552**
Brill authentic Chinese restaurant, always packed, with the best yum cha (dim sum) in town.

🏮 **STEPHANIE'S, 405 Tooronga Rd, Hawthorn East, Vic 3123**
☎ **(03) 208944**
The Berowra Waters of Melbourne, or as **Ken Hom** puts it, *"the Chez Panisse of Australia"*, based in a beautifully restored Victorian mansion. **Len Evans** backs the accolades already showered upon Stephanie Alexander, one of the most innovative chefs in Australia. Her fixed-price menus are created as an entity with complementary dishes. Home-made bread and petits fours to yearn for. *"The most unusual menus in Australia. Stephanie Alexander really is the most extraordinary lady; she has a great Victorian house, but she herself is very ungrand and down-to-earth. Everything she does is a mix of Australasia. It all comes out in a wonderfully light, adventurous way"* – **Robert Carrier.** *"Really delicious food. Although it's very grand, the service is quite unpretentious"* – **Ken Hom.**

TANSY'S, 555 Nicholson St, N Carlton, Vic 3054
☎ (03) 380 5555
A Victorian terrace with iron fretting. Both setting and food are fresh and light. Cuisine veers towards the nouvelle – deliciously frail mousses, warm salads; duck, quail and hare.

TSINDOS BISTROT, 100 Bourke St, Vic 3000
☎ (03) 663 3076
A fashionable, noisy (but not too noisy) bistro with marvellous food. Stylish sausages and fantastic veal that appeals to **Barry Humphries**: "*A scrumptious brasserie.*"

VLADO'S, 61 Bridge Rd, Richmond, Vic 3121
☎ (03) 428 5833
For serious carnivors. Vlado Gregurek is "*an absolute meat fanatic to the nth degree. After the meal, you must discuss the steak you have just eaten with Vlado – it's very serious. He also makes the finest sausages in Australia*" – **Len Evans**. A further meaty vote from **Lord Lichfield.**

SHOPS

FLEISCHER'S, 586 Chapel St, S Yarra, Vic 3141
☎ (03) 241 9606
The best continental cake shop in Melbourne, lined with lusciously calorific delicacies.

HAIGH'S, 521 Toorak Rd, Toorak, Vic 3142
☎ (03) 241 8713
The best chocolates. A speciality is segments of orange, lemon or grapefruit dipped in chocolate.

LIX, 396 Chapel St, S Yarra, Vic 3141 ☎ (03) 241 8396
"*The best ice cream in the whole world*" – **Lillian Frank.**

MYER'S, 314 Bourke St, Vic 3000 ☎ (03) 66111
"*Probably the best food shop in Australia*" – **Max Lake**. Particularly for cheese...

SAM'S CHICKEN BAR, 1115 Malvern Rd, Toorak, Vic 3142
☎ (03) 201540
Smart take-away chicken joint:

"*The answer to every society woman's prayers. Wonderful spiced chicken, roast spuds and corn on the cob*" – **Lillian Frank.**

VICTORIA MARKET, Cnr of Elizabeth and Victoria Sts, Vic 3000 ☎ (03) 658 9800
An exotic open-air mélange of stalls and stallholders – Turkish, Greek, Italian, Chinese, Indian. Excellent for cheese and meat.

PERTH
RESTAURANTS

CORZINO'S, 483 Beaufort St, Highgate, WA 6000
☎ (09) 328 1770
One of the best Italian eateries in Perth. Cuisine from the north of Italy, using lots of game and poultry.

ESTABLISHMENT, 35a Hampden Rd, Nedlands, WA 6009 ☎ (09) 386 5508
Both the restaurant and the clientele are well established, but they're anything but stuffy. Constantly changing, inventive cuisine; home-smoked meats, delicious salads.

IRWIN RESTAURANT, Ansett International Hotel, 10 Irwin St, WA 6000
☎ (09) 325 0481
Haute French gastronomy in a small, soft pink dining room seating only 38. Delicious seafood dishes such as fresh crab, scrambled eggs and caviare in a sea urchin; interesting game.

JESSICA'S FINE SEAFOOD, Shop 1, Merlin Centre, 99 Adelaide Terrace, WA 6000
☎ (09) 325 2511
"*The best fish restaurant in Western Australia*" – **Lord Lichfield**; and one of the trendiest eateries in Perth with views over the Swan River. Grilled dhufish (unique to the west), shark, whole Western Rock lobster and chowder.

ORD STREET CAFE, 27 Ord St, W Perth, WA 6005
☎ (09) 321 6021

Light modern cuisine is served in the drawing rooms or on the verandah of this old house which trebles up as a cosy, romantic evening dinery, smart business lunchery, and a cool place for power or leisure breakfasts.

OYSTER BEDS, 26 Riverside Rd, E Fremantle, WA 6158
☎ (09) 339 1611
Based on the Swan River, this is a "*superb seafood restaurant*" – **Lord Lichfield**. Nautical décor – timbered fittings, ships' memorabilia.

REST OF WA

LEEUWIN ESTATE RESTAURANT, Leeuwin Estate, Witchcliffe, WA 6286
☎ (097) 576253
The best country restaurant in the west, on Denis Horgan's booming wine estate, half a day's drive south of Perth. Table tops are slabs of Karri tree from the estate. The glassed-in restaurant has a verandah and sloping lawns leading to acre upon acre of vines. Superb wine list, natch.

SYDNEY
CAFES AND BARS

BAR ROMA, 189 Hay St, NSW 2000 ☎ (02) 211 3909
Some of the best iced coffees in Sydney, made with ice cream.

CAPPUCCINO CITY, 12 Oxford St, Paddington, NSW 2021 ☎ (02) 334543
For the best cappuccino, natch, and also wonderful iced coffee.

COLUZZI BAR, 322 Victoria St, Darlinghurst, NSW 2011 ☎ (02) 357 5420
An ultra-fash café-society haunt that does "*the very best espresso in Sydney*" – **Jane Roarty**. Latecomers have to quaff on the pavement, it gets so packed.

DEAN'S, 7 Kellett St, Kings Cross, NSW 2011
☎ (02) 358 2174
This late-night café skims

trendies with stamina from local nightclubs. Best hot chocolates in town – tall, with a dollop of cream and a sprinkling of cinnamon. Open until 6am on Fri and Sat; 3.30am weekdays.

GELATO BAR, 140 Campbell Parade, Bondi Beach, NSW 2026 ☎ (02) 304033
"Excellent coffee, pastries out of this world and a menu not many people know about – middle-European dishes, the best osso buco in Sydney – and it's BYO" – **Max Lake**. See also Shops.

LAMROCK CAFE, 72 Campbell Parade, Bondi Beach, NSW 2026 ☎ (02) 306313
Very casual, as close to the beach as you can be. Great Bloody Marys. Trendies like Stuart Membery and the Double Bay Ferrari set come here for breakfast on Sunday – fabulous eggs benedict.

SEBEL TOWN HOUSE, 23 Elizabeth Bay Rd, Elizabeth Bay, NSW 2011 ☎ (02) 358 3244
"The best bar in the whole of Sydney. It's so small, and you see so many interesting people

there" – **Jane Roarty**. *"A voyeur's paradise"* – **Dorian Wild**. *"I love to go there. John mixes the best Bloody Marys in town"* – **Elise Pascoe.**

TROPICANA COFFEE LOUNGE, 110 Darlinghurst Rd, Kings Cross, NSW 2011 ☎ (02) 331 6486
"When my fashion friends are over from Paris, this is where they go" – **Anne Lewin.**

RESTAURANTS

BALKAN, 209 Oxford St, Darlinghurst, NSW 2010 ☎ (02) 357 4970; BALKAN II, 215 Oxford St ☎ (02) 331 7670
Simple, cheapie haunt for barbecued hunks of meat and sausages, delicious thick bean soup, and, at the Balkan II, brilliant seafood specials. *"We love the open-fire grilling"* – **Max Lake.**

BANGKOK, 234 Crown St, Darlinghurst, NSW 2010 ☎ (02)334804
The stylish, consistently good top Thai favourite of **Elise Pascoe** (*"We're mad about Thai food, nuts about it. This is very good"*), and **Lord**

Lichfield's best bargain diner: *"As good as any Thai restaurant outside Thailand; unpretentious and small."*

BARRENJOEY HOUSE, 1108 Barrenjoey Rd, Palm Beach, NSW 2108 ☎ (02) 919 4001
Delightful, bright and buzzy. Best on a summer's evening, dining under a white awning on a plant-filled terrace. Inventive dishes such as quail foie gras with eggplant terrine; scrummy puddings such as chocolate millefeuille with blackcurrant sauce. One of Bryan Brown and Rachel Ward's fave locals.

BAYSWATER BRASSERIE, 32 Bayswater Rd, Kings Cross, NSW 2011 ☎ (02) 357 2749
Fashionable, lively haunt for media-style clientele. *"The Langan's of Sydney"* – **Lord Lichfield**. Simple, subtle, consistently good food. *"Great, a lot of fun to be in"* – **Jane Roarty**. *"Very, very charming – marvellous seafood, and lovely to look at"* – **George Melly**. No bookings, just diners with clout.

BEPPI'S, Cnr Stanley and Yurong Sts, E Sydney, NSW 2000 ☎ (02) 360 4558
Brilliant Italian restaurant, run by Beppi Polese for over 30 years. Lauded by **Len Evans** and **Max Lake**: *"The food has reached new heights. It is creative, new in style, yet manages to appear traditional regional Italian. One of the best wine lists in Australia."*

BLUEWATER GRILL, 168 Ramsgate Ave, Bondi, NSW 2026 ☎ (02) 307810
The new ultra-trendy Neil Perry (formerly of Perry's) eatery-with-a-view. Modern fishy cuisine with Californian-style char-grilling plus hints of Asia. Perry smokes his own ocean trout and salmon from Tasmania. *"The best restaurant view and the most adventurous seafood by miles"* – **Lord Lichfield**. *"The view is great. It's a little noisy but the food makes up for it – Atlantic salmon, char-grilled tuna and salads that are so fresh"* – **Jane Roarty**. *"An outdoor terrace*

FOOD AND DRINK

🕵 **Buzzzzzzzzz** ... So successful is **The Last Aussie Fishcaf** in Melbourne that it has sprouted a **twin in Sydney**, at 24 Bayswater Rd, Kings Cross. Is *this* the last word in innovative fish and seafood cuisine? 🕵 ...... **East Garden Shopping Centre**, Pagewood ☎ (02) 344 6766 is the best for **ethnic food** according to **Robert Burton**: *"It's the mind-blower of shopping developments"* 🕵 ...... The restaurant at the **Cricketers' Arms**, 106 Fitzroy St, Surry Hills ☎ (02) 331 6869 will **bowl you over**: Paul Merrony is using his experience at 3-star Le Gavroche, London, to create marvellous munch 🕵 ...... **Buzz ingredients** in Oz have **turned Thai**: sniff out makrut lime leaves, fresh lemon grass, and a dozen different strains of chilli and ginger 🕵 ...... Cool down with **S-R Juice**, the best **OJ**, extracted by ex-pat Pom David Smith-Ryland and available from most swanky Eastern Suburbs delis. Gets the A-OK from **Elise Pascoe.**

★ ★

> 66 *Australian cuisine means taking the best of the season's produce – as fresh as the day – and employing it simply but beautifully, not disguising it, not tricking it up, letting the food speak for itself. If you have produce as stunning as ours, why spoil it?* 99

🐾 ELISE PASCOE

with lovely views. Good fish and seafood, but the acoustics don't allow for any peace; also you can't book . . ." – **Elise Pascoe.**

🐾 **CHEZ OZ, 23 Craigend St, Darlinghurst, NSW 2010** ☎ **(02) 332 4866**
Bright, breezy, noisy, flower-filled, with a garden, it's a hybrid out of Fanny's and Glo Glo's (see Melbourne) crossed with the much-admired Spago in LA. Char-grilled fresh fish, quail, vegetables and fancy pizzas. *"Easily the best restaurant in Sydney itself"* – **Lord Lichfield**. *"The most chic and atmospheric restaurant. It's expensive and the food is terrific. A good-looking crowd goes there"* – **Leo Schofield**. *"The food is delicate, intelligent. It's very stylish – I love the darling little courtyard"* – **Elise Pascoe**. *"Their royal reds [special Australian prawns] are something to fight over. They also serve the best whiting fillets"* – **Michael Parkinson.**
Lady Susan Renouf, Dire Straits, Neil Diamond and Burt Lancaster have joined the throng.

CHOY'S JIN JIANG, 2nd Fl, Queen Victoria Bldg, Cnr Market and George Sts, NSW 2000 ☎ **(02) 261 3388**
An unrivalled setting filled with Ming dynasty antiques. *"Stunning Sichuan food showing the trend away from Cantonese cooking"* – **Elise Pascoe**. *"Excellent"* – **Len Evans**. Yin yang prawns in two sauces, pine-nut whole fish and other spicy dishes.

CLAREVILLE KIOSK, 27 Delecta Ave, Clareville, NSW 2107 ☎ **(02) 918 2727**
Down-to-earth Aussie noshery with fab fresh-from-the-surf fish, superb salads – a daily changing no-frills menu. *"So

good that we want to keep it to ourselves"* – **Jane Roarty.**

🐾 **CLAUDE'S, 10 Oxford St, Woollahra, NSW 2025** ☎ **(02) 331 2325**
After the tragic death of his wife (and chef) Josephine, Damien Pignolet and his team have reopened this intimate unlicensed restaurant that has played to packed houses for so long. Former exemplary standards have been maintained and this remains in the top league of Australian restaurants. As **Elise Pascoe**, an ardent fan of Claude's, says: *"Serious food lovers have continued to support Claude's and now I think it is even better than ever."*

DARCY'S, 92 Hargrave St, Paddington, NSW 2021 ☎ **(02) 323706**
Terrifically popular Paddo haunt, rather English in feel. Traditional Italianate salads and meat dishes and a sea of media faces such as Rupert Murdoch, Sam Chisholm, Jana Wendt, Mike Gibson, and Tony Greig – it's the Channel 9 canteen. *"A classic"* – **Dorian Wild.**

DOYLE'S ON THE BEACH, 11 Marine Parade, Watsons Bay, NSW2030 ☎ **(02) 337 2007**
Visitors love to love it. The problem is, there's too many of them loving it at once: *"It's become a tourist trap"* – **Lord Lichfield**. However, for a fish 'n' chippy, it's beautifully placed in a grand old waterfront house with tables overlooking the sea, and serves massive platefuls of exotic fish – barramundi, red snapper, John Dory – uniformly battered. Mud crabs and seafood chowder too. **Dorian Wild, Michael Parkinson** and **Prue Leith** are Doyle's fans.

EDOSEI, 74 Clarence St, NSW 2000 ☎ **(02) 298746**
"I love sitting at the sushi bar. Japanese food is all about fresh fish and you get the freshest there. I love the simplicity of it" – **Jenny Kee**. Indeed, watching the sushi chefs do their magic with prawn, sea urchin, squid and so on is a delight. Tempura and teriyaki too. **Jane Roarty** approves.

HANAYA, 42 Kellett St, Kings Cross, NSW 2011 ☎ **(02) 356 4222**
Individual Japanese epicure, appleciated velly much by Edmund Capon of the Art Gallery of NSW and **Lord Lichfield**: *"I rate it very highly. When I went, my companion and I were the only 2 non-Japanese, which says a lot."* Stylish setting in a renovated Victorian terrace.

IMPERIAL PEKING HARBOURSIDE, 15 Circular Quay W, The Rocks, NSW 2000 ☎ **(02) 277073**
A grand Chinese affair, expensive and superb, as **Len Evans** and **Michael Parkinson** will vouch. *"The Australians have some of the best Chinese restaurants in the world. This is a very good one"* – **Julian Lloyd Webber.**

🐾 **KABLE'S, Regent of Sydney, 199 George St, NSW 2000** ☎ **(02) 238 0000**
Len Evans's *"best hotel restaurant in town"*, with all the typical panache of a Regent Hotel. Elise Pascoe's No 1: *"Serge Dansereau makes the best main course in Sydney: supremes of quail – little quail breasts on an apple rösti with juice of calvados – divine. Kable's has probably the best cellar in Sydney, terrific service, regularly changing menus, the best table settings. Afterwards you can buy a toothbrush from the concierge and off you go!"*

FOOD AND DRINK

MACLEAY STREET BISTRO, 73a Macleay St, Potts Point, NSW 2011
☎ (02) 358 4891
A newish trend-spot that's *"absolutely brilliant"* – **Jane Roarty**. At lunchtime, Mark Armstrong (also of Pegrum's) cooks up typical Australian char-grills and scrumptious seafood, with wicked puddings to follow. A different team takes over for dinner. Eye-level mirrors all round for spying eyecatchers.

MARIGOLD, 299 Sussex St, NSW 2000 ☎ (02) 264 6744
Excellent, highly popular Chinese restaurant in Sydney's compact Chinatown. *"The best dim sum. Authentic Chinese food"* – **Lord Lichfield.**

MARIO'S, 73 Stanley St, Darlinghurst, NSW 2010
☎ (02) 331 4945
Wonderful Italiano teeming with life. *"I always have fun here. You always see someone you know"* – **Susie Stenmark**. Showbiz, fashion, ad and media types – Carla Zampatti, Maggie Tabberer and June McCallum join the mêlée.

🍴 **OASIS SEROS, 495 Oxford St, Paddington, NSW 2021**
☎ (02) 333377
Seros stuff. Confusing, too: formerly Perry's (Neil Perry has gone to the Bluewater Grill), this is now run by Phillip Searle (late of Possums, Adelaide), who was recently voted Great Chef of Sydney. Individual eclectic French-Oriental cuisine. *"Outstanding food, lovingly prepared. Stunning roast duck with baby Chinese steamed ginger buns. He makes the 2 best ices I have ever tasted: a pineapple and liquorice chequerboard; and one of champagne, raspberry and amaretto biscuit sorbets. It's the prettiest thing you ever saw and when you eat it, you're absolutely in seventh heaven!"*
– **Elise Pascoe.**

🍴 **PEGRUM'S, 36 Gurner St, Paddington, NSW 2021**
☎ (02) 357 4776
One of the very best – confident, cosy, eclectic, expensive (no prices on the menu – always a danger sign). Mark Armstrong presides over the kitchen, creating modern French cuisine with Japanese influences. **Elise Pascoe** applauds the excellent wine list.

SOMIS JITTRA THAI RESTAURANT, 14 South Steyne St at Victoria Parade, Manly, NSW 2062
☎ (02) 977 7220
With a magnificent view of the Pacific, no wonder **Max Lake** is a fan (he inscribed the first edition of this book for them: 'your warmest admirer'). Thai food with seafood specialities.

LA STRADA, 95 Macleay St, Potts Point, NSW 2011
☎ (02) 358 1160
Run by the Italian Topp family; swish, busy, entertaining. As well as local celebs, Spandau Ballet, George Michael and Julian Lennon have eaten there. It's tops for **Bruce Oldfield** when he's in this part of the world. Lady Susan

Renouf and **Barry Humphries** like it too: *"A delicious restaurant. The steak Diane and pasta are very good."*

SUNTORY, 529 Kent St, NSW 2000 ☎ (02) 267 2900
The best Japanese restaurant in Australia, savoured by **Edmund Capon** and **Len Evans**. Exceptionally good kaiseki. *"I've had some fine, fine dinners there. Their lobster sashimi is stunning. It's in a sea garden. You couldn't have anything fresher"* – **Elise Pascoe.**

TAYLOR'S, 203-205 Albion St, Surry Hills, NSW 2010
☎ (02) 335100
Based in a pair of colonial houses with a pretty garden where you can eat, this is a classy Italian ristorante. *"The only restaurant I'd give any praise to in Sydney. It's been revamped and they've reorganized the gardens. It's what I call going to dinner"* – **Robert Burton.**

🕵️ **Buzzzzzzzzz** the **BEST** 🍴 ...... **Sunday brunch** is to be had at the **Cruising Yacht Club** at Darling Point (go with a member) 🍴 ...... **mineral water**, says **Elise Pascoe**, is **Huon Valley** natural sparkling mineral water from Tasmania 🍴 ...... **burgers** for a dollar apiece can be bitten into at **Betty's**, Hastings St, Noosa: *"Absolutely stunning quality, brilliant"* – **Elise Pascoe** 🍴 ...... **pies** still come from **Harry's Café de Wheels**. Sadly, Harry is no longer there, but the all-night café-van lives on at Cowper Wharf Rd, Woolloomooloo: *"A great pie store for cabbies. You meet all sorts of people there late at night – MPs, socialites, frock-makers – it's very couth"* – **Dorian Wild**. Former pie-poppers include Robert Mitchum, Marlene Dietrich and George Hamilton 🍴 ...... **afternoon tea** is at the old colonial mansion **Yester Grange**, Yester Rd, Wentworth Falls ☎ (047) 571110, in the Blue Mountains. Beautifully restored into an art gallery / museum / antique shop / restaurant. Order tea, then go for a wander; lovely gardens and views too. Appetite worked up, dive into scones fresh from the oven, heavy cream and home-made jam, home-made choccie cake. Heaven on a plate.

★ ★

FOOD AND DRINK

FOOD AND DRINK

LE TRIANON, 29 Challis Ave, Potts Point, NSW 2011 ☎ (02) 358 1353
Run by Peter (*"probably the best dessert chef in Australia"* – **Elise Pascoe**) and Beverley Doyle, formerly of Reflections (and nothing to do with the fishy Doyle's). They've revamped what was *"the prettiest dining room in Sydney"* – **EP**, though not to everyone's taste. Never mind, it's bright and airy, and the minute those divine Doyle dishes hit the tastebuds, you'll be sent into blind ecstasy. **Len Evans** raves: *"Excellent, one of the best in Sydney."*

U-THONG, 433 Miller St, Cammeray, NSW 2062 ☎ (02) 922 6087
Another contender for the best Thai food (if not best décor) in town, according to **Elise Pascoe**: *"They do a stunning whole-fish dish with chillies."*

SHOPS

THE CHEESE SHOP, 797 Military Rd, Mosman, NSW 2088 ☎ (02) 969 4469
Owned by Rick Newman. *"I get coffee and chocolates from Rick; also vegetable lasagne and a few pestos ... and I wouldn't go to anyone else for parmigiano"* – **Elise Pascoe**.

CYRIL'S DELICATESSEN, 183 Hay St, City, NSW 2000 ☎ (02) 211 0994
A delectable array of poultry, cold meats, preserves and European specialities. *"The finest imported produce and fresh goose livers for pâté de foie gras"* – **Elise Pascoe**.

DAVID JONES, Market St, NSW 2000 ☎ (02) 266 5544
"The finest upmarket supermarket in Australia. A good selection of teas" – **Elise Pascoe**. *"The best food hall in the world. Superb, with white tiles, brass, glass and little bars all round where you can eat, say, a dozen oysters"* – **Glynn Christian**.

EUROPA EPIC CURE, 17 Kellett St, Kings Cross, NSW 2011 ☎ (02) 358 6266

For Tasmanian smoked trout from the Tasmanian Smoke House, and smoked salmon.

GELATO BAR, see Cafés & Bars
The best almond croissants – light, nutty, irresistible – and a particularly good apfelstrudel.

GEORGE'S DELICATESSEN, 2 Hopetoun St, Paddington, NSW 2021 ☎ (02) 332 3395
"A back-street deli where I get paper-thin, sweet, super-fresh prosciutto" – **Elise Pascoe**.

INTERNATIONAL CHEESE & GOURMET, 114 Willoughby Rd, Crows Nest, NSW 2065 ☎ (02) 436 3250
"Fantastic King Island brie. It's run by a young Greek family who are so knowledgeable" – **Elise Pascoe**.

OTELLO, 787 Military Rd, Mosman, NSW 2088 ☎ (02) 969 5662
"When they moved from Cremorne, they increased their production threefold in 3 months. That says a lot" – **Elise Pascoe**. Millie Sherman makes the freshest, finest handmade chocolates in Australia. Don't miss the unveiling of the Easter chocs. She is also a fine pâtissière.

PARIS CAKE SHOP, 91 Bondi Rd, Bondi, NSW 2026 ☎ (02) 387 2496
Prize pâtisserie – glazed fruit tarts and various creamy delicacies; yummy croissants. "Their chocolate cake is just fantastic" – **Jane Roarty**.

PASSELLO, 27 Bronte Rd, Bondi Junction, NSW 2022 ☎ (02) 389 3304
The best home-made pasta in Sydney, savoured by **Leo Schofield**. Wonderful sauces, too, plus imported goodies.

LE PATISSIER, 121 Military Rd, Neutral Bay, NSW 2089 ☎ (02) 953 8550
Owned by a French couple and open 7 days a week. *"Head and shoulders above the rest. They don't make a huge range, but what they do make is stunning.*

Croissants on Sunday!" – **Elise Pascoe**.

SYDNEY FISH MARKETS, Gipps St, Pyrmont, NSW 2009 ☎ (02) 660 1611
For the best fish and seafood in Sydney. **Elise Pascoe**'s a No 1 fan. *"They deserve a special mention"* – **Max Lake**.

REST OF NSW
RESTAURANTS

BEROWRA WATERS INN, Berowra Waters, NSW 2082 ☎ (02) 456 1027
Known universally as one of Australia's greatest, it is also one of the highest-priced – about A\$70 a head excluding drinks (except for a welcoming dram of champagne). Inventive cuisine – variations-on-a-veal-sweetbread school – under the direction of Gay Bilson. *"I think it's everyone's favourite restaurant in Australia. The marvellous thing is one lands by plane or comes up this little inlet by boat, and there we have absolutely fantastic food. One dish I had was sea scallops practically not cooked at all, served in cream sauce with white tree fungus mushrooms. The crispness and Chinesey look of the tree fungus with this very simple scallop dish is typical of Gay Bilson's cooking"* – **Robert Carrier**. *"A brilliant menu with lovely contrasts"* – **Elise Pascoe**. 10 out of 10 from **Lord Lichfield**: *"So sparse, with hardly a picture on the wall, yet the food is spectacular. Absolutely the best." "International class ... really innovative Australian cooking"* – **Leo Schofield**. *"A magnificent restaurant – people fly there specially"* – **Len Evans**. *"An unparalleled achievement, but I'm exhausted when I get there"* – **Max Lake**.

CARRINGTON HOUSE, 130 Young St, Carrington, NSW 2294 ☎ (049) 613564
"Stunning food, really excellent, run by one of those partnerships that works: Barry Michaeljohn is the chef, Paul

Garman runs the front of house. A very sleek operation" – **Elise Pascoe.**

CASUARINA, Hermitage Rd, Pokolbin, NSW 2321
☎ (049) 987562
"A very fine restaurant in the Hunter Valley" – **Len Evans.** *"The food is light and very well prepared. Peter Meyer really understands what he's doing. You can enjoy a 4-course meal and go away feeling just contented"* – **Murray Tyrrell.**

CLEOPATRA, Cleopatra St, Blackheath, NSW 2785
☎ (047) 878456
The best restaurant in this neck of the mountains, for unpretentious French country food. *"A wonderful experience to sit in the garden having lunch"* – **Jenny Kee.** *"Owned by 2 gorgeous girls, Dani Chouet and Trish Hobbs. Dani is one of the finest cooks in the country. You are pampered and cooked for beautifully. A few rooms – you stay in big beds with lovely linen. It's wonderful"* – **Elise Pascoe.**

POKOLBIN CELLAR RESTAURANT, Hungerford Hill Wine Village, Broke Rd, Pokolbin, NSW 2321
☎ (049) 987584
"Without doubt the best restaurant in the Hunter. A lovely place with a really laid-back country atmosphere. It's like being in a big greenhouse, with fresh flowers. Food depends on what's in season – game pies in autumn, wonderful soufflés in winter, sitting around a roaring log fire" – **Elise Pascoe**.

TERRIGAL RETREAT, 8 Ocean View Drive, Terrigal, NSW 2260 ☎ (043) 842503
Simple little BYO restaurant with an innovative menu.

TASMANIA
RESTAURANTS

DEAR FRIENDS, 8 Brook St, Hobart, TAS 7000
☎ (002) 232646
Upmarket restaurant in a cleverly converted warehouse. French-influenced cuisine with local and European wines.

PROSPECT HOUSE, Richmond, TAS 7025
☎ (002) 622207
A Georgian colonial building in the country outside Hobart. The best game in Australia, hung in the cellars of the house in company with some very good local and imported wines.

SHOPS

KING ISLAND DAIRY PRODUCTS, North Rd, King Island, TAS 7256
☎ (004) 621348
Some of the best dairy products. *"Surprise Bay Cheddar, big wheels of Brie . . . exceptional quality. The best butter in Oz, both unsalted and salted; double cream so thick and luscious you can stand the spoon in it, and a proper crème fraîche . . ."* – **Elise Pascoe.**

TASMANIAN SMOKE HOUSE, RSD 860, Beloraine, TAS 7304 ☎ (003) 622539
For special Tassie smoked trout and other fish.

AUSTRALIAN WINE

Australian vineyards are peppered (grapeshot, of course) across the bottom of the continent. There are a few wine-growing areas in Western Australia (*"one of the best is Margaret River"* – **Anthony Hanson**) and Tasmania; but South Australia, New South Wales and Victoria pouch the kangaroo's share. Aussie connoisseurs know their grapes.

Cabernet Sauvignon

Bordeaux, with a heavy Australian accent. The best Cabernets have emerged since tiny wineries such as **IDYLL** and **MOUNT MARY,** near Melbourne, started producing *"beautifully delicate French-style Cabernets"* – **Hugh Johnson.**
 At Clare and Coonawarra, SA, **WYNN'S, ROUGE HOMME, PENFOLD'S, HILL-SMITH, BRAND'S LAIRA** and **WOLF BLASS** fight for the crown. Grapies give Brand's Laira the Golden Mouton award: Wolf, too, likes to be seen in Mouton's clothing.
 In the Hunter, the small barrels used by Max Lake for his **LAKES FOLLY** wines earn **Hugh Johnson's** approval (*"splendid"*). **Max Lake** thinks 1969, 1972, 1978, 1980, 1981 and 1985 his best vintages.

Chardonnay

The great white wonder. It's done for Australian wine what waltzing did for Matilda. The HUNTER VALLEY, New South Wales, is one of the finest producers of Chardonnay, as **Hugh Johnson** will vouch. Particularly good are **ROSEMOUNT, TYRRELL'S** and **LINDEMAN'S.** Many back Brian Croser at **PETALUMA,** SA. Meanwhile, the rest of the best's in the west. Chardonnay from the **LEEUWIN ESTATE,** Margaret River, WA, is one of **Serena Sutcliffe**'s 2 best Aussie wines (*"but it's terribly expensive"*). Denis Horgan, the brains (and wallet) behind Leeuwin, chose the site on Robert Mondavi's recommendation. *"Leeuwin Estate Chardonnays have been*

FOOD AND DRINK

> **❝** *The most exciting wines are from the New World. The Australians are not afraid to experiment as they are not so tied by tradition* **❞**

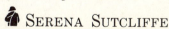 SERENA SUTCLIFFE

FOOD AND DRINK

GRAPIES' BEST WINERIES

The following wineries come out tops: **LINDEMAN**, Hunter Valley (*"the Lindeman wines are terrific"* – **Leo Schofield**). **PETALUMA**, South Australia (*"Outstanding whites. Stunning Chardonnays and Rieslings"* – **Serena Sutcliffe**). **TALTARNI**, Victoria (a fine pedigree – set up by Dominique Portet, brother of Bernard of Clos du Val, Napa, and son of André of Château Lafite. *"Dominique has the best of everything. Lovely soil in central Victoria, his French knowledge, daily contact with his brother in Napa. Taltarni makes the best rosé, in the French style but with different grapes"* – **Elise Pascoe**). **LEEUWIN ESTATE**, Western Australia (knock-out Chardonnays, think **Serena Sutcliffe** and **Hugh Johnson**. *"I consulted for them from 1970 to 1982 and they are making far superior wines today – richer, fuller, more elegant. Outstanding Chardonnay and Cabernet ... they're also some of the highest priced wines"* – **Robert Mondavi**.

sensational, with aromas, liveliness, richness and grip to outdo anything in Australia and most in California" – **Hugh Johnson**. TISDALL'S MOUNT HELEN is a winner with **Serena Sutcliffe**.

Muscat

Comes in two styles: light and aromatic, and thick and sticky. **Max Lake** eulogizes: *"I don't think there is a better drink than the Muscats from North Victoria which are equal to the best ports. MORRIS, BAILEY'S, CHAMBERS' ROSEWOOD, BROWN BROS and STANTON & KILLEEN are the best."* **Murray Tyrrell** agrees: *"Victoria certainly makes the greatest ports and Muscats comparable to anywhere in the world. BAILEY'S and BROWN BROS and CAMPBELLS all produce fabulous wines."* To which **Michael Broadbent** would add ALL SAINTS

VERY OLD RUTHERGLEN MUSCAT: on a par with Penfold's great GRANGE.

Sticky situation

"I'm a great believer in drinking the wines and eating the produce of the country you're in. Great Sauternes like Château d'Yquem are unbeatable, but an Australian sticky like Peter Lehmann's Riesling is nice and unctuous and goes well with pudding" – **Leo Schofield**. *"The best dessert wine is Petaluma Botrytis"* – **Elise Pascoe**.

Rhine Riesling

Its relatively undemanding flavour has always pleased punters. *"The best,"* says **Hugh Johnson**, *"are excitingly*

flowery, just off dry, satisfyingly acid and well worth several years' ageing." True Riesling does best when there's a nip in the air and where the grass stays green all summer: Tasmania's PIPER'S BROOK and MOORILLA are tipped and tippled by the best money. PETALUMA'S RHINE RIESLING (trucked home to the Adelaide Hills by Brian Croser) is 'outstanding', thinks **Serena Sutcliffe**.

Sparkling Oz

There is great snob value in 'French Champagne' (as against what **Dorian Wild** terms 'Aussie muck') but connoisseurs recognize the virtues of local sparklers. TALTARNI'S wines are recommended by **Max Lake** and **Len Evans**. The wines from YELLOWGLEN, Victoria (run by French-trained Dominique Landragin) are another **Lake** like. **Serena Sutcliffe** exclaims: *"The new rave sparkling wine is CROSER, from Petaluma/Bollinger. It beats the others into a cocked hat."*

Semillon

A white grape variety the French use for Sauternes and Graves. Australia has done something to it. No one quite knows what, but it works: *"A total triumph,"* says **Hugh Johnson**, *"light, dry, soft wine, Chablis-green when young, ageing superbly for up to 20 years."* The best area for these is the Hunter Valley: the catch is that the Semillon still sometimes gets called Riesling there (no one quite knows why). TYRRELL'S VAT 1 is the one to drown in. If you get pulled out, make for LINDEMAN'S BEN EAN. TISDALL makes a *"really intriguing Sauvignon Blanc/ Semillon blend"* – **Serena Sutcliffe**.

> **❝ The Australian white Chardonnays can be the best bargain in the world, they are absolutely brilliant ❞**

 AUBERON WAUGH

Shiraz (Hermitage)

The same red grapes that are used in the Rhône. The Rambo of the wine world: finds muscles in your mouth you never knew were there. Much admired by the best palates. PENFOLD'S GRANGE HERMITAGE is Australia's best of the best for **Hugh Johnson**: *"The one true first growth of the Southern Hemisphere"*, while **Auberon Waugh** has described it as *"Australia's equivalent of Château Latour"*. It is one of the two finest Australian wines **Michael Broadbent** has ever tasted (he remembers the 1955 vintage), while the best wine for **Dorian Wild** is: *"Grange Hermitage, any year you like. There's never been a bad year – just show me a bad year!"* Sparring partners include the **ROTHBURY ESTATE** (Hunter Valley), **TALTARNI** (Victoria) and **SEPPELT** (Barossa Valley).

Hair of the Dog

How to cure a hangover? *"Drink water. There is no cure. Resolve never to do it again,"* gabbles **Glynn Christian**. Then: *"I eat bacon and eggs, at lunchtime, never in the morning – then I'd be sicker than a dog. Speaking of which, hair of the dog is not stupid: the reason you have a hangover is that your body breaks down the complicated alcohol you drink (not poisonous) into simpler alcohols (poisonous). It's the expelling of them which takes so long. If you drink real alcohol again, you dilute them, and thus their effect. The body builds a tolerance. So the best hangover cure long-term is to drink every day."* **Keith Floyd** knocks back a bullshot or two: *"iced beef consommé with lots of vodka, tabasco, black pepper and lemon – it's brilliant."* **Elise Pascoe** takes the healthy approach: *"Freshly-squeezed juice – lots and lots of it! You've got to get that alcohol content down. A brisk walk, if summer, at sunrise, with lots of deep breathing and then a 2-minute swim. It will fix you every time."* *"A good meal"* gulps **Roy Ackerman**. *"Rest"* snoozes **Shakira Caine**. **Peter Ustinov** dismisses the question: *"I can't remember, thank God!"* Meanwhile, **Auberon Waugh** reveals smugly: *"Do you know, it's an amazing thing, I don't get hangovers. Touch wood."*

Austria

VIENNA

CAFES AND BARS

CAFE SPERL, Gumpendorfstrasse 11, A-1016 ☎ (01) 564158
"My favourite café – old marble tables, endless rows of newspapers, including The Times, *a billiard table, and it's full of artists and chess players . . . it's a great meeting place"* – **Cliff Michelmore.**

DEMEL, Kohlmarkt 14, A-1010 ☎ (01) 533 5516
Savour Sachertorte and Dobostorte in what was Emperor Franz Josef's favourite cake shop and tea salon. *"A pâtisserie frozen in the times of Franz Josef"* – **Egon Ronay**. *"Magnificent coffee house, full of pastries of every description"* – **Frank Bowling.**

HOTEL SACHER, Philharmonikerstrasse 4, A-1010 ☎ (01) 525575
Founded as a hotel-cum-pâtisserie in 1876, it is world-famous for its Sachertorte, a chocolate gâteau made from a special secret recipe. At Christmas, they send out up to 3,000 tortuously scrummy Sachertortes around the globe. See also Travel.

RESTAURANTS

ZU DEN DREI HUSAREN, Weihburggasse 4, A-1010 ☎ (01) 512 1092
One of the most internationally glamorous restaurants in Austria. Candlelight, antique furnishings, a piano tinkling away, and superb food.

Belgium

RESTAURANTS

🍴 COMME CHEZ SOI, 23 place Rouppe, 1000 Brussels ☎ (02) 512 2921
A 19th-century auberge with expensive but brilliantly orchestrated food. Pierre Wynants competes against Girardet for the title of best chef outside France. *"A great classic"* – **Bob Payton**. *"Without a doubt one of the best restaurants in the world. Sensational cooking"* – **Egon Ronay**. *"A very grand place with very grand food yet they manage to produce an atmosphere that's not intimidating. They greet you and are pleased to see you. It's a small, narrow dining room with a '30s interior. Madame is marvellous and keeps an eagle eye on things"* – **Roy Ackerman.**

SHOPS

GODIVA CHOCOLATIER, Grand Place, 1000 Brussels ☎ (02) 5112537
Inès de la Fressange's favourite chocolates.

MAISON LEONIDAS, 46 Blvd Anspach, 1000 Brussels ☎ (02) 720 5980
Reputed by globetrotting chocolate-lovers to be the best in the world.

FOOD AND DRINK

Britain

LONDON

MARKET

**BILLINGSGATE MARKET,
West India Docks, E14**
The fish market that supplies
the mongers. Fine if you're
nocturnal. *"I love it, I feel part
of it, I go there so often. I know
all the people. A tremendous
atmosphere. Everything's fresh
from the sea ... the best
oysters"* – **Anton Mosimann.**

RESTAURANTS

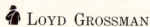 **ALASTAIR LITTLE, 49 Frith
St, W1 ☎ (01) 734 5183**
Where food's at – a small, spare
eatery where Alastair's much-
praised modern Anglo-eclectic
cuisine is served to an image-
conscious crowd. *"You could
not have had Alastair Little's
place (the most fantastic
restaurant) 5 years ago – you'd
have had 'Oh my dear, it's not
very comfortable'. But now, it's
frequented by media types who
can use it as their caff. It's so
good one's terrified it is going to
get spoilt"* – **Drew Smith.** *"The
best of the trendy restaurants.
It's book at birth at the
moment"* – **Robert Elms.**
Votes too from **Prue Leith,
Barbara Kafka** and **Stephen
Jones,** who is in a quandary:
*"My favourite would be
Alastair Little, but it's so noisy
and I'm deaf as a post – after
one drink I can't hear anyone
and I have to lip-read, which is
extremely tiring. Actually if
you write that they might do
something, I've told them, but
..."*

**L'ARLEQUIN, 123
Queenstown Rd, SW8
☎ (01) 622 0555**
Christian Delteil's fearsomely
French restaurant has a
charming little terraced-house
setting, terrific puddings –
some of the best home-made
sorbets in town. *"Top-quality
French food"* – **Steven
Spurrier. Serena Sutcliffe**
agrees.

**BAHN THAI, 21a Frith St,
W1 ☎ (01) 437 8504**
Raymond Blanc and **Drew
Smith** rate this the best Thai
restaurant in London. Philip
Harris spent many years in
Thailand and has a Thai wife.

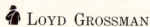 **BIBENDUM, Michelin
House, 81 Fulham Rd, SW3
☎ (01) 581 5817**
Simon Hopkinson departed
Hilaire to join Sir Terence
Conran in creating this
restaurant. It is the product
of caring restoration of the
Art Deco former Michelin
garage (M Bibendum is the
bubbly Michelin man), and
tuned-in design by Conran
himself. Through Bristol-blue
stained-glass windows (M
Bibendum with cigar and M
Bibendum on a bicycle) a
glorious dappled light falls on
lunchers. *"Seriously good – he
really is a talented cook"* –
Loyd Grossman. Ned Sherrin
is a Hopkinson fan. *"Superb
location, excellent chef – but
only time will tell ..."* – **Roy
Ackerman.** What will the
Michelin guide make of
Bibendum: will the 'family'
connection sway them?

**BLAKES HOTEL, 33 Roland
Gardens, SW7 ☎ (01) 370 6701**
Anouska Hempel's ritzy hotel
has an outstanding restaurant.
This is dining in exotica,
gorgeously black and mirrored,
with Oriental lacquer and
bamboo, and tables laid
alternately in black and white
with contrasting plates that
offset eclectic couture dishes
perfectly.

**BOMBAY BRASSERIE,
Bailey's Hotel, Courtfield
Close, Courtfield Rd, SW7
☎ (01) 370 4040**
The best Indian restaurant in
Britain. A slice of old colonial
life with ceiling fans and a
conservatory. *"My favourite*

*... always a good atmosphere,
good food"* – **Anton Mosimann.**
**Shakira Caine, Mark
McCormack** and **Madhur
Jaffrey** recommend it. *"The
food is excellent, the people are
nice and I don't care which
room I sit in"* – **Duggie Fields.**

**CAFE PELICAN, 45 St
Martin's Lane, W1
☎ (01) 379 0309**
Fine brasserie nosh in airy,
rather pretty, mottled peach
surroundings. A hit with **Prue
Leith** and **Joanna Lumley.**

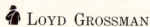 **LE CAPRICE, Arlington
House, Arlington St, SW1
☎ (01) 629 2239**
The most fashionable dinery in
town; glittering international
crew of film, fashion and media
stars. Dishes are of the light-
crisp-fresh kind, which appeals
to high-profile waistlines.
Bullshots and spritzers take
precedence over great
vintages. *"The people there are
so nice, which is the best asset
a restaurant can have"* –
Duggie Fields. *"There are
about 2 or 3 main courses
under £6 – it's remarkable. My
favourite dish is Caesar salad"*
– **Simon Hopkinson. Barry
Humphries** goes for the fish
cakes. **Harvey Goldsmith, Ned
Sherrin, Joanna Lumley** and
Jeffrey Archer go for all of it.
*"The most glamorous
restaurant in London. It
always feels like an event to go
to Le Caprice. You should go
there only once every 6 months
you should never become used
to it"* – **Stephen Jones.** *"I very
much enjoy the atmosphere"* –
George Melly. *"It
accomplishes everything pretty
well 90% of the time. The food
is always good, the service is
always good and the ambience
is always good. It's good for
slightly chic business lunches,
it's good for a romantic evening
for 2 and it's very good for*

> ❝ *In terms of dazzling technique,
> real love of food and innovation, it boils
> down to Alastair Little, La Tante Claire,
> Simply Nico and Bibendum* ❞
>
> LOYD GROSSMAN

LORD LICHFIELD'S BEST ETHNIC RESTAURANTS

Lord Lichfield, a keen connoisseur of ethnic restaurants around the globe, rounds up some of his London favourites: **AL HAMRA**, 31-33 Shepherd Market, W1 ☎ (01) 493 6934 (Lebanese; *"an absolutely wonderful place. They are very helpful and polite. There are something like 60 different starters, hot and cold, which are sensational"*). **JADE GARDEN**, 15 Wardour St, W1 ☎ (01) 439 7851 (*"unless you are Chinese, this is the best place for dim sum, because they actually understand what you're saying"*). **HIROKO OF KENSINGTON**, Kensington Hilton, 179 Holland Park, W11 ☎ (01) 603 5003 (*"affordable Japanese; very good sushi"*); also a favourite of **Michael Clark**. **HUNG TOA**, 54 Queensway, W2 ☎ (01) 727 6017 (*"the most unpretentious Chinese restaurant"*). **MALABAR**, 27 Uxbridge St, W8 ☎ (01) 727 8800 (*"a sweet, nice place. Anyone who is fond of Indian food I take there"*). **KOREAN HOUSE**, 10 Lancashire Court, W1 ☎ (01) 493 1340 (a grand, 3-floor affair with floodlit garden, and *"a great experience in Korean food"*). **TUI**, 19 Exhibition Rd, SW7 ☎ (01) 584 8359 (a chic but friendly, authentic little Thai restaurant).

immaculate. The restaurant and Grill serve both trad English and French cuisine. *"I love it. If I were going to spend £50 on dinner, I'd tend to go here or Le Gavroche because I'd be confident I'd get a good meal"* – **Drew Smith**. *"For a wonderful British meal the Connaught Grill is my favourite"* – **Jane Asher**. *"The best scrambled eggs and bacon – it's a wonderful place to have breakfast"* – **Ed Victor**.

THE DORCHESTER, Park Lane, W1 ☎ (01) 629 8888
Closed until 1990 for a £72 million facelift. How the Terrace Restaurant (French) and the Grill Room (English) will fare then, without the legendary Anton Mosimann (now at Mosimann's) is in the balance. If style and standards remain the same, the Dorchester will continue to be a great name in hotel dining.

L'ESCARGOT, 48 Greek St, W1 ☎ (01) 437 2679
The upstairs restaurant has long been a retreat for pleading-poor publishers, agents, filmy folk and other media types, though some regulars have defected to the Groucho Club. Downstairs is cheaper, relaxed and fashionable, with a nice brasserie menu. Appreciative habitués include grapies **Steven Spurrier** and **Auberon Waugh**. **Duggie Fields**, too, and **Ned Sherrin**: *"Like everybody else, I'm mad about Elena"* (the manageress).

FUNG SHING, 15 Lisle St, W1 ☎ (01) 437 1539
"Chef Wu Kwun started working near Canton as a young boy in 1948. His job was to carry water with a pole and 2 buckets from the river to the restaurant. His best dishes are stuffed almond chicken wings – quite delicious; chicken casserole with fermented clams; special abalone; lobster baked in prime stock (which is actually done in the wok) and casserole duck with plums" – **Yan-Kit So**.

celebratory gangs of 4" – **Loyd Grossman**.

CECCONI'S, 5a Burlington Gdns, W1 ☎ (01) 434 1509
One of the most authentic and expensive Italian restaurants in Britain (Harry's Bar takes the biscotti). Patronized largely by visiting Italian newspaper and publishing magnates, and American millionaires. Plus **Jeffrey Archer** plus **Robert Mondavi**: *"They make very good minestrone and very good pasta with truffles – it's outstanding."*

CHUEN CHENG KU, 17 Wardour St, W1 ☎ (01) 437 1398
On Sundays, 4 storeys-worth of mainly Chinese eaters tuck into some of the best dim sum in London. One of Chinese food-lover **Anton Mosimann**'s top 3.

CIBOURE, 21 Eccleston St, SW1 ☎ (01) 730 2505
French owners, English chef. The changing menu always includes some divine form of lamb and the cheeseboard is interestingly all-English. *"Very nice – it's quiet, it's*

attentive, it's French but not dismissive – you know sometimes the French can be very dismissive. A charming little restaurant"* – **George Melly**. *"It has a bit of a buzz"* – **Bruce Oldfield**.

♣ CLARKE'S, 124 Kensington Church Street, W8 ☎ (01) 221 9225
"An extraordinary place – Sally Clarke chooses the menu and it's like dining at home" – **Lord Lichfield**. This brilliant young chef, trained in Paris and California, takes a free-spirited approach towards cooking with the best market produce; she also bakes delicious herb and fruit breads. *"It's just great – there's a fixed menu, no choice, like going to a very special dinner party – absolutely brilliant"* – **Liz Smith**. *"One of the best, for her delightful cooking"* – **Robert Carrier**.

♣ THE CONNAUGHT, Carlos Place, W1 ☎ (01) 499 7070
The first great English hotel kitchen to be resurrected by a European – Michel Bourdin, whose style is classic and

♣ LE GAVROCHE, 43 Upper Brook St, W1 ☎ (01) 408 0881
"I honestly can't think of a

restaurant in this country that's more accomplished, more professional and less likely to fall down. The extent of Albert Roux's creative effort is unbelievable. Here, you do not have bad experiences – if you spill some ash on the tablecloth, whoomf, they change the tablecloth" – **Drew Smith**. Steep prices make you savour every precious mouthful, though the set lunch menu at £19.50 allows a few bargain swallows. "I think the Roux brothers are terribly good" – **Lord Montagu of Beaulieu**. But the Rouxs have sparked a foodie battle. Too much success and publicity? Those who boo hiss are Loyd Grossman (who dared omit it from his London's top 100 guide), Paul Levy, and **Frederic Raphael** ("3-star in a very, very poor constellation").

GAY HUSSAR, 2 Greek St, W1 ☎ (01) 437 0973

The owner of 35 years, 73-year-old pseudo-Hungarian mega-personality Victor Sassie, has sold up, but his devotees will keep on lunching as long as his spirit remains. A hotbed of Lefties and literati such as Michael Foot, Roy Hattersley and Lord Longford. "Far and away the best. It's a bit like the monarchy – it has to evolve, but I hope the atmosphere remains the same. I'd go here for a lively meal, surrounded by friends. (If I didn't like them I'd take them to the House of Lords. It has the worst food in London)" – **Lord Donoughue**. "Probably one of the best restaurants in London" – **Leo Cooper**. "Marvellous food" – **Ed Victor**. **Barry Humphries** loves it too.

GOLDEN CHOPSTICK, 1 Harrington Rd, SW7 ☎ (01) 584 0855

"One of the few female Chinese chefs, Yee-Kiu Choi. Her best dish is stuffed sea bass. I just marvel at the work it takes. Any damage to the skin and you've ruined it. I've had umpteen stuffed fish in my life but I've never had one so light and delicious. Her other specialities are soft-shell crabs and hand-torn chicken. You

DESIGNER DINING

In recent yuppie times, restaurateurs have been paying ever more attention to the design of their eateries. Reflecting the cold spirit of materialism, restaurants display minimalist monochrome chic. There's the black, white and chrome **Le Caprice** (designed ahead of the game by Eva Jiricna, who also fashioned Joseph's **Joe's Café**), and Julyan Wickham's grey and white constructivist **Kensington Place**. Tchaik Chassay is behind **192**, the **Groucho** and **Fred's** (see Social and Night Life) and the **Corney & Barrow** chain in the City. Rick Mather's cool **Zen**s with their running water and split levels are "wonderful, designed so that the customers are the décor" – **Drew Smith**. Rick also designed **Fifty-One Fifty-One**, the sparse Cajun eatery in Sloane Ave. The £2 million **Braganza** in Frith St is a lofty bi-level affair whose ceiling was painted by Ricardo Cinalli. And of course there's Sir Terence Conran's **Bibendum**. But state-of-the-art may soon be laid to rest – the newly impoverished yuppies profess a need for a warm, comforting environment rather than a stark, soulless space where champagne corks have ceased to pop.

must order these in advance" – **Yan-Kit So**. The POW and POWess have eaten here.

HARRY'S BAR, 26 South Audley St, W1 ☎ (01) 408 0844

Private dining club, owned jointly by Mark Birley and James Sherwood (Orient Express/Cipriani chief). Carefully designed à la Harry's in Venice, with all the hallmarks of Birley's taste, it has an idolatrous clientele of jetsetters. "My favourite. Lovely atmosphere and great, great food" – **Michael Grade**. "A restaurant must be an experience – the service must be very smooth, the waiters must be friendly but not too friendly and there must be a sense of busyness, energy. This works" – **Caroline Hunt**. "Unquestionably the best Italian food in London" – **Lord Lichfield**. "Good because of the staff – excellent service, and fun people go there" – **Robert Sangster**. A favourite of **Prue Leith**, **Michael Parkinson**, **Mark McCormack**, **Joan Burstein** and **Helen Gurley Brown**.

♠ HARVEY'S, 2 Bellevue Rd, Wandsworth, SW18 ☎ (01) 672 0114

"The new up-and-coming chef is young Marco Pierre White" – **Nico Ladenis**. An eccentric in the Nico mould (only much dishier), he worked his way through Le Gavroche, La Tante Claire and Le Manoir aux Quat' Saisons before setting up on his own. "He's had an absolute dream début and he's good. A lot of his menu is Best British Restaurants' Greatest Hits ... Harvey's is serious stuff" – **Drew Smith**. "Simply wonderful contemporary cuisine" – **Ned Sherrin**. But 'The Stallion' is known for being temperamental ... "Mad Marco! He works so hard and talks in such a crazy, passionate manner...! He's very young, enormously talented. He varies between amazingly good and just good" – **Alastair Little**. "One of the best natural cooks in the world ... but disorganized" – **Simon Hopkinson**. "Without doubt a very talented cook but he's too intelligent for the mass of his customers and cannot tolerate fools" – **Roy Ackerman**.

KALAMARAS, 76-78 Inverness Mews, W2 ☎ (01) 727 9122

"The best Greek restaurant –

> " *My favourite restaurants in London are Neal Street, Langan's, Gay Hussar and L'Escargot. All serve wonderful food, although sadly when I go there I'm always talking too much to really appreciate it. I like them because they all have impeccable manners* "

🕵 JILLY COOPER

for style of greeting. It's run by Stelios Platonos, who is amazing – his spirit's there even when he's not. He greets you with a warmth and sincerity and fusses over you. His all-girl staff have learnt his philosophy. It's taverna-style and to me typically Greek. Spit-roasted lamb with thyme, seafood wrapped in pastry, hot crab, calamari ... enlightened cooking, simple and fresh" – **Roy Ackerman**.

KENSINGTON PLACE, 201 Kensington Church St, W8
☎ (01) 727 3184
Coolly fashioned by architect Julyan Wickham, with Rowley Leigh (ex-Le Poulbot) heading the kitchen, this new glassily shop-fronted restaurant is one for people-watchers. Original, eclectic, highly seasoned dishes – salt cod soup, calf's liver with polenta and braised radicchio; exotic puddings such as baked tamarillo. **Alastair Little** is a Leigh admirer (and pal). **Roy Ackerman** ventures: *"Fashion can change, but wall-to-wall customers must be the proof of the pudding."*

LANGAN'S BRASSERIE, Stratton St, W1
☎ (01) 493 6437
Think of glitz and you think of Langan's, though the glamour is sometimes tarnished by a brassy sub-pop star set and, for novices, by the rumbustious proprietor Peter L. *A face is bound to be there; paparazzo Richard Young checks in most evenings for gossip-column fodder. Clock Mick Jagger, Jerry Hall, David Bowie, Bryan Ferry, **George Melly** or **Michael Parkinson**, tucking into his favourite starter – spinach soufflé with anchovy sauce. *"For its buzz, madness and craziness and for Peter*

Langan himself, one of my great friends"* – **Robert Carrier**.

LEITH'S, 92 Kensington Park Rd, W11 ☎ (01) 229 4481
Prue Leith's restaurant has been revamped and is *"even better than ever. I went there for dinner the other night and it was sensational"* – **Lord Lichfield**. Solid English/international fare including a gourmet vegetarian menu and an eye-popping hors d'oeuvre trolley.

LINDSAY HOUSE, 21 Romilly St, W1
☎ (01) 439 0450
In the style of a private house with an English menu. Private dining rooms, too. *"Smart, classy décor, chandeliers, silk curtains. It shows that Soho is becoming a gastronomic centre once again"* – **Richard Compton-Miller**.

MIYAMA, 38 Clarges St, W1
☎ (01) 499 2443; 17 Godliman St, EC4 ☎ (01) 489 1937
"The best Japanese in London, more interesting and accessible than Suntory. The City branch has a sushi bar and teppan-yaki bar" – **Drew Smith**. It's No 1 for financial whizzes.

MOSIMANN'S, 11b W Halkin St, SW1 ☎ (01) 235 9625
The place to watch: owner Anton Mosimann has left the Dorchester (after 12 years, during which time he was consistently voted one of the top chefs in Britain) and now presides over the kitchen here. He pioneered the low-fat cuisine naturelle. *"Anton Mosimann's food is very clean and wonderful, full of flavour, out of this world – very imaginative ... food that you can really eat all night"* – **Ken Hom**. Mosimann's, formerly a

---

BARGAIN BITES

ALBION PUB, 2 New Bridge St, EC4 ☎ (01) 353 8852: one of the best real meat bargains in London, accompanied by real beer. *"Not chic, but sells very good steak for about £5"* – **Drew Smith**. **UPPER STREET FISH SHOP**, 324 Upper St, N1 ☎ (01) 359 1401, probably the best fish 'n' chippy in London, run by chirpy Olga. Caviare starters; fresh, beautifully battered cod and plaice, fresh scallops, poached salmon; nursery puds to round off the evening (and the tum). Regulars bring their own wine and Hellman's mayonnaise. **NEW WORLD**, 1 Gerrard Place, W1 ☎ (01) 734 0677, for a good bargain Chinese nosh-up. *"The best dim sum"* – **Drew Smith**, while **WONG KEI**, 41-43 Wardour St, W1 ☎ (01) 437 3071, is best *"for everything else"* – **DS**. *"Great! So good for chips"* – **Robert Elms**. **POLLO**, 20 Old Compton St, W1 ☎ (01) 734 5917 is *"a little transport caff that gets its pasta from I Camisa, which is probably the best in London"* – **Drew Smith**. Dozens of permutations, from around £2. **GEALE'S FISH RESTAURANT**, 2 Farmer St, W8 ☎ (01) 727 7969 is another first-rate fish and chippery; good value, great wine.

FOOD AND DRINK

Scottish Presbyterian church, is a private dining club kitted out in country-house style.

ORSO, 27 Wellington St, WC2
☎ **(01) 240 5269**
Joe Allen's second string, a modern Italian eatery. *"Excellent quality of ingredients, wonderful mozzarella and prosciutto. Packed full and good after the theatre"* – **Prue Leith.**

PHOENICIA, 11-13 Abingdon Rd, W8
☎ **(01) 937 0120**
"The ethnic restaurant that seems the most satisfactory. It's Lebanese. People are becoming more and more interested in Middle-Eastern cookery and Lebanese along with Turkish is the highest expression of that. It's very

good and appears to be quite healthy, exotic enough to be interesting without keeping you awake all night" – **Loyd Grossman.** *"Spectacular"* – **Lord Lichfield.**

POONS, 4 Leicester St, W1
☎ **(01) 437 1528; 27 Lisle St, WC2** ☎ **(01) 437 4549**
Cheapie Chinese chain of varying grades. *"Wonderfully good. They broaden people's tastes in Chinese. I love Sichuan and you can have all that. For gritty authenticity go to the tiny original in Lisle Street"* – **Robert Elms.** *"Alastair [Little] and I used to meet every other Saturday for lunch at Leicester St. We'd always have fried squid with garlic, fried eel, noodle bean sprouts – it became a ritual"* – **Simon Hopkinson.**

SAN LORENZO, 22 Beauchamp Place, SW3
☎ **(01) 584 1074**
This glossy greenhousy Italian joint is a perennial trend-spot for the international fash. **Shakira Caine** and **Bruce Oldfield** love lunching there. So do the Duchess of York, Tina Turner, Jack Nicholson, **Marie Helvin**, Maggie Smith, Viscount Linley, Susannah Constantine, Rifat Ozbek and the Princess of Wales . . .

SANTINI, 29 Ebury St, SW1
☎ **(01) 730 4094**
Small, sublime, but astronomical. *"The best restaurant in London for Mr Santini himself, a fantastically agreeable patron who knows everything there is to know about Venetian food, and for its porcini and its polenta with game"* – **Robert Carrier. Lord Lichfield** and **Mark McCormack** recommend.

Buzzzzzzzzz The best **pie and mash shop** is known as **Manze's** in Chapel Market, Islington – *"It's the best preserved, all tiled with marble tables"* – **Robert Elms** . . . . . . Chefs to watch: **Brian Turner**, formerly of the Capital Hotel, now at **Turner's**, 87-89 Walton St, SW3 ☎ (01) 584 6711 (*"I think he will have a shot at the big time"* – **Barbara Kafka***; "a really good, interesting chef"* – **Prue Leith**); his successor at the Capital: **Philip Britten** (ex-Chez Nico) and **Nick Gill** (ex-Hambleton Hall), now at 190 Queen's Gate, SW7 . . . . . . the best **private dining room** is at the **Connaught** – it seats 24 and is *"enormously impressive"* – **Lord Lichfield** . . . . . . The **best breakfast** according to **Robert Elms** is from the **Riverside** restaurant in the **Savoy**: *"It's the one I always take foreigners to, to impress them. You're served in a style that is almost forgotten. Porridge and kippers or kedgeree or devilled kidneys. And that great view across the river"* . . . . . . the first British **designer water** is **Abbey Well**, whose label portrays David Hockney by Peter Blake. Arty smarty *and* a big seller to top restaurants like Le Manoir aux Quat' Saisons . . . . . . The greatest of the **great British caffs** is The **Chop House**, Farringdon Rd, EC1 – *"Probably the only remaining Victorian eating house. For £4 you can eat magnificently – lamb chops, toad-in-the-hole, steak and kidney pie, spotted dick and custard . . ."* – **Robert Elms.**

★ ★

SIMPLY NICO, 48a Rochester Row, SW1
☎ **(01) 630 8061**
Nico Ladenis is one of Britain's culinary kings, reigning once more in London. *"The best chef and restaurant in England. His pâté de foie is superb and better than anywhere in France"* – **Barbara Cartland.** *"His style is so totally different"* – **Simon Hopkinson.** *"It's terrific, and he seems much happier, as if at last he's found somewhere where he doesn't feel that he has to be prickly"* – **Andrew Lloyd Webber.** *"Fantastic now, cooking better and better"* – **Prue Leith.** One of **Loyd Grossman**'s top raters, for technique, and a **Ned Sherrin** fave.

LE SOUFFLE, Inter-Continental Hotel, 1 Hamilton Place, W1
☎ **(01) 409 3131**
Soigné hotel dining room named after Swiss chef Peter Kromberg's speciality (he can cope with 280 soufflés at a time). *"Very good and excellent service"* – **Barbara Cartland.**

LE SUQUET, 104 Draycott Ave, SW3 ☎ **(01) 581 1785**
A cheerful little seafood eatery,

where *"it's as if you're sitting in Monte Carlo harbour hearing the clinking masts. Their plateau de fruits de mer would rival any, even in France"* – **Richard Compton-Miller**. *"... For Pierre Martin's great platters of freshly grilled fish"* – **Robert Carrier. Lord Lichfield** and **Imran Khan** both savour the seafood.

TAI-PAN, 8 Egerton Garden Mews, SW3 ☎ (01) 589 8287
Lord Lichfield's Chinese restaurant attracts the ritzy Knightsbridge set. The Princess of Wales has been spotted here and **Mark McCormack** likes Tai-panning; **Serena Sutcliffe** hops along for the frogs' legs.

T'ANG, 294 Fulham Rd, SW10 ☎ (01) 351 2599
Sleek little restaurant with an eclectic though unadventurous Oriental menu, and designery black lacquer and cane décor. *"I love it – it's terrific"* – **Jane Asher**. *"For its unpretentious and yet unusually welcoming staff"* – **Robert Carrier**.

♣ **LA TANTE CLAIRE, 68 Royal Hospital Rd, SW3 ☎ (01) 352 6045**
Voted the best French restaurant in London. Kitted out in cool blue with bird's-eye maple. *"Has to be in the top 3 in the country – the best in my opinion. It's fabulous, the décor's great, very unusual. Pierre Koffmann won't come out front – he's a dedicated, very talented cook and he's there first thing in the morning making bread, etc. His maître d', Jean-Pierre Dorantet, is very very good"* – **Roy Ackerman**. *"The lunches are terrific and very good value"* – **Jane Asher**. *"The only restaurant I would really think 'Oh, yes please' if I were taken out to lunch. The service is extremely good, I don't find the maître d' overpatronizing in explaining dishes. As excellent as one would hope"* – **Frederic Raphael**. *"My favourite. Pierre Koffmann is one of my mentors. His food is simplicity; by capturing simplicity he captures elegance"* – **Marco Pierre**

White. Prue Leith and **Barbara Cartland** are fans, but **Andrew Lloyd Webber** takes a more sober stance: *"Absolutely fine, but it wouldn't cause too much of a stir in France."*

ZEN W3 83 Hampstead High St, NW3 ☎ (01) 794 7863; Zen Central, 20 Queen St, W1 ☎ (01) 629 8103; Zen Chelsea Cloisters, Sloane Ave, SW3 ☎ (01) 589 1781
"Zen W3 made the breakthrough. Michael Leung is a genius of a chef. He's developed Chinese food for a London market so it's unauthentic but very good" – **Drew Smith**. *"Zen W3 has interesting food, interesting people, excellent design, a good concept"* – **Anton Mosimann**.

"I like the style of Zen Central. It's so different from the normal Chinese restaurant. Smart staff, slick dining room" – **Roy Ackerman. Harvey Goldsmith** is keen. **Yan-Kit So** susses the chef: *"Leung goes to France and Italy to see what other cuisines are like. Many Chinese chefs are too narrow and unsophisticated to appreciate other cuisines. His quick-fried fillet of duck with ginger and coriander sauce is adapted from French cuisine. His fish cake with fresh coriander is adapted from Thai. The Chinese fondue is adapted from Japanese cuisine and incorporates the inner-*

Mongolia barbecue lamb. And he doesn't use MSG."

SHOPS

R ALLEN & CO, 117 Mount St, W1 ☎ (01) 499 5831
Old-fashioned Mayfair butcher, widely voted tops. *"The best rabbit and game"* – **Robert Carrier. Ed Victor**'s a fan.

BERNIGRA ICE CREAM PARLOUR, 69 Tottenham Court Rd, W1 ☎ (01) 580 0950
Superb smooth Italian ices in rich, tangy fruit flavours or creamy coconut, hazelnut ...

BOUCHERIE LAMARTINE, 229 Ebury St, SW1 ☎ (01) 730 4175
Owned by the Roux brothers.

TEATIME TREATS

Very genteel English teas are served in the salons of the best London hotels: Indian or China teas, mere slivers of cucumber sandwiches that make the daintiest of eaters seem ham-fisted, light scones, fresh cream and jam, delicate cakes and smooth, old-fashioned service. The best are: **CHINOISERIE**, Carlton Tower, Cadogan Place, SW1 ☎ (01) 235 5411, which sends **Glynn Christian** into ecstasies: *"When the scones went cold they baked us some more; instead of putting more water in the teapot, they kept bringing us a fresh pot"*; **BROWN'S**, 20-24 Dover St, W1 ☎ (01) 493 6020; **CLARIDGE'S** (see Travel); the **DORCHESTER** (see Restaurants); and – the most famous, most expensive and most tourist-ridden (so book) – **THE RITZ** (see Travel).

"Very chi-chi and expensive, but the most wonderful French breads" – **Sophie Grigson**. Recommended by **Jane Asher**.

I CAMISA & SON, 61 Old Compton St, W1 ☎ (01) 437 4686
The best Italian deli in London – a ceiling full of salamis and Parma hams, cheeses, fresh pasta and seasonal sauces (pesto genovese, hare, wild mushroom). *"Just unbelievable; wonderful spicy Italian sausage, an endless variety of salami"* – **Ed Victor**. *"The best fresh pasta in London"* – **Robert Carrier. Drew Smith** and **Loyd Grossman** agree.

FOOD AND DRINK

CHARBONNEL ET WALKER, 28 Old Bond St, W1 ☎ (01) 491 0939
Masters of presentation, the royal chocolatiers were established in 1875 and patronized originally by Edward VII. Top-quality dark chocs in floral mini hat-boxes or the famous boîte blanche, which gives you carte blanche to fill the box to your whim.

FORTNUM & MASON, 181 Piccadilly, W1 ☎ (01) 734 8040
Hushed, carpeted food hall, locked in a time warp, with a liveried doorman and black morning-coated attendants. Traditional English foods (*"the best cheese in the world"* – **Craig Claiborne**); mustard, preserves and chocolates under their own suave wraps. *"Great for things in tins and packages, but their fresh fruit and veg is exorbitant"* – **Sophie Grigson**. *"The best Beluga caviare in London. They pack it in lb white porcelain jars – if you can afford it"* – **Robert Carrier. Anton Mosimann, Giorgio Armani** and **Steven Spurrier** are Fortnum's fans, but **Loyd Grossman** finds it *"depressing: it's become like a smart shop that you see in a TV sit-com."*

HARRODS, Knightsbridge, SW1 ☎ (01) 730 1234
Still regarded as home of the most beautiful and comprehensive food halls in existence. *"I like the variety, the presentation, the cleanliness ... everything. The class, the décor, all that reminds you of a bygone age. It's like an outing, better than going to the cinema"* – **Nico Ladenis**. *"There's no place on earth like Harrods, for food or anything else"* – **Wolfgang Puck**. *"Absolutely wonderful – a great asset to London"* – **Loyd Grossman**. *"The best cheeses and smoked salmon – when freshly cut"* – **Robert Carrier**. *"You can't beat it. It's so corny but it's so lovely. Over-the-top charm"* – **Robert Elms**.

H R HIGGINS, 79 Duke St, W1 ☎ (01) 629 3913

BEST WINE MERCHANTS

Wine buffs have pet merchants; here are some of the best: **ADNAMS**, The Crown, High St, Southwold, Suffolk ☎ (0502) 724222 – wide range of interesting wines from the Old and New Worlds, selected by Simon Loftus. Mail-order service. The other half of the East Anglia wine mafia, **LAY & WHEELER**, 6 Culver St W, Colchester, Essex ☎ (0206) 67261 *"have probably the greatest all-round list in the country"* – **Serena Sutcliffe**. **HAYNES HANSON & CLARK**, 17 Lettice St, London SW6 ☎ (01) 736 7878 – fine affordable wines; specialists in Bordeaux and burgundy (Anthony Hanson wrote *Burgundy*). **LA VIGNERONNE**, 105 Old Brompton Rd, London SW7 ☎ (01) 589 6113 – run by Liz Berry, MW; a treasure trove of fine old wines. **O W LOEB & CO**, 15 Jermyn St, London SW1 ☎ (01) 734 5878 – top-quality stuff, **Auberon Waugh**'s choice for German and Alsatian wine. **YAPP BROTHERS**, The Old Brewery, Mere, Wiltshire ☎ (0747) 860423 – Rhône and Loire specialists. **AVERYS OF BRISTOL**, 7 Park St, Bristol, Avon ☎ (0272) 214141 – old burgundies (where lover of heavy-style burgundies **Auberon Waugh** would go for his tipple); also Spanish, German and Australian wines. **CORNEY & BARROW**, 118 Moorgate, London EC2 ☎ (01) 638 3125 (and branches) – expensive, but *the* place for clarets from St-Emilion or Pomerol, according to **Auberon Waugh**; C&B are also merchants to **Ed Victor** and **Lord Donoughue** (*"they look after me very well"*). **LES AMIS DU VIN**, 51 Chiltern St, London W1 ☎ (01) 487 3419 – the best source of California wines, a wine club too. They own **THE WINERY**, 4 Clifton Rd, W9 ☎ (01) 286 6475, which has an impressive range of American and Australian wines. As for the chains, **ODDBINS** is adventurous but reliable with a well trained staff and *"terrific for champagnes – the whole range at very ungreedy prices"* – **Serena Sutcliffe**. **WAITROSE** is *"the wine connoisseur's supermarket"* – **Serena Sutcliffe**. **PETER DOMINIC** is **Auberon Waugh**'s choice: *"Absolutely brilliant in offering a huge variety of moderately priced wines – interesting bottles from California, Chile, Australia, New Zealand – but not serious wines."*

The best coffee suppliers in London, full of beans from around the world; roast-to-measure and mail-order services. Tea, too.

JEROBOAMS, 24 Bute St, SW7 ☎ (01) 225 2232
A **Prue Leith** favourite, specializing in unpasteurized French cheeses and English farmhouse cheeses. Run by New Zealander Juliet Harbutt, who is *"very good"* – **Drew Smith**. Up to 120 varieties, including some from Androuet in Paris. Wines, too.

JUSTIN DE BLANK, 42 Elizabeth St, SW1 ☎ (01) 730 0605
A highly favoured deli/bakery for ready-made dishes – goulash, quiches, salads, meringues, tarts – special sausages, cheeses and home-baked breads from his Hygienic Bakery in Walton Street, SW3. *"Wonderful, very fresh"* – **Sophie Grigson**.

PAXTON & WHITFIELD, 93 Jermyn St, SW1 ☎ (01) 930 9892
200-year-old purveyors of

Gourmet to go

Carry-out cuisine is the new way to impress dinner guests, and a number of gastronomic take-away joints are springing up. **Mrs Stoke's Kitchen**, 1 Kensington Church Walk, W8, provides home-made soups, delicate main courses and hearty puds. Antony Worrall-Thompson (of Ménage à Trois) opened **KWT Food Show**, 4 Bellevue Parade, Wandsworth Common this summer, for tapas, terrines, casseroles, tarts, summer pudding. **Finns**, 4 Elystan Street, SW3, offers beef with mushrooms and Guinness and some fine fish dishes.

choice cheeses. Went through a crumbly phase but now has the cream of English and Continental cheeses. *"Wonderful shop, a beautiful selection"* – **Anton Mosimann**.

RANDALL & AUBIN, 16 Brewer St, W1 ☎ (01) 437 3507
"What a butcher's ought to be. I don't like most British butchers – they're mucky, smelly, bloody, very unpleasant. A butcher's shop in France is clean, things are nicely displayed, there is a pride. This is just like the ones in France and you walk out with much more than you intended" – **Sophie Grigson**.

LES SPECIALITES ST QUENTIN, 256 Brompton Rd, SW3 ☎ (01) 225 1664
French pâtisserie selling exquisite tartlets and flans that tug on the purse strings. The local trendies' lunchtime demi-baguettes stuffed with ripe brie

and finely sliced ham take some beating. *"You can forgive the expense when it's so good"* – **Drew Smith**.

STEVE HATT, 88 Essex Rd, N1 ☎ (01) 226 3963
A family business with the best-quality fresh and home-smoked fish. Alert them a day in advance, and your fish is their command: they'll scale the market next morning for anything you desire, and prepare it any way you ask – for sushi, say. *"The best fish"* – **Robert Carrier**.

REST OF BRITAIN

RESTAURANTS

Some of the best dining in the country is at country-house hotels. Exemplary standards are held at **Chewton Glen, Hambleton Hall, Miller Howe, Sharrow Bay, Homewood Park** (see Travel).

CARVED ANGEL, 2 South Embankment, Dartmouth, Devon ☎ (08043) 2465
The best of British ingredients prepared with Mediterranean flair in the Elizabeth David style by Joyce Molyneux. Garlicky provençale fish soup, Dart salmon with samphire and champagne. Strong wine list.

GIDLEIGH PARK, Chagford, Devon ☎ (06473) 2367
Modern British cuisine with Oriental tinges in a superb country-house hotel. Innovative handling of the freshest of ingredients, from duck and foie gras to scallops and herb ravioli filled with white truffles. Wonderful cream teas too. *"A cosy country house with the additional splendours of imaginative, tasty menus and an outstanding wine list"* – **Michael Broadbent**.

LE MANOIR AUX QUAT' SAISONS, Church Rd, Great Milton, Oxfordshire ☎ (08446) 8881
This 15th-century manor is one

SUPREME SUPERMARKETS

The British love their supermarkets. **MARKS & SPENCER** gets the majority vote: *"The best everyday foods, because they buy their goods from the best producers. Where they lead, others follow. They produced bottles of freshly squeezed orange and grapefruit juice and the others copied. They countered by producing mandarin juice, which is out of this world"* – **Lord Lichfield**. *"M&S's foods are impossible to beat in quality and packaging and price and cleanliness and freshness. They're cleaning up in the sandwich business (though I don't think their sandwiches are that great); they do fresh farm eggs"* – **Alastair Little**. *"Their ready-made dishes beat all other supermarkets' – especially the Moules Bonne Femme – that's smashing"* – **Jane Asher**. *"Some are good and some aren't. When you're stuck without a local fishmonger, they're the next best thing,"* says a cooler **Loyd Grossman**. But then he's a **SAINSBURY'S** man: *"I don't think in the foodie world it's the place – they like to go off and find the man with one leg who sells olive oil out of a tin can in Primrose Hill – but as a cornucopia of the most wonderful things, Sainsbury's does a terribly good job."* **WAITROSE** has an equally devoted following: *"The best food shop in England, accessible for everything. Vegetables are fantastic, spices, herbs and fruits very good"* – **Keith Floyd**. Shop-around **Jane Asher** thinks Waitrose is best for fresh food: *"They're adventurous and they do try new lines. They're also helpful, organized and efficient and I feel at home in them."*

FOOD AND DRINK

of the best restaurants in the world, with Raymond Blanc at the helm. It's also a small hotel, so that purring punters can make a weekend of it. Menus change with the seasons. *"I think Raymond is an extremely accomplished and brilliant cook, and so young. He has a very original mind; his combinations of flavours and textures are brilliant. It's like the difference between learning to play the piano and playing by ear"* – **Roy Ackerman**. For **Robert Carrier** it's *"my favourite restaurant in England. Raymond can do no wrong."* *"Excellent"* – **Serena Fass**. *"Delicious. The best. Very imaginative. The house is beautiful, exquisitely decorated, and very romantic"* – **Barbara Cartland**. *"Very good. You can all go and stare up Tim Rice's drive afterwards, as he lives opposite"* – **Andrew Lloyd Webber.**

MOREL'S, 25-27 Lower St, Haslemere, Surrey
☎ (0428) 51462
Quaint little restaurant with bow windows and hanging flower baskets. Modern French food from Jean-Yves Morel. *"I like it because it's got class, it's got style and you feel that you are in an exciting restaurant"* – **Nico Ladenis.**

THE OLD WOOLHOUSE, Northleach, Gloucestershire
☎ (04516) 366
A minuscule restaurant (seats 18) run by Jacques and Jenny Astic. *"One of my all-time favourites in this country. He's a great guy, his kitchen is extraordinary – tiny with 2 wooden tables, a stove and 2 sinks. No microwave, no washing-up machine – that's it. The food is brilliant. He's very French and a very talented cook. Not pretentious, not too pricy"* – **Roy Ackerman.**

L'ORTOLAN, The Old Vicarage, Church Lane, Shinfield, Berkshire
☎ (0734) 883783
John and Christine Burton-Race took over when Nico Ladenis found the country air disagreed with him and moved

---

♟ —*Britain's Best*— ♟

RESTAURANTS
1   **LE MANOIR AUX QUAT' SAISONS**, Great Milton
2   **LA TANTE CLAIRE**, London
3   **THE CONNAUGHT**, London
4   **SIMPLY NICO**, London
5   **LE GAVROCHE**, London

back to London. *"It is absolutely the best – extremely elegant. The food is sublime, the ambience is sublime, it's all decorated in pinks and greys and there's a garden"* – **Elisabeth Lambert Ortiz**. *"Burton-Race is arguably the best of the new generation of chefs. He's French in outlook and technically ahead of the field"* – **Drew Smith**. *"Very good"* – **Barbara Cartland**. *"It's terrific – very, very good news. They haven't changed it inside, but you feel more relaxed now"* – **Andrew Lloyd Webber**.

WATERSIDE INN, Ferry Rd, Bray, Berkshire
☎ (0628) 20691
In what is perhaps the most expensive restaurant in Britain, Michel Roux rouxles as his brother rouxles in London. 3 Michelin stars; food and clientele on the nouvelle side. *"Michel Roux's charm and deftness of touch and a beautiful riverside situation"* – **Michael Broadbent**. *"The Roux brothers were the first to give the English a taste for gourmet food. Waterside Inn has the advantage of the river, the boats and a dining room that can be opened completely to the fresh air"* – **Barbara Cartland**.

WELL HOUSE, St Keyne, Liskeard, Cornwall
☎ (0579) 42001
Newly established small country-house hotel that is already wowing visitors and locals alike for its marvellous modern British cooking.

Seasonal game, salads and vegetables, delicious home-made rosemary and walnut bread with the cheese, and an exemplary wine list.

SHOPS

COLCHESTER OYSTER FISHERY, North Farm, East Mersea, Colchester, Essex
☎ (0206) 384141
The best English oysters and clams. Mail-order service.

FITZBILLIES, 52 Trumpington St, Cambridge, Cambridgeshire ☎ (0223) 352500 **(shop); 50 Regent St** ☎ (0223) 64451 **(tearoom)**
Sticky cakes, brioches, buns, bread, croissants and the famous Chelsea bun are voted figure-licking good by **Prue Leith**. Go early . . .

MAISON BLANC, 3 & 3a Woodstock Rd, Oxford, Oxfordshire ☎ (0865) 54974
The best bread and croissants in the world according to, unsurprisingly, **Raymond Blanc**: *"Seriously the best bakery."* (PS Other foodies swear by it too.)

MINOLA SMOKED PRODUCTS, Kencot Hill Farmhouse, Filkins, Lechlade, Gloucestershire
☎ (036786) 391
Oak-smoked wild Scottish salmon with an almost buttery melt-in-the-mouth consistency. Smoke pots made from whole English oak logs give the salmon a delicate but distinct flavour – you can taste the smokiness; no sharpness and no cloying. Also other fish, poultry, game, nuts and cheeses. Mail-order service.

THE TOFFEE SHOP, 7 Brunswick Rd, Penrith, Cumbria ☎ (0768) 62008
The best fudge in England according to **Lord Lichfield**. Chocolate fudge, mint fudge, treacle toffee, butter toffee – mmmm. Mail order too.

WELLS STORES, Bull Corner, Reading Rd, Streatley-on-Thames,

Berkshire ☎ (0491) 872367
Patrick Rance (now retired) is
renowned for his finely tuned
nose, which has sniffed out a
brilliant and expansive range of
superb cheeses. His son Hugh
now runs the shop. Also the
best (French) olive oil.

SCOTLAND
RESTAURANTS

Dine finely also at top country-
house hotels **Inverlochy
Castle, Altnaharrie Inn,
Kinloch Lodge, Cromlix
House** and **Isle of Eriska
Hotel** (see Travel).

**CHAMPANY INN, Champany
Corner, Linlithgow, W
Lothian** ☎ (050683) 4532
The best steak and beef in
Britain. Clive Davidson
upholds an entire philosophy of
meat – cut, breed, thickness
and cooking.

**THE PEAT INN, Peat Inn,
Cupar, Fife** ☎ (033484) 206
This whitewashed inn is the
sum of the crossroads village.
Chef-owner David Wilson is
*"the most darling man. He
provides the most heavenly
food. Nouvellish but nice"* –
**Lady Macdonald of
Macdonald**. Real Scots food
fashioned à la française, and an
enviable wine list. Scallops
poached in Barsac, wild duck
with blueberries, grouse and
pigeon are regulars.

**LA POTINIERE, Main St,
Gullane, E Lothian**
☎ (0620) 843214
*"Certainly the best-value
restaurant in the country. It's
a bit potty, they only open
Mon, Tues, Thurs, Fri and
Sunday lunch, and dinner on
Saturday. I had mousseline of
lemon sole with hazelnuts,
orange stuffing and lemon
hollandaise – it worked really
well, wonderfully executed. I
would go so far as to say it's
the best, most interesting and
incredibly fairly priced wine
list in the land. Altogether as a
package it's extraordinary"* –
Simon Hopkinson. There's one

WHISKY GALORE

Whisky-lovers gather to distil their views. Grapies, move
over. *"I detest champagne, and don't particularly mind about
wine, but I like a good Scotch,"* declares **Douglas Fairbanks
Jr**. *"For non-purists, old Bushmills Irish whiskey is a treat. I
was given some in Dublin and was bowled over by it"* – **Serena
Sutcliffe**. *"I have the most frightfully expensive tastes. One of
the joys in my life is a good single malt whisky, Laphroaig.
Some people think it tastes like disinfectant"* – **Michael
Grade**. Others' votes go to these single malts: Glenlivet, Glen-
morangie, Lagavulin, Longmorn, Macallan and Talisker.

---

sitting for each meal and a set
menu with no choice.

SHOPS

**JENNERS, 48 Princes St,
Edinburgh** ☎ (031) 725 2442
Marvellous food halls
displaying Speyside smoked
salmon, smoked trout from
Mull, 70 different honeys, 68
cheeses, 112 teas, and bread
baked on the premises. *"Still
family-run. It has moved with
the times and has a wonderful
range"* – **Lady Macdonald of
Macdonald**.

**PINNEY'S OF SCOTLAND,
Brydekirk, Annan, Dumfries
& Galloway** ☎ (05763) 401
Superb salmon go through a
subtle smoking process and are
finely carved by hand. No
colouring or preservatives,
naturally. Suppliers to all the
best shops – Harrods,
Fortnum's, Marks & Spencer –
and a mail-order service. Also
gravadlax, smoked trout,
mackerel, eel, fish pâté ...

WALES
MARKET

SWANSEA MARKET
*"Wales has more genuine
markets than anywhere else in
Britain. Here you get Welsh
salted butter, Welsh unsalted
butter, Welsh bacon ..."* –
Glynn Christian. *"The best
market in Britain. Enormous,
extremely old-fashioned; you
get farmers bringing their own*

*butter and cheeses and
chickens. You get laverbread (a
type of seaweed, and the
caviare of Wales), cockles, very
good fish. Untainted,
uncorrupted, nothing tinned"* –
Drew Smith.

RESTAURANT

**WALNUT TREE INN,
Llandewi Skirrid, Gwent**
☎ (0873) 2797
French-trained Italian chef-
owner Franco Taruschio has
made this little pub a gourmet's
country retreat. Home-made
pasta, superb seafood, fresh
Piedmontese truffles, salmon
and wild game followed by rich
European puddings, washed
down with a rare Italian or
French wine. *"The most
economic way to eat white
truffles. You can have fresh
pasta with truffles for a song –
he shaves them like they're
going out of fashion – very
generous"* – **Simon Hopkinson**.
*"A great restaurant – the best
all round. Everything is very
fairly priced – you're not being
charged for elaborate service or
décor. Sensational olive oil, his
own wind-dried beef (which is a
revelation to me) and the best
gravadlax I have ever tasted"* –
Alastair Little.

SHOP

**VIN SULLIVAN, 11 High St,
Abergavenny, Gwent**
☎ (0873) 2331
A special fishmonger, gamery
and grocer (very fine fruit and

veg) that supplies fish to many top-class restaurants in Britain, from Miller Howe to the Walnut Tree. A Parisian agent sends fresh and unusual supplies across the channel twice a week. Isle of Man scallops, baby crayfish, Kenyan and Turkish écrevisse, Cornish and Canadian lobster, wild Wye salmon, and live sea urchins (collected at their peak, during a full moon).

Canada

MONTREAL

CAFES AND BARS

LUX, 5220 Saint Laurent Blvd, H2T 151
☎ (514) 271 9272
At 3am, any francophone worth his *sel* is sipping steamy coffee, tucking into a delicious breakfast, and flipping through the latest European mags at this 24-hour bookstore-cum-café-bar. One of **Tyler Brule**'s fave haunts.

RESTAURANTS

L'EXPRESS, 3927 Rue Saint Denis, H2W 2M4
☎ (514) 845 5333
"A wonderful little bistro in the heart of the city. Very fashionable and the perfect place to people watch" – **Bonnie Brooks-Young.**

LES HALLES, 1450 Crescent St, H3G 2B6 ☎ (514) 844 2328
A Montreal institution, *très français* and a hive of activity at night. Chef Crevoisier Dominique has been here from the beginning (some 16 years ago), turning out delicious gourmet cuisine. *"A very nice Parisian restaurant. Very beautiful, yet very informal"* – **Robert Ramsay.**

LA MAREE, 404 Place Jacques Cartier, H2Y 3B2
☎ (514) 861 8126
Brilliant, old-established seafood restaurant. *"A wonderful old favourite"* – **Bonnie Brooks-Young.**

LES MIGNARDISES, 2035 rue Saint Denis, H2X 3K8
☎ (514) 842 1151
The service is immaculate, the food spectacular and the linen luxurious. Bring beaucoup d'argent. Co-owner Jean Pierre Monnet is an alumnus of Les Halles's kitchens.

PREGO, 5142 Saint Laurent Blvd, H2T 1RB
☎ (514) 271 3234
A superb Italian restaurant. Black and white zebra-striped chairs, beautifully set dining tables, jump-to service and imaginative pastas. *"Definitely the place to be seen, the hottest"* – **Bonnie Brooks-Young.**

TORONTO

MARKET

ST LAWRENCE MARKET, cnr of Jarvis St and Front St
A wonderful old market for the best fish, game, beef, pasta and cheeses in the city. Everyone yelling in foreign languages adds to the ethnic atmosphere. A favourite of **Sondra Gotlieb** for *"great vegetables"*.

RESTAURANTS

LE BISTINGO, 349 Queen St W, M5V 2A4 ☎ (416) 598 3490
It's sooo cool to dine here amid slick, stark, modern design. *"It's very hot. The food is extremely good – it's country French, and that brings the 'haute' to Toronto"* – **Joyce Davidson.** *"One of my favourites. it's really kinda fun. Very French, good food, great service"* – **Sondra**

Gotlieb. *"Like a high-grade bistro. The food is wonderful. It has a real sense of action"* – **Robert Ramsay.** *"Another favourite . . . so French and wonderful"* – **Tyler Brule.**

CIBO RISTORANTE, 1055 Yonge St, M4W 2L2
☎ (416) 921 2166
Wonderful noisy Italian restaurant – always busy and always delicious. Open kitchens mean you can see what the chef's doing to your pasta (whatever he does, he gets it dead right).

FENTON'S, 2 Gloucester St, M4Y 1L5 ☎ (416) 961 8485
One of the prettiest restaurants in town, based in an old converted house. The garden room, a glass-roofed conservatory, is filled with fresh flowers and frondy trees all year and fairy-lit at night. In the drawing room, with its crackling fire in winter, you sit on small Chesterfield sofas rather than straight-backed chairs. The basement is slightly cheaper, but with the same soigné service and cuisine. *"Always a favourite . . . so beautiful, and the food is always good"* – **Tyler Brule.**

MASANIELLO, 647 College St, M6G 1B7 ☎ (416) 533 7046
An authentic trattoria in the heart of little Italy. They dish up healthy portions of country Italian cooking at its finest. Their simple mozzarella salad with fresh basil is perfection. *"The seafood risotto is wonderful, but whatever they make is super. You're really in an Italian restaurant – you could be the only table speaking English"* – **Joyce Davidson.**

IL POSTO, York Square, 148 Yorkville Ave, M4W 1L2
☎ (416) 968 0469
The best and most imaginative Italian food in Toronto – dishes such as sautéed fresh sardines

---

❝ *The ideal place to lunch in Montreal is on the terrace at the Ritz-Carlton. It's a fairytale. It has stayed the same for 30 years* **❞**

 SONDRA GOTLIEB

" *My favourite place to dine is the Chef's Table at Sansssouci at the Sutton Place Hotel [955 Bay St ☎ (416) 924 6068]. It is an actual table in the kitchen of the restaurant. You must book it weeks in advance; there are only 4 places. You sit there with all the pots and pans and you have no idea what they are going to serve. It's as good as any 4-star French restaurant* "

ROBERT RAMSAY

stuffed with parmesan, spinach, eggs, garlic and parsley. Clubby atmosphere, a favourite of **Peter Ustinov.**

PREGO, 150 Bloor St W, M5S 2X9 ☎ (416) 920 9900
"The Spago of Toronto. It's great, a wonderful new hot-spot to see and be seen at. I had a great pizza with sun-dried tomatoes and goat's cheese" – **Tyler Brule.**

THE ROSEDALE DINER, 1164 Yonge St, M4W 2L9 ☎ (416) 923 3122
"My favourite because it's so eclectic. The restaurant is really unique . . . the décor is a little offbeat but I love it. The food is great, very light cuisine. They have wonderful things like strawberry soup and swordfish and a huge selection of beers" – **Steve Podborski.**

SCARAMOUCHE, 1 Benvenuto Place, M4V 2L1 ☎ (416) 961 8011
"An old love for me – we go whenever we have something special to celebrate. The deserts are absolutely incredible" – **Karen Kain.**

SENATOR, 249 Victoria St, M5B 1T8 ☎ (416) 364 7517

"An old refurbished diner with the most extensive California wine list in the city. Everything from gourmet burgers to chicken in raspberry vinaigrette" – **Karen Kain.**
Tony Aspler is also impressed by the cellar.

TRUFFLES, Four Seasons Hotel, 21 Avenue Rd, M5R 2G1 ☎ (416) 964 0411
A super-smart hotel restaurant for award-winning 5-star French cuisine. The chef hosts a table once a month for enthusiastic diners.

WINSTON'S, 104 Adelaide St W, M5H 1S2 ☎ (416) 363 1627
Established and expensive, Winston's is part of the framework of Toronto, decorated in Belle Epoque style. Robust, gourmet French cuisine and a wine list beyond reproach. An old loyal clientele – lots of politicos and lawyers.

🕵 **Buzzzzzzzzz** The best **power lunchspot** in Toronto is **The Courtyard Café**, Windsor Arms Hotel, 22 St Thomas St, M5S 2B9 ☎ (416) 979 2212, for major mergers and amazing acquisitions in the business and film worlds 🕵 . . . . . . **Power meals 2**: meeting 1st thing over a boiled egg is common practice. Bleary-eyed execs gather in their hotel dining room – **King Edward (Café Victoria)**, 37 King St E, M5C 1E9 ☎ (416) 863 9700; **Park Plaza**, 4 Avenue Rd, M5R 2EH ☎ (416) 924 5471 and the **Four Seasons (Truffles)**, 21 Avenue Rd, M5R 2G1 ☎ (416) 964 0411 🕵 . . . . . . For the **best burgers** in Toronto, nothing licks **Lick's Burgers and Ice Cream Cones**, 2383 Kingston Rd, M1N 1V1 ☎ (416) 267 3248; try the Coney Island fries and listen to waiters singing your orders in brilliant melody 🕵 . . . . . . After watching the Leafs at home (that's the Maple Leafs ice hockey team), *the* place to celebrate/commiserate is **George Bigliardi's Dining Lounge** over a mammoth steak 🕵 . . . . . . the **best cabaret-dinner** is at the **Imperial Room of the Royal York Hotel**, with the great Louis Janetta maître d'-ing and the likes of Pearl Bailey, Tina Turner and Tony Bennett performing.

★ ★ ★ ★ ★ ★ ★ ★ ★ ★ ★ ★ ★ ★ ★ ★ ★ ★ ★

VANCOUVER

MARKET

GRANVILLE ISLAND MARKET
The yuppiest place to shop in the city. Fresh seafood, delicious fudge and other pricy produce. Good for browsing or simply sipping cappuccino. Watch out for **The Stock Market**, a tiny shop with a mint of different stocks – heaven in a cube.

RESTAURANTS

BRIDGES, 1696 Duranleau, Granville Island, V6H 3S4 ☎ (604) 669 2422
Romantic setting on the docks; superb seafood straight (almost) from the ocean.

FOOD AND DRINK

CAFE SPLASH, 1600 Howe St, V6Z 2L9 ☎ **(604) 582 5600**
Bright, light, cheerful café-restaurant in a wonderful, windowful West Coast setting. *"The place to be seen in the evening. The best of the freshest ingredients as well as innovative concoctions like artichoke and sun-dried tomato strüdel"* – **Beverley Zbitnoff.** *"A lot of fun"* – **Tony Aspler.**

LE CROCODILE, 818 Thurlow St, V6E 1W2 ☎ **(604) 669 4298**
Cosy and quaint, superb French food and excellent service. *"Every evening the handful of tables enjoys traditional French preparations served impeccably by waiters with* real *accents"* – **Beverley Zbitnoff.**

MILIEU, 1145 Robson St, V6E 1B5 ☎ **(604) 684 4600**
Cool café in the Euro-style mode. Nouvelle cuisine is counteracted by a bakery on the premises that ruins good intentions with exquisite but fattening delicacies.

THE TEAHOUSE, Ferguson Point, Stanley Park ☎ **(604) 669 3281**
Overlooking the ocean with mountains in the background, this restaurant is perfect for imbibing romantic sunsets in between nibbles of the best item on the menu – a wonderful West Coast salmon dish.

UMBERTO II GIARDINO, 1382 Hornby St, V6Z 1W5 ☎ **(604) 669 2422**
The best of foodie king Umberto's restaurants (**Umberto's** at 1380 is the original, for northern Italian cuisine; **La Cantina di Umberto** at 1376 serves fresh local seafood). This one dishes up delicious Italian cuisine, specializing in wild game.

BURMESE BERRIES

"The British left some odd notions behind, none more so than the idea of growing strawberries several thousand feet above sea level at Maymyo, Burma, the town which was hilly and spring-like enough to form a refuge from Rangoon's summer heat. These strawberries are at their peak in Feb/March, and what makes them so much better than our pampered, slightly soggy monsters is that they are closer to the original woodland strawberry – smaller, nuttier, tastier and infinitely more romantic. The central market at Maymyo (where you can also buy a buffalo cart in kit form), sells the best strawberry milkshake. I have always hated milkshakes before, but this was ambrosial" – **Miles Kington.**

China

BEIJING

RESTAURANTS

FENGZE YUAN, Zhushikou, No 83 ☎ **332828**
Expensive, prestigious place famed for its fine seafood.

HUAIYANG FANZHUANG, Xidan N, No 217 ☎ **660521**
Good rich seafood – crabs, prawns, eels and more.

SHAGUO JU, Xisi Kaijie, No 60 ☎ **663206**
This 300-year-old restaurant is the oldest in Beijing. Its Manchurian specialities centre around pork.

SICHUAN FANDIAN, Rongxian Hutong, No 51 ☎ **336356**
A 9-courtyard house with beautiful décor (rare in China). Excellent hot peppery Sichuan dishes.

TINGLI GUAN, Summer Palace ☎ **281276**
Formerly the private theatre of the Dowager Empress Ci Xi. Set on the north shore near the Marble Boat, it's a stunning place to eat Imperial dishes.

REST OF CHINA

DONG FENG, Dong Feng Lu, Chengdu, Sichuan ☎ **7012**
Tipped by Paul Levy as one of the best restaurants in the world. Zhou Bai Meng is the chef (he and Liu Chih are the 2 best in China). Both are elderly and walking encyclopaedias of their culinary tradition.

GOLDEN FLOWER HOTEL, 8 Chanan Xijie, Shaanxi Province ☎ **32981**
A contender for the best Sichuan food in China, by hand-picked first-class chefs. Fine international-class service. *"We ate there a lot – the chef had discovered a huge supply of écrevisse which the locals didn't like, so we were able to gorge ourselves"* – **Robin Hanbury-Tenison.** See also Travel.

SONG HE LOU, 141 Guangqian St, Suzhou
What this restaurant lacks in

> ❝ *The world's most exotic food market is the People's Free Market in Guangzhou at 6am. I stood entranced watching fish being boned with a cleaver, snakes, turtles, snails and civet cat ... the Cantonese are noted for their kinky carnivorous tastes!* ❞

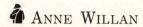 ANNE WILLAN

décor it makes up for in quality of food as Liu Chih, the chef, is one of the best in the world.

France

PARIS

CAFES AND BARS

Wine bars are the current rage in Paris. The old ones are always the best: both run by Englishmen, they are Steven Spurrier's **Blue Fox**, Cité Berryer, 25 rue Royale and Mark Williamson's **Willi's**, 13 rue des Petits Champs.

AUX DEUX MAGOTS, 170 blvd St Germain, 75006
☎ **(1) 4548 5525**
Very obviously on the tourist beat, but it's a fabulous place to sit and watch the world strut by, near the little cobbled place St Germain des Prés. A haunt of the Left Bank literati.

CAFE DE FLORE, 172 blvd St Germain, 75006
☎ **(1) 4548 5526**
La même chose, next door; preferred by **Steven Spurrier** (and formerly by Picasso, Sartre, Simone de Beauvoir and Albert Camus).

LA CALAVADOS, 40 ave Pierre Premier de Serbie, 75116 ☎ **(1) 4720 3139**
For a late late drink (or supper at 3am), a dark wood-panelled bar with a first-class old jazz pianist, Joe Turner. Americans-in-Paris-in-the-'50s nostalgia.

HEMINGWAY BAR, Hôtel Ritz, 15 place Vendôme, 75001
☎ **(1) 4260 3830**
The barman used to hunt with his old habitué, 'Papa' Hemingway lui-même. Scott Fitzgerald also drank here. Now it's one of **Charlotte Rampling**'s haunts. Also the Cambon bar and Vendôme bar.

LE VIEUX BISTROT, 14 rue du Cloître Notre-Dame, 75004
☎ **(1) 4354 1895**
A family restaurant,

remarkable for its kir royal à la mûre – champagne with blackberry liqueur. Wonderful curved, antique zinc bar. Great family cooking, too, and the best gratin dauphinois in town.

RESTAURANTS

LES AMBASSADEURS, Hôtel de Crillon, 10 place de la Concorde, 75008
☎ **(1) 4265 2424**
Not only the most beautiful hotel restaurant in Paris (deliciously marbled, mirrored and chandeliered), but also one of the best, with André Signoret heading the kitchen. **Lord Lichfield** and **Mark McCormack** recommend.

APICIUS, 122 ave Villiers, 75017 ☎ **(1) 4380 1966**
"I don't know of a restaurant in Paris that people are universally more fond of. Jean Pierre Vigato is the Tom Selleck of cooks – both he and his wife are very attractive. Beautiful décor; lots of attention to presentation. Plates are either black or white. It's startling" – **Robert Noah. Mark McCormack** is also keen.

L'ARPEGE, 84 rue de Varenne, 75007
☎ **(1) 4551 2002**
Chef Alain Passard used to work under Senderens at L'Archestrate and has now taken over the tiny premises.

"My favourite of the new ones. He uses sweet-sour more than most French chefs. One of his signature dishes is a lobster salad with a sweet-sour vinaigrette; he puts a streak of caramel on savoury dishes. It seems to be attracting the same crowd as Senderens – trendy and jetset" – **Robert Noah**.

AU TROU GASCON, 40 rue Taine, 70012 ☎ **(1) 4344 3426**
"A marvellous bistro" – **Egon Ronay**. Specialities include foie gras de canard and truffe de chocolat noir.

THE CULINARY ADVENTURES OF AUBERON WAUGH

*"In **Australia** I ate some **kangaroo** at the Adelaide Hilton which they served as a special. Not bad at all, tastes rather like magret de canard, which is the way nouvelle cuisine restaurants serve duck to make it taste like steak. I've eaten **crocodile** in **Cuba** which is quite nice; it tastes like a mixture of lobster and pork. In Saga, **Japan** I had raw **horse**, which is rather like that raw beef dish, carpaccio, but slightly saltier. I had **snake** in **Thailand**. It's very bony and crunchy and you have to suck the meat off. The skin is left on, which is very off-putting. It wasn't a big experience. I had **dog** in **Manila**. Dog is not interesting at all. One tries to experience whatever the country has to offer."*

FOOD AND DRINK

LE BRISTOL, 112 rue du Faubourg St Honoré, 75008
☎ (1) 4266 9145
Elegant hotel restaurant, a gastronomic winner.

LA BUCHERIE RESTAURANT, 41 rue de la Bûcherie, 75005
☎ (1) 4354 2452
For a romantic dîner à deux with a view of Notre Dame ask for a table next to the fireplace. Cuisine bourgeoise with flashes of genius such as mousse au chocolat aux oranges amères.

CARRE DES FEUILLANTS, 14 rue de Castiglione, 75001
☎ (1) 4286 8282
Formerly of Au Trou Gascon, the brilliant Alain Dutournier is inspired by cuisine of the south-west of France. *"Dutournier is a fabulous chef"* – **Robert Carrier**. Delicacies include ravioli stuffed with foie gras and truffles or with lobster; wild salmon cooked with smoked bacon.

CAVIAR KASPIA, 17 place de la Madeleine, 75008
☎ (1) 4265 3352
"Wonderful for its Russian atmosphere" – **Steven Spurrier**. Above the caviare shop is a romantic wood-panelled restaurant, where you can sample an ounce of Beluga, Oscietra, etc with a chilled glass of Sancerre or bubbly.

CHEZ L'AMI LOUIS, 32 rue du Vertbois, 75003
☎ (1) 4887 7748
An old-fashioned landmark in Paris, still going under the same chef, although owner M Magnin has sadly died. Fab foie gras, roast poultry and game, and gargantuan quantities of allumettes (matchstick chips). **Anne Willan** has always loved *"the finest of honest food."* **Prue Leith** says: *"Emphasis is all on food and atmosphere. The thing to eat there is scallops fried in garlic and butter."* A long-time favourite of the Hollywood set – Marlene Dietrich, Robert De Niro, Barbra Streisand, Roman Polanski.

CHEZ EDGARD, 4 rue Marbeuf, 75006
☎ (1) 4720 5115
Any night of the week you could form a new cabinet by walking into Paul Benmussa's red and black dining room. M. Paul's eatery is an institution for political and media Paris. Everyone is treated with the same warmth; there are good tables for all. You might rub épaules with Liza Minnelli, Mick Jagger, Alain Delon or Anouk Aimée. The food is good too – try tartare de saumon or selle d'agneau aux petits légumes. And save space for Paul B's delectable chocolates (see Shops).

LE COCHON D'OR, 192 ave Jean-Jaurès, 75019
☎ (1) 4208 3981
Some of the best steaks – and foie gras – in Paris. Huge 4-inch wedges of meat, scorched on the outside, red but warm inside. Serious eating in a working-class quartier (becoming hipper daily).

LA COUPOLE, 102 blvd du Montparnasse, 75014
☎ (1) 4320 1420
Recently acquired by the Flo chain, this famous brasserie is vast and airy, with row upon row of tables, and waiters in long white aprons. Totally trendy (more so at lunchtime), with a set menu that won't break la banque. *"I love the size of it, the bustle, the efficiency of the waiters – the staff are fantastic. I love the fact that it's le tout Paris. There's nowhere else like it"* – **Simon Hopkinson**. *"Everyone loves it, though not necessarily for the food. When you're there, you know you are in Paris and it's just an amazingly exciting place"* – **Loyd Grossman.**

DODIN-BOUFFANT, 25 rue Frédéric Sauton, 75005
☎ (1) 4325 2514
A grand bistro that has various toques and stars to its credit and diners such as Mitterrand and Lagerfeld. The best raspberry soufflé in town.

DUQUESNOY, 6 ave Bosquet, 75007 ☎ (1) 4705 9678
A former provincial chef who has moved up to town. *"He is concerned with flavour and body and substance. His signature dish is wonderful – cabbage stuffed with fish mousse and langoustine. One of my favourite restaurants"* – **Robert Noah.**

FAUGERON, 52 rue Longchamp, 75016
☎ (1) 4704 2453
The recently redecorated world favourite of **Peter Ustinov**: *"An agreeable place where the food is extraordinarily good."*

LE GRAND VEFOUR, 17 rue Beaujolais, 75001
☎ (1) 4296 5627
Grand is the word. It's owned

🕵 **Buzzzzzzzzz** The best place for **tea** is **Angelina's** salon de thé, 226 rue de Rivoli, where chic little old ladies and rock stars sip side by side at 4.30pm. Best pudding here is the Mont Blanc 🕵 . . . . . . Best **kitchen equipment** is found at **La Bovida**, 36 rue Montmartre – *"catacomb-like cellars with an amazing array of copper pans"* – **Alastair Little** 🕵 . . . . . . The best **aligot**, a dish from the Auvergne using fresh local cheese and mashed potato, comes from **Ambassade d'Auvergne**, 22 rue Grenier St Lazare, 75003 🕵 . . . . . . Ever popular is the chain of fashionable, value-for-money, classic **Art Deco brass-eries** Flo, Terminus Nord, Julien, Vaudeville, the newly acquired La Coupole, and Le Boeuf sur le Toit.

★ ★

> **❝** *I tend to like bourgeois cooking because it's an antidote to all this ludicrous nouvelle neologism. So I like rather modest restaurants like Chez André in the rue Marbeuf and Restaurant des Ampères in rue des Ampères where you get simple dishes like braised tongue and boeuf en gelée served up with tremendous ebullience and style* **❞**

🐾 LOYD GROSSMAN

by Claude Taittinger (who also owns the Hôtel de Crillon). *"That's what I would call smart, classical cooking in an unparalleled setting. It's probably the most beautiful restaurant in the world"* – **Loyd Grossman. Barbara Cartland, Alan Crompton-Batt** and **Simon Hopkinson** like it too.

GUY SAVOY, 18 rue Troyon, 75017 ☎ **(1) 4380 4061**
The eponymous chef is much toqued about (he's now gained a fourth from Gault Millau) for his fine combinations of poultry, fish, offal and vegetables, served in unusual ways. **Robert Noah**'s a fan and so is **Bob Payton** – *"My new favourite restaurant in Paris". "The most imaginative chef but never over the top. He never insults you with mango or kiwi on a duck breast. His marriages of flavour are so masterful – you wonder why they're not classic"* – **Prue Leith.**

🐾 **JAMIN (ROBUCHON), 32 rue de Longchamp, 75116** ☎ **(1) 4727 1227**
Joël Robuchon is voted best chef in the world. When he dishes up pig's head and mash his way, or the more traditional truffle, foie gras and seafood masterpieces, foodies dish out accolades (and the Michelin men, 3 stars). *"Everyone agrees it is the best. Whether it is total best for the wine, the food, the atmosphere and the service I'm not sure ... I think it has the best food"* – **Robert Noah.** *"For me it is No 1. It's out of this world, orgasmic. He takes simple things and adds a twist. The taste is very flavourful and solid and not gimmicky. He is not just well trained in techniques and*

skills, he is also intelligent and has impeccable taste – he's a genius. I eat there at least 2 or 3 times a year. It's a rare treat – like oxygen!" – **Ken Hom. Robert Carrier** describes the famous purée de pommes de terre: *"A concoction which is the best I've ever had – probably 2 potatoes, half a pint of cream and half a pound of butter whipped up – absolutely incredible." "The food vies with Taillevent"* – **Egon Ronay.** *"Among the best in Europe"* – **Barbara Kafka. Leo Schofield** and **Roy Ackerman** are also in favour. What price ecstasy? The cheaper set menu is FF590 a head, sans vin.

LE JULES VERNE, Tour Eiffel, Champ de Mars, 75007 ☎ **(1) 4555 6144**
It may sound like a tourist trap but it ain't. You arrive by private glass lift and enter one of the most striking salles in Paris, renovated in dark steel

tones to match the Tower's technological style. Breath-taking view and imaginative 2-star nouvelle cuisine by Louis Grondard. Françoise Dumas has given memorable parties here, and it's a top spot for **Barry Humphries.**

THE LANCASTER, 7 rue de Berri, 75008 ☎ **(1) 4359 9043**
The new chef produces some of the most subtly inventive nouvelle cuisine in Paris. Tables in the interior garden in summer.

🐾 **LUCAS CARTON, 9 place de la Madeleine, 75008** ☎ **(1) 4265 2290**
Inspiration and ingenuity have been breathed into this restaurant by the great chef, Alain Senderens (late of L'Archestrate). Praised by **Steven Spurrier, Michel Guérard** and **Robert Noah**: *"Very trendy modern cuisine."* An all-time best dish for

---

MARKETS I: AROUND PARIS

Rungis (the major wholesale food market of Paris – one for the professionals) is *"the only market I would wake up at 4 o'clock in the morning to go to"* – **Nico Ladenis**. *"Best of all is* **rue Lepic, Montmartre** *– it's fabulous on a Sunday morning, big and fun. Also* **rue Montorgueil** *near Les Halles: it's a bit bloody sometimes, but it's terrific"* – **Glynn Christian**. *"My favourite market is* **rue Mouffetard** *– for fish, vegetables, tea, fruit, the whole works. Also* **rue Daguerre**. *I like to go where the people shop; I'm interested in social patterns of eating; I like to see what people are buying that month"* – **Clare Ferguson. Rue de Seine** is unmissable if you're wild about wild mushrooms. A **Glynn Christian** tip for market-lovers is to obtain the leaflet *Les Marchés de Paris* from the Mairie. **Versailles** Sunday market is *"superb"* – **Frederic Raphael** and *"fabulous"* – **Paula Wolfert**. *"Fontainebleau is best because although it's French, there are African influences – an exciting food market"* – **David Litchfield.**

FOOD AND DRINK

AFTER THE REVOLUTION

What was nouvelle cuisine all about? Is there life after the kiwi fruit? **Raymond Blanc** elucidates: *"Nouvelle cuisine was a movement which was created as a reaction against the rule. The cuisine of the 19th century suited neither the physiology nor the needs of people today. In any revolution you get blood and paranoia and ecstasy! This movement was no exception. A lot of silly things were done. Now, especially in France, which is still the leader of gastronomy, nouvelle cuisine is better understood and there are beautiful things coming out. Cuisine is light – not deceitfully light, but* really *light. It's ever-changing with the seasons, it's curious, it's exciting!"* **Anton Mosimann** has known it for years: *"I believe cuisine naturelle is going far – flying my own flag, I know, but the lightness of food is popular. Excellent food with health in mind."* **Ken Hom** agrees: *"The trend for lighter food has spread everywhere. Portions have got bigger again but cream and butter have diminished, thank heavens."* As for the kiwi fruit, that's had its day, but the art of presentation remains.

Barbara Kafka was *"a whole roast foie gras – wonderful"*. *"For grandeur it's particularly beautiful. Modern interpretation of classic cuisine in classical surroundings"* – **Roy Ackerman**. *"Really quite delicious. It's like Cantonese food in that it has very little sauce"* – **Ken Hom**. *"Goes from strength to strength . . ."* – **Prue Leith**. Also from expense to expense.

LA MAREE, 1 rue Daru, 75008 ☎ **(1) 4763 5242**
One of the best fish and seafood restaurants in Paris owned by mother-son team Babette and Eric Trompier. Chef Gérard Rouillard knows how to pick the freshest fish and concocts new recipes – belons au champagne, suprême de turbot à la moutarde. Arguably the best rougets grillés in France (it vies with La Reserve de Beaulieu). **Mark McCormack's** No 1 in Paris.

MAXIM'S, 3 rue Royale, 75008 ☎ **(1) 4265 2794**
Exorbitant prices and fair cooking, but, most importantly, the Art Nouveau elegance of one of the world's best dining rooms. The glitzy clientele sit in the front room at lunchtime and at the back for dinner.

LA MIRAVILE, 25 quai de la Tournelle, 75005 ☎ **(1) 4634 0778**
Owner-chef Gilles Epié's tiny new restaurant attracts a branché crowd. Classical French cuisine. *"A good up-and-coming chef. He does a wonderful bread pudding"* – **Robert Noah**. Modest prices.

LE ROI DU POT-AU-FEU, 34 rue Vignon, 75009 ☎ **(1) 4742 3710**
For – you guessed it – pot-au-feu, the in thing in Paris. *"That's all they serve. It's wonderful, terribly simple. First they serve the broth from the meat and marrow bone, which is full of flavour, then everything that was cooked in it – beef, a big leek, carrots, potatoes, turnips, with coarse salt and mustard. It's marvellous"* – **Sophie Grigson**.

🍴 **TAILLEVENT, 15 rue Lamennais, 75008** ☎ **(1) 4561 1290**
A consistent front-runner. Among the experts who say so are: **Craig Claiborne** (*"The greatest restaurant in the world"*), **Ken Hom** (*"Original and imaginative. He tries to go beyond his métier into a realm that makes him a genius"*), **Steven Spurrier** (*"The best*

grand restaurant in Paris – one I'd cancel all appointments for"*), **Michael Broadbent** (*"Quietly elegant setting, consistently excellent food, faultless wine selection and immaculate service"*), **Thomas Hoving** (*"It's the greatest classic French restaurant, with one of the greatest wine cellars in the business"*), **Egon Ronay** (*"I love it"*), **Prue Leith** (*"Still the best"*), **Robert Noah** (*"The most beautiful, the best wine and service"*), **Simon Hopkinson, Mariuccia Mandelli** and **Serena Sutcliffe**: *"The one with the most class because it combines great quality with discretion – it's not flash. The owner, Jean-Claude Vrinat, is a civilized man of taste, and so his restaurant takes on his aura."*

🍴 **TAN DINH, 60 rue Verneuil, 75007** ☎ **(1) 4544 0487**
"Just amazing combinations of flavours, very unusual – different spices, interesting seafood, the treatment of raw foods is excellent, presentation very attractive. A French chef cooking Vietnamese is about as near as you will get to perfection" – **Roy Ackerman**. *"The most exquisitely flavoured food I have ever tasted, though it was its wine list that drew me there in the first place"* – **Michael Broadbent**. *"Fantastically delightful, with one of the best lists of claret in Paris"* – **Robert Carrier**.

LA TOUR D'ARGENT, 15 quai Tournelle, 75005 ☎ **(1) 4354 2337**
A string of bests keep this otherwise hackneyed restaurant in the top league: the best view, over the Notre Dame; the best wine cellar in Paris, if not the world; the most elegant setting – and a better-than-ever menu under new chef Manuel Martinez (Claude Terrail is still proprietor). Walls are graffiti-stricken with autographs of the *right* sort of diner – Princes of Wales past and present, Sir Winston Churchill, de Gaulle, Roosevelt . . . and it's next-best-thing-to-royalty Duke Jacques d'Orléans's favourite. *"The worst restaurant to be*

FOOD AND DRINK

DESERT ISLAND SURVIVAL KIT:

NICO LADENIS

"I think I would take a cookery book with me – probably Michel Guérard's La Cuisine Gourmande. I would take a pre-cooked, ready-to-consume bacon-and-egg breakfast with a hot cup of coffee and some toast; and a knife to enable me to fend for myself and exist on the desert island."

---

seen at with the best food" – **Anne Willan. Paula Wolfert** elaborates: *"Unless you've already been photographed and put up on the walls, forget it. They treat you like a spot on the carpet. What is so irritating is it* does *have wonderful food."* **Robert Carrier** reckons *"the new chef is bringing this world-famous restaurant back to a great, new life"*.

SHOPS

ANDROUET, 41 rue Amsterdam, 75008
☎ (1) 4874 2690
A fabulous fromagerie. Cheeses from all over the country are aged in cellars below the shop. About 4½ tons of 200 varieties are sold a month. **Robert Carrier** is a fan. Tuck into their 7-course fromage feast.

BARTHELEMY, 51 rue de Grenelle, 75007
☎ (1) 4548 5675; 92 rue Grande, Fontainebleau
☎ 6422 2164
The grandest cheese shop in town serves the crème of Paris society, including the Palais d'Elysée. It's le meilleur, according to Judith Krantz, **Azzedine Alaïa, Steven Spurrier** and **Don Hewitson.**

BERTHILLON, 31 rue St Louis en l'Ile, 75004
☎ (1) 4354 3161
The ices are a dream, although the queues and offhandedness of the staff can make it a nightmare. *"You find it by looking for the queue. The best flavour is fraises des bois, which doesn't taste of strawberries or of fraises des bois essence, it tastes of fraises des bois"* – **Frederic Raphael.**

Azzedine Alaïa and **Michel Guérard** line up; if you can't bear the wait, taste the ices at the café, **Le Flore en l'Ile.**

CHRISTIAN CONSTANT, 26 rue du Bac, 75007
☎ (1) 4296 5353
Le choix for chocolates, superb sorbets and ice creams. **Robert Carrier** goes for the pastries.

DALLOYAU, 101 rue du Faubourg St Honoré, 75008
☎ (1) 4359 1810
Established in 1802, they make the best macaroons in a zillion flavours, and other extravagant gâteaux. Hog a mogador – chocolate cake, mousse and

♣ —*Europe's Best*— ♣

	RESTAURANTS
1	**JAMIN (ROBUCHON)**, Paris
2	**GIRARDET** , Crissier, Switzerland
3	**MICHEL GUERARD**, Eugénie-les-Bains, France
4	**LE MANOIR AUX QUAT' SAISONS**, Gt Milton, England
5	**LUCAS CARTON**, Paris
6	**PAUL BOCUSE**, Lyons, France
7	**LA TANTE CLAIRE**, London
8	**SAN DOMENICO**, Bologna, Italy
9	**COMME CHEZ SOI**, Brussels
10	**DIE AUBERGINE**, Munich

♣ ———————— ♣

raspberry jam. Tops for **Charlotte Rampling.**

FAUCHON, 26 place de la Madeleine, 75008
☎ (1) 4742 6011
The grandest and most famous food hall in Paris. Over 20,000 products from home and abroad – exotic groceries (*"The best salad shop in the world and every kind of fresh herb, olive oil and flavoured vinegar"* – **Robert Carrier**), pastries, chocolates (**Charlotte Rampling**'s favourites), coffee, tea, spices and charcuterie.

HEDIARD, 21 place de la Madeleine, 75008
☎ (1) 4266 4436 and branches
A tremendous array of goods, down to their own spices, oils and vinegars. *"The world is divided into those who like Fauchon and those who like Hédiard. I like Hédiard"* – **Loyd Grossman**. *"Quite right too,"* exclaims **Anne-Elisabeth Moutet**: *"Fauchon is nouveau riche, Hédiard is BCBG."*

LAMAZERE, 23 rue de Ponthieu, 75008
☎ (1) 4359 6666
The best foie gras in town. A restaurant, too, with fine cuisine from the south-west. *"The only man who has ever patented a way of preserving truffles!"* – **Robert Carrier.**

LIONEL POILANE, 8 rue du Cherche-Midi, 75006
☎ (1) 4548 4259
His handmade sourdough pain de campagne, baked in wood-fired ovens, is known and loved the whole world over.

LA MAISON DE LA TRUFFE, 19 place de la Madeleine, 75008
☎ (1) 4265 5322
Among other delicious delicacies (caviare, terrine de foie gras, brimming hampers), the best and most expensive truffles can be sniffed out here between November and March.

LA MAISON DU CHOCOLAT, 225 rue du Faubourg St Honoré, 75008
☎ (1) 4227 3944; 52 rue François 1er, 75008
☎ (1) 4723 3825

Though Paul B... is the hot chocolatier of the moment, Robert Linxe has been No 1 for years. Golden platters piled high with sinful wafers, truffles and filled chocolates tempt **Michel Guérard. Sophie Grigson** chocs out the branch at rue François 1er: *"It's like a salon de thé serving only hot chocolate ... thick, rich mountains of whipped cream. It's wicked, sincerely bad for you and heavenly. After one I was sunk."*

PAUL B..., 4 rue Marbeuf, 75008 ☎ (1) 4720 8626
Next door to his Chez Edgard, this ivory-panelled shop is the latest from Paul Benmussa. All his chocs are fresh with no additives. The pralines are unsurpassable and the dark chocolate-coated *smoked* almonds are subtly sweet-savoury. M. Paul even closes during the hottest summer months rather than see his chocolates spoil.

PETROSSIAN, 18 blvd Latour-Maubourg, 75007 ☎ (1) 4551 5973
Cult caviare of the very best quality, sold in picturesque tins. Also very fine smoked salmon, foie gras, truffles, fresh blinis and Russian pastries. Also a grand restaurant in New York.

RAFFI, 60 ave Paul-Doumer, 75016 ☎ (1) 4503 1090; 60 rue Lafayette, 75009 ☎ (1) 4770 1292
The original branch of this Armenian grocer's is at rue Lafayette, but the seizième branch is smarter. Anything Middle Eastern – all sorts of olives, halva, sackfuls of Oriental spices and basketfuls of dried fruits. *"Just the* smell *of the place is fattening,"* sighs **Jean-Michel Jaudel.**

ROBERT & COESNON, 30 rue Dauphine, 75006 ☎ (1) 4326 5639
The best charcuterie in town – a small affair with the finest pâté en croûte, cervelas, rosette de Lyon, home-smoked bacon, foie gras cru, game terrines and a range of boudins noirs (black pudding).

REST OF FRANCE

RESTAURANTS

ALAIN CHAPEL, Mionnay, 01390 St-André-de-Corcy ☎ 7891 8202
Some of the best food in the world when Chapel's en forme. A complex menu offering the local cuisine Bressane – ragoût of cocks' combs, kidneys with truffles. However, the interior has been described as being as attractive as a motel in Tucson, Arizona. *"Maybe he's sincere but he's too intellectual for me"* – **Robert Noah.**

AUBERGE DE L'ILL, rue de Collonges, Illhaeusern, 68150 Ribeauvillé ☎ 8971 8323
Highly recommended by **Paula Wolfert** and **Craig Claiborne**, this restaurant sits by the river Ill, with a lovely flower garden full of willows. Sophisticated combination of haute cuisine and Alsatian regional cooking.

CHANTECLER, Hôtel Negresco, 37 promenade des Anglais, 06000 Nice ☎ 9388 3951
Jacques Maximin is one of the leading chefs in the world. But check he's still here – he may be opening his own restaurant in Paris.

LE CHATEAU EZA, 06360 Eze-Village ☎ 9341 1224
Brilliant young chef Dominique le Stanc's hotel-restaurant. *"He has taken the coast by storm and does some of the best food you will ever find. He's very inventive, one of those people who can do something extraordinary with the simplest pasta or potato. It's phenomenal to eat in the sun and look down at St Jean Cap Ferrat and the sea"* – **Andrew Lloyd Webber.** Closed in winter. See also Travel.

CLUB 55, plage de Pampelonne, 83350 Ramatuelle ☎ 9479 8014
The place to eat around St Tropez, set in two fishermen's cottages by the beach. *"The car park is crammed full with expensive machinery – the latest Ferraris. You go through a door and you're literally on the beach, covered a series of umbrellas. It's the Langan's of St Tropez"* – **Roy Ackerman.**

ESPERANCE, St Père, 89450 Vézelay ☎ 8633 2045
A classic restaurant tucked away in a small hotel. *"M. Meneau is self-taught. He cooks 'sexual cuisine' – the cromesquis de foie gras explodes in your mouth"* – **Robert Noah. Paula Wolfert** is another great admirer, and so is **Raymond Blanc:** *"His best dishes are fricassée de champignons des bois, the cromesquis, and for dessert just warm raspberries with vanilla ice cream.*

GEORGES BLANC, 01540 Vonnas ☎ 7450 0010
Run by one of the best chefs in the world, this restaurant is in **Ken Hom**'s and **Roy Ackerman**'s top 10.

JEAN BARDET, 57 rue Groison, 37000 Tours ☎ 4741 4111
Celebrated for his featherlight touch and gastronomic surprises. Recommended by **Roy Ackerman.**

LABORDERIE, Tamniès, 24620 Les Eyzies-de-Tayac ☎ 5329 6859
For one of the best wine lists in the country. *"It's exceptional, very very reasonable. While stocks last there is a Château Grand Barrail still at FF 125, which is a gift. All the grapies in the region go there"* – **Frederic Raphael.**

LEON DE LYON, 1 rue de Pleney, 69001 Lyons ☎ 7828 1133
Lyonnaise ambience and specialities. *"I love it, I love the continuity. When his father died the current chef was in his early 20s and everyone said that's the end of that, but he made it better than ever. The Lyonnaise still go there, it's not artificial"* – **Robert Noah.**

LOU MAZUC, 12210 Laguiole ☎ 6544 3224
Paula Wolfert rates this

FOOD AND DRINK

> 66 *Chefs are like authors – they don't write their best book at 19.*
> *Their peak comes later. In their 20s they show extreme talent, but*
> *they don't actually have an identity, and it's only when they're*
> *more mature that they refine and develop their own style* 99

🐾 DREW SMITH

restaurant among the top 10 in France. Michel Bras is certainly armed with a mass of new ideas. *"He has taken real peasant – not bourgeois but peasant – food and brought it to new heights. It's definitely worth the 3-hour trip from civilization – the food is that good"* – **PW.**

🐾 **MICHEL GUÉRARD, Les Prés et les Sources d'Eugénie, Eugénie-les-Bains, 40320 Geaune ☎ 5851 1901**
Michel Guérard's restaurant is a showpiece for his cuisine minceur and classic nouvelle cuisine. None-too-slender recommendations from **Barbara Kafka, Robert Mondavi** and **Robert Noah***:* *"His cuisine minceur has been misunderstood. He says it's a comma in the sentence of his life." "My favourite dessert, bar none, is Michel Guérard's pear soufflé, especially when eaten in the company of his eternally smiling, raven-haired wife"* – **Lady Mary Fairfax.**

MOULIN DE L'ABBAYE, 80310 Brantôme, Dordogne ☎ 5305 8022
An old mill with a riverside terrace. *"A wonderful restaurant in French peasant country; always packed"* – **Roy Ackerman.**

🐾 **MOULIN DE MOUGINS, Quartier Notre-Dame de Vie, 424 chemin de Moulin, 06250 Mougins ☎ 9375 7824**
Roger Vergé's famous restaurant has earned 3 stars from Michelin, 19/20 from Gault Millau, and now a head of Napoleon. Rich gourmet extravaganzas are served to a rich, ritzy clientele from the coast, who throng in at Film Festival time. **Joan Collins, Lord Lichfield** and **Barbara Kafka** love it.

LE MOUSTIER, 41 bis rue Langlois, Milly la Forêt, 91490 Essonne ☎ 6498 9252
"My son and I were extremely impressed with luncheon there. One of the most outstanding things they gave us was pâté with fig purée, which was delicious. As the restaurant is in the crypt, it is a very unusual position, and very romantic" – **Barbara Cartland.**

OUSTAU DE BAUMANIERE, Le Vallon, Les-Baux-de-Provence, 13520 Mausanne-les-Alpilles ☎ 9097 3307
Pretty hotel and restaurant with antique furniture and a flowery terrace, though expansions have slightly spoilt the atmosphere and it's over-crowded in summer. Still, **Robert Noah** thinks it's worth it *"because it's so beautiful and the view is so special"*. *"Marvellous"* – **Egon Ronay.**

🐾 **PAUL BOCUSE, 50 quai de la Plagne, 69660 Collonges-au-Mont-d'Or, Lyons ☎ 7822 0140**
An inspired master of cuisine ancienne – home cooking exquisitely executed. A favourite of **Michel Guérard** *("His roast chicken is one of the best I know"). "The Lourdes of gastronomy. Nevertheless the Bocuse ethic is 'don't let them out still able to walk if they don't want to'. He belongs to the tradition of French cooking where it's not at all*

FOOD AND DRINK

MARKETS II: SOUTHERN FRANCE

"My greatest pleasure in food shopping is at markets – **Nice** *for instance"* – **Barbara Kafka. Sophie Grigson** agrees: *"Nice general market is like dying and going to heaven. It has Provence encapsulated. 7 different types of peaches, wonderful provençale herbs in huge bunches, candied fruit. Marvellous fish markets. It smells of Provence, all the scents mingling – peaches, lavender, thyme."* **"L'Isle-sur-la-Sorgue** *in Provence has everything from fish to truffles, from peasant-made olive oil to bags of mint brought by the Arabs. It's in a beautiful market square of a very attractive town – good on every count"* – **Keith Floyd.** *"My favourite market is* **Périgueux** *on Saturday mornings. All regional products – you see anything from an octogenarian selling a dozen eggs and 2 home-reared ducks, to an assortment of foie gras, some of the finest herbs and the most amazing selection of olives"* – **Roy Ackerman.** *"On the waterfront at* **Ajaccio, Corsica** *there is so much home-made produce – pastries, cheeses, wonderful salamis and the best charcuterie in the world. This is because the pigs are extremely lean, eating only chestnuts and acorns"* – **Glynn Christian.** *"I think the picture postcard-sized jewel of France is* **Bandol.** *I love that market – it's perfection in miniature"* – **Paula Wolfert.**

FOOD AND DRINK

chancy – that's what professionalism is all about – and not trying to make the customer feel inferior" – **Frederic Raphael**. "I love it. Excellent food. He's always putting more money into it, whether it's changing colour schemes or buying more silver. His kitchen is one of the most beautiful I've ever seen" – **Robert Noah**. Craig Claiborne and **Robert Mondavi** are fans.

PIC, 285 ave Victor Hugo, 26000 Valence ☎ 7544 1532
"The food is absolutely superb – mousse of salmon done too beautifully like a flower. You can sit in the garden and the place is always packed" – **Barbara Cartland**. "Always full of locals not tourists. It still has a family feel to it. Lovely" – **Serena Sutcliffe**. "It's like the gastronomic civic centre for the whole Lower Rhône region. The wine people go there to entertain, the locals go" – **Robert Noah**. "The one French chef who never stirs from his restaurant. His soufflé orange glacé is the best pudding in the world" – **Quentin Crewe**.

PIERRE BENOIST, Croutelle, 86240 Ligugé ☎ 4957 1152
"The best one-star meal that I know. It's very simple cooking – very good salade tiède with chicken's livers and artichoke hearts" – **Frederic Raphael**.

LA RESERVE CHEZ LOULOU, 91 blvd de la Plage, 06800 Cagnes-sur-Mer ☎ 9331 0017
"A lovely restaurant. He has excellent ideals – he closes at weekends and in July and August because he doesn't like tourists. It's just fish brought in that morning" – **Andrew Lloyd Webber**.

ST HUBERT, St Saturnin d'Apt, 84490 Vaucluse ☎ 9075 4202
"The very best restaurant in the whole world. The chef draws heavily from regional sources. His roots are very much in Provence, but he cooks in his own very special modern way" – **Keith Floyd**.

TROISGROS, place de la Gare, 42300 Roanne ☎ 7771 6697
A long-standing family-run hotel-restaurant that has consistently been awarded the top foodie accolades. Unpretentious, bourgeois cooking at its very finest. "Better than ever. They're assured, calm. There's the same joking and enthusiasm, the same waiters. Bursting with new ideas" – **Robert Noah**.

VANEL, 22 rue Maurice-Fontvieille, 31000 Toulouse ☎ 6121 5182
"He is always overlooked. When I see the recipes from other chefs, I laugh: Vanel was doing that 10 years ago! The problem is he's too old, and he's not a designer cook. He's done for country cooking what Troisgros did for cuisine bourgeoise" – **Paula Wolfert**.

Monaco

LOUIS XV, Hôtel de Paris, place du Casino, 98007 Monte Carlo ☎ 9350 8080
The great Alain Ducasse (ex-Juana in Juan-les-Pins) has been installed with a top-notch staff and the restaurant has been renovated (ultra-grand Parisian rather than simple Côte d'Azur). The results are wowing the Riviera.

FRENCH WINE

ALSACE

"France is still undoubtedly the tops, but, with increasing world competition, it must keep looking to its laurels to see it isn't overtaken" – **Serena Sutcliffe**.

Aromatic, spicy, light white wines combine French and German character. These are far and away the best wines to order in a restaurant when nothing else on the list beckons; the finest – like the GEWURTZTRAMINER of

Théo Faller – deserve ordering in their own right.
Adventurous palates should seek out Hugel's Vendange Tardive and Selections de Grains Nobles: **Michael Broadbent** thinks the 1971 Vendange tardive wine the best Alsace wine he's sipped.

BORDEAUX

"Bordeaux remains the best and most reliable source of fine wine in the world" – **Anthony Hanson**. Thinkers pause over claret to sip and reflect: irrationalists and sensation-seekers gulp at burgundy. There are four main growing areas for red Bordeaux.

The Médoc

A small number of beautiful châteaux and a large number of valuable grapes redeem an otherwise dull landscape. The four 1ers crus classés – Baron Eric's LAFITE-ROTHSCHILD, MOUTON-ROTHSCHILD (formerly Baron Philippe's, now his daughter Philippine's), Laura Mentzelopoulos's MARGAUX and the English-owned LATOUR (Pearson Group) – dominate, and these are the wines that top the best lists. **Michael Broadbent** (whose gold-plated taste buds deserve mention in their own right: the world's best papillae) lists 2 vintages of each 1er cru among his greatest wines: 1899 and 1953 for Lafite, 1900 and 1961 for Margaux, 1924 and 1949 for Mouton, and 1929 and 1945 for Latour. **Charlotte Rampling** takes a broader view: "I like any Bordeaux from the Pauillac area."

LAFITE
Jeffrey Archer plumps for Lafite, "Of course, if I could, I'd be drinking Château Lafite!" **Lord Gowrie** agrees: "I have a few bottles left of a wine I'm very fond of, and that's Lafite 1953." Admired also by **Azzedine Alaïa** and **Inès de la Fressange**.

LATOUR
"I think Latour has come up

top more often than any other claret during my lifetime" – **Hugh Johnson** (now a director of the château). Tops also with **Lord Montagu of Beaulieu.**

MARGAUX
Perhaps the finest château. **Max Lake** fancies the vintages since 1978 (after Laura Mentzelopoulous took over and the wines improved).

MOUTON-ROTHSCHILD
According to **Joseph Berkmann**, "1949 Château Mouton-Rothschild is probably the greatest claret ever produced. It has a strong concentration of cassis-like flavour, clean, elegant, soft yet masculine." **Robert Mondavi** flocks to Mouton, "the best maintained château in the world."

Rest of Médoc

Joseph Berkmann rates highly the 1961 CHATEAU PALMER – "under the condition that it was cellared at the château, since quite a few cases in a much more tired version make the rounds of Christie's and Sotheby's. Not as rich and concentrated as Mouton and Latour, but tremendous finesse, marvellous flavour – everything great claret should be." **Serena Sutcliffe** notes: "Many classified châteaux of Bordeaux have recently been through a renaissance and are better than ever. These are some of the rising meteors of the '80s and are still bargains: CHATEAU D'ISSAN from the Margaux area and CHATEAU LAGRANGE (owned by Suntory) from the St Julien area." **Joseph Berkmann** rates another 2ème cru from St Julien, 1962 CHATEAU LEOVILLE-LAS CASES – "delicate now, yet surprisingly young and certainly much better than the fabled 1961. A hint of cigar box and a long silky finish." PICHON-LONGUEVILLE, Comtesse de Lalande (from Pauillac) and COS-D'ESTOURNEL (St-Estèphe) are mooted by **Anthony Hanson** to be among the "super-seconds" – the best

2ème cru neighbours to the four 1ers. LYNCH-BAGES (affectionately known as 'Lunch Bags') is relished by **Anthony Hanson** and **Max Lake.**

The Graves

HAUT-BRION
Although surrounded now by suburban Bordeaux, it maintains its long-held dominance. **Michael Broadbent** is haunted by 1945 and 1961 while **Hugh Johnson** votes an IMPERIALE of 1899 "the most spell-binding claret I have ever drunk." **Lord Gowrie** adds praise: "I like Haut-Brion '59 when you can get it (which is seldom!)."

St-Emilion

CHEVAL BLANC
Along with AUSONE (the name is associated with Roman poet and tippler Ausonius), this is the best in the region, producing soft, rich wines. Among those who dream of Cheval Blanc are **Lords Lichfield** and **Montagu of Beaulieu**, as well as **Michael Broadbent** ("the 1921 and the 1947"). "The '47 is one of the great classic vintages of all time: it is the marker for all claret lovers, a monolithic wine, like a pillar of marble. The moment you meet it, it grabs your attention and explodes with flavour. You just think: 'What is this thing?' Anybody would know that it was something quite out of the ordinary" – **Hugh Johnson.**

Pomerol

"John Armit taught me to love wines from Pomerol. I adore them all". – **Ed Victor.**

PETRUS
Hors concours, and nearly everything else. Tiny quantities of fabulous wine ("out of this world" – **Margaux Hemingway**) sell at double the price you first thought of and more. Pétrus '61 is the finest wine **Auberon Waugh** has ever tasted. **Michael Broadbent** sticks his neck out over the '45

and '71. It's **Stanley Marcus**'s "best wine."

Sauternes

CHATEAU D'YQUEM
To turn to sweeter things, as Pétrus to Pomerol, so d'Yquem to Sauternes: definition and epiphany in one. Tipplers include **Lord Lichfield, Steven Spurrier** ("the 1945"), **David Shilling** ("1925, iced, is my absolute favourite drink"), **Charlotte Rampling, Michael Broadbent** ("the 1847 – just about the greatest wine ever") and **Leo Schofield** ("the 1927").

CLIMENS, from Barsac, 1929 and SUDUIRAUT, Preignac, 1976 are alternative sweet-tooth soothers, votes **Michael Broadbent.**

BURGUNDY

Red burgundy is an unreasonable, irrational wine. The climate in the Burgundy region is of almost British unpredictability, and the grape they use (pinot noir) is a prima donna. The best red burgundies are wildly expensive. For **Sir Clive Sinclair**, any burgundy is the best red wine. White burgundy is more reliable (though no less expensive), a sage queen to its mad red consort.

Red Burgundy

BONNES MARES
Top-ranking grand cru. "Christopher Roumier of Chambolle-Musigny is now acknowledged one of Burgundy's rising stars, lifting Domaine Georges Roumier into the top league" – **Anthony Hanson.**

CHAMBERTIN-CLOS-DE-BEZE
"Domaine Louis Trapet, Joseph Drouhin, Joseph Faiveley and Ets Leroy consistently field top examples" – **Anthony Hanson.**

CLOS DE VOUGEOT
Here the growers' position on the hillside is paramount.

FOOD AND DRINK

Anthony Hanson advises: *"Choose from growers with their vines in the top section of the Clos touching the château: Domaine Jean Gros is one of the best."*

NUITS ST GEORGES

Joseph Berkmann recommends the *"1979 Les Chaignots, Domaine Alain Michelot, a glorious burgundy, rich in fruit, powerful stuff. The kind of wine that made Nuits St Georges famous the world over."*

RICHEBOURG

Expensive *grand-cru* wines. *"Rising stars of this great vineyard are Mongeard-Mugneret, Jean Grivot and Méo-Camuzet. Wines to watch are the '85 and '86 vintages"* – Anthony Hanson.

LA ROMANEE-CONTI

The best red burgundy with prices in the Pétrus league. Michael Broadbent cites the 1937 vintage as the one to sell your house to buy, while Steven Spurrier thinks the 1934 the best wine he's ever tasted. Quentin Crewe says: *"Burgundy is my favourite, and Romanée-Conti is the best. I'd be very happy drinking that for the rest of my life."* For Raymond Blanc, it's *"really the very best burgundy, still made in the traditional way – bare feet, treading the grapes."*

LA TACHE

Michael Broadbent recalls the 1945 with reverence; it would see Quentin Crewe happily through life if the Romanée-Conti ran dry. Both vineyards, unfairly enough, are owned by the Domaine de la Romanée-Conti, a partnership between vivacious Mme 'Lalou' Bize-Leroy, and Aubert de Villaine, urbane, scholarly, meticulous. In 1983 de Villaine had damaged grapes picked by tweezer.

VOLNAY

Lord Montagu of Beaulieu likes any Volnay. For Anthony Hanson, the 1966 VOLNAY TAILLEPIEDS Domaine de Montille is *"an immaculately fine, earthy, elegant burgundy."*

White Burgundy

Ed Victor says simply: *"I love white burgundies"*, while Serena Sutcliffe says that *"the most exciting whites are from Burgundy, with the New World not far behind."*

MEURSAULT

Topping, smooth dry whites, tipped by Lord Montagu of Beaulieu and Anthony Hanson. Of MEURSAULT-PERRIERES, Hanson says *"Comte Lafon has the deepest cellar in the village, and holdings in the best vineyards of Meursault."* Joseph Berkmann adds fruitily: *"The 1979 Meursault-Perriéres, Domaine Jean-François Coche-Dury, gives an impression of melon and mango enlivened by a touch of grapefruit, very fine; soft finish."*

MONTRACHET

Hugh Johnson, Raymond Blanc, Lord Montagu of Beaulieu, Michel Guérard and Anne Willan are united and positive: this is the best (*"all 9 acres of it"* – AW). Michael Broadbent thirsts after a 1952 (Laguiche) or a 1966 (Domaine de la Romanée-Conti).

PULIGNY- AND CHASSAGNE-MONTRACHET

Joseph Berkmann nominates the 1984 Puligny-Montrachet LA TRUFFIERE, Domaine Etienne Sauzet, as *"surely the greatest bottle of white burgundy for present day drinking. An exotic combination of cinnamon and cloves with hints of allspice, perfectly balanced by great elegance and tremendous length."* For Stirling Moss, Puligny-Montrachet (and CLOS DES MOUCHES – Beaune) are his favourite *"crisp white wines."* Anthony Hanson votes for CHEVALIER-MONTRACHET (*"the greatest wine in the Domaine Leflaive stable – elegant, complex, silky, exquisite"*) and BATARD-MONTRACHET (*"Etienne Sauzet makes delicious wine, so does Joseph Drouhin"*).

CHAMPAGNE

BOLLINGER

Non-vintage favourite, for its majesty and balance: it regularly has grapies such as Lord Montagu of Beaulieu groping for their flûtes. *"The best without a doubt"* – Elise Pascoe. *"Bollinger RD (recently disgorged) is for real aficionados with its extra bottle age and biscuity bouquet and flavour. Their Vieilles vignes Blanc de Noirs comes, remarkably, from non-grafted vines and tastes out of this world"* – Serena Sutcliffe.

DEUTZ & GELDERMANN

A small champagne house whose luxury brand is Cuvée William Deutz. *"I have a favourite champagne, which is not necessarily the most expensive. It's Deutz, it's a wonderful champagne, and I prefer it often to Roederer Cristal"* – Ed Victor.

DOM PERIGNON

Moët & Chandon's flagship, and the Cuvée de Prestige with the highest profile. Favoured by Lord Montagu of Beaulieu and Dorian Wild who reveals that in Australia, *"Dom Perignon is the yuppies' champagne, especially in Perth."*

❝ *The best red burgundy producers at the moment are Henri Jayer on the Côte de Nuits and Michel Lafarge on the Côte de Beaune. White burgundy is always easier to produce* ❞

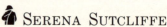

SERENA SUTCLIFFE

> 66 *Champagne to my mind isn't worth drinking. I think it's just a way of using up all the wine that isn't good enough to drink flat. It's the greatest bit of marketing in the world. Now they get racing drivers to squirt it all over each other* 99
>
> STIRLING MOSS

KRUG
The non-vintage Grande Cuvée is a match for anyone else's Cuvée de Prestige: *"The size of bubbles is very small and they almost seem to disappear as you taste – outstanding. It has a beautiful after-taste. I don't like champagnes that are too acid. Krug is beautifully harmonious and delicate"* – **Robert Mondavi**. *"The best-made champagne – one of the few remaining grandes marques that is made with proper hand-turning of the bottles. Magnificent"* – **Leo Schofield**. *"Their Blanc de Blancs, Clos du Mesnil, is fantastic"* – **Hugh Johnson**. **Margaux Hemingway**'s No 1. Meanwhile, **Serena Sutcliffe** votes Krug *"the best* vintage *champagne and the one that keeps for ever."*

LANSON BLACK LABEL
Frederic Raphael finds inspiration in its freshness and fruitiness. He was not the first. Edward and Mrs Simpson were partial to a drop of Lanson '15. Now it's in to drink pink.

LAURENT-PERRIER
The non-vintage is admired for its floweriness, lightness and delicacy. **Auberon Waugh** is *"very fond"* of the Cuvée Grande Siècle, while **Serena Sutcliffe** finds it *"remarkable for its depth of flavour, and a brilliant blend of 3 vintages."* The rosé was chosé by **Lady Elizabeth Anson** as her house bubbly to add froth to clients' parties.

PERRIER-JOUET
The luxury Belle Epoque comes in a painted bottle; together they please the eye and the palate of **Robert Mondavi**. **Serena Sutcliffe** divulges:*"The insiders' Cuvée de Prestige is Blason de France, a non-vintage blend that only* connoisseurs know about. It's also the bargain of the moment among luxury blends."

POL ROGER
Much support, including that of **Hugh Johnson** (*"My favourite champagne since I was born – their Cuvée de Prestige is the 'Sir Winston Churchill', but I think their rosé is fabulous. Very à la mode, the chic-est thing in town"*); **Lord Gowrie** (who also loves it in the pink); **Steven Spurrier** (*"delicious, elegant, perfect – lots of tiny bubbles"*), **Serena Sutcliffe** (*"one of the best non-vintages"*); **Lady Elizabeth Anson** and **Lord Montagu of Beaulieu.**

ROEDERER CRISTAL
Most people find the world looks best through a Cuvée de Prestige Cristal glass. *"I have to admit a weakness for Cristal – exquisite"* – **Michael Grade**. Also loved by **Serena Sutcliffe** (*"the best non-vintage"*), **Lord Lichfield**, **Quentin Crewe**, **Jeremiah Tower**, **Barbara Kafka**, **Lord Montagu of Beaulieu** and **Charlotte Rampling**, while **Raymond Blanc** enjoys the pink, in company with **Azzedine Alaïa.**

SALON LE MESNIL
The original Blanc de Blancs. Only appears about once every 5 years. *"The snobbiest of the lot"* – **Hugh Johnson.**

TAITTINGER
When you buy a bottle of bubbly you could also be getting a work of art: Taittinger Collection Champagne bottles are specially designed in a limited edition and wrapped around the latest vintage. The 1982 is housed in André Masson's 'early-morning blue' bottle with splashes of red and white (grape colours – geddit?) and another splodge of white on the top 'to evoke the sun on the vines and the champagne mousse'. **Inès de la Fressange** and **Lord Montagu of Beaulieu** like the *drink*, at any rate, while **Egon Ronay** and **Nico Ladenis** happily sip the Comte de Champagne.

VEUVE CLICQUOT
The well-known and well-loved yellow-label champers, named after the widow ('veuve') Clicquot herself, who discovered the method of producing uncloudy champagne.

Vintage Champagnes

Made from grapes picked in a single year and rich with the character of that year. (Non-grapies are sometimes disappointed by the un-bubbliness of their venerable beads.) Front runners are KRUG 1979, POL ROGER 1982, ROEDERER CRISTAL 1981 and BOLLINGER RD 1973.

> 66 *The best drink for me is champagne on the rocks. That way you never have a hangover in the morning, you can drink twice as much, and it always remains fresh and ice-cold* 99
>
>  LYNN WYATT

FOOD AND DRINK

FOOD AND DRINK

LOIRE VALLEY

A good MUSCADET is one of the best *petits vins* for seafood and a favourite of **Lady Elizabeth Anson** (though a cheap one can take on paint-stripper characteristics). POUILLY-FUME is the perfect complement to smoked food of all sorts. The best Loire wines are the sweetest: the ANJOU RABLAY 1928 is a **Michael Broadbent** best.

RHONE VALLEY

For those that like red wines that are big and unbridled, smell of earth, animals and leather, and taste of fruit and spice, the Rhône has at least three best wines.

CHATEAUNEUF-DU-PAPE

The knave: at its worst, infernal and head-splitting: at its best (like the 1969 Château Rayas that **Michael Broadbent** thinks the best Rhône wine he's

ever tasted), rich, herby and head-turning. *"An up-and-coming estate to watch, for its 1978 and 1983 vintages, is Châteauneuf-du-Pape, Domaine du Vieux Télégraphe"* tips **Anthony Hanson.**

COTE-ROTIE

The queen: it has a delicacy foreign to Hermitage that makes it *"the finest of all Rhône wines"* for **Hugh Johnson**. Etienne Guigal, Robert Jasmin and René Rostaing are the best names: **Steven Spurrier** reckons Guigal's 1978 'La Landonne' to be one of the finest young wines he's ever tasted.

HERMITAGE

The king. (It sold at FF 5 a bottle even in 1835, FF 1 more than Mouton and Latour.) The best names are Paul Jaboulet Aîné (Hermitage La Chapelle) and Gérard Chave. Impatient imbibers are warned away: no good Hermitage should even be approached before its 10th

Best Cognacs

COURVOISIER XO
DELAMAIN GRANDE
  CHAMPAGNE PALE
  AND DRY
HENNESSY PARADIS
RAGNAUD SABOURIN
  GRANDE
  CHAMPAGNE

birthday, and the best of the best only begin to learn manners at 15.

Grapies-in-the-know buy all the CORNAS they can lay their hands on, especially Jaboulet's or Clape's: it is Hermitage's considerably cheaper country cousin, though it needs nearly as long to mature.

Germany

RESTAURANTS

DIE AUBERGINE, Maximiliansplatz 5, D-8000 Munich 2 ☎ (089) 598171
The very best of the new French-influenced German nouvelle cuisine, based on trad national favourites, from game and mushrooms to quark. Gets **Barbara Kafka**'s vote.

GOLDNER PFLUG, Olpener Strasse 421, Merheim, D-5000 Cologne 91 ☎ (0221) 895509
They are certainly sold on gold here – gold chairs, gold curtains, gold ceiling. Despite the determinedly German name, there is a fine marriage of German taste and French genius. Dishes include seabass with truffles, and goose liver with lentils and cream.

LE MARRON, Provinzialstrasse 35, D-5300 Bonn 1 ☎ (0228) 253261
In a suburb of the capital, this old chestnut supplies adventurous German/French/ Italian dishes to off-duty politicians and diplomats.

COURVOISIER: A TRADITION OF XO-LENCE

Cognac Courvoisier continues to draw rich, fluid comments from the cognacenti, not just about the finest, XO, but at all levels. Of the Napoleon, contributors comment: *"If the book is one half as good as that bottle of Courvoisier, it ought to be a tremendous runaway best seller!"* – **Douglas Fairbanks Jr.** *"The best pre- or après-dinner drink is Courvoisier cognac"* – **Stanley Marcus**. *"I adore cognac – it's my drink – and Courvoisier is the best!"* – **Helen Gurley Brown. Glynn Christian** describes the XO: *"Courvoisier XO is one of the most fascinating and complicated experiences when drunk European-style in a balloon glass (as against Hong Kong-style over ice). Some of the XO cognacs have been aged in the cask for more than 60 years."* **Jacques Chirac** has this to say: *"The finest and noblest bouquets come from the Charente region, and from Jarnac in particular where Courvoisier is based. The Courvoisier products are of legendary quality. Each bottle bears a signature guaranteeing the uniqueness of the product."* You might think that **Paula Wolfert** is committing a sacrilege by *cooking* with Courvoisier, but why not make the whole meal taste as good as the digestif? *"Of course my favourite cognac is Courvoisier,"* she says. *"I represent them in the USA to show people how to cook with it – it's such a great flavour-enhancer."*

66 *The French have always dismissed the idea that there might be some great restaurants outside France. Well they've got to come to their senses, because if you go to Belgium, Germany, England, America, there is a new generation of chefs who are very bright, keen, ambitious and gifted* 99

RAYMOND BLANC

HOTEL VIER JAHRESZEITEN-KEMPINSKI,
Maximilianstrasse 17, D-8000 Munich 22 ☎ (089) 230390
The Walterspiel restaurant in this landmark hotel (see Travel) is one of the best and most beautiful in Germany.

GERMAN WINE

"Forget all those bland, sugary drinks from the supermarkets and go for the top estate Rieslings, which are currently the unsung beauties of the wine world" – **Serena Sutcliffe.**

MOSEL-SAAR-RUWER

DEINHARD
One of the best Mosel names, thanks initially to its 1900 acquisition of a portion of the Mosel's best vineyard: Doktor at Bernkastel. *All* its wines meet a very high standard: *'classic'* is the favoured description.

DER BISCHOFLICHEN WEINGUTER
Based in Trier. It may be a mouthful, but a sip of any of its elegant wines would be ample compensation for attempting to pronounce it.

EGON MULLER
The best name in the Saar: SCHARZHOFBERGERS-SCHWARZHOF has, for **Hugh Johnson**, *"as much penetrating perfume, vitality and 'breeding' as any wine in Germany."*

MAXIMIN GRUNHAUS
The best name in the Ruwer has a more musical ring: von

Schubert is the owner. Much loved for their fairytale label (more Perrault than Grimm) and for their magically haunting wines.

JJ PRUM
Their Sonnenuhr wines are among the Mosel's most voluptuous: **Hugh Johnson** enjoys their *"glorious honeyed ripeness."* It was their WEHLENER SONNENUHR FEINSTE BEERENAUSLESE of 1949 that **Michael Broadbent** noted in golden ink.

RHEINGAU

SCHLOSS VOLLRADS
One of the two best names in the Rheingau (and their labels harbour, in smaller print, one of the wine world's best names: owner Graf Matuschka-Greiffenclau). This is one of Germany's greatest private estates, from whose cellars came **Michael Broadbent**'s all-time Rhine wine: a 1947 TROCKENBEERE-NAUSLESE (TBA) – the sweetest and rarest grade of German wine. His sentiments are echoed by **Max Lake**: *"The great TBA is the best sweet wine in the world,"* and by a highly appreciative **Hugh Johnson**.

Among the other great Rheingau estates, all recommended by **Hugh Johnson**, are the RHEINGAU STATE DOMAIN at Eltville (*"one of the greatest wine estates on earth, historically amazing, going back to the Cistercian monks"* – **HJ**), SCHLOSS SCHONBORN, VON SIMMERN and WEGELER-DEINHARD.

NAHE

The best Nahe wines are often said to be between those of the Mosel and Rhine in character. This they are – with something more: *"To me, the great Nahe wines often have a hint of ethereal Sancerre, a delicate hint of the blackcurrant leaf with a delicious mineral undertone. In their delicacy yet completeness they make hypnotic sipping, far into the night"* – **Hugh Johnson**. Most hypnotic of all are CRUSIUS, HANS and PETER (*"among the best in Germany"* for **HJ**) and the STATE DOMAIN OF NIEDERHAUSEN-SCHLOSS BOCKELHEIM, mighty rival to Eltville.

RHEINPFALZ

Germany's sunny back garden produces much wine best drunk in sunny back gardens. The finest, though, are dining or drawing room affairs, and the three 'B's – VON BUHL, BASSERMANN-JORDAN and BURKLIN-WOLF – are among the names to go for. Burklin-Wolf is perhaps the best: **Hugh Johnson** can imagine drinking their Riesling Kabinett for breakfast: *"so pure and refreshing".*

Hong Kong

CAFES AND BARS

Also Browns Wine Bar and **Captain's Bar** (see Social & Night Life).

FOOD AND DRINK

BOTTOMS UP, 14-16 Hankow Rd, Tsimshatsui ☎ 3-721 4509
Not really the hostess bar it appears to be, this is in fact a raunchy, fun gweilo meeting-place, owned by expat Pat Sephton. All sorts jam in to sing 'yum sing' ('bottoms up').

DRAGON BOAT BAR, Hilton, 2 Queen's Rd, Central ☎ 5-233111
The best place in HK for strange, exotic cocktails.

MANDARIN COFFEE SHOP, 5 Connaught Rd, Central ☎ 5-220111
Where Tai-tais (grand Chinese ladies) reign at the morning-coffee hour, before going on to a hefty mahjong session.

RESTAURANTS

See also Social & Night Life for top gweilo haunts – the bar-café-disco-bistros **California Bar and Grill, Duddell's, 1997** and **Camargue.**

🍴 **AMIGO, 79a Wongneichong Rd, Happy Valley ☎ 5-772202**
"The best restaurant outside a hotel, as good as any of the top

🍴 Far East's Best 🍴

	ETHNIC RESTAURANTS
1	**FOOK LAM MOON**, Hong Kong
2	**KICCHO**, Osaka
3	**LEMON GRASS**, Bangkok
4	**FUKUZUSHI**, Tokyo
5	**KISSO**, Tokyo
6	**MAN WAH**, Hong Kong
7	**LAI CHING HEEN**, Hong Kong
8	**MIN JING**, (Goodwood Park Hotel), Singapore
9	**SANKO-IN-TEMPLE**, Koganei-chi
10	**INAGIKU**, Tokyo

JUNK FOOD

You can gollop down some of the best and cheapest seafood at ramshackle seaside restaurants on islands a mere ferry – (but preferably junk-) ride away: **Po Toi** is the current hit, where they actually *like* gweilos. Try salt-baked prawns, clams in black bean sauce, deep-fried squid and lobster. Or *"take a ferry to* **Lamma**, *to the village of Sok Ku Wan. There is a whole line of seafood restaurants. Excellent for lovely fresh prawns, crabs, lobsters, steamed fish ... Very easy to reach and a lot of fun"* – **Saul Lockhart**. Alternatively, and rather more touristy, from Oct-Apr: *"Floating sampan restaurants in the* **Causeway Bay Typhoon Shelter** *have excellent if slightly pricy seafood. Picture a sampan with table and chairs – the bar floats up to you, followed by the kitchen ... If you want, the world's most off-key band, who only know* The Yellow Rose of Texas *, will come up and play"* – **SL**. NB Go with a local and make sure you don't get in the wrong sampan – you could end up in a fish ball stall (floating brothel). For real street eats, **Robert Carrier** enjoys *"anything cooked in the great wide woks at the Poor Man's Nightclub"*, the open-air night market near the Macau ferry terminal.

Western hotel restaurants. Pure French, absolutely posh. A marvellous place" – **Saul Lockhart**. For post-races solace/self-congratulation.

BODHI, 56 Cameron Rd, Kowloon ☎ 3-739 2222; 388 Lockhart Rd, Wanchai ☎ 5-732155
One of the best Chinese vegetarian restaurants. *"You get things with lovely names like Three Marvels of the Hearts Desire – fried elm fungus with fresh dried mushrooms"* – **Saul Lockhart.**

🍴 **FOOK LAM MOON, 459 Lockhart Rd, Causeway Bay ☎ 5-891 2639**
Here is a test of whether you have 'face' with the Chinese: have you been taken to lunch at Fook Lam Moon? (You also pass if you've been taken to Gaddi's, Pierrot or Man Wah.) Superb for local specialities such as abalone and shark's fin at humbling prices – a bowl of shark's-fin soup could cost HK$1,000. Lord Hanson's sons Robert and Brooke eat here.

🍴 **GADDI'S, Peninsula Hotel, Salisbury Rd, Kowloon ☎ 3-666251**

One of the top restaurants in HK for Western food, in a dining room straight out of Edwardian England (though it opened in the '50s) – the same white damask napery, grand patterned carpet, and deferential service. Rolf Heiniger is the only maître d' in HK that matters: when he greets you by name, you've arrived. *"I love Gaddi's. Really fabulous food. Their roast pigeon breasts and salads are really wonderful – especially the foie gras salad"* – **Ken Hom**. A favourite of **Lord Lichfield.**

🍴 **LAI CHING HEEN, The Regent, Salisbury Rd, Kowloon ☎ 3-721 1211**
Chic setting behind the Regent's prized picture windows. Minimal, artistic modern Chinese cuisine.

🍴 **MAN WAH, Mandarin Oriental Hotel, 5 Connaught Rd, Central ☎ 5-220111**
Faultless Cantonese cuisine and through-the-roof prices. Voted by **Lord Lichfield** one of the best Chinese restaurants in the world. **Saul Lockhart**, however, finds *"it doesn't hold a cracker to the best Chinese*

FOOD AND DRINK (vertical margin text)

outside the hotels". These days, when a young gweilo's fancy turns to spring rolls, he may venture elsewhere.

🐟 **MARGAUX, Shangri-la Hotel, 64 Mody Rd, Tsimshatsui E ☎ 3-721 2111**
Along with the other hotel restaurants, it boasts first-class French cuisine in super-luxe surroundings, but here *everyone* is treated with the same deference. Mind-blowing pâtisserie. It also has an exceptionally good female Chinese sommelière (which caused shock-waves around the colony) and a fine cellar.

🐟 *Far East's Best* 🐟

WESTERN RESTAURANTS	
1	**MARGAUX**, Hong Kong
2	**PLUME**, Hong Kong
3	**GADDI'S**, Hong Kong
4	**PIERROT**, Hong Kong
5	**NORMANDIE GRILL**, Bangkok
6	**PRUNIER**, Tokyo
7	**JOEL**, Tokyo
8	**CAFE D'AMIGO**, Hong Kong
9	**L'ORANGERIE**, Tokyo
10	**LES CHOUX**, Tokyo

NORTH SEA FISHING VILLAGE CO, Auto Plaza, Tsimshatsui E, Kowloon ☎ 3-723 6843; G/F, 445 King's Rd, N Point ☎ 5-630187
Two of the finest restaurants in the Hong Kong area. At the centre of each is an authentic junk stacked with floodlit tanks of fishy victims (you choose your own). Excellent prawns, octopus, crab, lobster, shark's fin and dim sum.

🐟 **PIERROT, Mandarin Oriental Hotel, 5 Connaught Rd, Central ☎ 5-220111**
One of the best French restaurants in Hong Kong, frequented by bejewelled and

fashionable Chinese and bizmen out to impress. On the international itinerary for the world's best guest chefs. A favourite of **Diane Freis**.

🐟 **PLUME, The Regent, Salisbury Rd, Kowloon ☎ 3-721 1211**
Peep into this dining room in the daytime and you'll find it unremarkable. Go back at night and you'll draw breath: the décor is the harbour, with its fluctuating, twinkling lights, seen through a wall of picture windows. Fantastic French cuisine which starts with a complimentary steaming nan (bread) and pâté and a glass of pink bubbly. Dinner only.

SICHUAN GARDEN, 3/F, Gloucester Tower, The Landmark, Central ☎ 5-214433
"Authentic food and accommodating staff. The thing I like especially is the smoked tea duck which I have rarely had so good even in China. The chefs were trained in Sichuan province and are among the best in Hong Kong. This is one of the few Chinese restaurants that also does great desserts" – **Ken Hom**. Elegant sister restaurant, **Guangzhou Garden, Exchange Square ☎ 5-251163**, for Cantonese cuisine.

SUN TUNG LOK'S SHARK'S FIN RESTAURANT, Phase 3, Harbour City, 25-27 Canton Rd, Kowloon ☎ 3-722 0288
The place for unusual southern Chinese food at sky-high prices. *"What I like about this place is its Art Deco-ness. It looks like a setting for a Fred Astaire and Ginger Rogers film. Superb shark's-fin dumplings"* – **Ken Hom**.

🐟 **SUNNING UNICORN, 1 Sunning Rd, Causeway Bay ☎ 5-776620**
This is the place for the Sichuan speciality, drunken prawns. *"The prawns are alive in a glass bowl and Chinese yellow wine is poured over them. You can see them gradually getting drunk. Then they are put into a hotpot on the table and cooked. They're*

the freshest, most remarkable-tasting prawns I've ever had. Afterwards you have the broth with ginger and spring onion" – **Robert Carrier**. Not for the faint-hearted.

YUCCA DE LAC, Ma Liu Shui, Shatin ☎ 0-612011
One of the best restaurants in the New Territories – a favourite stop-off point on a 'let's see China' jaunt.

Ireland

BALLYMALOE HOUSE, see Travel

BEWLEY'S CAFE, Grafton St, Dublin ☎ (01) 776761
Legendary, lofty, clattery café with fabulous stained-glass windows. *"It has the best bread I know – you can buy bread, coffee and sweets, or you can have poached eggs on toast, tea and cakes. I love it"* – **Lord Gowrie**.

THE RAMORE RESTAURANT, The Harbour, Portrush, Co Antrim ☎ (0265) 824313
"The best restaurant in Northern Ireland. Seriously good food and not a main course above £9, fully garnished. That's turbot and lobster and things. We had chocolate or lemon soufflés and there was no fuss – no brackets '15 minutes and please order when you sit down' " – **Alan Crompton-Batt**.

Italy

BOLOGNA

RESTAURANTS

Some Italian restaurants close in the winter months, so it is worth telephoning first.

🐟 **SAN DOMENICO, via Gaspare Sacchi 1, 40026 Imola ☎ (0542) 29000**
Just outside Bologna, this is

FOOD AND DRINK

❝ *It was very fashionable to talk about cucina nuova, but it's fading away. People much prefer the real, traditional Italian food* **❞**

🥄 MARCELLA HAZAN

reckoned to be one of the best restaurants in Italy. Old-style and refined, serving duck, game, truffle pâté and Bolognese specialities.

DANTE, via Belvedere 2b, 40121 ☎ (051) 224464
A wonderful, dimly lit, avant-garde restaurant hidden in the maze of streets. Beautiful presentation in nouvelle cuisine style of Bolognese favourites.

FLORENCE

CAFES AND BARS

DONEY'S, via Tornabuoni 46, 50123 ☎ (055) 214348
In the best position for the evening passeggiata. Terrifically smart, a traditional writers-and-artists hang-out since the early 19th century. *"The café with the most relaxing atmosphere"* – **Giorgio Armani.**

GIACOSA, via Tornabuoni 83, 50123 ☎ (055) 296226
Exclusive café-bar for the young élite. Birthplace of the Campari-based Negroni.

RESTAURANTS

ANTICA TRATTORIA SANESI, via Airone 33, Lastra a Signa, 50055 ☎ (055) 872 0234
"A fine Tuscan trattoria; best traditional cuisine" – **Marchesa Bona Frescobaldi.**

IL CIBREO, via dei Macci 118r, 50100 ☎ (055) 234 1100
"Excellent – everyone is talking about it. No pasta at all, they use artichokes for the ravioli with bits and pieces inside" – **Andrew Lloyd Webber.**

COCO LEZZONE, via Parioncino 26, 50123 ☎ (055) 287178
Genuine Tuscan trattoria, teeming with cool types from film, finance and fashion; favourite of **Giorgio Armani.**

🐓 **ENOTECA PINCHIORRI, via Ghibellina 87, 50122 ☎ (055) 242757**
One of the best ristoranti in Italy. Superb cellars; very chic, very expensive. **Marchesa Bona Frescobaldi** is a fan.

TAVERNA DEL BRONZINO, via delle Ruote 25, 50129 ☎ (055) 495220
Smash hit in Tuscany, discovered by Denholm Elliott

during the filming of *A Room With a View* and canonized by gastronome Simon Callow.

SHOPS

VIVOLI, via Isola delle Stinche 7, 50122 ☎ (055) 292334
A gelateria of world renown – the very best creamy-textured Italian ice cream, tasting acutely of the fruit or chocolate that it's meant to taste of. It gets **Marchesa Bona Frescobaldi**'s vote.

MILAN

RESTAURANTS

ANTICA OSTERIA DEL PONTE, piazza Negri 9, 20080 Cassinetta di Lugagnano ☎ (02) 942 0034
In an old country villa on the bank of the Naviglio Milanese is this *"fantastic place – it's quite small, not luxurious, but*

🕵 **Buzzzzzzzzz** In FLORENCE, sniff out **Procacci Specialità Alimentari**, via dei Tornabuoni 64r ☎ (055) 211656, *"a marvellous grocery shop; in the back you can buy a glass of champagne and* **truffle sandwiches**. *At the end of the same street there's a lovely little fast food joint,* **Cantinetta Antinori**, *piazza Antinori 3* ☎ *(055) 292234. You can get a bowl of soup, a hunk of bread and a bottle of Tignanello for no money at all"* – **James Burke** 🐓 . . . . . . Melt-in-the-mouth handmade **chocolates and pastries** come from **Giacosa**, via dei Tornabuoni 83 ☎ (055) 296226 🐓 . . . . . . **ice cream** addicts can support their habit at **Perché No**, via dei Tavolini 19 ☎ (055) 298969 🐓 . . . . . . in MILAN, follow in **Marchesa Fiamma di San Giuliano Ferragamo**'s footsteps, to the **Antica Trattoria della Pesa**, viale Pasubio 10 ☎ (02) 655 5741 (a small trat that does delicious **risotto milanese** with osso buco); **Brasera Meneghina**, via Circo 10 ☎ (02) 803004 (lovely **garden dining** in summer, trad Milanese dishes, arty clientele); and the **utterly irresistible pastry** shop, **Pasticceria Marchesi**, via San Maria alla Porta 13 ☎ (02) 876730.

★ ★ ★ ★ ★ ★ ★ ★ ★ ★ ★ ★ ★ ★ ★ ★ ★ ★ ★ ★

one of the best restaurants anywhere in Italy, superb food" – **Egon Ronay.**

🐾 **BICE, via Borgospesso 12, 20121 ☎ (02) 702572**
It is this long-established eatery that spawned the ultra-fashionable one in New York. But Bice Milano has been chic for *years*. The smartest of the smart sit closest to the kitchen even though it's smoky and smelly – the owner keeps tables here for close friends who come in without a reservation. All the Milanese fashion designers lunch here. *"Without a doubt, the best restaurant in Milan. I like to eat at home, but if I can't I go to Bice. Simple, unaffected Italian cookery"* – **Gianni Versace.**

🐾 **LE IDEE DI GUALTIERO MARCHESI, via Bonvesin de la Riva 9, 20129 ☎ (02) 741246**
Perhaps the best restaurant in Milan, a temple of *cucina nuova*. Serious, expensive foodie stuff. Sig Marchesi, one of the top chefs in the world, has revolutionized Italian cuisine this decade. He has revived historical dishes and flavours with his own modern stamp, and launched his own classic Italian liqueurs, vinegars and olive oils.

🐾 **SAVINI, Galleria Vittorio Emanuele, 20121 ☎ (02) 805 6400**
One of the oldest and best restaurants in Italy (established 1867). Set in the historical glass gallery, it's got bags of style and zippy service. Giancarlo Guancioli serves a wide range of light dishes. Home-made pasta is fresh every day. Meeting point of international jetsetters, politicos and all-round VIPs such as Craxi, Agnelli and **Peter Ustinov**, for whom this is one of the top 3 restaurants in the world. Also a favourite of **Marchesa Fiamma di San Giuliano Ferragamo.**

EL TOULA, piazza Paolo Ferrari 6, 20123 ☎ (02) 870302
Top fashion and financial whizzes come to this '60s-style ristorante to tittle-tattle over dishes from the Veneto and Lombardy regions. *"Especially good after an evening at La Scala,"* thinks **Gianni Versace.**

SHOPS

PECK'S, via Spadari 9, 20123 ☎ (02) 871737
Superb displays of pastas, cheeses, a charcuterie, an amazing rotisserie and tavola calda. *"The best food shop"* – **Marchesa Bona Frescobaldi.** *"Truly wonderful, one of the most wonderful food shops I have ever been in – it's out of this world"* – **Ken Hom.**

ROME

CAFES AND BARS

ALEMAGNA, via del Corso 181, 00186 ☎ (06) 679 2887
The best sandwiches in Rome, superb fruit milkshakes and panettone.

ANTICO CAFFE GRECO, via Condotti 86, 00187 ☎ (06) 679 1700
Founded in 1742, with long-standing intellectual and literary connotations, it now plays host to an older establishment clientele. *"I like cafés to have historical or literary associations, like this one. But it's so full that it's unbearable"* – **Peter Ustinov.**

BARETTO DI VIA CONDOTTI, via Condotti 55, 00187 ☎ (06) 678 4566
So smart and exclusive, there's no sign to tell you this is Baretto. Only those in the know go.

DONEY'S, via Veneto 145, 00187 ☎ (06) 493405
Not as aristocratic as its Florentine counterpart but more trendy. *"I do like Doney's. It has excellent croissants and oustanding goodies"* – **Robert Mondavi.**

HARRY'S BAR, via Veneto 150, 00187 ☎ (06) 474 5832
Almost as famous and just as fashionable as the Venice Harry's.

SAN FILIPPO, via di Villa San Filippo 8, 00197 ☎ (06) 879314
The best ice cream in town. Their ice cakes are what the cognoscenti dish up for pudding; worth a pilgrimage for their zabaglione.

RESTAURANTS

ALBERTO CIARLA, piazza Cosimata 40, 00183 ☎ (06) 581 8668
Brilliant fish restaurant, probably the finest in Italy. *"It's very good, he does a lot of raw fish . . . the only good restaurant in Rome"* – **Barbara Kafka.** A favourite, too, of **Gianni Versace.**

OSTARIA DELL' ORSO, via Monte Brianzo 93, 00186 ☎ (06) 656 4250
The grandest restaurant in Rome, in a magnificent Renaissance building. Moltissimo chic for Roman nobility and other well-heeled diners.

LE RALLYE, Grand Hotel, via Vittorio Emanuele Orlando 3, 00185 ☎ (06) 4709
The best hotel restaurant in Italy. Outstanding classic Italian and international cuisine, recommended by **Gianni Versace.**

VENICE

CAFES AND BARS

BAR AI SPECCHI, Hotel Antico Panada, Calle Specchieri, San Marco 646, 30124 ☎ (041) 522 5824
'The Mirror Bar' is so named because its walls are a glassy tapestry of antique mirrors. *"It's cute and small and very nice after dinner because it has a large selection of grappa"* – **Marcella Hazan.**

CAFE FLORIAN, piazza San Marco 56159, 30125 ☎ (041) 528 5338
Established in 1720, the gilded and frescoed café-bar (rather than the restaurant part) is at the hub of Venetian social life

FOOD AND DRINK

Italy: Best Markets

For **James Burke**, a memorable market is *"the central food market in* **Vicenza***, a perfect medieval town. It has 20 different kinds of mushrooms."* **Sophie Grigson** nominates **Campo dei Fiori**, Rome, *"partly because of its location, in the medieval centre of Rome in a beautiful square with a statue of a monk. Very lively. Lovely fresh produce brought in from the countryside – fish, flowers, fruit and vegetables."* **Cagliari**, Sardinia, is an **Anton Mosimann** favourite, for *"gorgeous vegetables, fresh and tiny, small pigs as well – they have a recipe where they roast a pig in the earth. Moments in life like this you never forget – the atmosphere and freshness – just wonderful."* **AM** also loves **Rome**'s *"beautiful markets – you can smell tomatoes and basil from a mile away, they're so fresh. The sun shines, it's a gorgeous experience."* For **Marcella Hazan**, it's *the food markets in* **Venice**. *Here everything arrives by boat and it's fun to watch them unloading. The large fish market is in a very old loggia with beautiful columns, looking over the Grand Canal near the Ponte di Rialto. It is very lively. They also sell lots of vegetables, grown on the islands around Venice; they have a special flavour because of the salty breeze."* **Margaux Hemingway** isn't choosy: *"I'd go to an Italian market any day. You can go just to see the colours – marvellous. Sexy and delicious!"*

when you can't get near Harry's. Frothy cappuccinos and scrumptious pastries.

HARRY'S BAR, Calle Vallaresso 1323, 30124 ☎ (041) 523 6797
The most famous bar in the world. *Everyone* goes to Harry's to say 'I'm in town' and to suss out who else is. Home of the bellini (champagne and fresh peach juice). *"It's the best cocktail I've ever had in Europe. I just loved to bits sitting at that bar in the northern Italian summer ..."* – **Elise Pascoe**. They also do fine pastas and risottos. *"It's the best restaurant in the world for the cooking, its atmosphere and because it's in Venice!"* – **Giorgio Armani**. *"The best food and the most amusing place to go in Venice. They somehow cram in the most unbelievable number of people"* – **Mark Birley. Lord Lichfield** (*"wonderful Tizianos"*), **Steven Spurrier, Anton Mosimann, Jeremiah Tower** and **Helen Gurley Brown** fight to get in.

Restaurants

ANTICA LOCANDA MONTIN, Fondamenta Eremite, Dorsoduro 1147, 30100 ☎ (041) 522 7151
"A garden restaurant with a canopy of green leaves. Marvellous for lunch" – **Egon Ronay**.

OSTERIA DA FIORE, San Polo Calle del Scaleter 2202, 30125 ☎ (041) 522 3824
Venetian seafood and fish specialities. *"It is wonderful for any kind of seafood – they serve only fish – cappe lunge, razor clams, coquilles St Jacques, risotto ..."* – **Marcella Hazan**.

TRATTORIA CORTE SCONTA, Calle del Pestrin, Castello 3886, 30100 ☎ (041) 522 7024
"They don't have a menu – they tell you what is fresh that day; it is almost all fish and seafood. Very fashionable people go there. I like it very much" – **Marcella Hazan**.

Rest of Italy

BECCHERIE, piazza Ancillotto 11, Treviso ☎ (0422) 540871
Specialities from the Veneto region. *"They serve game and fowl, followed by tripe in broth. They do pheasant; and guinea fowl with pere sauce (made of marrowbone and a lot of pepper)"* – **Marcella Hazan**.

BOSCHETTI, piazza Mazzini 10, 33019 Tricesimo (Udine) ☎ (0432) 851230
"A very good restaurant in the north-east of Veneto. They serve things like pasta fagioli, tortelli ai formaggi, fish and lamb" – **Marcella Hazan**.

GIAPPUN, via Maonaira 7, Vallecrosia (Imperia) ☎ (0184) 290970
"The most fabulous Italian restaurant, just over the French border. I had the best Italian meal in 10 years there. I've been back several times since and every time it's been fantastic. The first restaurant I've ever been to which has 9 separate kinds of olive oil to dress your salad and 4 kinds of sugar. The quality of the seafood – and all they do – is unlike anything I've experienced. The wine cellar is infinite" – **Andrew Lloyd Webber**.

RISTORANTE FLORA, via Roma, Graniti (Messina) Sicily ☎ (0942) 29148
Simple peasant family restaurant in the hills behind Taormina. *"Quite the best food I've eaten in Italy"* – **Joanna Lumley**.

TRATTORIA LA BUCA, via Ghizzi 3, Zibello (Parma) ☎ (0524) 99214
"One of the best trattoria in the entire province, run by 3 women. Amazing food, including lingua in sugo di funghi (tongue in mushroom sauce)" – **Eric Newby**.

Italian Wine

Italian wines have suffered as the world's most maligned (and recently the most spiked), but the best are indeed as extraordinary as any work of art in Florence. Take GRECO DI GERACE CERATTI, one of the world's best sweet aperitif wines. **Simon Loftus** thinks: "*Italy is the most exciting part of the Old World at the moment. It's the California of Europe. The best thing about Italy is that most of their best wines are not based on clones of French varieties, but on their own ancient grapes.*"

PIEDMONT

"*For uninhibited exploration of the varieties of grape juice and what can be made of them, no part of Europe can compare with Piedmont*" – **Hugh Johnson**. Most of the grape juice is red, and the best ends up as Barolo and Barbaresco. The differences between the best of these are less important than their similarities: big wines, rich in fruit, extract and mysterious woodland smells, for long ageing.

BARBARESCO
One name dominates: GAJA. The label is the world's most megalomanic: the name hits the eye, 'Barbaresco' is lost in the small print. All of Gaja's wines are good: the best is the single-vineyard Sori San Lorenzo. The 1961 was one of the two best Italian wines **Michael Broadbent** has tasted. **Serena Sutcliffe** says: "*Watch out for GIACOSA, too.*"

BAROLO
"*There are some frightfully good Barolos coming in*" – **Auberon Waugh**. The best is Pio Cesare's all-conquering version. "*I like Barolo with my shepherd's pie or spaghetti bolognese*" – **Jeffrey Archer**.

TUSCANY

BRUNELLO DI MONTALCINO
Outprices any other wine in Italy (partly because, in poor years, the whole crop is declassified). **Robert Mondaví**

eyes their vineyards enviously: "*Montalcino has some very fine growing areas.*" CASTELGIOCONDO is another Brunello di Montalcino to reckon with.

CHIANTI
Florence's fruity red gets a puff from **Marchesa Bona Frescobaldi** for the Frescobaldi MONTESODI CHIANTI RUFINA 1982 (only ever bottled in the best years), while **Joanna Lumley** votes for the CHIANTI CLASSICO, Emilio Pucci '75. Antinori's Chiantis are tops, too.

POMINO
POMINO IL BENEFIZIO is one of Italy's most prestigious white Chardonnays, from the aristocratic Frescobaldi fold. The family owns 8 estates; their motto is: 'Our own wines from our own vines.' Also their fine red POMINO, a marriage of 4 noble grapes – Cabernet, Sangioveto, Pinot Noir and Merlot.

SASSICAIA
A red cabernet, and "*a fantastic wine – it has been the best red wine in Italy for the past 10 years*" – **Hugh Johnson**. In part responsible is Piero Antinori, "*the best and most interesting wine-maker in Italy. He has made the top reds in Tuscany*" – **Hugh Johnson**. (His own triumph is TIGNANELLO.)

VENETO

The best wine-makers of the Veneto all have big attics. In a good year, that's where they take their prize bunches of red grapes to have them wizen slowly in the warmth of the autumn. The resulting wines can be either very dry and very strong (AMARONE) or sweet and slightly less strong (RECIOTO DELLA VALPOLICELLA). Visiting grapies take home bottles of Tedeschi's RECIOTO CAPITEL MONTE FONTANA and any Giuseppe Quintarelli's AMARONE MONTE CA' PALETTA they can lay their hands on.

TOKYO

CAFES AND BARS

See also Social & Night Life.

FRANK LLOYD WRIGHT BAR, Imperial Hotel, 1-1-1 Uchisaiwai-cho, Chiyoda-ku ☎ (03) 504 1111
The equivalent of the Captain's Bar at the Mandarin Hong Kong: expats and smarties crowd in for pre-prandials.

RUNDELL, 8-3-7 Ginza, Chuo-ku ☎ (03) 572 3843
Wildly expensive cocktail club catering to Tokyo's top expense-accounters (a few hours for a party of 4 means a bill for at least 100,000 yen). Mainly Japanese male execs.

TON TON, 2-1 Yurakucho, Chiyoda-ku
This movable underneath-the-railway-arches café has been going since 1946 (it only 'happens' from 5 to 11 pm). Tables are made from stacked-up beer crates while overhead trains rumble. Fare is straight *yakitori* and sake.

MARKET

TSUKIJI FISH MARKET
"*The best market in the world for fish. A wonderful experience to be there at 4am. I'm a market man, I love markets. Tokyo is an eye-opener. Fish are still live in tanks. The freshness! The cleanness! The action! The auctions . . !*" – **Anton Mosimann.**

RESTAURANTS

In Japan, it is usually advisable to dine at lunchtime from the set menu. Forget paying *double* à la carte – expect to *add a nought* to your bill.

A TANTOT, Axis Bldg, 3F, 5-17-1 Roppongi, Minato-ku ☎ (03) 586 4431
In the middle of the ultimate

designer shopping arcade is the ultimate designer restaurant. Food is a bit designed too – French/japonais.

BODAIJU, Bukkyo Dendo Center Blg, 2F, 4-3-14 Shiba, Minato-ku ☎ (03) 456 3257
The official restaurant of the Buddhism Promotion foundation (the only place in Tokyo with ancient Chinese vegetarian cuisine). Excitingly different from the established Chinese cuisines.

**CHIANTI, 3-1-7 Azabudai, Minato-ku
B1 ☎ (03) 583 7546;
2F ☎ (03) 583 2240**
Smart Italian that's chocker with gaijin most evenings – spaghetti alla vongole is a fave, followed by the best chocolate mousse in town and *"the only decent espresso to be found in Tokyo"* – **Tina Chow**.

LE CHINOIS, Bianca Bldg, 3-1-26 Jingumae, Shibuya-ku ☎ (03) 403 3929
Tokyo's most strangely glamorous restaurant, drawing late-night city sleekers. Décor is Art Deco (it inspired Wolfgang Puck's Chinois on

Main in LA). The food is not wildly authentic Chinese, just clever-Zennish: the Restaurant-As-Theatre Experience.

LES CHOUX, Central Toriizaka, 5-11-28 Roppongi, Minato-ku ☎ (03) 470 5511
The Sunday lunchery for gaijin, who grab the rare chance of sitting at outdoor tables. Chef Makino makes regular trips to France and concocts incredible desserts; the best lemon tart in town.

FUKUZUSHI, 5-7-8 Roppongi, Minato-ku ☎ (03) 402 4116
Marvellous traditional sushi bar, recommended by **Bernard Cendron** as *"top of the tops for Tokyo sushi"*. Also tops for *chirashizushi*, a platter of rice with raw fish laid on top – the attraction of roll-your-own sushi for DIY freaks.

INAGIKU, 2-9-8 Nihonbashi Kayabacho, Chuo-ku ☎ (03) 669 5501
If you have a yen for tempura, this is the place – it has a list of 18 types. The height of luxury with hovering service.

INAKAYA, 7-8-4 Roppongi, Minato-ku ☎ (03) 405 9866
The place for *robatayaki* (roast-buttered-grilled) amid a barrage of screaming and shouting. This noisy 'hello/welcome/sit down' is the norm in such eateries, as is an elaborate clapping ceremony at each change of shifts. Food is served on long paddles. Great fun for visitors. Apart from grilled prawns, fish, meat, etc, try *nasu* (aubergine) and *jagaimo* (potato).

JOEL, Kyodo Building, 2F, 5-6-24 Minami-Aoyama, Minato-ku ☎ (03) 400 7149
Despite the external dinge (tatty plastic sign, faded Club Med poster, etc), this is one of the best French restaurants in Tokyo. Chef-owner Joel Bruants worked with Paul Bocuse at Collonges-au-Mont-d'Or. Superb à la carte menu (plus set meals at 10,000 yen-plus); first-rate wine list, proper cheeses. Seats 15.

KEIKA, 3-25-6 Shinjuku, Shinjuku-ku ☎ (03) 352 4836
Perhaps the very best ramen (robust, Chinese-style noodles) are those sold on street stalls under red lanterns. Such stalls are usually run by the *yakuza* (mafia) and it's not uncommon to find someone's little finger in your ramen. Beastly. However, if there is no red light in your district, Keika comes a close second for noodles – without the digits.

KICCHO, 8-17-4 Ginza, Chuo-ku ☎ (03) 541 8228
A branch of the great Osaki Kiccho. *"The best restaurant for* kaiseki *in Tokyo with food served on exquisite dishes"* – **Tina Chow**. But you'd be lucky to taste their kaiseki ryori (a delicate imperial food designed to be eaten before the tea ceremony), which is sampled by invitation only.

Buzzzzzzzzz Gorge sensational **shabu-shabu** at **Hassan**, 6-1-20 Roppongi ☎ (03) 403 8333 ...... Slurp tasty **noodles** – also the best bargain binge – at **Yabu Soba**, 2-10 Awajicho ☎ (03) 251 0287 ...... Try top-grade **tempura** at **Tenmasa**, 3-38-5 Hongo ☎ (03) 811 0607 ...... **Yakitori** ain't yukky if you eat it at **Nanbantei**, Mitake Bldg, B1, 5-6-6 Ginza ☎ (03) 571 5700 (also in Roppongi) or, as man-about-Tokyo Bill Wilk recommends, at the **Torigen** chain ...... Dip into the fluffiest of **soufflés** (a zillion sorts) at **Le Soufflé**, 4-5-9 Nishi-Azabu ☎ (03) 407 7344 ...... Thirsty for Mozart? Over coffee at **Casa Mozart**, 1-10-23 Jingumae ☎ (03) 404 7842, you can drink in any recording you care to specify – they stock the lot, along with Mozart memorabilia ...... Dive into designer den **Metropole**, 6-4-5 Roppongi ☎ (03) 405 4400 (a lofty Nigel Coates and Shi Yu Chen creation) for **drinks**, as Tina Turner, Eric Clapton and the in-crowd do.

★ ★ ★ ★ ★ ★ ★ ★ ★ ★ ★ ★ ★ ★ ★ ★ ★ ★ ★ ★

KISSO, Basement, Axis Bldg, 5-17-1 Roppongi, Minato-ku ☎ (03) 582 4191
Spurned by Kiccho? Come to Kisso. This modern, fashionable, gaijin-friendly eatery is the answer for those who are nervous of the

formality of *kaiseki ryori* (it can be a tense experience).

NODAIWA, 1-5-4 Higashi Azabu, Minato-ku ☎ (03) 583 7852
Established at the end of the Edo era, it has always fed a stash of celebrities, *thanks to* rather than despite the fact that its speciality is yummy *kaba-yaki* (broiled eel). A favourite of **Shizuo Tsuji**.

🍴 L'ORANGERIE, Hanae Mori Bldg, Omotesando, 3-6-1 Kita Aoyama ☎ (03) 407 7461
An elegant airy dining room, the place to be seen for brunch on Sunday. Fashion designers (including Madame Mori herself), architects, anyone who's in town, crowd in here informally for the brill buffet.

🍴 PRUNIER, Tokyo Kaikan, 2F, 3-2-1 Marunouchi, Chiyoda-ku ☎ (03) 215 2111
Very grand, very subdued, very Western fish restaurant, packed at midday by the out-to-lunch international banking set. French bourgeoise cuisine, dreamy bouillabaisse and bargain Beluga caviare.

SHIRUYOSHI, 6-2-12 Akasaka, Minato-ku ☎ (03) 583 0333
Tokyo's limo and table-telephone folk congregate here to toy with the *tempura* and *kaiseki* after a hard day's power-broking. Combines the Japanese food ethic with Western nouveau luxe. None of your tatami mats – here it's fitted carpets, crystal tumblers, buttoned leather loungers.

SPAGO, 5-7-8 Roppongi, Minato-ku ☎ (03) 423 4025
A branch of the LA original where Tokyo yuppies hang out (though it's not the same without the old maître d', Johnny Romoglio). Star culinary attractions are the marinated raw tuna with red caviare, and capelli di angeli (angel-hair pasta with goat's cheese and asparagus).

SUSHI BAR SAI, 2F, Dandling Core Andos Bldg, 1-7-5 Jinnan, Shibuya-ku ☎ (03) 496 6333
Sushi California-style in a cool Los Angeles setting. Combining the best of both sides of the Pacific, this is still the real, fresh-as-fresh Japanese thing. Also tofu and vegetable sushi. Gaijin love it.

TENMI, Shizen Shokuhin Centre, 1-10-6 Jinnan, Shibuya-ku ☎ (03) 496 9703
The best health-food restaurant in Tokyo. *Makunouchi* is a healthy hamper of seasonal ingredients presented in a handsome lacquered box. Draws the showbiz set.

TONKI, 1-1-2 Shimo-meguro, Meguro-ku ☎ (03) 491 9928
The best robotic dining experience in Tokyo (provided you like pork as that is all there is). Robotic means a blaze of white lights, a frighteningly clinical assembly-line eating bar and 15 white-shoed assistants slotting you and your order in with breathtaking timing.

REST OF JAPAN
RESTAURANTS

ARAGAWA, 2-15-18 Naka-yamate-dori, Chuo-ku, Kobe ☎ (078) 221 8547
Stupendous steakery, using beef from specially bred cattle. *"The tenderness and flavour of the meat is top quality; a truly perfect steak dinner"* – **Shizuo Tsuji**.

CHIHANA, Nawate-higashi-iru, Shijo-dori, Higashiyama-ku, Kyoto ☎ (075) 561 2741
Small *kappo* (top-grade restaurant for authentic Japanese cuisine) serving traditional Kyoto dishes. *"Beautiful presentation of food served on plates of super quality. In front of the clean cypress counter [for 9 at most], you can watch the chef deftly perform his art"* – **Shizuo Tsuji**.

🍴 KICCHO, 3-23 Koraibashi, Higashiku, Osaka ☎ (06) 231 1937
"My most favourite restaurant in Japan, because of its absolute perfection in all respects. Mr Teiichi Yuki is an exceptionally skilled chef held in the highest esteem. Superb food. Also the tableware and furniture – many are art treasures" – **Shizuo Tsuji**.

🍴 SANKO-IN-TEMPLE, 3-1-36 Hon-machi, Koganei-chi ☎ (0423) 811116
Book a month in advance if you want to sample Buddhism for an afternoon. At this peaceful Buddhist temple (the only one of its kind open to foreigners) nuns prepare *shojin ryori* (vegan Buddhist food). Float in to your private room, and await the understated mouthfuls.

Malaysia
RESTAURANTS

The best of Malaysia's smart bars and restaurants are in the top hotels (see Travel).

LE COQ D'OR, 123 Jalan Ampang, Kuala Lumpur ☎ (03) 429732
One of the most popular European restaurants in Kuala Lumpur, frequented by any expat who is anyone.

Morocco
MARKETS

TANGIER
"The fish market has not only the fish of the Mediterranean, but the Atlantic as well. Get there by 8am to get the fish cold and fresh as there is no refrigeration. By 10am it's still fresh, but it's warming up with the sun. It's a fabulous market. And the spice markets, and the olive markets ... They can't keep things so everything is much fresher" – **Paula Wolfert**.

MARRAKECH
"My favourite market is the

FOOD AND DRINK

FOOD AND DRINK

fish, fruit, vegetable, herb and spice market in the Gueliz area of Marrakech. When I'm in Morocco, I go every day, for the pleasure of enormous variety and quality. The fish come that morning from Safi, Agadir, etc; vegetables from the farms. Some of the best melons I've ever had; wonderful, irregular, almost square tomatoes; baby aubergines and courgettes; tangerines; lemons of every variety ..." – **Robert Carrier.**

FEZ
"This is the biggest covered market in North Africa. Go to buy spices – it's the best fun you'll ever have in a market. Morocco has the best mixed spice in the world, 'ras el hamout' – 'top of the shop'. It is a culinary representation of Arabic trading – they have a spice from virtually everywhere they've ever been. 5 types of pepper, lavender, rose petals, cinnamon, cascia, nutmeg, and cantharides (Spanish fly). It's best to buy the ingredients individually, and grind them yourself" – **Glynn Christian.**

New Zealand

AUCKLAND

ANTOINE'S, 333 Parnell Rd, Parnell 1 ☎ (09) 798756
Probably the best restaurant in New Zealand, based in one of the earliest colonial houses. *"I couldn't believe it. Here, in the middle of what we who live outside Australasia think of as*

the wilderness, there is this eccentric, passionate young man, Tony Astle, who is just crazy about food. Something as simple as a wonderful roast lamb – a thing you would think people are sick of eating in New Zealand – he does with imagination: he gets a very young lamb (which is difficult to find because most of them are sheep) and roasts it with fresh herbs ... not overwhelming, really delicate. When you eat this you think 'my God, I'm in France'. It's absolutely brilliant" – **Ken Hom. Don Hewitson** agrees.

CIN CIN ON QUAY, 99 Quay St ☎ (09) 376966
Warwick Brown's buzzy new brasserie offers Italian, French, Chinese and Japanese cuisine, plus char-grills and wood-fired pizzas.

FLAMINGO'S, 242 Jervois Rd, Herne Bay 2 ☎ (09) 765899
A BYO that's hot on presentation and service. Mainly ethnic European food. Top-rater for **Don Hewitson.**

LE GOURMET, 1 Williamson Ave, Ponsonby ☎ (09) 786499
Elegant little restaurant; 2 dining rooms with an open fireplace and a small garden bar. Warwick Brown is among the most celebrated chefs in the country. Small, seasonal menus of market-fresh food; great selection of wines. Rave reports from **Glynn Christian.**

RICKERBY'S, 83 Victoria Rd, Devonport ☎ (09) 457072
A restaurant that's popular with the yuppie community as well as older wine connoisseurs. Light cuisine.

HAVELOCK NORTH

ARDEN LODGE, PO Box 423, Havelock North, North Island ☎ (070) 777410
Vicki Bruhns-Bolderson was voted chef of the year in 1987. She now operates from this small tourist lodge, with 5 double bedrooms. Modern New Zealand cuisine – rabbit, venison, duck livers, wild mushrooms, crayfish. A beautifully balanced 6-course set menu is served to just one table of up to 14 diners. Vicki recommends wines (predominantly from New Zealand) for each course. **Don Hewitson** is a fan.

WELLINGTON

THE COACHMAN ON THE TERRACE, 46 Courtenay Place ☎ (04) 848200
The Coachman reincarnate, in beautiful new apparel and with lighter, more unusual food. *"Des Britten is the forerunner of the new-wave restaurants. He's been going over 20 years. Half of New Zealand [including Tony Astle of Antoine's] has done its apprenticeship at The Coachman. It seems to have captured both style and individuality. It's beautiful, fantastic"* – **Don Hewitson.**

COUNTRY LIFE, Main Rd, Waikanae ☎ (04) 36353
Just outside Wellington, this restaurant has been taken over by Herman Werth (who has always been chef) along with his wife Laraine, and Ian and Judith Spiller. New Zealand food cooked in the French

❝ *New Zealand has the best cake shops. It is the greatest repository of Scottish and Welsh home baking. It's not easy to hold up your head in the supermarket unless your cake tin at home is full ... kisses, butterfly cakes, Louise cakes, ladies' fingers, scones and lamingtons. You simply cannot get christened, married or die without those on the table* **❞**

 GLYNN CHRISTIAN

Australia and New Zealand are producing wines that belong in the company of the best wines in the world. I was tremendously impressed with New Zealand. It has very fine wines

Robert Mondavi

style. *"Not pretentious, lovely garden setting. The wine list is superb – they have wines no one else can get"* – **Don Hewitson**. Sir Frank and Lady Renouf had their wedding reception here.

GRAIN OF SALT, 232 Oriental Parade
☎ (04) 848642
Romantic restaurant with a fab view over Wellington Harbour, the city lights glimmering on the water. Candlelit tables with pink cloths, blue napkins, crystal, the whole special-occasion dîner-à-deux set-up. New Zealand food of the nouvelle kind. A winner with **Don Hewitson**.

PIERRE'S, 342 Tinakori Rd, Thorndon ☎ (04) 726238
A French bistro that has been polled best eatery in Wellington and best BYO in NZ. *"Still going strong, very good value for money"* – **Don Hewitson**.

NEW ZEALAND WINE

"In the next 3 years, we'll see New Zealand as the white wine producer challenging the very best in the world," declares **Simon Loftus. Hugh Johnson** elaborates: *"New Zealand's natural gift is what the wine-makers of Australia and California are constantly striving for: the growing conditions that give slowly ripened, highly aromatic rather than super-ripe grapes.*

At the north end of the South Island in the Marlborough, or Blenheim region, is the HUNTER ESTATE, whose Chardonnay and Sauvignon are staggeringly good and will be talked about in the future." In the same area is CLOUDY BAY, home of *"the best and*

most fashionable wines available in restaurants" – **Elise Pascoe.**
Vines are planted as far south as Christchurch. According to **Don Hewitson**, the other great areas are *"on the east coast of the islands".* And the best wines produced are their whites: the top New Zealand Sauvignon Blancs are the best white wines **DH** knows.

Names to watch for are the TE MATA ESTATE and MISSION VINEYARDS (both in Hawkes Bay), MATUA VALLEY WINES (Waimauku), and COOKS (Te Kauwhata, near Auckland). Look out, too, for the Gewürztraminer of MATAWHERO WINES (Gisborne) and the Chardonnay of MORTON ESTATE (on the Bay of Plenty: supplies are always good). MONTANA (Gisborne and Marlborough) is *"a very large winery with very good wine indeed"* – **Robert Mondavi**; they produce a spicy Riesling that is appreciated by **Hugh Johnson**, and a Lindauer that is, for **Glynn Christian**, *"the best champagne-style wine."*
The best reds are the TE MATA Cabernet/Merlot blend (*"a very fine wine,"* approves **HJ**); MCWILLIAMS's Cabernet Sauvignon and NOBILO'S Pinot Noir.

Portugal

RISTORANTE TAVARES RICO, Rua de Misericordia 37, Lisbon 1200 ☎ (01) 328942
"The most beautiful, exquisite restaurant. Very good for figs, smoked ham from the north of Portugal, and a wonderful soufflé of crystalized fruit" – **Barry Humphries**.

PORTUGUESE WINE

The Portuguese red wines are the best 'forgotten' wines of Europe. The Portuguese forgot about them, too, for as long as 10 years at a stretch, which is why, when they come to sell them, some of them are so good. *"Portuguese reds are very good and cheap – warm and velvety"* – **Serena Sutcliffe.** One of the best, BUCACO TINTO, can be tried only in Portugal. Nothing has changed in the way this wine is made for centuries. **Hugh Johnson** notes its *"exquisite handmade quality, great fragrance and depth".*

MADEIRA

Vintage Madeira is among the world's best fortified wines, and it will outlive vintage port. A vintage year, however, is rarer.
The best Madeiras – like the 1795 TERRANTEZ enjoyed by **Michael Broadbent**, or even the non-vintage COSSART GORDON SERCIAL DUO CENTENARY so liked by **Hugh Johnson** – command love, respect, devotion . . . and further purchases.

PORT

TAYLOR'S
The best: still foot-trodden, their wines are of *"unrivalled ripeness, depth and every other dimension"* – **Hugh Johnson. Michael Broadbent** thinks their 1935 the best he's ever tasted, while **Anton Mosimann** favours the 1945. Their top vineyard is the Quinta de Vargellas, released in lesser years as a single vineyard port and eagerly snapped up by

FOOD AND DRINK

Auberon Waugh *("about half the price of Taylor's vintage port and just as good")*.

Other houses worth a vintage detour are GRAHAM, DOW, FONSECA, COCKBURN, WARRE (**Joanna Lumley** goes for the 1977) and QUINTA DO NOVAL (**Michael Broadbent** enjoyed the 1955, 1963, 1908 and 1931 respectively, while **Joseph Berkmann** fell for the 1931: *"I had an entire case for birthday celebrations: the ultimate bottle of vintage port"*). Of recent years, 1977 is the one to invest in: just the thing for New Year's Eve 1999.

Singapore

RESTAURANTS

BANANA LEAF APOLLO, Race Course Rd ☎ 293 8682
Simple, excellent place where you eat with your fingers and food is served on a banana-leaf plate. Excellent Indian, fish and meat dishes (fish-head curry is a speciality).

CHAO PHAYA, 4272-A, Block 730, Ang Mo Kio Avr 6 ☎ 456 0119
First-rate Thai restaurant. You choose your garoupa, crab or

lobster and vegetables from the market display, then watch your dinner being broiled, fried or steamed behind huge glass windows. Specialities are *tom yam kung* (spicy prawn soup), hot and sour fish and green fish curry.

Street food

For typical ethnic cuisine at street level, go to the food markets, where hawkers each specialize in 1 or 2 dishes. The best are **Newton Circus** (over 100 different stalls; haunt of expat kids from the American School – all Coke and bravado); **Rasa Singapura** (wide selection of Asian foods), **Satay Club** and the **East Coast Lagoon Stalls**. Seek out spicy *laksa*, (fish and coconut soup with noodles); Hainanese steamed chicken and rice; chilli crabs; duck rice; oyster omelette; and banana fritters with fresh sugar-cane syrup. Few menus, no tablecloths – and don't mind the swill bins. Go with a local or prices will rise.

GREAT EXPECTATIONS BY FREDERIC RAPHAEL

"I expect not to be made ill in order to justify the chef's reputation for being luxurious – I do not regard not feeling able to eat or think about food for the next day as evidence of a good meal. On the other hand, one should have enough to eat and not feel that one is taking part in one of those ancient nouvelle cuisine jokes about dirty plates. I think the food should not be the only available subject of conversation – it should not draw attention to itself excessively. The price should be irrelevant – having gone to a great restaurant, you should not quibble about the price, only about the content – which should be beyond question. If I have any complaints, I expect to be dealt with courteously and not hosed down with offers of free drinks."

GOODWOOD PARK HOTEL, 22 Scotts Rd ☎ 737 7411
Excellent seafood barbecues at the **Garden Seafood Restaurant,** the best straight steaks in Singapore at the **Gordon Grill**, the best Sichuan food at **Min Jing** and the best coffees at **L'Espresso.**

OMAR KHAYYAM, 55 Hill St ☎ 336 1505
Sublime for seafood and the best tandoori chicken in town. Dine like a Moghul prince here. Menus are hand-painted with scenes from Indian mythology.

PINE COURT, Mandarin Hotel, 333 Orchard Rd ☎ 737 4411
Highly recommended for Beijing and Sichuan food (specialities include Peking duck and baked tench).

SUMMER PALACE, Pavilion Inter-Continental, 1 Cuscaden Rd ☎ 733 8888
For Chinese New Year, Singapore goes mad. Special New Year dishes include Prosperous Raw Fish – a spicy raw fish salad.

Spain

SPANISH WINE

RIOJA

MARQUES DE MURRIETA
"Powerful and altogether more serious stuff than the Marqués de Riscal" – **Hugh Johnson.**

MARQUES DE RISCAL
The best-known name, especially among claret-lovers, though its elegant modern wines are almost too light to take seriouly.

PENEDES

TORRES
In terms of the best table wines, Penedès means Torres. Every year, Torres produces a portfolio of wines from

different classic and native grape varieties, in different styles, that would leave a Californian breathless – and he then rushes off to the family's vineyards in Chile to do the same thing there. The best Torres wine is undoubtedly GRAN CORONAS 'BLACK LABEL'.

VEGA SICILIA
This wine is 10 years in the making. *"It's living dangerously – it's kept in the wood almost too long"* – **Hugh Johnson**. Valbuena, the junior version, makes less demands on time and wallet and, according to **HJ**, *"it's also better wine"*.

SHERRY

Just as mouldy grapes make some of the world's best sweet wines, so mouldy white wine makes one of the world's best apéritifs: dry sherry. The thicker the fur of *flor* across the wine in cask, the drier the finished sherry. BARBADILLO'S SANLUCAR MANZANILLA, DOMECQ'S LA INA and the famous TIO PEPE would make a Fino start to any meal. *"The truly great wines of Jerez, wines that can stand comparison in their class with great white burgundy or champagne, are absurdly undervalued. There is no gastronomic justification for the price of Montrachet being four times that of the most brilliant Fino – nor, at the other end of sherry's virtuoso repertoire, of the greatest Olorosos selling at a fraction of the price of their equivalent in Madeira"* – **Hugh Johnson**.

Switzerland

CAFES AND BARS

CAFE SCHOBER, Napfgasse 4, CH-8001 Zurich ☎ (01) 251 8060
"One of my favourites. Absolutely sensational because

it rambles all over the place. This kind of café develops a special kind of waitress who is maternal and feminine at the same time. Here you get the best chocolate cakes in the world. It's full of students and dour burghers reading newspapers on sticks"* – **Peter Ustinov**.

CONFISERIE SPRUNGLI, Am Paradeplatz, Bahnhofstrasse 21, CH-8001 Zurich ☎ (01) 221 1722
The biggest and best chocolatiers in Switzerland. *"You can't beat it. It's quality, made with fresh Swiss milk and cream – just gorgeous. Famous for their white truffles"* – **Anton Mosimann**. A celebrated coffee house and restaurant too.

RESTAURANTS

BUNDERHOLZ STUCKI, Bunderholzalle 42, CH-4059 Basle ☎ (061) 358222
Fine French cuisine by a rising chef, Hans Stucki. Fish and seafood are his love – rouget marinated in coriander, oyster consommé with ginger, frogs' legs in sweet peppers.

CHEZ MAX, Seestrasse 53, CH-8702 Zollekon ☎ (01) 391 8877
A synthesis of French and Japanese aesthetics, this is eye – and palate-stroking fodder. Wonderful use of fruits, Oriental seasonings and uncommon combinations.

LE DUC, 7 quai du Mont Blanc, CH-1201 Geneva ☎ (022) 317330
Run by the Michelli brothers, who hold the key to simplicity. Fish and shellfish are specialities.

GIRARDET, 1 rue d'Yverdon, Crissier, CH-1023 Lausanne ☎ (021) 341514
Still wrestling with Jamin, Paris, for No 1 slot. Super-fresh ingredients, brilliant inventiveness and perfectionist execution. Showered with approval from all the foodies – **Alan Crompton-Batt, Drew Smith, Ken Hom, Robert**

Mondavi, Barbara Kafka, Robert Carrier*: "The best restaurant in the world";* and **Egon Ronay***: "Certainly worth the flight, never mind the detour. It is recognized by some of the most prominent chefs to be the greatest in Europe."*

KRONENHALLE, Ramistrasse 4, CH-8001 Zurich ☎ (01) 251 0256
"Lovely place to be, lovely place to be seen. Very much a fashionable place, has been for the past 20 years. Nice atmosphere, gorgeous paintings" – **Anton Mosimann**. *"One of the very best restaurants. They have an exceptional collection of pictures. The restaurant is over 100 years old and it's still run in the old-fashioned way. All the staff have been there for donkeys' years and they're just satisfied – the service is absolutely effortless. Excellent cooking"* – **Mark Birley**.

TAVERNEN-LANDGASTHOF LOWEN, Heimiswil bei Burgdorf, Emmental ☎ (034) 223206
"I took a helicopter there from Berne just to have lunch. It was great fun, a wonderful experience. Peter Ludi's best dish is bernerplatte, a typical Emmental speciality. It's sauerkraut cooked with white wine, raw potatoes, beans, and about 12 different meats and sausages. You really get spoilt" – **Anton Mosimann**.

Thailand

BANGKOK

CAFES AND BARS

THE ORIENTAL, 48 Oriental Ave ☎ (2) 236 0400
Chic quaffing, indoors or out on the terrace. *"I love their Oriental Slings, made of Thai whisky and lime juice"* – **Auberon Waugh**. They also serve one of the most refined afternoon teas in the Far East, in the Authors' Lounge.

FOOD AND DRINK

THAI CUISINE

Thai cuisine is on everybody's lips right now. Thai, Thai, Thai. From New York to LA, London to Paris, Sydney to Perth, diners can't get enough of those spicy but pure flavours. International chefs are experimenting with Thai ingredients (coriander and lemon grass are almost ubiquitous), blending them into their own style of cooking. *"I think Thai food is one of the great cuisines of the world. I like it because it is such a wonderful combination of flavours – of hot, sweet, sour and salty and it is so aromatic. There are all kinds of aromatic herbs that go into Thai food and it really is an explosion of tastes and smells which is very unusual"* – **Madhur Jaffrey**.

RESTAURANTS

BUSSARACUM, 35 Soi Pipat 2, Convent Rd ☎ (2) 235 8915
A reliable old favourite for beautifully presented trad Thai food. Wonderful *tom yam kung*.

THE CUP, Peninsula Plaza, Rajadamri Rd ☎ (2) 253 9750
Where the fashionable, wealthy crowd lunch – the smart shoppers' stop-off. It's run by a group of well-known society ladies, all educated at international institutions – hence the French/English nosh such as roast beef and Fortnum & Mason Christmas pudding. Old School Thais love it.

GENJI, Hilton International, 2 Wireless Rd ☎ (2) 253 0123
One of the best Japanese restaurants in town.

HONG KONG PALACE, Chongkolnee Rd ☎ (2) 234 2389
Tiptop Chinese restaurant in authentic surroundings; frequented mainly by Thais.

KALAPRAPRUECK, 27/1 Pramuan Rd, Silom ☎ (2) 236 4335
Excellent Thai restaurant that only the in-crowd know about. Owned by a lady-in-waiting to the Queen. A cool dining room and garden.

🍴 **LEMON GRASS, 5/1 Soi 24 Sukhumvit Rd** ☎ (2) 258 8637
Arguably the best Thai restaurant in the country. Small, like dining in a private house, very 'in'. Consistently brilliant food – never an off-day nor an off-dish. Regional specialities, particularly from southern Thailand.

MAYFLOWER, Dusit Thani Hotel, Rama IV Rd ☎ (2) 233 1130
The best Chinese restaurant in Bangkok, in a grand Western-style environment.

🍴 **THE ORIENTAL, 48 Oriental Ave** ☎ (02) 236 0400
The **Normandie Grill** serves the most superb French cuisine in town. Beautifully presented, delicately sauced, fresh local fish and seafood are a speciality. The perfect, most impressive business lunchery. Rooftop view of the Chao Phya River. Munch on to the excellent **Lord Jim's** in the new wing. **Sala Rim Naam** the riverside restaurant opposite the main hotel, offers traditional temple-like Thai surroundings, a Thai classical dance show, great food, great views . . . the whole package.

THE REGENT, 155 Rajadamri Rd ☎ (2) 251 6127
3 fine eateries: the super-swish **Cristal**, offering French cuisine of the high standard you'd expect from a Regent restaurant. **La Brasserie** for moderately less formal dining. **Spice Market** is a reliable country Thai restaurant, done out in pseudo-rustic, earthy style. Classic national cuisine with fiery regional specialities. *"The most delicious Thai restaurant"* – **Lord Lichfield**.

SAVOURY, 60 Pan Rd, Silom ☎ (2) 236 4830
A restaurant of the same school as The Cup, only more intimate and more a dinner venue. English country-style décor with festoon curtains. The best sweet treat in Bangkok is their delicate meringue layer cake. The owners run a contemporary art gallery in the basement (see Culture).

TUMNAK THAI, 131 Ratchadapisek Rd ☎ (2) 276 1810
A phenomenon. This 10-acre complex seats 3,000, is served by waiters on roller-skates and run by computer. Set in Thai-style houses around a pond with a stage for classical dance shows. The most OTT eating experience in Bangkok.

A WOK IN BANGKOK

There are dozens of street stalls where they'll cook you up a tasty concoction in a wok. Don't expect them to understand any foreign tongue – just point to noodles/rice/soup and what you want in them (prawns, veg, etc) and prepare to be *spiced out*. Some of the best little stalls can be found off Silom Road; dead cheap at around 20 baht a bowl. At a slightly smarter level, Silom Village caters for Thais and tourists alike – pick dishes from various stalls, choose fish and seafood from a tank, then sit at proper laid tables. Fruit freaks can OD on pineapple, papaya and water melon, kept sliced on ice by street vendors. NB Mango is often served unripe and sour with a salt-spice mix that looks deceptively like demerera sugar.

INDEX